THE

WILLARD J. GRAHAM SERIES

IN ACCOUNTING

BOOKS IN
THE WILLARD J. GRAHAM SERIES IN ACCOUNTING

CONSULTING EDITOR ROBERT N. ANTHONY *Harvard University*

ANDERSON, SCHMIDT, & McCOSH *Practical Controllership* 3d ed.

ANTHONY *Management Accounting: Text and Cases* 4th ed.

ANTHONY *Management Accounting Principles* rev. ed.

ANTHONY, DEARDEN, & VANCIL *Management Control Systems: Text, Cases, and Readings* rev. ed.

BARR & GRINAKER *Short Audit Case* rev. ed.

FREMGEN *Accounting for Managerial Analysis* rev. ed.

GORDON & SHILLINGLAW *Accounting: A Management Approach* 4th ed.

GRIFFIN, WILLIAMS, & LARSON *Advanced Accounting* rev. ed.

GRINAKER & BARR *Audit Practice Case*

GRINAKER & BARR *Auditing: The Examination of Financial Statements*

HAWKINS *Corporate Financial Reporting: Text and Cases*

HENDRIKSEN *Accounting Theory* rev. ed.

HOLMES, MAYNARD, EDWARDS, & MEIER *Elementary Accounting* 3d ed.

HOLMES & OVERMYER *Auditing: Principles and Procedure* 7th ed.

HOLMES & OVERMYER *Basic Auditing Principles* 4th ed.

KENNEDY & McMULLEN *Financial Statements: Form, Analysis, and Interpretation* 6th ed.

LADD *Contemporary Corporate Accounting and the Public*

MAURIELLO *The Irwin Federal Income Tax Course: A Comprehensive Text*

MEIGS, LARSEN, & MEIGS *Principles of Auditing* 5th ed.

MIKESELL & HAY *Governmental Accounting* 4th ed.

MOORE & STETTLER *Accounting Systems for Management Control*

MURPHY *Advanced Public Accounting Practice*

MURPHY *Auditing and Theory: A CPA Review*

NEILSON *Interactive Computerized Accounting Problems Set*

NEUNER *Cost Accounting: Principles and Practice* 8th ed.

NICHOLS *Programmed Cost Accounting: A Participative Approach*

NIELSEN *Cases in Auditing*

O'NEIL, FARWELL, & BOYD *Quantitative Controls for Business: An Introduction*

PATON *Corporate Profits*

PYLE & WHITE *Fundamental Accounting Principles* 6th ed.

SALMONSON, HERMANSON, & EDWARDS *A Survey of Basic Accounting*

SCHAFER *Elements of Income Tax—Individual*

SCHRADER, MALCOLM, & WILLINGHAM *Financial Accounting: An Input/Output Approach*

SHILLINGLAW *Cost Accounting: Analysis and Control* 3d ed.

SPILLER *Financial Accounting: Basic Concepts* rev. ed.

STAUBUS *Activity Costing and Input-Output Accounting*

VATTER *Accounting Measurements for Financial Reports*

WELSCH, ZLATKOVICH, & WHITE *Intermediate Accounting* 3d ed.

WILLIAMS & GRIFFIN *Management Information: A Quantitative Accent*

FINANCIAL STATEMENTS
Form, analysis, and interpretation

Financial statements

Form, analysis, and interpretation

RALPH DALE KENNEDY, Ph.D.
Late Professor of Accounting and Chairman
Department of Accounting
The George Washington University

STEWART YARWOOD McMULLEN, M.B.A., C.P.A.
Executive Director
The American Group of C.P.A. Firms

Sixth Edition • 1973
RICHARD D. IRWIN, INC. *Homewood, Illinois 60430*
IRWIN-DORSEY LIMITED *Georgetown, Ontario*

© Richard D. Irwin, Inc., 1946, 1952, 1957, 1962, 1968, and 1973

All rights reserved. No part of this publication may be
reproduced, stored in a retrieval system, or transmitted,
in any form or by any means, electronic, mechanical,
photocopying, recording, or otherwise, without the prior
written permission of the publisher.

Sixth Edition

First Printing, February 1973

ISBN 0-256-01464-7
Library of Congress Catalog Card No. 72–93546
Printed in the United States of America

Preface

THE PRINCIPAL PURPOSE of this volume continues to be an explanation of techniques to use in analyzing and interpreting the financial statements of industrial and commercial business enterprises, plus certain special industries such as electric power companies and banks.

The authors continue to assume that the reader has a working knowledge of the fundamentals of accounting as reflected in financial statements. These concepts are reviewed in the first section of the book, which may be by-passed by the reader who has no need of such a review.

However, the chapters include new information about pronouncements of the Accounting Principles Board* of the American Institute of Certified Public Accountants affecting various aspects of the published financial statements of publicly held corporations, and current changes in financial statement practices as reviewed in Accounting Trends and Techniques.

Financial statement analysis techniques are useful to many different segments of the business community, including (1) company management, which uses them to test the soundness of present practices, (2) credit grantors and credit rating organizations, and (3) investors and their advisors.

The book is divided into four parts. Part I (Chapters 1 through 7) is

---

* In 1972 action was initiated to supersede the Accounting Principles Board (composed of part-time members) by a Financial Accounting Standards Board, the members of which will be full-time, and will be more representative of the various groups which are significantly concerned with the preparation and use of financial statements of U.S. organizations. As of January 1973 the Financial Accounting Standards Board is in existence and is preparing to begin its activities.

a review of the general principles governing the construction of financial statements of business organizations including a discussion of asset valuation, amortization and income determination problems. Chapter 7 discusses consolidated statements.

Part II (Chapters 8 through 16) is devoted to the techniques of financial statement analysis together with a discussion of various characteristics of financial statements related to an understanding of analytical methods, including working capital and the statements that report working capital changes and cash flows, and analytical tools such as ratios. The published statements of actual business concerns are used as examples throughout.

Part III (Chapters 17 through 21) discusses the problem of price level changes, their effects on financial statements, and methods of analyzing the effects of such changes on statement interpretation. The authors take no position, in this volume, in the controversy within the accounting profession over the extent to which the effects of changing price levels should be reflected in the accounts. However, they insist that, regardless of the methods followed in accounting and reporting, the financial analyst cannot afford to ignore the effect of changing price levels in his analyses of the reported figures. Of course, the seriousness of the distortion of the story told by a company's financial statements varies in proportion to the dynamics of the inflation during the periods in which the statement figures arose. The substantial and rapid increases in prices during the late 1940s, and to a lesser extent since, seriously impaired the value of reported accounting data. Examples are displayed in Part III.

Part IV considers the unique analytical problems encountered in the financial statements of special industries, such as airlines and banks.

This volume does not attempt to standardize financial statement analysis, as differing conditions require analytical flexibility. The techniques described should be regarded as a kit of tools that analysts use as the occasion warrants.

Extensive changes, necessary to keep pace with the rapidly changing worlds of business and accounting, will be found to have been incorporated in this new edition. Many of these changes have been brought about by the recent flood of Opinions issued by the Accounting Principles Board of the American Institute of Certified Public Accountants. The Accounting Principles Board has been awarded a considerable measure of authority over the attest function of auditors who are members of the American Institute of Certified Public Accountants. It also has the unofficial support of the Securities and Exchange Commission. In the last few years, the activities of the APB, which publishes a numbered series of Opinions under the imprint of The American Institute, have brought about many changes in the financial statement practices not only of the larger U.S.

corporations but also of smaller enterprises that use annual audits or follow the developing code of best financial statement practices.

New material has been added throughout the book. Especially noteworthy are new sections on Judging the Solvency of the Small Business in Chapter 11 and Appraising Bonds for Long-Term Investment in Chapter 15.

Questions, exercises, and problems for course use have been edited and moved into the body of the book. A book of suggested solutions is available. We are indebted to Professor Carson Cox of Loyola University, Chicago, for his assistance in updating the questions and problems and the proposed solutions.

It is hoped that the material changes made in this edition will be regarded by our users as substantial improvements.

January 1973   STEWART Y. McMULLEN

Contents

receivable. Accounts receivable. Valuation of notes and accounts receivable. Inventories. Valuation of inventories. Inventories—cost. Capital stock subscriptions receivable. Accrued receivables.

results of the equity method. Understanding consolidated statements. Amount paid for subsidiary capital stock. Minority interest in the owners' equity of the subsidiary. Intercompany receivables and payables. Intercompany unrealized profit. Factors limiting the usefulness of consolidated statements. Requirements of complete reporting. Difference between a consolidation and consolidated statements.

PART II

Analysis and interpretation of commercial and industrial financial statements

PART III

The effect of changing price levels on the interpretation of financial statements

The nature of the problem illustrated. The accounting conventions now in effect. The significance of price-level changes. The effect of price-level changes on fixed assets. Effect of price changes on inventories. Gains or losses on "monetary" (fixed dollar) items. The index number problem.

Monetary and nonmonetary items.

General steps to prepare general price-level financial statements.

Balance sheets. Statements of income and retained earnings. AN OVER-VIEW: Statement of income. Balance sheet. Both statements.

PART IV

Analysis and interpretation of the financial statements of several regulated industries

Uniform system of accounts. Comparison of balance sheets of air carriers and nonregulated business. ASSETS: Current assets. Investments and special funds. Operating property and equipment. Reserves for depreciation and maintenance. Nonoperating property and equipment. Deferred charges. Contingent assets and contingent liabilities. LIABILITIES AND CAPITAL: Current liabilities. Noncurrent liabilities. Deferred credits. Stockholders' equity. Comparison of operating statements of air carriers and commercial businesses. OPERATING REVENUES: Transport revenue; nontransport revenue. OPERATING EXPENSES: Flying operations. Maintenance. General services and administration. Depreciation and amortization. Nonoperating income and expense—net. Income taxes for current period. Special items.

dividends—form. Report of income and dividends—description of items. Current operating revenue. Current operating expenses. Net current operating earnings. Recoveries, transfers from valuation reserves, and profits. Losses, charge-offs, and transfers to valuation reserves. Net income.

PART I

Introduction to financial statements and accounting concepts

1

Introduction

THIS VOLUME is primarily concerned with financial accounting. Financial accounting deals with recording, analyzing, describing, and reporting the financial affairs of business corporations and other entities. Financial affairs are those affairs which are customarily summarized in dollars, recorded in double-entry accounts, and reported in financial statements and other summaries.

Financial reports are used by numerous interested recipients in our society including management (to operate the business), creditors (to appraise the possible results of credit granting), governments (for tax purposes), investors and their advisors, regulatory commissions (in connection with rate regulation for example), buyers and sellers of business concerns, and many others.

Accounting is sometimes called "the language of business" because it is a principal means of communicating business information, and particularly business information that can be quantified in dollars. Examples of business matters which are not usually stated in dollars are the backgrounds and capabilities of company officers and managers, and the morale and productivity of lower level employees; such nonquantified information is also of substantial importance.

Accounting is used (1) to measure the resources held by specific entities such as cash and inventories and plants; (2) to reflect the claims against and the interests in those entities such as unpaid taxes and capital stock outstanding in the hands of the public; (3) to measure the changes in those resources, claims and interests such as a decline of cash due to payment of current bills (accounts payable) or wages (accrued wages); (4) to assign the changes to specifiable periods of time thus yielding in dollars an amount of net income to be reported as earned in June or in the year ended June 30, 1972; and (5) to express the foregoing in terms of money as a common denominator.[1]

Managing a business, particularly a large business, is a complex task; and management finds many uses for financial reports including—

1. Formulating, implementing, and appraising policies.
2. Bringing about coordination of activities.
3. Planning for and controlling day-to-day operations.
4. Accounting for responsibilities within the business.
5. Studying specific projects or phases of a business.
6. Measuring the financial position and income of the business.
7. Reporting on the stewardship of the business to the owners and presenting accounting data to other interested groups outside of the business, including creditors, governmental agencies, prospective investors, trade associations, employees, and the general public.

Published financial statements

The principal financial statements published for the information of outsiders are the balance sheet, the income statement, the statement of retained earnings or owners' equity, and the statement of changes in financial position (formerly usually known as the statement of sources and applications of funds). This last named statement, which alternatively may be in the form of a statement of sources and uses of cash, has now been required in all published financial statements attested to by certified public accountants who are members of the American Institute of Certified Public Accountants (AICPA).[2]

As used in this volume, the word "funds" means working capital, the excess of current assets over current liabilities. *The balance sheet* portrays the financial condition of a business, as reflected in the accounting records, at one particular moment in time, usually the close of business on the day indicated by the date of the statement. The balance sheet lists the assets, liabilities, and owners' equity items. It contains the balances remaining in the accounts after the adjusting and closing processes in the general ledger have been completed. However, to make the resulting balance sheet more meaningful to the reader, groupings

---

[1] Maurice Moonitz, "The Basic Postulates of Accounting," *Accounting Research Study No. 1* (New York: American Institute of Certified Public Accountants, 1961), p. 23. For brevity, AICPA will be used in the text to identify the American Institute of Certified Public Accountants. The American Accounting Association will be identified as the AAA.

[2] The change of name was required by the Accounting Principles Board, AICPA, in *Opinion No. 19* (New York, March 1971).

and descriptions used on the balance sheet usually differ from those found on the records.

Various types of items are classified on a balance sheet as assets. Some have value in exchange, such as cash, while others are unamortized costs, which will be amortized over their useful lives and which may or may not have exchange value (such as buildings and equipment).

Liabilities represent legal obligations of the concern, usually to disburse assets. Ownership equity items represent the obligation of the concern, as an entity, to its owners. While ownership entitles the owner to certain rights, the resulting obligation is not ordinarily a liability in the legal sense. But the liabilities and owners' equity elements in a balance sheet are supposed to represent, collectively, the sum of all claims (by creditors and owners) against the enterprise.

The balance sheet (Illustration 1–1) is a statement of investment—a dual analysis and presentation of the sources of capital (borrowed funds and owners' equity) and the investment of the capital in assets. The net amount of capital obtained to date from each of several sources is classified according to the terms under which the capital was secured. The net amount of capital invested to date in each asset item is classified according to the nature of the commitment of capital and the frequency of opportunity to decide about the recommitment of capital into specific investments.

This approach to the balance sheet emphasizes that it is not and does not purport to be a statement of value; it is only a listing of the sources and investments of capital.

The income statement of a manufacturing or trading concern (Illustration 1–2) shows primarily the *revenue* realized from the sale of goods or services and the *costs* incurred in the process of earning the revenue. Also, the statement reveals the net income or net loss resulting from the operation of the business during the period covered by the report. It is a statement of activity and the results of that activity.

The statement of retained earnings (Illustration 1–3, which uses the title "Earned Surplus") prepared for corporations shows an analysis of changes in the stockholders' equity that have been recorded in the Retained Earnings (occasionally known as Earned Surplus or Retained Income) account during a stated period of time. The statement of owners' equity prepared for single proprietorships and partnerships summarizes the changes that have taken place in the capital investment account or accounts during a designated period of time.

The statement of changes in financial position (Illustration 1–4) shows the flow of working capital during a stated period of time. The statement summarizes the change in the working capital and accounts for this change by showing the sources from which working capital has been obtained and the uses to which it has been devoted.

ILLUSTRATION 1–1

MARSHALL FIELD & COMPANY
CONSOLIDATED BALANCE SHEET

ASSETS

	January 31, 1972	January 31, 1971
Current Assets:		
Cash..	$ 7,854,710	$ 9,557,624
Receivables from customers and others, less allowance for doubtful accounts of $1,595,577 and $1,512,300, respectively...................	78,423,490	81,858,620
Merchandise inventories (note 2)...................	77,750,563	73,732,240
Prepaid insurance, supply inventories, etc........	3,560,923	2,962,596
Total Current Assets.....................	$167,589,686	$168,111,080
Investments in Real Estate Ventures (note 3).........	$ 11,411,466	$ 7,345,409
Property and Equipment (at cost):		
Land...	$ 23,103,036	$ 23,105,480
Buildings..	111,368,139	104,094,856
Equipment.......................................	44,148,937	44,825,066
	$178,620,112	$172,025,402
Less accumulated depreciation...................	66,590,868	66,237,452
Net Property and Equipment............	$112,029,244	$105,787,950
	$291,030,396	$281,244,439

See notes to financial statements on page 19.

LIABILITIES

	January 31, 1972	January 31, 1971
Current Liabilities:		
Accounts payable..............................	$ 18,181,848	$ 17,466,068
Accrued income taxes—		
Current.....................................	5,866,368	6,195,079
Deferred (net), including deferral for income on uncollected installment sales................	9,178,639	8,307,902
Other accrued liabilities..........................	33,647,757	33,172,959
Current maturities of long-term debt............	1,772,996	745,565
Total Current Liabilities..................	$ 68,647,608	$ 65,887,573
Long-Term Debt, less current maturities:		
3¾% notes, payable $800,000 annually in 1973-1981 and $15,000,000 in 1982..............	$ 22,200,000	$ 23,000,000
4%-8% installment notes and bonds, payable 1973-1995.................................	5,937,563	6,910,559
Total Long-Term Debt....................	$ 28,137,563	$ 29,910,559
Stockholders' Equity:		
Preferred Stock—		
Authorized 1,000,000 shares of $1 par value, issuable in series; issued at par value:		
Series A, $2.40 cumulative; $52 per share redemption and liquidation value (aggregate $982,124); 19,719 and 21,706 shares, respectively....................................	$ 19,719	$ 21,706
Series B, $3.00 cumulative; $52 per share redemption and liquidation value (aggregate $1,060,800); 20,400 shares in both years.	20,400	20,400
Common Stock—		
Authorized 20,000,000 shares of $1 par value; 9,154,971 shares issued at par value.........	9,154,971	9,154,971
Paid-in Surplus....................................	31,138,537	31,215,436
Earned Surplus ($114,542,466 available for dividends on common stock under terms of long-term debt).....................................	154,735,918	145,826,443
	$195,069,545	$186,238,956
Less treasury stock, at cost—		
832 Series A preferred shares..................	31,671	—
32,706 common shares in both years.........	792,649	792,649
Total Stockholders' Equity...............	$194,245,225	$185,446,307
	$291,030,396	$281,244,439

Detailed financial and operating data, essential to a comprehensive analysis, are customarily shown in schedule form supplementary to the more condensed financial statements (Illustration 1–5). For example, schedules may be presented to show the details of land; buildings; equipment; natural resources; accumulated depreciation, depletion, and amortization of fixed assets; inventories; long-term investments; accrued liabil-

ILLUSTRATION 1–2

MARSHALL FIELD & COMPANY
CONSOLIDATED INCOME STATEMENT

	Fiscal Year Ended	
	January 31, 1972	January 31, 1971
Net Sales.	$466,688,654	$401,882,833
Deduct:		
Cost of goods sold and expenses, exclusive of items listed below.	$401 628,668	$347,478,258
Maintenance and repairs.	4,374,919	3,575,170
Depreciation (straight-line method).	6,183,380	6,069,561
Taxes other than income taxes.	13,581,217	10,929,164
Rentals paid.	2,944,286	1,888,004
Net interest expense (income).	924,442	(225,593)
Total costs (note 4).	$429,636,912	$369,714,564
Income before Income Taxes.	$ 37,051,742	$ 32,168,269
Income taxes (including net deferred taxes of $871,000 and $2,462,000, respectively).	18,000,000	16,089,000
Net Income.	$ 19,051,742	$ 16,079,269
Net Income per Common Share.	$ 2.08	$ 1.82

See notes to financial statements on page 19.

ILLUSTRATION 1–3

MARSHALL FIELD & COMPANY

EARNED SURPLUS

	Fiscal Year Ended	
	January 31, 1972	January 31, 1971
Balance at beginning of year	$145,826,443	$139,493,089
Net income	19,051,742	16,079,269
	$164,878,185	$155,572,358
Cash dividends declared on:		
Cumulative preferred stock—		
Series A, $2.40 per share	$ 46,575	$ 13,031
Series B, $3.00 per share	61,200	15,300
Common stock—$1.10 per share in each year	10,034,492	9,717,584
	$ 10,142,267	$ 9,745,915
Balance at end of year	$154,735,918	$145,826,443

PAID-IN SURPLUS

Balance at beginning of year	$ 31,215,436	$ 8,904,669
Excess of fair market value over par value of stock issued in acquisition	—	8,605,838
Excess of stated value over par value of common stock converted from no par value to par value	—	13,735,920
Excess of cost over par value of Series A and B preferred stock purchased and retired	(76,899)	(30,991)
Balance at end of year	$ 31,138,537	$ 31,215,436

See notes to financial statements on page 19.

ILLUSTRATION 1–4

MARSHALL FIELD & COMPANY
CHANGES IN FINANCIAL POSITION

	Fiscal Year Ended	
	January 31, 1972	January 31, 1971
Working Capital Provided:		
Net income......................................	$ 19,051,742	$ 16,079,269
Add depreciation, which does not use working capital...	6,183,380	6,069,561
Working capital provided from operations....	$ 25,235,122	$ 22,148,830
Stock issued in acquisition of The Halle Brothers Company..	—	9,045,690
Miscellaneous....................................	647,920	102,870
	$ 25,883,042	$ 31,297,390
Working Capital Used:		
Purchase of property and equipment of The Halle Brothers Company, less assumed long-term debt of $6,639,628...........................	$ —	$ 3,406,135
Investment in real estate ventures..............	4,066,057	7,345,409
Additions to property and equipment...........	13,072,593	9,795,393
Dividends to stockholders.......................	10,142,267	9,745,915
Purchases of Company stock....................	110,558	377,855
Decrease in long-term debt.....................	1,772,996	229,069
	$ 29,164,471	$ 30,899,776
Net Increase (Decrease) in Working Capital.......	$ (3,281,429)	$ 397,614
Increases (Decreases) in Working Capital:		
Cash and short-term investments................	$ (1,702,914)	$ (10,930,206)
Receivables.....................................	(3,435,130)	17,895,587
Merchandise inventories........................	4,018,323	8,099,771
Prepaid expenses...............................	598,327	1,291,300
Accounts payable...............................	(715,780)	(3,274,250)
Accrued income taxes..........................	(542,026)	(2,401,250)
Other accrued liabilities........................	(474,798)	(9,537,773)
Current maturities of long-term debt............	(1,027,431)	(745,565)
Net Increase (Decrease) in Working Capital....	$ (3,281,429)	$ 397,614

See notes to financial statements on page 19.

ILLUSTRATION 1–5

(4) Total costs as reported to the Securities and Exchange Commission are classified as follows:		
	Fiscal Year	
	1971	1970
Cost of goods sold, buying and occupancy expenses:.......	$329,272,392	$283,525,944
Selling, general and administrative expenses..............	99,440,078	86,414,213
Net interest expense (income).........................	924,442	(225,593)
	$429,636,912	$369,714,564

ities; long-term liabilities; cost of goods manufactured and sold; selling expenses; and general and administrative expenses. Analytical information is also presented in notes supporting the financial statements, referred to in statement captions.

Financial statements may be studied from the standpoint of construction and of analysis and interpretation. In earlier days, accountants were primarily concerned with the construction of the statements; today, they play an important part in the analysis and interpretation of financial and operating data. In fact, from management's point of view, the accountant's work is not complete until he has analyzed and interpreted the data presented in the statements. The process of analysis and interpretation should be carefully considered when the statements are prepared so that their content, arrangement, and form will contribute to the effectiveness of a study of the data.

Internal managerial accounting reports

Published financial statements are usually general-purpose entity statements, which present the financial position and operating results of an entire business for the period stated, usually a year. This overall information is historical in nature and does not purport to be in the best form for managerial control. Management needs a relatively large number of detailed and/or summarized accounting reports showing status or activity of parts or segments of the business. These internal managerial accounting reports are prepared on a daily, weekly, biweekly, monthly, bimonthly, quarterly, or on a when-requested basis.

Understanding financial statements

The AICPA has said this about financial statements:

Financial Statements are prepared for the purpose of presenting a periodical review or report on progress by the management and deal with the status of the investment in the business and results achieved during the period under review. They reflect a combination of *recorded facts, accounting conventions,* and *personal judgments;*[3] and the judgments and conventions applied affect them materially. The soundness of the judgments necessarily depends on the competence and integrity of those who make them and on their adherence to generally accepted accounting principles and conventions.[4]

The term *recorded facts* refers to the data drawn from the accounting records. For example, recorded facts include such data as the amount of cash on hand and in the bank, the amount of promissory notes and accounts receivable due from customers and other debtors, the cost of fixed assets, the amounts payable on promissory notes and to other creditors, and the amount of sales. The original *cost*—the amount paid when the fixed assets were acquired—is as a rule stated in the accounts rather than the reproduction or replacement cost. It should be clear, therefore, that the balance sheet does not show the financial position of a business in terms of current economic conditions because historical costs rather than current costs are given for most of the items. (See Illustration 1–1.)

Certain factors that may affect the financial position of a business may not be recorded in the accounting records or shown in the body of the balance sheet. Examples of such items, which sometimes appear as footnotes to the balance sheet, are unfilled customer orders, purchase and sales contracts and commitments, patent-infringement cases, claims for tax refunds, judgments, endorsements, and guaranties.

The term *accounting conventions* has reference to certain assumptions and procedures which will be discussed beginning on page 15.

It is assumed, for example, that the business is a going concern—that it will continue. Income determination requires that revenues and costs be properly matched within the time scale of a relatively short period, usually a year or less. Expenditures which give rise to assets, such as plant and equipment, which will have value for many years, are to be charged to expense only ratably during the periods which comprise the useful life. Assets are recorded at cost, and the costs of assets purchased at different price levels are lumped together without adjustment and, therefore, without regard to the unequal value of the dollar in different years of acquisition. (The price-level problem is discussed in depth in Part III).

Personal judgment is combined with recorded facts and accounting conventions in the financial statements when the accountant decides (1) to use one of several methods for estimating uncollectible receivables

---

[3] Italics supplied.

[4] *Examination of Financial Statements by Independent Public Accountants,* bulletin prepared and published by the AICPA, January 1936, p. 1. Certain words were italicized in the quotation in preparation for the following discussion of their meaning.

expense and for the determination of the depreciation and depletion charges for a particular year; (2) to write off intangible value within five years rather than a shorter or longer term; (3) to evaluate the merchandise inventory at cost or at the lower of cost or market; (4) to consider that cost will be applied on the theory that the first goods acquired are the first goods to be issued or sold, or that the last goods acquired are the first goods to be issued or sold; and (5) to record certain expenditures as capital (balance sheet) rather than revenue (income statement) expenditures, or vice versa.

ILLUSTRATION 1–6.   A CPA opinion showing a change

Accountants' Report   TO THE BOARD OF DIRECTORS AND STOCKHOLDERS OF TIME INCORPORATED

We have examined the consolidated financial statements of Time Incorporated and subsidiaries for the year ended December 31, 1970. Our examination was made in accordance with generally accepted auditing standards, and accordingly included such tests of the accounting records and such other auditing procedures as we considered necessary in the circumstances.

In our opinion, the accompanying balance sheet and statements of income, stockholders' equity and funds present fairly the consolidated financial position of Time Incorporated and subsidiaries at December 31,

1970, and the consolidated results of their operations, changes in stockholders' equity and sources and uses of funds for the year then ended, in conformity with generally accepted accounting principles, which, except for the change (in which we concur) in accounting for promotion costs as described in Notes to Financial Statements, have been applied on a basis consistent with that of the preceding year.

Ernst + Ernst   New York, New York,
                               February 18, 1971

CHANGES IN ACCOUNTING POLICY AND PRACTICE

Promotion costs of book and record series have been expensed as incurred, although resultant revenues have been realized over a period of years. Retroactively to January 1, 1970, this accounting policy was changed to expense these costs over a 12-month period, beginning with the month in which they were incurred. The effect of this change was to increase net income in 1970 by approximately $200,000.

Alternative methods of handling accounting data are sometimes permissible. An example would be various methods of computing depreciation, such as straight line or declining balance. (Whatever method is used, the total depreciation charged to expense must not exceed original cost). While it is permissible to change from one method to another, and companies sometimes do so, it is not acceptable practice to jump haphazardly, without disclosure, from one method to another. When a CPA (certified public accountant) signs his name to an opinion that attests that statements "present fairly" the financial condition (balance sheet) and results of operations (statement of income) of his client, he adds "in conformity with generally accepted accounting principles *applied on a consistent basis*" (italics supplied). If there has been a change, he says so and describes the change and its effect in his opinion (Illustration 1–6). An important method of analyzing financial statements is to compare two statements—for succeeding years, for example. By analyzing such a comparison it becomes possible to determine whether conditions have improved or deteriorated.

In the decade of the 1960s, and now in the 1970s, there has been a mounting volume of criticism concerning the availability of acceptable alternative accounting methods and the use of this leeway by some companies to improve the appearance of their annual reports. The so-called pooling of interests method of combining the accounting data of two merging concerns has been under particularly heavy fire because it has been used to maximize recorded net income.[5] The Accounting Principles Board (APB) of the AICPA, having been vested with the power to require disclosure of deviations from its opinions, has been valiantly attempting to narrow the range of permissible options in financial statements. The opinions which have so far been issued will be described and evaluated when the subject matter concerned comes up for discussion in later chapters.

Financial statements represent the summation of a variety of conventions governing the recording of financial transactions. Unless specially prepared, they do not customarily reflect current economic values.

Accounting concepts and principles

The nature and limitations of financial statements have been discussed above in some detail. To the extent that accounting functions are properly completed, the financial statements will contain objective and meaningful data for use (1) by management as the basis for financial and operating routine and policy decisions; and (2) by stockholders and bondholders, banks, creditors, government agencies, and labor unions for a variety of decisions.

Within the framework of "generally accepted accounting principles," the accountant has a set of guidelines[6] which are necessary to assure a desirable degree of consistency in accumulating financial and operating data; to provide comparability of accounting data that are presented to management, creditors, investors, the public, and governmental bodies; and to provide a basis for decision making and formulation of solutions to the many complex accounting problems encountered in the functioning of an accounting system.

The need for accounting concepts and principles has developed from the growing complexity of business and governmental affairs and an increasing recognition by those who are interested in these affairs that timely, reliable accounting data are essential to the complex operations of today. Chief among those who have formulated these concepts and principles, and who provide a constant search for means of improving

---

[5] To curb abuses associated with poolings of interests, the Accounting Principles Board of the AICPA issued *Opinion No. 16* (New York, 1970).

[6] Accounting concepts and principles represent uniform guides to action, while procedures are the methods by which action is taken.

them, are the professional accounting associations such as the American Institute of Certified Public Accountants, the American Accounting Association, and the National Association of Accountants. Also, the Securities and Exchange Commission and the stock exchanges have had a part in this effort.

Accounting principles, more properly associated with such terms as concepts, conventions, standards, and practices, are man-made in contrast to those created by natural law. When a distinction is made between accounting concepts and principles, emphasis is placed on the fact that underlying all accounting activity is a group of basic rules that may be referred to as fundamental concepts or assumptions such as the business (accounting) entity, going concern, unit of measurement, cost, realization, and stability of the unit of measurement conventions. Other accounting concepts that are not as basic but are fundamental to accounting practice are the time period concept, objective evidence, disclosure, consistency, conservatism, and the matching of revenue and cost.

The business (accounting) entity concept.   Basic to all accounting must be the establishment of boundaries for the accounting and reporting activity. The accounting assumption is that a business activity shall be accounted for separately from its owners. That is, accounting reports the financial position and operating results of the business entity rather than that of the owners or others who are associated with the business.

With the corporate form of business organization, the accounting entity approach generally corresponds with the legal concept of the corporation as an entity separate and distinct from its owners (the stockholders). However, even in this case, the accounting entity concept provides for legally treating separate corporations as one accounting entity for reporting purposes in those instances when the corporations are closely related. This would be the case when several corporations are carrying on related or complementary activities and are tied together by common ownership, in which instance the corporations would represent a business or economic entity even though they are each separate legal entities. Corporations forming an economic entity in this matter commonly prepare consolidated financial statements.

The business entity concept is probably most important in its application to the sole proprietorship and partnership forms of business organization, where the owners generally participate actively in the business. In these instances, the business entity concept requires that a distinct separation of the accounting and reporting of the business affairs be made from the personal affairs of the owners.

The going-concern, continuity of existence concept.   A going concern represents an established business being conducted with the expectation of continuing indefinitely. That is, when a business is organized, the going-concern concept of accounting assumes a continuity of existence for the accounting entity longer than that of any of its components. This affects the methods of valuation used. For example, many assets are shown on the records and financial statements at cost or cost less depreciation, and it is assumed that current fair market value and cost of replacement are not particularly relevant. In other words, going-concern values of assets and original costs, rather than liquidating values, are used.

The unit of measurement concept.   Accounting is based on the assumption that for accounting purposes, money (the dollar) is the unit of measurement to be used in recording, classifying, summarizing, and reporting business transactions and the results thereof. This concept provides a common denominator for which all transactions, whether past, present, or future, may be accounted for. The use of nonmonetary units for certain accounting records and reports is not in conflict with this concept.

The cost concept.   Accounting data are recorded at cost as of the date of acquisition, and these costs are maintained on the records and statements unless there is a write-down to recognize a loss or a write-up to record appreciation.[7] Substituting the cost of replacement or current market values for original cost represents a departure from cost. It is assumed that the recording of transactions at cost is a more objective approach.

Cost should include all expenditures incurred in obtaining and placing the asset in position or condition for business use. Costs are measured by the amounts invested on a cash or cash-equivalent basis. If cash is disbursed, the total amount paid to purchase the asset and prepare it for use represents the cost. If other than cash is given, the cash-equivalent value of the consideration or the fair appraisal value of the asset received should be recorded as the cost.

The realization concept.   Revenue is realized when a sale is completed or when a service is performed. That is, when a bona fide sale or exchange of economic values takes place between the business and an outside firm or individual, revenue is realized.

The stable-dollar concept.   Another assumption in accounting is that in primary statements of financial condition,[8] fluctuations in the value

---

[7] Under *Opinion No. 6* (October, 1965) of the APB of the AICPA, property, plant, and equipment "should not be written up . . . to reflect appraisal, market or current values which are above cost" except in reorganizations. If this is done nevertheless, auditors who are members of the organization must disclose the fact and its effect and state whether depreciation has been charged—as it should be—on the written-up amount.

[8] Primary statements should be distinguished from supplementary statements; the former are commonly published alone, whereas the latter always accompany (and supplement) the primary statements. See the discussion of the price-level problem in Part III.

of the dollar must not be permitted to affect the amounts shown. But to some extent the position of the AICPA has changed: in its *Statement No. 3* the APB has stated that supplementary data showing the effect of changes in the price level are information useful to management, investors, and others and has recommended that supplementary financial statements be prepared to display such data. This same recommendation was made by the Committee on Concepts and Standards of the American Accounting Association in 1951. At this writing a few—but very few—companies have done so.

The time period concept. While business activity is a continuous flow, the reporting process breaks up that flow into periods. A year, calendar or fiscal, usually serves as the basic accounting period. Interim periods such as quarters are also used. The recording process also relies on the establishment of reporting periods, and the revenue and expense accounts are closed periodically.

The objective evidence concept. An important reason for the confidence placed in the financial statements of a business is the fact that auditors require verifiable, objective evidence to support the accounting transactions that are recorded in the accounting records. The best evidence is that which is most objective, i.e., that which is least influenced by personal opinion and judgment.

For example, business documents give verifiable evidence of exchanged economic value (cost). Cash, other assets, or the businesses' capital stock of readily determinable market value exchanged for assets or the liquidation of a liability is accepted as evidence of the incurrence of transactions. Specific examples of objective evidence include invoices, canceled checks, legal contracts, employee timecards, formal actions by the board of directors, and copies of receipts issued to outsiders for collections of cash. Examples of the use of unacceptable evidence include recording sales based solely on a tally prepared by the salesmen, recording cash disbursements on the basis of telephone calls from the disbursing officers, and increasing the book value of real estate based on the opinion of a corporate officer that it is worth an amount greater than its recorded cost.

The disclosure concept. Among the most important products of an accounting system are the financial statements prepared from the accumulated and classified data. It is imperative that adequate disclosure of all material facts be made on the financial statements to make them as informative and meaningful as possible. Disclosure of certain facts should be made to avoid misleading statements.

Disclosures should generally be made in the body of the statement in the form of a description of each item or as a parenthetical remark. If this method is not feasible, footnotes may be appended to the statement.

On occasion there may even be disclosure of events which occurred after the closing date of the financial statements. If the statements are audited, the auditor will insist that post-statement-date events which are important in understanding the situation of the company be disclosed (Illustration 1–7).

ILLUSTRATION 1–7.   A financial statement note disclosing subsequent events

---

INDIANA & MICHIGAN ELECTRIC COMPANY

NOTES TO FINANCIAL STATEMENTS

Twelve
Months
Ended
August 31,
1971

NOTE 10—SUBSEQUENT EVENTS:

On September 23, 1971, the Company transferred at original cost its investment of approximately $240,000,000 in the Donald C. Cook Nuclear Plant, presently under construction and consisting of two generating units, to a newly-organized wholly-owned subsidiary, Indiana & Michigan Power Company, and in connection therewith the subsidiary issued 1,500,000 shares of its common stock and $130,000,000 principal amount of its subordinated promissory notes and assumed certain liabilities of approximately $1,800,000 (largely retained percentages). Any consolidated statements that might have been submitted, giving effect to this transaction as of August 31, 1971, would have been identical with those of the Company herein as of, or for the twelve months ended on August 31, 1971, except for costs incidental to the transfer of the property.

Also, in September, 1971, the Company entered into a nuclear leasing agreement and it has sold to the lessor certain uranium hexafluoride carried on its books at August 31, 1971, and relating to the first unit of the Donald C. Cook Nuclear Plant, for a cash consideration of approximately $20,100,000.

The consistency concept. Where there are several acceptable methods of performing certain accounting tasks, the accountant should apply the method best suited to each particular case and disclose the method being used. For example, one of several inventory cost-flow assumptions *or* various depreciation methods may be used. The selected method should be consistently applied year after year, and if there is a change it should be disclosed. In this manner, the financial statements are more comparable between time intervals as well as between businesses. The emphasis on consistency does not mean that accounting methods that have been adopted should be continued regardless of changed conditions. However, if a change is made to another generally accepted method, specific disclosure should be clearly made in a footnote, showing the dollar effect of the change.

The conservatism concept. The term *conservatism* usually means recording assets owned at a value lower than cost, or overstating liabilities. This valuation method, if carried to extremes, results in the understatement of asset value, misstatement of profits, and a temporary understatement of owners' equity. Such a result would be evident if the book value of a depreciable asset is arbitrarily written down to a nominal sum long before its useful life has lapsed.

On the other hand, reasonable conservatism is practiced when the accountant follows the "principle" of providing for all possible losses and anticipating no profit. For example, the valuation of an inventory on the basis of the lower of cost or market when market is lower than cost would result in recognizing an expected but unrealized loss that has taken place currently.

The matching of revenue and cost concept. The importance of the income statement and the periodic "test reading" of the flow of income that it provides have placed greater emphasis on income determination principles. These principles are applied to make the periodic amount of net income a meaningful figure that can be relied upon by management in formulating business decisions and by other interested parties in appraising the results of management's efforts.

Foremost among the income determination concepts is that referred to as *matching costs and revenues*. This concept has to do generally, but not entirely, with the periodic matching of the costs incurred in earning revenues in a particular period, with the revenues realized. To the extent that revenues and costs are not matched with precision, misleading results of operations will be reported to management, which in turn may use these data in making unwarranted decisions.

Certain phases of the matching process include the acceptance of the realization concept as discussed above, selection of an accounting period, adoption of the accrual basis of accounting, making a proper distinction between capital and revenue expenditures, and the recognition of losses but not the anticipation of profits. The last four principles will be discussed in chapters to follow.

When these "generally accepted accounting concepts" are appropriately recognized, the financial condition and operating results of each business entity may be more readily and accurately determined. Consequently, the reported data are more meaningful, comparable, and useful to both management and other groups that are interested in the affairs of the business.

The balance sheet and the income statement

A half century ago the balance sheet was regarded as more important than the income statement. But experience has taught the overriding importance of the income statement to investors and long-term creditors; short-term creditors retain their interest in the financial situation portrayed in the balance sheet (particularly current assets and current liabilities—working capital).

Both the balance sheet and the income statement are important to the analyst who should use all the information that he can obtain. Some of his information is derived from analyses of the trend of balance sheet items (Illustration 1–8), other information comes from comparisons of balance sheet and income statement details.

ILLUSTRATION 1–8.   A comparison of five-years' operations

WM. WRIGLEY JR. COMPANY
AND WHOLLY-OWNED ASSOCIATED COMPANIES

Five Year Financial Summary
(000 Omitted)

	1971	1970	1969	1968	1967
Net sales	$189,883	$176,832	$167,194	$159,504	$148,251
Earnings before income taxes	33,959	29,653	32,710	31,952	28,454
Income taxes	16,749	14,470	17,115	16,479	13,399
Net earnings for the year	17,210	15,183	15,595	15,473	15,055
Net earnings per outstanding share of capital stock	8.74	7.71	7.92	7.86	7.65
Dividends paid per share	5.00	5.00	5.50	5.50	5.50
Dividend payment % to net earnings	57.2%	64.9%	69.4%	70.0%	71.9%
Net current assets	$ 39,216	$ 50,986	$ 57,290	$ 60,174	$ 59,141
Total properties (net)	79,359	60,727	49,415	42,089	38,469
Stockholders' equity	121,348	113,980	108,639	103,871	99,225
Book value per share	61.65	57.90	55.19	52.77	50.41
Number of stockholders at year end	11,412	13,268	13,441	13,786	13,627
Number of employees at year end..	4,480	4,090	3,910	3,880	3,550

Thousands are omitted from dollar amounts except for per share comparisons.

Nevertheless, the income statement is of the highest importance; and if the analyst were forced to choose one statement or the other, he would probably choose an appropriately prepared comparative (two or more years) income statement. Even for credit purposes, the ability of the corporation to pay its debts may depend primarily on future profits. Certainly, bondholders are commonly dependent on earnings to secure payment of principal at maturity and interest during the term of the bonds.

The items included on a balance sheet[9] are customarily "valued" at historical dollar cost, with or without offsetting valuation and amortization accounts. The real value of such assets depends on the earning power of the business. Certainly, in a time of sharply rising prices, there is considerable doubt as to the usefulness of such "values" to an analyst who ignores the income statement entirely; and even if prices are relatively stable, the balance sheet items (which do not show liquidation values) get their going-concern meaning by relating them to earning power. The real value to a going concern of assets such as ending inventories, expense prepayments, and plant and equipment will depend on the amount realized on them in the course of future operations.

Although the statements are fundamentally related, the income statement is considered to be far more important today than formerly because of the greater emphasis upon earnings as compared with asset book values. Asset book values are relatively meaningless as absolute quantities; they have more meaning in comparative form, which permits analysis of changes and trends. A study of earnings provides a more effective analysis of economic conditions as affecting a business and, therefore, helps in estimating the future profitableness of operations.

Limitations of financial statements

Financial statements have the appearance of completeness, exactness, and finality. However, the statements have definite limitations. *First,* they are essentially interim reports and, therefore, cannot be final because the actual gain or loss of a business can be determined only when it is sold or liquidated. For various reasons, it is necessary to have an accounting in the form of financial statements at relatively frequent periods during the existence of a business. A period of 12 months, a year, has been generally adopted as the standard accounting period, since the year includes all four seasons.

The allocation of revenue and costs to an accounting period involves personal judgment. The problem involves the achievement of a satisfactory (but never a perfect) matching of costs with revenues.[10] In a cor-

---

[9] Assets, as shown on a balance sheet, can be usefully divided into three categories. Some balance sheet items (such as investment in subsidiaries) have elements of all three categories in them; but most assets can be classified as (1) revenue-stream items, such as receivables; (2) cost-stream items, such as expense prepayments, inventories, and plant; and (3) cash items, such as cash and government bonds, which constitute the connecting link between the two streams. An adequate understanding of the relationships between the balance sheet and the income statement will be promoted by considering the implications of this classification.

[10] For example, during the year a bridge-building company started to construct two bridges but completed only one. The bill for the completed bridge was $500,000. It is necessary for the company to see that the costs matched with the completed bridge (charged off as cost of goods sold) do not contain any of the costs incurred

poration, these judgments are a responsibility of the board of directors, although they may, in fact, be made by the officers or accounting supervisors of the company. For example, policy must be determined with respect to (1) the valuation method to apply to inventories; (2) the amounts of annual depreciation, depletion, amortization, and uncollectible receivables expenses; and (3) the proper treatment of capital expenditures and revenue expenditures. Revenue and cost transactions flow continuously throughout the life of a business enterprise; yet they must be "cut off" at each balance sheet date. Numerous differences of opinion are encountered in attempting to set policies under which the cutoff will be made. The responsible officials have freedom of choice within the boundaries of three restrictions: (1) the costs assigned or allocated to the period must have a logical relationship to the revenues allocated to the period; (2) the policies adopted must be consistently applied thereafter unless notice is given to the user of the statements that a change of policy has taken place; and (3) if they wish to obtain a "clean certificate" by means of an audit performed by a member of the AICPAs, they must conform to the published opinions of the Accounting Principles Board. Companies which issue securities to the public are subject to the regulations of the Securities and Exchange Commission which then exercises a type of control which is similar to and which complements the powers of the APB.

It is clear, therefore, that financial statement data are not exact—they cannot in all instances be measured precisely. Other factors that tend to make statement data uncertain include the existence of contingent assets and liabilities and deferred maintenance.

Second, the financial statements show exact dollar amounts, which give an impression of finality and precision. The reader may ascribe to these amounts his own concept of value, whereas the statements may have been set up on the basis of quite different value standards. Rarely does the stated value of an asset represent the amount of cash that would be realized on liquidation; even the cash balance would be reduced by the expenses incidental to the liquidation process.

The balance sheet is prepared on the basis of a going concern; it is assumed that the enterprise will continue in business. Fixed assets are customarily stated at historical cost, and a deduction is made for the amount already charged against revenue in the income statements (accumulated depreciation); the figures do not, as a rule, reflect either the amount for which the fixed assets could be sold or the amount that would have to be expended to replace them. Organization costs

---

in connection with the bridge still in process of construction, which should be carried over into the next period on the balance sheet (unless, of course, some income from the uncompleted bridge has been taken into the statement of income).

are listed with the assets on the assumption that a corporate charter or other form of organization has value *to the company.* In liquidation, this value would disappear. A patent, trademark, or organization costs may be stated by management policy at the conservative value of $1; in a liquidation a large sum might be realized on such assets.

Third, both the balance sheet and the income statement reflect transactions that involve dollar values of many dates. During the last 40 years the dollar has declined markedly in purchasing power; and unless prices decline substantially in the next few years, which does not now seem likely, the increase in the price level during the last two decades will have been particularly marked. Between 1939 and 1972, the general price level more than doubled. Many plants built in 1939 could not be replaced in 1972 for three times the original historical cost shown on the balance sheet. Under these circumstances, the depreciation charged against current revenues by companies using prewar plants is less than the depreciation appropriate on a replacement-cost basis. The balance sheet itself is not indicative of current economic realities.

Likewise, an increase in sales volume stated in dollars may or may not be the result of a larger number of units sold. All or a part of the apparent increase in volume may represent increases in selling prices, which may or may not have kept pace with the rising level of costs. Therefore, conclusions based on an inadequate analysis of comparative data may be quite misleading.

Fourth, financial statements do not reflect many factors which affect financial condition and operating results because they cannot be stated in terms of money. Such factors include sources and commitments for materials, merchandise, and supplies; the reputation and prestige of the company with the public; the credit rating of the company; and the efficiency, loyalty, and integrity of management and employees. Contingent assets and contingent liabilities customarily are not—and usually cannot be—stated definitely in dollars.

The foregoing discussion of the limitations of financial statements shows their tentative character under normal or peacetime conditions. It should be evident that financial statements are still more tentative when abnormal or wartime conditions prevail.

Parenthetical explanations and footnotes to financial statements

When adequate disclosure of pertinent information relative to financial condition and results of operations cannot be given merely by listing the financial statement items, additional data may be given parenthetically. More complete descriptions and extensive explanations may also be shown in footnotes, which are made an integral part of the financial statements (Illustration 1–7).

Examples of parenthetical explanations selected from unrelated published financial statements are as follows:

1. Marketable securities at cost (quoted market value, $20,175,140) . . . . $ 19,411,121
2. Receivables (estimated uncollectibles and sales discounts, $905,110 deducted) 20,134,514
3. Accounts receivable ($300,000 pledged as security for bank loans payable) 1,375,160
4. Inventories (Lifo) 11,235,111
5. Twenty-five-year 3½% debentures (due April 1, 1980, $250,000,000 original issue) 197,161,000
6. Capital stock, common (authorized 14,000,000 shares; par value, $20 per share; outstanding, 10,000,000 shares) 200,000,000
7. Capital stock, preferred ($3.75 cumulative no par value, authorized and outstanding, 161,522 shares; redemption, $107.50 per share) 16,610,235
8. Retained earnings ($60,175,000 restricted as to dividends until first-mortgage bonds are paid) 171,432,821
9. Retained earnings ($750,000 restricted as a result of the purchase of 7,000 shares of treasury stock) 2,160,192

Adequacy of disclosure is an important value in good financial reporting. Of course, judgment must be exercised both to determine what is important enough to require disclosure and to determine what is sufficiently unimportant to justify omission. Official bodies of the AICPA, and the Securities and Exchange Commission have been firm in their insistence on the need for adequate disclosure of important information. So has the New York Stock Exchange. If information cannot be adequately disclosed parenthetically, it is customary to do so in footnotes. Footnotes are an important part of published financial statements.

The Securities and Exchange Commission has enumerated some of the types of information that should be disclosed if the financial statements are to secure the approval of the Commission:

1. Changes in accounting principles employed.
2. Material retroactive adjustments.
3. Significant purchase commitments.
4. Long-term lease agreements.
5. Liens on assets.
6. Callable, convertible, or preference features of preferred stock.
7. Pension and retirement plans.
8. Provisions restricting the payment of dividends.
9. Contingent liabilities.
10. Depreciation and depletion policies.
11. Stock option and stock purchase agreements.

The financial statements in the annual reports of substantial U.S. corporations invariably include a variety of notes. A sampling of 125

annual reports issued in 1969 and 1970 yielded footnotes which included
the following subjects:

107 corporations (86% of the companies sampled) discussed various as-
     pects of the shareholders' equity (common stock, preferred stock,
     capital surplus, retained earnings, etc.)
103 (82%) were concerned with retirement plans
 90 (72%) reviewed their long-term debt
 75 (60%) disclosed the accounting principles used in preparing con-
     solidated statements
 74 (59%) discussed matters related to their federal income tax
 69 (55%) disclosed options granted to officers and others to purchase
     the company's stock
 54 (43%) reviewed the methods used in computing depreciation and
     amortization
 46 (37%) dealt with their inventories and disclosed the accounting
     methods used in arriving at balance sheet values
 37 (29%) discussed property, plant, and equipment
 35 (28%) were concerned with lease commitments
 31 (25%) disclosed how they computed earnings per share
 29 (23%) used footnotes to disclose contingent liabilities
 29 (23%) were concerned with domestic investments
 26 (21%) disclosed and discussed proposed mergers
 22 (18%) dealt with foreign investments
 20 (16%) discussed assets acquired by merger and purchase of
     companies
 18 (14%) disclosed events subsequent to the balance sheet date
 16 (13%) reviewed accounts receivable
 15 (12%) were concerned with extraordinary items
  8 (6%) disclosed suits in which they are defendants
  8 (6%) discussed deferred credits
  5 (4%) disclosed changes in accounting methods

Events subsequent to the balance sheet date (shown above) can
be important to analysts in assessing the operations for the coming year
or years. Examples of this type of disclosure include information relative
to a material decline in the market value of inventories and investments; settlement of income tax liability or lawsuit which was pending
at the balance sheet date; a material change in the capital structure
resulting from an issuance, conversion, or retirement of capital stock
or a stock split or stock dividend; cash dividend declarations; collection
of receivables; payment of debts; changes in personnel; incurrence or
reduction of indebtedness; unusual losses or gains; sale, purchase, de-
struction, or expansion of plant facilities; and plans for new financing.

Other matters sometimes discussed in footnotes are commitments to
purchase assets, restrictions on the unfettered use of working capital
(by bond indentures, etc.), pledges of assets to secure liabilities.

Audited financial statements

The external analyst does not have access to the accounting records
and, therefore, of necessity depends for his financial and operating infor-

mation on published financial statements. The statements presented to the Securities and Exchange Commission and a relatively large number of those submitted to commercial banks have been audited by independent public accountants. However, the greater proportion of financial statements used as a basis for credit extension have not been audited; in fact, many of these statements are quite loosely prepared.

Audited financial statements are of major importance because they have been compared with the accounting records by independent public accountants; and, in turn, the accounting records have been studied by them. After making his investigation in accordance with generally accepted auditing standards and procedures, the accountant indicates that in his opinion the financial statements present fairly the financial position and operating results in conformity with generally accepted accounting principles, consistently applied. The customary short form auditor's report is shown in Illustration 1–9. This particular certificate shows a qualification inserted by the auditor to modify his report. Auditors sometimes issue long-form reports which contain additional detailed information stretching over several pages.

It is customarily assumed by auditors that the management of the business is responsible for the form and adequacy of financial statements and the independent auditor is responsible for his report. Of course, public accountants do advise management regarding their financial statements, and also assist in other ways. But it is an ethical precept among CPAs that the auditor must not make decisions which are the province of management, on pain of losing his independence. If an auditor is not independent, he is forbidden to attest to the fairness of the financial statements.

In using the expression "present fairly the financial position," the

ILLUSTRATION 1–9. A qualified CPA opinion

Report of Independent Certified Public Accountants

Filter Dynamics-International, Inc.
Cleveland, Ohio

We have examined the consolidated balance sheet of FILTER DYNAMICS INTERNATIONAL, INC. AND SUBSIDIARIES as of November 30, 1971 and 1970, and the related consolidated statements of income, retained earnings, capital in excess of par value and changes in financial position for the years then ended. Our examination was made in accordance with generally accepted auditing standards and accordingly included such tests of the accounting records and such other auditing procedures as we considered necessary in the circumstances. We did not examine the financial statements of Sun Battery Company, Inc., Grand Safgard Automotive Products, Inc. and E-T Industries, Inc., for the current fiscal year or E-T Industries, Inc. for the period ended November 30, 1970, which statements represent total assets and sales constituting 23% and 27%, respectively, of the consolidated total for the current year and 10% and 3% for the prior year. These statements were examined by other auditors whose reports thereon have been fur-

nished to us and our opinion expressed herein, insofar as it relates to the amounts included for the above-mentioned subsidiaries, is based solely upon the report of the other auditors.

In our opinion, based upon our examination and the report of other auditors, and subject to the realization on certain receivables referred to in Note 8, the aforementioned financial statements present fairly the consolidated financial position of Filter Dynamics International, Inc. and Subsidiaries at November 30, 1971 and 1970, and the consolidated results of their operations and the consolidated changes in their financial position for the years then ended in conformity with generally accepted accounting principles applied on a consistent basis.

February 12, 1972   MEADEN & MOORE
Cleveland, Ohio

Certified Public Accountants

auditor has reference to the financial position as shown by the accounting records maintained in accordance with generally accepted accounting principles with due consideration being given to supplementary data which usually appear in footnotes. This opinion does not refer to the dollar amount of owners' equity that would be realized currently if the assets were sold and the liabilities were paid. The auditor does not indicate that the statements are "correct" or "true" in any absolute manner.

If the auditor qualifies his opinion relative to the financial statements, he usually does so by including in the "report" a paragraph to explain his reservations or exceptions as shown in Illustration 1–9.

The annual reports of large U.S. corporations

In the last 50 years the annual reports issued by the major U.S. corporations have developed into elaborate booklets embellished not only with the financial statements and the auditor's report but statistics, graphs, schedules comparing statistics for 5, 10, or even 25 years, and a discussion of the corporation's affairs such as a "President's Letter." It is suggested that the reader obtain the recent annual report of a large U.S. corporation, such as the General Motors Corporation or the American Telephone & Telegraph Company, and study it with care.

Sources of financial and operating data—miscellaneous

Moody's Manuals on railroads, public utilities, industrials, governments and municipals, banks, insurance, real estate, finance, and investment trusts furnish a valuable source of financial, operating, and other corporate data, although the condensed form is of limited value in making a detailed analysis of a business. *Standard & Poor's Corporation* publishes financial statements and financial operating statistics for businesses in general. *Fitch Investor's Service* includes a bond service, a statistical service, and an individual bulletin service, all of which present information and opinions to be used by investors as a basis for judging security values. The *Magazine of Wall Street*, the *Wall Street Journal*, the *Commercial and Financial Chronicle*, *Barron's*, and the *New York Times* supply additional material which is useful in the analysis of specific businesses.

Dun & Bradstreet publishes annually ratios which are drawn from a sampling of results in 125 lines of business; and the Robert Morris Associates, a banker-oriented service organization, publishes annually balance sheets which are reasonably representative of various lines of business. The Dun & Bradstreet ratios for 1970 are reproduced in Illustration 1–10.

ILLUSTRATION 1-10

RETAILING

Line of Business (and number of concerns reporting)	Current assets to current debt	Net profits on net sales	Net profits on tangible net worth	Net profits on net working capital	Net sales to tangible net worth	Net sales to net working capital	Collection period	Net sales to inventory	Fixed assets to tangible net worth	Current debt to tangible net worth	Total debt to tangible net worth	Inventory to net working capital	Current debt to inventory	Funded debts to net working capital
	Times	Per cent	Per cent	Per cent	Times	Times	Days	Times	Per cent	Per cent	Per cent	Per cent	Per cent	Per cent
5641 Children's & Infants' Wear Stores (43)	3.21	3.85	14.15	15.85	6.23	9.46	**	6.8	5.9	36.7	88.8	83.7	39.4	23.3
	2.58	2.49	9.18	10.17	4.44	5.50	**	4.9	11.6	57.9	106.0	124.8	68.3	27.6
	1.63	0.77	3.04	4.31	3.70	4.19	**	3.8	22.2	94.8	188.3	195.1	96.2	72.1
5611 Clothing & Furnishings, Men's & Boys' (205)	4.81	4.02	13.15	15.18	4.56	5.08	**	5.9	5.0	24.5	60.9	60.2	36.9	14.9
	2.84	2.36	6.62	7.29	3.11	3.54	**	4.0	11.3	44.8	107.1	94.2	63.6	27.7
	1.99	0.60	2.24	2.41	2.15	2.63	**	2.8	21.3	92.8	169.3	123.0	89.7	42.7
5311 Department Stores (243)	4.37	3.11	10.39	13.29	4.65	5.98	**	7.1	11.7	22.5	49.1	58.3	46.0	14.6
	2.82	1.91	6.04	7.69	3.30	4.15	**	5.6	25.4	40.7	78.1	80.2	69.3	37.3
	1.92	0.85	3.02	3.72	2.40	3.14	**	4.3	48.6	65.4	135.4	112.6	100.0	77.7
Discount Stores (224)	2.56	2.86	17.01	23.94	8.80	11.96	**	7.2	12.4	56.8	83.7	101.4	56.5	11.6
	1.87	1.63	11.54	15.67	6.10	7.64	**	5.3	24.0	88.1	128.3	157.9	75.0	29.0
	1.49	0.76	5.87	7.04	4.49	5.28	**	3.9	46.6	130.9	209.3	218.2	94.0	70.3
Discount Stores, Leased Departments (57)	2.14	2.70	15.76	22.53	9.19	10.73	**	7.0	13.2	64.8	82.3	108.7	58.0	7.7
	1.83	1.22	9.86	10.95	6.50	8.22	**	4.9	22.7	108.2	120.7	173.0	75.0	25.8
	1.45	0.16	2.97	3.47	5.16	5.53	**	3.0	39.0	169.7	247.3	237.8	97.4	42.3
5651 Family Clothing Stores (94)	4.56	3.92	14.53	15.08	5.68	6.83	**	6.4	6.7	23.4	54.4	59.2	38.7	17.1
	2.94	2.48	7.87	8.26	3.48	4.05	**	4.5	12.9	43.7	122.0	94.4	61.5	38.0
	1.91	0.80	3.53	4.79	2.38	2.79	**	3.4	33.4	89.2	172.2	151.4	85.2	59.6
5252 Farm Equipment Dealers (92)	2.50	3.07	15.67	19.29	7.06	8.50	17	4.6	7.8	65.0	119.5	96.2	62.6	17.5
	1.67	1.70	8.01	8.69	4.78	5.53	30	2.9	18.1	137.3	227.4	174.5	81.3	28.6
	1.35	0.81	2.50	3.46	2.64	3.15	55	2.1	28.7	242.8	374.8	294.2	100.7	60.7
5969 Farm & Garden Supply Stores (76)	3.95	4.49	16.13	28.27	4.91	12.27	**	17.1	20.0	21.0	55.0	45.2	54.5	19.9
	2.23	2.51	9.12	16.18	3.36	6.45	**	9.1	43.9	46.9	89.8	75.8	120.7	53.3
	1.50	1.42	4.29	7.56	2.30	4.06	**	5.7	64.1	73.4	116.4	114.9	213.3	124.2
5712 Furniture Stores (183)	6.33	4.38	10.10	12.34	4.37	5.58	46	6.2	3.6	19.7	52.6	34.3	50.2	8.5
	2.81	2.22	5.85	6.46	2.45	2.75	92	4.6	10.6	52.4	87.2	63.0	90.3	18.5
	1.76	0.64	1.77	2.03	1.67	1.69	202	3.6	21.8	91.8	163.9	121.8	129.5	39.3
5541 Gasoline Service Stations (70)	3.84	4.14	11.23	33.04	5.22	13.13	**	23.9	23.9	17.0	34.2	41.9	69.9	22.6
	2.33	2.51	7.82	19.93	3.22	6.93	**	9.9	46.6	32.4	61.8	82.6	128.2	56.2
	1.47	1.13	4.77	10.88	1.83	4.54	**	6.1	66.4	66.5	113.3	120.8	191.9	139.7
5411 Grocery Stores (137)	2.35	1.71	15.47	48.19	13.51	39.52	**	22.9	38.7	34.2	64.2	85.5	67.9	27.4
	1.66	0.99	10.30	23.12	9.70	21.65	**	16.8	67.4	58.3	106.4	136.1	94.0	72.6
	1.27	0.63	7.28	15.51	6.89	13.00	**	12.8	90.9	84.1	169.5	233.5	124.1	184.0
5251 Hardware Stores (97)	7.82	4.35	12.45	14.54	4.30	4.59	**	5.4	5.8	11.1	44.1	62.1	25.2	15.3
	3.81	2.52	6.94	8.80	2.59	3.15	**	3.9	14.7	25.3	63.0	82.7	46.0	31.4
	2.19	0.98	2.83	3.76	1.71	2.24	**	3.0	35.3	74.3	113.3	113.2	76.1	66.3
5722 Household Appliance Stores (92)	3.13	2.80	12.50	15.47	7.04	9.15	22	8.4	7.9	36.2	72.4	61.6	64.5	10.7
	2.12	1.61	8.09	9.80	4.21	5.44	35	5.6	15.7	77.8	144.1	101.7	103.6	23.7
	1.52	0.52	3.54	4.37	2.97	3.66	66	4.2	32.3	138.7	254.8	155.5	126.8	65.9
5971 Jewelry Stores (71)	5.93	5.08	11.82	12.41	3.06	3.20	**	4.0	2.8	19.4	40.6	59.0	30.4	10.3
	3.09	2.98	6.53	6.88	2.09	2.44	**	2.9	10.7	36.0	57.1	82.4	57.2	27.9
	2.34	1.34	3.87	4.18	1.53	1.73	**	2.2	28.7	73.4	124.0	118.8	81.5	45.4
5211 Lumber & Other Bldg. Mtls. Dealers (197)	5.61	3.28	8.98	12.56	4.15	5.86	41	8.5	13.7	16.9	55.9	49.5	38.9	15.0
	3.03	1.43	4.67	6.19	2.89	3.81	56	5.4	25.0	37.1	88.1	69.8	71.9	32.7
	2.10	0.41	1.21	1.71	1.91	2.58	79	4.0	47.5	66.4	126.8	98.4	119.7	61.7
5399 Miscellaneous General Mdse. Stores (84)	5.34	5.40	16.37	21.69	5.71	7.15	**	6.3	8.1	22.6	55.1	58.8	32.6	16.2
	2.91	2.92	10.16	12.83	3.46	3.91	**	4.3	16.0	41.3	101.1	89.3	60.5	34.5
	1.92	1.06	4.02	4.69	1.79	2.44	**	3.4	39.0	77.2	160.9	148.7	94.0	51.1
5511 Motor Vehicle Dealers (102)	2.53	1.60	12.44	20.33	12.19	17.99	**	12.6	9.3	50.3	79.3	93.1	66.5	10.4
	1.82	0.86	6.77	11.66	8.23	11.53	**	7.6	27.2	76.1	126.9	138.5	83.6	42.4
	1.40	0.21	2.15	3.27	5.34	8.37	**	5.6	53.3	157.3	278.8	228.5	104.7	87.0
5231 Paint, Glass & Wallpaper Stores (36)	4.64	3.38	12.83	17.54	5.15	6.22	**	10.7	11.4	18.9	36.2	34.3	44.4	12.8
	2.99	2.41	8.08	10.00	3.14	4.23	**	6.3	17.8	38.8	58.9	63.8	75.0	30.9
	2.28	0.80	3.23	5.61	2.34	3.13	**	5.2	33.0	62.1	86.6	98.9	126.6	49.6
5661 Shoe Stores (102)	6.04	4.44	12.16	13.84	4.45	5.66	**	5.0	4.3	15.7	50.2	71.9	26.4	6.6
	3.52	2.10	6.26	7.55	3.18	3.73	**	3.9	10.3	33.2	75.3	102.3	45.3	16.8
	2.38	0.78	2.85	3.28	2.14	2.65	**	2.9	23.1	61.5	141.4	134.1	69.1	38.3
5531 Tire, Battery & Accessory Stores (67)	3.28	4.50	15.63	19.13	5.38	9.48	**	8.9	13.6	27.5	68.1	64.0	51.7	19.4
	2.21	1.89	8.42	10.83	4.10	5.69	**	6.1	29.0	65.1	120.0	88.8	102.7	32.6
	1.31	0.86	4.01	4.59	2.48	3.24	**	4.4	57.1	141.6	199.8	160.1	169.0	57.8
5331 Variety Stores (68)	4.78	3.63	13.42	17.60	5.38	7.16	**	5.7	10.7	21.2	35.8	95.8	31.8	6.7
	2.97	2.12	8.55	9.83	3.75	4.67	**	4.5	22.2	39.1	61.1	113.2	45.7	17.6
	2.32	1.14	3.77	4.56	2.61	3.42	**	3.5	34.9	60.8	94.7	136.6	60.0	45.0
5621 Women's Ready-to-Wear Stores (181)	4.26	3.71	14.45	18.71	6.17	7.74	**	9.4	7.4	24.1	67.1	45.2	58.1	13.0
	2.38	1.86	7.14	9.98	3.76	4.90	**	6.7	17.5	54.5	124.1	71.1	93.9	34.0
	1.74	0.44	2.53	3.36	2.52	3.23	**	5.2	40.2	98.0	172.4	121.3	129.5	66.7

* Not computed. Necessary information as to the division between cash sales and credit sales was available in too few cases to obtain an average collection period usable as a broad guide.

ILLUSTRATION 1–10 (continued)

How the Ratios are Figured

Although terms like "median" and "quartile" are everyday working language to statisticians, their precise meaning may be vague to some businessmen.

In the various ratio tables, three figures appear under each ratio heading. The center figure in bold type is the **median**; the figures immediately above and below the median are, respectively, the **upper** and **lower quartiles**. To understand their use, the reader should also know how they are calculated.

First, year-end financial statements from concerns in the survey (almost exclusively corporations with a tangible net worth over $100,000) are analyzed by Dun & Bradstreet statisticians. Then each of 14 ratios is calculated individually for every concern in the sample.

These individual ratio figures, entered on data-processing cards, are segregated by line of business, and then arranged in order of size—the best ratio at the top, the weakest at the bottom. The figure that falls in the middle of this series becomes the **median** for that ratio in that line of business. The figure halfway between the median and the top of the series is the **upper quartile**; the number halfway between the median and the bottom of the series is the **lower quartile**.

In a statistical sense, each median then is the **typical ratio figure** for all concerns studied in a given line. The upper and lower quartile figures typify the experience of firms in the top and bottom halves of the sample respectively.

CURRENT ASSETS TO CURRENT DEBT
Current Assets are divided by total Current Debt. Current Assets are the sum of cash, notes and accounts receivable (less reserves for bad debt), advances on merchandise, merchandise inventories, and Listed, Federal, State and Municipal securities not in excess of market value. Current Debt is the total of all liabilities falling due within one year. This is one test of solvency.

NET PROFITS ON NET SALES
Obtained by dividing the net earnings of the business, after taxes, by net sales (the dollar volume less returns, allowances, and cash discounts). This important yardstick in measuring profitability should be related to the ratio which follows.

NET PROFITS ON TANGIBLE NET WORTH
Tangible Net Worth is the equity of the stockholders in the business, as obtained by subtracting total liabilities from total assets, and then deducting intangibles. The ratio is obtained by dividing Net Profits after taxes by Tangible Net Worth. Tendency is to look increasingly to this ratio as a final criterion of profitability. Generally, a relationship of at least 10 per cent is regarded as a desirable objective for providing dividends plus funds for future growth.

NET PROFITS ON NET WORKING CAPITAL
Net Working Capital represents the excess of Current Assets over Current Debt. This margin represents the cushion available to the business for carrying inventories and receivables, and for financing day-to-day operations. The ratio is obtained by dividing Net Profits, after taxes, by Net Working Capital.

NET SALES TO TANGIBLE NET WORTH
Net Sales are divided by Tangible Net Worth. This gives a measure of relative turnover of invested capital.

NET SALES TO NET WORKING CAPITAL
Net Sales are divided by Net Working Capital. This provides a guide as to the extent the company is turning its working capital and the margin of operating funds.

COLLECTION PERIOD
Annual net sales are divided by 365 days to obtain average daily credit sales and then the average daily credit sales are divided into notes and accounts receivable, including any discounted. This ratio is helpful in analyzing the collectibility of receivables. Many feel the collection period should not exceed

the net maturity indicated by selling terms by more than 10 to 15 days. When comparing the collection period of one concern with that of another, allowances should be made for possible variations in selling terms.

NET SALES TO INVENTORY
Dividing annual Net Sales by Merchandise Inventory as carried on the balance sheet. This quotient does not yield an actual physical turnover. It provides a yardstick for comparing stock-to-sales ratios of one concern with another or with those for the industry.

FIXED ASSETS TO TANGIBLE NET WORTH
Fixed Assets are divided by Tangible Net Worth. Fixed Assets represent depreciated book values of building, leasehold improvements, machinery, furniture, fixtures, tools, and other physical equipment, plus land, if any, and valued at cost or appraised market value. Ordinarily, this relationship should not exceed 100 percent for a manufacturer, and 75 percent for a wholesaler or retailer.

CURRENT DEBT TO TANGIBLE NET WORTH
Derived by dividing Current Debt by Tangible Net Worth. Ordinarily, a business begins to pile up trouble when this relationship exceeds 80 percent.

TOTAL DEBT TO TANGIBLE NET WORTH
Obtained by dividing total current plus long term debts by Tangible Net Worth. When this relationship exceeds 100 percent, the equity of creditors in the assets of the business exceeds that of owners.

INVENTORY TO NET WORKING CAPITAL
Merchandise inventory is divided by Net Working Capital. This is an additional measure of inventory balance. Ordinarily, the relationship should not exceed 80 percent.

CURRENT DEBT TO INVENTORY
Dividing the Current Debt by Inventory yields yet another indication of the extent to which the business relies on funds from disposal of unsold inventories to meet its debts.

FUNDED DEBTS TO WORKING CAPITAL
Funded Debts are all long term obligations, as represented by mortgages, bonds, debentures, term loans, serial notes, and other types of liabilities maturing more than one year from statement date. This ratio is obtained by dividing Funded Debt by Net Working Capital. Analysts tend to compare Funded Debts with Net Working Capital in determining whether or not long term debts are in proper proportion. Ordinarily, this relationship should not exceed 100 percent.

WHOLESALING

Line of Business (and number of concerns reporting)	Current assets to current debt	Net profits on net sales	Net profits on tangible net worth	Net profits on net working capital	Net sales to tangible net worth	Net sales to net working capital	Collection period	Net sales to inventory	Fixed assets to tangible net worth	Current debt to tangible net worth	Total debt to tangible net worth	Inventory to net working capital	Current debt to inventory	Funded debts to net working capital
	Times	Per cent	Per cent	Per cent	Times	Times	Days	Times	Per cent	Per cent	Per cent	Per cent	Per cent	Per cent
5077	3.34	4.35	18.56	19.22	8.20	8.87	37	9.0	4.2	39.2	58.6	63.8	57.6	10.5
Air Condtg. & Refrigtn.	2.13	2.78	13.91	14.23	4.64	5.60	50	6.3	11.3	66.4	99.9	90.9	88.6	23.8
Equipt. & Supplies (53)	1.57	1.58	7.89	9.84	3.25	3.84	64	3.9	25.6	184.4	270.8	134.7	165.6	57.0
5013	3.90	3.46	15.18	18.52	5.34	6.49	28	6.7	6.3	30.9	54.8	72.3	46.6	12.3
Automotive Equipment	2.62	2.20	9.21	11.28	3.92	4.59	34	5.1	13.1	50.4	90.4	92.6	65.2	28.1
(184)	1.95	1.15	4.76	5.78	2.90	3.52	45	3.9	26.9	81.0	145.8	129.0	97.4	53.2
5095	3.07	2.00	14.24	27.66	10.97	18.91	7	15.3	10.2	30.9	59.7	69.2	62.2	21.7
Beer, Wine & Alcoholic	1.87	1.11	8.21	13.19	7.38	10.94	24	9.6	26.7	77.9	138.7	114.1	99.7	41.2
Beverages (88)	1.41	0.43	3.29	5.67	5.11	7.58	36	6.3	54.0	162.5	241.3	197.3	132.3	61.8
5029	3.08	2.88	15.77	28.89	8.27	17.21	37	15.9	12.7	33.9	95.0	46.1	94.7	32.6
Chemicals & Allied	1.74	1.39	8.42	15.63	5.90	8.52	51	11.7	28.2	60.9	162.8	82.1	138.6	57.9
Products (49)	1.43	0.42	4.78	5.76	3.02	5.95	65	7.7	48.4	140.1	234.0	123.9	236.1	96.3
5037	4.32	2.43	12.97	15.87	8.60	11.11	30	20.5	1.9	26.8	84.1	40.3	60.8	14.7
Clothing & Accessories,	2.17	1.23	8.05	11.01	5.78	5.97	45	9.7	6.6	76.8	124.0	69.3	131.7	34.9
Women's & Child's (64)	1.73	0.23	2.07	2.34	3.65	3.88	59	5.6	19.7	128.8	196.8	104.6	212.0	47.3
5036	3.51	1.67	8.37	8.99	7.37	8.32	34	8.0	2.1	36.6	49.0	73.4	56.5	9.3
Clothing & Furnishings,	2.34	0.53	2.59	2.80	5.35	6.00	48	5.2	6.4	70.8	119.5	87.7	80.8	21.0
Men's & Boys' (51)	1.79	0.04	0.16	0.39	2.85	3.34	71	3.8	15.7	124.6	148.4	125.1	120.0	24.2
5081	3.66	2.60	14.36	15.74	7.49	7.68	45	10.3	4.8	30.9	78.0	57.6	66.1	6.7
Commercial Machines	1.98	1.36	6.47	8.32	4.98	5.82	59	7.7	12.6	77.2	101.7	73.2	109.0	18.6
& Equipment (54)	1.58	0.37	1.10	2.12	3.04	3.79	75	5.4	26.6	128.5	212.0	107.1	180.5	48.3

ILLUSTRATION 1–10 (continued)

WHOLESALING

Line of Business (and number of concerns reporting)	Current assets to current debt	Net profits on net sales	Net profits on tangible net worth	Net profits on net working capital	Net sales to tangible net worth	Net sales to net working capital	Collection period	Net sales to inventory	Fixed assets to tangible net worth	Current debt to tangible net worth	Total debt to tangible net worth	Inventory to net working capital	Current debt to inventory	Funded debts to net working capital
	Times	Per cent	Per cent	Per cent	Times	Times	Days	Times	Per cent	Per cent	Per cent	Per cent	Per cent	Per cent
5045	3.87	1.67	10.76	14.72	16.13	19.32	11	19.2	6.9	38.1	111.1	57.6	57.0	14.5
Confectionery	2.26	0.43	7.53	9.52	10.68	11.99	18	12.8	13.4	70.9	158.4	98.1	84.1	33.8
(35)	1.73	0.25	3.89	4.01	6.39	7.35	27	10.3	30.0	125.4	227.7	129.4	124.8	74.3
5043	3.10	2.00	14.87	26.81	11.88	26.22	21	56.4	11.2	27.5	52.7	23.1	101.5	18.2
Dairy Products	2.06	0.97	9.99	15.60	8.09	11.84	28	25.7	36.0	58.5	139.9	36.7	161.8	29.8
(54)	1.41	0.56	3.89	6.44	5.05	9.23	33	15.6	60.6	104.5	187.8	92.0	459.5	94.2
5022	3.17	1.70	10.33	12.29	8.53	8.75	27	8.0	7.0	40.3	76.5	75.8	58.6	15.1
Drugs & Druggists'	2.22	1.17	6.78	7.52	6.19	6.60	35	6.7	14.7	74.9	123.1	102.3	77.5	25.0
Sundries (103)	1.72	0.65	3.95	4.77	4.54	5.14	44	5.8	31.5	122.8	194.8	129.0	104.1	51.4
5064	2.70	1.97	9.88	11.50	7.70	9.83	33	7.2	4.2	48.3	95.4	76.9	74.2	12.2
Electrical Appliances, TV	1.96	1.16	6.35	7.16	5.85	6.45	42	5.8	9.0	90.3	152.0	115.0	101.5	27.7
& Radio Sets (94)	1.54	0.56	3.25	4.00	4.23	4.88	54	5.0	20.4	156.6	224.2	159.2	120.5	48.3
5063	3.01	2.27	13.29	15.65	8.33	9.49	35	9.9	5.3	42.9	72.7	72.5	71.2	6.6
Electrical Apparatus &	2.14	1.27	7.38	8.81	5.98	6.56	43	7.6	12.7	79.2	112.3	89.5	104.2	17.5
Equipment (150)	1.65	0.68	4.01	4.61	3.72	4.58	54	5.5	25.8	133.3	163.6	115.6	138.3	33.4
5065	2.96	3.55	12.48	13.00	6.30	7.06	30	5.5	6.1	47.8	85.2	81.5	52.1	8.8
Electronic Parts &	2.32	1.86	7.38	9.03	4.50	4.79	42	4.6	12.9	77.2	124.1	105.7	74.3	24.6
Equipment (47)	1.90	0.95	3.83	4.23	3.18	3.47	52	3.3	24.5	111.0	174.5	138.0	92.0	54.5
5083	3.70	2.89	13.97	17.67	6.70	7.95	32	7.5	7.0	28.7	54.2	65.0	62.7	4.7
Farm Machinery &	2.06	1.82	7.37	10.03	4.98	5.58	45	5.5	12.3	73.7	128.1	102.1	88.9	19.4
Equipment (56)	1.64	0.64	3.54	4.74	2.81	3.60	68	3.7	33.0	126.6	181.2	137.1	123.6	50.4
5039	2.54	3.31	14.48	15.77	7.27	8.00	41	9.9	1.1	62.9	85.5	57.5	71.9	6.7
Footwear	2.03	2.02	9.44	10.32	4.52	5.22	62	5.7	4.2	85.1	142.8	89.9	113.0	13.0
(58)	1.60	1.09	5.09	5.30	3.24	3.42	75	4.0	7.5	149.3	211.6	123.1	157.0	49.2
5048	3.11	2.03	15.32	44.37	12.66	22.34	13	103.0	17.1	23.9	48.9	15.7	138.3	16.9
Fresh Fruits &	2.11	1.14	7.81	14.87	8.67	12.67	21	43.0	37.0	53.3	82.5	38.4	268.1	29.7
Vegetables (64)	1.12	0.15	1.88	6.54	5.54	7.99	37	19.8	79.0	90.3	162.7	75.5	702.2	71.0
5097	3.22	3.08	11.15	15.50	7.29	8.25	38	10.4	6.6	39.2	75.2	50.9	72.0	14.2
Furniture & Home	1.78	1.50	6.85	7.52	4.68	5.34	51	7.1	15.8	79.0	133.8	81.2	107.3	23.1
Furnishings (78)	1.58	0.34	2.30	2.50	3.31	4.22	70	5.3	28.5	155.6	201.0	122.2	167.9	51.6
5041	3.26	1.09	12.47	17.90	21.15	26.66	7	17.5	10.6	35.9	89.0	88.6	50.3	16.9
Groceries, General	2.13	0.58	7.70	8.67	13.09	16.39	12	12.6	26.1	76.4	138.1	120.9	77.0	41.3
Line (199)	1.59	0.24	3.84	4.43	7.52	10.03	17	9.7	63.1	133.0	236.0	168.8	110.5	80.2
5072	4.30	2.45	8.02	10.09	5.86	6.98	33	6.3	6.2	24.8	45.8	75.7	40.2	6.1
Hardware	2.78	1.30	5.16	6.28	3.68	4.40	42	4.7	14.4	48.5	77.1	94.7	60.9	16.9
(181)	1.89	0.59	2.18	2.76	2.60	3.10	52	3.5	26.9	86.9	139.4	121.1	93.9	33.1
5084	3.01	2.65	11.84	14.73	7.24	9.45	31	10.1	9.8	39.7	72.4	58.5	65.5	10.3
Industrial Machinery	2.21	1.26	6.07	6.42	4.66	5.85	44	6.3	23.3	63.8	103.9	89.8	91.2	24.1
& Equipment (107)	1.61	0.41	1.18	2.11	3.12	3.81	54	4.2	41.5	132.1	203.9	111.6	144.8	77.8
5098	4.30	2.50	9.82	16.10	7.64	9.28	34	10.5	10.6	23.5	61.0	53.4	46.9	16.0
Lumber & Construction	2.71	1.29	5.89	7.28	4.40	5.14	43	6.9	22.0	51.5	109.7	80.0	95.1	28.4
Materials (153)	1.67	0.44	2.31	2.47	2.77	3.67	58	5.5	39.9	104.5	183.4	107.6	143.9	50.9
5047	2.67	1.81	21.12	30.13	23.84	35.10	13	100.4	10.2	36.2	78.7	24.2	133.1	19.9
Meats & Meat	2.01	0.86	11.58	19.05	16.01	23.45	19	44.9	28.8	76.3	107.4	57.7	210.0	31.7
Products (45)	1.48	0.27	6.63	9.87	9.80	15.15	24	29.9	50.7	116.0	277.4	79.5	329.2	69.2
5091	3.68	2.74	10.84	16.09	5.69	7.19	37	7.2	11.6	29.7	44.7	65.2	51.5	9.6
Metals & Minerals	2.37	1.95	7.11	9.17	4.05	5.12	44	5.0	30.1	54.4	84.8	89.5	87.5	22.7
(76)	1.56	1.06	4.09	5.28	2.64	3.72	57	4.1	46.9	110.9	145.1	129.4	114.5	45.0
5028	4.93	2.36	8.42	11.38	4.91	6.49	28	7.4	9.2	16.6	36.3	58.6	44.1	9.3
Paints & Varnishes	2.60	1.30	5.55	6.47	3.85	4.65	38	6.0	19.8	33.9	67.1	84.5	75.3	26.9
(41)	2.06	0.66	2.36	3.00	2.40	3.01	51	4.6	32.7	68.4	106.8	100.1	102.7	51.5
5096	3.49	2.21	11.22	13.10	7.85	10.19	29	11.8	6.5	31.3	61.6	56.8	59.1	12.5
Paper & Its	2.44	1.21	6.86	7.70	5.33	6.78	40	8.1	14.3	51.6	92.9	80.5	87.8	23.5
Products (120)	1.77	0.53	3.04	4.03	3.58	4.51	49	6.5	31.5	98.6	161.3	102.7	134.2	52.7
5092	3.10	3.13	14.39	41.55	8.01	18.64	23	33.7	35.3	24.2	44.5	28.4	112.1	20.2
Petroleum & Petroleum	2.01	1.68	8.80	22.34	4.29	10.02	33	21.8	56.6	38.1	76.3	56.7	188.3	46.7
Products (85)	1.37	0.78	3.44	9.81	3.09	6.07	48	12.4	86.1	85.9	160.1	93.7	327.6	128.6
5033	3.09	2.46	10.79	11.60	7.41	8.07	31	10.2	2.2	45.2	76.9	58.1	58.6	12.4
Piece Goods	2.11	1.25	5.87	6.54	4.48	5.23	47	6.3	5.8	80.4	111.6	87.8	94.6	22.3
(117)	1.69	0.45	2.48	2.87	3.36	3.51	65	4.3	17.0	117.6	174.9	126.5	165.9	46.0
5074	3.91	2.48	10.40	13.05	5.75	6.74	37	7.3	7.1	29.7	51.0	67.6	50.3	7.8
Plumbing & Heating	2.65	1.62	6.71	7.61	4.17	5.14	46	5.6	14.0	53.0	91.6	85.2	77.4	18.1
Equip. & Sup. (183)	1.90	0.78	3.12	3.64	2.90	3.53	58	4.4	27.8	95.1	156.6	112.5	107.3	33.7
5044	3.89	1.58	13.96	23.43	16.51	31.83	15	81.3	16.4	26.1	44.8	24.2	93.6	23.2
Poultry & Poultry	2.31	0.79	8.89	13.82	9.54	19.27	20	54.9	38.0	44.6	60.7	39.0	173.5	42.0
Products (42)	1.54	0.47	4.64	8.54	5.08	11.07	31	18.8	70.1	103.2	167.9	100.5	379.9	172.9
5093	3.78	3.74	13.87	26.60	6.91	12.78	16	26.4	13.8	18.6	52.8	25.3	75.1	17.9
Scrap & Waste	2.45	2.10	7.82	13.94	4.46	8.02	27	15.5	37.0	34.4	86.7	50.7	127.6	36.1
Materials (59)	1.71	1.06	4.47	6.36	2.87	5.20	35	10.0	63.1	78.0	176.5	91.3	252.9	74.5
5014	2.77	3.52	14.09	18.35	7.27	8.70	33	7.0	15.8	52.9	134.4	78.6	82.6	15.0
Tires & Tubes	1.81	1.74	8.36	9.97	5.34	6.22	42	5.3	25.9	111.7	164.9	112.3	118.8	55.5
(38)	1.47	0.66	2.21	3.67	3.59	4.33	62	4.3	57.5	147.2	193.3	157.0	161.7	73.9
5094	2.61	1.00	14.07	18.41	22.71	31.14	12	24.2	7.7	53.4	95.5	70.2	81.3	14.5
Tobacco & Its	1.88	0.72	8.00	10.98	14.08	18.20	16	18.7	14.9	86.2	141.8	95.4	116.6	25.4
Products (92)	1.43	0.30	4.36	6.22	9.16	11.54	24	14.0	30.3	159.3	225.7	165.2	175.1	46.4

ILLUSTRATION 1–10 (continued)

MANUFACTURING & CONSTRUCTION

Line of Business (and number of concerns reporting)	Current assets to current debt	Net profits on net sales	Net profits on tangible net worth	Net profits on net working capital	Net sales to tangible net worth	Net sales to net working capital	Collection period	Net sales to inventory	Fixed assets to tangible net worth	Current debt to tangible net worth	Total debt to tangible net worth	Inventory to net working capital	Current debt to inventory	Funded debts to net working capital
	Times	Per cent	Per cent	Per cent	Times	Times	Days	Times	Per cent	Per cent	Per cent	Per cent	Per cent	Per cent
2871–72–79 Agricultural Chemicals (43)	2.86	4.53	13.77	29.57	4.04	17.62	37	12.8	29.8	28.8	69.4	35.6	90.6	17.9
	1.84	2.05	8.24	14.00	2.49	5.35	59	8.7	47.5	52.7	135.0	89.6	135.3	118.3
	1.18	0.89	2.75	5.25	3.33	3.33	100	5.3	82.3	91.6	218.2	168.3	243.4	201.1
3722–23–29 Airplane Parts & Accessories (68)	3.43	3.73	9.16	13.59	3.37	5.94	38	8.1	36.7	23.0	51.7	59.0	68.2	27.6
	2.42	1.91	4.46	5.58	2.35	4.08	53	5.2	56.0	36.9	78.9	82.6	100.0	69.0
	1.59	0.07	0.20	0.27	1.89	3.04	74	3.8	81.9	80.0	135.6	135.6	126.7	98.9
2051–52 Bakery Products (65)	2.94	2.85	9.98	43.54	5.73	24.22	17	41.2	57.0	16.6	38.1	33.7	134.7	23.9
	1.94	1.22	5.85	22.02	4.22	13.20	22	30.0	71.6	29.9	52.6	60.3	196.8	63.0
	1.40	0.57	2.62	12.51	3.17	9.06	30	18.4	93.9	44.1	87.9	86.0	303.7	152.5
3312–13–15–16–17 Blast Furnaces, Steel Wks. & Rolling Mills (71)	3.31	5.81	10.54	23.42	2.92	5.56	38	7.5	31.5	14.9	38.8	72.5	57.2	31.8
	2.40	3.07	6.18	13.89	1.96	4.13	44	4.9	59.9	29.7	66.0	90.5	77.6	53.5
	1.50	1.34	3.01	6.19	1.50	3.18	58	4.0	79.8	47.7	99.3	114.0	102.1	132.5
2331 Blouses & Waists, Women's & Misses' (54)	2.13	3.19	23.82	28.84	11.96	16.12	33	22.6	4.4	72.5	86.7	53.3	126.3	7.8
	1.62	1.65	10.50	12.38	9.34	12.33	43	14.3	9.8	136.3	178.4	83.0	174.9	23.1
	1.40	0.64	3.43	4.67	5.85	6.48	56	7.9	18.2	210.5	269.8	120.8	273.2	34.0
2731–32 Books: Publishing, Publishing & Printing (54)	4.21	6.50	13.85	19.68	3.12	4.10	53	6.9	14.1	20.7	37.9	40.6	56.8	7.2
	2.86	3.92	8.22	10.60	2.04	2.86	65	3.9	36.0	43.6	71.7	63.8	81.0	24.2
	1.94	1.50	3.70	4.20	1.43	2.00	100	2.9	48.5	67.6	119.8	86.6	173.8	76.3
2211 Broad Woven Fabrics, Cotton (46)	3.97	3.93	8.68	19.14	2.26	5.79	46	7.7	43.4	12.3	36.7	58.6	50.6	25.6
	3.07	2.75	5.12	11.53	1.92	4.24	58	5.3	58.0	21.2	57.1	74.9	64.6	47.6
	2.13	1.62	2.44	5.32	1.66	3.43	72	3.9	67.1	37.9	97.6	107.3	87.7	71.1
2031–32–33–34–35–36–37 Canned & Preserved Frts, Vegs, Sea Fds (76)	2.93	4.10	14.24	26.51	5.28	12.14	18	7.6	38.1	27.5	73.7	96.8	59.7	21.1
	1.68	2.15	7.73	15.86	3.76	6.74	28	4.3	57.1	70.8	138.9	142.3	90.7	55.2
	1.23	0.84	3.65	4.88	2.20	4.14	37	2.9	88.5	140.9	229.2	294.3	113.2	164.2
2751 Commercial Printing except Lithograph (85)	3.17	3.35	10.46	18.76	4.66	10.82	35	**	41.8	21.5	72.2	**	**	33.8
	2.19	1.37	4.55	8.78	3.04	6.14	45	**	58.5	40.7	104.4	**	**	72.2
	1.62	0.50	1.01	2.41	1.91	4.02	58	**	89.2	69.9	120.9	**	**	159.7
3661–62 Communication Equipment (76)	3.86	4.30	12.61	16.31	3.75	4.83	52	7.0	20.6	24.6	43.1	55.0	56.1	17.4
	2.81	2.66	6.33	8.18	2.46	3.04	63	4.7	39.0	35.9	70.9	73.8	84.7	38.6
	1.65	0.19	0.48	0.59	1.88	2.27	96	3.5	66.4	64.1	131.4	102.7	124.3	76.7
3271–72–73–74–75 Concrete, Gypsum & Plaster Products (81)	3.80	4.79	9.68	36.57	2.93	9.12	36	19.7	42.9	12.0	31.2	33.4	68.2	13.1
	2.68	3.13	6.29	16.53	2.10	5.38	53	10.3	60.6	29.0	61.1	56.5	141.4	42.9
	1.56	1.42	3.66	8.63	1.53	3.77	74	6.2	80.2	57.1	106.2	84.8	328.6	136.6
2071–72–73 Confectionery & Related Products (51)	3.53	4.49	13.31	26.12	5.27	11.63	15	10.1	34.4	20.7	41.0	65.1	50.0	24.2
	2.31	1.78	4.96	9.61	3.65	7.32	24	7.7	55.7	35.9	70.7	94.4	69.5	70.6
	1.48	0.06	0.25	0.76	2.26	4.64	40	5.3	90.7	86.0	184.4	175.1	123.2	166.7
3531–32–33–34–35–36–37 Const., Min. & Hdlg. Machy. & Equip. (82)	3.40	5.01	13.09	21.49	4.26	5.13	39	7.6	20.8	24.5	44.9	68.6	51.9	19.2
	2.37	2.96	7.18	11.16	2.36	3.48	61	4.0	35.7	44.4	87.3	84.2	72.7	38.2
	1.68	1.32	3.47	4.96	1.90	2.50	79	2.9	51.6	96.5	155.6	118.9	128.0	70.9
2641–42–43–44–45–46–47–49 Converted Paper & Paperboard Prods. (76)	3.81	4.25	12.25	24.43	4.63	9.63	33	10.8	41.4	19.0	47.0	49.1	64.0	31.8
	2.70	2.48	7.77	12.26	2.87	5.32	42	7.8	61.1	34.3	75.3	74.6	90.9	62.0
	1.72	0.92	3.12	5.64	1.97	3.47	57	6.2	87.0	73.0	109.4	108.6	133.8	112.3
3421–23–25–29 Cutlery, Hand Tools & General Hardware (99)	5.86	5.57	12.32	19.50	3.20	4.51	33	6.7	27.3	13.2	31.8	56.4	35.9	6.9
	3.39	2.92	6.63	11.55	2.21	3.50	46	4.6	38.9	25.4	59.8	77.9	55.3	35.2
	2.15	1.03	2.17	3.47	1.69	2.70	60	3.3	53.9	47.7	105.2	95.4	86.6	58.4
2021–22–23–24–26 Dairy Products (120)	2.06	2.43	13.23	53.27	8.44	34.14	17	51.9	40.2	27.4	56.6	36.6	142.9	34.1
	1.52	1.22	7.32	23.04	6.07	19.59	26	28.7	61.5	58.4	88.6	66.6	257.1	68.0
	1.21	0.50	3.07	8.88	4.06	10.70	35	16.6	89.8	91.7	149.3	131.6	413.4	114.5
2335 Dresses: Women's, Misses' & Junior's (99)	2.14	2.05	15.99	20.90	11.64	15.08	34	19.3	4.5	66.0	83.2	54.7	124.4	11.8
	1.66	1.03	10.20	12.57	8.10	10.59	52	14.4	9.2	122.6	148.5	81.0	182.2	22.6
	1.39	0.37	2.80	3.45	4.70	6.21	60	7.5	20.0	208.3	216.9	124.6	277.1	43.7
2831–33–34 Drugs (66)	3.78	8.96	21.30	38.05	3.30	6.68	40	8.4	23.5	22.9	32.8	53.3	64.7	15.4
	2.36	4.77	12.19	18.59	2.14	4.20	58	6.0	38.6	31.4	56.9	67.1	96.9	34.0
	1.45	2.26	5.08	8.65	1.74	2.89	89	4.2	62.1	50.7	96.6	134.2	112.1	98.8
3641–42–43–44 Electric Lighting & Wiring Equipment (59)	4.32	4.40	12.94	17.54	3.87	6.79	38	7.6	14.9	19.5	37.7	57.0	44.7	11.3
	3.10	2.93	7.98	11.46	2.79	4.15	45	5.4	39.6	36.4	59.9	77.2	68.1	29.2
	1.88	1.02	3.22	5.59	1.95	3.07	55	4.0	58.5	54.8	101.4	107.8	107.1	54.9
3611–12–13 Electric Transmission & Distribution Equipment (61)	3.66	4.34	10.68	13.89	3.71	5.81	49	5.5	22.5	24.7	53.6	74.6	44.7	21.6
	2.77	2.81	6.69	9.02	2.52	3.31	61	3.8	40.9	41.6	82.6	90.1	73.2	37.7
	1.82	0.41	1.29	2.21	1.81	2.13	78	2.9	59.8	78.0	151.8	122.4	99.6	68.9
3621–22–23–24–29 Electrical Industrial Apparatus (54)	4.48	4.26	12.51	20.70	4.01	6.84	39	6.8	31.7	21.6	33.2	64.1	42.9	8.6
	2.64	2.78	7.63	10.73	2.80	3.69	51	4.8	45.2	34.5	72.8	84.8	73.8	46.8
	1.78	1.15	2.65	3.85	2.11	2.96	68	3.7	69.4	76.8	134.0	109.1	96.5	87.4
1731 Electrical Work (135)	3.21	3.51	15.17	20.50	8.53	13.30	**	**	11.8	35.0	50.0	**	**	6.7
	2.09	1.74	8.71	11.65	5.14	7.20	**	**	20.3	66.2	108.9	**	**	17.4
	1.44	0.67	3.72	5.60	3.43	4.56	**	**	38.8	134.2	205.0	**	**	41.4
3671–72–73–74–79 Electronic Components & Accessories (96)	3.34	3.41	9.85	16.22	4.29	5.87	42	6.8	27.0	30.8	64.9	62.3	62.0	28.0
	2.41	1.71	4.67	6.65	2.68	4.05	55	4.8	48.4	49.0	102.8	82.1	87.8	60.3
	1.79	(3.64)	(11.64)	(12.56)	1.89	2.87	71	3.4	79.1	77.3	160.4	107.4	128.5	92.6
3811 Engineering, Laboratory & Scientific Instruments (41)	5.18	5.83	11.40	15.43	2.57	3.36	52	4.7	28.0	15.9	47.6	54.6	34.9	16.7
	3.43	2.11	5.74	7.69	2.06	2.50	67	3.8	41.9	34.5	84.9	71.1	60.6	43.3
	2.31	(1.26)	(2.78)	(4.17)	1.78	2.16	86	2.8	61.1	65.2	136.0	90.8	81.7	70.1

** Not computed. Printers carry only current supplies such as paper, ink, and binding materials rather than merchandise inventories for re-sale. Building Trades contractors have no inventories in the credit sense of the term. As a general rule, such contractors have no customary selling terms, each contract being a special job for which individual terms are arranged.

ILLUSTRATION 1–10 (continued)

MANUFACTURING & CONSTRUCTION

Line of Business (and number of concerns reporting)	Current assets to current debt	Net profits on net sales	Net profits on tangible net worth	Net profits on net working capital	Net sales to tangible net worth	Net sales to net working capital	Collection period	Net sales to inventory	Fixed assets to tangible net worth	Current debt to tangible net worth	Total debt to tangible net worth	Inventory to net working capital	Current debt to inventory	Funded debts to net working capital
	Times	Per cent	Per cent	Per cent	Times	Times	Days	Times	Per cent	Per cent	Per cent	Per cent	Per cent	Per cent
3441–42–43–44–46–49 Fabricated Structural Metal Products (128)	4.02	3.52	11.04	17.28	4.82	6.95	42	12.1	24.1	26.3	51.5	46.9	62.5	16.1
	2.44	1.53	4.85	7.49	3.06	4.67	52	6.7	37.0	45.7	87.0	68.1	95.7	38.6
	1.78	0.32	1.06	1.91	2.41	3.40	73	4.8	64.2	79.1	184.6	105.0	171.9	72.2
3522 Farm Machinery & Equipment (80)	4.28	5.52	14.34	21.55	4.07	5.80	25	5.4	21.4	22.1	46.9	68.4	39.0	19.0
	2.59	2.91	8.05	10.65	2.67	3.71	43	3.8	42.6	39.1	80.7	89.8	65.8	36.7
	1.67	1.48	3.07	4.05	1.99	2.61	67	2.9	58.8	79.5	138.6	134.3	92.0	54.5
3141 Footwear (111)	3.75	3.43	12.71	17.21	6.00	8.37	41	9.4	11.8	31.3	66.5	60.0	59.9	8.7
	2.33	1.50	6.27	7.40	4.03	5.30	55	6.0	23.9	59.1	108.4	87.2	90.2	21.9
	1.66	0.42	1.61	2.58	3.07	3.48	67	4.1	38.5	118.0	192.8	139.7	136.8	46.2
2371 Fur Goods (41)	3.29	1.20	8.59	9.32	8.28	9.10	26	17.8	1.7	42.6	196.7	42.9	79.7	17.3
	1.91	0.35	1.62	1.74	5.86	6.24	53	6.0	4.0	97.4	266.8	83.7	135.0	18.3
	1.44	(1.71)	(3.44)	(5.45)	3.07	4.24	87	3.1	7.6	257.7	321.3	122.7	249.9	110.8
1511 General Building Contractors (194)	2.04	2.29	17.45	29.94	13.55	20.86	**	**	9.4	67.1	76.5	**	**	8.3
	1.45	1.20	9.10	14.20	8.19	12.54	**	**	24.1	124.8	180.7	**	**	30.8
	1.24	0.53	4.38	7.02	4.27	6.76	**	**	40.1	237.3	315.5	**	**	77.3
3561–62–64–65–66–67–69 General Industrial Machinery & Equip. (113)	4.38	5.50	12.16	19.09	3.46	5.76	44	7.6	27.6	22.6	45.3	52.6	53.5	19.6
	2.76	2.92	8.03	12.36	2.64	3.93	58	4.7	44.8	35.3	68.1	76.6	80.0	37.5
	1.98	0.79	1.98	3.93	1.81	2.91	72	3.6	63.9	62.1	126.0	99.6	128.0	67.9
2041–42–43–44–45–46 Grain Mill Products (71)	4.11	3.24	14.27	31.70	6.39	15.63	21	16.0	30.2	19.5	41.2	40.4	73.4	39.1
	2.11	1.96	7.85	15.44	4.47	9.16	27	11.8	51.0	32.3	78.7	77.3	107.3	65.5
	1.44	0.87	4.14	7.82	3.17	5.62	45	8.1	76.3	65.8	132.3	148.0	145.1	94.5
3431–32–33 Heating Apparatus & Plumbing Fixtures (47)	4.66	3.74	13.22	15.84	4.49	5.57	29	6.9	16.8	21.8	55.8	61.3	49.7	15.3
	2.45	1.84	6.17	8.63	2.81	3.95	46	5.1	37.2	36.8	88.2	88.8	77.1	45.5
	2.00	0.76	2.83	3.93	1.95	3.34	63	3.9	64.0	72.7	190.4	108.9	100.7	62.5
1621 Heavy Construction, except Highway & Street (105)	2.64	3.80	14.62	34.60	5.87	14.53	**	**	33.5	29.8	59.5	**	**	20.4
	1.68	2.08	7.91	19.32	3.96	7.43	**	**	54.5	54.4	107.5	**	**	65.9
	1.22	0.62	2.75	5.97	2.25	4.50	**	**	84.9	111.6	214.5	**	**	121.8
2251–52 Hosiery (57)	3.76	3.75	12.26	24.78	4.87	9.18	29	9.6	34.3	21.3	55.1	58.6	44.2	20.1
	2.10	2.19	6.63	10.95	3.19	5.30	40	5.5	47.7	42.1	85.3	94.3	90.3	45.3
	1.66	1.03	3.44	5.45	2.24	3.32	61	4.0	68.7	78.3	108.0	128.3	128.3	72.0
3631–32–33–34–35–36–39 Household Appliances (48)	3.85	4.71	13.89	31.20	4.44	6.71	42	6.4	18.9	26.5	45.1	71.8	53.9	16.8
	2.38	2.63	9.87	13.33	3.10	4.00	51	4.6	36.0	43.0	84.8	93.4	74.7	35.3
	1.59	1.12	2.72	3.95	2.27	3.19	73	3.5	56.1	86.6	127.9	155.2	100.0	58.6
2812–13–15–16–18–19 Industrial Chemicals (65)	3.04	5.31	10.71	33.97	2.87	10.40	47	10.0	40.9	18.2	46.1	63.4	62.2	44.9
	1.99	2.73	6.83	14.54	2.06	4.91	57	6.0	63.7	32.7	70.6	86.2	100.0	85.8
	1.34	0.88	2.64	3.65	1.65	3.64	100	4.9	81.7	55.8	107.1	138.5	151.3	166.3
3821–22 Instruments, Measuring & Controlling (52)	4.69	4.31	11.25	16.40	3.53	4.61	49	5.1	22.8	17.7	45.1	61.4	38.8	21.3
	3.38	3.21	6.08	7.39	2.34	3.01	61	4.1	37.3	32.3	75.4	77.3	59.8	36.9
	2.00	0.74	2.25	2.49	1.58	2.14	87	3.0	59.6	74.0	160.6	98.3	111.8	77.2
3321–22–23 Iron & Steel Foundries (61)	3.59	3.50	11.18	25.45	3.10	7.91	37	15.9	44.3	21.0	37.2	31.9	65.8	19.3
	2.36	2.52	6.14	13.04	2.23	5.67	45	10.2	60.5	28.8	57.8	66.2	104.2	41.8
	1.81	0.69	1.82	5.15	1.88	3.77	58	6.1	78.0	44.0	88.5	93.1	231.9	77.0
2253 Knit Outerwear Mills (53)	3.06	2.78	11.69	13.95	5.53	8.86	23	12.7	5.8	35.8	57.7	47.2	73.2	12.8
	2.45	1.10	4.41	5.33	4.03	5.51	43	6.9	23.7	55.3	80.9	68.2	109.7	22.5
	1.72	0.46	1.43	1.54	2.86	3.68	66	5.1	39.9	95.4	137.8	103.8	176.4	41.0
2082 Malt Liquors (34)	3.04	4.29	9.86	65.21	3.76	22.44	12	22.2	51.9	18.9	50.5	39.1	112.6	81.2
	2.04	1.31	4.48	17.79	2.69	11.03	17	14.4	75.0	28.9	58.5	77.0	159.7	99.0
	1.37	0.35	0.56	1.13	2.07	4.99	30	10.9	99.4	35.3	79.9	145.5	178.4	270.7
2515 Mattresses & Bedsprings (46)	4.90	3.47	9.57	15.85	5.32	7.68	34	10.4	13.2	13.9	55.7	49.7	49.9	25.1
	2.58	1.93	5.31	10.02	3.16	5.30	50	8.2	24.1	33.5	75.7	66.9	90.4	39.3
	1.92	0.73	3.31	5.85	2.14	3.77	56	5.8	41.4	66.9	136.0	99.5	153.9	64.9
2011 Meat Packing Plants (94)	3.85	1.52	13.75	36.01	15.84	33.69	10	52.6	41.0	19.7	53.3	40.6	79.7	19.8
	2.30	0.82	9.45	16.89	10.02	20.79	14	34.5	57.0	41.6	84.7	63.4	131.5	49.5
	1.39	0.35	3.72	7.92	7.25	12.65	20	22.3	79.6	84.7	153.4	117.0	214.6	121.6
3461 Metal Stampings (103)	3.88	3.50	9.27	18.26	4.66	8.30	29	12.6	36.8	17.9	42.6	48.9	57.5	24.8
	2.55	1.64	4.75	9.21	3.04	5.80	37	7.7	56.0	35.5	72.4	75.7	99.3	47.5
	1.67	0.39	1.18	3.33	2.07	4.04	46	5.9	81.9	63.5	139.5	106.4	165.2	94.4
3541–42–44–45–48 Metalworking Machinery & Equipment (124)	4.10	5.13	11.17	21.30	4.02	7.78	34	14.7	38.9	20.4	44.0	38.0	52.8	17.0
	2.45	2.25	5.88	9.52	2.30	3.89	51	6.4	49.2	33.6	81.9	81.4	91.2	42.1
	1.61	0.14	0.15	0.61	1.56	2.59	67	3.2	71.4	66.7	126.9	106.6	186.2	88.7
2431 Millwork (59)	5.26	4.03	12.39	19.13	5.16	6.87	33	9.8	19.9	17.4	46.1	42.4	40.6	16.6
	3.27	1.98	7.92	9.75	3.35	4.30	45	6.8	36.0	33.9	75.8	69.4	72.9	26.2
	2.04	1.05	2.93	4.42	2.37	2.99	57	5.0	54.6	71.7	184.3	102.0	130.8	42.4
3599 Miscellaneous Machinery, except Electrical (90)	4.09	5.28	13.07	26.51	3.25	7.24	30	24.4	29.0	15.2	38.7	21.6	64.9	8.3
	2.76	2.74	7.03	13.49	2.45	4.75	44	8.8	46.9	29.7	66.5	53.1	135.0	24.3
	1.99	1.60	2.68	2.68	1.74	3.36	55	5.2	69.8	50.3	104.2	91.4	272.3	87.9
3714 Motor Vehicle Parts & Accessories (88)	3.98	5.21	12.91	20.28	3.81	6.19	35	9.3	29.8	22.7	48.8	57.7	52.6	25.8
	2.87	2.73	7.74	11.67	2.73	3.94	44	5.7	45.8	34.1	77.1	76.8	73.7	44.2
	1.87	1.15	3.80	5.22	2.00	2.80	54	3.8	61.4	63.7	107.4	103.9	115.8	77.0
3361–62–69 Nonferrous Foundries (45)	3.94	4.34	9.44	21.42	3.89	8.54	32	19.7	36.7	18.4	36.0	42.6	82.1	19.5
	2.42	1.41	5.18	9.80	2.82	6.50	42	10.9	51.5	34.8	58.5	61.8	127.2	40.4
	1.73	(1.03)	(2.63)	(3.48)	2.17	3.77	49	7.0	88.7	56.7	114.3	106.4	180.3	129.1

** Not computed. Printers carry only current supplies such as paper, ink, and binding materials rather than merchandise inventories for re-sale. Building Trades contractors have no inventories in the credit sense of the term. As a general rule, such contractors have no customary selling terms, each contract being a special job for which individual terms are arranged.

ILLUSTRATION 1–10 (concluded)

MANUFACTURING & CONSTRUCTION

Line of Business (and number of concerns reporting)	Current assets to current debt	Net profits on net sales	Net profits on tangible net worth	Net profits on net working capital	Net sales to tangible net worth	Net sales to net working capital	Collection period	Net sales to inventory	Fixed assets to tangible net worth	Current debt to tangible net worth	Total debt to tangible net worth	Inventory to net working capital	Current debt to inventory	Funded debts to net working capital
	Times	Per cent	Per cent	Per cent	Times	Times	Days	Times	Per cent	Per cent	Per cent	Per cent	Per cent	Per cent
2541–42 Office & Store Fixtures (65)	3.94	5.09	15.12	24.15	5.11	7.38	31	13.2	17.0	24.1	41.4	36.1	74.3	22.0
	2.51	2.06	7.77	12.07	3.16	4.68	47	7.6	35.3	52.5	100.1	67.3	115.0	49.5
	1.75	0.55	1.71	2.70	2.18	2.80	78	4.8	57.9	96.1	149.4	94.9	188.8	83.5
2361–63–69 Outerwear, Children's & Infants' (57)	2.47	2.43	20.40	26.62	10.79	12.42	25	16.3	5.9	56.6	72.7	48.2	81.5	4.8
	1.88	0.99	10.08	12.95	7.21	8.09	38	9.1	15.0	93.6	128.5	76.3	151.5	15.7
	1.36	0.37	2.47	3.19	4.33	5.07	53	5.3	29.5	236.7	280.6	153.9	234.0	53.4
2851 Paints, Varnishes, Lacquers & Enamels (112)	4.83	3.86	10.16	16.58	3.93	6.00	34	8.4	19.7	18.0	39.3	54.2	46.0	20.2
	3.39	2.33	5.86	8.44	2.83	4.43	45	6.8	35.6	25.2	65.1	68.2	67.5	37.2
	2.44	0.79	2.60	4.27	2.13	3.16	60	5.1	56.3	46.6	100.0	87.4	92.2	58.2
2621 Paper Mills, except Building Paper (53)	3.46	4.89	8.99	29.53	2.40	6.18	32	10.4	41.9	17.9	33.5	53.1	65.7	28.9
	2.50	2.66	6.02	15.26	1.89	5.55	42	7.4	78.8	22.0	64.5	66.5	99.2	82.1
	1.55	1.30	2.78	5.10	1.51	3.68	53	5.8	105.7	32.6	88.2	92.9	139.0	179.2
2651–52–53–54–55 Paperboard Containers & Boxes (62)	5.39	4.83	13.13	28.30	4.23	7.76	30	16.8	34.3	12.5	52.4	33.0	53.7	40.3
	2.90	2.61	6.95	13.55	2.94	5.70	39	10.6	68.1	26.1	87.0	54.8	99.3	81.6
	1.86	0.40	2.19	5.62	1.98	3.47	47	5.8	101.2	59.7	128.0	96.8	165.0	142.6
3712–13 Passenger Car, Truck & Bus Bodies (47)	3.79	3.63	11.30	19.98	5.49	8.65	29	9.4	23.9	26.0	40.3	58.4	64.5	10.8
	2.11	1.95	7.07	12.21	3.86	5.60	47	6.6	38.4	54.6	96.6	95.2	102.5	19.8
	1.60	0.32	2.80	5.46	2.40	3.60	56	5.1	69.1	97.0	142.4	129.2	129.1	58.7
2911 Petroleum Refining (53)	1.76	6.80	11.62	68.89	3.39	19.07	44	30.1	7.1	6.6	12.8	40.6	100.0	33.3
	1.09	3.41	7.45	32.35	1.91	8.89	54	14.2	34.1	23.0	35.2	82.6	119.1	112.0
	1.00	1.74	3.62	21.59	1.36	4.70	66	9.0	79.2	62.0	120.1	204.2	184.1	262.9
2821–22–23–24 Plastics Materials & Synthetics (36)	2.58	5.53	17.13	51.64	4.87	11.40	40	11.7	32.4	26.6	43.5	62.5	79.8	30.6
	1.84	2.34	7.00	17.39	2.96	6.04	60	8.6	54.3	41.4	68.3	86.3	108.8	83.5
	1.27	0.88	3.10	5.50	2.08	4.59	70	6.7	89.7	78.6	135.3	122.2	214.2	137.8
1711 Plumbing, Heating & Air Conditioning (106)	2.82	2.72	18.22	23.30	9.91	13.55	**	**	10.9	41.2	59.9	**	**	10.3
	1.85	1.58	10.11	13.38	6.31	8.45	**	**	20.6	90.1	143.3	**	**	22.1
	1.37	0.57	3.26	4.78	4.31	5.30	**	**	30.8	172.7	250.6	**	**	48.1
2421 Sawmills & Planing Mills (84)	4.87	5.46	11.47	35.48	3.60	7.27	20	9.9	26.1	11.2	26.4	52.3	47.7	15.3
	2.58	2.29	5.32	17.25	2.35	4.97	29	5.6	48.6	26.4	55.3	74.9	73.4	43.0
	1.80	0.61	1.22	3.72	1.43	3.20	46	4.0	79.8	57.4	102.9	117.4	129.8	149.5
3451–52 Screw Machine Products (74)	4.73	5.15	10.37	22.37	3.31	8.04	26	11.6	37.1	14.7	42.5	50.7	54.3	22.8
	2.72	2.70	4.87	10.82	2.45	4.85	36	6.3	55.2	24.8	64.0	74.5	85.7	51.2
	1.95	0.51	1.33	2.50	1.70	3.04	49	4.8	78.3	48.4	84.1	109.5	123.2	89.5
2321–22 Shirts, Underwear & Nightwear, Men's & Boys' (62)	3.09	3.16	11.77	14.42	6.07	6.74	42	7.7	2.6	47.4	78.9	66.1	71.7	6.8
	1.98	1.79	7.04	7.91	4.34	5.02	55	5.3	12.9	93.2	104.3	95.2	102.2	21.4
	1.58	0.45	1.57	2.87	3.43	3.80	68	4.2	30.4	148.1	202.8	137.0	142.0	48.5
2841–42–43–44 Soap, Detergents, Perfumes & Cosmetics (71)	4.31	6.29	15.06	25.87	3.96	6.98	39	10.5	17.3	20.4	38.2	44.3	62.0	12.7
	2.40	3.23	10.04	15.93	2.90	4.40	52	7.3	26.9	34.5	56.2	61.5	95.5	21.8
	1.80	0.67	1.84	2.95	1.79	2.99	83	5.2	39.9	57.6	85.2	95.8	124.7	46.4
2086 Soft Drinks, Bottled & Canned (75)	3.04	6.06	16.35	73.59	4.55	17.68	14	20.3	50.3	19.0	34.8	46.6	97.2	25.3
	1.84	3.74	10.87	39.45	2.88	9.93	20	14.7	79.3	32.2	66.5	83.7	151.7	99.0
	1.42	1.76	7.27	18.92	1.97	5.69	31	10.7	120.6	51.1	119.7	120.6	222.8	276.9
3551–52–53–54–55–59 Special Industry Machinery (94)	5.27	5.42	10.91	16.67	3.04	5.50	42	6.4	25.0	16.3	48.4	51.4	48.4	12.9
	2.70	3.18	7.78	10.55	2.16	2.99	57	4.6	36.4	37.2	75.9	78.7	70.7	32.0
	1.91	0.69	1.28	1.49	1.59	2.12	78	3.1	50.0	63.8	124.6	104.5	111.1	63.2
2337 Suits & Coats, Women's & Misses' (81)	3.30	2.55	11.24	15.47	10.15	11.64	25	22.6	2.7	39.1	60.0	36.0	94.8	8.6
	2.14	1.03	5.33	6.38	5.76	6.58	44	13.4	5.5	69.5	122.0	61.5	139.1	17.2
	1.54	0.33	1.21	1.65	3.66	4.18	62	5.6	12.0	158.0	271.8	85.9	236.9	66.2
2311 Suits, Coats & Overcoats, Men's & Boys' (110)	2.83	2.53	12.10	13.43	6.26	7.50	24	7.9	3.9	47.2	77.0	58.1	67.1	9.0
	2.13	1.29	4.41	5.93	4.26	5.31	53	5.0	8.7	82.4	106.8	90.8	89.5	26.0
	1.68	0.24	1.32	1.59	3.02	3.50	83	3.6	22.1	140.4	172.7	140.4	127.9	40.2
3841–42–43 Surgical, Medical & Dental Instruments (62)	5.29	6.07	14.82	21.16	3.28	4.76	43	7.5	19.2	18.0	32.6	56.0	36.8	10.9
	3.20	4.21	9.97	11.82	2.62	3.52	56	4.8	35.3	30.8	59.4	72.2	62.2	29.5
	2.11	2.20	5.53	6.26	1.89	2.68	67	3.5	51.5	53.5	91.2	98.4	98.5	63.0
3941–42–43–49 Toys, Amusement & Sporting Goods (62)	2.74	4.82	16.66	23.26	4.63	8.79	46	6.9	19.6	41.0	71.7	77.1	77.0	22.6
	1.89	1.80	8.08	9.80	3.74	5.12	60	4.7	39.1	75.1	122.2	106.2	119.1	42.3
	1.35	0.53	2.16	2.92	2.28	3.30	92	3.6	65.5	132.3	176.3	165.7	147.6	61.5
2327 Trousers, Men's & Boys' (49)	3.58	2.95	15.29	15.78	8.22	9.30	36	11.4	4.7	41.0	68.9	50.8	71.9	10.5
	2.05	1.48	8.90	9.98	4.82	5.57	59	5.7	8.3	85.9	102.2	68.4	109.7	19.4
	1.56	0.91	3.04	4.35	3.31	3.45	.86	4.1	20.5	158.1	209.5	129.8	190.0	33.9
2341 Underwear & Nightwear, Women's & Children's (77)	3.37	3.40	13.96	19.69	7.45	9.73	32	10.7	8.1	36.4	57.2	60.1	64.2	8.9
	2.21	1.33	7.18	9.58	5.71	6.32	41	7.6	16.0	69.3	114.1	86.7	106.2	21.9
	1.50	0.40	2.20	3.18	4.00	4.67	54	5.2	32.6	132.7	178.6	134.9	162.8	63.1
2511–12 Wood Household Furniture & Upholstered (127)	4.70	3.95	11.89	19.23	4.34	6.77	31	8.8	24.0	19.0	37.7	52.3	44.2	10.0
	2.95	2.15	7.15	9.52	3.01	4.33	42	6.8	37.9	31.3	65.7	82.5	66.8	28.2
	1.94	0.46	2.21	3.78	2.23	3.16	56	4.3	50.2	62.5	112.9	110.3	101.8	58.4
2328 Work Clothing, Men's & Boys' (44)	5.30	4.02	12.89	13.20	4.86	5.24	37	6.6	7.7	23.2	62.0	67.1	43.3	5.3
	2.55	2.28	7.44	8.53	3.61	3.90	53	4.4	15.7	55.5	100.3	84.7	75.7	25.0
	1.95	1.04	3.77	4.82	2.51	2.74	81	3.0	25.4	92.7	129.5	125.2	104.6	39.0

( ) indicates less.

** Not computed. Printers carry only current supplies such as paper, ink, and binding materials rather than merchandise inventories for re-sale. Building Trades contractors have no inventories in the credit sense of the term. As a general rule, such contractors have no customary selling terms, each contract being a special job for which individual terms are arranged.

The Interstate Commerce Commission, the Federal Trade Commission, the Federal Power Commission, the Federal Communications Commission, the Securities and Exchange Commission, the Board of Governors of the Federal Reserve System, the Board of Directors of the Federal Deposit Insurance Corporation, and other governmental agencies also have made available to the public detailed annual reports of different types of businesses. Much related information may also be obtained from trade associations and from commodities and securities exchanges.

The Securities and Exchange Commission is a most important source of detailed financial and operating data on corporations that sell their securities in interstate commerce. Acting under the authority of several securities acts, the Securities and Exchange Commission now requires, and specifies the content of, annual reports from most concerns that market their securities publicly, in more than one state.

Although the Securities and Exchange Commission has prescribed neither a uniform system of accounts nor a uniform method for the preparation of financial reports, it has had a profound influence on accounting and on standardization of published financial statements. The statements of registrants are examined by the Commission to be certain that they have been prepared in accordance with recognized and accepted principles of accounting. These principles require adequate disclosure.

Internal and external analysis

There is a difference in the amount of information available for internal and external analyses of financial statements. The internal analysis, primarily for managerial purposes, is accomplished by those who have access to the detailed records and all other information relative to a business. In this group would be included the management and employees of the enterprise and governmental and court agencies that may have major regulatory or other jurisdiction over the business.

An external analysis, primarily for establishing credit and evaluating an investment, is made by those who do not have access to the detailed records of the company. This group, which must depend almost entirely on published financial statements, includes stockholders, bondholders, credit agencies, labor, and those governmental agencies regulating a business in a nominal way. The position of the external analyst has been improved in the last decade because of the detailed information that is made available to the public by the Securities and Exchange Commission and because of the growing practice of businesses to issue audited statements. Furthermore, in comparison with earlier practice, businesses now furnish their creditors with a larger volume of financial and operating data.

Analysis and interpretation of financial statements and internal managerial reports

The analysis and interpretation of financial statements including internal managerial accounting reports, which are an attempt to determine the significance and meaning of the financial and operating data, represent the last of four major steps in accounting. The first three steps, which involve the work of the accountant in the accumulation and summarization of financial and operating data and in the construction of financial statements, are:

1. Analysis of each transaction to determine the accounts to be debited and credited, and the measurement or valuation of each transaction to determine the amounts involved.
2. Recording of the information in journals, summarization in ledgers, and preparation of a work sheet.
3. Preparation of financial statements.

The fourth step—the analysis and interpretation of the financial statements—results in the presentation of information that will aid in decision making by business managers, investors, and creditors as well as other groups who are interested in the financial status and operating results of a business.

It is beyond the scope of the book to consider many problems of management and influencing factors of business enterprises such as location, history, general business and economic conditions, and the effects of governmental taxation and regulation, all of which must be taken into account in a complete analysis of a business. The analyst must always be on the alert to obtain pertinent data relating to the financial position and operating results that are not included in the financial statements.

The following chapters are devoted to a comprehensive presentation, accompanied by illustrations, of basic fundamentals involving (1) the arrangement, content, and form of the balance sheet, income statement, and statements of capital and retained earnings; and (2) the principles of asset valuation, amortization, and income determination.

QUESTIONS AND PROBLEMS

1-1. Distinguish between:
   a) The balance sheet and the income statement.
   b) Overall entity financial statements and internal managerial accounting reports.

1-2. Explain the following italicized terms: "Financial statements reflect a combination of *recorded facts, accounting conventions,* and *personal judgments.*"

1–3. Discuss what is meant by "an audited financial statement" and indicate its significance.

1–4. Explain the importance of *footnotes* and *parenthetical explanations,* relative to financial statements.

1–5. Make a list of sources of financial statement data to which you have access.

1–6. Compare, with reference to the contents, the annual reports of several corporations.

1–7. Do you consider a bank which loans funds on a short-term basis an investor in a business?

1–8. What is the function of accounting?

1–9. State the nature and function of each of the financial statements.

1–10. Discuss the limitations of financial statements and indicate whether or not these shortcomings could be corrected.

1–11. "The corporate form of business organization is more complex than the single proprietorship and partnership." Explain.

1–12. What are the objectives of a course in "analysis of financial statements"?

1–13. Discuss the advantages and disadvantages of the special-purpose balance sheet from the point of view of a banker who is reviewing a loan application.

1–14. Explain the meaning of the term "going concern" and discuss its significance in accounting.

2

The balance sheet:
General principles

IT IS the purpose of this chapter to explore the characteristics of properly prepared balance sheets.

Balance sheet—titles

Of the six hundred large U.S. corporations the financial statement practices of which are surveyed annually by the AICPA,[1] in 1970, 518 used the title "balance sheet," up from 466 in 1955; 57 used the title "statement of financial position," and 25 used the caption "statement of financial condition," both having declined from a combined total of 127 in 1955. Other descriptive terms that may be included in the statement title are condensed, comparative, and consolidated.

A *pro forma balance sheet* gives effect to proposed transactions such as acquisition of additional properties, new financing, consolidation, recapitalization, or reorganization. This giving-effect balance sheet reveals the anticipated results of the changes in assets, liabilities, and owners' equity.

The financial position of an insolvent company is sometimes shown by a *statement of affairs* prepared from the point of view of liquidation. This statement identifies the assets that have been pledged to creditors and reflects both going-concern and estimated realizable asset values. Liabilities are classified as prior or preferred, fully secured, partially secured, and unsecured creditor claims.

---

[1] AICPA, *Accounting Trends and Techniques* (25th ed.: New York, 1971).

Balance sheet—main divisions

The main divisions of the balance sheet are:

Assets. Assets represent economic resources which are owned by a business; more specifically, they are the properties and rights to properties or services that the enterprise owns. It is the service potential of any property or right owned by a business that makes it an asset of that business. The assets have three important characteristics: the service potential, monetary value, and ownership.

The word "asset" is not synonymous with or limited to property or claims to resources but includes also that part of any potential expense which is properly carried forward as an unconsumed cost applicable to a future period.[2] (See Illustration 2–1.)

An asset is usually defined as property owned, to which an individual or business holds legal title or in which the individual or business possesses some equity. Title to property in a single proprietorship is vested in one individual, the owner; in a partnership, in two or more individuals, the partners, or in one partner as trustee for all partners; and in a corporation, in the corporate entity. For balance sheet purposes the assets should be adequately described, measured dollarwise in conformity with generally accepted accounting principles, and arranged in the order of their probable availability in liquid form for reallocation by management to a going-concern purpose.

The balance sheet of a business conducted by an individual or partnership does not include, as a rule, all of the assets that may be subject to the claims of creditors of the business. In the event of insolvency of the business, and after the settlement of personal debts and the exclusion of exemptions allowed by law, the personal properties of the single proprietor or partners may be attached to satisfy the creditor claims of the business. Corporations enjoy limited liability, which means that this principle does not hold true for them since creditors have no legal right to attach the personal properties of stockholders in order to enforce payment of their claims.

Liabilities. Liabilities are amounts owed to creditors. Liabilities or debts owed by an individual or business represent sources of capital obtained from creditors; the detailed classification of the liabilities shows the extent to which each type of credit is being utilized. Unless a lien or mortgage is given when the liabilities are incurred, the *creditors* have claims against the total assets rather than against particular assets. When a lien or mortgage on a particular asset is given at the time the liability is incurred, the creditors have a prior claim on that asset

---

[2] Even the cost of washing windows could conceivably be an asset were it not for the fact that windows get dirty again so rapidly. And of course the sum involved is too small to justify capitalization as an asset.

ILLUSTRATION 2–1.   Asset side of a balance sheet

Ex-Cell-O Corporation and Subsidiaries
CONSOLIDATED BALANCE SHEET

ASSETS

	November 30	
	1971	1970
CURRENT ASSETS:		
Cash	$ 6,289,683	$ 9,377,280
Marketable securities, at cost (approximates market)...................	11,025,000	—
Accounts and notes receivable, less allowance for possible credit losses of $278,333 in 1971 and $342,100 in 1970	41,478,636	53,240,699
Other receivables and claims.......................................	5,841,339	4,626,695
Inventories, at the lower of cost (first-in, first-out and average) or market...	81,254,578	101,456,565
Prepaid expenses	2,229,209	2,386,292
Deferred income tax charges	—	1,795,206
Total current assets	148,118,445	172,882,737
INVESTMENTS IN AFFILIATED COMPANIES, note 1	5,716,707	4,603,227
SUNDRY RECEIVABLES	9,327,414	10,928,758
PROPERTY, PLANT AND EQUIPMENT, AT COST, note 3:		
Land	4,777,569	4,758,497
Buildings and improvements	49,104,775	47,948,122
Machinery and equipment	101,923,298	104,995,960
	155,805,642	157,702,579
Less accumulated depreciation	89,041,184	84,059,276
Net property, plant and equipment	66,764,458	73,643,303
RENTAL MACHINES, AT COST, note 3:		
Machines under lease and in construction	119,546,802	121,606,382
Less accumulated depreciation	67,761,680	66,762,360
Net rental machines	51,785,122	54,844,022
PATENTS AND DEFERRED CHARGES, AT COST, LESS AMORTIZATION	1,054,741	434,375
	$282,766,887	$317,336,422

Notes to financial statements on page 17.

and a general claim on the total assets. The liabilities, properly included and described, should be listed on a balance sheet in the order of their probable maturity (due date). (See Illustration 2–2.)

Creditors of a business may be classified as (1) secured, (2) partly secured, and (3) unsecured. A secured creditor is one who has received some lien on specified assets as security for the payment of the amount

ILLUSTRATION 2–2.   Liability and equity side of a balance sheet

Ex-Cell-O Corporation and Subsidiaries

LIABILITIES AND SHAREHOLDERS' EQUITY

	November 30	
	1971	1970
CURRENT LIABILITIES:		
Current portion of long-term debt and other loans	$ 11,210,114	$ 52,683,836
Accounts payable and accrued liabilities	34,550,996	42,800,718
Dividend declared	1,684,110	2,632,034
Income taxes	752,479	3,865,487
Deferred income taxes, note 5	368,106	—
Total current liabilities	48,565,805	101,982,075
LONG-TERM DEBT:		
Term loans, note 2...	51,725,000	27,500,000
Other	2,815,234	3,597,654
Total long-term debt	54,540,234	31,097,654
DEFERRED ITEMS:		
Rental income on leased machines	1,326,745	1,994,987
Deferred income taxes, note 5	142,791	838,500
Total deferred items	1,469,536	2,833,487
SHAREHOLDERS' EQUITY:		
Preferred stock, no par value:		
Authorized — 5,000,000 shares		
Issued — none	—	—
Common stock, par value $3 a share:		
Authorized — 25,000,000 shares		
Issued — 8,598,273 shares including treasury stock....................	25,794,819	25,794,819
Additional paid-in capital	26,313,214	26,313,214
Earnings reinvested in the business, note 2	131,720,840	134,952,734
	183,828,873	187,060,767
Less cost of 175,822 shares of treasury stock	5,637,561	5,637,561
Total shareholders' equity	178,191,312	181,423,206
	$282,766,887	$317,336,422

due him. If the pledged property is valued at less than the amount of the debt, the creditor is only partially secured. If the business becomes insolvent and the pledged property is insufficient to meet the debt in full, the creditor becomes a general creditor for the amount of the unpaid balance.

Unsecured creditors include all creditors who have not received a lien on property; these creditors may be classified as prior-claim (or preferred) creditors and general creditors. Prior-claim creditors are those who are entitled to receive payment for their debts before all other unsecured creditors. The right to prior payment is established by law. Preferred unsecured creditors include governments, for unpaid taxes;

employees, for unpaid wages; and creditors, for expense of liquidation and for court receivers' debts. General creditors include all creditors that have neither security nor priority for their debts. In the case of liquidation, these creditors share pro rata in the remaining assets or, in the event that there are sufficient assets, up to the amount of their respective claims. The balance sheet should reveal, with respect to all creditors, including bondholders, the creditor claims that are secured and the assets that have been pledged as security therefor.

Owners' equity. The owners' equity or interest in the business is known as stockholders' equity, shareholders' equity, capital,[3] net worth, proprietorship, or ownership. Ownership in a single proprietorship or a partnership business is evidenced by the capital investment accounts in the ledger; ownership in a corporation is evidenced by stock certificates, which show the kind of capital stock and the number of shares owned.

The term "net worth" bears a misleading connotation to individuals who do not have a knowledge of financial accounting practice, since it suggests present worth or readily realizable market value of the net assets. The book value of the assets represents a combination of cash values (cash and its equivalent), estimated realizable current values (receivables), lower-of-cost-or-market values (inventories), and unamortized costs (fixed assets).

The equity of the owners in a business as shown by the accounting records is determined by deducting the amount of capital obtained from creditors from the total amount of capital invested in the assets. The accounting equation, Assets *minus* Liabilities *equals* Owners' Equity, expresses this relationship. Therefore, the owners' equity shown on the balance sheet represents the residual book value of the assets after the creditor claims or liabilities have been deducted. The equity, determined on a worth-to-the-business rather than a cash-realization basis, thus shown does not express what the proprietors might realize if the business were to be sold or dissolved.

In brief, owners' equity represents the net dollar amount contributed by and earned in behalf of the owners of the business. The asset side of the balance sheet reflects how capital derived from creditors and owners is employed. The owners' equity serves as a margin of safety for the creditors, since losses are first charged against retained earnings. That is, in the absence of contracts to the contrary, creditors do not suffer loss until all of the owners' equity has been absorbed.

---

[3] The term "capital" has several meanings. In accounting, the word "capital" has reference to the owners' equity, or it may refer to the total amount of borrowed funds and owners' equity; in economics, capital represents productive goods, i.e., wealth employed in production of further wealth; in business, capital often means the assets of the business; and in the legal profession, capital generally has reference to capital stock.

Balance sheet—forms

There are two conventional and most commonly used forms of balance sheet—the account form and the report form. In the account form (Illustration 2–3), the assets are listed on the left side and the liabilities and the owners' equity on the right side. This arrangement makes pos-

ILLUSTRATION 2–3.   Account form of balance sheet

Assets	*Liabilities*
Current assets	Current liabilities
	Long-term liabilities
Long-term investments	*Owners' equity*
Fixed assets	Capital stock
Intangible assets	Paid-in capital in excess of par or stated value
	Retained earnings
Deferred charges	
Other assets	Appropriated retained earnings

sible the convenient comparison of current assets and current liabilities and of fixed assets, long-term liabilities, and owners' equity.

Of the six hundred balance sheets of large U.S. corporations, surveyed in *Accounting Trends and Techniques 1971*, 570 used the account form, up from 517 in 1955.

In the only version of the report form now in much favor, current liabilities are subtracted from current assets, yielding working capital, other assets are then added, and other liabilities are deducted, yielding owners' equity (Illustration 2–4). Of the six hundred large corporations, 26 used this form down from 70 in 1955.

The report form has an obvious advantage in that it facilitates comparisons between years. It also points up working capital.

ILLUSTRATION 2–4. Report form balance sheet

STATEMENT OF CONSOLIDATED FINANCIAL POSITION

Cluett, Peabody & Co., Inc. and Subsidiaries

	December 31 1970
Cash	$ 11,620,104
Marketable securities (at cost which approximates market)	16,903,836
Accounts receivable (less reserves)	87,590,146
Inventories	132,455,667
Current assets	248,569,753
Notes payable	48,041,657
Accounts payable and accrued liabilities	40,902,628
Accrued taxes	925,921
Current liabilities	89,870,206
Working capital	158,699,547
Plant and equipment (less depreciation)	49,460,690
Investments in and advances to subsidiary and associated companies	3,560,144
Excess of investment in acquired companies over amounts ascribed to tangible assets	6,358,943
Prepaid expenses, deferred charges, and other assets	5,227,047
Total assets less current liabilities	223,306,371
Long-term debt	55,210,140
Reserves, compensation awards, deferred income taxes, and minority interests	12,489,696
4¼% Convertible subordinated debentures	3,833,400
	71,533,236
Net assets	$151,773,135
7% Cumulative preferred stock	$ 636,600
$1 Cumulative convertible preferred stock	1,442,273
Common stock	9,418,658
Capital surplus	32,932,237
Earned surplus	108,846,421
	153,276,189
Treasury stock (at cost)	1,503,054
Shareholders' equity	$151,773,135

[Reference to the Notes to the Financial Statements has been deleted]

An alternative arrangement of the report form balance sheet merely moves the liabilities and owners' equity items to a position below the assets. This arrangement fails to capture the advantage of pointing up working capital which probably explains why it is currently out of favor.

All-purpose versus special-purpose statements

As already suggested, various groups for whom financial statements are prepared are interested in different types of information. The question frequently arises as to whether or not a special-purpose statement,

ILLUSTRATION 2–5

POTTER-ENGLEWOOD CORPORATION AND SUBSIDIARIES

PRO FORMA CONDENSED COMBINED BALANCE SHEET

The following balance sheet represents the combination of the financial positions of Potter-Englewood Corporation and Subsidiaries ("P-E") and The Muter Company ("Muter") as of December 31, 1970, after giving effect to the proposed merger as a pooling of interests and the additional consideration in the acquisition of a subsidiary.

ASSETS

	Potter-Englewood Corporation (unaudited)	The Muter Company	Pro Forma Adjustment Dr.(Cr.)(a)	Pro Forma Combined
Current assets	$15,741,928	$ 6,631,107	$ —	$22,373,035
Other assets	1,115,045	42,646	680,835 (3)	1,838,526
Properties, plant and equipment—net	1,801,825	3,895,108	—	5,696,933
	$18,658,798	$10,568,861	$ 680,835	$29,908,494

LIABILITIES AND STOCKHOLDERS' EQUITY

Current liabilities	$7,845,646	$ 4,575,687	$ (316,670)(3)	$12,738,003
Long-term indebtedness(b)	3,469,686	1,137,894	—	4,607,580
Stockholders' equity:				
Potter-Englewood Corporation:				
Preferred stock, no par value; authorized 1,500,000 shares; issued and outstanding 13,750 shares Series A (liquidation preference $1,375,000)	275,000	—	—	275,000
Common stock, $1.00 par value; authorized 3,000,000 shares; issued and outstanding 870,917 shares	870,917	—	{ (561,212)(2) { (63,333)(3)	1,495,462
The Muter Company:				
Common stock, $.50 par value; authorized 3,000,000 shares; issued 1,425,673 shares	—	712,836	{ 11,322 (1) { 701,514 (2)	—
Paid-in surplus	1,682,989	4,575,562	{ 72,687 (1) { (140,302)(2) { (300,832)(3)	6,626,998
Retained earnings (deficit)	4,514,560	(345,925)	3,184 (1)	4,165,451
	7,343,466	4,942,473	(276,972)	12,562,911
Treasury stock, 22,644 shares common	—	(87,193)	(87,193)(1)	—
Total stockholders' equity	7,343,466	4,855,280	(364,165)	12,562,911
	$18,658,798	$10,568,861	$ (680,835)	$29,908,494

(a) The pro forma condensed combined balance sheet combines the consolidated balance sheet of P-E with the balance sheet of Muter, treating the merger as a pooling of interests for accounting purposes, after giving effect to the following transactions since December 31, 1970, the date of the balance sheets:

(1) the retirement of 22,644 treasury shares of Muter.

(2) the proposed exchange of 4/10ths share of P-E common stock for each share of Muter common stock (1,403,029 shares outstanding at December 31, 1970). The excess of the par value of Muter common stock outstanding over the par value of the 561,212 common shares to be issued by P-E in the merger has been credited to paid-in surplus.

(3) the provision for issuance of 63,333 shares of P-E common stock and additional cash consideration of $316,670 payable in acquisition of Videocraft Manufacturing Co.—Note 2 to consolidated financial statements of P-E.

(b) Reference is made to Note 7 to the consolidated financial statements of P-E and Notes 5 and 6 to the financial statements of Muter for terms and restrictions incident to long-term indebtedness.

No effect has been given in the pro forma condensed combined balance sheet to expenses of the proposed merger, which are not expected to be material.

emphasizing data of main interest for each specific purpose, should be prepared. The arrangement of the items and presentation of facts may be changed to suit the needs of those who will use the statement. Such a statement would be substituted for the general all-purpose financial statement which follows some conventional or accepted form and is customarily used. The all-purpose statement meets reasonably well the needs of most interested persons, namely, the short- and long-term creditors, the stockholders, the employees, the management, and the government.

Special-purpose financial statements are required for many specialized purposes: internally, for the use of management; by regulatory authorities such as the Securities and Exchange Commission (public issues of securities), the Interstate Commerce Commission (railroads), the Federal Communications Commission (telephones), and the Comptroller of the Currency (commercial banks); state authorities regulating the insurance carriers; and many others. But financial statements for issuance to the public (including investors, employees, and credit grantors) for the purpose of informing them about present financial condition and the results of current operations have been shown by experience to be best when cast in the conventional all-purpose form.

Illustration 2–5 shows a special-purpose statement combining the financial positions of two corporations which are proposing to merge. This is a pro forma statement. Literally translated, pro forma means for form's sake. In other words, the statement shows not how things are but how they will be under given conditions.

The variations in method of presenting financial and operating data may be justified so long as the financial statements clearly indicate what they purport to present. Care is required to avoid misstatement of material fact and omission of information necessary to the clear understanding of the subject matter.

Best practice in preparing a balance sheet

In preparing a balance sheet, regardless of the type used, the following practices should be observed:

1. The heading should include the recognized name of the business and the name and date of the statement. Unless otherwise indicated, a balance sheet is assumed to be prepared as of the close of business on the date stated.

2. In an account form balance sheet the left-hand side is almost always headed "*assets*"; the right-hand side is headed "*liabilities*" (45 out of 125 balance sheets surveyed), "*liabilities and stockholders' equity*" (28 out of 125), and "*liabilities and shareholders' equity*" (also 28 out of 125). Some argue that the stockholders' (or shareholders') equity

is not a liability and therefore that the single word *"liabilities"* should not be used, but the statistics show that opinion is divided on the point.

3. The accepted method of valuing property on the balance sheet is cost. The APB, in *Opinion No. 6* (1965), stated categorically that "property, plant and equipment should not be written up . . . to reflect appraisal, market or current values which are above cost. . . ." There are exceptions in the case of reorganizations and quasi-reorganizations and in foreign operations where serious inflation has taken place. But "whenever appreciation has been recorded on the books, income should be charged with depreciation computed on the written up amounts." *Opinion No. 12* (1967) states that "because of the significant effects on financial position and results of operations of the depreciation method or methods used" it is desirable to disclose depreciable assets by classes, depreciation for the period, accumulated depreciation by classes, and methods used.

Accounting Trends and Techniques shows that by 1971 (reports for the year 1970) the major U.S. corporations were—in most cases though not universally—disclosing in detail their depreciation policies, methods, and results. On the balance sheet, 535 broke down their property by major classes, 38 divided it by line of business, and 27 presented no details. In connection with the statement of income, only 4 out of 600 did not disclose the amount of depreciation charged to expense. Different methods of disclosure were used: 341 in various ways on the income statement page; 148 in footnotes; and 106 in the statement of changes in financial position only. As to the depreciation methods used, 574 companies disclosed while 26 did not. Many companies used more than one method: the straight-line method was used by 531; the declining balance method by 74; the sum-of-the-years'-digits method by 53; and "accelerated" method by 75.

Since the American Institute Committee on Terminology recommended against the use of the word "reserve" as a title for accumulations of depreciation (and depletion), use of the word in this context has declined markedly (26 cases in 1970 statements). "Accumulated depreciation" was used by 473 companies.

Cost is also the accepted method to be used in valuing other assets such as securities and inventories. If the market value of inventories (replacement cost) is less than actual cost, most concerns value at market below cost. Securities too are written down to market when the decline in value has been material and promises to be of indefinite duration. Sometimes market values below cost are disclosed without charging the unrealized loss against income.

4. The items should be classified accurately and logically and in accordance with the purpose the statement is to serve. Generally speaking, assets in each group should be listed in the order of their liquidity

(availability) and the liabilities in the order in which they are payable in the ordinary course of business.

5. Dissimilar items should not be combined in the balance sheet. For example, combinations like cash and call loans, or property and goodwill, or marketable securities and sinking funds are to be avoided.

6. An asset and a liability should not be offset one against the other. This procedure, which is called "netting," is contrary to good accounting practice. An exception is the deduction of notes receivable discounted from notes receivable.

Current Assets:

Notes receivable........................ $25,000
Less: Notes receivable discounted 10,000 $15,000

A second example, which was restricted in 1966 by APB *Opinion No. 10,* involved applying U.S. government securities against federal income tax liability.

Current Liabilities:

Estimated federal income taxes payable $33,072
Less: U.S. government securities............. 33,072 None

Opinion No. 10 does specify an exception to this prohibition "when it is clear that a purchase of securities (acceptable for the payment of taxes) is in substance an advance payment of taxes that will be payable in the relatively near future, so that in the special circumstances the purchase is tantamount to the prepayment of taxes." The offsetting of U.S. government securities against federal income tax liability has virtually disappeared.

7. Totals for the various major groups and subdivisions of the balance sheet should be clearly displayed.

8. The statement should be correct mathematically.

9. The statement should be truthful and not misleading; there should be full disclosure of significant data. Additional information may be given parenthetically, in schedules, or in footnotes to the balance sheet for items that are not adequately explained in the body of the balance sheet.

10. Descriptive asset titles should be used, and detailed information not essential to clear and concise presentation should be shown in schedules and footnotes.

11. Cents may be omitted from the balance sheet; in fact, if the amounts are large, the statement may be stated in terms of hundreds, thousands, or millions of dollars. The practice of rounding the amounts requires the stating of each at the nearest dollar (or hundred- or thou-

sand-dollar) amount and the adjustment of one of the amounts to make the column add to the total shown. A few large businesses have adopted bookkeeping procedures omitting cents except for accounts having to do with the receipt or disbursement of cash.

Simplifying the published balance sheet

Sometimes companies depart from the customary forms of balance sheet terminology and arrangement in the attempt to make the report

ILLUSTRATION 2–6

LOCK CORPORATION
Simplified Report on Financial Position
As of December 31, 197x
(in thousands)

Investment in Assets:

Cash in banks and marketable securities	$ 5,781
Money due to the company, mostly from customers	29,123
Materials, parts in various stages of manufacture at plants, and finished products and service parts being held for sale.	54,247
Land, buildings, and equipment, less estimated wear and tear resulting from use of these properties.	31,461
Long-term investments	3,572
Total Investment in Assets.	$124,184

Sources of Capital:

Creditors:

To a group of institutions for money loaned to the company to help finance its operations.	$ 36,100
For materials, supplies, wages, salaries, employee benefits, dividends payable, and other normal business expenditures	15,701
For taxes on income and property.	4,923
Total We Owed to Others.	$ 56,724

Stockholders:

The difference between the investment in assets and the creditor claims represents the book value of our stockholders' investment in our business through their ownership of 2,237,846 shares of common stock	$ 67,460

more understandable to unsophisticated readers. Usually such "simplified" reports are included in the annual report along with a primary (more conventional) balance sheet. The wording and arrangement of one such statement are reproduced in Illustration 2–6.

Such a simplified report would not ordinarily be deemed useful by a professional analyst who is interested in as much information as he can obtain.

A second example of an unconventional report for the layman is shown in Illustration 2–7.

ILLUSTRATION 2–7

JAMISON CORPORATION
The Year in Brief—What We Had to Work with at End of Year

Our Net Working Capital:
Cash and items readily convertible into cash consisted of:

Money and short-term securities	$ 27,233
Amount due from customers and others.	41,211
Materials and products for use or sale.	131,600
In terms of cash, the above amounted to.	$200,044
Against this, we owed for bank borrowings, current bills, payrolls, taxes, and dividends.	101,135
After paying what we owed currently, the amount of net working capital left to run the business was	$ 98,909

Our Tools and Other Assets:

Land, buildings, and equipment, after allowances for wear and tear	235,611
Investments, advances, and other assets.	23,224
Total of What We Had to Work With	$357,744
Against this, we owed long-term debt payable over the next 20 years.	40,000
The Remaining Balance, representing the shareholders' investment, was.	$317,744
Of the above, the preferred shareholders' investment was.	15,000
This Left as the Investment of the Common Shareholders in the Company	$302,744

Adding to the usefulness of the primary balance sheet

For many years the Caterpillar Tractor Company has published a somewhat unconventional primary balance sheet, designed to make readily available to the reader basic information about how the statement amounts were computed. The company was also a pioneer in presenting a great deal of information in a form which compares the last 46 years. Its income statement and financial statement notes are also used as vehicles to transmit to the reader a wealth of detail about the company's condition and operations (Illustration 2–8).

Almost all of the substantial industrial and commercial U.S. corporations are now presenting in their annual reports a 10-year comparison of data reflecting their financial condition and results of operations, and are giving much other information in the financial statement notes and the president's report.

The accounting valuation problem

The valuation of items in the financial statements is a major problem for management, for their accountants, and for their auditors.

Many items affect both the balance sheet and the statement of income.

ILLUSTRATION 2–8

STATEMENT 1
Consolidated Results of Operations
(Millions of dollars)

	1971	1970
Sales	**$2,175.2**	**$2,127.8**
Costs:		
Inventories brought forward from previous year	678.1	599.0
Materials, supplies, services purchased, etc.	1,063.2	1,087.7
Wages, salaries and contributions for employee benefits	767.2	710.3
Depreciation (portion of original cost of buildings, machinery and equipment allocated to operations)	99.7	99.5
Interest on borrowed funds	31.3	36.9
Taxes based on income (note 7)	107.6	129.9
	2,747.1	2,663.3
Deduct: Inventories carried forward to following year	698.9	678.1
Costs allocated to year (1)	2,048.2	1,985.2
	127.0	142.6
Profit of subsidiary credit companies (note 4)	1.3	1.2
Profit for year—consolidated (per share (2): 1971—$2.25; 1970—$2.53)	**128.3**	**143.8**
Profit employed in the business at beginning of year	838.9	763.4
	967.2	907.2
Dividends paid in cash during year (per share: 1971—$1.35; 1970—$1.20)	76.7	68.3
Profit employed in the business at end of year	$ 890.5	$ 838.9
(1) Includes cost of goods sold	$1,707.5	$1,639.5

(2) Computed on weighted average number of shares outstanding.

See notes on pages 21, 22 and 23

Opinion of Independent Accountants

TO THE SHAREHOLDERS:

We have examined the financial statements of Caterpillar Tractor Co. and its subsidiaries for the years ended December 31, 1971 and 1970. Our examinations were made in accordance with generally accepted auditing standards and accordingly included such tests of the accounting records and such other auditing procedures as we considered necessary in the circumstances. We have made similar annual examinations since incorporation of the Company.

In our opinion, the accompanying statements present fairly (a) the financial position of Caterpillar Tractor Co. and consolidated subsidiaries at December 31, 1971 and 1970, the results of their operations and the changes in financial position for the years then ended, in conformity with generally accepted accounting principles consistently applied and (b) the historical financial data included therein.

Chicago, January 19, 1972   Price Waterhouse & Co.

For example, the amount of uncollectible receivables expense used in income determination affects the valuation of the balance sheet item accounts receivable; the amount of depreciation expense shown on the income statement reduces the cost of depreciable assets that is deferred for allocation to expense for future periods; and the cost assigned to the inventories affects both the balance sheet and the income statement.

ILLUSTRATION 2–8 (continued)

STATEMENT 2

Consolidated Financial Position at December 31

(Millions of dollars)

	1971	1970
Current assets:		
Stated on basis of realizable values:		
Cash	$ 49.3	$ 37.4
Receivable from customers and others (note 6)	224.4	274.8
Prepaid expenses and income taxes allocable to the following year	55.1	51.1
	328.8	363.3
Stated on basis of cost using principally "last-in, first-out" method:		
Inventories	698.9	678.1
	1,027.7	1,041.4
Deduct: Current liabilities:		
Notes payable	250.0	215.4
Payable to material suppliers and others . . . . : . .	219.6	234.2
Taxes based on income	56.6	72.2
Long-term debt due within one year	17.1	18.3
	543.3	540.1
Net current assets (statement 3)	484.4	501.3
Income taxes and other costs allocable to future years, etc.	16.5	15.6
Depreciable properties at original cost:		
Buildings	470.1	432.4
Machinery and equipment	891.0	819.1
	1,361.1	1,251.5
Deduct: Accumulated depreciation	673.1	582.7
Buildings, machinery and equipment—net	688.0	668.8
Land—at original cost	24.3	23.3
Investments in affiliated companies (note 3)	28.9	28.9
Investments in subsidiary credit companies (note 4)	25.7	23.8
Total assets less current liabilities	1,267.8	1,261.7
Deduct: Long-term debt due after one year (note 5)	237.0	283.9
Net assets	$1,030.8	$ 977.8
Ownership (statement 5):		
Preferred stock of no par value (note 8):		
Authorized shares: 5,000,000		
Outstanding shares: none		
Common stock of no par value:		
Authorized shares: 70,000,000		
Outstanding shares: 1971—56,952,105; 1970—56,897,154 (note 9)	$ 140.3	$ 138.9
Profit employed in the business (note 5)	890.5	838.9
	$1,030.8	$ 977.8

See notes on pages 21, 22 and 23

In general, companies tend to favor the income statement when confronted with a choice involving both the computation of income and the valuation of assets. For example, many companies elected to use Lifo (last-in, first-out) in arranging the sequence of actual costs out of inventory into cost of goods sold (however, its use is declining[4]). Lifo

[4] In 1970 reports, 146 companies (out of the 600) reported some use of Lifo, down from 202 in 1955.

ILLUSTRATION 2–8 (continued)

STATEMENT 3
Changes in Consolidated Financial Position
(Millions of dollars)

	1971	1970
Additions to working capital from:		
Operations:		
Profit.	$128.3	$143.8
Add: Provision for depreciation not involving use of working capital	99.7	99.5
	228.0	243.3
Deduct: Profit of subsidiary credit companies	1.3	1.2
Working capital provided from operations	226.7	242.1
Capital assets sold or scrapped	2.3	1.3
Common stock sold for cash under stock options	1.4	.2
Long-term debt.	-	1.5
Other.	.5	1.2
	230.9	246.3
Reductions of working capital for:		
Cash dividends	76.7	68.3
Land, buildings, machinery and equipment	123.6	113.2
Investments in affiliated companies	-	5.0
Investments in subsidiary credit companies	.6	4.0
Long-term debt	46.9	24.0
	247.8	214.5
Increase or (decrease) in working capital during year	(16.9)	31.8
Working capital at beginning of year	501.3	469.5
Working capital at end of year	$484.4	$501.3
Increase or (decrease) in components of working capital:		
Cash	$ 11.9	$ (.4)
Receivable from customers and others	(50.4)	40.2
Prepaid expenses and income taxes allocable to the following year	4.0	12.6
Inventories.	20.8	79.1
Net change in current assets	(13.7)	131.5
Notes payable	34.6	62.5
Payable to material suppliers and others	(14.6)	30.5
Taxes based on income	(15.6)	3.8
Long-term debt due within one year	(1.2)	2.9
Net change in current liabilities	3.2	99.7
Net change in working capital	$(16.9)	$ 31.8

tends to charge the highest costs into the income statement and leaves the lowest costs as residuals on the balance sheet, a result which many managements prefer for tax reasons.

"Valuation"[5] as the term is used here relates to the number of dollars

---

[5] Other purposes for the valuation of property or of a business include the following: (a) valuation for purchase or sale on the basis of either the replacement

ILLUSTRATION 2–8 (continued)

Notes to Financial Statements

1. Summary of Accounting Policies

A. Basis of Consolidation

All companies described as subsidiaries of Caterpillar Tractor Co. are wholly owned. The consolidated results of operations include all subsidiaries, but the consolidated financial position excludes Caterpillar Credit Corporation and Caterpillar Overseas Credit Corporation S.A. Investments in these credit company subsidiaries are carried at cost plus the profit retained by them. Affiliated companies (Note 3) are not consolidated and are carried at cost.

B. Translation of Foreign Currencies

Inventories, investments and properties carried in foreign currencies are translated at rates of exchange prevailing at dates of acquisition; other assets and liabilities are translated at the rates of exchange prevailing at the end of the year. Sales, costs and expenses are translated at the average rates of exchange prevailing during the year, except that cost of goods sold and depreciation are translated at the rates of exchange prevailing at the time the related assets were acquired.

The rates of exchange used at December 31, 1971 were those prevailing at that date in the countries where the principal assets and liabilities denominated in other currencies were located.

The net adjustment arising from the translation of foreign currency accounts to U.S. dollars is deferred and amortized over the term of foreign currency long-term liabilities. At December 31, 1971 $3.0 million of such adjustment had been charged to "Income taxes and other costs allocable to future years, etc." The impact on consolidated profit for 1971 resulting from the translation of foreign currencies was negligible.

C. Inventories

A major portion of the inventories is stated on the basis of the "last-in, first-out" method of inventory accounting adopted in 1950. This is a generally accepted accounting method designed to allocate incurred costs in such a manner as to relate them to revenues more nearly on the same cost-price level than would the "first-in, first-out" method used prior to 1950. The general effect is to determine reported profits without including therein a major portion of the increases in inventory costs which result from rising price levels.

If the "first-in, first-out" method had been in use, inventories would have been $241.8 million and $196.7 million higher than reported at December 31, 1971 and December 31, 1970, respectively.

D. Depreciation

Depreciation is computed principally using accelerated methods ("sum-of-the-years-digits" and "declining balance") for both income tax and financial reporting purposes. These methods result in a larger allocation of the cost of buildings, machinery and equipment to operations in the early years of the lives of assets than does the straight-line method.

When an asset becomes fully depreciated, its cost is eliminated from both the asset and the accumulated depreciation accounts.

If the straight-line method had always been in use, "Buildings, machinery and equipment—net" would have been $166.8 million and $155.2 million higher than reported at December 31, 1971 and December 31, 1970, respectively, and depreciation expense for 1971 and 1970 would have been, respectively, $13.3 million less and $18.9 million less.

For financial reporting purposes the depreciation rates used are principally based on the "guideline" lives established by the U.S. Internal Revenue Service. For income tax purposes the depreciation rates used are principally based on the "guideline" lives for assets acquired prior to 1971 and on the Class Life System as provided for in the Revenue Act of 1971 for 1971 additions.

The generally accepted accounting principle followed with respect to buildings, machinery and equipment is the systematic allocation to each year's operations of a portion of the *original* cost of these facilities. The plant assets currently in use were acquired over many years at price levels which were lower than current price levels. The portion of the original cost of these assets allocated to each year and used in determining profit was, therefore, substantially lower than if a provision had been made on the basis of current replacement price levels.

E. Research and Development Costs

Research and development costs related to both future and present products are charged against operations as incurred.

F. Investment Credit

Investment tax credits are accounted for on the "flow-through" method, which recognizes the benefit in the year in which the assets which gave rise to the credit are placed in service. This is consistent with the treatment for income tax purposes. The alternative method would allocate the credit over the depreciable lives of the related assets.

assigned to the asset, liability, owners' equity, expense, and revenue items so that the most informative balance sheet and income statement may be prepared.

cost or the capitalization of earnings, or a combination of the two; (*b*) valuation for taxation on the basis of policies established by a government agency; (*c*) valuation for fire or other loss adjustment on the basis of current replacement costs; and (*d*) valuation for liquidation based on probable realization prices.

ILLUSTRATION 2–8 (continued)

2. Subsidiaries outside the United States

The net assets of the subsidiaries outside the United States and included in the consolidation at December 31 were as follows:

Locations of subsidiaries	Net current assets	Non-current assets	Long-term debt	Net assets	1970 Net assets
		(Millions of dollars)			
Australia	$ 29.3	$ 7.3	$ 1.1	$ 35.5	$ 30.8
Belgium and France	19.2	96.3	24.6	90.9	80.6
Brazil	15.1	11.7	—	26.8	22.0
Canada	7.3	1.9	—	9.2	11.1
Great Britain	42.6	20.5	—	63.1	54.2
Hong Kong and Singapore	26.0	2.2	—	28.2	21.2
Mexico	1.7	1.5	—	3.2	3.8
South Africa	6.5	1.2	—	7.7	6.4
Switzerland	75.3	5.8	—	81.1	80.3
	$223.0	$148.4	$ 25.7	$345.7	$310.4
December 31,1970	$204.8	$148.5	$ 42.9	$310.4	

Sales to customers outside the United States were $1,058.0 million or 48.6% of consolidated sales for the year ended December 31, 1971 and $1,117.6 million or 52.5% for the year ended December 31, 1970. More than 68% of consolidated sales for 1971, and more than 70% for 1970, consisted of product manufactured in the United States on which the consolidated profit margin is substantially the same as on product manufactured and sold to customers in the United States.

The product of manufacturing subsidiaries located outside the United States in most instances consists of components manufactured or purchased abroad which are assembled with components manufactured in the United States and sold to the subsidiaries at intercompany prices. The profits of these subsidiaries do not bear any definite relationship to their total net assets and, consequently, are not reported separately.

3. Investments in affiliated companies

Investments in affiliated companies are carried at cost and consist of 50% equities in Caterpillar Mitsubishi Ltd., Japan ($28.3 million) and in Tractor Engineers Limited, India ($0.6 million). The other 50% owners of these companies are, respectively, Mitsubishi Heavy Industries, Ltd., Tokyo, Japan, and Larsen & Toubro Limited, Bombay, India.

Caterpillar Mitsubishi was organized in 1963 and, as anticipated, incurred normal start-up and pre-operating expenses in the early years of its operations. It has, however, operated profitably in recent years and for the fiscal years ended September 30, 1971 and 1970 reported profits of $9.3 million and $8.5 million, respectively, including extraordinary credits arising from the carry-forward of income tax losses of $2.1 million and $4.1 million, respectively. The carry-forward of tax loss was fully utilized as of September 30, 1971.

Beginning in 1972 the Company will include in consolidated results of operations its proportionate share of Caterpillar Mitsubishi's profits or losses. The effect of equity accounting on profit for 1971 and prior years would not be material.

At December 31, 1971, $44.4 million of bank loans to Caterpillar Mitsubishi and Tractor Engineers were guaranteed by Caterpillar Overseas S.A. and, partially, by Caterpillar Tractor Co.

4. Investments in subsidiary credit companies

The combined condensed financial statements of Caterpillar Credit Corporation and Caterpillar Overseas Credit Corporation S.A. are as follows:

Financial Position (Millions of dollars)	December 31, 1971	1970
Current assets:		
Cash	$ 5.5	$ 2.7
Receivables—including $8.1 and $12.6 due after one year	40.9	67.6
	46.4	70.3
Deduct: Current liabilities:		
Trade accounts	.4	.8
Notes payable	20.0	45.5
Taxes based on income	.3	.2
	20.7	46.5
Net current assets	$25.7	$23.8
Subordinated debentures and notes payable to consolidated companies	$11.3	$10.7
Ownership:		
Common stock	6.9	6.9
Profit employed in the business	7.5	6.2
	14.4	13.1
	$25.7	$23.8

Results of Operations (Millions of dollars)	Year ended December 31, 1971	1970
Interest income	$ 5.7	$ 6.7
Deduct:		
Expenses	3.5	4.7
Taxes based on income	.9	.8
	4.4	5.5
Profit for year	1.3	1.2
Profit employed in the business at beginning of year	6.2	5.0
Profit employed in the business at end of year	$ 7.5	$ 6.2

The valuation and amortization problem is essentially a matter of properly allocating revenue and costs to particular past and future, as well as present, accounting periods. The basis of the assignment of dollar amounts to the various assets should be clearly indicated on the balance sheet by parenthetical explanations, in footnotes appended to the balance sheet, or in the text of the annual report.

ILLUSTRATION 2–8 (continued)

5. Long-term debt

Debt due after one year at December 31, consisted of the following:

	1971	1970
By parent company:	(Millions of dollars)	
Notes—3⅞%, due 1972 . . . . $ —	$ 7.0	
Debentures—5%, due 1973-1977	28.5	32.5
Debentures—5⅛%, due 1974-1986	32.5	37.5
Debentures—5.30%, due 1975-1992	135.0	150.0
By subsidiaries —due 1973-1988		
(equivalent to)	41.0	56.9
	$237.0	$283.9

The foregoing long-term debt at December 31, 1971 was payable as follows:

	(Millions of dollars)
1973	$ 20.7
1974	6.5
1975	14.0
1976-1980	78.9
1981-1985	61.0
1986-1992	55.9
	$237.0

There are varying restrictions on the payment of cash dividends under the agreements and indentures relating to the long-term debt. As of December 31, 1971 and December 31, 1970, under the terms of the most restrictive agreement, approximately $230 million and $580 million, respectively, of profit employed in the business was not available for the payment of dividends.

6. Receivable from customers and others

Receivables at December 31, 1971 and December 31, 1970 included $58.9 million and $102.7 million, respectively, evidenced by promissory notes from dealers and customers. Approximately $19.2 million and $31.9 million, respectively, of these notes mature beyond one year but were included in current assets in accordance with the accounting practice followed within the industry.

7. Taxes based on income

Taxes charged against operations are comprised of the following:

	1971	1970
Income taxes currently paid or payable . .	$104.0	$131.9
Tax effect of timing differences	3.6	(2.0)
Taxes based on income	$107.6	$129.9

Investment credits were $1.9 million and $1.6 million for 1971 and 1970, respectively.

8. Preferred stock

The Board of Directors is authorized to issue up to 5,000,000 shares of preferred stock in series and to determine the number of shares and the dividend, conversion, voting, redemption, liquidation, and other terms of each series. As of December 31, 1971, none of the shares had been issued.

9. Stock options

In August 1959 and April 1970 shareholders approved plans providing for the granting to officers and other key employees of options to purchase common stock of the Company, and in April 1971 shareholders approved an amendment of the 1970 plan. Options granted under both plans carry prices equal to 100% of the market price on the granting date. Authority to grant options under the 1959 plan expired in 1969.

Changes during 1971 in shares subject to issuance under options were as follows:

	Shares
Options outstanding at December 31, 1970	326,014
Granted at average price of $51.96 per share . . .	195,450
Exercised	(54,951)
Lapsed	(11,528)
	454,985

Options outstanding at December 31, 1971:	
At average price of $34.65 per share	216,735
At average price of $51.65 per share	238,250
	454,985

At December 31, 1971, 607,050 shares were available for future grants of options.

10. Pension plans

The Company and its subsidiaries have several pension plans covering substantially all employees. Total pension expense for the years 1971 and 1970 was $46.1 million and $33.0 million, respectively, which includes amortization of prior service costs over periods not to exceed 30 years. The Company's policy is to fund accrued pension costs. Based on actuarial estimates, the computed value of vested benefits exceeded the totals of the respective pension funds at December 31, 1971 and December 31, 1970 by approximately $165 million and $90 million, respectively.

The higher pension expense for 1971 and the increase in the amount by which the actuarial estimates of vested benefits exceed the pension funds are due primarily to increases in pension plan benefits.

There is no one single measurement policy which may be applied to all financial statement items. As shown by the Caterpillar Tractor Company's statement of financial position (Illustration 2–8, statement 2), different accounting principles, explained in some detail later in this chapter, are used in assigning dollar amounts to the various items. For example: Temporary investments when lower than cost may be

ILLUSTRATION 2–8 (continued)

STATEMENT 4
Significant Trends Since Incorporation
(Dollar amounts in millions except those stated on a share basis)

Year	Sales	Profit Amount	Profit Percentage of sales	Profit Per share of common stock(1)(2)	Cash dividends on common stock Amount	Cash dividends on common stock Per share(1)	Materials, supplies, services purchased, etc. *
1925	$ 13.8	$ 3.3	23.7	$ .077	$ .7	$ .015	$ 5.1
1926	20.7	4.3	20.9	.102	1.6	.039	12.4
1927	26.9	5.7	21.3	.136	2.7	.064	14.9
1928	35.1	8.7	24.9	.196	4.2	.095	22.9
1929	51.8	12.4	24.0	.254	5.6	.116	28.1
1930	45.4	9.1	20.1	.186	7.5	.154	21.7
1931	24.1	1.6	6.5	.032	5.6	.116	7.6
1932	13.3	(1.6)	(12.2)	(.033)	1.2	.024	5.8
1933	14.4	.4	2.5	.007	.2	.005	7.7
1934	23.8	3.8	16.0	.078	2.4	.048	11.4
1935	36.4	6.2	17.2	.128	3.8	.077	18.0
1936	54.1	10.2	18.9	.209	3.8	.077(3)	27.7
1937	63.2	10.6	16.7	.210	3.8	.077(3)	33.5
1938	48.2	3.2	6.7	.054	3.8	.077	20.5
1939	58.4	6.0	10.3	.111	3.8	.077	30.0
1940	73.1	7.8	10.7	.160	3.8	.077	36.9
1941	102.0	7.7	7.6	.159	3.8	.077	57.6
1942	142.2	7.0	4.9	.143	3.8	.077	78.1
1943	171.4	7.6	4.4	.155	3.8	.077	87.5
1944	242.2	7.3	3.0	.150	3.8	.077	146.5
1945	230.6	6.5	2.8	.133	4.7	.096	139.4
1946	128.4	6.1	4.8	.125	5.6	.116	78.0
1947	189.1	13.5	7.1	.276	5.6	.116	110.4
1948	218.0	17.5	8.0	.357	5.6	.116	121.2
1949	254.9	17.2	6.7	.343	6.6	.135	147.4
1950	337.3	29.2	8.7	.577	8.5	.173	187.7
1951	394.3	15.8	4.0	.298	11.3	.228	279.6
1952	480.8	22.7	4.7	.437	11.5	.231	254.3
1953	437.8	20.6	4.7	.396	9.6	.194(4)	237.0
1954	406.7	25.9	6.4	.502	8.0	.162(4)	195.1
1955	533.0	36.0	6.8	.699	13.3	.266	306.3
1956	685.9	55.5	8.1	1.016	16.9	.315	381.3
1957	649.9	40.0	6.2	.725	21.6	.399	380.0
1958	585.2	32.2	5.5	.580	21.6	.400	275.5
1959	742.3	46.5	6.3	.842	24.4	.450	409.2
1960	716.0	42.6	6.0	.770	27.2	.500	383.5
1961	734.3	55.8	7.6	1.012	27.2	.500	370.6
1962	827.0	61.9	7.5	1.124	27.2	.500	415.5
1963	966.1	77.3	8.0	1.416	31.4	.575	491.7
1964	1,216.6	129.1	10.6	2.280	42.6	.750	623.0
1965	1,405.3	158.5	11.3	2.796	56.4	1.000	705.5
1966	1,524.0	150.1	9.9	2.643	68.0	1.200	784.8
1967	1,472.5	106.4	7.2	1.872	68.1	1.200	788.6
1968	1,707.1	121.6	7.1	2.139	68.1	1.200	845.6
1969	2,001.6	142.5	7.1	2.505	68.3	1.200	1,064.3
1970	2,127.8	143.8	6.8	2.527	68.3	1.200	1,087.7
1971	2,175.2	128.3	5.9	2.253	76.7	1.350	1,063.2

(1) After adjustment for stock splits and stock dividends.
(2) Computed on weighted average number of shares outstanding.

shown on the balance sheet at actual present realizable amounts. Accounts receivable are customarily stated at the estimated realizable amount by deducting estimated uncollectible receivables from the amount of gross receivables. Inventories, on the other hand, are not shown at either actual or estimated realizable amounts. Realizable amounts with reference to inventories mean selling prices. Inventories

ILLUSTRATION 2–8 (continued)

CATERPILLAR TRACTOR CO. AND CONSOLIDATED SUBSIDIARIES

Wages, salaries and contributions for employee benefits	Taxes based on income		Capitalized expenditures for land, buildings, machinery and equipment	Depreciation and amortization	Average number of employees	Number of shareholders of common stock at year end	Year
	Amount	Percentage of sales					
$ 2.9	$ .3	2.0	$ .6	$ .3	2,537	1,919	1925
4.8	.7	3.3	1.1	.5	2,931	2,556	1926
5.8	.9	3.3	2.3	.7	3,511	4,597	1927
7.8	1.1	3.2	5.6	.9	4,897	6,851	1928
11.5	1.5	2.8	7.1	1.3	6,875	10,820	1929
10.6	.9	2.0	2.8	1.7	6,282	12,812	1930
6.7	.2	.8	1.1	1.6	3,737	15,983	1931
5.3	—	—	.9	1.7	3,247	17,451	1932
5.2	—	.2	.9	1.8	3,501	15,668	1933
8.0	.5	2.3	1.0	1.8	5,586	15,014	1934
11.2	1.1	2.9	2.0	1.8	7,488	15,063	1935
17.4	1.8	3.3	4.7	1.9	11,168	15,062	1936
21.7	1.8	2.9	3.8	2.2	12,234	15,626	1937
16.7	.9	1.9	2.4	2.4	9,432	16,553	1938
19.7	1.3	2.3	2.2	2.5	10,671	16,838	1939
23.5	3.8	5.3	4.4	2.6	11,781	17,175	1940
34.0	8.4	8.2	5.0	3.7	15,292	17,224	1941
43.9	15.3	10.8	3.2	4.5	16,488	17,225	1942
51.4	18.2	10.6	1.2	4.9	18,252	17,455	1943
70.4	17.6	7.3	1.3	5.4	20,455	17,464	1944
62.2	9.3	4.0	3.7	4.6	18,609	18,383	1945
52.2	2.5	1.9	11.1	1.4	19,755	18,799	1946
65.0	7.9	4.2	21.7	2.3	20,925	18,991	1947
71.4	10.3	4.7	18.1	3.8	21,638	18,662	1948
76.8	10.8	4.3	8.3	4.9	22,795	18,863	1949
90.0	33.2	9.8	17.4	5.5	24,746	19,211	1950
111.3	20.5	5.2	26.5	7.9	28,633	19,171	1951
137.9	46.0	9.6	17.2	10.6	31,678	19,348	1952
135.0	36.3	8.3	33.9	12.8	29,643	19,597	1953
125.9	28.0	6.9	21.7	16.0	25,783	19,515	1954
174.2	39.3	7.4	30.9	18.6	31,400	21,274	1955
205.4	59.7	8.7	31.4	22.3	37,909	26,376	1956
216.5	40.1	6.2	73.6	21.8	39,491	27,555	1957
164.0	26.1	4.5	54.6	27.7	31,060	27,330	1958
245.6	39.7	5.4	59.1	28.0	42,120	28,694	1959
244.0	31.3	4.4	53.2	28.3	40,638	33,460	1960
229.2	51.6	7.0	27.9	31.6	35,810	34,262	1961
250.2	52.2	6.3	31.9	39.8	36,364	34,139	1962
280.9	81.6	8.5	44.9	41.2	38,527	33,138	1963
353.1	118.3	9.7	60.8	43.7	46,204	39,515	1964
408.2	130.3	9.3	98.1	46.2	50,800	47,840	1965
473.4	109.7	7.2	140.3	51.7	55,107	50,180	1966
490.0	61.0	4.1	219.9	64.0	56,635	48,910	1967
571.6	90.5	5.3	183.3	82.2	59,848	48,126	1968
652.9	130.6	6.5	110.0	95.9	63,939	47,178	1969
710.3	129.9	6.1	113.2	99.5	66,062	48,201	1970
767.2	107.6	4.9	123.6	99.7	62,528	46,726	1971

(3) In addition, dividends were paid of 7/200 of a share of preferred stock for each share of common in 1936 and 3/100 of a share of preferred stock for each share of common in 1937. A portion of the 1936 dividend was payable in cash at the option of the shareholder and in 1938 and 1939 the preferred stock was retired for cash.

(4) In addition, dividends of 4% were paid in common stock.

are traditionally stated on the balance sheet at cost or the lower of cost or market. Market refers to replacement cost and not to selling price.

Long-term investments and land are customarily stated on the balance sheet at cost. Prepaid expenses, deferred charges, and property, plant, and equipment (exclusive of land) are shown as unexpired costs, i.e.,

ILLUSTRATION 2–8 (concluded)

STATEMENT 5
Source of Consolidated Net Assets
(Millions of dollars)

CAPITAL STOCK, COMMON

Year		Number of shares	Amount paid in for stock	Profit employed in the business incorporated in capital accounts	Total in capital accounts
1925–26	Issued for net assets of predecessor companies	1,625,000(1)	$ 12.3	$ -	$ 12.3
1928	Issued for net assets of Russell Grader				
	Manufacturing Company	86,127	2.5	-	2.5
1929	Sold for cash	171,113	8.3	-	8.3
	Balance	1,882,240	23.1	-	23.1
1949	Exchange of two shares of $10 par value common				
	for each share of no par common	1,882,240	-	14.5(2)	14.5
	Balance after stock split	3,764,480	23.1	14.5	37.6
1951	Issued for entire capital stock of Trackson Company	54,000	2.2	-	2.2
1952–55	Sold for cash under stock options	38,372	1.7	-	1.7
1953–54	Issued as 4% stock dividends	311,785	-	16.9(3)	16.9
	Balance	4,168,637	27.0	31.4	58.4
1955	Issued one additional share for each share				
	outstanding	4,168,637	-	24.9(2)	24.9
	Balance after stock split	8,337,274	27.0	56.3	83.3
1955–59	Sold for cash under stock options	192,038	7.4	-	7.4
1956	Sold for cash	500,000	33.2	-	33.2
1956	Issued for entire capital stock of				
	Englehart Manufacturing Company	20,000	1.0	-	1.0
	Balance	9,049,312	68.6	56.3	124.9
1959	Exchange of three shares of no par value common				
	for each share of $10 par value common	18,098,624	-	-	-
	Balance after stock split	27,147,936	68.6	56.3	124.9
1959–64	Sold for cash under stock options	174,287	3.9	-	3.9
	Balance	27,322,223	72.5	56.3	128.8
1964	Issued one additional share for each share				
	outstanding	27,322,223	-	-	-
	Balance after stock split	54,644,446	72.5	56.3	128.8
1964–71	Sold for cash under stock options	415,981	8.2	-	8.2
1965	Issued for net assets of Towmotor Corporation	1,891,678	2.3	1.0	3.3(4)
		56,952,105	$ 83.0	$ 57.3	$ 140.3

PROFIT EMPLOYED IN THE BUSINESS

Year		Profit	Appropriations Cash Dividends	Incorporated in capital accounts	Amount at end of period
1925–69	. . . .	$1,589.1	$768.4	$ 57.3	$763.4
1970	. . . .	143.8	68.3	-	838.9
1971	. . . .	128.3	76.7	-	890.5
		$1,861.2	$913.4	$ 57.3	890.5
Source of consolidated net assets (statement 2)					$1,030.8

(1) At incorporation, 260,000 shares of common stock were issued for net assets of predecessor companies. In February, 1926, those shares were increased to 325,000 shares by a five-for-four stock split effected in the form of a 25% stock dividend. In December, 1926, a conversion of five shares for one share increased the issued shares to 1,625,000.
(2) Excess of par value of shares outstanding after stock split over amount carried in capital accounts prior to the stock split.
(3) Market value of stock at date issued as 4% stock dividends.
(4) Total of common stock and capital surplus accounts of Towmotor Corporation at the date of the merger.

the dollar amounts that are allocable to future accounting periods as operating costs.

As a result of the various methods of measuring or assigning dollar amounts to the assets as indicated above, it should be quite clear that the stated amount of owners' equity does not reflect "present worth." In fact, it is compounded of a variety of "values."

Distinction between capital and revenue expenditures

An expenditure is the incurrence of an obligation to pay immediately or in the future for a benefit received. Expenditures applicable to fixed assets are either capital or revenue expenditures. Purchases of properties such as buildings, machinery, fixtures, and equipment that are not consumed during the current accounting period represent capital expenditures that affect the income of future accounting periods. Purchases of properties, supplies, and services that are consumed during the current accounting period are revenue expenditures that affect only the income for the present period. These latter expenditures are for the most part repetitive in nature.

Therefore, the cost of washing windows, being of very short-lived value, is a revenue expenditure, not an asset. If the value derived from washing windows was longer lived, like a paint job, it could be a capital expenditure.[6]

Although most acquisitions are readily classified as either capital or revenue expenditures, the accountant is sometimes faced with difficult classifications. Fundamentally, the classification rests on the relation of the useful life of the property acquired and the length of the accounting period for which income is being determined. However, certain parts of an asset that are replaced may be of some benefit to future periods, but the cost might be too immaterial to be considered as a capital expenditure.

The distinction between capital and revenue expenditures is discussed in more detail below:

Additions to fixed assets result in adding quantity to the existing property that will benefit future accounting periods, and their cost should be treated as capital expenditures. That is, the total cost of acquiring an entirely new unit, enlarging a building by adding an additional story or a new wing, or of acquiring and installing a new machine should be charged to specific asset accounts.

Expenditures for improvements and betterments to fixed assets result in increasing the efficiency, productivity, life, or durability of a plant facility. The physical quantity of the property is not changed—there is an increase in quality. The foregoing capital expenditures if material in amount should be charged to accumulated depreciation unless the expenditures result in increasing the cost of the asset above that which was originally incurred. In this case the expenditure is charged to the asset account. For example, the replacement of a wooden or composition

---

[6] But painting costs are frequently charged to expense. Technically they should be capitalized but they are usually short-lived (though more than a year) and are "charged off" as a convenience. Even the Internal Revenue Service usually accepts this procedure.

shingle roof with a tile roof represents an improvement since the durability of the building is greater and the life of the asset in all probability would be extended. Furthermore, the cost of the improvement would be in excess of the original cost of the old covering of the roof. The cost of the old roofing should be eliminated from the asset account, and the amount of depreciation accumulated on the old roofing should be removed from the accumulated depreciation account.

"Used" property that is acquired usually requires expenditures for rehabilitation or reconditioning to restore its efficient operating state. Such costs should be treated as capital expenditures.

Ordinary repairs and minor replacements of parts maintain a fixed asset in an efficient operating condition. These revenue expenditures are proper charges to expense accounts because only the current accounting period is affected; the original cost or the estimated service life of the assets is not changed.

A theoretical distinction usually not reflected in the accounts may be made between repairs and maintenance. Maintenance such as oiling, painting, and adjusting maintains the operating efficiency of assets; this is a type of work directed to prevent substandard efficiency. Repairs such as minor replacements when a machine breaks down or is less efficient because of worn parts restores the asset to normal operating condition; this is a curative type of work. The term "deferred maintenance and repairs" has reference to maintenance and repair work that has been delayed until some accounting period subsequent to the time that the cost should have been incurred.

Major (extraordinary) repairs and replacement of parts result in increasing, i.e., prolonging, the service life of a fixed asset or its efficiency, productivity, or utility. A replacement may be a substitution of a similar part or installation of a new part that is better than the old one when the asset was acquired. The latter type of replacement represents an improvement or betterment. Theoretically, such expenditures should be capitalized by charging the specific asset involved. This would also require the removal of the cost of the replaced part from the asset account; the related accumulation of depreciation should also be eliminated. In most cases the foregoing "removal" is not practicable; therefore, an alternative procedure is customarily followed—the capitalization of the expenditure by charging the accumulated depreciation. In effect, such a charge cancels recorded depreciation. The problem of accounting for repairs and replacements must be viewed from a practical point of view. Additions and improvements to fixed assets are readily classified as capital expenditures. Expenditures that definitely result in prolonging the life of an asset or increasing its usefulness, utility, or efficiency beyond the original estimates can also be considered capital expenditures. Costs for repairs and replacements in addition to the foregoing cannot be logically separated into capital (large) and revenue (small) expenditures except on the bases of a planned relationship to the annual depreciation charge in terms of dollar amounts or units of plant.

For example, a 5 percent depreciation rate may be established, with the understanding that all of the cost of repairs and replacements is to be treated as *revenue* expenditures. A 10 percent depreciation rate may be established on the assumption that the cost of all of the repairs and replacements is to be capitalized by charging the *accumulated depreciation* account. In the latter case, the annual depreciation charge represents a combination of depreciation and repairs and replacements expense. In between these two extremes, management may establish minimum dollar costs that may be charged to the accumulated depreciation amount.

Therefore, management may establish a 7 percent depreciation rate and decide to charge major repairs and replacements in excess of $1,000 to the accumulated depreciation. According to this plan the annual depreciation charge should be sufficient to absorb the foregoing expenditures and also to provide for the full depreciation of the asset (less salvage value) during its estimated service life. If a 5 percent depreciation rate is established, the minimum amount for repairs and replacements to be charged to the accumulated depreciation account might be raised to $1,500; if a 9 percent rate is set, the minimum may be lowered to $500. In the foregoing cases the cost of repairs and replacements in excess of a minimum dollar amount is capitalized by charging accumulated depreciation and the cost below the minimum is debited to expense.

Some businesses account for units of property in terms of physical units and use these property units as bases for computing the amount of the annual depreciation. For a telephone company, the telephone is a unit of property; for an air carrier, an aircraft engine, propeller, and radio and radar equipment are units of property.

When a physical unit is replaced, the cost is capitalized and the cost of the discarded unit is eliminated from the asset, and the related amount of accumulated depreciation is also removed. When repairs or replacements are made, the cost is considered a revenue expenditure.

In distinguishing between capital and revenue expenditures, units of property may be defined in terms of dollars rather than physical units. In this instance the units of property must be coordinated with the annual depreciation charge—the larger the depreciation charge, the smaller the "unit of property."

QUESTIONS AND PROBLEMS

2–1. In financing a business, funds are obtained from several sources. In what manner does a balance sheet show the sources of these funds? How does the balance sheet reflect the investment of these funds?

2–2. Explain the term "accounting equation." Formulate an accounting equation to illustrate each of the following situations:
  a) The closing process has not been completed.
  b) The closing process has been completed.

2–3. *a*) Distinguish between capital and revenue expenditures.
  b) When does the accountant make the distinction between capital and revenue expenditures?
  c) Does the element of time enter into the problem of making a distinction between capital and revenue expenditures?
  d) What is the practical significance of making such a distinction?
  e) Explain: "Expenditures that are *capital expenditures* are referred to as capitalized items."

2–4. Discuss the accounting valuation and amortization problem and show how the financial statements are affected.

2–5. An accountant indicated to his staff that it is necessary to comply with the following practices:
  (1) Distinguish clearly between capital and revenue expenditures.
  (2) Allocate revenue and expense to the appropriate accounting periods.
  (3) Recognize losses but do not anticipate profit.
  Required:
  You are requested to answer the following questions relative to the foregoing:
  a) In what way would the results of matching revenue and expense be affected if the listed practices were disregarded?
  b) Would the financial statements be stated correctly if the practices were not considered? Explain.
  c) If the practices are not followed, would the company's accounts be maintained on the cash-basis of accounting?

2–6. Define a balance sheet.

2–7. List the major divisions of the balance sheet and explain their meaning.

2–8. Distinguish between the various forms of balance sheets.

2–9. List practices that should be observed in balance sheet preparation.

2–10. What is meant by the term "valuation" as used in this text?

3

The balance sheet: Current assets

THE ARRANGEMENT of items on a balance sheet depends largely on the purpose it is to serve. Listing the items in only three groups—assets, liabilities, and owners' equity—is not adequate for a satisfactory analysis, since relationships between individual items or groups of similar items cannot be conveniently determined. Therefore, it is customary to subdivide the main divisions of the balance sheet into sections. Typical balance sheet sections are as follows

Assets	*Liabilities*
Current assets	Current liabilities
Long-term investments	Deferred credits
Fixed assets	Long-term liabilities
Intangible assets	
Deferred charges	*Owners' Equity*
Other noncurrent assets	Capital stock*
	Capital contributed in excess
	of par or stated value
	Retained earnings:
	Unappropriated
	Appropriated

* In some states, *capital stock* is designated *stated capital,* which represents the par or stated value of shares of stock or the amount received for the stock when sold.

The caption "other noncurrent assets" or "miscellaneous assets" is used frequently in balance sheets for classifying such assets as cash in closed bank, miscellaneous investments not included as temporary or long-term investments, and other assets that cannot be properly classified according to the groups used.

Current assets

Assets may be usefully classified as current and noncurrent. Liabilities are also current and noncurrent. The distinction between current and noncurrent items is encountered on almost all published balance sheets, but opinions differ as to the classification of some of the items. The basic underlying difference between current and noncurrent assets is the frequency of opportunity for managerial decision relative to recommitment of capital to other uses. This opportunity arises when an asset is converted into cash. Current assets are converted into cash with far greater frequency than are noncurrent assets. Cash becomes available for payment of liabilities to the extent that management decides not to *reinvest* the capital in some form of asset. Therefore, the sources of cash for payments on debt are other borrowings (for example, incurring long-term debt to pay current debt), profits, depreciation, and contributions of additional capital.

Of course, depreciation does not in fact really produce cash. The cash comes from gross revenue, and the depreciation serves to bar it from being counted as profit. This is one of the principal reasons why the incoming flow of cash is often in excess of net income; but not always, as when expenditures for equipment or other assets are heavy.

The distinction between current and noncurrent items is relative; classification depends on the period of time that will elapse before the asset is converted into cash or completely consumed or before the liability matures. Current receivables will soon be converted into cash; cash will be applied to the acquisition of inventory, to the payment of short-term debt, or to other purposes depending upon management's decision. All of these items—cash, receivables, inventory, short-term debt—are current because they turn over at a relatively high rate during a short period of time. The circulating nature of current asset items is as follows: Cash and trade credit are used to acquire materials, goods, and supplies that are sold after processing, without processing, on credit or for cash. The receivables are eventually collected in cash, which is used in part at least to pay current liabilities and for additional inventory.

Plant facilities may be currently salable, but they are not held for that purpose; therefore, they are properly classified as noncurrent (fixed) assets. U.S. government obligations usually represent a temporary investment that is readily available for conversion into cash and may be used to meet current liabilities or for other corporate purposes; such items are current assets. Bonds payable in 10 years do not represent a burden on current assets; therefore, such bonds are noncurrent liabilities. Inventories and prepaid expenses, such as unexpired insurance and prepayment of rental charges, will be sold or consumed in current operations; their availability makes it unnecessary to incur additional current liabilities and expend available cash; therefore, these items are current.

The Committee on Accounting Procedure of the AICPA, *Accounting Research Bulletin No. 43*,[1] stated that for accounting purposes "the term current assets is used to designate cash or other assets or resources commonly identified as those which are reasonably expected to be realized in cash or sold or consumed during the normal operating cycle of the business." The normal operating cycle may be defined as the average time intervening between the expenditure for merchandise or for materials and labor for the production of finished goods and the collection of cash from sales. A one-year time period is to be used as a basis for the segregation of current assets in cases where more than one operating cycle occurs within a year. However, where the period of the operating cycle is more than 12 months, as in the tobacco, distillery, and lumber businesses, the longer period should be used.[2]

Current assets[3] consist, in general, of such resources as:

1. Cash available for current operations and other corporate purposes.
2. Marketable securities or other temporary investments of cash which normally will be available for current operations or for use in emergencies.
3. Inventories including factory supplies and ordinary maintenance material and parts.
4. Trade accounts, notes, and acceptances receivable.
5. Receivables from officers, employees, affiliates, and others if collectible in the ordinary course of business within one year.
6. Installment or deferred accounts and notes receivable if they conform generally to normal trade practices and terms within the industry.
7. Prepaid expenses such as insurance, interest, rents, taxes, unused royalties, current payment for advertising service not yet received, and operating supplies.

The following items should be excluded from current assets,[4] since it is not expected that they will become available for the payment of current debt within the normal operating cycle or one year, whichever is longer.

1. Cash and claims to cash that are restricted as to withdrawal, or clearly intended for use for other than current operations, are designated for expenditure in the acquisition or construction of noncurrent assets, or are segregated for the liquidation of long-term debts.
2. Investments in securities (whether marketable or not) or advances

---

[1] Page 20.

[2] AICPA, *Accounting Research Bulletin No. 43* (1953), p. 21, in *Accounting Research and Terminology Bulletins, Final Edition* (New York, 1961).

[3] Ibid., p. 20.

[4] Ibid., p. 21.

which have been made for the purposes of control, affiliation, or other continuing business advantages.

3. Receivables arising from unusual transactions (such as the sale of noncurrent assets, or loans or advances to affiliates, officers, or employees) that are not expected to be collected within 12 months.
4. Cash surrender value of life insurance policies.
5. Plant, property, and equipment used in regular operations.
6. Land and other natural resources.
7. Long-term prepayments that are fairly chargeable to the operations of several years, or deferred charges such as unamortized debt discount and expense, bonus payments under a long-term lease, costs of rearrangement of factory layout or removal to a new location, and research and development costs.

Whenever current assets are pledged they should be shown under a separate title, or the pledge should be indicated by parenthetical comment or by a footnote to the balance sheet. Such information is pertinent to making an analysis of the financial condition of any business.

Current asset items should be listed on the balance sheet according to their liquidity, i.e., in the order in which they normally will be converted into cash. The usual order of presentation is:

Cash on hand and in bank	
Special deposits for payment of interest and dividends (for current use)	Cash and its equivalent
Temporary investments of cash	
Notes receivable	
Accounts receivable	One step removed from cash
Accrued revenue receivable	
Inventories	
Prepaid expenses	Two steps removed from cash

In the following pages the nature and the valuation problems of individual current asset items are discussed.

Cash on hand and in banks

Cash consists of coins, paper money, demand deposits, checking accounts in banks, express and postal money orders, customer checks, and bank drafts, all of which are unrestricted and therefore available immediately for general business purposes. Any item accepted for deposit at its face value by a bank may be included as *cash*. Deposits in savings accounts may be included as cash inasmuch as banks seldom demand notice of withdrawal. Demand certificates of deposit may also be classified as cash. Petty cash and payroll funds may be included in cash or shown separately. Cash should not include such items as postdated or dishonored customer checks, or time certificates of deposit, or deposits in closed banks.

Cash should not include segregated funds earmarked for specific purposes that make the money not available for current purposes, such as the payment of current debt. Examples are cash segregated for plant modernization and expansion; or for payment of long-term debt; or retirement of preferred stock; or on deposit with utility companies; or in escrow. Therefore, cash earmarked for the payment of dividends would not be included in unearmarked cash; nor would it be included in current assets unless the liability created by the declaration of a dividend is listed as a current liability.

An overdraft in a bank account is a current liability, and it should not be included as a negative element in cash in banks unless there is an offsetting positive balance in the same bank.

Valuation of cash

The valuation of cash is relatively simple since it has a definite assigned value. Problems do arise, however, in connection with valuing cash balances in closed banks[5] and converting balances in foreign banks in terms of U.S. dollars.

Unless otherwise stated, one should be able to assume that the amount of cash shown in the balance sheet is available for immediate application to payment of current debt.

Temporary investments of cash

Temporary investments of cash are usually moneys not needed currently for the operation of the business, but which should remain part of working capital, readily available should a need for cash arise. U.S. government obligations are a favorite investment of such funds.

The following should not be included as marketable securities in the current asset section of the balance sheet: (1) the company's own stocks or bonds that have been reacquired; (2) stocks or bonds of a subsidiary or affiliated company unless the securities can be and are held to be used if necessary for current operations or emergencies; (3) securities that are earmarked for specified funds; (4) securities of uncertain value; and (5) securities not readily marketable.

Valuation of temporary investments of cash

Temporary investments of cash are most commonly shown on balance sheets at cost with a parenthetical notation relative to the current market

---

[5] When the bank is a member of the Federal Deposit Insurance Corporation, deposits up to $20,000 are protected by insurance.

value; but if convertibility into cash can be reasonably assured, current assets can be valued at market.

The AICPA's *Accounting Research Bulletin No. 43*,[6] which carries the approval of the Accounting Principles Board, says:

The amounts at which various current assets are carried do not always represent their present realizable cash values.

. . . However, practice varies with respect to the carrying basis for current assets such as marketable securities and inventories. In the case of marketable securities where market value is less than cost by a substantial amount and it is evident that the decline in market value is not due to a mere temporary condition, the amount to be included as a current asset should not exceed the market value. . . .

It is important that the amounts at which current assets are stated be supplemented by information which reveals, for temporary investments, their market value at the balance sheet date. . . .

Of the 600 large corporations surveyed in *Accounting Trends and Techniques 1971*, 376 listed marketable securities in the current assets section of their balance sheets. Those stating that their stated value, at cost, approximated market value, numbered 211. Those stating market value above and below cost numbered 30. The remainder, 140, made no mention of market.

If marketable securities are pledged or otherwise encumbered, it is of course necessary to disclose that fact parenthetically or in a footnote. Sometimes, if marketable securities are expected to be carried for a relatively short period, discount or premium is not amortized.

When the market value of temporary cash investments is lower than cost, the difference may be recorded in a valuation account deducted from the cost of the asset. This device makes it possible to show both the original cost and the present value on the face of the statement.

If a valuation account is not created, securities that are worth less than their cost may be shown as follows:

Marketable securities (cost, $1,619,000) $1,515,000

Cost includes brokers' commissions, postage, insurance, and taxes.

Notes receivable

A promissory note is "an unconditional promise in writing made by one person to another, signed by the maker, engaging to pay on demand or at a fixed or determinable future time a sum certain in money to order or to bearer."[7] Promissory notes may or may not be interest bearing; U.S. Treasury bills include an amount for interest in the face value. If a material amount of interest has been earned on notes receiv-

---

[6] Chap. 3, "Working Capital," Sec. A, par. 9.

[7] Uniform Negotiable Instruments Law.

able as of the balance sheet date, it should be shown as accrued interest receivable. Notes receivable are frequently called bills receivable. Since the instruments have substantially the same characteristics, drafts receivable, trade acceptances, and bills of exchange are usually shown under the title of notes receivable. Bonds, notes, bills—all negotiable instruments—that mature within a year (or within the operating cycle) are current assets.

Promissory notes received in payment of current sales of merchandise are more desirable than accounts receivable, since they usually bear interest and represent written evidences of indebtedness, a characteristic that improves their enforceability in court; they are signed by the debtor. Furthermore, in most instances, promissory notes may be discounted more readily and conveniently than accounts receivable.

Drafts receivable and trade acceptances are time drafts drawn on customers and accepted by them. Drafts may not represent a current transaction but, instead, the formalization of a past-due account receivable.

A trade acceptance is customarily preferable to a draft receivable because it is a time draft accepted by the purchaser at the time the sale is made and is, therefore, more readily approved for discount purposes at a bank. When discounted, this instrument is two-name paper; the acceptor has a primary liability, and the drawer has a secondary liability. A trade acceptance is known as "self-liquidating paper" because it is given by the customer for merchandise that is to be resold in the ordinary course of business. The proceeds of these sales will often serve to pay the trade acceptance at maturity.

The notes receivable item on the balance sheet should reflect only regular trade notes. Promissory notes that have been received from officers, employees, and others for loans and the sale of capital stock should be shown separately rather than as notes receivable. So should past-due or dishonored notes, and an adequate amount for estimated uncollectible receivables should be provided; worthless promissory notes should be written off.

A business sometimes discounts (borrows on) notes receivable. This creates a contingent liability. A contingent liability is one that may or may not have to be met. If the maker of a note or the acceptor of a draft pays the discounted obligation at maturity, the endorser is not liable. If the person or company primarily liable does not pay, the contingent liability becomes a real liability, and the endorser may have to pay it.

Notes receivable discounted also represent a *contingent asset.*[8] That is, if the note is dishonored at maturity, the endorser is required to

---

[8] Contingent assets may also be present in connection with claims for infringement of patent rights, claims for income tax refund, and receivables that have been written off but have some prospects of being at least partially collected.

pay the holder of the instrument. The endorser receives the promissory note, which represents a claim on the maker. Therefore, the contingent asset (from date of discount to date of dishonor) has become a real asset (as of date of payment by endorser). The actual value of the asset depends upon the probability of receiving final payment from the maker. Contingent assets are not usually mentioned on the balance sheet.

The contingent liability for notes receivable that have been discounted may be shown on the balance sheet (1) as a footnote indicating that the company is contingently liable for notes receivable discounted ($10,000) or (2) in this way:

Current Assets:
Notes receivable $30,000
Less: Notes receivable discounted 10,000 $20,000

It is desirable also to state parenthetically or in a footnote that "the company is contingently liable as endorser of these notes."

Accounts receivable

Accounts receivable should include only claims against customers for merchandise sold on credit. This item, sometimes called trade debtors, customers' accounts, or trade accounts receivable, should not include such items as promissory notes, loans to officers or employees, advances to salesmen, advances to agents or affiliated companies, transfers of merchandise to branches, amounts receivable from sales of noncurrent assets or other nonmerchandise assets, advances on contracts to buy merchandise, or sales of capital stock on a subscription plan. These miscellaneous receivables, in general, do not arise in the ordinary course of business; and they will not be collected in accordance with the regular credit terms. Sometimes a merchant includes in accounts receivable advances or deposits made to suppliers on contracts or purchases. These items are properly shown separately as advances on purchases.

Accounts receivable that are collectible within one year or within the operating cycle should be shown on the balance sheet as current assets at book value. A valuation account, representing the estimated uncollectible total included in the receivables shown, is deducted from the asset.[9] The terminology currently in use for this valuation account by 600 companies is shown in *Accounting Trends and Techniques 1971*. Since the AICPA's Committee on Terminology stated that it is undesirable to use the term "reserve" except in connection with appropriations of retained earnings,[10] the title "reserve for doubtful accounts," and simi-

---

[9] Accounting Principles Board, AICPA, *Opinion No. 12.*

[10] Committee on Terminology, AICPA, "Review and Resumé," *Accounting Terminology Bulletin No. 1* (New York, 1953). (Republished in AICPA, *Accounting Research and Terminology Bulletins, Final Edition* (New York, 1961).

lar headings has declined from 181 in 1955 to 71 in 1970. "Allowance for doubtful accounts" was used in 1970 by 235 companies out of the 573 that indicated the existence of such a provision. There has been a 50 percent increase in the use of the word "allowance" since 1955. The terms "provision" and "estimates" were each used by only 21 companies: both titles have declined steadily.

Credit balances in customer accounts may be caused by overpayments, returns or allowances made after full payment of invoice, or advance payments for goods not billed. These credit balances are current liabilities. Accounts receivable that are not due within one year or within the operating cycle should be shown as noncurrent assets immediately below the current asset section. However, if according to generally recognized trade practice all such accounts receivable are shown as current assets, the amount collectible after one year should be clearly shown in a parenthetical statement.

Frequently, accounts receivable and notes receivable are pledged as collateral for loans or credit. Such pledged assets, which are subject to the prior claim of the creditor or creditors, should be shown as a separate item on the balance sheet. Alternative methods of presentation are by way of parenthetical comment or by footnote.

Collateral or other pledged assets may be held as security for the payment of notes and accounts receivable. In such instances the current market value, or a brief description of the pledged assets, should be noted.

Accounts receivable may also be assigned. Unless the assignment was made on a *without-recourse basis,* the assigning company has a contingent liability, which should be shown on the balance sheet.

In the majority of published reports, notes receivable and accounts receivable are listed in one amount, and a valuation account is deducted. It is important that there be an adequate and informative disclosure of the nature of receivables and the basis of their valuation.

Valuation of notes and accounts receivable

Accounts and notes receivable, commonly referred to as trade receivables, should be shown on the balance sheet at face value less the related valuation account, Allowance for Doubtful Accounts. It is the best practice to list the accounts and notes as separate totals and to state the total allowance provided.

Debit balances in creditors' accounts are receivables and should be reclassified as assets.

At the end of the accounting period, the uncollectible receivables expense and the increase in the allowance account is often computed as a percentage of the total net sales, the credit sales, or the balance of receivables. Two other bases may be mentioned: an arbitrary amount, or an aging of receivables. Experience in collecting is the real criterion in determining the estimated amount of uncollectible receivables.

Customer accounts are *aged* by listing all accounts receivable and classifying the amounts as "not due," "one to 30 days past due," "31 to 60 days past due," and so forth. From this information the estimated uncollectible receivables item may be established or its accuracy gauged. Obviously, the external analyst would not have the detailed records for the purpose of aging the accounts.

Inventories

"The term inventory is used to designate the aggregate of those items of tangible personal property which (1) are held for sale in the ordinary course of business, (2) are in the process of production for such sale, or (3) are to be currently consumed in the production of goods or services to be available for sale."[11]

A merchandise inventory represents the stock in trade of a retail or wholesale business that does not engage in manufacturing. This inventory should include (1) the stock of goods on hand and out on consignment and (2) merchandise in transit if the title to the goods has passed to the purchaser. The inventory should not include goods received on consignment[12] or unsalable goods. Obsolete, shopworn, broken, or damaged goods should be excluded from the inventory if they are unsalable or included at their current realizable value (after allowance for selling expense and a normal profit).

A manufacturing company has three important inventories—materials,[13] work in process, and finished goods—which under the caption "inventories" are shown as current assets on the balance sheet.

These inventories should be distinguished from inventories of factory, store, and office supplies. Factory supplies do not ultimately become a measurable, integral part of the finished goods but are essential to production and the general operation of the factory. Store and office supplies are not used in production or in the operation of the factory. The inventories of factory, store, and office supplies are properly shown as prepaid expenses in the current asset section of the balance sheet.[14]

---

[11] AICPA, *Accounting Research Bulletin No. 43*, p. 27.

[12] When goods are sent on consignment, ownership remains in the sender.

[13] Raw materials, indirect materials, and/or articles partially or fully fabricated by others.

[14] However, the accounting executives of *Accounting Trends and Techniques'* 600 companies did not agree with this dictum. In 1970, manufacturing supplies were disclosed in the inventories section by 173 corporations. In a number of instances the supplies inventory was merged into raw materials. [The data reported in *Accounting Trends and Techniques 1971* is from 1970 reports.]

The work-in-process inventory represents an accumulation of material costs, direct labor costs, and indirect manufacturing costs applied to the manufacture of products that have not been finished. Indirect manufacturing costs include all costs of production that cannot be classified as direct material or direct labor.

The finished goods inventory represents the total cost of manufactured goods on hand. Finished goods consist of the dollar amount of direct material, direct labor, and indirect manufacturing cost that has been applied to completed goods.

Inventoriable goods must be distinguished from such assets as plant, property, and equipment. The cost of the latter expires during their service life; the cycle of investment, expiration, and reinvestment is much longer than for inventories; and there is no continual change in the physical items as in the case of inventories. An inventory may be distorted by the evaluation method adopted, by inclusion of intercompany profits, by inclusion of merchandise or materials the liability for which has not been recorded, and by inclusion of inventory that is on consignment to the company (belongs to someone else).

The reader of a balance sheet is concerned with the following inventory information, which may be disclosed (though frequently is not) by parenthetical notations, in footnotes, or in the auditor's report:

1. The major classes of inventory.
2. The method that has been used in valuing the inventory.[15]
3. Whether or not any of the inventory has been pledged as security for loans.
4. The replacement cost of the inventory if it is substantially above or below the cost figure shown.

Under generally accepted accounting principles the basis of stating inventories should be disclosed in the financial statements; whenever a significant change is made therein, there should be a disclosure of the nature of the change and, if material, of the effect upon income.

Advance payments on purchases of raw materials or ·merchandise to be delivered in the future should not be shown as inventory. These payments are properly shown as advance payments, a receivable item.

Purchase commitments, i.e., where goods have been contracted for but neither the goods nor the title to the goods has been received, should not be included in the inventory. However, prospective net losses

---

[15] Of the *Accounting Trends and Techniques 1971* corporations, 120 did not disclose fully their methods of computing cost of inventories. The balance, 480 firms, stated the cost methods used for their entire inventories in accordance with Chapter 4 of *Accounting Research Bulletin No. 43* which states that "the basis of stating inventories must be consistently applied and should be disclosed in the financial statements; whenever a significant change is made therein, there should be disclosure of the nature of the change and, if material, the effect on net income."

on purchase commitments, measured in the same way as inventory losses, should be recognized, if material in amount. Information relative to purchase commitments may be given in a footnote.

Valuation of inventories

A major objective of accounting for inventories is the proper determination of income through the process of matching appropriate costs against revenue. At the same time the proper valuation of inventories is of significance from the point of view of both the balance sheet and the income statement. Unless inventories are evaluated appropriately, the assets and the owners' equity, as well as the current net income, will be either overstated or understated. An overstatement of the ending inventory value results in an understatement of cost of goods sold, an overstatement of net income, an inflated working capital, and possibly, excess dividend and tax payments. An understatement of the ending inventory value results in an overstatement of cost of goods sold, understatements of net income and working capital, and higher income tax at a later time if the tax rates increase when the corrected income is reported.

Inventories should not be valued on the basis of estimated cash realizable value similar to accounts receivable. To do so would violate the concept of revenue recognition and would normally result in anticipating profit. Revenue from merchandise is not realized until a bona fide sale is made. Consequently, a profit should not be recognized until the sale is consummated.

The most commonly used methods of costing the goods that have been sold and determining the residual cost to be assigned to the inventory include cost and lower of cost or market. Cost has reference to specific identification or an assignment of cost using one of the following methods: first-in, first-out (Fifo); last-in, first-out (Lifo); and average.

Cost or market whichever is the lower means that market will be used instead of cost whenever it yields a lower inventory value. Market means the cost to replace. This is an anticipate-all-losses approach to inventory valuation. The ways in which the value of inventory at market is calculated vary; the comparison of cost with market may be made on an as-a-whole basis, or by groups.

The *Accounting Trends and Techniques* companies in their 1970 reports disclosed 704 methods: cost without mention of market was reported 72 times; the lower of cost or market was reported (using a variety of wordings) 622 times.

Cost is calculated in four different ways:

1. Identifying the specific items sold or alternatively, retained in inventory (this method can be used only with high-value items; real estate for example):

2. Charging to cost of goods sold the items longest in the inventory (first-in, first-out: Fifo);
3. Charging out to cost of goods sold on an average cost basis;
4. Charging out to cost of goods sold the most recent inventory costs (last-in, first-out: Lifo).

The 600 companies reported the use in 1970 of 765 methods: Fifo was reported 292 times (38 percent); average cost was reported 203 times (27 percent); Lifo, 146 times (19 percent). The balance was made up of standard cost, retail method, production cost, replacement cost, and specific cost, which between them accounted for about 16 percent. In 1955 Lifo was the major method and has declined 21 percent since that time; average cost was second (as it still is) and it has gone up 33 percent; Fifo was third (now first) and it has risen 80 percent. Presumably these results reflect some disillusionment with the complexities of Lifo in particular, and also average cost.

Inventories—cost

Cost means the total expenditure incurred in procuring an inventory. The cost of a materials inventory includes the invoice price;[16] transportation, purchasing, receiving, storage, and handling costs; import duties; and other costs involved in the acquisition of the goods purchased. Purchases cash discounts are most commonly treated as adjustments to purchases cost. The foregoing cost items, except for the invoice price, are customarily charged as indirect manufacturing costs rather than attempting to allocate them to inventory items. Theoretically, all costs that can be associated with the acquisition and maintenance of inventory should be allocated to specific goods in order to state more accurately income measurement and inventory valuation. However, from a practical point of view it is difficult to assign acquisition and maintenance of inventory costs to specific inventory items. Therefore, there is a common acceptance of procedure of recording these costs as period costs (under production costs).

When the specific-cost basis of inventory valuation is used, each individual item is identified and priced at its actual cost. This method is not practical when the inventory contains a large number of items and when purchases at different prices are numerous. It is not practical when the concern sells a continuous stream of fully interchangeable items of product. Whenever it is not practical or meaningful to identify each item of the inventory with respect to its specific (actual) cost (which is the usual situation), inventory cost must be assigned or computed in accordance with one of several available assumptions.

---

[16] Trade discounts are deducted in computing the invoice price.

First-in, first-out inventory method. When the first-in, first-out method (Fifo) of pricing withdrawals of raw materials or stores from stock is used, the materials or stores that are issued or sold are priced at the unit cost of the oldest items in stock. When the most remote acquisition has been completely exhausted, additional issues are priced at the unit cost of the next purchase, and so on. Therefore, the inventory on hand as of the balance sheet date would be priced at the unit costs of the most recent acquisitions. This inventory method of costing issued goods represents an incurred (original, historical) cost method since the costs—which, note, are actual, incurred, costs—are assigned to cost of goods sold in the order that the goods were actually acquired.

Of course, the actual flow of costs is almost certainly not on a first-in, first-out or last-in, first-out, or any other arrangement, consistently. In many instances first-in, first-out is most likely to approximate actual inventory behavior as management usually assumes that obsolescence and spoilage will be minimized by shipping out the items which have been longest in the inventory. But the reason for the method selected is most likely to have to do with the assumed effect on net income and the federal income tax.

The first-in, first-out method of maintaining a perpetual inventory record during the accounting period is applied as shown in Illustration 3–1. It should be noted that the first 5,000 units cost $1 per unit and that the first 5,000 units actually issued were costed out at $1 per unit. The ending inventory of 6,100 units consists of 5,000 units at a cost of $1.40 per unit and 1,100 units at a cost of $1.20 per unit. The book value of the inventory as of June 30, on the cost basis of first-in, first-out, is $8,320. Inventories valued on this basis reflect most recent costs, while the cost of goods sold includes the earliest costs.

When the first-in, first-out assumption is used, a rise in prices will tend to inflate income and a decline in prices will tend to deflate income.

ILLUSTRATION 3–1. Perpetual inventory (first-in, first-out method of pricing withdrawals)

Date	Particulars	Received Units	Received Unit cost	Received Cost	Issued Units	Issued Unit cost	Issued Cost	Balance Units	Balance Cost
January 1	Inventory	5,000	$1.00	$5,000				5,000	$ 5,000
25	Purchase	2,000	1.10	2,200				7,000	7,200
31	Issued				2,000	$1.00	$2,000	5,000	5,200
February 1	Purchase	7,000	1.20	8,400				12,000	13,600
28	Issued				2,200	1.00	2,200	9,800	11,400
March 31	Issued	*5,000*			800	1.00	800		
					1,300	1.10	1,430	7,700	9,170
April 30	Issued				700	1.10	770		
					1,600	1.20	1,920	5,400	6,480
May 1	Purchase	5,000	1.40	7,000				10,400	13,480
31	Issued				2,200	1.20	2,640	8,200	10,840
June 30	Issued				2,100	1.20	2,520	6,100	8,320

This effect on income is a result of increasing sales prices, in accordance with the changing price level, against which would be offset earlier costs of the inventory that is sold. If "market" (replacement cost) is less then the cost assigned to inventory, there is a potential loss which is not reflected on the income statement under the Fifo method.

When Fifo is used, reported profits may include price profits, an element of profit that is tied up in maintaining the same physical quantity of inventory acquired at higher costs. These price profits will not be repeated in following periods unless prices continue to increase. Such price profits will be followed by future losses if prices decline.

Last-in, first-out inventory method. When the last-in, first-out method (Lifo) of costing withdrawals from stock is used, the stores issued are priced at the cost of the materials most recently acquired. The unit cost of the most recent acquisition is used in pricing withdrawals. The *newest* dollar cost is used to price withdrawals; the *oldest* dollar cost remains in the inventory. Under this pricing method, inventories of goods in process and of finished goods include material cost on the basis of last-in, first-out, plus direct labor and factory overhead applicable thereto. Finished goods, when sold, are priced on the basis of last-in, first-out production costs.

As previously pointed out, the Fifo and Lifo inventory pricing methods reflect the "flow," i.e., the assignment, of costs, and not necessarily the actual flow of goods. The choice between Fifo and Lifo should be made in accordance with management's concept of profit. Under Fifo, gross margin represents the excess of revenue over the original cost of the goods sold; consequently, gross margin arises after the recovery of the dollars invested in the inventory. Under Lifo, gross margin represents the excess of revenue over the cost of goods recorded on the records as of the date of sale; therefore, profit arises after recovery of the replacement cost (or approximately thereof) of the goods sold. Lifo is considered to be a replacement cost (incurred cost) method. However, if acquisition costs are increasing, the cost of the most recent purchase may not match the cost when the goods are actually replaced. This lag becomes more significant as purchases are made at infrequent dates and prices are moving upward rather rapidly.

Under Lifo, profits may be distorted (understated) by large end-of-the-year purchases of inventory items having the highest price increases. Such a pricing policy results in reported profits that neither reflect a realistic situation of the past nor a sound basis for estimating future profits.

The last-in, first-out pricing method of maintaining a perpetual inventory record during the accounting period is applied as shown in Illustration 3–2. It should be observed that the first withdrawal of stock of 2,000 units is priced at $1.10 per unit, since that represents the cost of the most recent purchase as of the date of withdrawal. For each of the subsequent issues the latest unit cost is used. Cost of Goods Sold is charged with approximately the cost of replacing the items sold.

The ending inventory (perpetual inventory, Illustration 3–2) of 6,100 units consists of 5,000 units at $1 per unit, 400 units at $1.20 per unit, and 700 units at $1.40 per unit. The book value of the inventory as of June 30, on the last-in, first-out unit-cost basis, is $6,460.

ILLUSTRATION 3–2. Perpetual inventory (last-in, first-out method of pricing withdrawals)

Date	Particulars	Received			Issued			Balance	
		Units	Unit cost	Cost	Units	Unit cost	Cost	Units	Cost
January 1	Inventory	5,000	$1.00	$5,000				5,000	$ 5,000
25	Purchase	2,000	1.10	2,200				7,000	7,200
31	Issued				2,000	$1.10	$2,200	5,000	5,000
February 1	Purchase	7,000	1.20	8,400				12,000	13,400
28	Issued				2,200	1.20	2,640	9,800	10,760
March 31	Issued				2,100	1.20	2,520	7,700	8,240
April 30	Issued				2,300	1.20	2,760	5,400	5,480
May 1	Purchase	5,000	1.40	7,000				10,400	12,480
31	Issued				2,200	1.40	3,080	8,200	9,400
June 30	Issued				2,100	1.40	2,940	6,100	6,460

When perpetual inventories are not maintained or the cost of the units issued or sold is not recorded until the end of the accounting period, the units on hand at that time may be valued at the earliest costs. The units issued would be priced at the latest costs.

Under these circumstances the 6,100 units of stock shown by a physical inventory at the end of the accounting period would be valued (under Lifo) at $6,210 (5,000 units at $1 and 1,100 units at $1.10). The units of stock issued would be priced at $16,390 (5,000 units at $1.40, 7,000 units at $1.20, and 900 units at $1.10).

The discrepancy in the dollar amount of the perpetual inventory, $6,460, and the physical inventory, $6,210, is a result of pricing withdrawals during the accounting period on the basis of new acquisitions. For example, on a perpetual inventory basis the ending inventory is valued according to the *dollar* amount left in the inventory. Illustration 3–2 shows that unit costs not used in recording issues during the accounting period were (1) 5,000 units at $1, (2) 400 units at $1.20, and (3) 700 units at $1.40. The application of the Lifo method to a physical inventory at the end of the accounting period would result in an ending inventory valuation of $6,210 (5,000 units at $1 and 1,100 units at $1.10).

Sometimes the perpetual inventory record is adjusted to correspond to the periodic inventory concept of last-in, first-out, i.e., to reflect in the ending inventory only the costs obtaining at the beginning of the period. To adjust the perpetual inventory shown in Illustration 3–2, the following entry might be used:

```
Inventory Adjustment . . . . . . . . . . . . . . . . . . . . . . . . . . . . . 250
     Inventory . . . . . . . . . . . . . . . . . . . . . . . . . . . . . . . . . . .          250
     To reduce inventory as shown on the books to Lifo:
                Inventory per books . . . . . . . . . . . . . .    $6,460
                Physical inventory per Lifo . . . . . . . . . .     6,210
                Required adjustment . . . . . . . . . . . . .     $  250
```

The Inventory Adjustment should be shown as an addition to Cost of Goods Sold.

Average cost inventory methods.   The term "average cost" includes two different methods of evaluating an ending inventory and costing the goods that have been sold. These methods are (1) the moving weighted-average method usually associated with a perpetual inventory and (2) the simple weighted-average method which is sometimes used in connection with a periodic physical inventory.

Moving weighted-average inventory method.   When the moving weighted-average inventory method, Illustration 3–3 is used, the stores withdrawn from stock are priced at the average unit cost of the goods on hand as of the withdrawal date. Under this pricing method, inventories of goods in process and of finished goods include material cost on the basis of average unit cost, plus direct labor and overhead costs applicable thereto. Finished goods, when sold, are withdrawn from stock on the basis of average unit cost of production. It is necessary to use perpetual inventory records in order to maintain unit costs up to date. The moving weighted-average method is applied as shown in Illustration 3–3.

The first withdrawal of 2,000 units was priced at $1.0286 per unit, the average cost of the 7,000 units on hand as of January 31, the withdrawal date ($7,200 divided by 7,000). The second withdrawal of 2,200 units on February 28 was priced at $1.1286, the average cost of the 12,000 units on hand as of the withdrawal date ($13,543 divided by 12,000).

The moving weighted-average cost method, sometimes referred to as the during-the-period-weighted-moving-average method, of pricing withdrawals theoretically requires the determination of a new average unit cost whenever a purchase is made at a price higher or lower than the existing average cost. When purchases at different prices are very numerous, a modification of the moving weighted-average method may be used to avoid an excessive number of computations. The commonly accepted practice is to determine a new average unit cost at the beginning of each month or quarter. If the withdrawals during the month or quarter exceed the inventory at the beginning of the month or quarter or if the price fluctuates materially, a new average unit cost should

ILLUSTRATION 3–3.   Perpetual inventory (moving weighted-average method of pricing withdrawals)

Date		Particulars	Received			Issued			Balance	
			Units	Unit cost	Cost	Units	Unit cost	Cost	Units	Cost
January	1	Inventory	5,000	$1.00	$5,000				5,000	$ 5,000
	25	Purchase	2,000	1.10	2,200				7,000	7,200
	31	Issued				2,000	$1.0286	$2,057	5,000	5,143
February	1	Purchase	7,000	1.20	8,400				12,000	13,543
	28	Issued				2,200	1.1286	2,483	9,800	11,060
March	31	Issued				2,100	1.1286	2,370	7,700	8,690
April	30	Issued				2,300	1.1286	2,596	5,400	6,094
May	1	Purchase	5,000	1.40	7,000				10,400	13,094
	31	Issued				2,200	1.2590	2,770	8,200	10,324
June	30	Issued				2,100	1.2590	2,644	6,100	7,680

be computed during the period. It should be clear that the foregoing variation is not strictly a moving weighted-average method and that a practical difficulty arises in the use of average costs due to the clerical effort required.

The book value of the inventory as of June 30 on the moving weighted-average unit-cost basis is $7,680. This amount is less than the most recent costs, since the last 6,100 units now in the inventory cost $8,320—5,000 units at $1.40 per unit and 1,100 units at $1.20 per unit.

If the unit price had declined during the six-month period under review, the book value of the inventory on an average unit-cost basis would be higher than current replacement.

The moving weighted-average method tends to level off short-term price fluctuations. As new purchases are made at higher or lower prices, average unit costs move upward or downward, but slowly.

Simple weighted-average inventory method. The closing inventory may be valued by determining the simple weighted-average unit cost for a month, quarter, or year. This cost is computed at the end of the accounting period as follows:

Units	Unit cost	Cost
5,000	$1.00	$ 5,000
2,000	1.10	2,200
7,000	1.20	8,400
5,000	1.40	7,000
19,000		$22,600

Weighted average = $22,600 ÷ 19,000 = $1.18947
Inventory value = 6,100 × $1.18947 = $7,256
Cost of goods sold = 12,900 × $1.18947 = $15,344

The simple weighted-average method sometimes referred to as the end-of-the-period-weighted-average method is not satisfactory if unit cost must be available during the accounting period. Furthermore, this method, the use of which is not practical when a perpetual inventory is maintained, involves a large amount of detailed work in pricing the issuances of material at the end of the accounting period.

Inventories may be priced by using a *simple unweighted average* of invoice unit costs. For example, if three purchases are assumed to be made at $1.10, $1.15, and $1.20, the simple average would be $1.15. The inventory value would be determined by evaluating the units at $1.15 each. This method is unsatisfactory unless all purchases are for substantially equal physical quantities.

Whichever of these assumptions is used as a basis for costing the goods that have been sold and determining the cost of the ending inventory, replacement costs may at times be less than the book value of inventories. Under current practice, inventories are commonly written down to "market," below cost.

Standard cost inventory method. Standard costs represent what a particular unit of material or product should cost or is expected to cost under certain assumed conditions. The American Institute of Certified Public Accountants states: "Standard costs are accepted if adjusted at reasonable intervals to reflect current conditions so that at the balance sheet date standard costs reasonably approximate costs computed under one of the recognized bases. In such cases descriptive language should be used which will express this relationship, as, for instance, 'approximate costs determined on the first-in, first-out basis,' or if it is desired to mention standard costs, 'standard costs, approximating average costs.' "[17]

Lower-of-cost-or-market inventory methods. The rule of valuing inventory at the lower of cost or market is applied most commonly, as shown in Illustration 3–4, by pricing inventory items at both cost and market. The lower of cost or market for each item is extended to the final money column on the inventory sheet, and the total of this column is shown on the financial statements. For purposes of inventory valuation

ILLUSTRATION 3–4.   Physical inventory (lower of cost or market)

Product	Units	Unit cost	Cost*	Unit replace- ment	Market	Lower of Cost or Market
A. . . .	5,000	$1.40	$7,000	$1.50	$7,500	$7,000
B. . . .	1,100	1.20	1,320	1.00	1,100	1,100
	6,100		$8,320		$8,600	$8,100

* First-in, first-out basis of pricing withdrawals of stores is assumed here.

[17] AICPA, *Accounting Research Bulletin No. 43*, p. 30, fn.

on the basis of the lower of cost or market, the term "market" has reference, in most cases, to the cost—invoice price plus transportation and other necessary expenses—of replacing the goods on the date of the inventory and in the volume usually produced or purchased.

The term "market" may also refer to the net realizable value of goods, i.e., the estimated selling price in the ordinary course of business less all directly identifiable costs yet to be incurred prior to sale. A more conservative valuation is obtained by also deducting from the estimated selling price the normal profit margin realized on sales.[18]

In determining the market value of inventory, the lower of cost of replacement or net realizable value may be used.

An alternative method, not approved for federal income tax computation, of evaluating an inventory at the lower of cost or market is to apply the rule of "cost or market, whichever is lower," to the total of the components of each major category or to the totals of the entire inventory. For example, following this procedure, the valuation of the inventory, Illustration 3–4, would be $8,320, the lower of total cost or total market. This method of applying the rule of the lower of cost or market is acceptable when the inventory items involve one end product or when they may be classified logically in one or more major categories.[19]

In valuing the goods-in-process and finished goods inventories at the lower of cost or market, it is necessary to show separately the cost and the market value of the raw material, labor, and factory overhead. When an adequate cost system is not being used, costs are estimated.

The lower of cost or market is the most widely accepted method for evaluating inventories. For balance sheet purposes, the lower-of-cost-or-market method results in a conservative valuation of inventory, since prospective losses, due to a decline in market value below cost, are recognized in the period of market decline rather than in the period of sale. Items written down to market are thereafter carried at that value until sold, whether or not replacement costs rise.

Dealers in marketable securities are permitted to value their inventory of securities for federal income tax purposes at market, whether above or below cost.

To reflect the lower of cost or market on the books when a perpetual inventory is maintained, (1) the controlling account, Inventory, as well as the subsidiary stores record may be adjusted, or (2) a valuation account titled Estimated Market Decline in Inventory may be established. The following journal entry would record the inventory value at the lower of cost or market:

---

[18] Ibid., pp. 31 and 33.

[19] Ibid., p. 32.

Dec. 31   Inventory Market Decline   30,000
                    Inventory   30,000
            Loss in inventory value due to market decline.

The balance of the Inventory Market Decline account may be transferred to Revenue and Expense Summary as a debit and shown on
the income statement immediately following the gross margin on sales
figure or in the section in which extraordinary items are included.[20]
In this way, price losses are specifically shown on the statement instead
of being permitted to distort cost of goods sold. Each individual item
in the subsidiary inventory ledger affected by the decline in the market
would be adjusted.

An alternative and less costly plan of showing the lower of cost or
market is to set up a valuation account, Estimated Market Decline in
Inventory, instead of changing the costs shown in the Perpetual Inventory controlling account and the subsidiary accounts. The following general journal entry, debiting Inventory Market Decline and crediting Estimated Market Decline in Inventory, would record the difference between
cost and the lower of cost or market:

Dec. 31   Inventory Market Decline   30,000
                    Estimated Market Decline in Inventory . . .   30,000
            Loss in inventory value due to market decline.

The inventory valuation account is properly deductible from the inventory item on the balance sheet.

If an inventory valuation account is created, it should be disposed
of during the subsequent accounting period. Theoretically, when inventory items having market prices below cost are sold, the actual loss
should be debited to the Estimated Market Decline in Inventory and
credited to Inventory. The foregoing procedure results in recording and
beginning inventory items which have been transferred to Cost of Goods
Sold, at the lower of cost or market.

On the assumption that most, if not all, of the beginning inventory
has been sold, a preferable method is to transfer the inventory at cost
to the Cost of Goods Sold or to the Revenue and Expense Summary
account and to credit the same account with the Estimated Market
Decline in Inventory. This procedure avoids the necessity of analyzing
each individual sale to determine the difference between cost and the
lower of cost or market.

A third and probably the most practical procedure to follow at the

---

[20] In December 1966 the Accounting Principles Board of the AICPA issued *Opinion No. 9*, "Reporting the Results of Operations," in which it adopted the substance
of the "clean retained earnings" theory of income statement construction. *Opinion
No. 9* states that extraordinary items be included in a special section of the income
statement; extraordinary items are, therefore, elements entering into the computation
of net income. Only "prior period adjustments" may be charged against the opening
balance of Retained Earnings.

end of the subsequent accounting period is to transfer the inventory at cost to the Cost of Goods Sold account and to adjust the valuation account to its new required amount. If a larger valuation amount is necessary as a result of market decline of the ending inventory, Inventory Market Decline is debited and Estimated Market Decline in Inventory is credited. If a smaller valuation amount is required because of lower price declines of the ending inventory, Estimated Market Decline in Inventory is debited and Gain on Inventory Market Recovery is credited.

The Estimated Market Decline in Inventory account, established and disposed of in the preceding example, was designed to reflect an actual market decline which can be determined by using quotations current at the balance sheet date. A different procedure is appropriate when a concern desires to reflect an *anticipated* future decline in market prices.

A loss to be suffered on an anticipated future decline in market prices is conjectural and should not be taken into the income statement. Although there is considerable doubt as to the value of adjusting the books to give effect to a conjectural loss of this type, the adjustment, if made, should take the form of an appropriation of retained earnings—debit the Retained Earnings account, and credit the Provision for Anticipated Market Decline in Inventory.

The Estimated Market Decline in Inventory account is a valuation item which should be deducted from inventory on the balance sheet. A Provision for Anticipated Market Decline in Inventory retains its status as retained earnings and should be classified in the proprietary section as appropriated retained earnings. In the subsequent period, if a loss is caused by a market decline, it is charged to Market Decline in Inventory rather than to the retained earnings provision. The proper way to dispose of such a provision is to restore it to retained earnings.

Base-stock inventory method. The base-stock or normal-stock method of valuing inventories involves (1) the determination of the minimum quantity of goods or material that should be on hand at all times, regardless of business activity; and (2) the assignment of a cost to this stock. The minimum inventory may be valued at an average of minimum costs, using the data for a period of several years, or at a unit cost below which it is not expected that replacement costs will fall. The base-stock method of inventory valuation is neither in general use nor acceptable for income tax purposes. Therefore, it will not be discussed further.

Inventory—retail method. The retail inventory method is frequently used by retail stores, especially by department stores in order to control merchandise on the basis of retail prices. This method, which is not suitable for manufacturing businesses, provides a means of obtaining at any time and without a physical inventory, an estimate of the cost of goods on hand. Inventory records are maintained at retail prices, and each item of the goods available for sale is marked at retail. The total cost of the beginning inventory and of purchases and all markups and markdowns must be known. The fundamental objective of the retail inventory method in addition to facilitating merchandise control is its use in computing the approximate ratio which cost bears to the *total* retail price of the ending inventory so that this inventory, priced item by item at retail, may be converted to an estimated cost.

The following terms are used in connection with retail inventory computations:

1. Markup (mark-on)—the amount added to the cost of purchases (including transportation) in setting original sales prices to cover operating expenses and profit margin.
2. Original sales price—the sales price at which merchandise is first offered (cost of purchases [including transportation] plus original markup or mark-on).
3. Additional markup—an increase above the original sales price.
4. Markup cancellations—a decrease in the additional markup which does not reduce sales price below original sales price.
5. Markdown—a decrease of markup below the original sales price.
6. Markdown cancellation—a decrease in the markdown that does not result in increasing the sales price above the original sales price.

An example will clarify the way the above terms are used in practice. An article costing $10 per unit is *marked up* 40 percent, or $4, above cost to determine the *original sales price* of $14. That is, the purchase cost, $10, plus the initial markup of 40 percent, $4, equals original sales price, $14. The markup of $4 is referred to as a "40 percent markup on cost" or a "28.6 percent mark-on on sales price." Subsequently, because of higher or lower cost or weaker or stronger demand for such goods, changes were made in the original sales price. For instance, the original sales price was increased to $15 which represented an *additional markup*. At a later date the merchandise manager decided to reduce the sales price from $15 to $14.50. This change represents a *cancellation of 50 cents of the additional markup* of $1. It is not to be referred to as a markdown because the original sales price was not reduced.

If the original sales price of $14 had been reduced to $12, a *markdown* of $2 would have resulted. A later change of sales price to $13 would represent a *cancellation of markdown* of $1 since the new sales price did not exceed the original sales price.

Estimating cost of ending inventory. The cost of the ending inventory on hand may be estimated without taking a physical inventory, as illustrated below:

	Cost	Retail selling price
Beginning inventory.	$ 5,000	$ 7,333
Net purchases during the period.	17,000	24,333
Transportation on purchases	600	
		$31,666
Net additional markups*		3,500
Retail price after additional net markups, before markdowns	$22,600	$35,166
Less: Retail price of goods sold (returned sales deducted)		$22,400
Net markdowns†.		400
		$22,800
Inventory of goods on hand at retail price		$12,366
Inventory of goods on hand approximating the lower of cost or market		$ 7,957‡

* Increases in retail price after original selling price was established minus markup cancellations.
† Decreases in the original retail price.
‡ The merchandise available at calculated cost is 64.27 % of its selling price (cost, $22,600 divided by retail price after net markups, before net markdowns, $35,166); 64.27 % of the ending inventory at retail, $12,366 equals $7,957—the approximate lower of cost or market value of the ending inventory.

The ratio of cost to retail price may be computed using three different retail figures taken from the foregoing illustration:

Retail price of goods to be accounted for	Retail price	Cost of goods to be accounted for	Cost of goods as a percent of retail price	Cost of ending inventory	Valuation of ending inventory approximates
1. Before additional markups and markdowns	$31,666	$22,600	71.37	$8,826	Market
2. After additional markups and before markdowns	35,166	22,600	64.27	7,957	Lower of cost or market
3. After additional markups and markdowns	34,766	22,600	65.01	8,039	Cost

Method 1 results in showing the ending inventory at estimated market—the retail sales price less the original markup.

Assuming prices have increased, Method 2 shows the ending inventory at cost since the original and the additional markups are deducted from retail prices. This cost is lower than market. If prices have declined, the ending inventory is stated at market since the additional markups will have been canceled and the original markup is deducted from the sales price. Therefore, Method 2 shows the ending inventory on the basis of lower of cost or market.

Under *Method 3*, if prices are increasing, the result is approximate cost—retail less all markups. If prices are declining, the result is again approximate cost—retail less a percentage of net markup.

The assignment of $7,957 as the cost of the ending inventory is the most conservative. It approximates the lower of cost or market. This method, using markups and excluding markdowns, is the one most commonly used.

Advantages of retail inventory method. The advantages of the retail inventory method are:

1. Interim inventories may be estimated without incurring the cost of a physical inventory.
2. Time and expense may be saved in pricing a physical inventory—the inventory is taken and priced at retail (by reference to the tags attached to the articles) and then converted to cost without reference to individual costs and invoices.
3. Information is available for determining appropriate amount of insurance coverage and for establishing claims for fire and/or storm loss.
4. The movement of merchandise out of stock may be checked by comparing a physical count at retail with the perpetual inventory record at retail and, therefore, shortages may be detected.
5. A workable basis for the dollar control of the merchandise inventory is given.
6. Detailed control over profit may be exercised to an advantage because the rate of markups and markdowns is known currently.

Among the well-known companies which report that they are using the retail inventory method are F. W. Woolworth and R. H. Macy, a leading New York City department store.

Inventory valuation and income-determination summary

The selection of an inventory valuation method is of major importance because of the effect upon both the balance sheet and the income statement. The dollar amount of inventory and net income will vary in accordance with the method used in determining the cost of goods sold. For example, the following residual costs were assigned to the ending inventory of 6,100 units of material, under different costing methods:

1. The market value method	$9,150
2. The first-in, first-out method	8,320
3. The lower-of-cost-or-market-value method	8,100
4. The moving weighted-average method	7,680
5. The single weighted-average method	7,256
6. The last-in, first-out method	6,460

It will be observed that the foregoing inventory valuation figures have a range of $2,690, from $6,460 to $9,150. Since most inventories have a much larger number of items, the differences may become greatly magnified and, therefore, far more significant.

Inasmuch as wide variations in inventory valuation are possible, it is essential that the financial and operating reports indicate clearly the method used in determining the cost of the goods sold and, therefore, the cost that remains in the ending inventory. Unless the same method has been used, relationships and ratios of inventory, cost of goods sold, and other related items of different companies will not be comparable; and statements of the same company will not be comparable unless a method has been used consistently. A change in the cost of inventory alters cost of goods sold, net income, total current assets, and the owner's equity.

Of course, these are all methods of determining "cost," and in the long run, total cost will be the same whatever method is used, but nevertheless material variations in currently reported results will be encountered.

The federal income tax regulations permit the use of cost (Lifo or Fifo), the lower of cost (Fifo only) or market, and the retail method. To be acceptable, Lifo must also be used on the taxpayer's financial statements.

The regulations require the taxpayer to use the best accounting practice of the particular trade or business. Consistency of inventory valuation from year to year is of prime importance and is a basic requirement for both federal income tax and financial statement purposes.

The analyst who is determining a short-term credit rating for a manufacturing company (for which purpose liquidity is important) considers the nature of the items making up the inventories. Frequently, the finished goods inventory consists of specialized products the value of which, in case of liquidation, may be much less than that of the staple items in the raw material inventory. Furthermore, the work-in-process inventory is customarily valued at a heavy discount for short-term credit purposes because partly finished products are difficult to turn into cash.

Capital stock subscriptions receivable

Subscriptions receivable represent enforceable contracts with subscribers who have agreed to purchase a specified number of shares of capital stock at a designated price. Subscriptions receivable may be shown as a current asset, assuming that the amount is to be collected within one year from the date of the balance sheet. If the period of time involved is substantially more than one year, the subscriptions may be listed under the caption "other noncurrent assets." If there is no intention of collecting the balances due on the subscriptions, or if collection is doubtful, the amount should be shown in the owners' equity section as a deduction from capital stock subscribed. This latter method of showing subscriptions receivable is preferred by many accountants, even though current collection is anticipated.

Accrued receivables

The allocation of revenue to its proper account period is a major part of the accrual method. Revenue that has been earned in the current accounting period but has not been recorded should be accrued. Examples of accrued revenue items are accrued rent receivable, accrued interest receivable, and accrued royalties receivable. When accrued revenue is not recorded, the net income, the current assets, and the owners' equity are understated. Accrued revenue receivables are customarily shown as miscellaneous current assets or included in other or miscellaneous accounts receivable.

Prepaid expenses

Office and selling supplies, fire insurance premiums, interest expense, rent expense, and various other expense items which have been paid for but not consumed, or the benefit of which has not been fully realized by the end of the accounting period, represent prepaid expenses. Prepayments should be shown on the balance sheet as current assets; an alternative method is to show them separately following the current asset section. There is a definite trend toward classifying prepayments of expense items such as insurance, interest, rents, and operating supplies as current assets. These prepayments are not current in the sense that they will be converted directly into cash but in the sense that if not paid in advance they would require the use of current assets during the operating cycle. Prepaid expenses, carried over at the end of the period on the balance sheet, will be charged to expense accounts in the following accounting period or periods. Expenses properly matched against future revenue are balance sheet items; expenses properly matched against revenue on or before the balance sheet date must be charged off, since their asset cost has expired. Unconsumed portions of expense items are shown on the balance sheet at cost. If these items are not properly "costed," current assets and net income will be either overstated or understated.

The prepaid expense category does not include deferred charges such as discount on bonds payable and organization expense. Long-term prepayments of expense such as fire insurance may be shown partly as a current asset and partly as a noncurrent asset.

QUESTIONS AND PROBLEMS

3–1. What is the difference between current and noncurrent assets?

3–2. The valuation of cash is relatively simple as a general rule. List some exceptions.

3–3. Promissory notes may be considered more valuable than accounts receivable. Explain.

3–4. What may be included in accounts receivable?

3–5. What is the basis of valuation of accounts and notes receivable?

3–6. Explain the meaning of the term "inventory."

3–7. Proper valuation of inventories is of significance from the point of view of both the balance sheet and the income statement. Explain.

3–8. Explain the effect of Fifo and Lifo inventory pricing methods on the balance sheet and the income statement.

3–9. What is the objective in using the lower-of-cost-or-market inventory method for balance sheet valuation?

3–10. Under what circumstances is the retail inventory method used? Explain.

3–11. What is meant by the term "operating cycle" as defined in *Accounting Research Bulletin No. 43?*

3–12. Comment on the following statements:
   a) Any asset that may be readily converted into cash should be classified as a current asset.
   b) A note receivable is preferable to an account receivable.
   c) There is no such thing as a contingent asset.
   d) Inventories are preferably shown at cost.
   e) In a rising market, the use of Lifo assures that current replacement cost will be used in computing the cost of goods sold (when a perpetual inventory is maintained).
   f) All prepayments of expense are most logically classified as current assets.
      The questions *(g)*, *(h)*, and *(i)* which follow are based on the following items:
   (1) Estimated market decline of inventory.
   (2) Estimated uncollectible receivables.
   (3) Notes receivable discounted.
   (4) Estimated market decline of temporary investments.
   g) How should the foregoing items be classified on a balance sheet?
   h) How are the dollar amounts determined?
   i) What disposition is made of the items?

3–13. Relative to inventory:
   a) Distinguish between a perpetual inventory and a physical inventory.
   b) When a perpetual inventory is maintained is it necessary to take a physical inventory? Discuss.

c)   In comparison with the Lifo inventory pricing method, would the application of the Fifo inventory pricing method result in higher or lower cost of goods sold? Explain.

3–14.   Relative to cash:

a)   What items are properly included as cash?

b)   Distinguish between a petty cash fund and funds advanced to employees.

c)   What is the difference between a demand deposit and a certificate of deposit?

d)   How should a credit balance in the Cash account be classified on the balance sheet?

e)   Why is it necessary to reconcile the bank balance?

3–15.   The Flintkote Company presents the current asset section of its balance sheet as of December 31, 1971. Upon investigation, you obtain the supplementary data supplied herewith. Prepare a revised current asset section for the company and answer the questions listed below.

Current Assets (in thousands):

Cash on hand and in bank	$3,800
Marketable securities, at market	2,767
Accounts receivable, trade, net	630
Inventories, lower of cost or market	2,418
Cash surrender value of life insurance	375
Notes receivable, trade	360
Sinking fund cash and investments	385

Additional data:

(1)   IOUs received from employees have been included as cash, $2,000. *add to A/R*

(2)   Checks sent to creditors on December 31 were debited to Accounts Payable but not credited to Cash in Bank, $42,000.

(3)   Working funds and advances to salesmen included as cash amounted to $22,000.

(4)   Marketable securities cost the company $2,500,000.

(5)   Customer accounts receivable in the amount of $200,000 were pledged as security for a bank loan.

(6)   Raw materials in transit were included in the inventories, but the liability was not recorded, $154,000.

(7)   Notes receivable in the amount of $110,000 were discounted; Notes Receivable was credited. Maturity dates are in 1972.

(8)   Only $125,000 of the Sinking Fund Cash and Investments is to be used currently to pay current liabilities.

Required:

a)   What valuation principles are applicable to the current asset items?

b)   Is it proper to classify prepayments of expense as current assets? Explain.

3–16.   The Steel Corporation presented the following data relative to raw materials:

1971		Units	Unit cost	Materials issued		Units
July 1	Inventory	5,000	$1.10	July 31		2,000
20	Purchase	3,000	1.20	August 31		4,000
August 10	Purchase	8,000	1.30	September 30		3,000
October 28	Purchase	4,000	1.35	October 31		5,000
December 28	Purchase	2,000	1.45	November 30		1,000
				December 31		3,000
		22,000				18,000

Required:

a) Compute the December 31 raw materials inventory on the basis of the following valuation methods:

Perpetual inventory:

(1) First-in, first-out,

(2) Last-in, first-out,

(3) Moving average.

b) How is the income statement affected by the inventory valuation method selected?

3–17. The information shown below was obtained from the Boyd Department Stores, as of December 31, 1971. You are requested to select the items and their values that should be included in the current asset section of the balance sheet.

	December 31, 1971 (000's)
Cash in bank.	$10,113
Cash on hand	72
Working funds advanced to employees	56
U.S. government securities:	
At cost or current redemption amount	6,782
At market value (December 31).	6,971
Property, fixtures, and equipment—net	78,203
Intangible assets (including leases)	2,708
Unamortized debt discount	431
Due from customers:	
Regular accounts—net	10,120
Installment accounts (part due after one year)	8,250
Marketable securities:	
Cost	1,760
Market (December 31).	1,825
Prepaid expenses:	
Cost	2,570
Replacement (December 31).	2,630
Long-term investments (cost)	8,950
Merchandise inventory:	
Lifo	26,432
Replacement	27,680
Petty cash fund.	5

3–18. The Barry Corporation requests you to study the following information and determine in each case the classification of the item and the amount that should be shown on the balance sheet. If individual amounts are to be omitted, indicate the disposition to be made of them. Assume the date of December 31, 1971.

a) Cash and cash items, $41,600, includes, in addition to the regular bank account: IOUs received from employees and due January 20, 1972, $2,600; funds deposited in foreign banks, withdrawal of which is presently restricted, $11,500; time deposits, $3,000.

b) Temporary investment of cash, $74,780 (to be converted into cash within 90 days), includes: preferred stock of Company A at cost, $50,000 (current market value, $45,000); unsecured bonds of Alex Company, which is hopelessly insolvent, at cost, $1,250; U.S. government bonds, acquired December 30, 1966, purchase price, $11,460, shown on the books at face value, $13,000 stock of General Electric Company at current market value, $10,530 (cost, $9,400).

c) Receivables, $251,300, includes: notes receivable, $170,000; accounts receivable, $50,000; accrued receivables, $1,000; and accounts receivable due from Subsidiary D, $30,300 (current).

Notes receivable in the amount of $25,000 were discounted December 1, 1971; the maturity dates fall within the months of January and February, 1972; Notes Receivable was credited when the notes were discounted.

The Estimated Uncollectible Receivables, $25,600, which applies to both notes and accounts receivable, is overstated. The bookkeeper during the last two years wrote off $14,600 of worthless receivables against Retained Earnings.

Included in Notes Receivable is a six-month, $40,000 note, due April 10, 1972, from the president of the company and a $5,000 customer note which is six months' past due and in all probability is worthless.

Included in accounts receivable are four customer accounts amounting to $1,600 which cannot be collected.

d) Inventories, $505,900, includes: raw materials at cost, $270,000 (market value, $320,000); work in process, at cost, $60,000; finished goods, at market, $130,000 (cost, $110,000); factory supplies, at cost, $43,600; and office supplies, at cost, $2,300.

Raw materials costing $32,000 are in transit; the purchase was recorded by debiting Raw Material Purchases and crediting Vouchers Payable. The material was not included in the inventory.

Factory supplies inventory is a perpetual inventory which was not checked by physical inventory until after the books were closed for the year, 1971. The physical inventory stated at cost amounted to $21,400, the market value amounted to $25,800.

e) Prepaid expenses, $2,400, includes a one-year insurance policy which expired December 31, 1971; the premium, $500, has not been charged off.

3–19. From the data given below, select the proper items and prepare the current asset section of the Lemon Company's balance sheet; change the titles to coincide with the terminology most commonly adopted (December 31, 1971).

Accounts receivable	$ 36,300
Buildings	200,000
Cash	11,210
Land	30,110
Merchandise inventory	137,500
Notes receivable	2,700
Notes receivable discounted	1,900
Office supplies inventory	600
Prepaid insurance	1,200
Reserve for bad debts	1,300
Reserve for market decline of inventory	12,000
Reserve for market decline of temporary investments	1,000
Securities for building fund	51,210
Temporary investments	6,000

3–20. The following information appears on the books of Roberts Retail Stores:

	Cost	Retail
Inventory at January 1	$ 15,000	$ 21,000
Purchases during the year	110,000	200,000
Freight-in	8,000	
Purchase returns	4,000	6,000
Sales		19,000

Required:
Estimate inventory at December 31 at cost and retail.

4

The balance sheet: Noncurrent assets

Long-term investments

A BUSINESS invests resources in current and fixed assets which are used in connection with regular operations. The business may also invest resources in assets that are classified as long-term investments. Long-term investments may be made (1) to obtain control of another company, (2) to have the benefit of the revenue from the investments, (3) to create funds for various purposes, (4) to establish business relationships with other companies, and (5) to promote diversification of business activities.

Accounts pertaining to investments (both short-term and long-term) and transactions relating thereto should be maintained to measure original investment and subsequent revenue, gains, and losses in order to evaluate investment performance and the desirability of continuing such investments.

Accounting problems concerning investments include measuring (1) the original cost of the acquisition, (2) the revenue and expense during the period of possession, and (3) the value received at the time of disposition.

The usual balance sheet caption for noncurrent investments is "investments" or "other investments." Its noncurrent character is shown by its exclusion from the current assets section. Among the assets found under this title are:

1. Capital stock and bonds of, and loans to, other companies.
2. Properties not related to the regular operations of the business.

3. Funds earmarked for specific purposes other than the payment of current liabilities.
4. Other assets that are not intended for current operating purposes or that may not be readily convertible into cash.
5. Life insurance on officers, with the company as the beneficiary.
6. Loans to subsidiary or affiliated companies.

These items are excluded from current assets because there is no intention to have them available for the payment of current liabilities or for use in connection with regular current operations. Long-term investments may or may not be readily converted into cash.

Common stock of a subsidiary company is not a current asset, whether readily marketable or not, because the investment was made to secure control of the company; in view of this policy the investment is not available to meet current liabilities. Cash in closed banks is not a current asset unless a settlement of the bank's affairs is to be completed within a short time, and then only to the extent that recovery is likely. On the other hand, U.S. Treasury obligations are current assets unless the company has restricted their use to nonworking capital purposes.

Some corporations show treasury stock which has been acquired for a specific short-term purpose (such as employee bonuses) as a long-term investment at cost. Unless the current use of the treasury shares is probable, it is better practice to deduct the cost of the treasury stock in the owners' equity section of the balance sheet.*

In analyzing the long-term investments of a company, it is desirable to determine, if possible, (1) the marketability of the securities or their availability for use as collateral to secure short- or long-term loans; (2) the present market value of the securities in relation to cost; (3) the extent that the securities represent speculative or conservative investments, and whether they are likely to fluctuate widely in market value with variations of business conditions; (4) the extent to which the securities might be sold without affecting regular business operations; (5) the extent to which the investments represent advances of cash or merchandise to, or the ownership of capital stock or bonds of, subsidiary companies; and (6) the extent to which the securities or other investments are profitable.

One way to determine the profitability of an investment in a subsidiary company is to examine the statements of that concern, but of course they are not always available. If the financial statements of a subsidiary have been consolidated with those of the parent, then the reported results of both are inherent in the consolidated results. If the subsidiaries are not consolidated with those of the parent, the

---

* The 455 companies disclosing treasury stock in 1970 reports surveyed in *Accounting Trends and Techniques 1971* showed 499 deductions in the net worth section, and 52 classifications elsewhere.

parent will carry its investment on its balance sheet. It has been customary for concerns to carry their investments in unconsolidated subsidiaries on their balance sheets at cost which makes it difficult or impossible to assess their profits, if any. In December 1966 the Accounting Principles Board issued *Opinion No. 10* which stated in paragraph 3:

If . . . a domestic subsidiary is not consolidated . . . the investment in the subsidiary should be adjusted for the consolidated group's share of accumulated undistributed earnings and losses since acquisition. This practice is sometimes referred to as the "equity" method. In reporting periodic consolidated net income, the earnings or losses of the unconsolidated subsidiary . . . should generally be presented as a separate item.

Accounting Trends and Techniques 1971 reports that in 1970 statements slightly less than 25 percent of the companies reporting investments in unconsolidated subsidiaries (259) did not disclose the basis used in valuing the investment. Two thirds of the U.S. and Canadian subsidiaries were valued using equity in net assets while one third were valued using cost plus share of earnings. One third of other foreign subsidiaries were valued at equity in net assets, one sixth at cost plus equity in earnings, and one half at cost. Of course, many countries restrict the export of locally earned profits.

In March 1971 the Accounting Principles Board issued *Opinion No. 18* which reaffirmed *Opinion No. 10* and extended the application of the equity method to virtually all companies in which the parent company has substantial interests.

If a long-term investment has declined materially in market value since acquisition and the new lower value appears to be for the long term, a valuation provision should be deducted from the asset value (cost). If this is not done, the situation should be described parenthetically or in a footnote. If the long-term investment is in the stock of a subsidiary, it is customary to ignore fluctuations of market value.

Cash and other liquid assets earmarked to be used for plant expansion, bond and capital stock retirements, pension and contingent (noncurrent) liability payments, replacement of assets that may be destroyed by fire or other casualties, and for other similar reasons should be classified as long-term investments. Payroll, petty cash, and dividend funds established to pay current liabilities should be shown as current assets. A fund or a portion of a fund should be classified as a current asset only when it is to be used in current operations or in the payment of a debt that is shown as a current liability.

Funds for use in expanding or acquiring plant and equipment are sometimes included with fixed assets. However, this classification is not sound because the *investment* is not yet actually devoted to regular operations. Such inclusion would distort certain ratios used in the analysis of statements. Furthermore, the fund may possibly be devoted to some other purpose.

Funds may be in the custody of the company or a trustee. The existence of a trustee should be noted on the balance sheet. Funds may be established by the company on a voluntary basis or in accordance with the requirements of a trust indenture or other agreement. An important problem relative to these funds is the investment in income-producing securities which will insure the safety of the principal and which can be converted into cash when needed to pay debts or other uses.

Funds consisting of capital stock should be valued at cost unless the investment represents control of a subsidiary, in which event the investment account should be adjusted to show the increase in value due to the income of the subsidiary not distributed; funds consisting of bonds and mortgages should be valued at cost, with periodic adjustments for discount and premium. In the event that apparently permanent market declines have taken place, the excess of cost over market may be set up in a valuation account. The market decline should be shown as an extraordinary loss item on the income statement.

Sometimes a company will buy its own bonds and hold them as long-term investments. The preferable practice is to value the acquired bonds at the same amount shown as bond liability on the balance sheet, but this is not always done. Sometimes the bonds are carried at cost, or at market value. Neither of these practices is desirable unless it is known that the bonds are to be disposed of soon in the open market, in which case cost is the preferable value standard.

If the bonds are canceled, the Sinking Fund and the Bonds Payable accounts should be reduced accordingly. The result will be an extraordinary gain or loss on the item on the income statement.

Cash surrender value of life insurance. Frequently, a business insures the life of its partners, managers, or officers; the business is the named beneficiary in the policy. After the policy has been in effect for a few years, it acquires a cash surrender value which may be shown in the long-term investments section of the balance sheet. Many businesses consider this item as one of the most liquid or current assets; when cash is needed, the cash surrender value of the life insurance policy may be pledged as security for a loan. However, the classification as a current asset is not accepted practice because the insurance policy will not be converted into cash in the usual course of business. As a matter of fact, the life insurance policy normally would not be surrendered except in the event of the insured's death or when a financial emergency arose; generally, there is no intention to convert the insurance policy into cash currently. Consequently, the cash surrender value of this asset is properly classified as a long-term investment.

Annual premiums on the policies should be charged (1) to Cash

Surrender Value of Life Insurance in the amount of the increase in cash surrender value of the policy and (2) to Life Insurance Expense for the excess of the premium over the increase in the cash surrender value.

Capital stock owned. Investments in the capital stock of other companies may represent either a minority interest, a controlling majority interest in the company (more than 50 percent of the voting stock), or a one-half interest. Sharing a half-interest in a subsidiary with another corporation has become more and more common on the current business scene in the United States. When the ownership is shared equally with another, neither one has unquestioned legal authority; actual operating authority will be determined by agreement and may reside in one, or the other, or be shared. Of the 600 companies studied in *Accounting Trends and Techniques 1971,* 132 disclosed half-interests (exactly 50 percent) in shared subsidiaries. Over half of the owning companies use the equity method of valuation.

The basis of recording the investment in capital stock and, therefore, the method used in assigning the dollar amount for balance sheet purposes should be disclosed by parenthetical notation or footnote.

Stock rights or warrants may be received in connection with the ownership of capital stock. A certificate (warrant) given by the stock issuing corporation indicates the number of shares of new stock that the stockholder may buy (the preemptive right at a specific price).

Bonds owned. A bond is a promise by the issuer to pay the principal of and interest on a loan—it is a formalized promissory note. If the bond has no specific property assigned as security, it is a debenture bond. If the bond is secured by pledged collateral, it is a collateral trust bond. If the bond is secured by real property, it is a mortgage bond.

Mortgages may be used with notes or bonds. The mortgage is primarily a security device, as it creates a lien on specified property. The bond or note represents the promise to pay. When a corporation borrows from one lender and gives a mortgage note, the obligation is most likely to appear as a mortgage note payable. When many investors are involved, the obligation usually is shown as bonds payable. Long-term investments in the bonds of other corporations should be shown in the Bond Investment account at cost adjusted for the amortization of bond premium or bond discount.

When nonspeculative bonds have been purchased for an amount other than face value, the premium or discount if material in amount should be amortized over the remaining life of the bond so that the current Interest Income account may be stated properly. When the market interest rate is higher than the formal interest rate, the bonds will sell at a discount; when the market interest rate is lower than the formal interest rate, the bonds will sell at a premium. In other words, the market value of a high-grade bond depends on the yield for such a bond in the current bond market.

Fixed assets

Fixed assets represent tangible "physical" properties which are to be used for more than one year in the regular operations of a business and which normally are not intended for resale. Fixed assets, with the exception of nondepreciable or nonwasting land, which should be shown separately on the balance sheet, are consumed with respect to their service or useful life in the production of goods and services; therefore the cost is recovered through sales revenue. That is, the investment in fixed assets is converted into working capital through the process of recognizing depreciation, depletion, and amortization. Note that in a manufacturing concern, depreciation related to manufacturing becomes an asset (inventory) before it is transferred to cost of goods sold.

Leased property that is used in the regular operations of the business is not shown on the balance sheet unless the rental has been paid for in advance or improvements to the leased property have been made. In *Opinion No. 5* (September 1964) the Accounting Principles Board of the AICPA held that the details concerning noncancellable leases, if material in amount, should be disclosed, usually by footnote, and leases which are in fact purchases give rise to property and liability entries on the balance sheet.

From the point of view of most effective analysis, fixed asset items should be listed in separate classifications on the balance sheet or in a schedule because:

1. Land does not depreciate.
2. Buildings, furniture and fixtures, and equipment depreciate at different rates.
3. Though the Accounting Principles Board disapproves, appreciation may have been recorded.
4. Some of the assets may be highly specialized or of a wasting-asset type.
5. Some of the assets may be fully depreciated; others may be newly acquired.

The bases used in stating the book values of fixed assets on a balance sheet should be disclosed. The most important fixed assets are discussed below.

Machinery and plant equipment. Machinery and equipment may consist of the fixed assets that are not included within the classifications of buildings, land improvements, or land. Machinery and equipment includes airplanes, automobiles, trucks, tractors, electric motors, machine and hand tools, presses, lathes, cranes, office machines, and furniture and fixtures. Individual accounts for the foregoing are maintained in subsidiary ledgers. Sometimes the balance sheet shows delivery equipment and furniture and fixtures separately from machinery and plant equipment.

Buildings. A business may own buildings that are used in the regular operation of the business and that have been constructed either on owned land or on leased land. If the buildings have been constructed on owned land, the cost should be reflected in the Buildings account; depreciation should be based on the estimated service life of the buildings. If the buildings have been constructed on leased land, the cost should be included in an account called "Improvements to Leaseholds"; the amortization of cost to expense should be based on the life of the buildings or the life of the lease, whichever is shorter. The apportionment of cost to expense is known as (1) depreciation when the service life of the asset is shorter than the term of the lease or (2) amortization when the term of the lease is shorter than the service life of the asset.

The item improvements to leaseholds is customarily classified on the balance sheet as an intangible asset because from a technical point of view the company possesses only a "right to the use" of the property. Legal title is vested in the owner of the land. However, for purposes of statement analysis, this item should be treated in the same manner as other similar properties which are classified as fixed assets.

Standby equipment and idle facilities which are held with reasonable expectation of future use in the regular operations of the business may be included as fixed assets.

A company may also own buildings and land that are not used in the regular operations of the business. In such cases the property is usually designated as real estate and shown in the long-term investments section of the balance sheet.

Land. Land that is currently used in the regular operations of the business should be shown separately from buildings because ordinarily depreciation affects only buildings. Land that is to be used for future expansion or that is held for investment purposes should be classified as a long-term investment. Land improvements such as fences, paving, bridges, sewers, and drainage lines should be shown separately from land because the items are subject to amortization.

Natural resources. A business may own natural resources such as mines, oil and natural gas wells, timberlands, fruit groves, and sulphur deposits. These assets, which are referred to as wasting assets because physical elements are actually removed and in most instances cannot be replaced, are subject to depletion.

Amortization (valuation) of fixed assets

Fixed assets are generally shown on the balance sheet at cost;[1] cost less *accumulated* depreciation, depletion, or amortization; at appraised reproduction cost less depreciation; or at appraised sound value.[2] The preferred balance sheet caption is "accumulated depreciation"; or, if appropriate, "accumulated depletion" or "accumulated amortization." The title "reserve for depreciation" has been steadily declining and is now used by only 33 of the 600 *Accounting Trends and Techniques 1971* companies.

The determination of annual depreciation, depletion, or amortization and, therefore, the total amount of the cost that has been allocated to expenses are of major significance from the point of view of both the income statement and the balance sheet. The book value (the remaining undepreciated, undepleted, and unamortized cost) of fixed assets shown on the balance sheet is *going-concern* "value," i.e., the amount of cost yet to be recovered through charges to the revenue of future periods. Unless proper principles are applied in determining the allocation of fixed asset cost to expense, the expenses, net income, assets, and owners' equity will be either overstated or understated. The real value of fixed assets to the business is dependent upon their usefulness in future operations.

The accounts Accumulated Depreciation and Allowance for Doubtful Receivables reflect different values when deducted from their related assets. The doubtful receivables item (a valuation account) represents the estimated amount of uncollectible receivables; when this balance is deducted from accounts receivable, the remainder represents the estimated realizable amount to be collected from customers on a going-concern basis. The accumulated depreciation, depletion, and amortization reflect the portion of the cost of fixed assets included on the balance sheet that has been allocated to expense. When these accumulated amounts of depreciation, depletion, and amortization are deducted from the related assets, the remaining balances, exclusive of residual value, if any, represent the cost of the assets to be allocated to expense in the future. These balances do not show liquidation or sales value or replacement cost.

The amount of annual depreciation may be different for companies in the same industry because of differences in the composition of depre-

---

[1] Cost includes the invoice or the contract price plus all costs necessary to place the asset in usable condition. Cash discounts taken on purchases of fixed assets should be recorded as cost deductions in determining cost. If consideration other than cash is given for the asset, the cost depends upon the dollar value of the consideration exchanged.

[2] Sound value represents the replacement cost of an asset less observed depreciation and deferred maintenance, or present value as determined in an appraisal.

ciable assets, in the methods of depreciation adopted, and in the maintenance and repair policies. A liberal maintenance and repair policy may be accompanied by the recognition of less depreciation expense. On the other hand, some companies may adopt an extreme depreciation policy and write off the asset cost (or other basis) over a relatively short period of time. Such a policy cannot be justified if it materially understates asset values and current income; furthermore, excessive depreciation will overstate income in subsequent periods, which will be charged with an inadequate amount for depreciation.

Frequently, and contrary to the cost-less-depreciation amortization convention, assets acquired in exchange for bonds and capital stock are valued by management at an excessively high or low amount.

Fixed assets should show the cost as of the date of acquisition. Property that is constructed by the business should be charged with all costs incurred, including an equitable amount of overhead attributable to the project. If assets are acquired by exchanging other property or capital stock, the property acquired may be valued at the fair market value of the property received or the value of the consideration given for the purchase. The cost of property additions should be capitalized and included in the asset account. Betterments and improvements to fixed assets provide greater productivity, less costly production, higher asset cost, and/or a longer service life. Those expenditures that result in adding new cost to the asset should be debited to the asset account; other expenditures which restore previously depreciated service usefulness should be charged to the related accumulated depreciation account. If a portion of an old asset is removed when a betterment or improvement is completed, the original cost and the accumulated depreciation should be eliminated from the related accounts.

Land is sometimes donated to a business by a municipality in order to encourage it to locate in the community. Such assets should be shown on the records at a nominal value of $1. Such a donation is frequently subject to severe restrictions. It can be used only for a plant site; the land is not a "free" asset, and, therefore, cannot be sold by the grantee. The external analyst has no evidence relative to the amount of "value" placed by management on the property. In accepting the grant of land, management has decided that the advantages outweighed the disadvantages.

Sometimes a business may discover valuable natural resources on its property. Such assets may be entered on the records at appraised value; the unrealized owners' equity is appraisal capital. The valuation at appraised value should be disclosed.

Information with respect to the current appraised commercial value of the fixed asset would be useful to the analyst, but it is rarely shown.

Although fully depreciated assets that are still in use are often written off completely, it is better practice to continue to show the gross amount of property, plant, and equipment as well as the amount of the related accumulated depreciation.

Fixed assets and their book values may be incorrectly presented if a proper distinction is not made between capital and revenue expenditures; if the policy with reference to depreciation, depletion, and amortization is excessive, inadequate, or inconsistent from year to year; and if the book values of property accounts have been arbitrarily increased or decreased. Fixed assets are a difficult problem for the analyst.

Appreciation of fixed assets

Buildings and especially land often appreciate in dollar value because of increases in price levels or because of greater usefulness than is reflected by the book values of the assets.

In October 1965, in *Opinion No. 6,* the Accounting Principles Board stated that "The Board is of the opinion that property, plant and equipment should not be written up by an entity to reflect appraisal, market or current values which are above cost to the entity. This statement is not intended to change accounting practices followed in connection with quasi-reorganizations[3] or reorganizations. . . . Whenever appreciation has been recorded on the books, income should be charged with depreciation computed on the written up amounts."

Although, as the above quotation shows, the accounting profession strongly disapproves, appreciation is sometimes recorded by writing up the book value of assets to reflect the present *sound values.* The present sound value of a property is its reproduction cost new, less the accumulated depreciation on the replacement basis.[4]

There have been times in the past when writeups of asset values have been fairly common, but today they are very uncommon where substantial corporations with audited financial statements are involved.

Information about current value of fixed assets is of obvious value to analysts but it is rarely provided in published annual reports. Of course, such values are not easy to establish; they rest on highly subjective appraisals.

---

[3] A quasi-reorganization is a recognized accounting procedure by which the accounts of a corporation may be restated to the same extent as they properly would be if a new corporation were created and acquired the business of the existing corporation. It is essential that formal disclosure be given to the stockholders because a quasi-reorganization establishes a new basis of accountability for assets and liabilities. During a quasi-reorganization, all remaining retained earnings must be transferred to Paid-In Capital according to Committee on Accounting Procedure, AICPA, *Accounting Research Bulletin No. 43* (1953), pp. 45–47, in *Accounting Research and Terminology Bulletins, Final Edition* (New York, 1961).

[4] The term "condition percent" is used to denote the percentage of the sound value to the appraised value new.

A knowledge of the current appraised values is also useful for insurance[5] purposes and for furnishing data for taxation. However, such write-ups are not subject to income tax; nor do they increase depreciation allowable for income tax purposes.

The accounting profession does not object in the same way to asset, including fixed asset, writedowns. In fact these are required if there have been losses of value which appear to be permanent. In the case of a plant, for example, write-downs do not take place unless there is objective evidence of loss of going-concern value (usefulness in a going business) such as abandonment or offering for sale. Such a loss is treated as an element in the computation of net income, classified on the income statement as extraordinary.[6]

Fixed assets—effect of changes in the price level on "cost"

Assigning dollar amounts of "cost" to fixed assets, as currently practiced, is based on the traditional assumption that "cost" is historical cost, measured by the number of dollars invested in the asset.

However, from the standpoint of the analyst, the assumption is not necessarily correct. In accounting, as in other aspects of life, a different purpose may require a change of approach.

Between 1940 and 1970 the purchasing power of the dollar declined markedly. Measured by an index of plant construction costs, this decline has been 70 percent; measured by a general wholesale price index, the decline has been 66 percent. Whatever measure is used, the decline has been material in amount.

To the extent that the Plant account includes 31-year-old assets, it includes cost stated in 1940 ("big") dollars. Prepaid expenses (also stated at "cost") are in current ("small") dollars. Cash and receivables are in current dollars. Inventories may be in dollars of various sizes, depending on the inventory method in use, length of turnover, and so forth.

A Plant account stated in 1940 dollars bears no relation to replacement cost. If it takes three current dollars to equal one 1940 dollar, what was the "actual cost" of the plant for current balance sheet and income statement purposes? If depreciation is in 1940 dollars and sales are in current dollars, has a proper matching of cost and revenue been attained? If an analyst is analyzing "earning power," should depreciation be adjusted to reflect current price levels, or should historical cost be used?

---

[5] Fire insurance contracts are based upon current sound values rather than book values.

[6] Accounting Principles Board, AICPA, *Opinion No. 9*, (New York, December 1966), par. 20.

Since statements are being currently prepared under the historical cost assumption, these questions will be discussed in the second part of this book, in connection with the problems of the statement analyst.[7]

Intangible assets

An intangible asset, from an accounting point of view, is an asset (1) the value of which resides in the rights which its possession confers upon the owner and (2) that does not represent a claim against an individual or business. Of the 600 companies studied in *Accounting Trends and Techniques 1971,* approximately half (334) presented 587 intangible asset titles on their balance sheets.

Goodwill (usually acquisition costs in excess of values assignable to
   individual asset items), up from 183 in 1960 286
Patents, down from 150 in 1960 106
Trademarks, brand names, copyrights, down from 98 in 1960 59
Licenses, franchises, memberships, up from 14 in 1960 24
Formulas, processes, designs, down from 18 in 1960 8
Various other intangibles, described and not described, down from
   83 in 1960 74

In August 1970 the Accounting Principles Board issued *Opinion No. 17* on "Intangible Assets." The opinion distinguishes between the costs of intangible assets acquired from other enterprises or individuals— which should be recorded as assets—and the costs of developing, maintaining, or restoring intangible assets, which are not specifically identifiable, have indeterminate lives, or are inherent in a continuing business and related to an enterprise as a whole (such as goodwill)—which should be deducted from income when incurred.

The value at which specifically identified assets should be recorded is cost at date of acquisition. The cost of intangible assets should be amortized systematically, using straight-line methods, over the period which it is estimated the intangible asset will benefit—but not over 40 years. Factors which will affect such an estimate are numerous and include legal life, contractual provisions, and obsolescence.

Current trends in valuation practices of the 600 companies are shown in the following results:

The formerly popular practice of presenting intangibles at a nominal value has declined from 136 instances in 1965 to 36 in 1970. And carrying such assets at an unamortized value (presumably cost) has increased from 106 to 169. Corporations whose stocks are held by investors at large are becoming increasingly sensitive to practices which decrease their reported annual earnings.

On the other hand, 230 balance sheet intangible asset items were dis-

---

[7] The effect of changing price levels on the interpretation of financial statements is studied in Part III.

closed to be valued net of amortization (up from 167 in 1965), and the basis used in valuing 91 others was not disclosed, down from 120 in 1965.

An intangible asset, from a legal point of view—a view not adopted for purposes of accounting—is one that has no material existence. According to this definition, intangibles include, in addition to those already mentioned, property rights represented by accounts receivable, notes receivable, stocks, and bonds, which, in accounting, are otherwise classified.

Nature and valuation of specific intangibles

The initial amount assigned to all types of intangibles should be cost.[8] In case intangibles are acquired in exchange for securities or property other than cash, cost may be considered as being either the fair value of the consideration given or the fair value of the property or right acquired, which presumably are approximately identical. The nature of, and the valuation principles applicable to, intangible asset items are discussed in the following pages.

Copyrights. A copyright is the exclusive right, conferred upon the owner by the federal government, affording monopolistic protection to writings, drawings, and literary productions. The original grant is made for a term of 28 years and may be renewed for a like term. If the copyright cost is small, it should be charged against the first edition. When the copyright is obtained from a grantee, the cost, if a considerable sum, should be prorated over the period of time during which the sales are expected to continue.

Leaseholds. A leasehold represents a long-term lease on property, usually land or buildings. When rentals for the use of land and buildings are paid in advance, the payments should be shown on the balance sheet as leaseholds. In such a case the prepaid rental, the leasehold, is amortized over the life of the lease.

The existence of long-term leases should be disclosed in a footnote to the balance sheet. The amount of the annual rent, together with other information relative to obligations and/or guaranties assumed or to be assumed in the future, is of considerable importance to the analyst.[9]

Leasehold improvements. Leasehold improvements represent improvements made on leased property; these improvements may consist of new buildings and structures or additions to buildings already con-

---

[8] Accounting Principles Board, AICPA, *Opinion No. 17* (New York, August 1970).

[9] Accounting Principles Board, AICPA, *Opinion No. 5* (New York, September 1964). This opinion also points out that some leases are tantamount to purchases and the resulting asset and liability balances should be displayed on the balance sheet.

structed. Leaseholds and improvements to leaseholds are intangible assets because they represent *rights* to the use of the property for a period of time. When the lessee improves leased property, the cost of improvements is capitalized. This amount is amortized over the remaining life of the lease or the life of the improvement, whichever is shorter. For example, assume that improvements have been made on property that has been leased for a period of 20 years. If the improvements will have an economic life of 25 years, the cost should be written off over a 20-year period—the life of the lease. On the other hand, if the improvements have an economic life of 15 years, the cost should be written off over a 15-year period—the life of the asset, since it is less than the life of the lease.

Any residual value to be allowed the lessee, by agreement on the part of the lessor, should be taken into consideration in determining the annual write-off of improvements to leaseholds.

Leaseholds and leasehold improvements consisting of property used in regular operations are frequently shown as fixed assets on balance sheets. The depreciation of fixed assets and the amortization of leaseholds and leasehold improvements are therefore similar expense items. In analyzing financial statements, the total cost (less accumulated amortization and depreciation) of the foregoing assets, including regularly classified fixed assets, should be used as a basis in evaluating the adequacy of operating income.

Franchises.   A franchise is a privilege granted by a governmental unit to an individual, a partnership, or a corporation to use a public property, street, or highway, or the space above or below the street or highway. The franchise may be for a fixed term of years, for an indeterminate period of time, or in perpetuity.

The valuation of a franchise is dependent upon its original cost and its term. Under present-day conditions, franchises are obtained, in most cases, directly from public utility commissions; only a nominal cost is involved. This cost is customarily treated as a current expense.

A perpetual irrevocable franchise which costs a considerable sum should be capitalized and not amortized. If the perpetual franchise is revocable, the cost should be amortized over a relatively short period of time. When the franchise has been purchased and has a fixed term of years, the cost should be amortized over the life of the franchise.

Patents.   A patent is an exclusive right granted by the federal government to an inventor to manufacture, sell, or use his invention or process for a period of 17 years. This term may be extended only by an act of Congress.

The value of a patent is dependent upon its revenue-producing capacity. The cost of developing a patent or its purchase price should be capitalized. The cost of a patent should be amortized over its legal life, a period of 17 years, or its economic life, which in many cases is less than its legal life.

When a patent infringement lawsuit is lost, the cost of the lawsuit and the book value of the patent should be treated as an extraordinary loss item. If the lawsuit is won, the cost of defending the patent rights may be recorded as an additional cost of the patent. Such a capital expenditure is justified since the validity of the patent is thereby established.

Trademarks and trade names. A trademark or a trade name is any distinguishing label, symbol, or name used by a business concern to mark its product. Trademarks and trade names are factors in creating customer goodwill. Trademarks, unlike trade names, can be registered. When trademarks are not registered, they have common-law protection if the claimant can prove his prior use of the mark. The legal life of a trademark does not expire.

Goodwill. Goodwill is generally considered to consist of those intangible elements connected with a going concern, such as name, personality, or reputation; favorable and convenient location of the business; capability of management; quality of merchandise and demand for a certain product; favorable prices; good labor relations with employees; and efficient, fair, and courteous methods of treating customers.

Goodwill is customarily shown on the accounting records and, therefore, on the balance sheet only when it has been purchased. In the final analysis the real test of the existence of goodwill is the ability to earn a rate of return higher than is usually realized in the industry.

Some companies write off the cost of goodwill over a period of a few years as a special item on the statement of income. A charge-off in the year of acquisition is not considered good practice.[10] If the excess profits which originally gave evidence of the existence of goodwill have been maintained, the goodwill asset has not diminished in value; therefore, if the value of goodwill is written down, the assets and owners' equity will be understated. If the goodwill asset no longer has value, the write-off corrects the asset and owners' equity values.

Deferred charges

Accounting Research Bulletin 43, Chapter 3, Section A, in discussing deferred charges describes them as—

long term prepayments which are fairly chargeable to the operations of several years, or deferred charges such as unamortized debt discount and expense, bonus payments under a long-term lease, costs of rearrangement of factory layout or removal to a new location, and certain types of research and development costs.

---

[10] Accounting Principles Board, *Opinion No. 17.*

Accounting Trends and Techniques 1971 points out that 529 companies (out of 600) presented 852 cases of deferred charges or "other assets." Of these balance sheet items, 585 were not otherwise described. Of the remainder, 64 were described as prepaid expenses; debt discount and expense, 51; taxes,[11] 44; financing or organization expense, 16; start up and tooling, 23; and a variety of other infrequent examples. Organization expense also is sometimes classified as an intangible asset.

While expenses arising from the sale of capital stock are legitimate deferred charges, discount on stock is not. This latter should be carried as a deduction in the net worth section of the balance sheet, offsetting against the total of all items in that section or against a specific item such as the stock issue involved.

Prepaid expenses and deferred charges are often shown on published balance sheets in one amount under a common heading as deferred expenses, deferred assets, deferred charges, prepaid expenses, prepaid expenses and deferred charges, or deferred charges to future operations. This is not the best practice, since different types of assets are involved.

Sometimes the item, development of inventions, appears on a balance sheet as a deferred charge. If this is a bona fide expenditure and there seems to be hope for the success of the invention, this temporary classification is justifiable. Naturally, if there is no hope of developing the invention profitably, the total cost should be written off.

Experimental and development expense is frequently charged off in the year in which incurred. Sometimes it is capitalized as an asset and amortized over a (usually short) term of years. The guiding generally accepted accounting principle is the matching of cost and revenue—against what revenues should the costs be charged? In dealing with deferred charges the problem is to determine how much is properly includable on the balance sheet and how much is it appropriate to charge off on the statement of income? Thus the expense incurred in connection with the issuance of debt, and the discount, if any, suffered on the notes or bonds, give rise to costs which properly relate to all of the years until maturity. Bond expense and bond discount should pair up with interest expense to yield the total annual cost of the borrowing.

An unamortized balance of bond discount or premium may be (1) written off in full at the time bonds are refunded or retired before maturity, (2) amortized in future periods according to the original amortization plan, or (3) amortized over the life of the new issue. This last treatment is controversial: both the American Accounting Associa-

---

[11] For example, in its 1968 annual report the American Saint Gobain Corporation reported a deferred charge of $775,581 with the caption "future income tax benefit relating to provisions for pensions." The postponement of income tax effects is the subject of Accounting Principles Board, AICPA, *Opinion No. 11* (New York, December 1967).

tion, in its *Statement on Concepts and Standards Underlying Corporate Financial Statements,* and the American Institute's *Accounting Research Bulletin No. 43* declared it unacceptable. But in its *Opinion No. 6* the Accounting Principles Board says that "the third method, amortization over the life of the new issue, is appropriate under circumstances where the refunding takes place because of currently lower interest rates or anticipation of higher interest rates in the future. . . ."

For analytical purposes, financial statement analysts usually heavily discount deferred charges and "other assets" as their value is conjectural. Prepaid expense items, such as insurance premiums paid in advance of the period in which the company will benefit, are an exception as they carry an assurance of benefit without additional cost.

Summary

In the foregoing discussion of *assets,* emphasis has been given to the present-day traditional methods of balance sheet presentation. In brief, the following accounting practices have been stressed:

1. Provide for loss, but do not anticipate profit.
2. Value receivables at the face amount less a valuation account, and value inventory and marketable securities at the lower of cost or market.
3. Consistently apply a reasonable method of distinguishing between capital and revenue expenditures.
4. Allocate revenue and expense to proper accounting periods by such means as will keep them matched.
5. Show long-term investments at cost or at cost adjusted for periodic amortization of discount and premiums.
6. Record assets, when acquired, at cost.
7. If appreciation is recorded, enter the unrealized value in an Appraisal Capital account.
8. Recognize depreciation on the basis of the cost of the asset or, if appreciation has been recorded, which the accounting profession frowns on, on the basis of the appraised value.
9. Do not record assets unless they have been acquired or developed at some cost, have been "discovered" (natural resources), or have been donated to the business.

QUESTIONS AND PROBLEMS

4–1. Explain the difference between:
    a) A patent and a franchise.
    b) Accounts receivable and intangible assets.

c) The legal life and the economic life of an intangible asset.

d) Leaseholds and improvements to leaseholds.

4–2. Discuss the problem of determining the appropriate measurement (dollarwise) of the following, for balance sheet purposes:

a) Accounts receivable.

b) Machinery and the mine itself.

c) Improvements to leaseholds.

d) Temporary investments.

e) Land.

f) Long-term investments.

g) Life insurance policies.

4–3. The Marvin Corporation included the following in its balance sheet under the heading of long-term investments. You are requested to discuss the propriety of including these items as long-term investments.

a) Land purchased for future plant expansion, used currently as a parking lot.

b) Cash on time deposit in the Kearney National Bank.

c) Travel advances to employees.

d) Cash surrender value of life insurance policy on the life of the president of the corporation.

e) Land and buildings rented to other companies.

f) Unsecured, two-year, loan to the secretary of the corporation.

g) Securities purchased with cash not needed for regular operations during off-season period.

4–4. Comment on the following statements:

a) Depreciation should be computed on original cost even though the asset has been written up.

b) Discount and premium on bonds purchased as long-term investments should be shown in separate accounts.

c) Treasury stock should be classified as a long-term investment.

d) Cash surrender value of life insurance may be classified as a current asset.

4–5. Distinguish between:

a) An expenditure and a disbursement.

b) Capital and revenue expenditures.

c) Temporary and long-term investments.

d) Long-term investments and fixed assets.

e) Fixed assets and intangible assets.

4–6. Identify, define, or indicate the nature of the following items selected from the published balance sheets of various corporations. State the proper classification of each item.

a) Accumulated obsolescence.

b) Capital expenditures.

c) Cash set aside for modernization and expansion programs.

d) Cash surrender value of life insurance.

e) Land improvements.

f) Cost of contracts in progress (less: billings on contracts in progress).

g) Costs applicable to future periods.
h) Deferred charges to future operations.
i) Deferred debenture bond issue expense.
j) Federal income taxes recoverable.
k) Fund for redemption of 7 percent preferred stock.
l) Common stock in treasury (at cost).
m) Material and supplies.
n) Miscellaneous investments, less estimated losses.
o) Operating parts and supplies.
p) Ores, by-products, metals in process and on hand.
q) Prepaid and deferred charges.
r) Prepaid expenses applicable to future periods.
s) Receivables from subsidiaries not consolidated.
t) Reserves for depreciation, depletion, and amortization.
u) Timberlands, less depletion.
v) Unamortized debt discount and expense.
w) U.S. government securities set aside for property additions and replacements.

4–7.

T. R. HARTER CORPORATION

December 31, 1971

Accounts receivable	$ 70,200
Accrued interest receivable	500
Accumulated depreciation of buildings	35,750
Accumulated depreciation of delivery equipment	2,000
Accumulated depreciation of furniture	1,000
Accumulated depreciation of improvements to lease-holds	10,500
Accumulated depreciation of machinery and equipment	10,600
Advances to Subsidiary A	7,000
Buildings	187,000
Cash	50,000
Delivery equipment	3,400
Discount on bonds payable	1,500
Estimated uncollectible receivables	8,500
Finished goods inventory	80,700
Furniture and fixtures	4,500
Goods in process	26,000
Goodwill	1
Improvements to leaseholds	70,800
Land	150,200
Leaseholds	9,000
Machinery and equipment	210,000
Marketable securities	25,000
New York Telephone bonds	10,000
Notes receivable	20,000
Notes receivable discounted	18,000
Office supplies inventory	100
Organization expense	600
Patents, trademarks, and copyrights	500
Petty cash fund	2,000
Prepaid interest expense	100

Prepaid insurance	1,000
Raw material inventory	32,100
Real estate	110,000
Stock of Subsidiary A	400,000
Subscription receivable, common	20,000
Tools inventory (cost)	9,000

Required:

Prepare the asset side of the corporation's balance sheet.

4–8. The following unrelated groups of items were classified as noncurrent assets on published balance sheets; the supplementary data for footnotes in each case were obtained by studying the companies' annual reports and by special inquiry. After having analyzed the data for each company, present the items properly classified as to balance sheet sections. (Assume the date December 31, 1971.)

a) Noncurrent Assets:

Due from subsidiaries (current)	$ 1,460,942
Stocks of companies owned, 90% or higher, located in foreign countries, at estimated current value[1]	2,891,411
Loans and investments, net[2]	5,057,063
Pension funds, at cost[3]	8,157,176
Plant and equipment, less accrued depreciation, depletion, and amortization to date, $32,565,139[4]	67,196,055
Goodwill, patents, and licenses[5]	1
Other assets, including claims for refund of income taxes based on carry-back provision, $1,670,141[6]	4,134,553

[1] Cost, $4,615,322.
[2] A reserve for possible future decline in value, $200,000, has been deducted.
[3] Amortization of debt discount to date has not been recognized, $2,475.
[4] Land has been appreciated, $1,000,000.
[5] Patents and licenses have an estimated present value of $1,260,000.
[6] Prepaid expenses amount to $815,613.

b) Investments:[1]

U.S. government securities set aside, at cost, for property additions and replacements	$ 2,840,910
Miscellaneous security investments, at cost[2]	132,153
Life insurance policy (life of president)[3]	1,000,000

Property and Equipment:

Land, buildings, leaseholds, fixtures, and equipment less accumulated depreciation and amortization	56,608,444

Other Assets:

Special deposits and funds[4]	2,413,100
Operating parts and supplies, at cost	810,250
Patterns, patents, and goodwill	52,470
Accrued interest on U.S. government securities	2,440

[1] The current asset section includes a sinking fund, $124,500, which is being accumulated to pay long-term debt in 1975.
[2] Approximate quoted market, $325,000.
[3] The company capitalized the face of the policy during 1950 the annual premiums have been charged to expense. The cash surrender value as of December 31, 1966, was $429,471.
[4] Includes funds to be used during 1972 to pay debts now shown as current liabilities $361,492.

5

The balance sheet: Liabilities and owners' equity

THE AUTHORS' study of 125 annual reports issued by large U.S. corporations for the year 1968 revealed that the right-hand, liabilities and owners' equity, side of their account form balance sheets most often bore the heading "liabilities" (45 balance sheets), "liabilities and stockholders' equity" (28), and "liabilities and shareholders' equity" (also 28). A substantial minority (17) started the section with the heading "current liabilities." Eleven other headings were counted. Legally the obligation of a corporation to its shareholders is not a liability so in this book we will use the caption "liabilities and stockholders' equity."

Liabilities

A major problem relative to liabilities is their possible omission. All liabilities should be shown on the balance sheet properly labeled, classified, and valued. Contingent liabilities are ordinarily disclosed by footnotes. The dollar amount of most liabilities is readily determined at the time of their incurrence, although some, such as tax liabilities and those arising from litigation, have to be estimated.

In December 1967 the Accounting Principles Board of the AICPA issued *Opinion No. 11*, "Accounting for Income Taxes." This opinion deals with differences between the financial statements and the federal income tax returns in the way accounting charges and credits are handled. Simply stated, if there are tax deductions which do not have their counterpart in the financial statements, there has been a reduction in tax liability which will give rise to additional tax payments in future years. These potential tax payments are set up on the balance sheet as liabilities, current or long-term as the case may be. Other combinations of circumstances can give rise to current or long-term asset items. Such assets and liabilities are somewhat different in their character than the more usual asset and liability amounts.

Of the 600 *Accounting Trends and Techniques 1971* companies, all but 79 reported interperiod tax allocations and 360 of these showed resulting noncurrent liabilities only; 56 showed a variety of liability and asset items.

Pension and retirement plans can also give rise to liabilities, in this case to employees. Accounting Principles Board *Opinion No. 8*, "Accounting for the Cost of Pension Plans," was issued in November 1966. In 1970, 538 out of 600 companies disclosed pension plans in their annual reports. Many of these plans were supported by assets set aside as funds and no liabilities were set up on the balance sheet, but about 70 companies did show such liabilities.

Contingent liabilities were disclosed by 414 out of the 600 companies, arising from litigation (240 presentations), guarantees (152), tax assessments (60), agreements to purchase (131), sales of receivables (47), and other (120). Only 93 companies made their disclosure on the face of the balance sheet, while 321 used as a vehicle balance sheet notes or the president's letter. While notes to the balance sheet are regarded as integral parts of the statement, the president's letter is not, and disclosure only in the latter is believed by the authors to be substandard reporting.

Current liabilities

A current liability is an obligation that normally will require, within approximately one year of the balance sheet date, the use of current assets or the creation of other current liabilities.[1] This classification is also intended to include (1) obligations for items which have entered into the operating cycle, such as payables incurred in the acquisition of materials and supplies to be used in the production of goods or in providing services to be offered for sale; and (2) other debts which arise from operations directly related to the operating cycle. Current liabilities are customarily incurred in connection with regular current operations of the business. Adequate explanation should be given when assets have been pledged as security for debts and obligations. Mention should be made of the specific asset that has been pledged and whether the liability has been fully or partly secured.

---

[1] AICPA, *Accounting Research and Terminology Bulletins, Final Edition* (New York, 1961), chap. 3, sec. A, par. 7 and 8.

Accounts and notes payable

Accounts payable should include only amounts due creditors for merchandise or materials purchased from them on credit. Amounts due partners, officers, stockholders, employees, or affiliated companies should be shown separately or as miscellaneous accounts payable. Many businesses maintain a voucher system; consequently, vouchers payable may be used instead of accounts payable to show the current liability for credit purchases of assets, raw materials, merchandise, supplies, and services such as light, power, and transportation.

Notes payable are written promises, signed by the makers, to pay a sum certain in money on demand or at a definite or determinable date in the future. Promissory notes, which are assumed to be current unless otherwise indicated, may have been issued to banks, to merchandise creditors, or to others for cash, services, equipment, or merchandise. Drafts and trade acceptances are often included in notes payable, and justifiably, since these instruments, when "accepted," also represent written promises to pay and can be treated similarly from an accounting point of view. Notes payable issued to banks for current loans are often listed as bank loans. Notes payable, sometimes called bills payable, usually bear a definite rate of interest; and if interest has accrued as of the balance sheet date, it should be shown in the currently liability section as accrued interest payable. For more complete analytical purposes, notes payable should be classified on the balance sheet or on a supporting schedule as follows: notes payable—trade; notes payable—banks; notes payable—officers; notes payable—stockholders; notes payable—employees; notes payable—partners; notes payable—miscellanous.

Notes payable should also be classified as secured and unsecured. Unless notes payable are classified in some manner as suggested above, the nature of the obligation cannot be determined from the balance sheet.

Deposits

Frequently, the item, deposits, appears as a current liability. This item may represent either cash advances by customers on goods ordered or deposits made by employees. In the former case the title should be "advances on sale contracts"; in the latter case, "funds deposited by employees." If the loans by employees are not payable within approximately a year, they should be classified as long-term liabilities.

Dividends payable

Dividends payable represent unpaid cash dividends that have been declared by the board of directors. In the event of insolvency the stockholders entitled to these declared dividends would share pro rata with other unsecured creditors of the corporation. On the other hand, if a dividend fund has been established, the stockholders are entitled to the full dividend payment. Dividends do not represent a liability until the board of directors has formally declared them. Dividends, unlike revenue and expense items, do not accrue until declared.

The balance sheet item, dividend scrip, indicates that the company has issued promissory notes (*scrip*) in payment of a dividend. This type of obligation, which frequently bears interest, may be issued when sufficient cash is not currently available for the dividend. This handling of dividends is not common practice as most corporate managements regard a shortage of cash as a reason to reduce or suspend dividends.

Stock dividends which are to be paid in the company's own stock represent the capitalization of a portion of retained earnings. This type of dividend should not be listed as a liability, since it does not require the use of assets. Stock dividends payable should be added to capital stock outstanding or classified as appropriated retained earnings. The effect of a stock dividend is to bring about a rearrangement of the stockholders' equities; it decreases retained earnings and increases outstanding capital stock. Cash dividends reduce retained earnings and cash.

Bank overdraft

When cash disbursements exceed bank deposits, there is an overdraft; it should be listed on the balance sheet as a current liability. Some accountants approve showing an overdraft in one bank deducted from a cash balance in another bank if the balance is readily transferable. However, this practice may constitute "netting," which is poor practice unless the debt and the balance due from the bank can be offset.

Payroll taxes and income tax withholdings payable

Employees are required by law (Federal Insurance Contributions Act) to pay 5.85 percent of their first $10,800 of annual gross earnings as a social security or F.I.C.A. tax; employers withhold from paychecks and remit the funds to the federal government. The law provides that employers pay a like amount which cannot be charged against the employees. Employers also must pay an unemployment compensation insurance tax equal to 3.28 percent of the first $4,200 of annual gross earnings paid each covered employee. The federal government tax is reduced to .58 percent if similar taxes are paid to state governments.

Since 1943 employers have been required to withhold federal income taxes from wage and salary payments to employees. Some states now require the withholding of state income taxes.

As a result of these laws, employers may have current liabilities at the end of the accounting period as follows:

F.I.C.A. taxes payable.
State unemployment taxes payable.
Federal unemployment taxes payable.
Employees' federal and state income tax withheld payable.

Estimated federal income taxes payable

The estimated liability for federal income taxes should be included in the current liabilities section of the balance sheet. This is true although final payment may be as much as $15\frac{1}{2}$ months away and although the final adjustment of the tax has not been made. U.S. Treasury obligations should not be offset against the income tax liability unless their purchase was under such circumstances as to constitute payment of the tax.[2] Inasmuch as Treasury obligations are temporary investments of cash, they should be listed as current assets.

Accrued liabilities

Wages, interest on notes payable and mortgage notes payable, pensions, property taxes, and other similar items accrue or accumulate from day to day. Consequently, at the date of the balance sheet, there is almost certain to be some expense accrued but not yet payable.

If the amount of the accrued item can be exactly determined, as in the case of unpaid wages and interest, the liability should be shown as an accrued payable in the current liability section on the balance sheet. If the amount cannot be exactly determined, as in the case of property taxes, an account entitled Estimated Property Taxes Payable (or just Property Taxes) may be set up and shown as a current liability. The words, "estimated" and "reserve" (except in the owner's equity section) have been declining in popularity. In keeping with his trend the caption "income taxes" (with or without a designation of the governments involved) is now customary.

Sinking fund installments due within one year should be included as a current liability unless current assets have been earmarked for the purpose.

Accrued expense liabilities arise naturally from the entries used to accrue expenses at the end of the reporting period.

---

[2] Accounting Principles Board, AICPA *Opinion No. 10* (New York, December 1966), p. 147.

Serial bonds and maturing long-term debt

When current assets are to be used to pay serial bonds or long-term debts which are payable within one year, the amounts currently due should be shown as current liabilities, as illustrated below:

Current Liabilities:
First-mortgage bonds, payable during 1972 . . . . $ 100,000
Long-Term Liabilities:
First-mortgage bonds (less: amount payable in 1972,
$100,000).   1,100,000

If these debts are not so classified, the current debt-paying ability will be overstated. Maturing long-term debts should be continued as long-term liabilities (1) if the debt is to be refunded or renewed; or (2) if a fund, which is not classified as a current asset, is to be used in payment of the debt.

Of the 600 *Accounting Trends and Techniques 1971* companies, 139 showed long-term debt maturities as current liabilities, if due currently.

Miscellaneous current liabilities

Liability for workmen's compensation, injuries and damages, pensions, guaranties of service and replacements, claims for tokens, tickets, and gift certificates, and similar estimated items should be included as current liabilities if it is probable that the amounts will be paid out within one year of the balance sheet date. It may be impossible to divide the amounts into current and long-term liabilities except on a purely estimated basis.

Long-term leases

Long-term leases are frequently used as substitutes for ownership. Sometimes, the character of the lease agreement is such that the transaction may be tantamount to purchase. The problems involved in adequately reflecting on financial statements the asset, liability, income, and expense factors arising from long-term leases have long posed difficult problems.

In September 1964 the Accounting Principles Board of the AICPA published *Opinion No. 5* on "Reporting of Leases in Financial Statements of Lessee." This *Opinion* says, among other things, that when a lease has the essential characteristics of a purchase it should be treated as such on published financial statements which would, therefore, reflect ownership and related liabilities, and the expenses of ownership such as depreciation. However, leases which are not tantamount to purchases should be treated as leases, but relevant details sufficient to enable the reader of a statement to assess the situation should be disclosed—the minimum rents due, for instance, and the period during which payable. Furthermore, if rental payments in any year differ materially from the minimum disclosed above, the amounts involved should be stated. Other features which should be disclosed when they are important include guarantees, restrictions on dividends or debt, and so on. If rentals can be expected to vary materially from year to year, it may be desirable to show the amounts involved in a schedule. The test is whether information is needed by the reader of the statement to assess the effect.

Of the 600 *Accounting Trends and Techniques 1971* corporations, 141 capitalized obligations arising out of leases (up from 26 in 1965) while 362 more disclosed leases without capitalizing them.

Unearned revenue and deferred credits

Unearned revenue, which is revenue that has been collected in advance of the performance of a service or the delivery of a commodity, includes such items as rent, interest, and income from subscriptions to newspapers and magazines received in advance. The revenue is unearned because a service must be performed or merchandise must be delivered in the future; revenue and costs cannot yet be matched. These items are liabilities and are usually current because (1) current assets will be used in providing goods or services in the future or (2) cash will be refunded if the goods or services for which payment has already been received are not delivered or performed.

Deferred profit on installment sales is not a liability. The deferment of this profit (over a series of collections) is usually justified by pointing to the risk of uncollectible accounts and potential collection expense. In *Supplementary Statement No. 1,* issued in 1948, the American Accounting Association Committee on Concepts and Standards recommended that installment sales basis not be used. In December 1966, in *Opinion No. 10,* the Accounting Principles Board of the AICPA came to the same conclusion—unless special circumstances make the determination of income by the accrual method impractical.

Other captions commonly used are as follows: deferred liabilities, deferred income, deferred credits, and deferred credits to income. There is a distinction between unearned revenue or deferred credits to revenue and deferred credits to expense. Unearned revenue will be recorded as revenue in a subsequent accounting period, whereas a deferred credit to expense will bring about the reduction of an expense account. For example, premium on bonds payable is a deferred credit to the Interest Expense account. It is sometimes classified as an adjunct to bonds payable.

Unearned revenue which is to be realized within one year by performing services or furnishing materials should be classified as a current liability. Publishers of magazines and newspapers that receive payment of subscriptions in advance should distinguish between amounts to be earned within one year and the portion applicable to later years. The latter portion should be classified as a noncurrent liability. Deferred credits to expense are commonly shown in a separate section following the current liabilities.

Long-term liabilities

A long-term liability, frequently referred to as a fixed liability (a less desirable practice), is an obligation that normally will not be paid within approximately one year of the balance sheet date. Long-term liabilities are incurred to finance additional plant, equipment, or land; to obtain additional working capital; to meet a current debt; or to pay off another long-term debt.

Long-term obligations maturing within one year of the balance sheet date should be shown as current liabilities unless the debts are to be refunded or paid by using funds listed as noncurrent assets. A parenthetical statement should be given in connection with the portion of the long-term debt that is to be paid within one year.

From the standpoint of most effective analysis, financial statements should contain an adequate description of long-term obligations, including disclosure of interest rates, maturity dates, nature of the asset given as security for each obligation, sinking fund or other similar provisions for debt reduction or payment, and any other features of special significance to creditors and stockholders. This information may be given in supplementary schedules, explanatory comments, or footnotes.

Sometimes debts are payable serially or in installments, a certain amount being payable each year. The amount of the debt to be paid during the ensuing year should be shown as a current liability; the balance of the obligation should be shown as a long-term liability. The long-term liabilities include long-term promissory notes, mortgage notes payable, bonds payable, and advances from affiliated companies which are not subject to current settlement.

Mortgage notes payable

When money is borrowed or property is purchased and real estate or other assets are pledged as security for payment, two instruments are issued: (1) a promissory note, which is evidence of the obligation of the debtor to repay the loan; and (2) a mortgage, which is evidence that the obligation is secured by specific property. A mortgage represents a conditional deed transferring a conditional title to the mortgagee; however, the instrument provides that it shall be null and void if the mortgagor repays the loan at maturity. In effect, the mortgage creates a lien on the property to secure the payment of the obligation when it matures. It is customary to record the obligation as a mortgage note payable when a single promissory note is issued. Also, in this case the mortgage is issued to the holder of the promissory note. Accrued interest on the mortage note should be shown as a current liability.

Bonds payable

Bonds payable represent long-term promissory notes which may be secured or unsecured. If the bonds are unsecured, they are known as "debentures" and depend for value, in the final analysis, upon the general credit of the issuing company. If the bonds are secured, there may be a pledge of collateral or a mortgage on various types of properties. In the latter event a mortage is issued to a trustee or trustees who represent the interest of the numerous bondholders. It is customary to show the obligation as bonds payable rather than mortgage notes payable because the money is borrowed from the bondholders. Accrued interest on bonds payable should be shown as a current liability.

Corporate bonds may be classified with respect to security as:

1. *Mortgage bonds—senior and junior liens.* Senior-lien bonds have a prior claim on mortgaged assets in the event of dissolution of the business. Junior-lien bonds have a claim on assets secondary to senior-lien bonds. In the event that the bond interest is not paid when due, the mortgage may be foreclosed.

2. *Collateral trust bonds.* These bonds have as security stocks and bonds of other corporations. The pledged collateral is customarily turned over to a trustee.

3. *Debenture bonds.* These bonds have no specific security and, therefore, have the same status as unsecured promissory notes, since both rely on the general credit of the issuing company. Debenture bonds often include a provision for a sinking fund.

4. *Guaranteed bonds.* A corporation may gurantee the interest and principal of bonds issued by its subsidiary. Such bonds may have as security pledged assets of the issuing company as well as the general credit of the parent company which has guaranteed them. To the guaranteeing company, this obligation represents a contingent liability.

5. *Income bonds.* Although income bonds are sometimes secured by a mortgage, they are commonly backed solely by the general credit of the issuing company. The payment of interest on the bonds is contingent upon its being earned.

6. *Equipment trust bonds.* Issued primarily by railroad and utility companies, equipment trust bonds are secured by property other than real estate, such as railroad rolling stock. These obligations are as a rule paid off in series or annual payments.

Corporate bonds may be classified on the basis of how interest is paid:

1. *Registered bonds.* A registered bond is registered on the records of the issuing corporation. The transfer of title to these bonds is accomplished by recording the transfer on the books of the corporation. The title to the bonds cannot be transferred merely by delivering the bonds to another person. Bonds may be registered either as to principal and interest or as to principal only. If the bond is registered as to both principal and interest, the interest is paid by the corporation by check. If the bond is not registered as to interest, the interest is paid by means of coupons that are detached from the bonds at each interest date and presented to a designated bank for payment.

2. *Coupon bonds.* In the event that the bond is not registered as to either principal or interest, it is referred to as a "coupon bond." Coupon bonds are bearer paper and, therefore, can be transferred by delivery and without endorsement. Interest is collected by clipping the coupons and presenting them to a designated bank for payment.

If bonds payable have been sold at less or more than the face value, the discount or premium should be amortized over the life of the bonds.[3] The effect of this amortization is to increase or decrease the current interest expense. Unamortized discount on bonds payable is shown on the balance sheet as a deferred charge and the unamortized premium on bonds payable as a deferred credit to expense.

The best method of presenting a bond on a balance sheet is to give a description of the security, the interest rate, and the maturity date.

Long-Term Liabilities:

First-mortgage, 5% bonds payable, due on July 1, 1970;
authorized, $300,000; outstanding $200,000

These details are sometimes carried in a note to the balance sheet.

Sometimes unissued bonds are pledged as collateral; if so, this fact should be noted on the balance sheet, as follows:

---

[3] In *Opinion No. 12* (1967) the Accounting Principles Board ruled that the "interest" method of amortizing discount, premium, and expense (in such a way as to substantially level the impact on the annual statement of income) is acceptable. In *Opinion No. 6* (October 1965) it stated that discount and premium unamortized at the time of refunding bonds may be amortized over the new issue if "the refunding takes place because of currently lower interest rates or anticipation of higher interest rates in the future."

Long-Term Liabilities:

First-mortgage, 5% bonds payable, due on July 1, 1970;
authorized, $300,000; issued as collateral on bank loans,
$40,000; unissued, $60,000; outstanding $200,000

Reacquired bonds which are held for resale are sometimes shown on the balance sheet as an investment, but the best practice is to deduct them from bonds payable issued unless they are to be resold currently.

The amount of unissued bonds payable should be shown so that those concerned may know (1) that more funds may be raised without obtaining further authorization and (2) that additional bonds may be issued under the same mortgage. The security of the present bondholders may be adversely affected if subsequent to the original sale, bonds are sold at a discount or if the proceeds of the new bond issues are not properly expended.

The principal of mortgage notes and bonds becomes due and payable at once if there is a default in the interest payments.

Purchase-money notes and mortgage notes payable

Purchase-money notes and mortgage notes payable are issued in partial payment for property or equipment. These promissory obligations, which have a term of more than one year, are secured by the property acquired. For example, equipment costing $25,000 may have been purchased and paid for by issuing a $15,000 check and a $10,000 purchase-money note or mortgage note. Since a direct lien, in the amount of $10,000, has been issued against this equipment, only the balance, $15,000, becomes subject to any existing mortgage containing an "after-acquired property clause." This mortgage provision grants as security for a loan not only the property owned by the corporation at the time the bonds are issued but also property acquired later which is not subject to a lien or mortgage.

Notes payable—term loans

Term loans represent loans made by banks to businesses for a term of years. These obligations mature serially or in installments, usually making possible the repayment out of earnings of the full amount during the term of the loan. Certain protective measures, which may be required by the bank, include the maintenance of a minimum ratio of current assets to current liabilities and the agreement by the borrower not to mortgage or pledge any asset during the life of the loan.

Long-term promissory notes appear on published balance sheets as follows:

1. Unsecured promissory notes (sinking fund starts in 1970).
2. Notes payable, banks, $400,000, due serially on each June 1, 1977 to 1987, inclusive; and $60,000, due on June 1, 1988.
3. Term bank loans, 2¼ percent, maturing serially from December 1972, to June 1977.
4. Fifteen-year, 3¼ percent debenture notes, due on August 1, 1985.

Estimated long-term liabilities

A company should make provision for liabilities that are certain to occur within a period of several years, although the amounts to be paid may not be determinable in advance. By making provision for such liabilities on an annual basis through charges to appropriate expense accounts and credits to specially designated liability accounts, the total cost is spread over the accounting periods involved. In this manner, any one accounting period will not be unduly burdened when payments are made. Such obligations arise from many items such as workmen's compensation premiums payable, product and service guarantees and pensions.

The word "reserve" should not be used in connection with liabilities.[4]

Owners' equity

Liabilities to outsiders are legally different from accountabilities to the owners for their capital stock investment and accumulated earnings. In the event of liquidation, outside creditors must be paid in full before any distribution of cash or property is made to the owners.

The method of showing owners' equity on the balance sheet depends upon the type of business organization. In a single proprietorship, which is a business owned by one individual, owner's equity is commonly reflected in one account, as shown in the following illustration:

Owner's Equity:
A. J. Rex, capital[5] $91,468

In a partnership, which is an association of two or more individuals who as co-owners operate a business for profit, owners' equity is shown in several capital accounts, one for each partner:

---

[4] American Accounting Association, *Accounting Concepts and Standards Underlying Corporate Financial Statements, Supplementary Statement No. 1;* and Committee on Terminology, AICPA, "Review and Résumé," *Accounting Terminology Bulletin No. 1* (New York, 1953), pp. 26–28.

[5] A more informative presentation of the individual capital investment accounts of a single proprietor and a partnership would show for each owner the original and subsequent capital contribution, salaries, withdrawals of capital, and the amount of earnings retained in the business. A statement of owners' equity for several years would supply this information.

Owners' Equity:

E. F. Randall, capital....................	$141,920
W. F. Reese, capital.....................	102,400
J. R. Hanks, capital.....................	94,450
Total Owners' Equity	$338,770

In a corporation, which is a form of business organization authorized and incorporated by law, the owners' equity appears on the balance sheet in several capital stock and other capital accounts including earnings. The owners' equity section of a corporation's balance sheet is illustrated below.

Owners' Equity:

Capital stock:
Preferred stock, 6%, cumulative, $100 par; authorized, 1,000 shares; in treasury, 10 shares; outstanding, 790 shares		$ 79,000
Common stock, $100 par; authorized, 3,000 shares; in treasury, 100 shares; outstanding, 1,900 shares		190,000
Total Capital Stock		$269,000
Capital contributed in excess of par value:		
Premium on preferred stock.............	$ 1,100	
Donated capital	16,000	17,100
Retained earnings:		
Unappropriated	$110,000	
Appropriated for:		
Plant extension	24,000	
Sinking fund.....................	15,000	149,000
Total Owners' Equity		$435,100

The caption "tangible capital" or "tangible owners' equity" is sometimes used in balance sheets. This term signifies that intangible assets have been eliminated from the assets and deducted from retained earnings. This procedure is customary in analyzing financial statements because of the uncertain value of intangible assets.

Contributed capital also includes dollar amounts received in excess of the cost of treasury stock when the latter is sold.

It should be observed that the name or names of the owners are revealed on the balance sheet of a single proprietorship and a partnership but not on the balance sheet of a corporation. There are two reasons for this difference: *First,* the names of the stockholders of a corporation are too numerous to be shown conveniently on the balance sheet; and, *second,* and most important, creditors of the corporation have no claim to the personal property of the stockholders except, in some states, when the capital stock has been sold at a discount. The corporation is a separate and distinct legal entity; consequently, creditors transact business only with the corporation and must look only to it for payment.

Capital stock

The capital stock of a corporation represents the ownership interest in the corporation; this interest is divided into shares or units. The ownership of shares of capital stock is evidenced by stock certificates; the owners of stock are known as "stockholders," or "shareholders." The amount shown as capital stock, capital paid in in excess of par or stated value, and retained earnings (appropriated and unappropriated) comprises the stockholders' equity.

The capital stock of a corporation may be par value or no par value. If stock has a par value, each share has a nominal or arbitrary valuation, which is fixed by the charter. If stock is sold for less than its par value, the purchaser or subsequent holder may be liable to the creditors of the corporation for the amount of the discount if the corporation is unable to pay its debts; this is a matter of state law.

If stock is of no par value, an arbitrary or nominal valuation has not been established in the charter and does not appear on the certificates. However, state laws may (or may not) require the establishment of a stated value or a minimum issuing price. Some states permit a corporation to increase the stated value of no-par stock by transfers from the Retained Earnings account. No-par-value stock may be sold at any price, or at any price above a minimum issuing price when such a figure is required. Since a par value is not assigned, no-par-value stock may be sold without the purchaser incurring a discount liability.

A few states require the corporation to credit the full proceeds received for the capital stock to the Capital Stock account. On the other hand, most states prescribe that only a stated minimum or a declared stated value must be credited to the Capital Stock account; the balance of the issue price may be credited to Capital Paid-In in Excess of Stated Value.

The total amount paid in by the stockholders (par value and no-par-value stock) should be regarded as a contribution of owners' equity with which to pursue corporate purposes and as a base for measuring future performance.

The par value assigned to capital stock lacks real significance because it usually does not indicate either the book or the real value of the stock. Par value establishes a minimum price for which the stock should be sold. The following reasons may account for a difference between the par value of capital stock and its book value:

1. The stock may have been sold originally at a discount or a premium.
2. There may be accumulated earnings or deficits.
3. The valuation of assets acquired in exchange for capital stock is frequently arbitrary.

4. Anticipated future earnings or losses may result in a real value higher or lower than the par value.
5. The net asset value as shown on the books may be overstated or understated in relation to the current reproduction cost or replacement value.

The analyst studies the assets and the earning power of a corporation in relation to the number and kind of shares outstanding.

Many corporations give key officers and other employees the right to buy stock at a bargain if good management has pushed up the value of the stock (or so it is assumed).

Capital stock distinguished from bonds payable

Capital stock represents ownership; the principal amount is not payable at a designated time; there is no specified security back of the investment; in the event of dissolution the stockholders' equity is paid only after all creditors' claims have been paid; dividends are paid on the stock;[6] and the omission of dividends does not lead to foreclosure by the investors.

Bonds payable involve a creditor relationship; the principal is payable at a designated time; there may be specified assets pledged as security for the principal, and in the event of dissolution the principal and accrued interest are paid in full before stockholders may receive a return of their investment; interest[7] is payable at regular intervals of time; and the omission of interest payments customarily leads to foreclosure of mortgages or liens. Income bonds have some of the characteristics of stock, since failure to pay principal or interest may not result in foreclosure or receivership. The payment of the interest may require a declaration by the board of directors; deductibility for income tax purposes may be questioned.

Capitalization

The capitalization[8] of a corporation is the sum of par value of outstanding capital stock and the face amount of mortgages, term loans,

---

[6] Cash dividends represent a distribution of earnings and, therefore, cannot be deducted for income tax purposes.

[7] The payment of interest on bonds payable represents an expense and can be deducted for income tax purposes.

[8] The accountant also uses the word "capitalization" to refer to the process of recording assets. When an expenditure is made in acquiring an asset and it is recorded in an asset account, the expenditure has been "capitalized" rather than recorded as an expense. "Capitalization" may be used in another sense: income may be capitalized to estimate the present value of a property. Furthermore, when a stock dividend is declared, a portion of the retained earnings is "capitalized."

and bonds outstanding. If the stock does not have a par value, the capitalization may best be referred to in terms of number of shares of stock and the dollar amount of bonds. In analytical work, it is common to use the amount of the capital structure (in the broad sense)—long-term debt, capital stock, and other owners' equity items—rather than the capitalization figure.

A business is said to be "overcapitalized" (1) if the capitalization exceeds the real economic value of the net assets, (2) if a fair return is not realized on the capitalization, or (3) if the business has more net assets than it needs.

Rights of stockholders

When only one class of stock is authorized, it is usually called "common stock." Each share of such stock legally entitles its holder (1) to have an equal voice in the management through the election of the board of directors; (2) to have an equal share of the distributed profits, in the form of dividends declared by the board of directors; (3) to subscribe to a proportionate share of new issues of stock; and (4) to receive a proportionate share of the assets at the dissolution of the corporation after the creditors have been paid. The legal right to subscribe to new issues of stock of the kind already held—the preemptive right—is designed to prevent the dilution of the stockholders' equity.

It is a well-known fact that small (and not infrequently large) minority shareholders have no voice in the management through the election of directors or otherwise; the legal presumption of power inherent in the right to vote shares of stock is substantially modified by the proxy system and management's control of it.

If more than one class of capital stock is issued, it is customarily classified as "preferred" and "common." However, common stock may be classified as "Class A" and "Class B." Class A common stock may be a no-par issue, preferred as to dividends and assets, without voting rights, and noncumulative. In effect, Class A stock may have most of the characteristics of preferred stock.

Preferred stock has some specific preference over the common stock as a result of the assignment by contract of rights or privileges. Preferred stock may be issued in two or more classes, and these classes may have successive or equal claims upon earnings for their dividends. Thus, the rights of the two groups of stockholders depend upon the special rights assigned to the preferred stock.

The relative rights of various types of stock depend on the provisions of the pertinent contracts (indentures) and vary from company to company.

Dividends

A dividend is a pro-rata distribution to the stockholders. The term, unless qualified, customarily refers to a *cash dividend* declared out of current or accumulated earnings. If a dividend is paid in property (a distillery paid a dividend in whiskey), it is called a property dividend. In most states, all types of "surplus," regardless of source, may be used legally for dividend purposes; however, disclosure of the type of dividend may be required. When the corporation's own capital stock is used for dividend purposes, the transaction is referred to as a *stock dividend.*

Dividends paid out of contributed capital are known as *liquidating dividends.* Such dividends may be paid by a going concern to reduce the capital invested in the corporation; they are also paid by a concern that is being dissolved.

Preferred stock—voting rights

Inasmuch as the right to vote is one of the basic rights of stockholders, they cannot be deprived of the privilege unless a specific limitation has been agreed upon. Therefore, preferred stock carries voting privileges unless specifically denied. Most preferred stock is nonvoting except in states (such as Illinois) where laws require that it have voting power.

Preferred stock—preferred as to dividends

When stock is preferred as to dividends, the stockholders are entitled to a dividend of a specified percentage of the par value of the stock, or a prescribed amount per share if the stock has no par value, before a dividend is paid to common stockholders. Stockholders, including preferred stockholders, are not entitled to dividends unless there are current or accumulated prior earnings available for .dividend declaration and the board of directors has actually declared dividends.

Preferred stock—cumulative as to dividends

Unless expressly stated to be noncumulative, the courts ordinarily hold the preferred stock to be cumulative, in which case dividends not paid for prior years accumulate and must be declared and paid or otherwise provided for before a dividend may properly be declared and paid to common stockholders. However, there is no uniformity of law on this point in the various states. If dividends on 6 percent cumulative preferred stock, par value $100,000, have not been paid for two years, the preferred stockholders are entitled to dividends of $12,000, in addition to those for the current year, before any dividends can be paid on the common stock. Interest does not accrue on dividends that accumulate.

Dividends to not accrue in the way that interest accrues because it is necessary for the board of directors formally to declare dividends before they become liabilities of the corporation. Therefore, failure to declare dividends on cumulative preferred stock does not create a liability; it merely establishes a priority on retained earnings and future income. Dividends in arrears on cumulative preferred stock constitute a contingent liability. A footnote should indicate the full amount of the arrearage in cumulative preferred dividends. Noncumulative preferred stockholders are not entitled to dividends of prior years unless fraud can be proved. Most preferred stock is cumulative.

Preferred stock—participating as to dividends

Preferred stock is participating, unless specifically designated to be nonparticipating, because of the fundamental right of all stockholders to share in profits on a pro-rata basis. The holders of fully participating preferred stock are entitled to receive their regular fixed dividend; and after the common stockholders have received a prescribed or an equal rate, both common and preferred stock share pro rata or equally as to rate of dividend in any additional declaration of dividends.

To illustrate, assume that (1) a corporation has $100,000 of 6 percent, cumulative, fully participating preferred stock and $500,000 of common stock; (2) the corporation neither declared nor paid dividends during the year 1971, (3) the board of directors declared dividends for the year 1972, and (4) $72,000 of the retained earnings were used for dividend purposes. The dividend distribution is presented below:

		Year 1972		
Class of stock	Year 1971	Regular dividend	Participating dividend	Total dividend
Preferred stock	$6,000 (6%)	$ 6,000 (6%)	$ 5,000 (5%)	$17,000
Common stock		30,000 (6%)	25,000 (5%)	55,000
Total	$6,000	$36,000	$30,000	$72,000

The preferred stock is cumulative and fully participating; therefore, it is necessary to provide first for the 1970 and 1971 dividend on preferred; next, the common stock is assigned a 6 percent dividend for 1971. The balance of the retained earnings available for dividends ($30,000) is then divided pro rata between the two classes of stock.

If only $25,000 of retained earnings were available for distribution in the form of dividends, preferred stockholders would be entitled to receive $12,000; and the balance, $13,000, since it is not in excess of 6 percent, would go to common stockholders.

In the event that the preferred stock had been partially participating, i.e., participating up to 10 percent, the preferred stockholders would be entitled to a 6 percent dividend for the year 1970 and a maximum dividend of 10 percent for the year 1971. The common stockholders would receive the balance of the available retained earnings, or an 11.2 percent dividend. A summary of the distribution of the $72,000 retained earnings follows:

Preferred dividend for 1970 and 1971..................	$12,000
Preferred participating dividend for 1971 (4%—from 6% to 10%).....................................	4,000
Total Preferred Dividend.........................	$16,000
Common dividend for 1971—balance of retained earnings available for dividends ($56,000 ÷ $500,000 = 11.2%)......	56,000
Total Dividends.............................	$72,000

If the preferred stock had been nonparticipating, the preferred stockholders would be entitled to a 12 percent dividend only—6 percent for 1970 and 6 percent for the current year, 1971.

Most preferred stock is nonparticipating.

Preferred stock—preferred as to assets in dissolution

In the event of dissolution the holders of stock preferred as to assets are entitled to receive liquidating dividends equal to the par value of their stock before the holders of common stock are paid. Regular dividends in arrears on cumulative preferred stock would be paid only when there are retained earnings remaining after the par value of the preferred and common has been returned to the stockholders, unless otherwise provided for in the charter or in the preferred stock contract. Unless preferred stock is stated to be preferred as to assets, it does not possess this advantage.

For illustrative purposes, assume that (1) a corporation has $100,000 of 6 percent, cumulative, fully participating preferred stock, $500,000 of common stock, and retained earnings amounting to $60,000; (2) dividends have not been declared for the years 1970 and 1971; and (3) the corporation assets are sold at their book values for cash. The cash would be distributed as of December 31, 1971 as shown below:

Class of stock	Par value	Dividends in arrears, 1970	Current dividend, 1971	Participating dividend, 1971	Total cash
Preferred.....	$100,000	$6,000 (6%)	$ 6,000 (6%)	$ 3,000 (3%)	$115,000
Common.....	500,000		30,000 (6%)	15,000 (3%)	545,000
Total	$600,000	$6,000	$36,000	$18,000	$660,000

If the preferred stock, in the foregoing example, had been noncumulative and nonparticipating, the preferred stockholders would have received the par value of their capital stock and not more than a 6 percent dividend for the current year.

If the preferred stock is preferred as to assets in dissolution, an existing deficit would be borne entirely by the common stockholders, unless the deficit exceeded the par value of the common stock. If the preferred stock is not preferred as to assets in dissolution, the net assets would be distributed on a pro-rata basis between preferred and common stock. In other words, an existing deficit would be charged to both preferred and common stock.

Preferred stock—convertible and redeemable

Preferred stock may be convertible into common stock. The stockholder may have the option of exchanging his preferred stock for common stock following a specified plan agreed upon by contract. For example, the preferred stock may be converted into common stock at $40. This means that for each $40 of preferred stock par value the stockholder is entitled to one share of common stock.

Such a provision is usually made to improve the marketability of the preferred stock.

The preferred stock certificate may make provision for the stock to be redeemed at the option of the corporation. Usually, a premium is provided for upon the redemption of preferred stock.

Capital stock and other capital items on the balance sheet

Par-value capital stock accounts customarily show the par value of the stock. Discount and premium on capital stock should be recorded in separate accounts.

No-par value capital stock may be carried on the books at the amount for which it is sold; at the minimum issuing price, if one is established by state laws; at the stated value, if one is assigned to this class of stock; or at the amount determined by the board of directors. When no-par-value stock is sold for an amount above a declared value or a minimum selling price, the excess may be credited to a paid-in capital account, titled Additional Paid-In Capital (or some minor variant of that title) or Capital in Excess of Par (or Stated Value).

Separate ledger accounts should be maintained for each class of par-value, as well as no-par-value, capital stock, and each individual class of stock should be shown on the balance sheet. To be most informative, the balance sheet should show for each class of stock the par value; the number of shares authorized, issued, and outstanding; and the total dollar amount of the outstanding shares of stock. For no-par-value stock there should be shown the declared or stated value. Special features of preferred stock should also be given.[9] Capital stock items include the following:

Capital stock, authorized.   Authorized capital stock represents the total amount of stock that may be sold as provided for in the charter.

Unissued capital stock.   The amount of the authorized capital stock that has not been issued is known as "unissued capital stock." The difference between the amounts of authorized and unissued stock represents the amount of issued stock.

Authorized no-par-value stock is recorded only in terms of shares in a memorandum entry in the journal and in the Capital Stock account; issued shares are noted in the Capital Stock account.

Treasury stock.   Treasury stock is the company's own stock which (1) has been issued, (2) has been reacquired through purchase or donation, and (3) has not been retired. Treasury stock may be donated to the company to reduce or eliminate a deficit, to provide working capital, or for other general or specific corporate purposes. The purchase by a corporation of its outstanding stock amounts, in effect, to a reduction of owners' equity.

If the reacquired stock was originally sold at less than par value, it is subject to the discount liability. Treasury stock, if originally fully paid, in contrast to unissued capital stock, may be sold below par value without creating a discount liability.

When a corporation reacquires its capital stock through purchase, most state laws require that the stock be "purchased out of retained earnings"; legal capital should not be impaired. This stipulation means that retained earnings equal to the cost of the treasury stock became unavailable for dividends. In this event, some corporations show the

---

[9] In December 1966 the Accounting Principles Board of the AICPA ruled that when preferred stock has a preference in liquidation considerably in excess of par or stated value, disclosure should be made (*Opinion No. 10*, p. 148). Of the 600 corporations in *Accounting Trends and Techniques 1971*, 159 disclosed details concerning liquidation value. Only 78 did so on the face of the statement as urged by *Opinion No. 10*.

cost of treasury stock as a deduction from retained earnings. An alternative plan of showing the restriction of retained earnings is as follows:

Retained earnings ($125,000 restricted, cost of treasury stock). $527,468

Most corporations now show treasury stock as an offset in the owners' equity section, either as a deduction at cost from total owners' equity or at par value as a deduction from issued stock of the same class. Of the 600 corporations in *Accounting Trends and Techniques 1971*, 455 corporations showed treasury stock: 436 deducted it in the net worth section; 19 showed it as an asset. Some corporations carry the treasury stock at cost until it is sold or retired; others carry it at par and show the difference as Capital Contributed in Excess of Par Value; if the difference is a debit, it represents a distribution of owners' equity in excess of par to reacquire the stock. The amount paid for the treasury stock in excess of the par value may be charged to Retained Earnings in its entirety, or in part to Capital in Excess of Par Value.[10]

Treasury stock is sometimes acquired by corporations for immediate sale or for distribution as a bonus to employees. Although such treasury stock is occasionally classified as an asset, it preferably should be shown at cost as an offset in the owners' equity section.

Capital stock subscribed. Capital stock subscribed is the amount of the stock subscribed for but not yet issued. Subscriptions receivable are ordinarily shown as an asset, a current asset if collectible within a short period of time. However, if there is no intention of collecting the balance of the subscription receivable, or if there is any doubt as to its collectibility, the unpaid balance should be deducted from capital stock subscribed, thereby showing the amount of owners' equity paid in.

Dividends to be paid in capital stock. A corporation may declare a dividend payable in capital stock. The effect of such a dividend is the capitalization of a portion of the retained earnings. Unless restricted by law, the corporation may also declare the *stock dividend* from donated capital or appraisal capital. Stock dividends are not considered as income to the recipient but merely a further division of his ownership share. Until the stock certificates are issued, capital stock dividends payable should be shown on the balance sheet as an addition to capital stock outstanding or as appropriated retained earnings. Stock dividends payable is not a liability, since the use of assets is not required.

Discount on capital stock. Capital stock is sold at a discount if the cash or the fair market value of the services or property received is less than the par value. Discount on capital stock often results in a discount liability which may be collected from the stockholders for the benefit of the creditors in the event of the insolvency of the corpora-

---

[10] Accounting Principles Board, AICPA, *Opinion No. 6* (New York, October 1965).

tion. The contingent liability follows the stock in case of transfers.

The discount on capital stock is in most cases written off against Retained Earnings. Other treatments of the discount include (1) retaining it on the books permanently and (2) writing it off against Capital in Excess of Par (or Stated) Value. If Capital Stock Discount is written off against Retained Earnings, the distinction between paid-in and earned owners' equity is obscured. A stock dividend has a similar effect.

The write-off of discount on capital stock to Retained Earnings does not eliminate the stockholders' liability to the creditors of the corporation, unless the law in the state involved specifically legalizes such action. The stock discount liability may be discharged by the return of dividends formally declared and paid to stockholders.

When discount on capital stock is continued on the books, it may be shown on the balance sheet in such a way as to modify the showing of (1) capital stock, par value; (2) total surplus; or (3) total owners' equity. Discount on capital stock may logically be offset by premiums received on shares of stock of the same class but not by premiums on other classes of stock.

Frequently, capital stock which would sell for cash only at a discount is issued in exchange for property.[11] If the asset is recorded in the amount of the par value of the capital stock issued, the asset is inflated in value to the extent of the concealed discount. This is known as *stock watering*—the issuance of an excess of securities in relation to the actual cost of the asset—and results in overcapitalization when the surplus is not sufficient to absorb the inflated asset value resulting from the failure properly to record discount on capital stock. The practice is undesirable.

Retained earnings. Retained earnings, an owners' equity item, arises from the profitable sale of goods or services in the normal course of business, from gain on the sale of fixed or other assets such as investments, and from irregular revenue transactions such as retirement of liabilities for less than their face amount. Retained earnings may be appropriated or unappropriated.

An appropriation of retained earnings indicates that part of the earnings are made unavailable for dividends or purposes other than that specified by the *appropriation*. Working capital or other assets equivalent to the appropriation are retained in the business. That is, this portion of the earnings and the equivalent amount of working capital and other assets are not to be used for dividend or other purposes.

Retained earnings may be appropriated at the discretion of the board of directors, i.e., earmarked, so that the resources arising from retained earnings will be used:

---

[11] Most states permit great latitude to the directors in exercising their discretion as to the value of property acquired in exchange for capital stock.

1. To cover a loss occurring in the future—appropriation for possible future decline in inventory, for flood loss, and for unfavorable decision of a lawsuit.
2. To expand plant, retire preferred stock, or pay long-term debt— appropriation for plant extension, for retirement of preferred stock, and for sinking fund.
3. To replace assets at a higher cost—appropriation for asset replacement at a higher price level.
4. To practice self-insurance—appropriation for self-insurance.
5. To maintain a larger amount of current assets necessitated by a substantial increase in sales volume—appropriation for working capital.

Other appropriations of retained earnings reflect restrictions imposed by law or by contract such as bond indentures. For example, a corporation may enter into agreements with creditors, bondholders, preferred stockholders, or others to restrict the payment of dividends or other charges against retained earnings or by voluntary agreement of the board of directors. The existence of such an agreement should be disclosed by footnote or parenthetical explanation in the balance sheet. This disclosure can be accomplished by appropriating retained earnings, but this is not preferred practice.

Appropriations of retained earnings shown on published statements are declining in number, for two reasons: (1) appropriations of retained earnings to restrict dividends are unnecessary because dividends are controlled by the policies of the board of directors and because the assets restricted by such appropriations are not usually in liquid form, and (2) the accounting profession is less inclined currently to provide for appropriations as freely as it did formerly. The American Accounting Association recommends doing away with all appropriations. Actually, the appropriations of retained earnings convey to the statement reader only some of the reasons for not using the entire amount of retained earnings for dividends. Conservative financial management requires the accumulation of retained earnings for the same reasons, although specific appropriations may not necessarily be made.

Frequently, appropriated retained earnings items are listed between liabilities and owners' equity; this is not good practice, since it is confusing to the user of the balance sheet. Too often, valuation and amortization accounts and even liabilities are similarly shown without classification.

If appropriations of retained earnings are made and shown on the balance sheet, they should be classified in the owners' equity section and clearly described so that their nature and purpose are apparent. Such appropriations, when restored to retained earnings, should not affect the net income; nor should expenses or losses be charged against such appropriations.

Unappropriated retained earnings represent that portion of retained earnings which has not been appropriated for specific use and which is available for general corporate purposes, including dividends.

The appropriation of retained earnings does not necessarily restrict the payment of dividends; it is an accounting device to indicate that a portion of the retained earnings, although legally available for dividends, will not be used for that purpose for the time being because the directors consider it financially inexpedient to do so. The directors have the right to return the appropriation to unappropriated retained earnings at any time unless otherwise specified in the bond indenture.

A debit balance in the Retained Earnings account is known as a "deficit" and should be shown on the balance sheet as a deduction in the owners' equity section. A deficit may be deducted (1) from the total of capital stock and other owners' equity items or (2) the total of owners' equity items exclusive of capital stock. If total owners' equity is less than the par value or stated value of the capital stock outstanding, there is an *impairment of legal capital.*

A deficit does not represent actual insolvency unless the corporation is unable to pay its liabilities in full. A company is said to be "technically insolvent" when it is unable to meet its obligations as they become due, a situation that may exist when there are retained earnings or may not exist when there is a deficit.

Capital (or stated) in excess of par (or stated) value. This class of capital represents that portion of the stockholders equity, in excess of the capital stock, which has arisen from sources other than realized profits and appreciation of assets. The term Capital (or stated) in Excess of Par Value is often used as an account title, or it may appear as the caption of a group of capital items. The latter usage is preferable because it makes possible an analysis of this class of paid-in capital items. Examples of Additional Paid-in Capital, a title which is also popular, are:

Premium on capital stock (excess of issuing price received above the par value).

Excess of the issuing price of no-par-value stock over its stated value.

Donation from stockholders or others (capital stock or property).

Capital arising from treasury stock transaction.

Capital arising from forfeited stock subscriptions.

Capital arising from stock redemption, stock conversion, or reduction in value assigned outstanding stock.

Capital arising from stock assessments.

In some cases the higher present value of property in relation to the book value is due to excessive provisions for depreciation, depletion, and amortization, or to errors in charging asset items to expense. If so, adjustment of the asset and amortization accounts is necessary to correct the book value.

Reserves

The word "reserve" has various meanings. Because of the confusion with respect to the use of the term, the Committee on Terminology of the AICPA recommended[12] in 1953 that the word be used only in connection with owners' equity items. The Committee on Concepts and Standards of the American Accounting Association[13] recommended that the term be abandoned. This latter recommendation has been followed in this volume.

Since 1953 the use of the word in the asset and liability sections of the 600 balance sheets surveyed in *Accounting Trends and Techniques 1971* has steadily declined, though 227 companies still refuse compliance. The use of "reserve" in connection with uncollectible accounts declined from 155 instances in 1960 to 71 in 1970; use in connection with depreciation declined from 118 to 33; inventories, from 42 to 10; taxes from 19 to 5.

Because so many concerns still use the word "reserve," its various meanings are described below.

Balance sheet "reserves" are of three basic types: (1) retained earnings (owners' equity), (2) asset, and (3) liability.

Retained earnings (owners' equity) "reserves". "Reserves" of the owners' equity type include such items as the reserve for sinking fund, the reserve for contingencies, and the reserve for plant extension. In this book the earmarking of retained earnings is referred to as Appropriation of Retained Earnings for Plant Expansion or similar titles.

Valuation and amortization "reserves." Valuation "reserves," which are properly shown as deductions from the assets they evaluate,[14] include the reserve for uncollectible receivables and the reserve for sales discounts. Amortization reserves, which are also properly deductible from the assets to which they relate, include the reserve for depreciation and the reserve for depletion. There is a growing tendency at the present time to use the word "accumulated" instead of "reserve" in these titles: 477 companies in 1970, up from 266 in 1960.

Liability "reserves." Liability reserves, which are actually liabilities and are properly shown as such, include the reserve for pensions, the reserve for workmen's compensation, the reserve for incentive compensation, the reserve for employees' retirement benefits, and the reserve for replacement of guaranteed products.

---

[12] AICPA, *Accounting Terminology Bulletin No. 1*, pp. 26–28.

[13] American Accounting Association, *Supplementary Statement No. 1.*

[14] Accounting Principles Board, *Opinion No. 12.*

These accounts are established by debiting expense accounts. Frequently, accrued liabilities, the amounts of which are uncertain, are shown on the balance sheet as reserves. It is apparent that when used in the liability section, the word "reserve" means "estimated." This use of the word "reserve" is not good practice. It is becoming rare in published statements and is not used in this book in connection with commercial and industrial financial statements.

Sometimes it is difficult to distinguish between liabilities and owners' equity. If a lawsuit is lost, a liability results; if a favorable decision is obtained, owners' equity remains undisturbed or may increase. In the past, so-called "reserves for contingencies" or "general reserves" have been established to "disclose" a wide range of possible hazards, some of which might appear to be so imminent as to warrant classification as liabilities, whereas others are no more than vague fears. Because the caption "reserve for contingencies" is so ambiguous, it has no precise meaning for the analyst; balance sheets would be improved if the caption were either abandoned or supplemented by a full explanation such as by footnotes.

Since the issuance in 1953 of *Accounting Research Bulletin No. 43*, which ruled against establishing such reserves by charges in the income statement, they have disappeared from the statements of publicly held companies except for a small number created out of retained earnings.

QUESTIONS AND PROBLEMS

5–1. Explain the difference between liabilities and owners' equity.

5–2. What is a contingent liability? How should it be shown on the balance sheet?

5–3. Explain the difference between a current and a long-term liability.

5–4. Certain liabilities are incurred in connection with payroll transactions. Explain the nature of these liabilities and indicate proper financial statement presentation.

5–5. How should the liability for current year's income tax be shown on the balance sheet?

5–6. Why is income tax sometimes deferred?

5–7. What are the basic rights of a stockholder?

5–8. What valuation principle is followed when capital stock is issued in exchange for property?

5–9. Explain what is meant by treasury stock and describe correct financial statement presentation.

5–10. Explain the difference between par and no-par stock. How important are these values?

5–11. Give a brief explanation of the nature of the following and indicate how each item should appear on a balance sheet:

a)   Deficit.
b)   Stock dividend payable.
c)   Accumulated amortization.
d)   Bank overdraft.
e)   A valuation account.
f)   An owners' equity appropriation.
g)   Cumulative preferred stock dividends in arrears.
h)   Treasury stock.
i)   Discount on capital stock.

5–12.   The following items appeared in the owners' equity and reserve section of a balance sheet published in 1935. Discuss terminology and classification of these reserves.

a)   Capital stock and surplus.
b)   Reserve for bad debts.
c)   Reserve for depreciation.
d)   Reserve for plant expansion.
e)   Reserve for contingencies.
f)   Reserve for federal income tax.
g)   Reserve for pensions.
h)   Reserve for salaries.

5–13.   Distinguish between:

a)   Deferred charges and deferred credits.
b)   Unissued capital stock and treasury stock.
c)   Appropriation for contingencies and unappropriated retained earnings.
d)   A bond sinking fund and a bond sinking fund appropriation.
e)   The treatment of discount on bonds payable and discount on capital stock.
f)   An earnings dividend and a liquidating dividend.
g)   An accounts payable item and an unearned revenue item.
h)   Redeemable preferred stock and convertible preferred stock.

5–14.   The owners' equity section of the James Corporation is as follows:

Preferred stock, 5%, par value $100, cumulative,
nonparticipating. $500,000
Common stock, $100 par value 800,000
Retained earnings 500,000

Required:

Compute the book value of the common stock assuming the three separate cases stated below. In each case the regular cash dividend is to be paid on preferred stock.

(1)   A 20 percent stock dividend is declared and distributed to common stockholders.

(2)   A 20 percent cash dividend is declared and paid.

(3)   A two-for-one common stock split is approved and consummated.

5–15.   Prepare the long-term liabilities and owners' equity sections of Corporation A's balance sheet from the following group of items. Indicate the appropriate classification of items not included.

Accumulated depreciation	$ 40,000
Appreciation surplus (land)	5,000
Bonds payable	150,000
Capital stock outstanding	500,000
Dividends payable	15,000
Estimated federal income taxes payable	30,000
Estimated liability for pensions	25,000
Estimated uncollectible receivables	30,000
Notes receivable discounted	20,000
Premium on bonds payable	3,000
Premium on capital stock	3,000
Purchase money notes payable	25,000
Rent received in advance	1,000
Reserve for contingencies	25,000
Reserve for possible future market decline of inventories	8,000
Reserve for sinking fund	24,000
Retained earnings	110,000
Stock dividend payable	10,000
Treasury stock (at cost)	7,000
U.S. government obligations	31,000

5–16. The accountant of the Morrow Corporation prepared the following data for purposes of showing the financial position of the company (December 31, 1971):

(1)	Cash, which includes $500 of postage stamps and a 6-month $1,000 certificate of deposit	$ 4,800
(2)	Temporary investments in securities ($10,000 of the securities have been pledged on a bank note payable of $9,000) current market value $12,300	10,800
(3)	Petty cash, including $300 of employees IOUs and $50 of expense receipts	650
(4)	Notes receivable not yet due: (a) in the portfolio, $5,000; and (b) discounted, $2,000	7,000
(5)	Accounts receivable including (a) customer credit balances, $1,100; (b) advances to creditors, $2,500; (c) past-due accounts, $6,070 of which $2,890 is doubtful of collection	13,500
(6)	Merchandise inventory including goods received on consignment, $1,200; and merchandise in transit the liability for which has not been recorded, $1,800	20,500
(7)	Prepaid expenses, which includes cash surrender value of insurance policies on the life of the president, $7,200	8,000
(8)	Plant, property, and equipment including delivery equipment (cost, $5,000) which has been fully depreciated and disposed of (accumulated depreciation deducted, $31,600). Land was appreciated $10,000	80,000
(9)	Notes and accounts payable, including creditor accounts with debit balances, $750	50,000
(10)	Preferred stock, 6%, cumulative, $100 par value authorized, $100,000, outstanding (dividends have not been paid for 1970 and 1971)	10,000
(11)	Common stock, $100 par value, authorized, $300,000, outstanding	100,000
(12)	Premium on preferred stock, $2,000, discount on common stock ($16,500)	(14,500)
(13)	Retained earnings	8,700

Required:

Study the foregoing information and list the appropriate dollar amounts to assign to the items.

5–17. Study the following balance sheet and supplementary information and present a reconstructed statement.

PARK COMPANY

Balance Sheet Items as Shown on the Ledger
December 31, 1971

Assets

Cash		$ 45,000
Receivables (notes receivable discounted, $24,000 deducted).		186,000
Merchandise inventory (lower of cost or market)	$310,000	
Less: Reserve for possible future decline in inventory value	10,000	300,000
Marketable securities (cost, $71,500)		70,000
Prepaid expenses.		1,000
Deferred charges		6,000
Investments		200,000
Delivery equipment		7,000
Furniture and office equipment		8,000
Buildings		200,000
Land.		100,000
Intangibles.		50,000
		$1,173,000

Liabilities and Owners' Equity

Payables (trade and bank).	$ 210,000
Bonds and mortgage payable	210,000
Reserves	170,100
Preferred stock (issued)	200,000
Common stock (issued)	300,000
Retained earnings	22,900
Premium on preferred	10,000
Reserve for appreciation.	50,000
	$1,173,000

Additional data:

(1) The Cash balance includes a time deposit in the amount of $4,000 and Officers' IOUs, $10,000.

(2) Notes receivable in the amount of $12,000 which have been discounted matured December 30, 1971 and were paid by the individuals primarily liable. The Park Company was not notified until January 5, 1972.

(3) A warehouse receipt for $25,000 of the merchandise shown in the inventory has been given to the bank as collateral on notes payable.

(4) Investments which were purchased during the year 1966 include:

Stock of X-Y Corporation (current market value,
$35,000) . . . . $ 55,000
Bonds of R-J Corporation (current market value,
$28,000)   29,000
Real estate (current appraised value, $140,000) . . .   116,000

(5)   Intangibles recorded on the books January 2, 1967 at cost:

Goodwill . . . . $ 40,000
Trademarks.   10,000

(6)   Land was appreciated as of December 30, 1971.
(7)   The reserves consist of:

Reserve for bad debts . . . . $ 3,700
Reserve for depreciation   100,000
Reserve for contingencies.   23,000
Reserve for taxes   1,400
Reserve for sinking fund   27,000
Reserve for decline in inventory, December 31,
1970.   15,000

(8)   A mortgage in the amount of $30,000 is due July 1, 1972.
(9)   Total authorized stock amounts to:
   Six percent cumulative nonparticipating preferred 2,500
      shares, par value $100
   Common 4,000 shares, par value $100
(10) A stock dividend amounting to $20,000 was declared on De-
      cember 31, 1971, payable January 31, 1972, to common stock-
      holders of record January 15, 1972.
(11) Dividends on preferred stock in arrears for two years and for
      the year 1971 were declared December 31, 1971, payable Jan-
      uary 31, 1972, to stockholders of record on January 15, 1972.

6

Statements of income, retained earnings, and owners' equity

WHILE THERE is no standardized form of income statement, the issuance in December 1966 of *Opinion No. 9* of the Accounting Principles Board served to delineate the general approach. The most important provision of that opinion forbade—subject to a very small number of exceptions—the charging of expired costs (expenses) and losses directly to retained earnings, bypassing the income statement and the net income for the period.

Because of its effect on professional auditors, and their influence on corporate financial statements, *Opinion No. 9* served to establish as standard practice the "all-inclusive" or "clean retained earnings" approach to income statement construction and to obsolete the so-called "current-operating-performance" type of earnings report.

The opinion does this by specifying that "net income should reflect all items of profit and loss recognized during the period except for prior period adjustments. . . . ." "Prior period adjustments" which may be charged directly against retained earnings are carefully defined and circumscribed by the opinion as will be explained in a subsequent paragraph.

The opinion also describes "extraordinary items" and provides that they are to be separately classified at the bottom of the income statement, but are included in the computation of net income for the period.

Prior period adjustments and extraordinary items

Pursuant to an obvious intention to severely restrict items which may legitimately be carried directly to retained earnings, *Opinion No. 9* set up the following criteria:

a) Items which "can be specifically identified with and directly related to the business activities of particular prior periods;" and (not or)
b) Which "are not attributable to economic events occurring subsequent to the date of the financial statements for the prior period;" and
c) Which "depend primarily on determinations by persons other than management;" and
d) Which "were not susceptible of reasonable estimation prior to such determination."

"Examples," says *Opinion No. 9*, "are material, non-recurring adjustments or settlements of income taxes" or "amounts resulting from litigation. . . ." The opinion offers as an additional example, changes in the application of accounting principles such as a change in the basis of carrying investments in subsidiaries (e.g., from cost to the equity method).[1]

Extraordinary items recognized on the financial statements for the current period are separately classified on the income statement, but in such a way that they enter into the determination of net income. Extraordinary items are of a character significantly different than the customary business activities of the organization and which are material enough in effect to justify separate classification (either individually or in the aggregate as may be appropriate under the circumstances).

Examples offered by *Opinion No. 9* include a loss from the sale or abandonment of a plant, or a segment of the business, or an investment not acquired for resale; or a write-off of goodwill; or a loss arising from the expropriation of properties or from the devaluation of a foreign currency.

Items which are typical of the operations of a business are not extraordinary even though they may be very large.

The amount to be separately classified and displayed is the gross amount of extraordinary gain or loss, adjusted for applicable income tax effect. In other words, if a loss is $3,920,000, but its deduction will

---

[1] When the equity method is used in carrying an investment in a subsidiary on the balance sheet, the investment is valued at cost plus or minus income and losses since acquisition. The equity method was made mandatory by Accounting Principles Board, AICPA, *Opinion No. 10* and *Opinion No. 18* (New York, March 1971).

reduce federal income tax by $1,880,000, the net extraordinary loss, separately classified, will be $2,040,000.

The form to be used in preparing an income statement and a statement of retained earnings (or, if preferred, these statements combined) is shown in Illustrations 6–1, 6–2, and 6–3. Illustration 6–4 shows a five-year comparative statement, in thousands of dollars. All of these exhibits have been taken from *Opinion No. 9*, which states that they "illustrate the treatment of extraordinary items and prior period adjustments in financial statements" but "the format of the statements is illustrative only, and does not necessarily reflect a preference by the Accounting Principles Board for the format or for the intermediate captions shown."

ILLUSTRATION 6–1

STATEMENT OF INCOME

Years Ended December 31, 1967 and December 31, 1966

	1967	1966 (Note 2)
Net sales	$84,580,000	$75,650,000
Other income	80,000	100,000
	84,660,000	75,750,000
Cost and expenses —		
Cost of goods sold	60,000,000	55,600,000
Selling, general and administrative expenses	5,000,000	4,600,000
Interest expense	100,000	100,000
Other deductions	80,000	90,000
Income tax	9,350,000	7,370,000
	74,530,000	67,760,000
Income before extraordinary items (per share: 1967 — $1.73; 1966 — $1.37)	10,130,000	7,990,000
Extraordinary items, less applicable income tax in 1967 (Note 1) (per share: 1967 — $(.34); 1966 — $(.22))	(2,040,000)	(1,280,000)
Net income (per share: 1967 — $1.39; 1966 — $1.15)	$ 8,090,000	$ 6,710,000

Note 1

During 1967 the Company sold one of its plants at a net loss of $2,040,000, after applicable income tax reduction of $1,880,000. During 1966 the Company sold an investment in marketable securities at a loss of $1,280,000, with no income tax effect.

Note 2

The balance of retained earnings at December 31, 1966 has been restated from amounts previously reported to reflect a retroactive charge of $3,160,000 for additional income taxes settled in 1967. Of this amount, $1,400,000 ($.24 per share) is applicable to 1966 and has been reflected as an increase in tax expense for that year, the balance (applicable to years prior to 1966) being charged to retained earnings at January 1, 1966.

ILLUSTRATION 6–2

STATEMENT OF INCOME AND RETAINED EARNINGS
Years Ended December 31, 1967 and December 31, 1966

	1967	1966 (Note 2)
Net sales	$84,580,000	$75,650,000
Other income	80,000	100,000
	84,660,000	75,750,000
Cost and expenses —		
Cost of goods sold	60,000,000	55,600,000
Selling, general and administrative expenses	5,000,000	4,600,000
Interest expense	100,000	100,000
Other deductions	80,000	90,000
Income tax	9,350,000	7,370,000
	74,530,000	67,760,000
Income before extraordinary items	10,130,000	7,990,000
Extraordinary items, net of applicable income tax of $1,880,000 in 1967 (Note 1)	(2,040,000)	(1,280,000)
Net Income	8,090,000	6,710,000
Retained earnings at beginning of year —		
As previously reported	28,840,000	25,110,000
Adjustments (Note 2)	(3,160,000)	(1,760,000)
As restated	25,680,000	23,350,000
	33,770,000	30,060,000
Cash dividends on common stock — $.75 per share	4,380,000	4,380,000
Retained earnings at end of year	$29,390,000	$25,680,000
Per share of common stock —		
Income before extraordinary items ..	$1.73	$1.37
Extraordinary items, net of tax	(.34)	(.22)
Net income	$1.39	$1.15

Note 1

  During 1967 the Company sold one of its plants at a net loss of $2,040,000, after applicable income tax reduction of $1,880,000. During 1966 the Company sold an investment in marketable securities at a loss of $1,280,000, with no income tax effect.

Note 2

  The balance of retained earnings at December 31, 1966 has been restated from amounts previously reported to reflect a retroactive charge of $3,160,000 for additional income taxes settled in 1967. Of this amount, $1,400,000 ($.24 per share) is applicable to 1966 and has been reflected as an increase in tax expense for that year, the balance (applicable to years prior to 1966) being charged to retained earnings at January 1, 1966.

Referring to Illustration 6–1, we should note the following characteristics of a well-prepared income statement:

1. An income statement prepared for an actual business firm should be headed with the legally correct name of the organization, the title of the statement, and the period(s) covered.

2. Disclose the sources of revenue and the costs and expenses of the principal business operations. Reacting to the trend in large businesses toward "conglomerate" operations (engaging in several dissimilar

ILLUSTRATION 6–3

STATEMENT OF RETAINED EARNINGS

Years Ended December 31, 1967 and December 31, 1966

	1967	1966
Retained earnings at beginning of year —		
As previously reported	$28,840,000	$25,110,000
Adjustments (Note 2)	(3,160,000)	(1,760,000)
As restated	25,680,000	23,350,000
Net income	8,090,000	6,710,000
	33,770,000	30,060,000
Cash dividends on common stock —		
$.75 per share	4,380,000	4,380,000
Retained earnings at end of year	$29,390,000	$25,680,000

See accompanying notes appearing on Statement of Income, Illustration 6–2.

lines of business), the Accounting Principles Board issued, in September 1967, a statement[2] on "Disclosure of Supplemental Financial Information by Diversified Companies." In it, after announcing its intention to study the problem and perhaps issue a statement in the future, the Board "urges diversified companies to review their own circumstances carefully and objectively with a view toward disclosing voluntarily supplemental financial information as to industry segments of the business."

Accounting Trends and Techniques 1971 (600 annual reports for 1970) shows that profit was shown by division or product line in 301 instances as compared with 175 instances in 1967. In addition, 55 other statements disclosed that a segment of the business operated at a loss.

3. Indicate clearly the operating income or operating loss (preferably from principal activities) and the net income or loss for the period.

4. State specifically the federal income taxes.

5. Show separately and describe gain and loss items which are extraordinary and items which are related to prior periods.

6. Give comparative data (in comparable form) for prior periods.

7. Disclose in parenthetical or footnote form important explanatory informations such as amount and method of depreciation, inventory pricing method, effect on net income of changes made in accounting practices during the period, etc.

---

[2] Accounting Principles Board Statements are not "opinions" of the Board. They do not impose obligations to disclose on auditors who are members of the American Institute.

ILLUSTRATION 6–4

STATEMENT OF INCOME

For the Five Years Ended December 31, 1967

	1963	1964	1965	1966	1967
			(In thousands of dollars)		
Net sales	$67,100	$66,700	$69,300	$75,650	$84,580
Other income	80	80	60	100	80
	67,180	66,780	69,360	75,750	84,660
Costs and expenses:					
Cost of goods sold	48,000	47,600	49,740	55,600	60,000
Selling, general and administrative expenses	4,300	4,200	4,500	4,600	5,000
Interest expense	120	100	90	100	100
Other deductions	80	80	60	90	80
Income tax	7,340	7,400	7,490	7,370	9,350
	59,840	59,380	61,880	67,760	74,530
Income before extraordinary items	7,340	7,400	7,480	7,990	10,130
Extraordinary items, net of applicable income tax (Note A)	–	760	–	(1,280)	(2,040)
Net income (Note B)	$ 7,340	$ 8,160	$ 7,480	$ 6,710	$ 8,090
Per share of common stock:					
Income before extraordinary items	$1.26	$1.27	$1.28	$1.37	$1.73
Extraordinary items, net of income tax	–	$ .12	–	$(.22)	$(.34)
Net income	$1.26	$1.39	$1.28	$1.15	$1.39

NOTE A

The extraordinary items consist of the following: 1964 – gain as a result of condemnation of idle land, less applicable income tax of $254,000; 1966 – loss on sale of investment in marketable securities, with no income tax effect; 1967 – loss on sale of plant, less applicable income tax reduction $1,880,000.

NOTE B

The amounts of net income for 1963, 1964 and 1966 have been restated from amounts previously reported to reflect additional income taxes for such years settled in 1967. These retroactive adjustments reduced net income for such years by $860,000 ($.15 per share), $900,000 ($.15 per share) and $1,400,000 ($.24 per share), respectively, as follows:

	1963	1964	1966
		(In thousands of dollars)	
Previously reported	$8,200	$9,060	$8,110
Adjustments	860	900	1,400
As adjusted	$7,340	$8,160	$6,710

The income statement, when properly arranged, indicates the source of and the cost of obtaining current revenue; it is also useful in the process of estimating the future income[3] of the business.

Accounting period—calendar year versus natural business year

Most businesses adopt the calendar year as their fiscal year for purposes of determining annual net income or net loss. At the end of the accounting period, December 31, the books are adjusted and closed, and the accounting reports are prepared. For internal purposes, statements are usually prepared each month; many corporations publish quar-

---

[3] It is not possible to forecast with precision the future income of a business; all that the analyst can hope to do is to secure an indication of the prospects of earnings.

terly reports.[4] Some businesses have adopted a fiscal year of 52 weeks, divided into 13 periods of 4 weeks each. This scheme, which is not acceptable under the federal income tax law which requires that the fiscal year for which the taxpayer reports must end on the last day of a calendar month, was introduced to avoid noncomparability of monthly financial reports using the irregular calendar months, varying in length from 28 to 31 days.

Still others concerns have chosen the natural business year for their accounting period. The natural business year coincides with the annual cycle of the company's operations. The annual operating cycle[5] ends when the business activities of the company are at the lowest ebb and when inventories, receivables, and current liabilities have been reduced to a low point.

Income statement—titles

Most of the 600 companies surveyed in *Accounting Trends and Techniques 1971* (reporting on 1970 statements) use the term "income" (380 in 1970, down from 393 in 1965) or "earnings" (178 in 1970 up from 174 in 1965). The word "operations" was used by 37 (up from 24 in 1965).

These words are combined with others in a variety of ways in actual practice, such as "statement of" or "income statement," "statement of earnings and retained earnings," or "statement of net earnings."

Income statement—revenue and cost

Revenue. The term "revenue" is defined by the American Institute of Certified Public Accountants as follows:[6]

Revenue results from the sale of goods and the rendering of services and is measured by the charge made to customers, clients, or tenants for goods and services furnished them. It also includes gains from the sale or exchange of assets (other than stock in trade), interest and dividends earned on investments, and other increases in the owners' equity except those arising from capital contributions and capital adjustments.

Revenue is most commonly recognized at the time of completing sales. However, the revenue is *earned* in several stages, i.e., the purchase

---

[4] When monthly or quarterly interim financial statements are analyzed, it is necessary to be acquainted with and take into account the seasonal variations of the business.

[5] The operating cycle is less than one year for most businesses and more than one year for the distillery, lumber, and tobacco industries.

[6] AICPA, *Accounting Terminology Bulletin No. 2*, March 1955, p. 2.

and/or production, sales, shipping, and collection. It should be recognized that the revenue is not completely earned nor completely realized at the time credit sales are consummated. The actual asset and revenue *values* depend upon the conversion of the receivables into cash. The accountant customarily provides for estimated uncollectible receivables, and consequently reduces the book value of receivables and the sales revenue.

Earned revenue such as gain on sale of noncurrent assets should be reported as extraordinary nonoperating gain in order to avoid the impression that it is related to current operations.

Cost. "Cost" represents the dollar amount of cash expended or other property transferred, capital stock issued, services performed, or a liability incurred, in consideration for goods or services received or to be received. Costs can be classified as unexpired or expired.

Costs related to the activities or functions of a business that have not expired are carried forward as assets. For example, plant facilities that will benefit future accounting periods, inventories of goods or merchandise that remain on hand, and costs pertaining to manufacturing, selling, administrative, financial activities that will benefit a future period are treated as assets, i.e., unexpired costs.

Expired costs assigned to operations and shown on the income statement include:

1. *Cost of goods sold[7] or of services performed for the accounting period.* The cost of goods sold (frequently referred to as *cost of sales*) for a mercantile business consists of the cost of the goods purchased that were sold. The cost of goods sold for a manufacturing business includes the cost of the materials, labor, and indirect manufacturing items that has been incurred in producing the goods sold. The cost of performing services consists of the cost of supplies, labor, and other elements incurred in rendering services.

2. *Cost of activities of the operating and financial departments.* Costs incurred in carrying on the selling and general and administrative functions of a business are classified as operating expenses. Usually two groups of operating expenses are recognized: (1) selling expenses which include the expenses directly related to the sale and delivery of goods and (2) general and administrative expenses which involve the entire business. Financial department costs include those incurred in connection with planning for, receiving, and disbursing funds for the business. Although not specifically mentioned, it is assumed that expired cost

---

[7] Of the 600 1970 income statements surveyed in *Accounting Trends and Techniques 1971*, 110 used the multiple step form with an intermediate showing of gross profit after the deduction of cost of goods sold; in 1955, 107 used this form. However, 457 firms disclosed total cost of goods sold or cost of goods manufactured in one way or another, up from 373 companies in 1960.

of plant facilities (depreciation, depletion, and/or amortization) has been appropriately included in the foregoing costs for the accounting period. Expenses related to production should be included in cost of goods sold and inventories.

Costs related to the activities or functions of a business that have not expired are carried forward as assets. For example, plant facilities that will benefit future accounting periods, inventories of goods or merchandise that remain on hand, and costs pertaining to manufacturing, selling, administrative, and financial activities that will benefit a future period are treated as assets, i.e., unexpired costs.

Current large corporation income statements

The Hercules, Incorporated, consolidated statement of income reproduced in Illustration 6–5 shows the maximum amount of detail usually found in the best published income statements. Note that cost of goods sold and operating expenses are shown as separate totals with no detail given for either category; the total costs and expenses associated with those two lines are over $700,000,000, over 85 percent of gross revenue. The balance of the statement is concerned with $40 million of income tax and sundry other items, mostly $15,000,000 of interest, making up a net deduction of $47,000,000. This is typical of current statements.

Note the separate handling of profit from operations, income before income taxes, net income before extraordinary item (in accordance with APB *Opinion No. 9*), and net income. Note also the elaborated earnings per share data (APB *Opinion No. 15*).

Income statements displaying greater detail

Smaller concerns, particularly those not seeking a wide distribution of their securities, and those desiring more detail on statements used internally, supply more adequate income statements. A description of information which can be usefully displayed on such statements follows.

Sales or operating revenue section and the showing of net sales

The sales of goods or services are shown at their gross amount, with deductions for sales returns and allowances and cash discounts specifically listed; the resulting figure is net sales. Cash discounts are frequently shown as other expense on the basis that they are given for prompt payment of accounts receivable and, therefore, represent a cost of obtaining funds. Trade discounts are reductions of the price and are properly eliminated from gross sales.

ILLUSTRATION 6–5

HERCULES

CONSOLIDATED STATEMENT OF INCOME

| | (THOUSANDS OF DOLLARS) Year Ended | |
	Dec. 31, 1971	Dec. 31, 1970
Net Sales and Operating Revenues	**$811,884**	$798,608
Cost of goods sold and operating expenses	596,744	582,323
Selling, general, and administrative expenses	112,827	111,065
	709,571	693,388
Profit from Operations	102,313	105,220
(After depreciation and amortization: 1971—$57,524,000; 1970—$53,583,000)		
Other income—net	3,577	6,580
Interest and debt expense	(15,167)	(21,894)
Equity in net earnings of affiliated companies	3,244	4,977
Income Before Taxes on Income	93,967	94,883
U. S., foreign and state taxes on income	40,588	43,303
(Includes deferred taxes: 1971—$4,567,000; 1970—$4,897,000)		
Net Income Before Extraordinary Item	53,379	51,580
Net gain on realignment of currencies	1,736	—
Net Income	$ 55,115	$ 51,580
Earnings per share of common stock (Average shares outstanding: 1971—19,836,536; 1970—19,734,906)		
Income before extraordinary item	$ 2.69	$ 2.61
Net gain on realignment of currencies	.09	—
Net income	$ 2.78	$ 2.61

The accompanying notes are an integral part of the consolidated financial statements.

The revenue from only the regular and most significant source or sources are shown in this section.

Revenue derived from the ordinary, i.e., principal, business operations includes sales of goods for merchandising and manufacturing businesses, sale of services for public utilities, and commissions for brokerage firms. In many manufacturing businesses, special attention is given to sales of scrap and by-products. If the material is scrap, the revenue is recorded as a reduction in the cost of manufacture. If the material is a by-product resulting from the manufacture or processing of raw materials, the revenue is shown separately in the sales section.

The excess of gross sales revenue over the sales deductions for returns, allowances, and cash discounts is captioned as "net sales."

Frequently, sales, service, and other revenue items are combined and only the total revenue is given. However, for analytical purposes the various sources of revenue are better itemized, and cost of goods sold and operating expenses should be related to the sales revenue exclusive of the other revenue and gain on the sale of noncurrent assets.

Cost of goods sold section and the showing of gross margin on sales

For a mercantile business, this section shows the cost of goods available for sale during the period and the cost of goods that have been sold. The beginning and ending inventories, as well as the accounts dealing with the goods purchased—such as Purchases, Transportation on Purchases, and Purchase Returns, Allowances, and Discounts—are itemized. Cost of goods sold does not include the operating expenses. Purchases discounts are proper deductions from purchases, although, primarily to save clerical effort, many concerns show them as other revenue. When perpetual inventories are maintained, purchases discounts are generally not deducted directly from the invoice cost figure because of the necessity of recording fractional unit prices.

For a manufacturing business, the cost of goods sold section is expanded to show the cost of goods manufactured and sold. However, to relieve the income statement of details, the cost of goods manufactured is customarily itemized in a schedule, as shown in Illustration 6–6. Most companies do not show the details of manufacturing costs in their published statements.

The principal elements of manufacturing costs are direct material, direct labor, and indirect manufacturing cost. Indirect manufacturing costs includes all costs incurred in production which cannot be classed as direct material or direct labor. For companies performing services

ILLUSTRATION 6–6

THE RAY MANUFACTURING COMPANY
Statement of Cost of Goods Manufactured
For the Year Ended December 31, 1971

Raw Materials:			
Inventory, December 31, 1970			$ 13,100
Purchases	$96,200		
Less: Purchases returns and allowances. . . $1,700			
Purchases discounts. 1,000	2,700		
	$93,500		
Add: Transportation on purchases.	1,000	94,500	
		$107,600	
Less: Inventory, December 31, 1971		15,800	
Raw Materials Used			$ 91,800
Direct labor			77,600
Factory Overhead:			
Depreciation of buildings		$ 4,900	
Depreciation of machinery and equipment.		8,100	
Factory supplies expense		4,200	
Heat, light, and power expense		3,100	
Indirect labor expense		10,400	
Insurance expense.		1,200	
Repairs to buildings.		200	
Repairs to machinery and equipment		500	
Taxes expense		1,700	
Miscellaneous factory expense.		1,300	
Total Factory Overhead Costs			35,600
Total Material, Labor, and Factory Overhead			$205,000
Add: Goods-in-process inventory, December 31, 1970			12,600
			$217,600
Less: Goods-in-process inventory, December 31, 1971			7,345
Cost of Goods Manufactured for the Year 1971			$210,255

such as transportation, an operating expense section is substituted for the cost of goods sold section.

The excess of net sales over cost of goods sold is most commonly captioned "gross profit on sales" or "gross profit." Although not widely used, the caption "gross margin," as used above, is preferable because gross profit is a contradiction of terms inasmuch as a "profit" cannot be realized until all costs relating to operations have been covered. If the cost of goods sold exceeds net sales, the amount may be captioned "excess of cost of goods sold over net sales."

In published income statements the cost of goods sold is often shown in one account rather than in detail. It is also frequently combined with selling, general, and administrative expenses, thereby making it impossible to distinguish production from distribution costs in analyzing the data.

Some manufacturing businesses show cost of goods sold without including depreciation, depletion, or amortization expense; these items of expense are then specifically listed and deducted before stating the net income. This method of disclosing the items results in understating the cost of goods sold, selling expenses, and general and administrative expenses, but it has the virtue of making disclosure of the total amounts of these expenses. When this procedure is followed, specific mention should be made of the omission. For example, captions similar to the following would be appropriate:

1. Cost of goods sold exclusive of depreciation, depletion, and amortization.
2. Gross margin on sales, exclusive of depreciation, depletion, and amortization.

And the dollar amounts should be disclosed.[8]

Cost of goods sold customarily contains the amount of loss resulting from inventory write-downs to market below cost. While the best practice is to disclose the amounts involved in such write-downs, this is rarely done. If anticipated losses on contractual commitments to make future purchases are recorded, these too are usually included in the total cost of goods sold amount, unfortunately without disclosure.

Operating expense section and the showing of operating income

Expenses incurred in carrying on the buying, selling, and general administrative functions of the business are frequently classed together as operating expenses. Strictly, there are only two principal types of costs incurred by a manufacturing or merchandising concern in carrying on its major activities: the cost of the goods that it sells and the cost of selling them. But there are two major difficulties in the way of a classification of all costs in these two categories: (1) the clerical expense involved and (2) the arbitrary allocations which are required. The cost of carrying on the purchasing function is clearly an element in the final cost of the goods purchased, but the clerical burden involved in dis-

---

[8] Accounting Principles Board, AICPA, *Opinion No. 12* (New York, 1967), specifies the following should be disclosed: amount of depreciation expense, balances of classes of depreciable assets, accumulated depreciation, and depreciation methods. *Accounting Trends and Techniques 1971* reports that (out of 600 statements) 65 did not give information about classes of assets (but 38 gave totals by product lines), 4 gave no information on depreciation expense (a wide variety of methods were used to disclose), and 26 did not reveal depreciation method used.

tributing such costs to inventories and cost of goods sold is generally regarded as excessive. General and administrative expenses are related to the acquisition of goods for sale or to selling them, but there is no clear-cut measure of the amounts to be allocated to each category. For these reasons, income statements frequently show two subdivisions in the operating expense section:

1. *Selling expenses,* which include the expenses directly connected with the sale and delivery of goods are:

Advertising and publicity expense.
Delivery expense (delivery wages, gasoline and oil, equipment repair, depreciation of delivery equipment, and taxes related to delivery).
Sales building expense.
Sales managers' salaries expense.
Sales office expense.
Salesmen's salaries expense.
Salesmen's traveling expense.
Shipping expense.
Transportation on sales.
Miscellaneous selling expense.

2. *General and administrative expenses,* which include the expenses of general supervision and administration, maintenance of the accounting records, purchasing, general correspondence, and credits and collections:

Administrative and office building expense.
Auditing and other accounting fees.
Credit and collection expense.
Depreciation of furniture and office equipment.
Directors' compensation.
Donation expense.
Legal expense.
Office salaries.
Office supplies and expense.
Postage, stationery, and printing expense.
Telephone and telegraph expense.
Uncollectible receivables expense.
Miscellaneous general expense.

Such items as rent, depreciation, property taxes, telephone and telegraph, postage, printing, and stationery should be allocated among the production, selling, and administrative functions involved.

Some businesses show transportation on sales as an offset to sales on the assumption that sales prices have been increased by the amount of these shipping costs. On the other hand, most companies show transportation on sales as a selling expense on the basis that it represents a cost of delivering the goods. Both of these methods can be logically supported; the one used should be consistently followed.

Special attention should be given to the classification of uncollectible receivables expense. This expense item is variously shown as a selling, general and administrative, or financial expense. The department that is responsible for sales should probably not have jurisdiction over credits and collections; but in some cases, it does. In some firms, credits and collections are considered to be directly related to the general administration of the business and not primarily a responsibility of the financial department. In such cases, uncollectible receivables expense may be classified as a general and administrative expense. In many firms the credit and collection function is under the treasurer. Here, it is logical to classify uncollectible receivables expense as a financial expense. Some accountants deduct uncollectible receivables expense from sales on the theory that this portion of the sales revenue will not materialize.

Some companies classify income taxes as general expense; however, most businesses deduct income taxes as a separate item after showing other revenue and other expense near the bottom of the income statement.

The analyst should give special consideration to the following expense items that are subject to managerial discretion:

Depreciation	Depletion
Amortization	Uncollectible receivables
Maintenance and repairs	Contingencies
Bonuses	Management and service contract fees

A statement of policy with reference to the foregoing items is needed if the analyst is to interpret properly the operating results.[9] Any departure from the established policy of recording and presenting these items should be disclosed in the financial statements. For analytical purposes, it is desirable to have available the amounts of the expense items listed above that have been distributed to the manufacturing, selling, and general and administrative functions. It would be helpful if these amounts were shown separately in the various expense and cost classifications; otherwise, they should be disclosed in footnotes or in a schedule. It is accepted practice to report the amount of depreciation which has been charged to manufacturing costs and to expense for the year; some of this cost is in inventories.

Repairs and maintenance, like depreciation and amortization, are sometimes shown as individual items of cost and not distributed to cost classifications. When this method is used, it is impossible to determine the total cost of goods manufactured and sold, selling expenses, and

---

[9] In 1972 the Accounting Principles Board issued, as of April 1972, its *Opinion No. 22* on "Disclosure of Accounting Policies." This pronouncement requires disclosure of all significant accounting policies including those relating to basis of consolidation, depreciation methods, amortization of intangibles, inventory pricing, accounting for research and development costs (including basis for amortization), translation of foreign currencies, recognition of profit on long-term construction-type contracts, and recognition of revenue from franchising and leasing operations.

The ruling applies to profit and nonprofit organizations and to all significant policies even though they are predominantly followed in the industry. Policy changes should be reported in accordance with APB *Opinion No. 20,* "Accounting Changes" (New York, July 1971).

general and administrative expenses; however, because of the importance to the analyst of this total, which frequently varies according to management policy, the undistributed total is better than no information.

The Securities and Exchange Commission requires registrants to show details of the following items in the income statement or supporting schedules:

Cost of goods sold.
Maintenance and repairs.
Amortization—depreciation, depletion, and expiration of service life of intangibles.
Taxes.
Management and service contract fees.
Rents and royalties.

Many companies report items of revenue and cost for income tax purposes on a basis different from that followed for accounting purposes. Therefore, "estimated federal income taxes payable" for the current period as shown on an income statement does not necessarily pertain exclusively to the reported current income. This is especially true when extraordinary gains and losses and other special items are included in determining the amount of income tax. In this event the income tax should be allocated between ordinary and extraordinary items to avoid the distortion of income before extraordinary items.

Income reported for income tax determination may differ from the net income from operations shown on the accounting records because:

1. Provision may have been made on the income statement for such items as maintenance and repairs deferred to future years and additional costs arising out of activities which are not deductible for income tax purposes.
2. Different rates of depreciation and of amortization may be reflected in the income statement and in the income tax report.
3. Income that has been received but not yet earned is taxed in the year of receipt.
4. A loss of a preceding year may have been carried forward to the current year, or a loss for the current year may have been carried back to a preceding year.
5. Income from installment sales or from long-term contracts may be taken up currently, although the income may not be taxable until a later accounting period.

As mentioned heretofore the accounting profession has worked out an elaborate system of income tax allocation in financial statements so federal income tax due and payable in the current year may be divided between operating and extraordinary items on the income statement. It may also be deferred to the income statements of future periods if the income or expenses to which it relates, though currently reported to the Internal Revenue Service, are deferred on published financial statements.[10]

The amount of federal income taxes for the year should be specifically disclosed because the analyst may wish to analyze and perhaps reclassify the item. He would be aided in this analysis by a description of the difference between net income for statement purposes and net income for income tax purposes, but this information is rarely provided.

An example of an item handled differently on tax returns than on financial statements is in the area of depreciation. An accelerated depreciation method may be used for computing income tax, and a straight-line method for accounting for regular income. The annual depreciation charge reported for income tax purposes would be higher and the resultant income tax lower than is recorded for accounting income determination. In order to record the difference in income taxes, Deferred Federal Taxes on Income may be credited at the time of recording Estimated Federal Income Taxes Payable. The latter item, a liability, is payable currently; the former would be amortized in subsequent years as smaller amounts of depreciation are recognized for income tax purposes. This procedure results in disclosing on the books the difference between accounting income and taxable income and the income taxes resulting therefrom.

Accounting Trends and Techniques 1971 reported that in 1970, 516 companies of the 600 surveyed showed interperiod allocations of current federal income tax. The primary cause was differences in depreciation methodology.

Depreciation methodology

Because of the importance of depreciation, not only in income tax allocations but in the computation of net income, it will be analyzed in some detail at this time.

Nature of depreciation

Fixed assets such as buildings, machinery, and equipment have a limited productive life; these lives are estimated for book and statement purposes. The total cost or other basic value, less salvage or residual proceeds, of these assets is distributed or allocated as expense over their estimated useful lives. The portion of the total charge allocated each year to expense is known as depreciation for the year. In accounting, the term "depreciation" does not refer to decay, deterioration, or loss of market value or price decline. It does not measure loss in efficiency

---

[10] Accounting Principles Board, AICPA, *Opinion No. 11* (New York, December 1967).

of a particular asset; it does represent an annual allocation of cost in recognition of the exhaustion of the service life of the asset. The annual depreciation charge is intended to amortize the cost, less salvage value, of the depreciable assets over their useful or service lives. Depreciation accounting represents a process of cost allocation, not of valuation. The title "depreciation expense" might well be changed to "depreciation allocated to operations of the year" in order to emphasize the fact that depreciation accounting is a process of cost allocation to the accounting period. Depreciation is a real (although, in the short run, not a working capital) cost; unless depreciation is recorded for every accounting period, the operating income or operating loss is misstated.

The fact that depreciation has been recognized does not guarantee, nor is it intended to represent, funds that will be available to replace the asset. Depreciation does not provide funds since it is merely a cost expiration. Funds to replace depreciated equipment will flow into the business through sales, but whether such funds are in fact available for fixed asset replacement will depend on the policies followed by management; if the funds are applied to other purposes, such as bond retirements or plant extension, they will not be on hand when replacement of fixed assets is required. Inasmuch as depreciation is a nonworking capital cost, the funds from sales revenue, after covering other costs, will be greater than the reported net income; and the reduction of net income by means of the charge for depreciaton may serve to discourage dividends.

Current assets may be segregated as a fund provided for the replacement of fixed assets. However, this approach ties up assets that might be more effectively utilized for other purposes in the business and is not commonly encountered. Modern business management prefers to handle the problem by forecasts (budgets) as to funds that will be needed for various purposes; such forecasts commonly are made, tentatively, five years in advance.

During periods such as the present, when prices have risen steadily and substantially, there is always considerable discussion of the disparity between accumulated depreciation and the cost of replacing the assets. Some critics argue that unless the depreciation policy is realistic with regard to current construction costs, selling prices cannot be properly evaluated. This argument is not conclusive because separate cost computations, divorced from published statements, have always been appropriate in evaluating selling prices and for other specialized purposes.

It is also argued that depreciation should be high enough to "provide for" the replacement of the assets. This is an involved matter which seems to the authors to turn on the question of whether the annual depreciation charge is intended to provide or assure replacement funds or whether this purpose is the proper function of the company's budget.

The recording of depreciation is a process of matching "actual" costs with revenues, whereas the replacement of the asset is a financial process which involves allocating available funds to the most productive uses.

The most serious indictment against depreciation based on historical cost is the claim that revenue and cost are not properly matched in dollars of the same size and that the reported net income may be seriously overstated due to inadequate depreciation when prices have risen steadily and substantially.

Many professional accountants are now of the opinion that the deterioration in value of the dollar has seriously impaired the usefulness of conventional depreciation allowances. *Certainly the analyst, who is attempting to forecast future revenues and costs, cannot ignore the steady deterioration of the value of the dollar.* For him, a plant which in 1940 dollars cost $100,000, in current dollars actually may cost over $300,000. The problems of the analyst in adjusting for this factor will be discussed at length in Part III of this book.

"All machinery is on an irresistible march to the junk heap, and its progress, while it may be delayed, cannot be prevented by repairs."[11] The determination of when and at what rate the service life of a fixed asset will expire represents a rather complicated problem. Factors that are considered in determining the service life of assets include wear, tear, usage, the action of the elements, inadequacy, obsolescence (commonly due to development of superior machines), and the passage of time. The first four causes of depreciation represent physical depreciation, and the last three are functional depreciation.

In estimating the service life of a depreciable asset and the annual depreciation charge, it is assumed that the asset will be adequately maintained and kept in good repair. To the extent that the asset is not properly maintained and repaired, it will become inefficient and will have to be abandoned sooner than anticipated. When repairs and maintenance are not made currently, *deferred maintenance* exists. Maintenance may be deferred because of a manpower shortage; insufficient earnings; excessively high costs; inability to obtain materials and repair parts; and undesirability of closing down for repairs, even temporarily, the productive facilities.

Depreciation methods

Although there are several methods of recognizing depreciation, as explained below, no one method is completely appropriate for all of the various kinds of assets owned by a business.

1. The straight-line method of determining depreciation, which relates depreciation expense to the passage of time, is most commonly

---

[11] Henry Rand Hatfield, *Accounting* (New York: Appleton & Co., 1932), p. 130.

used because (a) it is readily understood and easily applied and (b) it results in a uniform charge for each accounting period, which fact presumably makes for more comparable data. However, it should not be assumed that there is uniformity with respect to the number of service units derived from the asset during each accounting period. In determining the "time" or life of the asset, all causes of depreciation are considered.

2. The working- or production-hours depreciation method requires an estimate of the total number of hours that the asset will be used during its service life. This method recognizes the use that is made of the asset, i.e., the amount of depreciation varies depending upon whether the asset is used part time, full time, or overtime. However, if the asset is idle, no depreciation is recorded. If the asset is used somewhat continuously, the working-hours or production-units method provides a more equitable charge to expense as compared to the straight-line method.

3. The units-of-production or output depreciation method requires an estimate of the total number of units of product that an asset will produce during its economic life. This method has the same advantage and disadvantage as the working-hours method. If use or production is continuous, there would be an appropriate recognition of depreciation and, therefore, a proper matching of cost and revenue. However, during idle time, depreciation is not recorded.

4. The reducing-charge depreciation methods are based on the assumption that a greater amount of depreciation takes place during the first years of use as compared with the last years of service life. These methods—sum of the years' digits, fixed percentage of diminishing book value, and arbitrary diminishing percentages of cost—result in relatively high depreciation charges during the early years of the asset while efficiency is at a peak and maintenance and repair expense is relatively low. During the later years of service life the depreciation charge is comparatively low, while the efficiency is decreasing and maintenance and repair expense is relatively high. In other words, these methods result in higher depreciation charges during the early life of the assets when presumably the revenue is highest. From an income tax point of view these "rapid or accelerated amortization methods" permit deducting larger amounts of depreciation expense for each accounting period during the early life of the asset, thereby making available more working capital for fixed asset replacement or other corporate purposes.

5. The composite depreciation method requires the determination of a single rate which is applied to the total plant or, preferably, to a group of similar assets. The composite rate is based on the average life of the individual assets.

Permissible depreciation methods under the federal income tax code differ in detail as successive laws are enacted, but in general and subject to specific restrictions the methods enumerated above are allowed for income tax reporting as well as for financial statement purposes. Depreciation computed for both purposes is subject to an overall limitation: total depreciation may not exceed historical dollar cost.

Depletion

Natural resources, often referred to as *wasting assets*—such as coal, ore, and gold mines; quarries; timberland; oil wells; and sulphur deposits—are subject to *depletion*. Depletion represents the amount of the cost of the land, including the mineral content, which is charged to an accounting period as a result of the "depletion" of the available natural resource. That is, the natural resource is converted into inventory as a result of the removal of portions of the total supply. It should be evident that assets that are "depleted," unlike those that depreciate, do not remain intact so far as physical quantity is concerned.

The depletion charge for an accounting period in the case of a coal mine may be determined as follows:

$$\frac{\text{Cost of coal mine, less any residual value assigned}}{\text{Estimated tons of coal in the coal mine}} = \frac{\text{Unit cost of one}}{\text{ton of coal}}$$

Tons of coal removed from mine during the accounting period	*times*	Unit cost of one ton of coal	*equals*	The depletion charge for the accounting period

An alternative method of computing depletion is referred to as the percentage-of-revenue method, which is permitted for many natural resources under the Federal Income Tax Law. Depletion expense is determined by applying a fixed percentage (fixed by law) to the gross revenue.

When this method is adopted, the total depletion charge during the life of the natural resource may be in excess of its cost, which is contrary to conventional accounting principles. This provision is regarded by many, including the authors, as a method of subsidizing the development of natural resources; its legitimacy or illegitimacy is a matter of public policy, not accounting theory.

Amortization

Assets, the term of existence of which is established by law, regulation, or contract, include patents, copyrights, leases and improvements to leaseholds, fixed-term franchises, and, during periods of war or defense production, plant facilities authorized by the federal government under certificates of necessity. Such assets are "written off," i.e., amortized by allocating cost to expense, over their fixed term or economic life, whichever is shorter. The term "amortization" also refers to the gradual reduction of a deferred charge (discount on bonds, page 123) and a deferred credit (premium on bonds payable).

The word "amortization" is sometimes used as a general term in referring to depreciation and depletion as well as to amortization of intangible assets, which are special cases of amortizing or spreading costs over a series of time or other units.

Distinction between depreciation expense and other expenses

Depreciation, like supplies and salaries, represents an expense of operating a business. When supplies and salaries expense items are recorded, either current assets are reduced or a current liability, which later will require the use of working capital, is created.

When depreciation expense is recorded, the Accumulated Depreciation account is credited. This entry does not bring about a reduction of net working capital.

Depreciable assets may be considered to be a special type (long-term) of prepaid expense or deferred charge to expense. Therefore, the current recognition of depreciation expense involves neither the use of working capital nor the incurrence of a current liability. Expenditures already incurred are recovered through the depreciation process. The annual depreciation charge, less expenditures for replacements, is a conversion of fixed assets into working capital. This expression is useful and not misleading so long as it is borne in mind that the working capital actually arises from sales revenue. When expenditures for replacements exceed the depreciation charge, the conversion process is reversed, unless funds for the replacements are secured from other than current sources.

Intangible assets that are subject to amortization and natural resources that are subject to depletion are similar to depreciable assets, since the recognition of amortization and depletion expense does not involve the use of current working capital.

Distinction between capital and revenue receipts

A capital receipt as distinguished from a revenue receipt is one derived from (1) the collection of future revenue, (2) the sale of a fixed asset, (3) the issuance of capital stock, (4) additional investment by a single proprietor or by partners, and (5) the issuance of bonds or other long-term evidences of debts. These receipts of cash or the equivalent must be properly accounted for as capital receipts rather than as revenue.

A revenue receipt is one which legitimately may be treated as income, such as a gross receipt derived from the sale of merchandise or services in which the business deals regularly. The effect of recording a revenue receipt as a capital receipt would be to understate the income for the current accounting period and to understate some asset or overstate some liability, and to understate owners' equity.

Distinction between a profit and a saving

Businesses frequently construct their own buildings and other fixed assets. A saving, but not a profit, results when the cost of construction is lower than the price at which the assets could have been purchased. The amount of the saving should not be considered a profit because there has been no realization. The business realizes its profit on future sales, against which a smaller amount of depreciation will be charged.

Revenue and expense should be properly allocated to accounting periods—matching of revenue and expense

In small businesses a cash basis of accounting is sometimes used: revenue and expense are reflected on the income statement for the accounting period in which cash is received or paid out. If sales are made for cash, if bills are paid promptly on receipt, and if inventories are small or nonexistent, the cash basis may give a satisfactory result. Sometimes cash basis recording is modified to give effect to adjustments that increase its usefulness; for example, cash-basis income tax returns include deductions for depreciation.

In larger concerns cash recording is not considered adequate because it does not properly match revenue and expense. The necessity for an adequate matching of revenue and expense is a generally accepted accounting principle on which the accrual basis of accounting is founded. For example: If a concern buys three items and sells two, the cost of goods sold for the period is the cost of the two items; to charge the cost of one item or of three against revenue from two is a mismatching of revenue and expense. The expense of insurance premiums should be charged against revenue for the period in which the insurance protection is received.

The net income for an accounting period is summarized on the income statement. Expenditures and revenues that will affect future income statements are included on the balance sheet until allocation to the income statement becomes appropriate. The balance sheet also includes other assets (such as cash and land) and other liabilities (such as bank loans) which will never be shown on the income statement.

QUESTIONS AND PROBLEMS

6–1. Distinguish between operating expenses, extraordinary items, and prior period adjustments.

6–2. How should extraordinary items be presented on the income statement?

6–3. What is the suggested treatment of prior period adjustments?

6–4. How should earnings per share be computed and reported?

6–5. Explain briefly:
- *a)* Different ways of showing sales and purchases discounts on the income statement.
- *b)* The proper classification of uncollectible receivables expense on the income statement.
- *c)* Depreciation of capital assets has been charged on the basis of the cost of such assets and not on the appreciated values.
- *d)* Why the recognition of depreciation is not directly related to the replacement of the asset.
- *e)* Why dividend declarations should not be shown on the income statement.
- *f)* Is it possible to maintain a fixed asset in such excellent repair as to make unnecessary recording depreciation expense?
- *g)* Do you consider federal income taxes an operating expense?

6–6. Distinguish between:
- *a)* A single-step and a multiple-step income statement.
- *b)* Depletion and depreciation.
- *c)* A liability of a business to its creditors and to the owners.
- *d)* Ordinary and extraordinary revenue and expense.
- *e)* Depreciation expense and salaries expense.
- *f)* Nominal and real accounts.
- *g)* Realized retained earnings and unrealized retained earnings.

6–7. Classify the following income statement items; give reasons.
- *a)* Sales discount.
- *b)* Purchases discount.
- *c)* Uncollectible receivables expense.
- *d)* Amortization of bond discount.
- *e)* Amortization of patents.
- *f)* Write-down of goodwill.
- *g)* Depreciation expense.
- *h)* Depletion expense.

6–8. As required by APB *Opinion No. 9,* the Brian Corporation is adopting the clean-retained earnings theory. The company requests you to prepare for the year 1971:
- *a)* The final section of its income statement following the caption, "income before federal income taxes."
- *b)* The statement of retained earnings.

The following list of items is presented:

Appropriation for plant expansion	$ 10,000
Loss on sale of bond investments	2,000
Refund of federal tax payments of 1970	15,000
Storm loss not covered by insurance	30,000
Dividends declared.	35,000
Federal income taxes for the year.	20,000
Understatement of depreciation expense of 1970 . .	2,000
Loss on disposition of fixtures	10,000
Income before federal income taxes	100,000
Write-off of goodwill	5,000
Gain on the sale of land	40,000
Additional appropriation for plant expansion to correct error made in prior years	8,000
Retained earnings, January 1, 1971.	200,000

6–9.

THE SCOTT COMPANY
Summary of Consolidated Earnings
For the Year Ended December 31, 1971
(in thousands)

Cost of sales	$381,201
Depreciation and depletion	40,150
Dividends and interest from subsidiaries not consolidated . .	1,972
Domestic and Canadian taxes on income	52,130
Interest expense	2,103
Other charges—net deduction.	350
Other earnings	4,600
Other taxes	10,700
Sales.	587,312
Selling, general, and administrative expenses.	82,516
Net earnings after income tax	?

Required:

Prepare an income statement and determine net income after taxes.

6–10.   The statement of earnings presented below was included in the annual
report to stockholders by the Strain Corporation for the year 1971.

Statement of Earnings
(in thousands)

Net sales		$23,863
Less: Cost of goods sold and buying, advertising, and occupancy expenses	$16,842	
Selling, general, and administrative expenses	4,205	
Depreciation and loss resulting from abandonments for the year.	182	
Property taxes	469	
Repair and maintenance expense	174	21,872
Income before federal and state taxes		$ 1,991
Federal and state income taxes.		821
Income for the Year, Transferred to Retained Earnings		$ 1,170

Required:

What improvements would you suggest in the above statement?

6–11.   The Sharp Corporation presented the following summary of items selected from its income statements for the years 1969, 1970, and 1971.
The additional data were provided by the accountant after the first
audit since the business was established.

	1969	1970	1971
Net sales	$100,000	$125,000	$175,000
Inventory, January 1	15,000	55,000	57,000
Net purchases.	100,000	73,000	113,000
Inventory, December 31.	55,000	57,000	70,000
Selling expenses	20,000	28,000	35,000 —
General and administrative expenses	6,000	10,000	12,500
Other revenue	3,000	8,000	19,000
Other expense	5,600	3,000	6,000

Additional data:
(1)   Annual depreciation on the building in the amount of $5,000
has not been recorded.
(2)   Administrative expenses include the write-off of uncollectible
receivables of $3,000 for 1970 and $5,000 for 1971. Four fifths
of these amounts were on the books prior to 1971. It is estimated that annual uncollectible receivables expense approxi-
mates ¾ of 1 percent of net sales.
(3)   Office supplies inventories were not recorded for the year 1970,
$100, and for 1971, $200.
(4)   Interest earned but not recorded amounted to $200 for 1971.
(5)   A three-year fire insurance policy was paid for on January 1,
1970, $520. Insurance expense was debited.
(6)   The closing inventories for 1969 and 1970 were valued at the
lower of cost or market. The lower of cost or market was
$60,000.
(7)   The company constructed a building during the year 1971 at
a cost of $100,000. A saving of $8,000 in construction costs
was realized. The building value was established at $108,000,
the $8,000 saving being included in other revenue as profit on
plant construction.
(8)   Delivery equipment costing $6,800 and having a resale value
of $800 at the end of five years was purchased January 1, 1970.
This equipment was fully depreciated on the records during
1970 and 1971.
(9)   Ten-year bonds payable were issued at a discount on January 2,
1969. This discount ($2,600) was shown on the income state-
ment as other expense for 1969.
(10) $8,000 of merchandise in transit, December 31, 1971, was
included in the inventory, but the invoice was not recorded.

(11)   Temporary investments were evaluated, December 31, 1971, at market value; this value exceeded cost in the amount of $600. Profit on temporary investments was shown as other revenue.

(12)   Ordinary repair and maintenance on buildings were charged to the accumulated depreciation: $550 for 1969, $600 for 1970, and $575 for 1971.

Required:

Prepare revised income statement for one, two, or three years as instructor assigns.

7

Consolidated statements and unconsolidated stock interests

A CORPORATION that controls the policies of other corporations through the ownership of their "voting" capital stock is known as a parent company. A company that does not operate properties but only controls and directs the operations of other corporations is known as a *"pure" parent* or *holding* company. From a legal point of view, the "pure", parent company is merely an investor in certain capital stocks. A corporation that operates property of its own in addition to controlling the policies of other corporations through voting-stock ownership is known as a *parent-operating* company.

The company holding the capital stock is the *parent,* and the company issuing the stock is the *subsidiary.* The term "affiliate" is used to indicate any one company in the parent company system. When a majority of the voting stock of the subsidiary is held by a parent company, it is known as the *controlling interest;* the remaining interest is known as the *minority interest.* In the event that a large portion of a corporation's capital stock is widely distributed and held in small amounts, the ownership of less than a majority of the shares of voting stock may make possible the control of the business. The Public Utility Holding Company Act of 1935 defines a utility parent company as one owning 10 percent of the voting securities unless the Securities and Exchange Commission declares otherwise.[1]

---

[1] Accounting Principles Board, AICPA, *Opinion No. 18* (New York, March 1971), requires that the equity method of accounting be used for reporting if 20 percent or more of the voting stock of a company is controlled by the "parent" unless there is persuasive evidence of a lack of "parent" influence.

Frequently, a number of corporations are merged or consolidated into a single unit. In these instances the various corporations lose their individual identity, and their properties and liabilities become the assets and obligations of the newly organized corporation. The new corporation may exchange shares of its capital stock for the properties, or it may raise funds by selling its capital stock.

The parent-subsidiary company device may be utilized to bring about the common control[2] of the companies without the actual consolidation or merger[3] of the properties of the individual companies. The identity of the respective corporations is maintained, but unified control of the independent companies is thereby effected.

Reasons for the parent company

The parent company may desire to control subsidiaries for many reasons, some of which are suggested below:

1. Subsidiary companies are frequently established to bring about the complete separation of manufacturing and selling functions and, at the same time, to maintain common control over both activities.

The parent company may control, through the formation of individual subsidiaries, the various stages of production from the mining of coal and ore to the manufacture of finished products. The parent company may obtain subsidiaries to be assured of the control of sources of supplies, parts, and materials at favorable prices without having to depend on outsiders.

The parent company may bring about either horizontal or vertical combinations of operating companies. A combination of properties producing like products or performing like services is a *horizontal combination*. The operation of a number of coal mines or a chain of retail stores exemplifies this type of parent company.

A *vertical combination* involves the control of subsidiary corporations engaged in successive stages of production or the performance of services. For example, the parent may have subsidiaries engaged in the mining of coal and iron ore; production of steel and steel products; and the manufacture of refrigerators, automobiles, airplanes, and/or tractors. A vertical combination may involve the control, by the parent, of manufacturing, wholesaling, and retailing functions.

---

[2] Common control has reference to the legal right of the parent company to elect the board of directors and to control fully the policies and activities of the subsidiary company or companies.

[3] A *consolidation* takes place when a corporation is organized to acquire the assets and to assume the liabilities of two or more previously existing companies. A *merger* is effected when the properties of one or more companies are acquired by an existing corporation. In both instances the properties are brought under a unified management.

2. Separate corporations with unified common control may be desirable from several points of view. The parent-subsidiary company device makes possible the incorporation of properties by states. In this way the assets located in each state and the business performed are organized in legally separate units. This facilitates the determination of, and sometimes minimizes, the amount of taxes and tends to eliminate double taxation, which often results when consolidated properties are operated in several states.

The organization of a subsidiary company may be useful if a new business is to be undertaken, the risk of which is not fully known. If creditors will advance funds, the amount of owners' equity may be kept at a minimum until the profitability of the operation can be determined.

The maintenance of separate and distinct legal entities facilitates financing. Funds may be raised more readily and at less cost, in most cases, if mortgages are issued on the separate properties of the subsidiaries rather than on the combined properties. In other words, a general first mortgage covering all of the properties should be less economical and useful as a means of financing than mortgages issued on the separately incorporated properties.

Another advantage of maintaining the individual identity of the subsidiary companies is that the net income or net loss for each property may be determined.[4] Unprofitable business may be discontinued or given special attention in eliminating financial and operating weaknesses.

3. The parent-subsidiary company device has been used extensively to obtain control of large corporations through a relatively small investment. In fact, the control of companies may be pyramided to such an extent that the control of the top parent company may be maintained by an investment entirely out of proportion to the total property value of the subsidiaries.

For example, observe the pyramiding of control by Companies A and B (Illustration 7-1). Company B, the intermediate parent company, owns 51 percent of the voting stock of Companies C, D, E, and F. In turn, Company A, the top parent company, owns 51 percent of the voting stock of Company B. The common stockholders of Company A, therefore, control a total asset book value of $10,696,100[5] with a par value investment of $100,000. In fact, a 51 percent or lower percentage control of the voting stock of Company A would be sufficient to

---

[4] On the other hand, the net income for each property can be determined on a departmental basis if the subsidiary's identity is eliminated.

[5] Total asset book value of Companies C, D, E, and F $10,000,000
Other assets of Company B.   592,000
Other assets of Company A.   104,100
                                                              $10,696,100

ILLUSTRATION 7–1

COMPANY A—THE PARENT COMPANY
Balance Sheet
As of December 31, 1971

Assets		Liabilities and Owners' Equity	
Investment in Company B*	$669,375	Current and other liabilities	$228,000
Other assets	104,100	5% bonds payable	200,000
		Preferred stock (6%)	100,000
		Common stock	100,000
		Retained earnings (common stock equity)	145,475
Total Assets	$773,475	Total Liabilities and Owners' Equity	$773,475

COMPANY B—THE INTERMEDIATE HOLDING COMPANY
Balance Sheet
As of December 31, 1971

Assets		Liabilities and Owners' Equity	
Investment† in:		Current liabilities	$ 150,000
Company C	$ 561,000	Bonds (4%)	1,000,000
Company D	816,000	Preferred stock (6%)	600,000
Company E	255,000	Common stock	1,000,000
Company F	688,500	Retained earnings (common stock equity)	162,500
Other assets	592,000		
Total Assets	$2,912,500	Total Liabilities and Owners' Equity	$2,912,500

* Equals 51 % of the voting stock (common) of Company B.
† Equals 51 % of the voting stock of the subsidiary companies.

ILLUSTRATION 7-1 (continued)

COMPANIES C, D, E, AND F
Comparative Balance Sheet
As of December 31, 1971

Items	Companies			
	C	D	E	F
Assets				
Current assets	$ 200,000	$ 300,000	$ 250,000	$ 500,000
Noncurrent assets	1,800,000	3,700,000	750,000	2,500,000
Total Assets	$2,000,000	$4,000,000	$1,000,000	$3,000,000
Liabilities and Owners' Equity				
Current liabilities	$ 50,000	$ 250,000	$ 100,000	$ 150,000
Bonds (4%)	700,000	1,750,000	300,000	1,200,000
Preferred stock (6%)	150,000	400,000	100,000	300,000
Common stock*	900,000	1,200,000	400,000	1,050,000
Retained earnings (common stock equity)	200,000	400,000	100,000	300,000
Liabilities and Owners' Equity	$2,000,000	$4,000,000	$1,000,000	$3,000,000

* 51% of this voting stock held by Company B.

ILLUSTRATION 7–1 (concluded)

SUMMARIZATION, AND DISTRIBUTION, OF INCOME FOR COMPANY A AND ITS SUBSIDIARIES, YEAR 1971

Subsidiaries C, D, E, and F

Net income before bond interest and preferred stock dividend		$600,000
Less: Bond interest ($3,950,000 at 4%)	$158,000	
Preferred stock dividend ($950,000 at 6%)	57,000	215,000
Net Income*		$385,000

Distribution of net income:

Company B—51%	$196,350
Minority interest	188,650
	$385,000

Intermediate Holding Company, Company B

Net income from subsidiary Companies C, D, E, and F		$196,350
Less: Bond interest ($1,000,000 at 4%)	$ 40,000	
Preferred stock dividend ($600,000 at 6%)	36,000	76,000
Net Income*		$120,350

Distribution of net income:

Company A—51%	$ 61,378.50
Minority interest	58,971.50
	$120,350.00

Parent Company, Company A

Net income from Company B		$61,378.50
Less: Bond interest ($200,000 at 5%)	$ 10,000	
Preferred stock dividend ($100,000 at 6%)	6,000	16,000.00
Net Income*		$45,378.50

* After federal income taxes.

control the $10,696,100 investment because of the wide distribution of the voting stock.

The principle of *leverage*, i.e., trading on the equity, is illustrated in the foregoing example of pyramiding. Since bonds and preferred stock bear a fixed interest and dividend rate, respectively, any excess income earned on these funds accrues to the common stockholders. Thus, as long as the operating companies are successful, the use of the parent-subsidiary company device makes it possible to reap the maximum rewards of trading on the equity. This is shown in the summarization of the earnings of Company A and its subsidiaries (Illustration 7–1). The income data are for the year 1971. It is assumed that no other change took place in the investment during the year 1971.

Company B, the intermediate parent company, is entitled to 51 percent, or $196,350, of the net income of Companies C, D, E, and F. Company A, the top parent company, is entitled to 51 percent, or $61,378.50, of the net income of Company B. The net income realized by Company A after providing for the bond interest and preferred stock dividend requirement represents a return of 43.4 percent on the common stock, par value. The foregoing income figures do not include income on the other assets for Companies A and B.

Unprofitable operations would result in a dangerous financial conditions for the parent companies. For example, assume that the subsidiaries C, D, E, and F (Illustration 7–1) had a net income of $85,000 instead of the $385,000. Fifty-one percent, or $43,350, of this amount which accrues to Company B, the intermediate parent company, is insufficient to meet in full the preferred stock dividend requirement. Since Company B has not realized a return on its common stock, there will be no income accruing to Company A. Therefore, as a result of the decrease in income of the operating companies, Company B's preferred stock dividend requirement and Company A's bond interest and preferred stock dividend requirement are unearned. If such a condition were to continue for a number of years, a financial reorganization of the parent companies would be necessary.

The general advantage of a parent-subsidiary company[6] system over a complete merger of the affiliated companies is that common control is accomplished and at the same time the individuality—and in many cases the valuable goodwill of the various affiliates—is maintained. Furthermore, a corporation may be able to acquire a controlling interest in another corporation by acquiring its stock more easily than it could obtain stockholder authorization for the sale of the company's assets.

---

[6] The parent company is not liable for the debts or other obligations of subsidiaries, except when specifically assumed or guaranteed. It is also true that the legal obligations of the parent company are not those of the subsidiary, unless otherwise arranged.

The major disadvantage inherent in the parent-subsidiary company device is the increased taxation and the other expenses of maintaining the affiliated corporate organizations. Many abuses, several of which are stated below, have been practiced in connection with the parent-subsidiary company device:

1. Concealment of financial condition and operating results by the preparation of uninformative and misleading consolidated statements.
2. The development of an unsound financial policy and the creation of top-heavy capital structures. *Pyramiding*, discussed on page 175, in many cases in the past has been most vicious.
3. Excessive service charges and profits on intercompany transactions have been charged against subsidiary companies.

The "pure" parent company's bonds and stocks, as a class, are junior to the securities issued by the subsidiary. Subsidiary interest charges, federal income taxes, preferred stock dividend requirements, and minority interest (if any) must all be provided for before the parent can determine its share of the subsidiary income.

Interest charges and preferred stock dividend requirements of the parent should be related to the total of the subsidiary and parent's earnings (after federal income taxes and minority earnings, before fixed interest charges) to determine the number of times the parent's fixed charges have been earned.

Consolidated statements

A consolidated balance sheet is a financial statement which shows the combined assets and liabilities, exclusive of intercompany transactions and account balances, of a group of closely related corporations, i.e., of the parent company and its subsidiaries. A consolidated income statement shows the combined revenue and expenses, exclusive of intercompany transactions, of various companies in the parent-subsidiary system. In other words, the consolidated statements show a broad overall picture of the financial position and operating results of the parent and subsidiary companies, which are operated under a common or unified control, as though they were one business organization or economic entity. For purposes of the consolidated statements, the independent legal existence of the separate companies is disregarded. The consolidated statements do not present the financial position and operating results of *a single legal entity;* these statements show the data of a business entity or economic unit consisting of a *group of legal corporate entities.* Each subsidiary corporation is a legal entity with distinct and separate legal rights and obligations.

APB *Opinion No. 10,* affirmed by APB *Opinion No. 18,* stated that "the usefulness of consolidated financial statements has been amply demonstrated by the widespread acceptance of this form of financial reporting" and quoted with approval *Accounting Research Bulletin No. 51* in which the predecessor committee stated that "there is a presumption that consolidated statements . . . are usually necessary for a fair presentation when one of the companies in the group directly or indirectly has a controlling financial interest in the other companies."

However, there are situations in which the financial statements of a subsidiary are much superior to a consolidated statement; for example, when a creditor of the subsidiary is looking to the financial statements to inform him about the backing of his receivable.

The Accounting Principles Board makes the equity method a requirement

Unless the statements of the parent and its subsidiaries are consolidated or the equity method is used, the parent company's statement of income will not yield any information about the profits or losses of the subsidiaries. The balance sheet will show an investment (at cost) in, and perhaps advances to, one or more subsidiaries (as in Illustration 7–2 on p. 187). If the investments in subsidiaries are carried on the balance sheet at original cost, the information given is not informative about the profit or loss characterstics of the subsidiaries. Under this "cost" method, dividends declared by the subsidiary, payable to the parent, are added to the investment in subsidiary account on the parent company balance sheet, and dividend payments received are deducted. The equity method, discussed below, gives more information—though not as much as consolidation—and in December 1966 the Accounting Principles Board issued *Opinion No. 10* (an omnibus opinion) which stated, in paragraph 3:

If, in consolidated financial statements, a domestic subsidiary is not consolidated, the Board's opinion is that, . . . the investment in the subsidiary should be adjusted for the consolidated group's share of accumulated undisturbed earnings and losses since acquisition. This practice is sometimes referred to as the "equity" method.

APB *Opinion No. 10* was followed in March 1971 by *Opinion No. 18*, "The Equity Method of Accounting for Investments in Common Stock," which superseded some of the wording of APB *Opinion No. 10* but not its essential meaning.

APB *Opinion No. 18* states categorically that investments in common stock of all unconsolidated subsidiaries (foreign as well as domestic) should be accounted for by the equity method. The Board also stated that "the equity method is not however a valid substitute for consolidation and should not [must not] be used to justify exclusion of a subsidiary when consolidation is otherwise appropriate."

Specifically, subsidiaries "whose principal business activity is leasing property or facilities to parent or other affiliated companies should be [must be] consolidated."

There are circumstances under which subsidiaries should not be consolidated. "Even though a group of companies is heterogeneous in character, it may be better to make a full consolidation than to present a large number of separate statements. On the other hand, separate statements or combined statements would be preferable . . . if . . . more informative to shareholders and creditors. . . . For example, separate statements may be required for a subsidiary which is a bank or an insurance company and may be preferable for a finance company where the parent and the other subsidiaries are engaged in manufacturing operations." Furthermore "a subsidiary should not be consolidated where control is likely to be temporary, or where it does not rest with the majority owners (as for instance, where the subsidiary is in legal reorganization or in bankruptcy). There may also be situations where the minority interest in the subsidiary is so large, in relation to the equity of the shareholders of the parent in the consolidated net assets, that the presentation of separate financial statements for the two companies would be more meaningful and useful. However, the fact that the subsidiary has a relatively large indebtedness to bondholders or others is not in itself a valid argument for exclusion of the subsidiary from consolidation" (*Accounting Research Bulletin No. 51*, cited by APB *Opinion No. 18*). "In view of the uncertain values and availability of the assets and net income of foreign subsidiaries . . . careful consideration should be given to the fundamental question of whether it is proper to consolidate the statements of foreign subsidiaries with the statements of United States companies. Whether consolidation . . . is decided upon or not, adequate disclosure of foreign operations should be made (*Accounting Research Bulletin No. 43*, chap. 12, also cited by APB *Opinion 18*).

When the equity method is in use, on the parent company's balance sheet subsidiary company earnings are added to the investment in subsidiary account when earned (reported on the subsidiary company financial statements) and dividends in cash are treated as withdrawals of capital.

Presumably, APB *Opinion No. 18* serves to eliminate an opportunity to mislead the readers of financial statements which existed when the cost method could be used by any company that wished to do so. By its nature the cost method served to conceal the existence of retained earnings of the subsidiary. Or, a subsidiary might have been operating at a loss and borrowing money from the parent company to get by.

In that case, the investment shown at cost and the advances shown as valid receivables could be misleading.

To the same end, APB *Opinion No. 18* sets out in considerable detail the following disclosure requirements:

1. The name of each investee and percentage of common stock owned.
2. The accounting policies of the investor with respect to investments in common stock.
3. The difference, if any, between the amount at which an investment is carried and the amount of underlying equity; and the accounting treatment of the difference.
4. If current value quotations are available, the present value of the investment (not required for subsidiaries).
5. If investments in unconsolidated subsidiaries are material in the aggregate, summarized information as to assets, liabilities, and results of operations. The same requirement may apply to investments which are less than 50 percent owned (See Illustration 7–3 on p. 188).
6. Material effects of possible conversions, exercises, or contingent issuances of convertible securities, options, warrants, etc., disclosed in notes.

APB *Opinion No. 18* also set down the following required procedures in calculating the financial statement amounts to be shown when using the equity method:

19. *Applying the equity method.* The difference between consolidation and the equity method lies in the details reported in the financial statements. Thus, an investor's net income for the period and its stockholders' equity at the end of the period are the same whether an investment in a subsidiary is accounted for under the equity method or the subsidiary is consolidated (except as indicated in paragraph 19 i). The procedures set forth below should be followed by an investor in applying the equity method of accounting to investments in common stock of unconsolidated subsidiaries, corporate joint ventures, and other investees which qualify for the equity method:

a) Intercompany profits and losses should be eliminated until realized by the investor or investee as if a subsidiary, corporate joint venture or investee company were consolidated.
b) A difference between the cost of an investment and the amount of underlying equity in net assets of an investee should be accounted for as if the investee were a consolidated subsidiary.
c) The investment(s) in common stock should be shown in the balance sheet of an investor as a single amount, and the investor's share of earnings or losses of an investee(s) should ordinarily be shown in the income statement as a single amount except for the extraordinary items as specified in (d) below.
d) The investor's share of extraordinary items and its share of prior-period adjustments reported in the financial statements of the investee in accord-

ance with APB Opinion No. 9 should be classified in a similar manner unless they are immaterial in the income statement of the investor.

e) A transaction of an investee of a capital nature that affects the investor's share of stockholders' equity of the investee should be accounted for as if the investee were a consolidated subsidiary.

f) Sales of stock of an investee by an investor should be accounted for as gains or losses equal to the difference at the time of sale between selling price and carrying amount of the stock sold.

g) If financial statements of an investee are not sufficiently timely for an investor to apply the equity method currently, the investor ordinarily should record its share of the earnings or losses of an investee from the most recent available financial statements. A lag in reporting should be consistent from period to period.

h) A loss in value of an investment which is other than a temporary decline should be recognized the same as a loss in value of other long-term assets. Evidence of a loss in value might include, but would not necessarily be limited to, absence of an ability to recover the carrying amount of the investment or inability of the investee to sustain an earnings capacity which would justify the carrying amount of the investment. A current fair value of an investment that is less than its carrying amount may indicate a loss in value of the investment. However, a decline in the quoted market price below the carrying amount or the existence of operating losses is not necessarily indicative of a loss in value that is other than temporary. All are factors to be evaluated.

i) An investor's share of losses of an investee may equal or exceed the carrying amount of an investment accounted for by the equity method plus advances made by the investor. The investor ordinarily should discontinue applying the equity method when the investment (and net advances) is reduced to zero and should not provide for additional losses unless the investor has guaranteed obligations of the investee or is otherwise committed to provide further financial support for the investee.[7] If the investee subsequently reports net income, the investor should resume applying the equity method only after its share of that net income equals the share of net losses not recognized during the period the equity method was suspended.

j) The guides in paragraph 16 of ARB No. 51 for income taxes on undistributed earnings of subsidiaries in consolidation remain in effect as provided in paragraph 39 of APB Opinion No. 11 until the Board issues an Opinion on that subject. The guides should also apply (1) to investments in common stock of unconsolidated subsidiaries, corporate joint ventures,[8] and other investee companies accounted for by the equity method

---

[7] An investor should, however, provide for additional losses when the imminent return to profitable operations by an investee appears to be assured. For example, a material, nonrecurring loss of an isolated nature may reduce an investment below zero even though the underlying profitable operating pattern of an investee is unimpaired. [Footnote from *Opinion No. 18.*]

[8] Certain corporate joint ventures have a life limited by the nature of the venture, project or other business activity. Therefore, a reasonable assumption is that a

in consolidated financial statements and (2) to investments accounted for by the equity method in parent-company financial statements prepared for issuance to stockholders as the financial statements of the primary reporting entity.

k) When an investee has outstanding cumulative preferred stock, an investor should compute its share of earnings (losses) after deducting the investee's preferred dividends, whether or not such dividends are declared.

l) An investment in voting stock of an investee company may fall below the level of ownership described in paragraph 17 from sale of a portion of an investment by the investor, sale of additional stock by an investee, or other transactions and the investor may thereby lose the ability to influence policy, as described in that paragraph. An investor should discontinue accruing its share of the earnings or losses of the investee for an investment that no longer qualifies for the equity method. The earnings or losses that relate to the stock retained by the investor and that were previously accrued should remain as a part of the carrying amount of the investment. The investment account should not be adjusted retroactively under the conditions described in this subparagraph. However, dividends received by the investor in subsequent periods which exceed his share of earnings for such periods should be applied in reduction of the carrying amount of the investment (see paragraph 6a).

m) An investment in common stock of an investee that was previously accounted for on other than the equity method may become qualified for use of the equity method by an increase in the level of ownership described in paragraph 17 (i.e., acquisition of additional voting stock by the investor, acquisition or retirement of voting stock by the investee, or other transactions). When an investment qualifies for use of the equity method, the investor should adopt the equity method of accounting. The investment, results of operations (current and prior periods presented), and retained earnings of the investor should be adjusted retroactively in a manner consistent with the accounting for a step-by-step acquisition of a subsidiary.

n) The carrying amount of an investment in common stock of an investee that qualifies for the equity method of accounting as described in subparagraph (m) may differ from the underlying equity in net assets of the investee. The difference should affect the determination of the amount of the investor's share of earnings or losses of an investee as if the investee were a consolidated subsidiary. However, if the investor is unable to relate the difference to specific accounts of the investee, the difference should be considered to be goodwill and amortized over a period not to exceed forty years, in accordance with APB Opinion No. 17.

20. *Disclosures.* The significance of an investment to the investor's financial position and results of operations should be considered in evaluating

---

part or all of the undistributed earnings of the venture will be transferred to the investor in a taxable distribution. Deferred taxes should be recorded at the time the earnings (or losses) are included in the investor's income in accordance with the concepts of APB Opinion No. 11. [Footnote from *Opinion No. 18.*]

the extent of disclosures of the financial position and results of operations of an investee. If the investor has more than one investment in common stock, disclosures wholly or partly on a combined basis may be appropriate. The following disclosures are generally applicable to the equity method of accounting for investments in common stock:

a) Financial statements of an investor should disclose parenthetically, in notes to financial statements, or in separate statements or schedules (1) the name of each investee and percentage of ownership of common stock, (2) the accounting policies of the investor with respect to investments in common stock,[9] and (3) the difference, if any, between the amount at which an investment is carried and the amount of underlying equity in net assets and the accounting treatment of the difference.

b) For those investments in common stock for which a quoted market price is available, the aggregate value of each identified investment based on the quoted market price usually should be disclosed. This disclosure is not required for investments in common stock of subsidiaries.

c) When investments in unconsolidated subsidiaries are, in the aggregate, material in relation to financial position or results of operations, summarized information as to assets, liabilities, and results of operations should be presented in the notes or separate statements should be presented for such subsidiaries, either individually or in groups, as appropriate.

d) When investments in common stock of corporate joint ventures or other investments of 50% or less accounted for under the equity method are, in the aggregate, material in relation to the financial position or results of operations of an investor, it may be necessary for summarized information as to assets, liabilities, and results of operations of the investees to be presented in the notes or in separate statements, either individually or in groups, as appropriate.

e) Conversion of outstanding convertible securities, exercise of outstanding options and warrants and other contingent issuances of a investee may have a significant effect on an investor's share of reported earnings or losses. Accordingly, material effects of possible conversions, exercises or contingent issuances should be disclosed in notes to the financial statements of an investor.

Presenting the results of the equity method

In Illustrations 7–2, 7–3, and 7–4 the reader will find reproduced portions of the balance sheet, statement of income, and notes to the financial

_____
[9] Disclosure should include the names of any significant investee corporations in which the investor holds 20% or more of the voting stock, but the common stock is not accounted for on the equity method, together with the reasons why the equity method is not considered appropriate, and the names of any significant investee corporations in which the investor holds less than 20% of the voting stock and the common stock is accounted for on the equity method, together with the reasons why the equity method is considered appropriate. [Footnote from *Opinion No. 18.*]

ILLUSTRATION 7–2

Consolidated Statement of
FINANCIAL CONDITION
Food Fair Stores, Inc. and Subsidiaries

July 31, 1971 and August 1, 1970

ASSETS	1971	1970
		(Restated, Note 2)
Current assets:		
Cash	$ 16,033,000	$ 18,765,000
Marketable securities, at cost	487,000	461,000
Accounts receivable, net of allowance for doubtful		
accounts: 1971, $1,026,000; 1970, $559,000	58,028,000	54,059,000
Inventories, at lower of cost (first-in, first-out or average)		
or market	173,123,000	151,130,000
Prepaid expenses	10,043,000	9,714,000
Real estate in the process of development and		
sale, net of payments received on account;		
1971, $7,475,000; 1970, $6,250,000	2,756,000	4,676,000
Total current assets	260,470,000	238,805,000
Investments:		
Affiliates, at equity in net assets:		
Food Fair Properties, Inc. (Note 2)	8,355,000	7,876,000
Other subsidiaries (Note 1)	3,529,000	3,279,000
Other, at cost	1,824,000	2,787,000
	13,708,000	13,942,000

Note: Only part of the balance sheet has been reproduced.

statements of Food Fair Stores, Inc., a grocery chain. These figures show the presentation of the relationship to two unconsolidated subsidiaries in the parent company's financial statements. Note the presentation in the balance sheet at "equity in net assets" and the references to notes 1 and 2. Note the item in the statement of income for income from nonconsolidated subsidiaries. Finally note the explanations in notes 1 and 2 including the statements of Food Fair Properties, Inc. and the explanation of the effect on income of the change to the equity method in accordance with APB *Opinion No. 18.*

Many sets of published financial statements do not give all the information supplied by notes 1 and 2, in which case the information given may be confined to the bare bones of the investment section of the balance sheet and a single amount of income from nonconsolidated subsidiaries and affiliates in the income statement

So long as the parent-subsidiary relationship exists, the subsidiary continues to own its assets and to owe its liabilities. Its income becomes legal income of the parent only when formally declared by the subsidiary's board of directors, but of course the parent company has legal control and will have its way in the end.

ILLUSTRATION 7–3

Food Fair Stores, Inc. and Subsidiaries

NOTES TO FINANCIAL STATEMENTS

Fifty-two Weeks Ended July 31, 1971

1. The consolidated financial statements include the accounts of the Company, its wholly owned Subsidiaries and its majority owned Subsidiaries, except its wholly owned life insurance company.

Investments in the life insurance company and in 50% owned companies are stated in the Company's equity in net assets.

The accounts of majority-held foreign Subsidiaries are consolidated for the year ended July 31, 1971. These companies were previously reported on the equity method. The effect of this change is not material.

2. In the year ended July 31, 1971, the Company changed its method of accounting for its investment in Food Fair Properties, Inc. from the cost, to the equity method, in accordance with Opinion No. 18 of the Accounting Principles Board. Under the new method, the investment is carried at cost plus equity in undistributed earnings since dates of acquisition. As a result of this change, net earnings of the Company for the years ended in 1971 and 1970, capital in excess of par and retained earnings at the beginning of these years were increased by the following amounts:

	1971	1970
Net earnings ($.06 and $.04, per share, respectively)	$ 444,000	$ 331,000
Capital in excess of par	2,407,000	2,407,000
Retained earnings	1,137,000	806,000

Financial statements for the year ended August 1, 1970 have been restated to reflect the change.

The Company owns all of the preferred stock and 40% of the common stock of Food Fair Properties, Inc. At July 31, 1971, the aggregate value of this preferred stock was $2,000,000 and the aggregate market value of this

common stock was $13,333,000, based on a quoted bid price of $4 per share.

The consolidated financial statements of Food Fair Properties, Inc. and its Subsidiaries are as follows:

		(000 omitted)
Consolidated financial position		December 31,
	1970	1969
Assets		
Investment in property and equipment at cost, net of depreciation	$166,624	$134,551
Other	8,952	8,613
	$175,576	$143,164
Liabilities		
Notes, mortgages and debentures payable	$104,305	$102,022
Construction loans payable	38,075	13,996
Other	15,360	10,505
	157,740	126,523
Shareholders' equity	17,836	16,641
	$175,576	$143,164

	(000 omitted, except per share amounts)	
	Years ended December 31,	
Consolidated statement of income	1970	1969
Income	$18,301	$15,951
Net expenses	15,866	13,963
Income before income taxes	2,435	1,988
Income taxes	1,122	978
Net income	$ 1,313	$ 1,010
Earnings per common share and common share equivalent	$.14	$.11

Note: Not all footnotes are shown.

Under a rule of the Securities and Exchange Commission, consolidated statements should not be prepared unless the parent company owns, directly or indirectly, more than 50 percent of the voting stock of the subsidiary. In practice, self-imposed rules require voting stock ownership in the amount of 60 to 100 percent. Frequently, a parent company exercises effective managerial control of a subsidiary through lease and interlocking directorates. Such subsidiaries may be consolidated by some corporations even though less than 50 percent of the voting stock is owned.

A corporation may own more than 50 percent of the common stock of a company without possessing 50 percent of the voting stock. Preferred stock may have voting rights; and common stock (A), nonvoting, and common stock (B), voting, may be outstanding.

A corporation may own less than 50 percent of the voting stock of another company and because of widespread dispersion of the latter

ILLUSTRATION 7–4

Consolidated Statement of

INCOME

Food Fair Stores, Inc. and Subsidiaries

Fifty-two weeks ended July 31, 1971 and August 1, 1970

	1971	1970
		(Restated, Note 2)
Sales	$1,928,179,000	$1,762,005,000
Cost of sales	1,550,901,000	1,419,120,000
Gross profit	377,278,000	342,885,000
Operating expenses	350,425,000	317,626,000
Income from operations	26,853,000	25,259,000
Income from nonconsolidated subsidiaries	717,000	968,000

Note: Only a part of the statement of income has been reproduced.

company's capital stock may control the subsidiary. The consolidated statements should show, either in the heading or in a footnote or appended schedule, the names of the subsidiary companies and the respective degrees of legal control possessed.

In recent years there have been a number of instances of joint ownership and control of a subsidiary by two large corporations, neither owning over 50 percent of the voting stock. There have also been many instances of actual control of a subsidiary though the proportion of voting stock owned is less than 50 percent, sometimes substantially less. In APB *Opinion No. 18* the Accounting Principles Board decreed that if the parent company owns at least 20 percent of the voting stock, and there is no persuasive evidence to show lack of influence, the equity method must be used in accounting for the reporting on the parent company's unconsolidated investment.

Understanding consolidated statements

It is not a purpose of this chapter to teach in detail the preparation of consolidated financial statements. This is done as a customary feature of advanced accounting courses. But the analyst must understand certain fundamental principles with respect to consolidated financial statements. Consolidated statements reflect the financial condition and operating results of the parent and subsidiary company in their relation to outsiders. Therefore, it is necessary in preparing a consolidated balance sheet to eliminate intercompany relationships, i.e., intercompany transactions and account balances which do not affect outsiders. Such relationships include intercompany holdings of capital stock and other securities and intercompany current receivables and payables. In preparing a consolidated income statement, intercompany transactions such as purchases and sales, profit or loss, interest, rents, and other revenue or expense items must be eliminated.

The consolidated balance sheet should show all of the assets and liabilities of the parent company and of its subsidiary that are not affected by intercompany transactions, on the theory that the various companies represent a single business unit or organization.

What happens in the process of consolidating the statements can be well illustrated by presenting and explaining a consolidating work sheet (Illustration 7–5).

Note that Company A has an investment of $500,000 in its subsidiary and owns 100 percent of the subsidiary's capital stock. Subsidiary B has owners' equity of $500,000. In this case the investment in the subsidiary is shown on the books of the parent at the book value of the subsidiary's stock.

From the point of view of the stockholders of Company A, a consolidated balance sheet should be prepared, showing the assets and liabilities, exclusive of intercompany transactions, if any, of both the parent and the subsidiary. That is, for the purpose of the consolidated balance sheet, the assets, $900,000, and the liabilities, $400,000, of Subsidiary B are substituted for the Investment in Subsidiary B account, $500,000, which appears on the records of the parent. The owners' equity, $500,000, of the subsidiary is eliminated since it is already reflected in the owners' equity of the parent.

Illustration 7–6 shows the resulting balance sheet. Note that Company A's $500,000 investment in Company B has disappeared; so have Company B's capital stock and retained earnings. The disappearance of Company B's retained earnings deserves comment. It is because when Company A bought Company B, B's past earnings ceased to be earnings in the hands of A and became merely assets bought and liabilities assumed.[10]

---

[10] Of late years a method known as "pooling" has developed. Under the reasoning behind this approach, the parent does not buy the subsidiary; instead, they "pool." Therefore, the prior earnings of A and B would be added together. This approach has been very popular with some financial managers, who have used it to create what is sometimes known as "instant earnings," an outgrowth of today's pressure for constantly increasing earnings per share. In August 1970, the Accounting Principles Board of the AICPA moved, in *Opinion No. 16*, "Business Combinations," to obtain a measure of control over the abuses practiced under the guise of pooling. The provisions of *Opinion No. 16* will be described where appropriate to the purposes of this volume, but a comprehensive discussion of *Opinion No. 16* will be left to more advanced texts. While restrictive rules have been laid down, pooling is still possible and may be encountered by the analyst. When this happens, *Opinion No. 16* requires disclosure.

ILLUSTRATION 7-5

COMPANY A AND SUBSIDIARY B
Consolidated Work Sheet
Date of Acquisition

Items	Company A	Company B	Eliminations	Consolidated balance sheet items
Assets				
Cash	50,000	25,000		75,000
Receivables, net	100,000	50,000		150,000
Inventories	275,000	150,000		425,000
Miscellaneous current assets	25,000	10,000		35,000
Land, buildings, and equipment, net	1,200,000	650,000		1,850,000
Investment in Subsidiary B*	500,000		500,000	
Other noncurrent assets	150,000	15,000		165,000
Total Assets	2,300,000	900,000	500,000	2,700,000
Liabilities and Owners' Equity				
Payables	250,000	75,000		325,000
Long-term liabilities	150,000	325,000		475,000
Capital stock—Company A	1,500,000			1,500,000
Retained earnings—Company A	400,000			400,000
Capital stock—Company B		325,000	325,000	
Retained earnings—Company B		175,000	175,000	
Total Liabilities and Owners' Equity	2,300,000	900,000	500,000	2,700,000

* 100 % ownership of subsidiary stock.

ILLUSTRATION 7–6

COMPANY A AND SUBSIDIARY B
Consolidated Balance Sheet
Date of Acquisition

Assets

Current Assets:		
Cash.	$ 75,000	
Receivables, net	150,000	
Inventories	425,000	
Miscellaneous current assets	35,000	
Total Current Assets		$ 685,000
Noncurrent Assets:		
Land, buildings, and equipment, net.	$1,850,000	
Other noncurrent assets	165,000	
Total Noncurrent Assets		2,015,000
Total Assets		$2,700,000

Liabilities and Owners' Equity

Current Liabilities:		
Payables	$ 325,000	
Long-term liabilities.	475,000	
Total Liabilities.		$ 800,000
Owners' Equity:		
Capital stock	$1,500,000	
Retained earnings	400,000	
Total Owners' Equity		1,900,000
Total Liabilities and Owners' Equity.		$2,700,000

Amount paid for subsidiary company capital stock

The parent company may acquire the stock of a subsidiary company by cash purchase or in exchange for its own securities. When capital stock and long-term debt obligations are issued by the parent company in exchange for subsidiary stock, the market value of the parent's stocks and bonds represents the cost of the subsidiary stock. The investment in the subsidiary usually represents (1) capital stock at par or stated value, (2) acquired retained earnings, and (3) an excess of investment over capital stock and retained earnings or an excess of capital stock and retained earnings over investment.

The assets of the subsidiary are usually included in the consolidated balance sheet on the same basis as shown on the books of the individual company. However, the amount paid for the stock of a subsidiary is seldom exactly equal to the book value of the stock. Therefore, the investment in a subsidiary's capital stock as shown on the holding company's books may be greater or less than its book value as shown on the subsidiary's books.

1. *Investment in excess of book value.* The amount paid for subsidiary stocks may exceed their book value for various reasons:

   a) When the assets of the subsidiary are properly valued, the excess payment may represent the purchase of "goodwill" identified with the subsidiary, a value which has not been recorded on the subsidiary's books. The commonest titles used by large corporations to caption this intangible asset are "excess of cost over book value of acquisitions" (or equivalent) and "goodwill." Intangible assets are frequently "buried" in fixed asset captions.

   b) The purchase price may exceed the book value of the subsidiary's stock because of the understatement of the asset accounts on the books of the subsidiary. That is, valuation and amortization accounts may be excessive or the present market or replacement value of the assets may be higher than the cost as shown on the subsidiary books. APB *Opinion No. 16* requires that the individual tangible assets be valued at their current fair value and any excess investment be allocated to "goodwill" ("excess of cost over book value of acquisitions"). APB *Opinion No. 17*, "Intangible Assets" (also August 1970) requires that this intangible asset be amortized against income for an appropriate period not exceeding 40 years; the straight-line method is to be used unless an alternative method can be demonstrated to be more appropriate under the circumstances. In the 1970 financial statements surveyed in *Accounting Trends and Techniques 1971*, more (230) showed an amortized balance than showed an unamortized balance (200), but 91 did not say how they valued their intangible assets and 36 used nominal value.[11]

   c) The excess payment may be the result of an unfortunate purchase. If this is a fact, the excess payment would appear to be a current extraordinary loss. However, it is unlikely that management will voluntarily admit this which would lead to a charge-off against current net income. It will probably be amortized over a period not exceeding 40 years.

2. *Investment less than book value.* A parent company may pay less than book value for the subsidiary stock for various reasons:

   a) The book value of the subsidiary assets may be overstated. If so, these assets should be adjusted on the books of the subsidiary to reflect present market or replacement values. In this way the cost of the stock and the book value of the stock may be brought into agreement.

   b) A difference between the payment for the stock and the book equity applicable to the subsidiary stock may be considered as *negative goodwill* sometimes referred to as a *bargain purchase credit*. In spite of the long-standing prohibition in accounting theory against showing income from bargain purchases, some financial managers in search of

---

[11] In its 1969 income statement, the Celanese Corporation wrote off an "Excess of Cost of Investments Over Related Equities" amounting to $22,700,000.

"instant earnings" have amortized negative goodwill into annual income. In *Opinion No. 16* the Accounting Principles Board prohibited this practice, requiring that tangible assets be reduced in value to an extent sufficient to eliminate the so-called negative goodwill.

Minority interest in the owners' equity of the subsidiary

If the parent company owns less than 100 percent of the subsidiary stock, the equity applicable to the stock owned by outsiders is known as the *minority interest*. This interest represents ownership by outsiders in the subsidiary's assets which have been included in the consolidated assets; it does not represent a liability. The minority interest does not appear as such in the ledger of the subsidiary company; it is shown on the consolidated balance sheet under a separate caption, "minority interest," just preceding the owners' equity section. Minority interest in capital stock and retained earnings should be listed separately.

The consolidated balance sheet includes (1) all of the assets and liabilities, exclusive of intercompany transaction, of the subsidiary being consolidated, as well as those of the parent company; and (2) the owners' equity of the nonvoting stockholders, the minority interest stockholders, and the majority interest stockholders.

Intercompany receivables and payables

Intercompany sales and purchases of goods create intercompany receivables and payables. The parent company may loan cash or sell merchandise or other assets to its subsidiary, and the debt may be evidenced by open accounts or by promissory notes. Therefore, either or both accounts receivable and notes receivable may appear on the parent company's books, and accounts payable and notes payable on the subsidiary's books. In preparing the consolidated statements, intercompany reciprocal accounts are eliminated.

Intercompany unrealized profit

When intercompany sales of merchandise are made at a profit and merchandise is in the possession of one of the affiliated companies as of the consolidated balance sheet date, it is necessary to eliminate the profit from inventories. So far as outsiders are concerned, profit on intercompany sales is not realized. The unrealized profit should be eliminated from the beginning as well as the ending inventories and from retained earnings. A valuation account, Estimated Unrealized Profit on Inventories, may be created on the books of the parent company to show the unrealized profit; or the elimination may be accomplished on the work sheet.

Fixed assets are frequently purchased by a parent company from its subsidiary at an amount above their cost to the subsidiary. In preparing a consolidated balance sheet, this intercompany unrealized profit should be eliminated from both the individual asset account and the retained earnings account. To the extent that the accumulated depreciation includes depreciation on the unrealized profit, elimination is required.

Factors limiting the usefulness of consolidated statements

Consolidated statements show the overall financial position and operating results of a group of affiliated companies. The analyst will sometimes need in addition to consolidated statements, the individual or legal statements of the parent and of each subsidiary within the holding company system. The individual statements may be essential to obtain a fuller and more adequate composite picture of the holding company economic unit. The distortion of pertinent facts and the concealment of individual company differences may be discovered through the scrutiny of the legal statements. Although the individual statements do not separate intercompany transactions or segregate intercompany profits, they do reveal the separate legal relationships by listing different creditor and ownership groups. The most important factors which limit the usefulness of consolidated statements are discussed below:

1.   The consolidated balance sheet does not reflect the financial position of each individual subsidiary. In fact, in most instances published corporate reports neither include the legal statements of the parent or the various subsidiaries nor any comprehensive data relative to the affairs of these companies. The status of bondholders and other creditors and the assets against which their claims rank cannot be shown clearly by the consolidated statement. The position of minority stockholders cannot be determined from consolidated statements, inasmuch as such statements do not detail the assets, liabilities, revenue, and expenses of the legal entities. The volume of business transacted among the different affiliates is not revealed. The variations in the net working capital position and the long-term debt and financial condition of the different subsidiaries and of the parent company are not revealed by the consolidated statements. In fact, an insolvent company may be hidden in these statements.

The consolidated balance sheet gives the impression that all of the assets shown are available to meet all of the debts and equity interests reflected on the statement; however, this is not the situation. The consolidated statements are prepared with reference to an economic entity, but the liabilities shown on the balance sheet rank on the basis of the legal entities and not the economic entity. In order to evaluate the position of creditors and minority stockholders, it is necessary to refer to the individual statements of the subsidiaries, since the creditors of each company have a claim against only the assets of that company. The parent company's equity in each of the subsidiary's assets ranks after the subsidiary's legal liabilities and preferred stock.

2. The consolidated statements do not provide information to determine the prospects of dividend declarations. Dividend policy for each legal entity is dependent upon its cash position, the amount of retained earnings, state laws, amount of current earnings, and present and prospective corporate plans. The consolidated statements show, relative to the economic entity, the total cash, retained earnings, and amount of current income. They do not reveal provisions of state laws pertaining to subsidary dividends or present and future corporate plans. A large consolidated retained earnings balance and a favorable consolidated working capital position should not be used as a basis for judging that dividends can or should be declared by any of the individual companies included in the consolidation. The dividend policy of the parent company will depend upon the composition of its own retained earnings, the nature of its assets, the laws of the state in which it is incorporated, and its future financial needs and prospects.

3. The consolidated income statement combines the operating results of profitable companies with those of unprofitable companies. These strong and weak links in the parent-subsidiary company system cannot be identified without reviewing the individual subsidiary statements.

Some consolidated income statements reveal priority of subsidiary preferred dividends in relation to the parent's bond interest. However, as a general rule the consolidated income statement does not reveal the priority of claims on the income. The claims of the bondholders and preferred stockholders, and the minority common stockholders of each individual subsidiary must be satisfied before determining the amount of net income that is earned by the parent on its investments in the subsidiaries. In a very real sense the preferred stock dividend of a subsidiary is senior to the interest on the parent company's bonds, since this interest is paid chiefly from dividends received on the investments in the subsidiaries.

The subsidiary bondholders and preferred stockholders are interested in knowing the number of times that the bond interest and preferred dividend have been earned, while the common stockholders are interested in relating the remaining earnings to common shares.

4. The accounting data of the various subsidiary companies may not be comparable because of differences such as the following:

a) Methods of estimating uncollectible receivables.
b) Valuation of temporary investments.
c) Inventory pricing policy.
d) Methods of computing depreciation and depletion.
e) Treatment of extraordinary gains and losses.
f) Accounting for intangibles.
g) Treatment of capital expenditures and revenue expenditures.
h) Substitution of appreciation or appraisal values for cost.
i) Classification of accounts.
j) Accounting periods.

5. The current and long-term financial conditions of each legal entity are not revealed by a consolidated balance sheet. Inasmuch as creditors' claims can be related only to the assets of the legal entity, the safety of the claims cannot be ascertained by analyzing the statement of the economic entity. The total assets shown by a consolidated balance sheet are not available on a pro-rata basis for the payment of the liabilities of all of the affiliated companies. It is difficult to reflect the liens or bond indenture requirements in a consolidated statement except by lengthy footnotes. The parent may have issued its own collateral notes or bonds by pledging the capital stock of a wholly or partially owned subsidiary which is consolidated. Furthermore, there may be pledged various other assets and the securities of companies not consolidated.

Bond indentures of subsidiary companies may (*a*) require the maintenance of specified ratios of current assets to current liabilities or (*b*) restrict dividends when retained earnings amount to less than a stated minimum.

6. Ratios computed from consolidated statements are averages, since they represent summations of various underlying situations set forth on the legal statements of the parent and the subsidiaries. The individual statements should be analyzed so that important variations may be detected and more thoroughly studied.

Requirements of complete reporting

The foregoing discussion of limitations of consolidated statements suggests that full disclosure insofar as that is possible by means of financial statements and supporting schedules requires:

1. Separate statements of the parent company, to show legal liability to subsidiaries and to the outside world.
2. Separate statements of each subsidiary, to reveal legal liability to other subsidiaries, to the parent and to the outside world.
3. Consolidated statements of the entire group of companies, to present

the financial position and operating results as a single economic entity.

However, it is currently customary to issue only a consolidated statement.

Difference between a consolidation and consolidated statements

When a consolidation takes place, assets and usually liabilities are transferred from one or more companies to a newly organized company or to one of the existing companies. All except possibly one of the companies are commonly terminated. The financial statements of the surviving company or of the new company would show the financial condition and operating results of a single *legal entity;* these statements would not be consolidated statements.

Consolidated statements are a result of combining the data contained in separate legal-entity financial statements after intercompany asset, liability, revenue, and expense items have been eliminated. The assets and liabilities of the subsidiary are not transferred to the parent company, and the subsidiary does not lose its identity as a legal entity.

In combined statements, intercompany transactions and balances are not eliminated.

QUESTIONS AND PROBLEMS

7-1. Discuss the nature of consolidated financial statements and indicate the purpose of preparing such statements.

7-2. Under what circumstances would the financial statements of a subsidiary be superior to a consolidated statement?

7-3. Distinguish between:
  a) Controlling interest and minority interest.
  b) A "pure" parent company and an operating company.
  c) A merger and a consolidation.

7-4. Discuss the following briefly:
  a) Does the parent company have a legal obligation with respect to the liabilities of its subsidiary companies?
  b) What factors are considered in determining whether or not to consolidate subsidiary companies?
  c) How does the consolidated balance sheet differ from a balance sheet prepared from the books of the parent company?
  d) "The amount of retained earnings shown on a consolidated statement and on a parent company's statement may be different." Discuss.
  e) What would be the effect upon the income and owners' equity values of pyramided parent companies (1) if the operating companies experience a major decline in income or a net loss and (2)

the value of the assets of the operating companies decline substantially? Would the position of creditors of the holding companies be affected?

7–5. Is minority interest a liability? Explain.

7–6. Balance sheet items of Corporation A and Company B are:

	A	B
Assets	$800,000	$150,000
Liabilities	$250,000	$ 50,000
Common stock ($100 par)	400,000	50,000
Retained earnings	150,000	50,000
Total Liabilities and Owners' Equity	$800,000	$150,000

How would the foregoing items appear on a consolidated balance sheet if—

a) Corporation A buys all of the stock of Company B for (1) $120,000, (2) $90,000, and (3) $100,000?

b) Corporation A buys 90 percent of Company B's stock at (1) $80,000, (2) $100,000, and (3) $150,000?

7–7. How should investments in common stock of unconsolidated subsidiaries be accounted for?

7–8. What are the disclosure requirements set out by APB *Opinion No. 18?*

7–9. What procedures are required by APB *Opinion No. 18* in calculating the financial statement amounts to be shown when using the equity method?

7–10. Company R purchased 90 percent of the stock of Company N on January 1, 1971, for $250,000. Company N had common stock of $160,000 and retained earnings of $90,000. How should the foregoing and following transactions be recorded if (*a*) the equity method or (*b*) the cost method of recording the investment in the subsidiary is adopted?

Transactions

(1) N had a net loss of $20,000 for 1971.
(2) N declared a dividend of 10 percent in 1971.
(3) N paid dividends (declared above) in 1972.
(4) N had a net income of $35,000 for 1972.
(5) N declared and paid a dividend of 15 percent in 1972.
(6) N declared and distributed a 10 percent stock dividend in 1973.
(7) N had a net income of $40,000 in 1973.

PART II

Analysis and Interpretation of
Commercial and Industrial
Financial Statements

8

Comparative financial statements

THERE ARE no standardized financial statement forms used by all industrial and commercial businesses. Furthermore, the classification of some of the financial statement items varies widely. These variations are frequently a result of (1) management's wishes; (2) the intended use of the statements; (3) the opinion of those who prepared the statements; (4) the accountants' knowledge, training, and experience; and (5) failure to adopt generally accepted accounting concepts and current changes in terminology and classifications. Frequently the analyst will wish to review and recast, i.e., rearrange or, occasionally, reconstruct, the financial statements in accordance with his views and purpose of making the study before he begins the work of ratio computation, analysis, and interpretation. The objectives of the review are to determine whether there has been a full disclosure of all relevant financial and operating data, whether proper accounting procedures have been employed, whether financial statement items are properly classified, and whether appropriate valuation and amortization methods have been adopted and followed. A study of explanatory notations, accountants' reports, footnotes, and other supplementary information frequently reveals changes in, or departures from, the consistent application of generally accepted accounting concepts or changes in the reclassification of items. One of the most important problems of the analyst is to have available comparable financial statements. The purposes of reconstructing the statements are (1) to combine similar items, thereby reducing the number of figures to be studied; (2) to include, classify, and arrange the items according to the concepts developed in the preceding chapters; and (3) to have available selected key totals as well as detailed amounts for purposes of computing trend percentages, common-size percentages, and individual ratios.

In many instances, the analyst obtains additional financial and operating data from the annual reports to stockholders and from other sources which should be incorporated in the reconstructed statements. Intangible assets and deferred charges, exclusive of prepaid expenses, are commonly eliminated from the assets and owners' equity for analytical purposes.

The analyst may find that the following and similar practices result in noncomparable statement information:

1. Including advance customer payments as credits in Accounts Receivable rather than as a current liability.
2. Valuing inventories on different bases of cost (Fifo, Lifo, or moving weighted average), the lower of cost or market, standard costs, or on the basis of direct costing (work-in-process and finished goods inventories include cost of direct material, direct labor, and variable indirect manufacturing costs—the fixed indirect manufacturing costs are shown as period costs and charged off).
3. Listing treasury stock as an asset rather than as an offset in the owners' equity section.
4. Including advance payments to creditors as debits in Accounts Payable rather than as a current asset.
5. Offsetting marketable government securities against estimated federal income taxes accrued rather than showing them as a current asset.[1]
6. Stating depreciation on varying bases: straight line, fixed percentage of diminishing balance, sum-of-the-years' digits, or other methods.
7. Including extraordinary gains and losses in the determination of net income.
8. Expensing or capitalizing research and development costs as well as other expenditures.
9. Evaluating intangible assets at a nominal sum ($1) or at total cash cost less amortization.[2]

---

[1] Of the 600 large corporations surveyed in *Accounting Trends and Techniques 1971*, only two deducted government securities from their income tax liability, down from 80 in 1960 and 50 in 1965. The offsetting of government securities against tax liabilities was discouraged in APB *Opinion No. 10* (December 1966) except where the securities were issued in a form that made the purchase tantamount to a prepayment of taxes.

[2] Of the 600 corporations in *Accounting Trends and Techniques 1971*, 334 showed intangible assets and used the following valuation methods: amortized balance, 230; unamortized value, 200; nominal value, 36; not determinable, 91.

10. Including write-up of noncurrent assets to recognize higher appraised replacement costs or higher price levels.[3]

If any of the foregoing differences are discovered, appropriate adjustments may be made to achieve comparability.

Analytical methods and techniques used in analyzing financial statements

The analysis of financial statements consists of a study of relationships and trends to determine whether or not the financial position and results of operations and the financial progress of the company are satisfactory or unsatisfactory. The analytical methods and techniques, i.e., analytical tools, listed below, are used to ascertain or measure the relationships among the financial statement items of a single set of statements and the changes that have taken place in these items as reflected by successive financial statements. The objective of any analytical method is to simplify or reduce the data under review to more understandable terms. The analyst first computes and organizes his data, and then analyzes and interprets them to make them more meaningful.

Analytical methods and techniques used in analyzing financial statements include the following:

1. Comparative balance sheets, income statements, and statements of retained earnings, showing:
   a) Absolute data (dollar amounts).
   b) Increases and decreases in absolute data (dollar amounts).
   c) Increases and decreases in absolute data (percentages).
   d) Comparisons expressed in ratios.
   e) Percentages of totals.[4]
2. Statement of changes in financial condition[5]
3. Trend ratios[6] of selected (related) financial and operating data.
4. Common-size percentages[7]—balance sheets, income statements, and individual sections of these statements.
5. Ratios expressing the relationships[8] of items selected from the balance sheet, the income statement, and both statements.
6. Composite industry ratios.
7. Statement of variation in net income[9] or gross margin.

---

[3] Auditors who are members of the AICPA will take exception to this in their audit reports but it occasionally happens nevertheless.

[4] See discussion of common-size percentages in Chapter 10.

[5] Chapter 12.

[6] Chapter 9.

[7] Chapter 10.

[8] Chapters 15–18.

[9] Pages 379–81.

The analyst should be aware of the misleading and distorting effects of price-level changes on the relationship of items, trends, and ratios from period to period. The subject of the influence of price-level changes on accounting data is discussed in Part III.

Statement-analysis techniques may be used (1) by the external analyst to measure the profitability of operations and the financial condition of the business in order to determine the desirability of investing in or extending credit to the business and (2) by the internal analyst to determine the efficiency of management and operations and to explain changes in the financial position. Internally, statement-analysis techniques are used to interpret data for use by management to measure progress against planned operations and to achieve control.

The term "financial strength" has reference to the ability of a business (1) to meet the claims of creditors not only under current economic and business conditions but also under unfavorable situations that may occur in the future; (2) to take advantage of business dealings or expansion which require presently owned resources, additional funds obtained through the sale of long-term debt obligations and capital stock, or a favorable credit rating; and (3) to continue interest and dividend payments without interruption. Financial strength should be studied from both a short-term and a long-term point of view.

When the financial statements for a number of years are reviewed, the analytical measures are often called "horizontal or dynamic measures and ratios." This term is applied because the analysis, which suggests probabilities, weaknesses, or strength, includes data from year to year rather than as of one date or period of time as a whole. The term "vertical or static measures and ratios" is frequently used in referring to ratios developed for one date or for one accounting period. These, in turn, can be compared over a number of periods. However, whatever methods or bases of analysis are employed, they are merely preliminary to the all-important mental processes necessary in analyzing financial statements. The objective of any analytical method is to make the data more understandable by significant rearrangement and simplification.

Money data in thousands or millions

In analyzing dollar data, it is frequently desirable to eliminate unimportant details like fractions of a dollar (cents). On occasions amounts may be rounded to thousands, or even millions, of dollars. The showing of financial and operating data in thousands or millions of dollars does not interfere with the preparation of ratios, percentages, and comparisons because the relationships remain unchanged.

Balance sheet form

When comparing balance sheets for two or more years, the account form balance sheet, with the assets and liabilities in a vertical column, is often preferable as it facilitates columnar presentation. An example of an account form balance sheet appears on page 43.

Comparative statements—absolute data

A balance sheet shows the assets, liabilities, and owners' equity of a business as of a specified date. A comparative balance sheet (see the illustration in Chapter 1) shows the assets, liabilities, and owners' equity of a business as of two or more dates and may also show increases and decreases in the absolute data in terms of dollars and percentages. Changes are important because they give an indication of the direction in which a business and its financial characteristics are developing.

The changes in the balance sheet items during an accounting period, as explained in Chapter 12, are a result of (1) operating profits and losses and extraordinary (nonoperating) gains and losses, (2) the acquisition of assets or the conversion of assets into a different form (usually current assets), (3) the conversion of one form of liability into another form, (4) the incurrence or payment of liabilities, or (5) the issuance or retirement of bonds and capital stock.

An income statement shows the net income or net loss resulting from the operation of a business for a designated period of time; it may include extraordinary gains and losses. A comparative income statement (see Chapter 1) shows the operating results for a number of accounting periods. The comparison may be of dollar amounts, or of percentages, or both, and the amount of change may be set up in an adjoining column, thus:

	December 31		Amount of change	
(Thousands)	1971	1970		
Net sales	$892	$947	$55	6.2%

Comparative statements are useful to the analyst because they contain not only the data appearing on single statements but also information necessary to the study of financial and operating trends over a period of years. These statements bring out more clearly the nature and trends

| | 1970 | | | | 1971 | | | |
Items	January	February	Total 2 months	Average per month	January	February	Total 2 months	Average per month
Net sales...............	$12,100	$14,900	$27,000	$13,500	$11,200	$15,500	$26,700	$13,350
Cost of goods sold.......	7,800	10,100	17,900	8,950	7,300	10,700	18,000	9,000
Gross margin on sales.....	$ 4,300	$ 4,800	$ 9,100	$ 4,550	$ 3,900	$ 4,800	$ 8,700	$ 4,350

of current changes affecting the enterprise—they indicate the direction of movement with respect to financial position and operating results.

When the financial statements are prepared at monthly or quarterly intervals, comparisons may be made with the corresponding month or quarter of the preceding fiscal year or years. Cumulative figures for the elapsed portion of the current year, with corresponding totals of the preceding year or years, may also be given or computed by the analyst. Averages may be computed and compared as shown on page 208.

Comparisons lose their value and tend to become misleading if the data being studied do not reflect the consistent application of generally accepted accounting principles from date to date or period to period. The reasons for the noncomparability of statements should be indicated in the footnotes that accompany the financial statements, as well as in the accountant's report.

The analyst should constantly keep in mind that accounting data are recorded as of the date of transaction incurrence; and, therefore, the accounts usually reflect a great variety of price levels. Consequently, each year's income statement includes items such as supplies and salaries expressed in terms of the current price level, as well as items such as depreciation, depletion, amortization, and beginning inventories which reflect past price levels. When the price level has fluctuated substantially during the period under review, the analyst must exercise caution in interpreting the trends expressed by the comparative statements.

Comparative statements—comparing dollars and percentages

Most people find it difficult to grasp the significance of changes in dollar amounts though they do emphasize major shifts. The extent of net changes in the absolute data from year to year may be observed more readily if relative changes in terms of percentages are determined. For example, the receivables and payables may have increased $25,000 each; the change in receivables may represent a 10 percent increase, whereas the change in payables may represent a 50 percent increase.

The following table shows changes in both dollars and percentages. A final column shows the relationship in ratio form.

| | December 31 | | Increase (decrease*) | | |
Items	1970	1971	Amount	%	Ratio
Cash	$ 8,000	$16,000	$ 8,000	100	2.00
Merchandise inventory	40,000	30,000	10,000*	25*	0.75
Notes payable.	20,000	5,000	15,000*	75*	0.25
Mortgage note payable	4,000	9,000	5,000	125	2.25
Retained earnings	37,500	51,375	13,875	37	1.37

The ratios are determined by dividing the dollar amount for the current year by the dollar amount for the preceding year or base year. A ratio of less than 1 means that the amount for the current year is less than the amount for the base year. For example, in the foregoing illustration, notes payable for December 31, 1971 were 0.25, or one fourth of the total for December 31, 1970. Cash increased $8,000, or 100 percent, during 1971. The cash, as of December 31, 1971 was 2 times the balance as of December 31, 1970 retained earnings as of December 31, 1971 were 1.37 times the balance as of December 31, 1970. The use of the ratios avoids the necessity of showing minus or decrease signs.

When the financial statements for a series of years are being analyzed, one of two bases of comparisons may be used:

1. Comparisons may be made with the data for the earliest date or period, as shown below (dollars in thousands):

| | | | | Increase (decrease*) | | | |
| | | | | 1970 | | 1971 | |
Items	1969	1970	1971	Over 1969		Over 1969	
Net sales	$791	$833	$935	$42	5.3%	$144	18.2%
Income before federal							
income taxes	48	38	62	10*	20.8*	14	29.2
Merchandise inventory . .	170	160	130	10*	5.9*	40*	23.5*
Current assets.	502	519	343	17	3.4	159*	31.7*

2. Comparisons may be made with data for the immediately preceding date or period, as shown in the following illustration (dollars in thousands):

| | | | | Increase (decrease*) | | | |
| | | | | 1970 | | 1971 | |
Items	1969	1970	1971	Over 1969		Over 1970	
Net sales	$791	$833	$935	$42	5.3%	$102	12.2%
Income before federal							
income taxes	48	38	62	10*	20.8*	24	63.2
Merchandise inventory . .	170	160	130	10*	5.9*	30*	18.7*
Current assets.	502	519	343	17	3.4	176*	33.9*

When negative amounts appear in the base year, no percentage change will be shown. For example, if the cash balance in the current year is $500 and in the preceding year there was an overdraft of $1,000, the net change represents an increase in cash of $1,500. This change in cash cannot be expressed in percentage form. When percentages cannot be computed for particular items, no amounts are shown. When an item has a value in the base year and none in the following period, the decrease is 100 percent. A percentage is not given for an item after the base year when there is no figure for the base year.

The foregoing procedures may be exemplified by the following illustration:

Items	Year		Increase (decrease*) during 1971	
	1970	1971	Amount	Percentage change
Cash (overdraft†)	$ 1,000†	$ 500	$ 1,500	. . .
Long-term investments.	-0-	15,000	15,000	. . .
Notes payable.	10,000	-0-	10,000*	100*
Operating loss.	1,000	4,000	3,000	. . .
Net income (loss ‡).	500	1,500‡	2,000	. . .

Comparative income statements—cumulative and average amounts

A comparative income statement may be expanded to show, in addition to the data for several consecutive periods, the cumulative figures and the annual average for the period. The condensed statement in Illustration 8–1 shows this form. The problem of the analyst is to determine whether or not the annual data appear to be out of line with the average amounts, to discover the factors responsible for the changes, and to decide whether favorable or unfavorable tendencies are reflected. The comparative income statement which shows annual averages is valuable from the point of view of "leveling" the items over several years— i.e., the data for periods of high and low business activity are averaged.

Comparative statements—analysis and interpretation

When comparative statements showing the net changes in absolute amounts or in percentages have been completed, it is necessary to select for study those items showing important changes. The analyst should consider these changes individually—and jointly where they are directly related—to determine, if possible, the reasons for the variations and whether or not the changes are favorable. For example, inventories may have been increased by 15.4 percent during the year. The increase may be a result of changes in quantity or price, or a combination of the two factors. The quantity increase may have been a result of larger sales volume and/or of acquisitions to obtain a better balance of inven-

ILLUSTRATION 8–1

Items	1969	1970	1971	Cumulative amount	Annual average amount
Net sales	$250	$390	$425	$1,065	$355
Cost of goods sold.	163	258	290	711	237
Gross margin on sales.	$ 87	$132	$135	$ 354	$118
Operating Expenses:					
Selling expenses	$ 60	$ 91	$101	$ 252	$ 84
General and administrative					
expenses	20	33	34	87	29
Total Operating Expenses	$ 80	$124	$135	$ 339	$113
Operating income	$ 7	$ 8	$ 0	$ 15	$ 5
Other revenue.	25	36	32	93	31
	$ 32	$ 44	$ 32	$ 108	$ 36
Other expense.	4	20	12	36	12
Income before federal income					
taxes	$ 28	$ 24	$ 20	$ 72	$ 24
Federal income taxes	6	5	4	15	5
Net Income Transferred to Retained					
Earnings	$ 22	$ 19	$ 16	$ 57	$ 19

tory items. An increase in accounts receivable may have been a result of a larger sales volume, a change in terms granted customers, or ineffectiveness of the collection department.

Comparative data—charts

Comparative information selected from financial statements may be shown graphically. The old saying, "a picture tells more than a thousand words," has significance in analyzing and presenting financial and operating data. By studying charted data, the analyst may obtain an idea of changes that have taken place in dollar amounts. That is, in comparison with reading a table of figures, a chart is much more meaningful since variations in dollar amounts are more noticeable.

Charts may be used in the original analysis in an attempt first to determine key variables and second to provide clues to their significant relationships. Charts may also be used in presenting the results of special studies or in reviewing and interpreting regular financial and operating reports.

Illustration 8–2 shows in bar chart form selected financial data for the Collins Department Stores as of December 31, 1970 and 1971. Although both the current assets and current liabilities were reduced, the current liabilities decreased at a more rapid rate and consequently the current financial position improved during 1971. The chart also reveals that total liabilities decreased and owners' equity increased. This is a favorable tendency because there was less dependence on financing from outside sources. The margin of safety for creditors has improved. The chart also shows the relationship between the sources of funds invested in total assets. The strengthening of the financial position during 1971 is reflected by the fact that total liabilities represented a smaller proportionate part of the total liabilities and owners' equity.

ILLUSTRATION 8–2

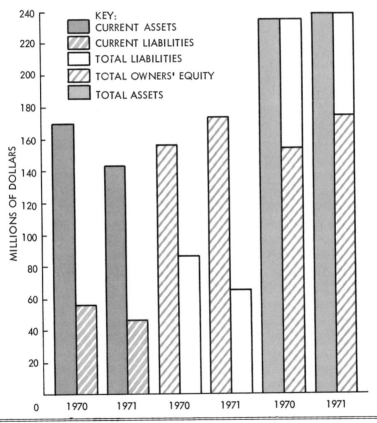

COLLINS DEPARTMENT STORES
Selected Balance Sheet Data
As of December 31, 1970 and 1971

| Items | Year | | Increase (decrease*) during 1971 | |
	1970 (000s)	1971 (000s)	Amount	% Change
Current assets	$169,335	$146,340	$22,995*	13.6*
Current liabilities	55,919	45,752	10,167*	18.2*
Total liabilities	84,059	67,082	16,977*	20.2*
Total owners' equity	153,545	171,605	18,060	11.8
Total assets	237,604	238,687	1,083	.5

QUESTIONS AND PROBLEMS

8–1. Company A had the following items on its balance sheet as of December 31:

	1970	1971
Marketable securities		$ 1,560
Cash . . . . . . :	$ 5,632	435*
Mortgage note payable	15,000	
Unappropriated retained earnings	25,770†	10,432

    * Overdraft.
    † Deficit.

Is it possible to compute percentage changes in the foregoing items? If not, what do you suggest?

8–2. Comment on the following statements:

a) An increase in dollar sales should always be viewed favorably.

b) The influence of price-level changes cannot be detected by using a comparative statement.

c) An expansion of plant, property, and equipment should be financed by sales of capital stock.

d) Intangible assets should be eliminated when the balance sheet is reconstructed for analytical purposes.

e) An increase in liabilities should be viewed with alarm.

8–3. The AICPA[10] states that:

"The presentation of comparative financial statements in annual and other reports enhances the usefulness of such reports and brings out more clearly the nature and trends of current changes affecting the enterprise. Such presentation emphasizes the fact that statements for a series of periods are far more significant than those for a single period and the accounts for one period are but an installment of what is essentially a continuous history." Discuss.

8–4. Give brief answers to the following questions:

a) When the analyst has available the percentage changes in financial statement items, would he also require the absolute data?

b) Inasmuch as the fixed assets are usually stated at "cost less depreciation" rather than at realizable values, are the values of importance in an analysis?

c) Is the analyst more interested in absolute changes in financial statement data than in percentage changes? Explain.

d) What is the significance from the point of view of statement analysis of extraordinary items shown on the income statement?

e) What treatment should be given to intangible assets in analyzing financial statements?

---

[10] *Accounting Research and Terminology Bulletins, Final Edition* (New York, 1961), p. 15.

8–5. It is better to compare financial statements of a company for succeeding years, or financial statements of two companies for the same year?

8–6. List five analytical methods and techniques used in analyzing financial statements.

8–7. The York Department Store was organized during the year 1942. The classification of accounts, the statement forms, and records have remained unchanged since that time. The company undertook an extensive expansion program during 1968 and completed its plan during 1971. The company presents below its comparative statements for 1968 and 1971 and requests you to:

a) Reconstruct the statements using the most commonly accepted terminology and classification.

b) Show dollar and percentage changes in the amounts for 1971 in comparison with 1968.

c) List and discuss favorable and unfavorable financial and operating tendencies.

YORK DEPARTMENT STORE
Comparative Balance Sheet
As of December 31, 1968 and 1971
(in thousands)

	December 31 1968	December 31 1971
Assets		
Current Assets:		
Cash.	$ 80.6	$ 210.7
Marketable securities.	75.3	100.2
Treasury stock at cost	50.0	88.5
Notes receivable	30.8	41.3
Accounts receivable	100.7	350.8
Merchandise inventory.	200.0	310.0
Accrued receivables.	5.6	7.1
Total Current Assets	$543.0	$1,108.6
Long-term investments.	$175.0	$ 75.0
Fixed Assets:		
Property, plant, and equipment.	$210.5	$ 388.6
Intangible assets	18.5	25.4
Total Fixed Assets.	$229.0	$ 414.0
Prepaid expenses.	$ 10.7	$ 19.1
Total Assets	$957.7	$1,616.7
Liabilities, Reserves, and Net Worth		
Current liabilities	$238.6	$ 340.8
Unearned income	9.5	13.9
Premium on bonds payable	9.8	9.8
Bonds payable	150.0	60.0
Total Liabilities.	$407.9	$ 424.5

(continued)

	December 31	
Liabilities, Reserves, and Net Worth	1968	1971
Reserves for:		
Bad debts	$ 3.4	$ 13.7
Decline in price of marketable securities	4.2	4.2
Depreciation	85.6	170.0
Federal income taxes payable	48.7	169.8
Future decline of inventory	6.2	8.7
General contingencies	45.0	45.0
Guarantee of product and services	25.0	50.0
Notes receivable discounted	9.8	13.6
Pensions	30.0	42.8
Plant replacement	20.0	105.0
Sales discounts	4.0	5.7
Sales returns and allowances	9.1	12.3
War loss (1943)	95.5	95.5
Total Reserves	$386.5	$ 736.3
Net Worth:		
Capital stock, common	$100.0	$ 240.0
Capital stock, preferred	120.0	95.0
Earned surplus (deficit*)	130.0*	25.9
Stock dividends payable (common)		60.0
Capital surplus	15.0	15.0
Appraisal surplus	58.3	20.0
Total Owners' Equity	$163.3	$ 455.9
Total Liabilities, Reserves, and Net Worth	$957.7	$1,616.7

YORK DEPARTMENT STORE
Comparative Profit and Loss Statement
For the Years 1968 and 1971

	1968	1971
Sales	$1,980.8	$2,610.3
Less: Sales returns and allowances	70.6	138.9
Net sales	$1,910.2	$2,471.4
Cost of sales, selling, and administrative expenses (exclusive of items shown below)	$1,610.2	$1,999.8
Depreciation and amortization	28.0	54.2
Maintenance and repairs	14.1	33.3
Rent expense	24.6	33.1
Taxes (exclusive of federal income taxes)	20.2	31.5
Other revenue (additions)	(18.3)	(35.4)
Interest and other fixed charges	25.0	35.0
Federal income taxes	48.2	170.8
Gain on sale of long-term securities (credit)	(29.7)	(180.0)
Revenue and expense on long-term investments (net credit)	(36.7)	(70.3)
Total Costs (Income and Gain Deducted)	$1,685.6	$2,072.0
Net Profit	$ 224.6	$ 399.4

8–8.

FIELD MANUFACTURING CORPORATION
Balance Sheet Data
December 31, 1970 and 1971
(manufacturers of glass and glassware)

	December 31		Increase (decrease*) during 1971	
	1970	1971	($)	(%)
Assets				
Current·Assets:				
Cash.	$ 26,472	$ 32,883	6,411	24.2
Time deposits	5,129	6,310	1,181	23.0
Marketable securities.	18,874	26,074	7,200	38.1
Notes receivable	488	13	475*	97.3*
Accounts receivable (net).	19,536	23,145	3,609	18.5
Inventories	50,104	51,714	1,610	3.2
Other current assets	2,412	2,260	152*	6.3*
Prepaid expenses	2,966	2,727	239*	8.1*
Total Current Assets	$125,981	$145,126	19,145	15.2
Land, plant, and equipment (net).	153,037	147,057	5,980*	3.9*
Intangibles	15,055	14,773	282*	1.9*
Long-term investments	16,128	16,444	316	2.0
Total Assets.	$310,201	$323,400	13,199	4.3
Liabilities				
Current Liabilities:				
Accounts payable.	$ 6,223	$ 8,140	1,917	30.8
Notes payable	453	503	50	11.0
Accrued payables, including income taxes	12,151	17,405	5,254	43.2
Unearned revenue.	463	464	1	
Total Current Liabilities	$ 19,290	$ 26,512	7,222	37.4
Long-term liabilities	14,260	11,192	3,068*	21.5*
Total Liabilities	$ 33,550	$ 37,704	4,154	12.4
Owners' Equity				
Capital stock	$149,504	$149,806	302	.2
Retained earnings†	127,147	135,890	8,743	6.9
Total Owners' Equity.	$276,651	$285,696	9,045	3.3
Total Liabilities and Owners' Equity.	$310,201	$323,400		
† Entries in retained earnings:				
Net income after federal income taxes . .	$38,715	$36,343	2,372*	6.1*
Dividends declared	32,600	27,600	5,000	15.3*

a)   Analyze the foregoing data and point out favorable and unfavorable financial tendencies.

b)   Should the analyst have available data from the income statement?

8–9.   After analyzing and interpreting the following statements, present a written report on favorable and unfavorable financial and operating tendencies.

KOHL DEPARTMENT STORE
Comparative Statement of Financial Condition
As of July 31, 1970 and 1971
(in thousands)

	July 31 1970	July 31 1971	Increase (decrease*) during 1971 $	Increase (decrease*) during 1971 %
Assets				
Current Assets:				
Cash..............................	$ 7,699	$ 9,077	1,378	17.9
U.S. government obligations...............	10,537	5,126	5,411*	51.4*
Receivables—trade......................				
Regular accounts.....................	10,960	10,051	909*	8.3*
Installment accounts..................	16,034	7,892	8,142*	50.8*
Merchandise inventory..................	24,839	25,357	518	2.1
Prepaid expenses......................	2,344	2,487	143	6.1
Other current assets...................	2,372	2,389	17	.7
Total Current Assets.................	$ 74,785	$ 62,379	12,406*	16.6*
Fixed Assets:				
Land, buildings, leaseholds, fixtures, and equipment........................	$ 60,805	$ 77,182	16,377	26.9
Less: Accumulated depreciation and amortization	21,611	20,574	1,037	4.8
Total Fixed Assets..................	$ 39,194	$ 56,608	17,414	44.4
Leases, copyrights, trademarks, goodwill, and other similar assets—at cost	$ 2,692	$ 2,692		
Less: Accumulation of amortization	403	484	81	20.1
	$ 2,289	$ 2,208	81*	3.5*
Other Assets:				
Overpayment of federal taxes on income for years ended January, 1964.............	$ 6,916	$ 6,916		
Miscellaneous investments at cost...........	2,001	1,799	202*	10.1*
Unamortized debt expense................	437	420	17*	3.9*
Total Other Assets..................	$ 9,354	$ 9,135	219*	2.3*
Total Assets.....................	$125,622	$130,330	4,708	3.7
Liabilities and Owners' Equity				
Current Liabilities:				
Accounts payable......................	$ 15,369	$ 13,261	2,108*	13.7*
Accrued liabilities......................	4,261	6,282	2,021	47.4
Estimated federal taxes payable	8,244	8,259	15	.2
Other current liabilities	13,068	2,000	11,068*	84.7*
Total Current Liabilities	$ 40,942	$ 29,802	11,140*	27.2*
Long-Term Liabilities:				
Twenty-five-year, 3% sinking fund debentures, amortization beginning 1968	$ 20,000	$ 20,000		
Notes payable, maturing semiannually	9,500	16,000	6,500	68.4
Total Long-Term Liabilities.............	$ 29,500	$ 36,000	6,500	22.0
Total Liabilities	$ 70,442	$ 65,802	4,640*	6.6*
Owners' Equity:				
Preferred stock, 4¼%, cumulative, $100 par value per share......................	$ 16,560	$ 16,560		
Common stock, stated value $25 per share......	25,790	25,790		
Additional paid-in capital.................	10,373	10,373		
Total Capital	$ 52,723	$ 52,723		
Retained earnings......................	2,457	11,805	9,348	380.5
Total Owners' Equity.................	$ 55,180	$ 64,528	9,348	16.9
Total Liabilities and Owners' Equity......	$125,622	$130,330	4,708	3.7

[1] Dividend declaration and net income entries were made in this account during the two years.

KOHL DEPARTMENT STORE
Comparative Income Statement
Years Ended July 31, 1970 and 1971
(in thousands)

	1970	1971	Increase (decrease*) during 1971 ($)	Increase (decrease*) during 1971 (%)
Net retail sales (including leased departments).........	$315,035	$308,119	6,916*	2.2*
Less: Cost of Sales and Operating Expenses:				
Cost of sales, buying, publicity, selling, occupancy, and administrative expenses.......	$289,444	$283,649	5,795*	2.0*
Taxes (other than federal income tax)......	4,123	4,217	94	2.3
Maintenance and repairs......	3,603	3,410	193*	5.4*
Rent expense less rent income......	2,839	3,374	535	18.8
Depreciation and amortization......	2,154	2,568	414	19.2
Total Cost of Sales and Operating Expenses......	$302,163	$297,218	4,945*	1.6*
Operating income......	$ 12,872	$ 10,901	1,971*	15.3*
Other expense:				
Interest and debt expense......	542	969	427	78.8
Income for the year before federal income taxes......	$ 12,330	$ 9,932	2,398*	19.4*
Federal income taxes......	5,400	4,186	1,214*	22.5*
Net income after federal income taxes......	$ 6,930	$ 5,746	1,184*	17.1*
Additions to Net Income:				
Income from nontrading sources......	$ 1,119	$ 888	231*	20.6*
Income from sales of property......	696	4,200	3,504	503.4
Total Additions......	$ 1,815	$ 5,088	3,273	180.3
	$ 8,745	$ 10,834		
Deduction from net income:				
Provision for federal income taxes for years prior to 1970......	500			
Net Income Transferred to Retained Earnings......	$ 8,245	$ 10,834	2,589	31.4

9

Trend percentages

Financial statements for a number of dates or years may be analyzed by determining and studying the trends of the data shown on the statements. This method of analysis is one of direction—upward or downward—and involves the computation of the percentage relationship that each statement item bears to the same item in the "base year," which may be the earliest year involved in the comparison, the latest year, or any intervening year. Generally, the first year is selected as the base year unless the amounts for that year are clearly not typical of those that follow. Trend percentages or relatives to the base year (see Illustration 9–1) emphasize changes in the financial and operating data between specific dates or period and make possible a horizontal analysis and study of comparative financial statement data. The analyst compares the trends of related financial and operating data in forming an opinion as to whether favorable or unfavorable tendencies are reflected by the data. The data may reflect conditions existing during a war period, postwar reconversion, recession, depression, or recovery.

Trend percentages—computation

Trend percentages, which may be thought of as index numbers showing relative changes in financial data resulting with the passage of time, are computed as follows (data in the statements in Illustrations 9–1 and 9–2 are usd for illustrative purposes):

ILLUSTRATION 9–1

SNYDER CORPORATION
Comparative Balance Sheet
As of December 31, 1966–71
(dollars in millions)

Items	December 31 1966 ($)	1967 ($)	1968 ($)	1969 ($)	1970 ($)	1971 ($)	Trend percentages Base date: December 31, 1966 = 100% 1967 (%)	1968 (%)	1969 (%)	1970 (%)	1971 (%)
Assets											
Current Assets:											
Cash	15.4	18.2	16.0	14.3	14.5	11.8	118	104	93	94	77
Marketable securities	7.2	5.5	4.4	5.6	6.9	2.7	76	61	78	96	37
Trade receivables, net	30.3	29.7	28.8	25.1	29.4	29.7	98	95	83	97	98
Inventories (Fifo)	39.4	37.4	35.9	36.2	42.6	41.8	95	91	92	108	106
Other current assets	1.8	.5	.5	4.4	2.6	.6					
Total Current Assets*	94.1	91.3	88.5	85.6	96.0	86.6	97	94	91	102	92
Long-term investments	1.2	4.9	5.3	6.8	1.3	11.6	408	442	567	108	967
Property, plant, and equipment (cost)†	121.6	141.1	156.9	170.2	187.3	206.7	116	129	140	154	170
Less: Accumulated depreciation and amortization	49.7	58.4	63.4	70.3	72.3	80.9					
Net	71.9	82.7	93.5	99.9	115.0	125.8	115	130	139	160	175
Total Assets	167.2	178.9	187.3	192.3	212.3	224.0	107	112	115	127	134
Liabilities and Owners' Equity											
Current liabilities	35.0	38.2	31.5	28.7	34.0	29.4	109	90	82	97	84
Long-term liabilities	22.4	22.0	21.1	20.2	19.3	18.1	98	94	90	86	81
Total Liabilities	57.4	60.2	52.6	48.9	53.3	47.5	105	92	85	93	83
Owners' Equity:											
Preferred stock	16.3	16.3	16.3	16.3	16.3	16.3	100	100	100	100	100
Common stock	22.5	28.8	32.0	38.0	50.0	52.9	128	142	169	222	235
Total Capital Stock	38.8	45.1	48.3	54.3	66.3	69.2	116	124	140	171	178
Capital paid-in excess of par value	42.7	46.1	47.8	52.1	57.2	58.9	108	112	122	134	138
Retained earnings	28.3	27.5	38.6	37.0	35.5	48.4	97	136	131	125	171
Total Owners' Equity	109.8	118.7	134.7	143.4	159.0	176.5	108	123	131	145	161
Total Liabilities and Owners' Equity	167.2	178.9	187.3	192.3	212.3	224.0	107	112	115	127	134

* Working capital (current assets less current liabilities)............ 59.1 53.1 57.0 56.9 62.0 57.2
† Current year capital expenditures............ 14.2 22.3 16.8 14.1 21.3 25.6

ILLUSTRATION 9–2

SNYDER CORPORATION
Comparative Income Statement
For the Years Ended December 31, 1966–71
(dollars in millions)

Items	Amounts						Trend percentages base year, 1966 = 100%				
	1966 ($)	1967 ($)	1968 ($)	1969 ($)	1970 ($)	1971 ($)	1967 (%)	1968 (%)	1969 (%)	1970 (%)	1971 (%)
Net sales	252.8	245.2	247.7	255.3	298.3	303.4	97	98	101	118	120
Less: Costs and expenses (depreciation and amortization not distributed):											
Cost of goods sold	173.1	169.6	174.8	171.4	195.6	204.3	98	101	99	113	118
Selling and administrative expenses	41.4	41.0	43.9	43.1	46.4	50.9	99	106	104	112	123
Depreciation and amortization expense	8.4	8.7	9.7	10.2	11.9	12.4	104	115	121	142	148
Total Costs and Expenses	222.9	219.3	228.4	224.7	253.9	267.6	98	102	101	114	120
Operating income	29.9	25.9	19.3	30.6	44.4	35.8	87	65	102	148	120
Add: Other revenue and other expenses, net	1.8	1.9	3.3	.9	1.2	1.1					
Income before federal income taxes	31.7	27.8	22.6	31.5	45.6	36.9	88	71	99	144	116
Federal income taxes	15.2	14.2	10.3	14.7	22.0	17.6	93	68	97	145	116
Net Income before Extraordinary Items	16.5	13.6	12.3	16.8	23.6	19.3	82	75	102	143	117

1.   In the statement that is to be used as the base, state the amount of each item as 100 percent. If the amount of an item in another statement is less than that in the base statement, the trend percentage will be below 100 percent; if the amount is more than the base amount, the trend percentage will be above 100 percent.

2.   Compute trend ratios, as illustrated below and on page 224 by dividing each amount in the statements by the corresponding item in the base statement. In determining the trend percentages, fractions of a percent may be disregarded or rounded; for example, 125.5 percent may be stated as 126 percent, and 125.4 percent may be stated as 125 percent. This rounding is justified because the financial statement items do not reflect precise measurements and the potential variations are greater than the fractional amounts eliminated.

$$\frac{\text{Ending inventories (1969), \$36,200,000}}{\text{Ending inventories (1966), \$39,400,000}} = 92\% \ldots$$

Inventories for December 31, 1969 were 92 percent of the inventories of December 31, 1966; ending inventories for 1969 represented a decrease of 8 percent of the ending inventories for 1966; December 31, 1969 inventories were 8 percent less than those at the close of 1966.

$$\frac{\text{Ending inventories (1970), \$42,600,000}}{\text{Ending inventories (1966), \$39,400,000}} = 108\% \ldots$$

Inventories for December 31, 1970 were 108 percent of the ending inventories for 1966; ending inventories for 1970 represented an increase of 8 percent of the 1966 inventories; ending inventories for 1970 were 8 percent more than those at the close of 1966.

$$\frac{\text{Ending inventories (1971), \$41,800,000}}{\text{Ending inventories (1966), \$39,400,000}} = 106\% \ldots$$

Inventories for December 31, 1971 were 106 percent of inventories for December 31, 1966; ending inventories for 1971 represented an increase of 6 percent of the December 31, 1966 inventories; ending inventories for 1971 were 6 percent more than those at the close of 1966.

$$\frac{\text{Sales (1969), \$255,300,000}}{\text{Sales (1966), \$252,800,000}} = 101\% \dots$$

Sales for 1969 were 101 percent of the sales for 1966; it will be observed that the 1969 sales were \$2,500,000 more than the sales for 1966.

$$\frac{\text{Sales (1970), \$298,300,000}}{\text{Sales (1966), \$252,800,000}} = 118\% \dots$$

Sales for 1970 were 118 percent of the sales for 1966; 1970 sales represented an increase of 18 percent of 1966 sales; 1970 sales were 18 percent greater than in 1966.

$$\frac{\text{Sales (1971), \$303,400,000}}{\text{Sales (1966), \$252,800,000}} = 120\% \dots$$

Sales for 1971 were 120 percent of the sales for 1966; 1971 sales represented an increase of 20 percent of 1966 sales; 1971 sales were 20 percent greater than in 1966.

It should be observed by the foregoing computations that the trend ratios for December 31, at the close of 1969, 1970, and 1971, represent percentages of the base statement amounts (for the year or as of December 31, 1966) rather than increases or decreases during the period. They do not indicate the amount of increase unless 100 is deducted from the percentage or the ratio is subtracted from 100. For example, the inventories for December 31, 1969, were 92 percent of the amount for December 31, 1966; the inventories for December 31, 1969, were 8 percent less than for December 31, 1966. The sales for 1971 were 120 percent of the sales for 1966; the sales for 1971 were 20 percent higher than for 1966.

The two comparative statements, i.e., the statements showing (1) increases and decreases in dollars and percentages from year to year and (2) the trend percentages for a number of years, have the same advantage in that they focus attention on year-to-year or date-to-date changes. The same information may be obtained from the trend-ratio statement and the statement showing the increases and decreases in terms of percentages, assuming that the latter contains the same years and the increases and decreases are in relation to the same base year as used for the trends. The trend ratios may be obtained by adding 100 to the percentage increases and decreases. The percentage increases may be determined by subtracting 100 from the trend percentages; percentages decreases may be obtained by deducting the trend percentage from 100. It is advantageous to prepare trend ratios rather than percentage increases and decreases because the former are simpler: it is not necessary (1) to determine the dollar increases and decreases and (2) to reduce these to percentages.

Trend percentages—evaluation

Trend ratios generally are not computed for all of the items on the statements, since the fundamental objective is to make comparisons between items having some logical relationship to one another. Any one trend alone is not informative; however, the comparison of related trends is valuable to the analyst. For example, sales may have increased $100,000, or 100 percent, over a five-year period. This percentage becomes meaningful when it is compared (1) with operating assets, which may have increased 200 percent during the same period; (2) with the cost of goods sold, which may have increased 150 percent; or (3) with operating expenses, which may have increased 170 percent. An upward trend for inventories, notes receivable, and accounts receivable, accompanied by a downward trend for sales, would usually reflect an unfavorable condition. Such a situation would indicate an overinvestment in inventories and receivables which may be results of inefficient inventory acquisition and control policies and ineffectiveness of the credit and collection department. A continued downward trend of sales volume, accompanied by a marked increase in plant investment, especially if this increase in plant has been made possible by issuing fixed interest obligations, would represent an unhealthy financial development. Such a condition would reflect an overinvestment in plant facilities, i.e., an excess capacity in relation to current sales prospects. An increase in the trend of total current assets, accompanied by a downward trend of current liabilities, would usually be viewed favorably if the changes reflected a greater liquidity of the former.

An upward trend of owners' equity would usually be considered with favor especially so if there is a downward trend or an upward trend at a much slower rate for total liabilities. Such a situation would reveal a growing financial strength and a greater margin of safety for creditors.

It should always be remembered that although trend ratios show whether an item has increased or decreased as well as the degree of change, they are valuable only to the extent to which they give clues to favorable or unfavorable tendencies and point the way to further analysis. In other words, a comparison of the trends of one activity as a group of related activities reveals facts as to growth or shrinkage in volume, variations in products, changes in the relationship between costs and expenses, and sales revenue.

The comparability of trend ratios is adversely affected to the extent to which accounting principles and policies reflected by the accounts have not been followed consistently throughout the period being studied. Comparability of the data is also adversely affected when the price level has changed materially during the years under review.[1] For example, if the price level increased 25 percent, the dollar sales for 1966 and 1971 would not be comparable unless the influence of the price-level change has been eliminated. Some analysts adjust the statement data, dividing the dollar amounts by a related price index, thereby providing figures that will give a rough picture of changes in physical quantity and volume exclusive of price changes. Analysts having access to the books can use unit sales data.

It is important to consider all trend percentages in connection with the absolute data on which they are based. For example:

1. The selected base year may not be typical or representative of some of the items on the statements. The amount of cash shown for the base statement might be $4,475,682 and all subsequent amounts less than $2,000,000. The base statement amount is not typical of the other amounts, and, therefore, subsequent variations in percentage form might give evidence of extreme conditions which did not actually exist.

2. One item may increase from $10 to $20 and another from $50,000 to $100,000. In each case a 100 percent increase has taken place, although the first-mentioned increase is insignificant.

3. Undue emphasis might be given to a 100 percent change as compared with a 10 percent variation. Prepaid expenses may have increased 100 percent while inventory increased only 10 percent. Obviously, in most instances the inventory dollar variation would require more detailed attention than the change in prepaid expenses. In the foregoing instance the major increase percentagewise is insignificant from a dollar standpoint.

4. An undesirable tendency may be reflected by the trend ratios but not actually evidenced by the dollar data. Long-term liabilities and owners' equity may have increased 100 percent and 50 percent, respectively. However, the dollar increase in long-term liabilities may have been from $10,000 to $20,000 and in owners' equity from $120,000 to $180,000. In instances like the foregoing, in order to avoid an exaggerated idea that might be given by the percentage change, it is necessary to study the dollar variations as well as the relationship of the items after changes have taken place before finally deciding whether favorable or unfavorable tendencies are present. Such relationships are discussed in later chapters.

---

[1] For financial analysis using data adjusted for changes in the general price level, see Part III.

Interpretation of trends—Snyder Corporation

As indicated above, trend-percentage analysis is most valuable when various related trends for a number of years are compared and interpreted. In order to give additional explanation of this method of analysis, the dollar and trend data for the Snyder Corporation, producers of building materials and supplies, are presented (Illustrations 9–1 and 9–2). The following favorable and unfavorable tendencies may be noted:

1. The current financial condition of the Snyder Corporation has improved, as reflected by the relationship between the current assets and current liabilities; although both of these items have decreased during the six-year period, the current liabilities declined at a more rapid rate. Current assets declined from $94.1 million to $86.6 million, or 8 percent; current liabilities declined from $35.0 million to $29.4 million, or 16 percent. The improvement in the current financial condition is also indicated by the fact that the current assets were 2.69 times the current liabilities as of December 31, 1966 and 2.94 times at the most recent date.

The trend data reveal that declines took place in cash, marketable securities, trade receivables, and total current liabilities. The decline in trade receivables from $30.3 million to $29.7 million, or 2 percent, and the increase in inventories from $39.4 million to $41.8 million, or 6 percent, is favorable because net sales increased from $252.8 million to $303.4 million, or 20 percent. This favorable tendency indicates that more effective credit, collection, and merchandising policies have been established and made effective. The relatively smaller amounts of trade receivables reflect more rapid turnover of customer accounts and possibly a large increase in cash sales. A change in credit terms may have resulted in the more favorable collection experience. Assuming that the inventories are typical of the year's average, the turnover of the inventories has improved during the six-year period.[2] It should be observed that working capital decreased from $59.1 million to $57.2 million during the period under review, while the sales increased from $252.8 million to $303.4 million. These trends in different directions reflect on balance an increasing efficiency of working capital management.

2. Property, plant, and equipment, net (fixed assets), new construc-

---

[2] The assumption that the inventory at the end of the year is typical of the inventory throughout the year may well be unsound. Most businesses are subject to seasonal variation; the inventory varies in size at different seasons of the year. This may be due to variations in monthly sales volume or, in a manufacturing concern, to the production-scheduling policy. Nor will an average of inventories at the beginning and end of the year necessarily give a more satisfactory result; after all, the beginning and end of a year fall in the same season. An average of monthly or quarterly balances, if available, is preferable. This average should be computed by taking the average of the inventories at the beginning and end of the year, averaging the result with the remaining (monthly or quarterly) amounts.

tion or acquisitions, increased from $71.9 million to $125.8 million, or 75 percent, from December 31, 1966 through December 31, 1971; during the same period, net sales increased from $252.8 million to $303.4 million, or 20 percent. The evaluation of the increase in property, plant, and equipment in relation to the improvement in sales is difficult if not impossible with the limited data available. The new acquisitions or construction may have brought about the reduction in the cost of goods sold. New functions, as well as methods of assembling, may have been introduced. Greater capacity to serve a larger number of customers has in all probability been acquired. The increase in sales dollar volume may be the result of an increase in the price level, greater sales promotional programs, more efficient and effective salesmanship, and an increase in productive facilities to serve a larger number of customers. The trend of physical volume of sales should be studied.

The sources of working capital used for the expansion of the property, plant, and equipment during the period under review included the proceeds from common stock sales and net working capital derived from current operations. In fact, a portion of the foregoing funds was also used to acquire additional long-term investments and to reduce both current and long-term liabilities.

A comparison of dollars (in millions) and trend data for Snyder Corporation's annual capital expenditures and depreciation and amortization charges is given below:

Items	1966	1967	1968	1969	1970	197
Capital expenditure. . . . . ($)	14.2	22.3	16.8	14.1	21.3	25.
Trend. . . . . (%)	100	157	118	99	150	180
Depreciation and amortization charges . . . . ($)	8.4	8.7	9.7	10.2	11.9	12.
Trend. . . . . (%)	100	104	115	121	142	148

The foregoing data show that working capital derived from current operations in the amount of the depreciation charges was used in acquiring new assets. The balance of the capital needed for the new assets in excess of the depreciation dollar recovery was obtained from the sale of capital stock and the net income.

3. A comparison of the trends for total liabilities and owners' equity reveal that the former declined and the latter increased. Total liabilities declined from $57.4 million to $47.5 million, or 17 percent, while owners' equity increased from $109.8 million to $176.5 million, or 61 percent. As a result of these variations the creditors' margin of safety has been increased substantially. As of December 31, 1971, owners' equity was over 3.7 times the total liabilities. The trends also clearly indicate that

the asset expansion and liability reduction has been accomplished through owners' equity.

The trend of the dividends appears to be justifiable from the points of view of the cash position, current earnings, and the status of the retained earnings. It will be noted that stock dividends are combined with regular cash dividends as reflected by the statement of retained earnings, Illustration 9–3. (The amount of each type of dividend should

ILLUSTRATION 9–3

SNYDER CORPORATION
Comparative Statement of Retained Earnings
For the Years Ended December 31, 1966–71
(in millions)

Items	1966 ($)	1967 ($)	1968 ($)	1969 ($)	1970 ($)	1971 ($)
Balance, January 1	17.9	28.3	27.5	36.6	37.0	35.5
Add: Net income	16.5	13.6	12.3	16.8	23.6	19.3
Extraordinary gain			3.8		3.0	3.5
	34.4	41.9	43.6	53.4	63.6	58.3
Deduct: Dividends (including stock dividend)	6.1	12.5	7.0	14.1	19.2	9.9
Extraordinary losses*		1.9		2.3	7.9	
	6.1	14.4	7.0	16.4	27.1	9.9
Balance, December 31	28.3	27.5	36.6	37.0	36.5	48.4

* Losses are result of fires and disposal of property.

be disclosed.) The net income exclusive of extraordinary items for the six years amounted to $102.1 million; dividends in the amount of $68.8 million of retained earnings were declared. Of the net income, 67.4 percent was used for dividend purposes.

4. It will be observed that the trends for sales and cost of goods sold and operating expenses increased at approximately the same rate. Sales increased 20 percent, while total costs and expenses also increased 20 percent. These data reflect a favorable situation from the point of view of managerial ability to control costs and expenses relative to changes in sales volume. Operating income increased 20 percent, a change which was the same as the increase in sales. The less favorable trend of operating income may be a result of one or a combination of factors similar to the following: increase in retail prices accompanied by a greater proportionate advance in cost of goods purchased, less rapid turnover of inventory accompanied by a less favorable markup, more special sales at unprofitable prices, a lower proportion of higher-margin sales, and less favorable purchases.

An unfavorable tendency is reflected by the fact that the trends for operating expenses increased at a greater rate than the net sales. Generally, selling expenses increase in about the same proportion as net sales; general and administrative expenses remain somewhat constant or increase more slowly.

5. Unfavorable tendencies are reflected by the extraordinary losses included in the statement of retained earnings, Illustration 9–3. These data may reveal an ineffective fire insurance plan and an adequate depreciation policy. These properties may not have been properly maintained, which necessitated replacement sooner than anticipated when the depreciation policy was established.

QUESTIONS AND PROBLEMS

9–1. Discuss or give a brief answer to the following statements or questions:
  a) Should the analyst compute trend percentages for all items on the financial statements?
  b) Should the analyst have available trend percentages for tonnage or physical volume of business?
  c) What year should be selected as the base for computing trends?
  d) Is the trend of total liabilities of significance in analyzing the financial condition of a business? If so, what other trends should be used in connection therewith?
  e) Should the analyst obtain trend percentages of price levels?

9–2. Discuss the following statements:
  a) Trend ratios show whether an item has increased or decreased and the rate of increase or decrease; they do not reveal whether the change is favorable or unfavorable.
  b) Trend percentages for an industry would be of value in analyzing financial and operating data for a particular company.
  c) The analyst should study footnotes to the financial statements in connection with trend percentages.

9–3. With reference to trend ratios, suggest related data which should be studied in connection with each of the following items:

  Current assets
  Total assets
  Long-term liabilities
  Sales
  Selling expenses
  Net income

9–4. Comment on the following statements:
  a) The trend percentages should be computed for all items on the financial statements.
  b) Trend percentages are more useful than the absolute data which they measure.
  c) One of the major problems of a trend percentage study is the selection of the base year.
  d) Inefficiency of management is difficult to detect by trend percentages.

9–5. Study the following trend percentages together with the dollar amounts and indicate whether or not illogical conclusions might result if the trends are used without reference to the dollar data. Explain.

		1967	1968	1969	1970	1971
Cash	($000)	984	287	260	271	256
Trend	(%)	100	29	26	28	26
Notes receivable	($000)	1	1	2	1	2
Trend	(%)	100	100	200	100	200
Merchandise inventory	($000)	410	500	600	730	820
Trend	(%)	100	122	146	178	200

9–6. Should the analyst compute the trend percentages for federal income taxes? Explain.

9–7. *Required:*

a) Prepare comparative financial statements for the Ellis Company, manufacturers of office equipment.

b) Compute trend percentages for the major items.

c) Write a report evaluating the current and long-term financial condition and operating results of the company.

ELLIS COMPANY
Balance Sheet Data
As of June 30
(in thousands)

	1967	1968	1969	1970	1971
Assets					
Cash	$ 1,000	$ 1,200	$ 400	$ 350	$ 320
Marketable securities	1,550	1,110	200	180	170
Receivables (net)	1,300	1,750	2,120	2,680	3,785
Inventories	3,500	4,710	6,950	7,690	7,810
Prepaid expenses	10	12	13	10	6
Property, plant, and equipment, net	6,810	6,980	9,550	9,465	10,100
Long-term investments	500	510	1,010	1,200	1,250
Intangibles	10	10	225	240	250
Deferred charges	750	775	910	900	900
Total Assets	$15,430	$17,057	$21,378	$22,715	$24,591
Liabilities and Owners' Equity					
Trade payables	$ 2,010	$ 2,180	$ 3,210	$ 3,400	$ 3,750
Other current liabilities	990	1,010	2,050	2,140	2,420
Long-term liabilities	5,800	5,800	7,000	7,000	7,000
Preferred stock	800	800	2,600	3,000	4,800
Common stock	4,000	4,000	4,000	4,000	4,000
Premium on stock	810	810	280	300	300
Reserve for sinking fund	215	275	275	300	300
Appraisal surplus	55	55	260	260	260
Retained earnings	750	2,127	1,703	2,315	1,761
Total Liabilities and Owners' Equity	$15,430	$17,057	$21,378	$22,715	$24,591

ELLIS COMPANY
Income Statement Data
Years Ended June 30, 1967–71
(in thousands)

	1967	1968	1969	1970	1971
Sales	$10,200	$15,615	$16,895	$10,562	$ 9,980
Cost of goods sold	6,670	8,765	9,810	7,561	6,782
Maintenance and repairs	470	685	830	504	480
Depreciation.	385	380	489	489	510
Taxes, including federal income taxes	270	510	850	416	390
Uncollectible receivables expense.	40	55	65	47	38
Selling, general, and administrative expenses	1,846	3,810	3,950	1,965	2,125
Other revenue, including extraordinary items.	270	280	909	1,450	280
Other expense, including extraordinary items.	289	290	300	235	1,041

Retained Earnings Data for the Years
(in thousands)

	1967	1968	1969	1970	1971
Refund of federal income tax		$ 85			$ 800
Net income (loss*)	$ 500	1,400	$ 1,510	$ 795	1,106*
Dividends declared	48	48	138	158	248
Appropriation of retained earnings		60		25	
Accumulated depreciation (credit).			1,796		

9–8.   The accompanying financial statement dollar and trend percentage data were presented by the Steel Products Corporation. The company requests you to analyze the data supplied and interpret the changes that have taken place in the current and long-term financial status and in the operating results.

STEEL PRODUCTS CORPORATION
Financial Statement Data
As of, or for the Years Ended, December 31, 1968–71
(dollar amounts in thousands)

	1968 ($)	1969 ($)	1969 (%)*	1970 ($)	1970 (%)*	1971 ($)	1971 (%)*
Balance Sheet Data (as of December 31)							
Cash	2,600	4,555	175	1,859	71	1,878	72
Receivables—net (trade)	4,637	3,687	80	5,829	126	5,930	128
Inventory	14,904	16,183	109	20,460	137	20,790	139
Other current assets	1,215	1,011		980		992	
Total Current Assets	23,356	25,436	109	29,128	125	29,590	127
Long-term investments	423	660		1,080		2,165	
Property, plant, and equipment—net	8,200	9,915	121	15,825	193	20,910	255
Other noncurrent assets (exclusive of intangible assets)	125	151		243		123	
Total Assets	32,104	36,162	113	46,276	144	52,788	164
Current liabilities	11,823	12,913	109	14,237	120	14,153	120
Long-term debt (5%)†	4,750	5,234	110	8,821	186	10,011	211
Total Liabilities	16,573	18,147	109	23,058	139	24,164	146
Capital stock (common) 791,500 shares of $10 stated value	7,915	7,915		7,915		7,915	
Retained earnings	7,616	10,100	133	15,303	201	20,709	272
Total Owners' Equity	15,531	18,015	116	23,218	150	28,624	184
Total Liabilities and Owners' Equity	32,104	36,162	113	46,276	144	52,788	164
Income Statement Data (for the Year)							
Net sales	57,783	60,703	105	75,298	130	55,086	95
Cost of goods sold	47,705	52,055	109	65,890	138	47,190	99
Gross margin on sales	10,078	8,648	86	9,408	93	7,896	78
Operating expenses	4,185	4,814	115	5,275	126	5,731	137
Operating income	5,893	3,834	65	4,133	70	2,165	37
Other items (net deduction)	160	212		203		226	
Income before federal income taxes	5,733	3,622	63	3,930	69	1,939	34
Federal income taxes for the year	2,300	1,511	66	1,542	67	842	37
Net income after federal income taxes	3,433	2,111	61	2,388	70	1,097	32
Extraordinary items, net addition	102	1,560		4,002		5,496	
Net Income Transferred to Retained Earnings	3,535	3,671	104	6,390	181	6,593	187
Retained Earnings Data (for the Year)							
Dividends Declared	1,187	1,187		1,187		1,187	

* Balance sheet amounts for December 31, 1968 and income statement items for the year 1968 equal 100 %.

† Principal increased on, and interest paid, January 2.

10

Common-size statements

THE METHODS of analyzing financial statements as presented in the preceding chapters have, in general, one common shortcoming—the inability of the analyst to comprehend or visualize, except casually, the dollar changes in individual items that have taken place from year to year in relation to the total assets, total liabilities and owners' equity, or total net sales. This criticism is particularly true when a comparison is being made of two or more companies, or of one company with the statements for an entire industry, since there exists no common base for comparison when dealing with absolute figures. However, if the balance sheet and income statement data are shown in analytical percentages—i.e., percentages of total assets, total liabilities and owners' equity, and total net sales—a common base for comparison is supplied. The statements in this form are designated as "common-size statements."

Common-size statements—computation and evaluation

Common-size statements (examples are shown in Illustrations 10–1 and 10–2) are often called "component percentage" or "100 percent" statements because each statement is reduced to the total of 100 and each individual item is stated as a percentage of the total of 100. Each percentage shows the relation of the individual item to its respective total. Therefore, the common-size percentage (analytical) method represents a type of ratio analysis because each individual item on a statement is expressed as a percentage of the total. The common-size statements

Comparative Balance Sheet, Including Common-Size Percentages
As of December 31, 1970–71
(dollars in thousands)

Items	Amounts, December 31						Common-size percentages December 31					
	1966 ($000)	1967 ($000)	1968 ($000)	1969 ($000)	1970 ($000)	1971 ($000)	1966 (%)	1967 (%)	1968 (%)	1969 (%)	1970 (%)	1971 (%)
Assets												
Current Assets:												
Cash	62.1	28.2	58.6	59.0	74.2	83.4	6.1	2.6	4.3	4.0	4.7	5.2
Marketable securities	33.7	105.1	39.6	39.8	39.5	44.9	3.4	9.7	2.9	2.7	2.5	2.8
Trade receivables, net	263.1	261.1	203.3	230.3	269.9	291.9	25.7	24.1	14.9	15.6	17.1	18.2
Inventory	182.4	197.2	219.6	241.9	268.3	253.4	17.8	18.2	16.1	16.4	17.0	15.8
Other current assets	25.6	60.7	50.5	51.6	52.1	35.2	2.5	5.6	3.7	3.5	3.3	2.2
Total Current Assets	566.9	652.3	571.6	622.6	704.0	708.8	55.5	60.2	41.9	42.2	44.6	44.2
Land, buildings, and equipment, net	433.5	426.9	682.2	690.4	715.1	720.1	42.4	39.4	50.0	46.8	45.3	44.9
Other noncurrent assets	21.6	4.3	110.5	162.3	159.4	174.8	2.1	.4	8.1	11.0	10.1	10.9
Total Assets	1,022.0	1,083.5	1,364.3	1,475.3	1,578.5	1,603.7	100.0	100.0	100.0	100.0	100.0	100.0
Liabilities and Owners' Equity												
Current Liabilities:												
Accounts payable	184.4	187.5	181.4	172.6	151.5	160.4	18.0	17.3	13.3	11.7	9.6	10.0
Notes payable	52.7	56.3	105.1	88.5	61.6	43.3	5.2	5.2	7.7	6.0	3.9	2.7
Other current liabilities	26.3	73.7	19.1	25.1	34.7	28.8	2.6	6.8	1.4	1.7	2.2	1.8
Total Current Liabilities	263.4	317.5	305.6	286.2	247.	232.5	25.8	29.3	22.4	19.4	15.7	14.5
Long-term liabilities (4%)	150.0	162.5	266.0	240.5	228.9	200.5	14.7	15.0	19.5	16.3	14.5	12.5
Total Liabilities	413.4	480.0	571.6	526.7	476.7	433.0	40.5	44.3	41.9	35.7	30.2	27.0
Owners' Equity:												
Capital stock ($100 par) common	400.0	425.0	525.0	620.0	620.0	620.0	39.1	39.2	38.5	42.0	39.3	38.7
Capital paid-in in excess of par value	60.0	70.0	120.0	160.0	160.0	160.0	5.9	6.5	8.8	10.8	10.1	10.0
Retained earnings	148.6	108.5	147.7	168.6	321.8	390.7	14.5	10.0	10.8	11.5	20.4	24.3
Total Owners' Equity	608.6	603.5	792.7	948.6	1,101.8	1,170.7	59.5	55.7	58.1	64.3	69.8	73.0
Total Liabilities and Owners' Equity	1,022.0	1,083.5	1,364.3	1,475.3	1,578.5	1,603.7	100.0	100.0	100.0	100.0	100.0	100.0

ILLUSTRATION 10-2

LYNN-DALE COMPANY

Comparative Income Statement, Including Common-Size Percentages
For the Years Ended December 31, 1966-71
(dollars in thousands)

	($000)						(%)					
	1966	1967	1968	1969	1970	1971	1966	1967	1968	1969	1970	1971
Net sales	812.5	853.7	859.8	1,201.2	1,341.3	1,491.8	100.0	100.0	100.0	100.0	100.0	100.0
Cost of goods sold	598.0	624.1	627.7	861.3	964.4	1,054.7	73.6	73.1	73.0	71.7	71.9	70.7
Gross margin on sales	214.5	229.6	232.1	339.9	376.9	437.1	26.4	26.9	27.0	28.3	28.1	29.3
Operating Expenses:												
Selling expenses	107.2	115.2	116.1	182.6	210.6	253.6	13.2	13.5	13.5	15.2	15.7	17.0
General and administrative expenses	43.9	49.5	54.1	79.2	81.8	92.5	5.4	5.8	6.3	6.6	6.1	6.2
Total Operating Expenses	151.1	164.7	170.2	261.8	292.4	346.1	18.6	19.3	19.8	21.8	21.8	23.2
Operating income	63.4	64.9	61.9	78.1	84.5	91.0	7.8	7.6	7.2	6.5	6.3	6.1
Other revenue and expense, net (deduct)	(10.6)	(10.3)	(8.5)	(13.2)	(10.7)	(7.5)	(1.3)	(1.2)	(1.0)	(1.1)	(.8)	(.5)
Income before federal income taxes	52.8	54.6	53.4	64.9	73.8	83.5	6.5	6.4	6.2	5.4	5.5	5.6
Federal income taxes	25.2	25.6	26.7	32.5	26.9	31.3	3.1	3.0	3.1	2.7	2.0	2.1
Net income*	27.6	29.0	26.7	32.4	46.9	52.2	3.4	3.4	3.1	2.7	3.5	3.5

	1966	1967	1968	1969	1970	1971
Note: Dividends declared ($000)	12.8	12.1	19.8	20.9	22.0	25.
Other expense includes:						
Interest on long-term liabilities ($000)	6.0	6.5	10.6	9.6	9.2	8.0

* Extraordinary items charged and credited directly to Retained Earnings. This is not good practice.
See page 147.

are miniatures of the originals; the "dollar" statements and the common-size statements are identical in proportion.

The method of converting dollar amounts into percentages of statement totals may be summarized as follows (data from the statements in Illustrations 10–1 and 10–2):

1. State the total assets, total liabilities and owners' equity, and net sales as 100 percent.
2. Compute the ratio of each statement item to the statement total by dividing individual dollar amounts by the statement total.

The computation of common-size percentages for the Lynn-Dale Company is illustrated below:

$$\frac{\text{Merchandise inventory (December 31, 1971), \$253,400}}{\text{Total assets (December 31, 1971), \$1,603,700}} = 15.8\% \ldots$$

The ending merchandise inventory for December 31, 1971 represents 15.8 percent of total assets; for each $100 of total assets, there were $15.80 of ending merchandise inventory.

$$\frac{\text{Accounts payable (December 31, 1971), \$160,400}}{\text{Total liabilities and owners' equity (December 31, 1971), \$1,603,700}} = 10.0\% \ldots$$

Accounts payable for December 31, 1971 represents 10.0 percent of total liabilities and owners' equity; for each $100 of total liabilities and owners' equity, there were $10 of accounts payable.

$$\frac{\text{Cost of goods sold (1971), \$1,054,700}}{\text{Net sales (1971), \$1,491,800}} = 70.7\% \ldots$$

Cost of goods sold for 1971 represents 70.7 percent of net sales; the cost of goods sold amounted to $70.70 per $100 of net sales.

$$\frac{\text{Selling expenses (1971), \$253,600}}{\text{Net sales (1971), \$1,491,800}} = 17.0\% \ldots$$

Selling expenses for 1971 represent 17.0 percent of net sales; selling expenses amounted to $17 per $100 of net sales.

The common-size statements are most valuable to the analyst in studying the current financial position and operating results of a business and especially in making comparisons between companies in the same industry and with industry standards. To a lesser extent, this method of analysis may be used in making a historical study of a particular

ILLUSTRATION 10–3

LYNN-DALE COMPANY
Retained Earnings
For the Six-Year Period Ending December 31, 1971

	1966	1967	1968	1969	1970	1971
Balance, January 1	$133.8	$148.6	$108.5	$147.7	$168.6	$321.8
Add:						
Net income before extraordinary items	27.6	29.0	26.7	32.4	46.9	52.2
Extraordinary gains:						
Refund of federal income taxes for 1966					16.8	
Gain on disposal of long-term investments				32.3		42.5
Gain on disposal of long-term lease					128.3	
	$161.4	$177.6	$167.5	$196.9	$343.8	$416.5
Deduct:						
Loss on disposal of other assets				$ 7.4		
Additional federal income tax assessment for 1964–65		$ 57.0				
Dividend declarations	$ 12.8	12.1	$ 19.8	$ 20.9	$ 22.0	$ 25.8
	$ 12.8	$ 69.1	$ 19.8	$ 28.3	$ 22.0	$ 25.8
Balance, December 31	$148.6	$108.5	$147.7	$168.6	$321.8	$390.7

NOTE: Total net income (6 years), $214,800: 52.8 % declared in dividends.
Total net income and extraordinary items (net) (6 years), $370,300; 30.3 % declared in dividends.
Total dividends declarations (6 years), $113,400: rate of dividends on owners equity (net income and extraordinary items) 1966, 210 %; 1967, 20.0 %; 1968, 25.0 %; 1969, 22.0 %; 1970, 20 %; 1971, 22.0 %.

business because major changes in the distribution of the individual items are revealed.

Common-size percentages, balance sheet—evaluation

A business invests capital in various forms of assets which are classified on its balance sheet. A common-size statement shows the percent of total assets that has been invested in each type or kind of asset. A study of these common-size percentages in comparison with those for a competitor or the industry should reveal whether or not the firm has an out-of-line investment in one or more of the assets. That is, an analysis may reveal that the firm has too large an amount invested in receivables or inventories or that the total current assets are lower and the fixed assets are higher than the industry. In addition to studying the dollar amounts that are invested in receivables and inventories in relation to the total asset investment, the analyst should study the turnover of the foregoing items in connection with sales. Therefore, it should be emphasized that a detailed study would include turnover and other statistics as well as the common-size percentages.

The common-size statement will also show the distribution of liabilities and owners' equity, i.e., the sources of the capital invested in the assets. It may be concluded that too large a percentage of the total liabilities and owners' equity has been obtained from creditors. This situation which reveals debt pressure for the company and a relatively low margin of safety for creditors would require additional detailed study.

The common-size balance sheet percentages show the relation of each asset item to total assets and of each liability and owners' equity item to total liabilities and owners' equity. For example, the Lynn-Dale Company's balance sheet (Illustration 10–1, page 235) shows that as of December 31, 1966 and 1971, cash was equal to 6.1 and 5.2 percent, respectively, of total assets. As of December 31, 1966 and 1971, capital stock was equal to 39.1 percent and 38.7 percent, respectively, of total liabilities and owners' equity. (An analysis of the changes in the retained earnings portion of owners' equity will be found in Illustration 10–4.)

ILLUSTRATION 10–4

LYNN-DALE COMPANY
Selected Balance Sheet Ratios as Percentages
As of December 31, 1966 and 1971

	December 31	
Items	1966 (%)	1971 (%)
Current assets to total assets	55.5	44.2
Fixed assets to total assets.	42.4	44.9
Current liabilities to total liabilities and owners' equity.	25.8	14.5
Long-term liabilities to total liabilities and owners' equity.	14.7	12.5
Owners' equity to total liabilities and owners' equity	59.5	73.0

Inasmuch as these percentages show relationship to balance sheet totals, variations from year to year do not necessarily indicate changes in dollar amounts. In fact, the balance sheet common-size ratios may reflect a change in the individual item, a change in the total, or a change in both.

Observe in another company, the Ball Corporation as shown in the following table, that the dollar amount of long-term investments remained constant over a period of four years, while total assets increased appreciably:

Items and computation	1968	1969	1970	1971
Long-term investments (a).	$ 40,000	$ 40,000	$ 40,000	$ 40,000
Total assets (b)	1,069,000	1,300,000	1,485,000	1,550,000
Percentage of long-term investments to total assets (a ÷ b)	3.74%	3.08%	2.69%	2.58%

ILLUSTRATION 10–5

LYNN-DALE COMPANY
Balance Sheet Dollar and Trend Data
For the Years Ended December 31, 1970–71

Items	1966 ($000)	1967 ($000)	1968 ($000)	1969 ($000)	1970 ($000)	1971 ($000)	Trends—1966 = 100%				
							1967 (%)	1968 (%)	1969 (%)	1970 (%)	1971 (%)
Assets											
Current Assets:											
Cash.	62.1	28.2	58.6	59.0	74.2	83.4	45	94	95	119	134
Marketable securities.	33.7	105.1	39.6	39.8	39.5	44.9	312	118	118	117	133
Trade receivables (gross)	270.9	269.1	211.9	240.8	282.2	306.6	99	78	89	104	113
Estimated uncollectible receivables . . .	7.8	8.0	8.6	10.5	12.3	14.7	103	110	135	158	188
Trade receivables, net	263.1	261.1	203.3	230.3	269.9	291.9	99	77	88	103	111
Inventory	182.4	197.2	209.6	241.9	268.3	253.4	108	120	133	147	139
Other current assets	25.6	60.7	50.5	51.6	52.1	35.2	237	197	202	204	138
Total Current Assets	566.9	652.3	571.6	622.6	704.0	708.8	115	101	110	124	125
Land, buildings, and equipment . . .	534.9	570.3	893.5	970.2	1,006.9	1,145.7	107	167	181	199	214
Accumulated depreciation	101.4	143.4	211.3	279.8	351.8	425.6	141	208	276	347	420
Land, buildings, and equipment, net . . .	433.5	426.9	682.2	690.4	715.1	720.1	98	157	159	165	166
Other noncurrent assets	21.6	4.3	110.5	162.3	159.4	174.8	20	512	751	738	809
Total Assets.	1,022.0	1,083.5	1,364.3	1,475.3	1,578.5	1,603.7	106	133	144	154	157
Liabilities and Owners' Equity											
Current Liabilities:											
Accounts payable.	184.4	187.5	181.4	172.6	151.5	160.4	102	98	94	82	87
Notes payable	52.7	56.3	105.1	88.5	61.6	43.3	107	199	168	117	82
Other current liabilities	26.3	73.7	19.1	25.1	34.7	28.8	280	73	95	132	110
Total Current Liabilities	263.4	317.5	305.6	286.2	247.8	232.5	121	116	109	94	88
Long-term liabilities.	150.0	162.5	266.0	240.5	228.9	200.5	108	177	160	153	134
Total Liabilities	413.4	480.0	571.6	526.7	476.7	433.0	116	138	127	115	105
Owners' Equity.											
Capital stock.	400.0	425.0	525.0	620.0	620.0	620.0	106	131	155	155	155
Capital paid-in in excess of par value . .	60.0	70.0	120.0	160.0	160.0	160.0	117	200	267	267	267
Retained earnings	148.6	108.5	147.7	168.6	321.8	390.7	73	99	113	217	263
Total Owners' Equity	608.6	603.5	792.7	948.6	1,101.8	1,170.7	99	130	156	181	192
Total Liabilities and Owners' Equity . . .	1,022.0	1,083.5	1,364.3	1,475.3	1,578.5	1,603.7	106	133	144	154	157

The trend of the percentage of long-term investments to total assets, shown above, would mean something different than the trend of the absolute data because the total assets have changed rather than the long-term investments.

The balance sheet common-size percentages represent component parts of the *totals;* therefore, a horizontal comparison from year to year would result only in a study of the *trends of relationships.* In other words, growth or decadence in the financial position—i.e., the year-to-year trend of the dollar data—cannot be detected from the common-size percentages; changes in the data relative to a total for a particular date or period can be determined. A statement item that has increased in dollar amount will show a decreased percentage if the total has increased at a greater rate than the individual item. An item that has decreased in dollar amount will show an increased percentage if the total has decreased at a lower rate than the individual item. The ratios shown as percentages in Illustration 10–5 have been taken from the statement for the Lynn-Dale Company in Illustration 10–1.

An inspection of the data presented below for the Lynn-Dale Company reveals that there has been a substantial change in the proportions of current and fixed assets and current and long-term liabilities during the period from December 31, 1966 to December 31, 1971. In studying these changes, the analyst should refer to the absolute data (Illustration 10–1, page 235), since the variation may actually involve only the current or fixed items; current assets may have remained the same, while fixed assets may have increased. When the current assets are related to total assets under these circumstances, an apparent variation in current assets is indicated.

The usefulness of the common-size balance sheet can be enhanced by providing an additional column for each year to show the percentages of each item within a group to the total of the group. For example, cash may be shown as a percentage of both total assets and total current assets. The common-size balance sheet in Illustration 10–3 is presented to demonstrate this method.

The common-size percentages of balance sheet section items shown in Illustration 10–6 give useful data because it is easier to determine a normal relationship between similar group items and their total.

Common-size percentages, income statement—evaluation

The income statement common-size percentages show the amount or percentage of the net sales that has been absorbed by each individual cost or expense item and the percentage that remains as net income. For example, the Lynn-Dale Company's income statement (Illustration 10–2, page 236) reveals that for the years 1966 through 1971, cost of

ILLUSTRATION 10–6

LYNN-DALE COMPANY
Balance Sheet
As of December 31, 1971
(in thousands)

Items	($000)	% of subtotals	% of totals
Assets			
Current Assets:			
Cash.	83.4	11.8	5.2
Marketable securities	44.9	6.3	2.8
Trade receivables, net	291.9	41.2	18.2
Inventory	253.4	35.8	15.8
Other current assets.	35.2	4.9	2.2
Total Current Assets.	708.8	100.0	44.2
Land, buildings, and equipment, net	720.1		44.9
Other noncurrent assets	174.8		10.9
Total Assets	1,603.7		100.0
Liabilities and Owners' Equity			
Current Liabilities:			
Accounts payable	160.4	69.0	10.0
Notes payable	43.3	18.6	2.7
Other current liabilities	28.8	12.4	1.8
Total Current Liabilities	232.5	100.0	14.5
Long-term liabilities (4%)	200.5		12.5
Total Liabilities	433.0		27.0
Owners' Equity:			
Capital stock, common ($100 par)	620.0	53.0	38.7
Capital paid-in in excess of par value.	160.0	13.7	10.0
Retained earnings	390.7	33.3	24.3
Total Owners' Equity	1,170.7	100.0	73.0
Total Liabilities and Owners' Equity. . . .	1,603.7		100.0

goods sold absorbed 73.6, 73.1, 73.0, 71.7, 71.9, and 70.7 percent, respectively, of the net sales. These ratios reflect a favorable situation because a successively smaller amount of the sales dollar was absorbed except in 1970 by cost of goods sold. This favorable result is also reflected in gross margin percentages for the same years of 26.4, 26.9, 27.0, 28.3, 28.1, and 29.3 percent, respectively. The company may have been successful in (1) improving its markup policy, (2) selling a larger volume of higher profit items, (3) increasing economy in procurement, and (4) adopting other effective and more profitable merchandising policies.

A comparison of the year-to-year income statement common-size ratios is significant because they show that a larger or smaller relative amount of the net sales figure was used in meeting particular costs or expenses. It must be remembered that the percentages may be influenced by variations in sales prices, higher or lower costs of goods acquired, or both.

Common-size percentages must be supplemented if a detailed analysis is to be made of financial and operating data; it is necessary to study trends and to make comparisons of items on the financial statements. Therefore, in addition to the common-size percentages, there should be available trend ratios as well as individual ratios showing relationships between balance sheet and income statement items.

Common-size percentage analysis is used by most companies in connection with studies of revenue, cost, and expense. Less extensive use is made of balance sheet common-size percentages. The reason for the greater use of common-size percentages for income statement items is the close relationship of sales, cost of goods sold, and operating expenses. In other words, all of the items on the income statement through the operating income figure relate to sales and to current operations.

The common-size percentages for a balance sheet are determined by stating total assets as 100 percent and each of the individual assets as a percentage of total assets. The percentages of the individual asset items may be somewhat distorted when the long-term investments, deferred charges, and other assets that are not used in connection with regular operations are included in total assets. That is, the balance sheet common-size percentages are not too significant because of the inclusion of the "nonoperating" assets. This is especially true when two or more companies having different amounts of the foregoing asset items are being compared, or when the same company has major increases or decreases in the items during the period under review.

The balance sheet common-size percentages may be somewhat misleading, at least without further study, because the dollar amount of some of the individual items may have remained about the same while total assets either increased or decreased.

In the following pages, common-size percentage financial statements are illustrated and discussed. Other percentages and ratios are used to a limited extent. In later chapters, individual ratios and complete and detailed analyses are presented.

Interpretation of common-size statements—Lynn-Dale Company

The common-size balance sheet for the Lynn-Dale Company (Illustration 10–1, page 235) shows that substantial dollar and percentage changes took place in several of the items, especially during the years ending December 31, 1968, 1969, and 1970, which may be considered as a period of expansion of land, plant, and equipment and other noncurrent assets, probably consisting mainly of long-term investments. This asset expansion was financed by increasing long-term liabilities, issuance of capital stock (at a premium), and working capital derived from current operations. The following summary of dollars and percentages shows for the Lynn-Dale Company the relative importance of balance sheet items as of December 31, 1966 and 1970:

| | December 31 | | | |
| | 1966 | | 1970 | |
Items	($000)	(%)	($000)	(%)
Assets				
Current assets........................	566.9	55.5	704.0	44.6
Land, plant, and equipment, net............	433.5	42.4	715.1	45.3
Other noncurrent assets	21.6	2.1	159.4	10.1
Total Assets	1,022.0	100.0	1,578.5	100.0
Liabilities and Owners' Equity				
Current liabilities	263.4	25.8	247.8	15.7
Long-term liabilities....................	150.0	14.7	228.9	14.5
Owners' equity.......................	608.6	59.5	1,101.8	69.8
Total Liabilities and Owners' Equity	1,022.0	100.0	1,578.5	100.0

The foregoing data reveal as of December 31, 1970, in comparison with the data for December 31, 1966, that a larger number of cents of each asset dollar was invested in land, plant, and equipment and other noncurrent assets and a smaller number in current assets. In other words, the expansion has resulted in a realignment or redistribution of the asset dollar: the noncurrent assets were relatively larger and the current assets relatively lower.

The percentage data also reveal that as of December 31, 1970, the owners' equity represented a relatively more important source of the capital invested in the assets. For example, the owners provided, through contributions and retained earnings, 69.8 percent of the capital in the assets as of December 31, 1970, in comparison with 59.5 percent four years earlier. A greater reliance on owners' equity funds rather than on creditor funds increases the margin of safety of the creditors and strengthens the financial position of the company. It will be observed, Illustration 10–1 (page 235), that subsequent to December 31, 1967, there was little change, percentagewise, in the asset distribution. However, both the current liabilities and long-term liabilities represented fewer cents of the total liabilities and owners' equity dollar while the cents of the owners' equity dollar increased.

The overall analysis of the balance sheet common-size percentages for the six-year period reveals many significant changes in the relative importance of the various sources and uses of funds.

It is quite clear, from a study of the common-size percentages shown in Illustration 10–7, that the Lynn-Dale Company has materially strength-

ILLUSTRATION 10–7

LYNN-DALE COMPANY
Comparative Balance Sheet—Common-Size Percentages
As of December 31, 1966 and 1971

	December 31	
	1966	1971
Assets		
Current Assets:		
Cash.	6.1	5.2
Marketable securities.	3.4	2.8
Trade receivables, net	25.7	18.2
Inventory	17.8	15.8
Other current assets	2.5	2.2
Total Current Assets	55.5	44.2
Land, plant, and equipment, net.	42.4	44.9
Other noncurrent assets	2.1	10.9
Total Assets.	100.0	100.0
Sources of Capital Invested in Assets		
Current Liabilities:		
Accounts payable.	18.0	10.0
Notes payable	5.2	2.7
Other current liabilities	2.6	1.8
Total Current Liabilities	25.8	14.5
Long-term liabilities.	14.7	12.5
Total Liabilities.	40.5	27.0
Owners' Equity:		
Capital stock	39.1	38.7
Capital paid-in in excess of par value.	5.9	10.0
Retained earnings.	14.5	24.3
Total Owners' Equity.	59.5	73.0
Total Liabilities and Owners' Equity.	100.0	100.0

ened its financial position during the period from 1966 through 1971, the current and long-term liabilities are relatively lower, and the owners' equity relatively higher. Therefore, the ratios between (1) current assets and current liabilities, (2) current assets and total liabilities, and (3) total liabilities and owners' equity have become much more favorable.

Individual ratios of balance sheet and income statement items should be computed and analyzed to determine whether or not the changes in the distribution of asset items have proven to be more or less profitable.

It is true, as indicated in Illustration 10–7, that the Lynn-Dale Company "strengthened" its financial position. This fact is especially favorable from the point of view of the creditors' margin of safety. However, this is not necessarily the most profitable financial plan. That is, up to a certain point, leverage—"trading on the equity"—is a sound source of higher return on owners' capital. As the percentage of owners' equity increases, it becomes "safer" but less profitable; and as it decreases, it customarily becomes more profitable but more dangerous—less conservative. It is quite probable that the Lynn-Dale Company could finance to a greater extent with creditor funds.

The Lynn-Dale Company's common-size income statement (Illustration 10–2, page 236) shows that the cost of goods sold consumed a decreasing percentage of net sales, from 73.6 percent to 70.7 percent, which resulted in an increasing percentage of gross margin to net sales, from 26.4 percent to 29.3 percent. These data reflect greater profitability of sales because of more effective merchandising policies. More specifically, this more desirable percentage may have been the result of one or more factors, such as favorable price-level changes, more effective markup policies, more effective selling of higher margin items, greater efficiency in purchasing, and changes in inventory valuation methods.

A larger proportion of the net sales dollar was consumed by selling expenses each year following 1966. Possibly a greater and more costly sales effort was necessary to obtain the larger and—from the standpoint of gross margin on sales—more advantageous sales volume. It will be noted that general and administrative expenses absorbed more of the sales dollar each year following the year 1966, but the increase was substantially less than that for selling expenses. This is characteristic because a greater portion of selling expenses varies directly with sales volume. The income, before estimated federal income taxes, for each succeeding year increased in dollars. The improved gross margin was offset by relatively higher operating expenses which absorbed a larger part of the sales dollar. During 1966 the operating expenses were equal to 18.6 percent of net sales and 23.2 percent for 1971. The sales cents remaining as operating income increased but at a lower rate.

A company is most fortunate when it can regulate cost of goods sold and operating expenses so that changes in sales dollar volume will be accompanied by proportionally similar changes in the costs. Many costs are relatively fixed and do not decline proportionately with volume. Certainly, an unfavorable situation exists when sales volume remains at the same level while cost of goods sold and especially selling expenses increase or when sales volume declines without a proportionate reduction in the cost of goods sold and operating expenses. Under these circumstances the company would encounter difficulty in maintaining a profitable sales volume.

The analyst should study both the trend and the common-size ratios as well as the absolute data in his attempt to determine favorable or unfavorable proportions. The trend-ratio analysis, a dynamic type of analysis, indicates the changes that have taken place in the statement items for a period of years; the rate of change in terms of percentages may be readily computed. The common-size percentage analysis, a static type of analysis, reveals the relationship between each individual statement item and the respective totals.

QUESTIONS AND PROBLEMS

10–1. Distinguish between (*a*) common-size and trend data; (*b*) ratios and common-size percentages; (*c*) comparative statement percentages and trend percentages.

10–2. "Common-size percentages are valuable in comparing the relative distribution and proportions of financial and operating data for one company from year to year and for several companies for a single year." Explain.

10–3. What information is provided by:
a) Comparative statements?
b) Trend percentages?
c) Common-size percentages?

10–4. Is it advantageous to compare the common-size income statements of two different businesses? Explain.

10–5. To what extent are common-size percentages useful in studying financial and operating data for a period of years?

10–6. Should the analyst compute common-size percentages for nonrecurring items shown on income statement? Discuss.

10–7. How can the analyst detect favorable and unfavorable financial and operating tendencies by using common-size statement percentages? Discuss.

10–8. Comment on the following statements:
a) Common-size percentages should be computed for all items on the income statement.
b) Common-size percentages are useful in showing the distribution of owners' equity items.
c) Common-size percentage analysis is more useful for studies of balance sheets than for income statements.
d) Common-size percentages indicate the trend of financial statement items.

10–9. Study the following data and suggest reasons for the variations among the companies.

	A		B		C	
	($)	(%)	($)	(%)	($)	(%)
Assets						
Current assets..............	860,000	33.3	500,000	20.1	1,500,000	57.5
Noncurrent assets	1,720,000	66.7	1,990,000	79.9	1,110,000	42.5
Total...............	2,580,000	100.0	2,490,000	100.0	2,610,000	100.0
Liabilities and Owners' Equity						
Current liabilities...........	400,000	15.5	350,000	14.1	1,200,000	46.0
Long-term liabilities.........	800,000	31.0	1,000,000	40.1	500,000	19.1
Owners' Equity.............	1,380,000	53.5	1,140,000	45.8	910,000	34.9
Total...............	2,580,000	100.0	2,490,000	100.0	2,610,000	100.0

10–10. Study the following data and indicate which company has the most favorable distribution of borrowed funds and owners' equity. What additional information should be available to solve the problem more completely?

	A		B		C	
	($)	(%)	($)	(%)	($)	(%)
Liabilities and Owners' Equity						
Current liabilities...........	160,000	9.9	400,000	25.5	380,000	23.7
Long-term debt.............	300,000	18.5	50,000	3.2	350,000	21.8
Total Liabilities	460,000	28.4	450,000	28.7	730,000	45.5
Preferred stock	250,000	15.4	20,000	1.3	400,000	24.9
Common stock	500,000	30.9	1,000,000	63.6	500,000	31.1
Paid-in surplus	225,000	13.9	5,000	0.3	1,000	0.1
Appropriated retained earnings	75,000	4.6	20,000	1.3	2,000	0.1
Retained earnings (deficit*).....	100,000	6.2	25,000	1.6	30,000*	1.9*
Appreciation surplus	10,000	0.6	50,000	3.2	3,000	0.2
Total Owners' Equity	1,160,000	71.6	1,120,000	71.3	876,000	54.5
Total Liabilities and Owners' Equity	1,620,000	100.0	1,570,000	100.0	1,606,000	100.0

10–11. The Doris Manufacturing Company requests you to:

   a) Prepare comparative statements showing dollar amounts and common-size percentages.

   b) Write a report evaluating the financial position and operating results.

Selected financial and operating data as of December 31, or for the year:

	1970	1971
Assets		
Cash	$ 15,100	$ 16,665
U.S. Treasury Bills.	30,000	38,521
Trade receivables—net	45,210	41,800
Inventories.	90,600	75,676
Other current assets.	1,510	1,366
Long-term investments.	7,550	6,284
Fixed assets—net	75,800	82,233
Other noncurrent assets	28,750	10,655
Liabilities		
Current liabilities.	64,790	45,898
Long-term debt.	89,825	87,151
Owners' Equity		
Capital stock, $25 par value, common	84,230	81,687
Retained earnings	29,745	31,691
Appropriated retained earnings	25,930	26,773
Revenue, Expense, and Dividends		
Net sales	1,854,600	1,036,800
Cost of goods sold and operating expenses.	1,813,799	1,010,880
Other revenue (recurring)	7,418	6,221
Other expense (recurring)	9,273	5,184
Estimated federal income taxes	18,546	10,368
Dividends paid	13,800	13,800

10–12.

   a) Compare, analyze, and interpret the following data for Companies A and B, manufacturers of similar iron and steel products.

   b) Write a report in which you list and discuss favorable and unfavorable financial and operating tendencies.

COMPANIES A AND B
Balance Sheet Data
December 31, 1966 and 1971
(in thousands)

	Company A				Company B			
	1971		1966		1971		1966	
	($)	(%)	($)	(%)	($)	(%)	($)	(%)
Assets								
Current Assets:								
Cash	860	2.0	1,730	10.2	2,371	5.3	1,027	2.2
Marketable securities	214	0.5	406	2.4	59	0.1	845	1.8
Accounts receivable—trade (net)	4,078	9.4	1,675	9.9	3,090	6.9	1,691	3.6
Notes receivable—trade	500	1.1	200	1.2	400	1.0	100	0.2
Merchandise inventory	11,057	25.4	3,308	19.5	9,949	22.2	7,782	16.4
Other current assets	34	0.1	14	0.1	60	0.1	24	0.1
Total Current Assets	16,743	38.5	7,333	43.2	15,929	35.6	11,469	24.2
Long-term investments	124	0.3	65	0.4	4,516	10.1	1,953	4.1
Land, buildings, and equipment (net)	26,477	60.8	9,428	55.5	23,822	53.3	33,484	70.7
Other assets	193	0.4	153	0.9	436	1.0	460	1.0
Total Assets	43,537	100.0	16,979	100.0	44,703	100.0	47,366	100.0
Liabilities and Owners' Equity								
Current Liabilities:								
Notes payable, bank	450	1.1	25	0.2	1,500	3.4	700	1.5
Accounts payable—trade	3,326	7.6	1,818	10.7	1,819	4.0	396	0.8
Other current liabilities	2,013	4.6	644	3.8	1,887	4.2	947	2.0
Total Current Liabilities	5,789	13.3	2,487	14.7	5,206	11.6	2,043	4.3
Long-term liabilities	343	0.8	343	2.0	4,733	10.6	6,955	14.7
Total Liabilities	6,132	14.1	2,830	16.7	9,939	22.2	8,998	19.0
Owners' Equity:								
Preferred stock	3,000	6.9	3,000	17.7	10,471	23.4	9,475	20.0
Common stock	20,855	47.9	3,820	22.5	9,816	22.0	25,350	53.5
Capital in excess of stated value	6,027	13.8	5,527	32.5	13,000	29.1	1,000	2.1
Retained earnings	7,523	17.3	1,802	10.6	1,477	3.3	2,543	5.4
Total Owners' Equity	37,405	85.9	14,149	83.3	34,764	77.8	38,368	81.0
Total Liabilities and Owners' Equity	43,537	100.0	16,979	100.0	44,703	100.0	47,366	100.0

COMPANIES A AND B
Income Statement Items
For the Years Ended December 31, 1966 and 1971
(in thousands)

	Company A				Company B			
	1971		1966		1971		1966	
	($)	(%)	($)	(%)	($)	(%)	($)	(%)
Net sales	37,332	100.0	17,091	100.0	28,571	100.0	12,896	100.0
Cost of goods sold	27,492	73.6	12,539	73.4	21,166	74.1	7,154	55.5
Gross margin on sales	9,840	26.4	4,552	26.6	7,405	25.9	5,742	44.5
Maintenance and repairs	1,732	4.6	1,912	11.2	2,337	8.2	1,862	14.4
Depreciation	1,348	3.6	771	4.5	1,362	4.8	1,235	9.6
Rents	279	0.7	118	0.7	110	0.4	80	0.6
Taxes (other than income)	815	2.3	146	0.9	862	3.0	398	3.1
Uncollectible receivables expense	69	0.2	14		42	0.1	23	0.2
Other selling expenses	2,019	5.4	515	3.0	1,312	4.6	1,020	7.9
Other administrative expenses	865	2.3	220	1.3	563	2.0	400	3.1
Total operating expenses	7,127	19.1	3,696	21.6	6,588	23.1	5,018	38.9
Operating revenue	2,713	7.3	856	5.0	817	2.8	724	5.6
Other income	62	0.2	53	0.3	793	2.8	233	1.8
Other expense	56	0.2	20	0.1	562	2.0	381	3.0
Net Income*†	2,719	7.3	889	5.2	1,048	3.6	576	4.4
Dividends paid for current year †	1,000		410		600		400	

* Estimated federal income taxes recorded in retained earnings.
† Dividends paid for current year.

10–13. *Required:*

a) Analyze and interpret the financial statement dollar and percentage data presented below for Companies A, B, C, and D, manufacturers of similar steel products.

b) Write a report discussing the relative financial condition and operating results of the several Companies.

COMPANIES A, B, C, AND D
Comparative Balance Sheet
As of December 31, 1971
(in thousands)

	A		B		C		D	
	Amount	Per-cent of totals	Amount	Per-cent of totals	Amount	Per-cent of totals	Amount	Per-cent of totals
Assets								
Current Assets:								
Cash.................	$ 21.6	2.0	$ 10.1	.8	$ 15.2	1.2	$ 4.1	.3
Notes receivable	50.2	4.6	80.4	6.2	60.1	4.9	100.4	7.4
Marketable securities....	4.1	.4	1.2	.1	5.4	.4	1.0	.1
Accounts receivable.....	$ 280.6	25.7	$ 360.5	27.7	$ 290.4	23.5	$ 300.6	22.2
Less: Estimated uncollectible receivables...	15.4	1.4	20.2	1.6	10.1	.8	4.3	.3
	$ 265.2	24.3	$ 340.3	26.1	$ 280.3	22.7	$ 296.3	21.9
Inventories	202.7	18.6	99.7	7.7	160.4	13.0	97.7	7.2
Other current assets.....	5.6	.5	3.1	.2	4.2	.3	2.1	.2
Total Current Assets..	$ 549.4	50.4	$ 534.8	41.1	$ 525.6	42.5	$ 501.6	37.1
Long-term investments....	$ 100.0	9.2	$ 236.0	18.1	$ 10.5	.8	$ 200.4	14.8
Fixed assets:								
Fixed assets..........	$ 461.8	42.3	$ 494.9	38.0	$ 670.3	54.3	$ 452.0	33.4
Less: Accumulated depreciation.......	41.6	3.8	14.7	1.1	70.1	5.7	1.2	.1
	$ 420.2	38.5	$ 480.2	36.9	$ 600.2	48.6	$ 450.8	33.3
Intangible assets	$ 20.6	1.9	$ 50.0	3.9	$ 100.0	8.1	$ 200.2	14.8
Total Assets	$1,090.2	100.0	$1,301.0	100.0	$1,236.3	100.0	$1,353.0	100.0
Liabilities and Owners' Equity								
Current Liabilities:								
Accounts payable	$ 91.6	8.4	$ 110.4	8.5	$ 105.7	8.6	$ 201.4	14.9
Notes payable	45.2	4.2	217.3	16.7	145.3	11.7	192.0	14.2
Other current liabilities ..	4.7	.4	12.5	1.0	5.8	.5	16.8	1.2
Total Current Liabilities	$ 141.5	13.0	$ 340.2	26.2	$ 256.8	20.8	$ 410.2	30.3
Long-term liabilities......	$ 125.0	11.4	$ 458.4	35.2	$ 300.0	24.2	$ 580.4	42.9
Total Liabilities.....	$ 266.5	24.4	$ 798.6	61.4	$ 556.8	45.0	$ 990.6	73.2
Owners' equity:								
Capital stock:								
Preferred stock ($100, par)........	$ 60.0	5.5	$ 100.0	7.7	$ 50.0	4.0	$ 200.0	14.8
Common stock ($100, par)........	500.0	45.9	300.0	23.0	300.0	24.3	100.0	7.4
Total Capital Stock	$ 560.0	51.4	$ 400.0	30.7	$ 350.0	28.3	$ 300.0	22.2
Surplus:								
Unappropriated retained earnings	$ 53.7	4.9	$ 95.4	7.3	$ 218.1	17.6	$ 58.4	4.3
Appropriated retained earnings	200.0	18.4	5.0	.4	95.8	7.8	3.0	.2
Capital in excess of par value	10.0	.9	2.0	.2	15.6	1.3	1.0	.1
Total Owners' Equity	$ 823.7	75.6	$ 502.4	38.6	$ 679.5	55.0	$ 362.4	26.8
Total Liabilities and Owners' Equity ..	$1,090.2	100.0	$1,301.0	100.0	$1,236.3	100.0	$1,353.0	100.0

	A		B		C		D	
	Amount	Per- cent of sales	Amount	Per- cent of sales	Amount	Per- cent of sales	Amount	Per- cent of sales
Sales.	$1,822.8		$1,656.2		$1,948.9		$1,201.2	
Less: Sales returns and allowances	21.6		35.8		28.1		40.5	
Net sales	$1,801.2	100.0	$1,620.4	100.0	$1,920.8	100.0	$1,160.7	100.0
Cost of goods sold	1,186.4	65.9	1,182.5	73.0	1,321.5	68.8	641.7	55.3
Gross margin on sales	$ 614.8	34.1	$ 437.9	27.0	$ 599.3	31.2	$ 519.0	44.7
Operating expenses:								
Selling expenses	$ 408.9	22.7	$ 350.0	21.6	$ 423.9	22.0	$ 360.0	31.0
General and administrative expenses.	114.8	6.4	101.6	6.3	112.8	5.9	108.3	9.3
Total Operating Expenses.	$ 523.7	29.1	$ 451.6	27.9	$ 536.7	27.9	$ 468.3	40.3
Operating income (loss*) . .	$ 91.1	5.0	$ 13.7*	.9*	$ 62.6	3.3	$ 50.7	4.4
Other revenue:								
Income on investments . .	$ 16.4		$ 5.5		$ 1.4		$ 1.8	
Miscellaneous other income.	12.1		7.4		10.8		1.1	
Total Other Revenue	$ 28.5	1.6	$ 12.9	.8	$ 12.2	.6	$ 2.9	.2
	$ 119.6		$ .8*		$ 74.8		$ 53.6	
Other expense:								
Interest on fixed liabilities	$ 7.1		$ 30.5		$ 17.2		$ 40.1	
Expense on investments . .	1.5		40.2		1.1		25.4	
Miscellaneous other expenses.	12.0		21.6		15.8		30.9	
Total Other Expenses	$ 20.6	1.1	$ 92.3	5.7	$ 34.1	1.8	$ 96.4	8.3
Net Income (Loss*)†	$ 99.0	5.5	$ 93.1*	5.8*	$ 40.7	2.1	$ 42.8	3.7*

* Federal Income Taxes recorded in Retained Earnings.

10–14. The Baltimore Company, manufacturers of office equipment and supplies, presents financial and operating data:

    a)   Analyze and interpret the company's financial position and operating results.

    b)   Write a report of your conclusions.

BALTIMORE COMPANY

Comparative Income Statement

For the Years Ended December 31, 1968–71

(in thousands)

	1968 Amount	1968 Percent of net sales	1969 Amount	1969 Percent of net sales	1970 Amount	1970 Percent of net sales	1971 Amount	1971 Percent of net sales
Net Sales	$1,125.6	100.0	$1,748.4	100.0	$1,813.1	100.0	$1,881.4	100.0
Less: Cost of goods sold	784.1	69.6	1,149.1	65.7	1,186.2	65.3	1,241.6	66.0
Gross margin on sales	341.5	30.4	599.3	34.3	629.9	34.7	639.8	34.0
Operating expenses:								
Selling expenses	214.8	19.1	388.5	22.2	406.5	22.4	405.2	21.5
General and administrative expenses	85.2	7.6	111.6	6.4	112.2	6.2	118.7	6.3
Total Operating Expenses	300.0	26.7	500.1	28.6	518.7	28.6	523.9	27.8
Operating income	41.5	3.7	99.2	5.7	111.2	6.1	115.9	6.2
Other revenue:								
Income on investments . .	6.4		14.1		17.2		20.2	
Miscellaneous other income	18.4		10.2		11.4		12.7	
Total Other Revenue. . .	24.8	2.2	24.3	1.4	28.6	1.6	32.9	1.7
Other Expense:								
Expense on investments. .	2.1		1.8		1.6		1.9	
Interest on fixed liabilities	5.9		8.2		8.2		8.2	
Miscellaneous other expense	3.2		14.7		22.1		24.7	
Total Other Expense. . .	11.2	1.0	24.7	1.4	31.9	1.8	34.8	1.8
Income (before federal income taxes)	55.1	4.9	98.8	5.7	107.9	5.9	114.0	6.1

BALTIMORE COMPANY
Comparative Balance Sheet
As of December 31, 1968–71
(in thousands)

	1968 Amount	1968 Per-cent of total	1969 Amount	1969 Per-cent of total	1970 Amount	1970 Per-cent of total	1971 Amount	1971 Per-cent of total
Assets								
Current Assets:								
Cash.	$ 10.8	1.2	$ 20.1	1.9	$ 23.4	2.2	$ 26.1	2.4
Notes receivable	50.1	5.4	46.3	4.4	40.4	3.7	35.3	3.3
Marketable securities. . . .	1.4	.1	2.4	.2	3.8	.3	8.1	.8
Accounts receivable.	$228.3		$ 270.4		$ 280.5		$ 290.6	
Less: Estimated uncol- lectible receivables. .	24.1		20.3		14.5		12.8	
	$204.2	22.1	$ 250.1	23.9	$ 266.0	24.5	$ 277.8	25.9
Merchandise inventory. . .	$121.6	13.2	$ 185.7	17.8	$ 194.8	17.9	$ 195.4	18.2
Total Current Assets. .	$388.1	42.0	$ 504.6	48.2	$ 528.4	48.6	$ 542.7	50.6
Long-term investments. . . .	60.0	6.5	70.0	6.7	100.0	9.2	100.0	9.3
Fixed assets, net	476.6	51.5	470.9	45.1	458.6	42.2	430.0	40.1
Total Assets	$924.7	100.0	$1,045.5	100.0	$1,087.0	100.0	$1,072.7	100.0
Liabilities and Owners' Equity								
Current Liabilities:								
Accounts payable	$ 61.4	6.7	$ 84.6	8.1	$ 94.3	8.7	$ 110.4	10.3
Notes payable	95.6	10.3	90.2	8.6	80.5	7.3	71.4	6.7
Other current liabilities . .	13.8	1.5	10.7	1.0	21.4	2.0	19.6	1.8
Total Current Liabilities	$170.8	18.5	$ 185.5	17.7	$ 196.2	18.0	$ 201.4	18.8
Long-term liabilities.	$225.0	24.3	$ 260.0	24.9	$ 255.0	23.5	$ 245.0	22.8
Total Liabilities.	$395.8	42.8	$ 445.5	42.6	$ 451.2	41.5	$ 446.4	41.6
Owners' equity:								
Capital stock:								
Common stock	$400.0	43.3	$ 450.0	43.0	$ 450.0	41.4	$ 450.0	42.0
Preferred stock	50.0	5.4	50.0	4.8	50.0	4.6	50.0	4.6
Total Capital Stock . .	$450.0	48.7	$ 500.0	47.8	$ 500.0	46.0	$ 500.0	46.6
Surplus:								
Appropriated retained earnings.	$ 55.0	5.9	$ 60.0	5.7	$ 62.0	5.7	$ 70.0	6.5
Paid-in capital in excess of stated value	25.0	2.7	25.0	2.4	25.0	2.3	25.0	2.4
Retained earnings (deficit*).	1.1*	.1*	15.0	1.5	48.8	4.5	31.3	2.9
Total.	$ 78.9	8.5	$ 100.0	9.6	$ 135.8	12.5	$ 126.3	11.8
Total Owners' Equity	$528.9	57.2	$ 600.0	57.4	$ 635.8	58.5	$ 626.3	58.4
Total Liabilities and Owners' Equity. . . .	$924.7	100.0	$1,045.5	100.0	$1,087.0	100.0	$1,072.7	100.0

BALTIMORE COMPANY
Comparative Statement of Retained Earnings
For the Years Ended December 31, 1968–1971
(in thousands)

	1968	1969	1970	1971
Retained Earnings,				
January 1............	$35.9	$ 1.1*	$ 15.0	$ 48.8
Add: Income before federal				
income taxes.........	55.1	98.8	107.9	114.0
	$91.0	$97.7	$122.9	$162.8
Deduct: Fire, flood, and				
other loss.........	$ 2.10	$37.9	$ 6.9	$ 38.8
Dividends paid.......	50.0	26.0	40.0	60.0
Federal income taxes ..	30.0	13.8	25.2	24.7
Appropriations				
retained earnings	10.0	5.0	2.0	8.0
	$92.1	$82.7	$ 74.1	$131.5
Retained Earnings,				
December 31............	$ 1.1*	$15.0	$ 48.8	$ 31.3

* Deficit.

BALTIMORE COMPANY
Selected Trend Percentages
1968 = 100 percent

	1969	1970	1971
Balance Sheet Items			
Cash..............................	186	217	242
Notes receivable	92	81	70
Marketable securities	171	271	579
Accounts receivable, net...............	122	130	136
Inventories.........................	153	160	161
Total current assets	130	136	140
Long-term investments.................	117	167	167
Fixed assets, net	99	96	90
Total assets, net	113	118	116
Accounts payable	138	154	180
Notes payable.......................	94	84	75
Total current liabilities...............	109	115	118
Long-term liabilities..................	116	113	109
Total liabilities	113	114	113
Appropriated retained earnings	109	113	127
Total retained earnings and capital in excess....	127	172	160
Total Owners' Equity.................	113	120	118
Income and Retained Earnings Items			
Net sales	155	161	167
Cost of goods sold....................	147	151	158
Gross margin on sales.................	175	184	187
Selling expenses	181	189	189
General and administrative expenses	131	132	139
Total operating expenses	167	173	175
Income before federal income taxes	179	196	207
Estimated federal income taxes	46	85	82
Net income after federal income taxes........	339	329	356
Dividends paid	52	80	120

10–15. Financial data for Companies L and M, manufacturers of similar iron and steel products, are presented below. You are requested to:
a) Compare, analyze, and interpret the data.
b) Write a report discussion your evaluation of the relative financial position and operating results of the two companies.

	L Amount	L Per-cent	M Amount	M Per-cent
Balance Sheet Data, December 31, 1971 (in thousands)				
Cash	$ 3,532	12.1	$ 620	2.6
Receivables—trade (net)	2,076	7.1	1,367	5.7
Inventories.	3,815	13.1	4,039	16.8
Marketable securities	208	.7	100	.5
Other current assets.	20		27	
Total current assets	9,651	33.0	6,153	25.6
Long-term investments.	210	.7	104	.5
Land, buildings, and equipment (net)	18,642	63.8	17,272	71.9
Other assets	724	2.5	485	2.0
Total assets	29,227	100.0	24,014	100.0
Trade payables	413	1.4	596	2.5
Notes payable, bank.	353	1.2	200	.8
Other current liabilities.	1,043	3.6	455	1.9
Total current liabilities.	1,809	6.2	1,251	5.2
Long-term debt.	1,778	6.1	8,396	35.0
Total liabilities	3,587	12.3	9,647	40.2
Preferred stock	1,000	3.4	5,000	20.8
Common stock	12,524	42.9	8,219	34.2
Paid-in surplus	1,584	5.4	473	2.0
Retained earnings	10,532	36.0	675	2.8
Total owners' equity	25,640	87.7	14,367	59.8
Total liabilities and owners' equity	29,227	100.0	24,014	100.0
Income Statement Items for the Year 1971 (in thousands)				
Net sales	$13,878	100.0	$13,766	100.0
Cost of goods sold	8,150	58.7	9,539	69.3
Gross margin on sales.	5,728	41.3	4,227	30.7
Maintenance and repairs	635	4.6	603	4.4
Depreciation	460	3.3	399	2.9
Taxes (other than income)	286	2.1	236	1.7
Rent.	150	1.1	442	3.2
Uncollectible receivables expense	13	.1	47	.3
Other selling expenses	1,498	10.8	1,156	8.4
Other general and administrative expenses.	630	4.5	510	3.7
Total operating expenses*.	3,672	26.5	3,393	24.6
Operating income	2,056	14.8	834	6.1
Other and extraordinary revenue	225	1.6	133	1.0
Other and extraordinary expense	240	1.7	519	3.8
Net income*.	2,041	14.7	448	3.3

* Federal income taxes recorded in retained earnings.

COMPANY M
Selected Trend and Common-Size Percentages
As of, or for the Years Ended December 31, 1966–1971

Balance sheet items (December 31)	Trend data 1966=100 percent					Common-size data** Total assets=100 percent					
	1967	1968	1969	1970	1971	1966	1967	1968	1969	1970	1971
Assets											
Cash and cash items	196	29	52	55	70	17.5	29.0	3.5	6.1	6.7	7.2
Marketable securities	50					10.5	4.4	.1	.1	.1	.1
Trade receivables, net	143	184	113	99	205	4.8	5.7	6.0	3.6	3.3	5.7
Inventories	144	171	207	198	270	13.3	16.1	15.7	18.4	18.2	21.0
Prepaid expenses	151	493	191	135	95	.4	.6	1.5	.5	.4	.2
Total current assets	142	83	92	89	126	46.5	55.8	26.8	28.7	28.3	34.2
Long-term investments	131	127	157	194	185	.8	.9	.7	.9	1.1	.9
Land, buildings, and equipment, net	98	200	201	194	211	52.5	43.2	72.4	70.3	70.2	64.9
Total assets	119	145	150	145	171	100.0	100.0	100.0	100.0	100.0	100.0
Liabilities											
Notes payable	252	358	72	180	318	1.4	2.9	3.9	5.1	7.2	2.7
Accounts payable	168	166	148	117	185	2.1	2.9	3.3	.7	1.7	2.5
Accrued payables	201	601	343	450	382			2.4	2.1	1.7	2.2
Total current liabilities						3.5	5.8	9.6	7.9	10.7	7.4
Long-term debt	100	127	87	101	134	2.0	1.7	4.6	10.9	7.7	21.1
Liability "reserves"								1.8	1.1	1.4	1.6
Total liabilities	164	425	547	525	951	5.5	7.5	16.0	19.9	19.8	30.3
Owners' Equity											
Capital stock, common	119	139	139	139	139	61.4	61.4	59.1	57.2	59.2	50.1
Capital in excess of stated value	100	100	100	100	100	23.1	19.5	16.0	15.5	16.0	13.6
Retained earnings	137	129	111	73	101	10.0	11.6	8.9	7.4	5.0	6.0
Total owners' equity	116	129	127	123	126	94.5	92.5	84.0	80.1	80.2	69.7
Total liabilities and owners' equity	119	145	150	145	171	100.0	100.0	100.0	100.0	100.0	100.0

Income Statement Items
(for the year)

Net sales	156	195	255	123	197	100.0	100.0	100.0	100.0	100.0	100.0
Cost of goods sold	158	217	286	135	196	74.6	75.8	82.9	83.6	82.2	74.2
Gross margin	149	132	164	86	200	25.4	24.2	17.1	16.4	17.8	25.8
Maintenance and repairs . . .	136	178	239	130	216	6.1	5.3	5.6	5.7	6.5	6.7
Depreciation	100	100	127	131	207	7.0	4.5	3.6	3.5	7.4	7.3
Taxes (other than income) . . .	103	156	308	252	273	1.5	1.0	1.2	1.8	3.1	2.1
Uncollectible receivables expense . . .	243	57	200	100		.1	.2		.1	.1	
Selling, general, and administrative expenses	126	124	136	114	131	6.0	4.9	3.8	3.2	5.6	4.0
Total Operating Expenses	119	134	177	135	191	20.7	15.9	14.2	14.3	22.7	20.1
Income (loss*) before federal income taxes	260	116	102	Loss	198	5.1	8.4	7.9	6.3	5.3*	5.1
Federal income taxes	269	120	131		200	1.3	2.2	2.0	2.0		1.3
Net income (loss*) after federal income taxes	256	115	92	Loss	196	3.8	6.2	5.9	4.3	5.3*	3.8
Net income transferred to retained earnings	91	40	34	Loss	66						
Note: Dividends declared	100	138	169	19	19						

** Totals do not check in all cases because minor items have been omitted.

COMPANY M

Selected Ratios and Percentages

As of, or for the Years Ended December 31, 1966–1971

	1966	1967	1968	1969	1970	1971
Current ratio (%)	1,357	958	188	366	269	448
Quick ratio (%)	956	671	67	124	94	169
Net sales to receivables (%)	1,104	1,206	1,170	2,488	1,368	1,058
Cost of goods sold to ending inventory (times)	2.9	3.2	3.7	4.1	2.0	2.1
Days' sales uncollected	33.1	30.3	31.2	14.7	26.7	34.5
Net sales to working capital (times)	1.21	1.38	5.61	4.27	2.46	2.26
Net sales to total operating assets (%)	52.8	69.4	71.0	90.0	44.8	60.8
Net sales to owners' equity (%)	55.4	74.4	83.9	111.4	55.3	86.5
Operating income (loss*) to total operating assets (long-term investments excluded)(%)	2.47	5.82	2.06	1.83	2.22*	3.48
Income before federal income taxes and fixed interest charges to total debt and owners' equity (%)	2.65	5.80	2.13	2.35	1.98*	4.11
Net income to owners' equity (%)	6.09	4.77	1.87	1.63	2.86*	3.20
Maintenance and repairs to fixed assets (cents)	6.1	8.5	5.5	7.3	4.1	6.3
Depreciation to fixed assets (cents)	6.9	7.1	3.5	4.4	4.7	6.8
Dividends to net income (%)	44.7	49.2	155.3	221.6		12.7

Required:

a) Analyze and study all data provided and evaluate the financial strength—current and long-term—of Company M.

b) Write a report on your conclusions.

11

Working capital and a section on judging the solvency of the small business

A STUDY of working capital is of major importance to internal and external analysts because of its close relationship to current day-to-day operations of a business. Inadequacy or mismanagement of working capital is one of the leading causes of business failures.

Working capital defined

There are two definitions of working capital that appear to have generally accepted usage:

1. Working capital is the excess of current assets over current liabilities, the amount of the current assets that has been supplied by the long-term creditors and the stockholders. In other words, working capital represents the amount of current assets that have not been supplied by current, short-term creditors. This definition is qualitative in character, since it shows the possible availability of current assets in excess of the current liabilities; it represents an index of financial soundness or margin of protection for current creditors and future current operations.

The immediate availability of working capital depends upon the type and liquid nature of current assets such as cash, temporary investments of cash, receivables, and inventories. When working capital is defined in this way, it cannot be increased by current loans from banks or extension of credit by trade creditors.

2. Working capital is the amount of the current assets. This inter-

pretation is quantitative in character, since it represents the total amount of funds used for current operating purposes. In this definition the current assets are considered to be gross working capital, and the excess of current assets over current liabilities is the net working capital. Net working capital represents the amount of the current assets which would remain if all the current liabilities were paid, assuming no loss or gain in converting current assets into cash.

The term "circulating capital" is frequently used to designate those assets that are changed with relative rapidity from one form to another, i.e., from cash to cost of operations and inventories, to receivables, to cash. When this term is used to designate the current assets, the amount of net current assets is thought of as net working capital.

In the following discussion, *working capital* denotes the excess of current assets over the current liabilities. A working capital deficit exists if current liabilities exceed current assets.

The working capital cycle

The working capital of a business enterprise circulates continuously to finance the current operations of the company. This process has come to be known as the *working capital cycle*. The cycle is, of course, circular and has no beginning or end as long as the enterprise is a going concern. However, in analyzing the nature of the cycle it is useful to start with cash. The cash is invested in merchandise inventory and various kinds of operating supplies and services. Inventory, supplies, and services are also acquired from suppliers on credit which later require payment in cash. The merchandise is sold to customers for cash or on open-account credit or in exchange for promissory notes. Cash is received from customers in payment of their accounts and notes. The cycle is repeated on a continuous basis.

It is useful in understanding enterprise finance to see that this cycle involves both of the basic "streams" inherent in the generation of net income—the revenue stream and the cost stream. Goods or services are sold at sales prices, and accounts receivable and cash receipts from cash sales are both on the higher, revenue stream level. On the other hand, expenses and purchases for inventory, on account, or for cash, are on the lower, cost level. Of course, it is from the difference between these two levels that a business derives its net income. Cash is the hinge or pivot on which a company's profit-making activities turn. From this can be seen the intimate relationship between the income statement's sales and the balance sheet's accounts receivable and, ultimately, debits to cash. Note also the close relationship between debits to inventory—which ultimately flow into cost of goods sold—and expenses (both are income statement) and accounts payable and credits to cash (balance sheet).

The magnitude of the investment in working capital is an important managerial problem. By increasing the turnover of working capital items, the same amount of working capital becomes more productive (i.e., can support larger operations).

Working capital should be adequate

Working capital should be sufficient in amount to enable the company to conduct its business on the most economical basis and without financial stringency and to meet emergencies and losses without danger of financial disaster. More specifically, adequate working capital:

1. Cushions the business from the adverse effect of a shrinkage in the values of current assets, such as from bad debts or losses of inventory value due to price declines.
2. Makes it possible to pay promptly all current obligations and to take advantage of cash discounts.
3. Insures to a greater extent the maintenance of the company's credit standing and provides for meeting emergencies such as strikes, floods, and fires.
4. Permits the carrying of inventories at a level that will enable the business to serve satisfactorily the needs of customers.
5. Enables the company to extend favorable credit terms to customers. Sometimes suppliers extend credit terms to six months or even longer to help good customers to finance their operations.
6. Enables the company to operate its business more efficiently by avoiding delays in obtaining materials, services, and supplies due to credit difficulties.

Adequate working capital also enables a business to withstand periods of recession or depression.

To the extent that the current assets exceed the working capital requirements, the business has *excess working capital*. Excessive working capital may be a result of:

1. The issuance of bonds or capital stock in larger amounts than necessary.
2. The sale of noncurrent assets which are not replaced.
3. Operating income or profits not devoted to cash dividends, acquisition of fixed assets, or other similar purposes.
4. The conversion, not accompanied by replacement, of operating assets into working capital through the process of depreciation, depletion, and amortization.
5. Temporary accumulation of funds pending investment, expansion, etc.

During and after World War II and the Korean war, a relatively large part of the working capital derived from current operations was retained by many companies in liquid form until repairs, supplies, and parts, equipment, and construction materials were removed from government control and became available in larger quantities at lower prices. The policy of accumulating and maintaining large amounts of current assets not required for regular current operations may be adopted to take advantage of technological improvements, to provide for future expansion, and to purchase property and equipment when such acquisition seems appropriate.

Excessive working capital, especially in the form of cash and marketable securities, may be as unfavorable as inadequacy of working capital because of the large volume of funds not being used productively. Idle funds involve a lower amount of income and often lead to investments in undesirable projects or in unnecessary plant facilities and equipment. In fact, the availability of excess working capital may lead to carelessness about costs and, therefore, to inefficiency of operations.

In accordance with the Internal Revenue Code, corporations are subject to a penalty tax on "undue accumulation of retained earnings." The tax is actually levied as a percent of taxable net income. The purpose of the tax is to encourage the payment of dividends (taxable to the recipients) and penalize corporations that in the opinion of the government are seeking to unduly minimize income tax.

Reasons for inadequacy of working capital

Inadequacy of working capital, one of the most important ailments of businesses that are unable to meet their current liabilities, may be caused by one or more of several circumstances:

1. *Operating losses.* Working capital may be inadequate as a result of operating losses as shown by the income statements. A business may incur operating losses because of (*a*) insufficient sales volume relative to the cost of obtaining sales, (*b*) depressed sales prices due to competition or "hard times" without a proportionate decrease in the cost of goods sold and expenses, (*c*) excessive current uncollectible receivables expense, (*d*) increases in expense not accompanied by a proportional increase in sales or revenue, and (*e*) increases in expense while sales or revenue decrease.

Operating losses, as shown by income statements, do not always bring about a reduction of working capital. There are some "noncash expenses" which do not reduce working capital in the period in which they are reported on the income statement. Examples are depreciation, depletion, and amortization. Usually, the assets from which these expense items come have reduced working capital in a prior period (when the depreciable asset was acquired and placed on the balance sheet as an asset for example).

Whether or not working capital is affected, net operating losses decrease retained earnings.

2. *Extraordinary losses.* An inadequacy of working capital may be caused by extraordinary losses such as a decline in market value of inventory; storm, flood, fire, defalcation, or burglary not covered by insurance; an adverse court decision; or an unfavorable income tax decision. An extraordinary loss will usually result in a reduction of current asset values or the incurrence of a current liability.

3. *Failure to obtain additional working capital when the business expands.* Working capital may be inadequate because of the failure of management to obtain from other sources funds needed to finance an expanding business. This expansion may include such activities as the development of new sales territories, the sale of new products, more intensive development of the present sales territory, adoption of new manufacturing as well as extensive sales programs, or the adoption of a new merchandising policy.

Inadequacy of working capital to finance an expanding business is a frequent cause of company failure. The problem is due in part to failure to understand what is involved in financing an expanding enterprise. Cash must be in proportion to the level of expenses (it is desirable that cash approximate total expense for a month). As sales volume grows, receivables (which must be financed) increase. So do inventories. It should not be difficult to visualize why enterprise growth causes financial problems.

4. *Unwise dividend policy.* An inadequacy of working capital may be caused by an unwise dividend policy. To maintain the appearance of a favorable financial record or in anticipation of selling new securities, corporation directors sometimes continue dividend payments although such dividends are not warranted. The dividend policy should be based on the current earnings, the amount of retained earnings, the cash position, and the anticipated need of the business for cash.

5. *Using working capital to acquire noncurrent assets.* Working capital may be inadequate as a result of the investment of current funds in noncurrent assets. This may be due to the replacement of a fixed asset (even though it is fully depreciated, cash to replace it will come out of working capital), purchase of new assets, or the acquisition of long-term holdings of securities in other companies. Working capital is similarly affected when the company pays current liabilities which arose out of the acquisition of noncurrent assets.

6. *Payment of maturing debt and meeting sinking fund requirements.* Working capital may be inadequate (*a*) if management does not accumulate funds for a necessary liquidation of bonds or preferred

capital stock and (*b*) if there is a rigid sinking fund provision, excessive in relation to the net income from year to year. The management may retire stock and bonds during periods of business inactivity by using idle funds. If these funds are not replaced when business activity increases, the working capital may be inadequate.

7. *Increasing price level.* Working capital may be inadequate because of increasing prices, requiring the investment of more dollars to maintain the same physical quantity of inventories and fixed assets and to finance credit sales of the same physical volume of merchandise. Since net income—as ordinarily computed on the basis of original dollar costs —does not exclude so-called "price profits," sufficient earnings should be retained in the business to finance these higher costs, or a shortage of working capital may be the result.

Factors affecting the amount of working capital

Many factors affect the amount of the various types of working capital items such as cash, temporary (cash) investments, receivables, and inventories. The working capital requirements of a particular business depend upon major determinants such as the following:

1. *The general nature or type of business.* The working capital required by a public utility is relatively low because investments in inventories and receivables are rapidly converted into cash. In fact, inventories, which consist mainly of coal and fuel for production of services and material and supplies necessary for repair and construction work, are negligible; receivables are usually collected within 10 to 15 days after the customers have been billed. Some public utilities obtain much of their working capital by billing customers in advance of performing service. For example, telephone bills, except for long-distance charges, are for the succeeding month. The working capital (current assets) of public utilities and railroads constitutes only a relatively small percentage of the total assets. An outstanding characteristic of these industries is the heavy investment in plant and equipment used in performing service for the public.

An industrial company has the problems of large investments of capital in, and relatively slow turnovers of, inventories and receivables. Therefore, in comparison with a public utility the industrial concern requires a much larger amount of working capital. A company that manufactures or processes goods requires a larger amount of working capital than a company that operates a retail store because of the relatively greater investment in raw materials, work in process, and finished goods. The retail store purchases goods ready for sale.

Fluctuations in the net income of public utilities are relatively small, even in times of slow business in general, compared with the ordinary industrial or commercial enterprise.

2. *The time required to manufacture or to obtain the goods for sale and the unit cost of the goods.* The amount of working capital is directly related to the period of time elapsing from the date on which the raw materials or finished goods are purchased to the date on which the goods are sold to the customer. That is, the longer the time required for the manufacture of the goods or the longer the time required to obtain the goods, the larger the amount of working capital that will be needed. Furthermore, the working capital requirements will vary, depending upon the volume of purchases and the unit cost of the goods sold.

For example, a company that manufactures railroad diesel locomotives will have work in process over a much longer period of time than a company that manufactures office equipment. A company that can replenish its stock of goods ready for sale within a 24-hour period will require a smaller inventory than the company that requires several weeks to replace its stock of goods. Also, the company that deals in air-conditioning systems will have a larger working capital requirement than the company that deals in fountain pens. A company engaged in producing a commodity that involves an aging or drying process—such as tobacco, lumber, or liquor—requires a large amount of working capital.

This phenomenon is known as the "inventory turnover," an element of the "working capital turnover." The inventory turnover phenomenon can be measured by dividing total inventory (average for the period is better) into cost of goods sold. If cost of sales is for a year and inventory is half of it, the inventory turnover is twice a year (once in six months). In a manufacturing concern the inventories are more complex, involving raw materials, work in process, and finished goods, and the turnover measurement must be by appropriate segments.

3. *Terms of purchase and sale.* The working capital requirements of a business are affected by the terms of purchase and sale. The more favorable the credit terms on which purchases are made, the less cash is invested in inventory; i.e., the creditors finance the inventory for a shorter or longer period of time. When payment for merchandise is required within a short time after its delivery, a larger amount of cash is necessary to finance a given volume of business. Purchases may or may not be self-financed. For example, a business that purchases merchandise on a 60-day credit basis may acquire cash from the sale of the goods before the debt becomes due. On the other hand, the business may extend longer credit terms to customers than it receives from creditors. The more liberal the credit terms granted to customers, the larger the amount of working capital that will be represented by receivables. In establishing credit terms, it is necessary to consider prevailing trade practices, local economic conditions, and the stage of the business cycle. Credit terms are usually modified during periods of business depression.

When cash discounts are allowed customers, the receivables tend to be collected sooner, resulting in a lower investment in receivables and fewer uncollectible accounts. This is because the financial benefit of the cash discount tends to be substantial and failure to take cash discounts is regarded as a sign of financial stringency. For example, if terms are 2 percent 10 days, net 30 days, by paying 20 days earlier the concern saves 2 percent which is 3 percent a month or 36 percent a year.

4. *The turnover of inventories.* The greater the number of times that the inventories are sold and replaced (the inventory turnover), the lower the amount of working capital that will be required. Effective inventory control is necessary to maintain adequate amounts, kinds, and quality of goods and to regulate the investment in the inventory. An efficient inventory and merchandise program results in a higher rate of turnover of inventory. The more rapid the inventory turnover, the less risk of loss due to decline of price, changes in demand, or changes in style; also, there is less cost involved in carrying the inventory.

Working capital in the form of cash may be obtained by pledging inventories (merchandise, raw materials, work in process, and finished goods) for loans. However, borrowing on inventories does not affect the inventory turnover.

5. *The turnover of receivables.* Working capital requirements depend on the period of time necessary to convert receivables into cash. The less time required to collect receivables, the lower the amount of working capital that will be required. Effective control of receivables is accomplished by wise administration of policies relating to credit extension, terms of sale, establishment of customer maximum credit, and collections. Efficient credit administration results in a higher turnover of receivables. A high turnover of inventory should be accompanied by a relatively prompt collection of receivables. Otherwise, working capital is tied up for a longer period of time and therefore is not available for immediate use in the operating cycle.

The turnover of receivables may be increased by selling or assigning accounts receivable as security. It has long been the practice in the textile industry to sell accounts outright, a process known as "factoring." This practice has been adopted by other industries.

The most effective modern managements place equal emphasis on percentage of net profit on sales and speed of turnover. These collateral factors together produce the amount of return on invested capital.

6. *The business cycle.* In periods of prosperity, business activity is expanded and there is a tendency for business to purchase goods in advance of their current needs in order to take advantage of lower prices and to be more certain of adequate inventories. In this event, a larger amount of working capital is required.

In periods of depression or business inactivity, as business volume declines, the most successful business will convert excess inventories and receivables into cash. Excess cash balances may be (a) accumulated, (b) used to purchase marketable securities, (c) used to pay liabilities, or (d) consumed if the business is operated at a loss.

7. *The degree of risk of possible value decline in current assets.* A decline in the real value in comparison with the book value of marketable securities, inventories, and receivables will result in decreased working capital. Consequently, the greater the risk of such loss, the larger the amount of working capital which should be available in the interest of maintaining the company's credit. To meet such contingencies and thereby prevent possible disaster, the company may maintain a relatively larger amount of cash or of temporary investments.

8. *Whether the sales are uniform throughout the year or are seasonal.* Many businesses have a more or less uniform volume of sales from month to month; whereas other businesses, seasonal in nature, have a concentration of sales during a few months each year. The company having a seasonal business requires a maximum amount of working capital for a relatively short period of time. If the goods are manufactured or processed, the investment of working capital in inventories will gradually increase during the months of preparation for the selling period.

A business having a seasonal demand for its merchandise normally has an excess of working capital during the period of least sales activity. Many businesses, formerly seasonal, have diversified their product lines to solve the problem of seasonal variation. This may accomplish a more effective utilization of working capital, reduce employee turnover, and spread overhead costs.

As discussed below, a seasonal need for credit is commonly satisfied by borrowing from banks.

9. *Credit rating of the company.* The amount of working capital, in the form of cash including temporary cash investments that a company should have available to meet operating requirements, depends upon the established cash policy. For example, management may decide to maintain the equivalent of three to five weeks' requirements for this type of working capital. In turn, the "cash policy" may depend upon:

a)   The credit rating of the business (can it borrow on short notice?)
b)   The conversion (turnover) period for receivables and inventory.
c)   The practice of taking advantage of purchases discount opportunities.

Who should supply working capital

Working capital may be divided into two parts: (1) a basic (relatively permanent) sum equal to the minimum amount of current assets required to conduct the business during the year; and (2) a variable amount of *current assets* (cash, receivables, and inventory), the sum varying with the seasonal activity and emergency and extraordinary needs of the business. The amount of regular, as well as seasonal, working capital will vary, depending upon the stages of the business cycle. That is, during periods of prosperity, working capital needs of both types are greater; and during depressions the needs are much reduced.

A larger proportionate part, if not all, of the basic or permanent working capital should be supplied by the stockholders, either through sales of capital stock or through the reinvestment of earnings in the business or both. The larger the amount of the permanent working capital that is obtained through the investment of the owners (capital stock or earnings), the more favorable will be the credit rating of the business. Also, under these circumstances, the business will be able to finance much more readily its needs for temporary working capital.

The sale of bonds or issuance of term loans or other long-term debt obligations represents other sources of permanent working capital.

These obligations almost always have a fixed maturity, which involves an element of risk affecting the survival of the enterprise. However, if the business is able to earn more on the borrowed funds than is demanded in interest, the excess earnings can be used for the benefit of the stockholders; this is called "trading on the equity."

Customarily, short-term bank loans, commercial paper, trade acceptances, and open-account credit may be depended upon as sources of the variable or temporary working capital. In practice, the last-mentioned sources frequently furnish a relatively large amount of the permanent working capital. This is especially true of businesses that have a relatively low amount of owners' equity and a weak credit rating.

Sources of working capital

The common sources of working capital include the following:

1. Current operations—current income before deducting nonworking capital items such as depreciation, depletion, and amortization. (Net income *plus* conversion of noncurrent assets into working capital via the depreciation, depletion, and amortization processes. In other words, the net income as shown by the income statement *plus* depreciation, depletion, and amortization represents the amount of working capital provided by current operations.)

2. Profit on the sale of marketable securities or other temporary cash investments.

3. Sale of fixed assets, long-term investments, or other noncurrent assets.

4. Federal income tax refunds and other similar extraordinary "gain" items.
5. Proceeds from sales of bonds payable and capital stock, and contributions of funds by owners.
6. Short-term and long-term unsecured loans from banks, insurance companies, or other private lenders.
7. Loans secured by real estate mortgages, chattel mortgages on equipment, or warehouse receipts.
8. Factoring or sale of accounts receivable.
9. Loans against the cash value of life insurance.
10. Loans from the Small Business Administration or from small business investment companies.
11. Sale and lease-back arrangements involving plant and equipment.
12. Trade creditors (accounts, trade acceptances, and notes payable).

A discussion of the sources of working capital follows. (Items 8 through 12 are assumed to be self-explanatory.)

1. *Working capital provided by current operations.* Working capital is provided by sales and other revenues which increase cash and receivables. However, some of this working capital must be devoted to the costs and expenses required to produce the revenues, including cost of goods sold and selling and administrative expenses. Therefore, net income is a source of working capital, and the amount of working capital provided by current operations is determined by analyzing the income statement.

The income statement includes two types of items: (a) cost and expense items, such as merchandise or raw materials purchases, salaries, wages, and insurance, that actually consumed working capital or caused the incurrence of a current liability which later will require the use of working capital; and (b) cost and expense items, such as depreciation, depletion, and amortization of bond discount, bond premium and intangible assets, that have not consumed current working capital or resulted in the incurrence of a current liability which will later reduce the working capital. In order to determine the amount of working capital that has been provided by current operations, it is necessary to eliminate this second group of cost and expense items from the income statement. Although the cost and expense items of the second type must be considered in determining the net income for the year, they are omitted in computing the amount of working capital derived from current operations because they are not *current* charges against working capital. (As previously noted, depreciation for example is generally a gradual transfer of the cost of fixed assets carried on the balance sheet to the income statement.)

It is frequently stated that depreciation and similar costs which are not a current burden on working capital represent sources of working capital. This is not literally true. Revenues, such as sales, interest, and dividends, are the real sources; and depreciation is eliminated from the computation because, unlike wages, working capital is not affected currently. Nevertheless, one may say that through the process of charging depreciation, depletion, and amortization of noncurrent assets against revenue, the fixed and intangible assets are, in a sense, converted into working capital.

Should uncollectible receivables expense be treated in a manner similar to depreciation expense in determining the amount of working capital obtained from current operations? No, because uncollectible receivables expense reduces receivables (working capital); whereas depreciation expense, being related to fixed assets, does not affect working capital. Uncollectible receivables expense is estimated in an attempt to state correctly the operating expenses and to evaluate receivables. Uncollectible receivables expense reduces the book value of receivables which are current assets, and, therefore, diminishes net working capital.

Illustration 11–1 shows the method of adding depreciation and other similar expense items to net income to determine the amount of working capital derived from current operations.

2. *Profit on the sale of marketable securities.* Marketable securities, a current asset item, may be sold, and a profit may be realized on the conversion. The sale of marketable securities represents a substitution of working capital items, i.e., cash, for marketable securities. The profit on the sale represents a source of additional working capital. On the other hand, a loss would constitute a reduction in working capital.

3. *Sale of fixed assets, long-term investments, and other noncurrent assets.* Another source of additional working capital is the proceeds from the sale of fixed assets, long-term investments, and other noncurrent assets which are no longer required by the business. The conversion of these assets into cash results in increasing the working capital in the amount of the net proceeds from the sale. The gain or loss on the sale of long-term investments and other noncurrent assets may qualify as extraordinary items but in any event they must be included in the computation of net income. Since the issuance of the Accounting Principles Board's *Opinion No. 9* carrying the results of such transactions directly to retained earnings is not permitted.

In preparing a report showing the sources of working capital, it is desirable to show clearly the various types of transactions which have affected working capital such as current operations and sales of noncurrent assets.

4. *Federal income tax refunds and other similar extraordinary "gain" items.* Frequently, a refund is made to a business by the state or federal government because of overpayment of income tax during prior years.

ILLUSTRATION 11–1.   The effects on working capital of the various items commonly encountered in income statements

Items			*Effects on working capital*
Sales		$100,000	Increases
Less: Cost of goods sold (except noncash items below)		75,000	Decreases
Gross margin on sales		$ 25,000	Increases
Less: Depreciation	$ 2,000		No effect
Bond discount amortization	200		No effect
Amortization of patent	300		No effect
Other operating expenses	17,250		Decreases
Other expense less other income	1,000		Decreases
Federal income tax	750	21,500	Decreases
Net Income		$ 3,500	Increases ($6,000*)

* Analysis of the $6,000 increase in working capital:

Gross working capital increase from sales.		$100,000
Working capital decrease from:		
Cost of goods sold (no noncash items).		75,000
		$ 25,000
Operating expenses.	$17,250	
Other expense over other income.	1,000	
Federal income tax.	750	19,000
		$ 6,000

The difference between net income ($3,500) and the increase in working capital ($6,000) = $2,500:

Depreciation.	$2,000
Amortization.	500
	$2,500

The more customary computation to arrive at the $6,000 increase is:

Net income.	$3,500
Noncash items.	2,500
	$6,000

A business may also obtain a favorable decision in a lawsuit. The tax refund (a reimbursement of working capital used in prior years) and proceeds from a favorable lawsuit decision (a source of new working capital) may be shown on the income statement or, if the circumstances qualify under APB *Opinion No. 9* as legitimate "prior period adjustments" (see Chapter 6, page 147), as credits directly to Retained Earnings. However, as the "clean retained earnings" concept is now the prevailing policy in the financial statements of major U.S. corporations, it would seem preferable to include such items in the computation of net income. The income from the lawsuit would appear to be best placed in the extraordinary income category. Inasmuch as the items are gains, not losses, it would seem probable that corporate managements would usually prefer to use them to augment profits. Both items should have adequate disclosure, probably by description in a footnote.

5. *Sales of bonds and capital stock and contributions of funds by owners.* Long-term mortgage notes, bonds, and capital stock may be sold to obtain and to increase the initial working capital, to increase

the working capital when expansion is undertaken, or to replenish working capital in the event of exhaustion or depletion. An excessive issue of interest-bearing obligations is undesirable because of risk arising from interest which must be paid on time and the eventual necessity for payment of the principal (or arrangement for its renewal).

In proprietorships and partnerships the owners of the business are the primary source of both the initial and the additional working capital.

6. *Bank and other short-term loans.* Short-term loans are depended upon by most businesses as an important source of current assets, especially when additional working capital is necessary to meet seasonal, emergency, or other short-term and temporary requirements. Because of this dependence on banks and creditors for short-term loans, it is of the utmost importance for the business to maintain its credit rating at a high level.

7. *Trade creditors (accounts, trade acceptances, and notes payable).* One of the most important sources of working capital is the credit extended by suppliers. Materials, goods, supplies, and services are customarily purchased on account or obtained in exchange for promissory notes. In certain lines of business, as in some branches of the textile trade, direct cash loans are made by suppliers to selected customers. An ideal situation exists when a business is able to sell merchandise and to collect receivables before payables are due. A lower total amount of working capital is then required.

Ideally, only temporary (seasonal) working capital should be obtained from short-term creditors, with the exception of customary trade credit under usual terms.

Uses (applications) of working capital

The uses or applications of working capital result in changing either the form or the amount of current assets. The most important uses made of working capital are as follows:

1. Uses or applications of working capital resulting in a reduction of current assets:
   a) Payments of current expenses and payables (including dividends payable).
   b) Withdrawals of profits in single proprietorships and partnerships.
   c) Operating losses or extraordinary losses that require the use of cash.
   d) Retirements of long-term liabilities and capital stock.
   e) Establishment of funds for such purposes as pensions for employees, retirement of capital stock, payment of bonds at maturity or when called, or replacement of noncurrent assets.

  f) Replacement or purchase of additional fixed assets, intangible
      assets, and long-term investments.
2. Transactions resulting in a change in the form of current assets:
  a) Purchase of marketable securities with cash.
  b) Purchase of merchandise with cash.
  c) Exchange of one form of receivable for another.

The use of working capital in 1 (e) above represents a transfer
from current assets to noncurrent assets, and in 1 (f) represents a reduction in working capital and an increase in noncurrent assets. The use
of working capital in 1 (a) above does not change working capital
when the items have been recorded as current liabilities; the use of
working capital in 1 (b) through 1 (f) reduces working capital.

JUDGING THE SOLVENCY OF THE SMALL BUSINESS

Measured by a simple count of the *number* of business organizations
in the United States, the majority of them are small. For example, income
tax statistics show that over one third of the retail hardware stores
have less than $50,000 of total assets and over two thirds have less
than $100,000 of assets. Over 90 percent have assets less than $250,000.
Drugstores and clothing stores show similar characteristics; jewelry stores
run 10 percent to 15 percent larger. Over half of the grocery stores
have less than $50,000 of assets; and restaurants, bars, and other such
establishments run even smaller, as do gasoline service stations. A few
types—department stores, for example—run larger, but half have total
assets under $250,000.

While these small retail stores bulk large when counting the number
of establishments, their proportion of the total sales volume is much
less impressive. Clothing stores with assets under $50,000 sold only 7
percent of the total apparel sold at retail; furniture and household equipment stores sold 9 percent; and jewelry sold 3 percent.

A substantial number of manufacturing and wholesaling enterprises
are also small. Of manufacturers of clothing, canned and frozen foods,
and dairy products, one out of four have total assets of less than $50,000;
so do wholesalers of meat. And their sales are less than 3 percent of
the total.

Whereas large corporations customarily use long-term debt as one
of the means to finance their operations, the small concern may not
have access to this type of financing. In fact, a substantial proportion
of the smallest enterprises do not have access to bank credit and rely
on their owners and on the concerns that sell them their stock in trade.

If there is little or no long-term debt, an analysis of the financial
soundness of the enterprise turns on its ability to pay its current debts.

The considerations discussed heretofore in this chapter are pertinent here but there may be certain aspects requiring special emphasis when the concern is very small. In addition to having little or no long-term debt, it may sell wholly or largely for cash. If so, receivables are not important and current assets are primarily inventory, plus cash—the latter frequently is less than adequate for the operating needs of the business. Current liabilities of the small enterprise consist of accruals (current payables arising from day-to-day running expenses, including taxes) and accounts payable—trade (sums due to suppliers for purchases of stock in trade).

Usually wages and taxes and other current-expense payables are paid first, and if cash is short, the suppliers of stock in trade are expected to wait for their money. Of course, the patience that suppliers are willing to display varies, but it is not uncommon for them to realize that they are suppliers of both merchandise and credit.

Under these circumstances, as small enterprises are often inadequately supplied with owner-contributed funds (equity capital), the current status of amounts payable to suppliers is of critical importance. The acid-test ratio (cash, cash equivalents, and receivables) of small retail stores is typically 50 cents for each dollar of current liabilities—or less. As a going business must have working funds on hand at all times, and as expense accruals usually receive preferred treatment, the trade supplier must look for his money to future sales. If there are accounts receivable, this will slow down the flow of cash and may raise the question of collectibility.

Under these circumstances, therefore, a critical question is: if the cash which will be forthcoming from sales is going to first be applied to pay off current-expense accruals, how long will it take to pay off accounts payable—trade? An approximate answer can be found by going through the following steps (see table on page 281).

1. Estimate the flow of cash which will be derived from sales. This estimate should show when the cash inflow can be expected to take place. If sales are for cash (there are no accounts receivable) sales will equate with cash receipts. If a material portion of the sales are on credit, the length of the typical interval between sale and collection will have to be estimated and consequently taken into account.

2. Apply (deduct from) the incoming cash the amount required to pay off the current-expense accruals. A refinement at this point would take into account the estimated net income (if it can realistically be concluded that the owner can wait until the debts already on the books have been paid). Of course, taxes, including income taxes, must be provided for as an element of current expense.

3. The balance is the sum available to pay the current, but longer term, accounts payable—trade. How many months of sales will it take?

Evaluation of the result reached in step 3 will be affected, of course, by the terms under which the accounts payable—trade are supposed to be paid. A knowledge of the history of financial relations with suppliers would be useful if available.

The following table shows the customary relationships between net sales and current liabilities in a few types of retail stores (the ratios are sales to current liabilities, the latter expressed as 1).

| | Total assets | | Average of all sizes |
	Under $50,000	$100,000–$250,000	
Clothing stores	3.2 to 1	4.0 to 1	2.2 to 1
Hardware.	2.4 to 1	3.5 to 1	2.9 to 1
Home furniture and			
equipment.	3.9 to 1	4.2 to 1	2.4 to 1

To understand these figures one must realize that if clothing stores with total assets under $50,000 typically have $1 of current liabilities for each $3.20 of net sales, and if the enterprise is habitually short of working capital (cash), it will take almost 4 months of sales to pay off the current liabilities (divide 12 months by 3.2). So, as pointed out above, the question now is, how patiently will the suppliers wait? Even if some cash can be squeezed out of the typical "quick" ratio of .5 to 1, the overall payment period can be expected to exceed two months.

We have been discussing this matter in terms of averages and some small stores will be more liquid than this, others will be less. If the business being analyzed will have current payables still outstanding after several months, it would be wise to be very cautious about advancing credit to the enterprise.

An example: A neighborhood food store

Earl and Amy Johnson own and operate a neighborhood grocery store which at the end of 1970 showed the financial condition reflected in the financial statements in Illustration 11–2.

Notice the following things about these statements:

1. A $973 profit in 1970 changed into a $651 loss in 1971 in spite of a reduction in operating expenses of $272. The net book value of store fixtures and equipment was identical in these two years which

ILLUSTRATION 11–2

	December 31	
	1971	1970
Assets		
Current Assets:		
Cash.	$ 925	$ 739
Inventory	4,122	4,397
Total Current Assets	$5,047	$5,136
Store fixtures and equipment.	3,052	3,052
Total Assets.	$8,099	$8,188
Liabilities and Net Worth		
Current Liabilities:		
Accounts payable*	$5,146	$4,584
Total Current Liabilities	$5,146	$4,584
Other payables (to owners)	465	465
Total Liabilities.	$5,611	$5,049
Net worth	2,488	3,139
Total Liabilities and Net Worth	$8,099	$8,188

* Analysis of accounts payable:		
Expense related	$1,226	$1,194
Inventory related.	3,920	3,390
Total.	$5,146	$4,584

	1971		1970	
	($)	(%)	($)	(%)
Net sales	97,489	100	97,251	100
Cost of goods sold	77,017	79	74,883	77
Gross margin	20,472	21	22,368	23
Operating expenses	21,123	22	21,395	22
Profit or (Loss).	(651)	Loss	973	1

seems to indicate that depreciation was not taken in 1971. While sales rose slightly ($238), cost of goods sold went up from 77 percent to 79 percent ($2,134). Of course, this was the major factor producing the 1971 loss, and the problem may (or may not) have been in inventory-taking rather than in operations. Inventory declined slightly as sales rose (also slightly).

2.   While net worth was going down, due to the loss, accounts payable went up by about the same amount. This is expectable as the funds have to come from somewhere. Inventory dropped slightly and cash rose by about the same amount.

3. We are now ready for the final step, the analysis explained on page 276.

Estimated inflow of cash from sales (all sales are for cash).		$97,500
Deduct, expense-related accounts payable		1,226
		$96,274
Add, estimated net income	Conjectural	....
		$96,274
To get estimated cash inflow for the first month divide by		12
		$ 8,023

Inventory-related payables are $3,920 so only one half of a month will be required to pay off all liabilities except the $465 due to the Johnsons. Consequently it would seem that they do not have any very severe problem currently.

A second example: A retail jewelry store

Measured by total assets, Charles Hale's jewelry store is about three times the size of the neighborhood grocery analyzed in the first example, but dollars of sales are smaller. Food stores are high turnover, relatively low gross margin establishments, whereas jewelry stores have high gross margins to support relatively low volume.

We have been supplied with the financial statements shown in Illustration 11–3 but we have not been able to secure comparative figures. Notice the following things about these statements:

1. Mr. Hale sells on credit as well as for cash, and the terms of sale were about half in each category. This will affect the interval between sale and collection of cash, as will be discussed below. Mr. Hale's gross margin and operating expense percentages are normal for retail jewelry stores as shown in the Robert Morris Associates *Annual Statement Studies 1970* and reflected in Illustration 11–4. The net profit margin is thin and seems to point to a need for better operating expense control.

2. To estimate the cash inflow from sales we must first determine the average collection interval on accounts receivable. Of approximately $30,000 of annual sales on account, $3,736 remains on the balance sheet as accounts receivable, uncollected at December 31, 1971. This is slightly over 12 percent and 12 percent of 365 days (in the year) is 44 days, the average collection period. As retail accounts, on the average, are customarily collected in less than 30 days, the result of this calculation makes one somewhat suspicious of the quality of the accounts receivable and of Hale's effectiveness as a collector.

3. $30,000 of cash sales means a cash inflow from that source of

ILLUSTRATION 11-3

CHARLES HALE JEWELRY
Balance Sheet
December 31, 1971

Assets			Liabilities and Net Worth	
Current assets:			Current Liabilities:	
Cash.		$ 1,478	Accounts payable	$13,127
Accounts receivable		3,736	Total Current	
Inventory		13,777	Liabilities	$13,127
Total Current Assets.		$18,991	Net worth:	
Fixed assets $5,712			Original capital.	7,500
Depreciation 810		4,902	Retained earnings	3,266
Total Assets.		$23,893	Total Liabilities and	
			Net Worth	$23,893

Income Statement
1971

Net sales: Cash	$29,982	
On account	29,998	
	$59,980	100%
Cost of goods sold.	33,067	55
Gross margin	$26,913	45
Operating expenses*	25,978	43
Net Income	$ 935	2% (actually 1.6%)

* Includes depreciation: $600.

$2,500 per month plus, after a month and a half, another $2,500 a month (this is actually an average result). Not much help can be expected from the cash account which at December 31st stood at about ⅝ths of a desirable balance for operating purposes (one month's operating expenses).

4. Accounts payable at December 31, 1971, stood at $13,127, and we do not know how that amount should be divided between expense-oriented payables and inventory-oriented payables. But we do know that on the average the accounts payable cannot be paid off any faster than is shown in the following table:

January.	$ 2,500
February.	3,750
March.	5,000
April (the balance)	1,877
	$13,127

While in the above calculation cash inflow which can be expected from 1972 cash sales has been fully taken into account, the receipts from sales on account would not be exactly as shown: there would also be receipts from 1972 sales on account. The effect of this factor can be measured by assuming that on $60,000 of total annual sales ($5,000 per month), cash inflow will be $5,000 per month. On this basis it will take about 2⅔ months to pay accounts payable of $13,127. And if one also takes into account that expense-oriented payables tend to be paid first, the suppliers for inventory will wait, on the average, about 55 days for their money—much too long unless the suppliers are willingly helping Mr. Hale to capitalize his business.

ILLUSTRATION 11–4. Factors to use in testing the ability of small businesses to pay their debts (except current expense accruals) (from *Financial Statement Studies, 1970* edition, by special permission of the Robert Morris Associates)

Retail business total assets under $250,000	Net profit before income tax	Esti- mated income tax (25%)	Net profit after income tax	Other ex- penses	Total ex- penses less profit	Available for current debt except expense accruals (including income tax)
Family clothing	4.2%	1.0%	3.2%	29.9%	26.7%	73.3%
Furs	3.9	1.0	2.9	36.1	33.2	66.8
Infants' clothing	4.3	1.1	3.2	34.1	30.9	69.1
Men's and clothing	4.4	1.1	3.3	34.6	31.3	68.7
Shoes	4.5	1.1	3.4	36.2	32.8	67.2
Women's ready-to-wear	3.7	.9	2.8	34.3	31.5	68.5
Books and stationery	3.8	.9	2.9	31.1	28.2	71.8
Office supplies and equipment	3.3	.8	2.5	32.8	30.3	69.7
Building materials	2.9	.7	2.2	25.7	23.5	76.5
Hardware	3.4	.8	2.6	28.0	25.4	74.6
Heating and plumbing equipment	3.9	1.0	2.9	23.5	20.6	79.4
Lumber	2.6	.6	2.0	23.1	21.1	78.9
Paint, glass, wallpaper	2.8	.7	2.1	27.5	25.4	74.6
Photographic equipment and supplies	1.9	.5	1.4	25.1	23.7	76.3
Dry goods and general merchandise	4.9	1.2	3.7	27.8	24.1	75.9
Drugs	3.0	.7	2.3	29.6	27.3	72.7
Farm equipment	1.8	.4	1.4	17.1	15.7	84.3
Feed, seed—farm and garden supplies	2.6	.6	2.0	23.6	21.6	78.4
Flowers	3.3	.8	2.5	46.3	43.8	56.2
Dairy products	2.2	.5	1.7	17.7	16.0	84.0
Groceries and meats	1.3	.3	1.0	18.3	17.3	82.7
Restaurants	4.0	1.0	3.0	52.4	49.4	50.6
Fuel except oil	2.9	.7	2.2	28.5	26.3	73.7
	1.3	.3	1.0	28.8	27.8	72.2
Floor coverings	2.8	.7	2.1	28.1	26.0	74.0
Furniture	3.8	.9	2.9	33.8	30.9	69.1
Household appliances	2.6	.6	2.0	22.9	20.9	79.1
Radios, TV, record players	3.1	.8	2.3	29.7	27.4	72.6
Jewelry	6.4	1.6	4.8	39.0	34.2	65.8
Liquor	2.3	.6	1.7	15.9	14.2	85.8
Luggage and gifts	5.4	1.3	4.1	33.4	29.3	70.7
Marine hardware, boat, supply	2.8	.7	2.1	20.6	18.5	81.5
Automobiles	1.7	.4	1.3	14.5	13.2	86.8
House trailers	2.8	.7	2.1	14.9	12.8	87.2
Tire, battery, accessories	3.0	.7	2.3	29.3	27.0	73.0
Trucks	2.0	.5	1.5	16.0	14.5	85.5
Musical instruments and supplies	3.7	.9	2.8	33.4	30.6	69.4
Road machinery equipment	2.1	.5	1.6	20.0	18.4	81.6
Sporting goods	3.0	.7	2.3	26.1	23.8	76.2
Vending machine merchandise	3.1	.8	2.3	38.4	36.1	63.9

* The small business enterprises summarized in this category are corporations, partnerships and proprietorships. Consequently, the federal income tax expense varies and, except for those which are incorporated, cannot be determined. For use in this table, an estimate of 25% has been made, based on the data for corporations summarized in Part IV of the Robert Morris Associates *Annual Statement Studies 1970*. While this estimate cannot be expected to be accurate, it is better than no adjustment at all, and is adequate for the use to which these data are put.

QUESTIONS AND PROBLEMS

11-1. Discuss the two definitions of working capital.

11-2. Should the amount of working capital increase or decrease in proportion to changes in sales volume? Explain.

11-3. What is the significance of working capital from the point of view of the bondholder, the stockholder, and the management?

11-4. Comment on the following statements:
 a) Inadequate as well as excessive working capital is unfavorable.
 b) The establishment of a sinking fund results in a reduction of working capital.
 c) Should noncurrent liabilities ever move to the current liabilities section? If so, when and why?
 d) Depreciation and amortization provide working capital.
 e) The adequacy of working capital depends upon the turnover of receivables and inventories.

11-5. Give a brief discussion of the following:
 a) What disposition should be made of excess working capital?
 b) In determining working capital, should U.S. government securities be classified as a current asset or shown as an offset to "estimated federal taxes liability"?
 c) Study the following data and give reasons which may account for the changes in the amounts:

	1970	1971
Marketable securities	$ 90,700	$ 88,330
Notes receivable	15,000	28,150
Merchandise inventory	751,320	841,940
Notes payable	5,000	150,000

11-6. Explain the meaning of the working capital cycle.

11-7. What determines the adequacy of working capital?

11-8. List several causes of inadequacy of working capital.

11-9. What are the uses of working capital?

11-10. Determine whether each of the following transactions would:
 a) Increase working capital.
 b) Decrease working capital.
 c) Have no effect on working capital
 (1) Paid $4,000 cash for merchandise.
 (2) $1,000 of trade accounts receivable were written off.
 (3) Borrowed cash from the bank; issued a 6 percent, $10,000, 60-day note.
 (4) Recorded estimated doubtful accounts expense at the end of the accounting period, $1,000.

(5) Declared and distributed a $20,000 stock dividend.
(6) Sold marketable securities which cost $7,500 for $9,000.
(7) Paid trade creditor accounts, $55,000, discount allowed, 2 percent.
(8) Recorded estimated depreciation of buildings at the end of the accounting period, $8,000.
(9) Borrowed cash from the bank; issued a $10,000, 90-day, noninterest-bearing note; the bank discount rate was 6 percent.
(10) Received a 60-day, 6 percent, $1,000 promissory note from a customer to apply on account.
(11) Fixed assets were sold for $11,000 cash.
(12) A $10,000 cash dividend on common stock was declared.
(13) The declared dividend (above) was paid.
(14) Purchased delivery equipment, $18,500; issued a check for $15,000 and a 90-day promissory note for the balance.

12

Statement of changes in financial position

In March 1971, the Accounting Principles Board issued *Opinion No. 19*, "Reporting Changes in Financial Position." In it, the Board, which had previously recommended (in *Opinion No. 3*) that a "funds statement be regularly included with other financial statements," changed the recommendation to a requirement. It also expanded the scope of the statement and set down guidelines concerning its form.[1]

Opinion No. 19 also changed the name of the "funds statement" to "statement of changes in financial position." This change was made because the content of the statement was broadened. The Board prescribed that all important events during the year having a bearing on the financial and investing activities of the concern must be included in the statement or disclosed in connection with it. Heretofore, many funds statements disclosed only events which affected working capital (current assets and current liabilities) or—in an alternative form of statement—cash.[2] For example, in the diagram shown, capital paid in by share-

---

[1] Much of the material in this chapter has been drawn from *Opinion No. 19*. The discussion of how to prepare such a statement, included in previous editions, has been removed because these mechanics are widely taught in other texts and will now, of course, be even more commonly explained.

[2] The "dotted line" is an imaginary line which might be drawn on any balance sheet immediately below the current assets and current liabilities sections. In other words, it is a sort of boundary mark delineating "working capital" (current assets less current liabilities). In the past, "funds statements" have shown where "funds" have come from and where "funds" have gone during the period—in other words, how "funds" have crossed the dotted line, coming and going. They still do, but now they show other transactions as well.

holders would give rise to a debit to cash and a credit to capital stock, and the transaction obviously would "cross the dotted line"—a source of funds. So would an investment of cash in a new plant. But the payment of a current liability by a draft on cash would cause a rearrangement of items within working capital but would not affect its total. Finally, consider the effect of acquiring a subsidiary company in exchange for the parent company's stock. All elements of this transaction are "below the dotted line," and working capital is not affected. Nevertheless, it is an important financial transaction and *Opinion No. 19* requires that the details be disclosed.

While *Opinion No. 19* does not prescribe any particular form, it does establish guidelines, explanation of which will begin in connection with a before–*Opinion No. 19* funds statement of the Hershey Foods Corporation, selected for its simplicity.

Opinion No. 19 specifically requires that "one statement should clearly disclose":

a)   Outlays for purchase and proceeds from unusual sales of long-term assets (identifying investments, property and intangibles, etc.).
b)   Conversion of debt or preferred stock to common stock.
c)   Long-term debt and capital stock transactions.
d)   Distributions to shareholders not otherwise disclosed.

Many companies made these disclosures in connection with their funds statements prior to the issuance of APB *Opinion No. 19*. For example, Xerox did so in a footnote (not reproduced) which disclosed that "the Company's voting rights in Rank Xerox Limited increased from 50% to 51% for which it agreed to issue . . . 142,956 shares of Xerox common stock . . . ; the value of such shares ($12,500,000) is included in . . . intangible assets and will be amortized to income over a 25-year period." Note that this transaction did not affect working capital or cash. It did affect investment in a subsidiary, capital stock and, ultimately, net income.

Statement of changes in financial position—nature and purpose

The statement of changes in financial position gives a picture of management's handling of circulating capital. It is, therefore, a "window" through which the analyst can closely examine one phase of management's planning and decision making. The statement provides answers to several questions which cannot be supplied by the conventional financial statements, such as those listed below. Questions may be raised by management, stockholders, creditors, and others.

1. What has caused the change in the working capital position?
2. How much working capital was provided by current operations, and what disposition was made of it?
3. What was the amount of capital derived from the sale of capital stock or through long-term borrowing, and what use was made of these funds?
4. Did the company dispose of any of the noncurrent assets, and if so, what were the proceeds?
5. What additional plant and equipment or other noncurrent assets were acquired by using working capital?

It should be clear then that the statement of changes in financial position summarizes the results of financial activities of a business for the current year and presents reasons for the net change in its financial position. It gives insight into the financial policy of management. The statement is useful to management as an important aid in controlling working capital and in effective utilization of resources in the future. It is of equal importance to credit grantors and others. This is why the Accounting Principles Board has added it to the basic financial statements, whether or not audited by certified public accountants.

Using budget procedures, the statement of funds may be projected into the future, in which event it becomes a working capital budget. Therefore, through disclosure of the factors affecting working capital in the past, the statement is an important instrument in the control of working capital and in the effective utilization of resources in the future.

Examples—how transactions affect working capital

As pointed out above, this volume no longer proposes to teach the technical details involved in constructing a statement of changes in working capital. But a few additional transactions will be discussed to strengthen the reader's theoretical comprehension.

The statement of funds is prepared from comparative balance sheets together with supplementary explanations of changes in the noncurrent items. Comparative balance sheets reveal net changes in dollar amounts from one date to another, but there is no indication as to either the amount of resources obtained by the business or how resources were used. For example, a comparative balance sheet may show that real estate decreased $100,000, buildings and equipment increased $481,000, land increased $10,000, and retained earnings appropriated for sinking fund increased $10,000. Questions may be raised relative to these changes as follows:

1. Was the real estate sold at cost, at a gain, or at a loss; or was it transferred to a fixed asset classification? In the first instance the transaction would represent a source of working capital because cash or the equivalent would be received in exchange for the real estate. In the second, the transaction would represent a nonworking capital entry; i.e., a transfer from one classification to another without affecting working capital. The decrease in real estate of $100,000 represents the net change during the period. Possibly additional real estate was acquired at a cost of $400,000 and $500,000 of owned real estate was sold.

2. Does the increase in building and equipment represent new acquisitions (a use of working capital), a transfer from the long-term investment category, the recording of appreciation (working capital not affected), or the net result of both acquisition and disposal? Did the company write off any of its old properties and trade in or sell other portions (working capital may have been affected)?

3. Does the increase in land reflect a new acquisition of land, a transfer from real estate, or the net result of both acquisition and disposal? A purchase of land would usually require the use of working capital; a transfer from one classification to another would not affect the working capital.

4. Does the increase in retained earnings appropriated for sinking fund represent a source of working capital, or does it reflect only a transfer from another account? An increase in this item is a result of transferring an amount from retained earnings; and, therefore, working capital is not affected.

It should be clear that the net changes reflected by the noncurrent sections of a comparative balance sheet represent (1) a source or a use of working capital, i.e., an increase or decrease in working capital; (2) account adjustments or transfers from one account to another by journal entries which neither increase nor decrease working capital; or

(3) a combination of the two. The exact nature of the net changes shown by noncurrent sections of the comparative balance sheet are determined by analyzing the transactions that have been entered in the noncurrent accounts.

The adjustment of accounts and the transfer entries concern the original recording of the following or similar types of transactions (so-called "nonworking capital items" or bookkeeping entries) which neither increase nor decrease working capital:

Item	Effect of original entry	Effect on working capital
Depreciation—*adjusting entry*	Increase: Depreciation Expense Increase: Accumulated Depreciation	No effect
Depletion—*adjusting entry*	Increase: Depletion Expense Increase: Accumulated Depletion	No effect
Amortization—*adjusting entry*	Increase: Amortization Expense Decrease: Intangible Assets or Increase: Accumulated Amortization	No effect
Declaration and issuance of stock dividends—*transfer entry*	Decrease: Retained Earnings Increase: Outstanding Capital Stock	No effect
Issuance of capital stock in exchange for outstanding bonds—*transfer entry* (conversion of bonds into capital stock)	Decrease: Bonds Payable Increase: Capital Stock	No effect
Issuance of capital stock in exchange for noncurrent assets—*transfer entry*	Increase: Noncurrent Assets (specifically) stated) Increase: Outstanding Capital Stock	No effect
Appropriation of retained earnings—*transfer entry*	Decrease: Retained Earnings Increase: Appropriated Retained Earnings or specific appropriated accounts	No effect
Appreciation of asset—*adjusting entry*	Increase: Asset (specific asset stated) Increase: Appraisal Capital	No effect
Write-off noncurrent asset—*transfer entry*	Decrease: Retained Earnings Decrease: Asset (specific asset stated)	No effect

The above transactions do not affect working capital. Nevertheless, to the extent that they are of enough importance to require attention (affect the judgment of an investor for example) APB *Opinion No. 19* requires that they be disclosed.

"Working capital flow per share"

In section 15 of *Opinion No. 19*, the Accounting Principles Board voices its disapproval of *isolated* statistics purporting to show "working capital flow per share" resulting from operations. In the past such statistics have sometimes been displayed without benefit of adjustments for noncash or nonworking-capital items and without incorporating the full story lying behind the actual flow of working capital during the period. In 1970, 109 of the 600 *Accounting Trends and Techniques* corporations mentioned cash flow, some of them several times, down from 113 in 1969.

The cash flow form of statement

The objective of a statement of changes in working capital is the summarization and disclosure of financial operations for a period. There are two conventional forms of such a statement: one focusing on the sources and uses of working capital discussed above, and the other focusing on cash (including securities which are the equivalent of cash).

APB *Opinion No. 19* has this to say about the format of a statement of changes in financial position.

9. The Board recognizes the need for flexibility in form, content, and terminology of the Statement to meet its objectives in differing circumstances. For example, a working capital format is not relevant to an entity that does not distinguish between current and non-current assets and liabilities. . . .

11. . . . the Statement may take whatever form gives the most useful portrayal of the financing and investing activities and the changes in financial position of the reporting entity. The Statement may be in balanced form or in a form expressing the changes in financial position in terms of cash, or cash and temporary investments combined, of all quick assets, or of working capital.

The cash flow form has never enjoyed great popularity. Prior to the effective date of APB *Opinion No. 19* (years ending after September 30, 1971), 529 corporations used the working capital form in their 1970 annual reports and 39 used the cash flow form; 5 used miscellaneous forms and 27 of the *Accounting Trends and Techniques 1971* companies did not present the statement.

The Colgate-Palmolive Company prepares its statement in this form (see Illustration 12–2 on page 291). Note that the statement displays changes in the following working capital items which, in the working capital form, would be merged in one amount, increase or decrease in working capital:

Under funds provided by:
(Increase) decrease in receivables
Increase in accounts payable
Increase (decrease) in other accrued current
  liabilities net of prepaid income taxes
Increase in accrued United States and
  foreign income taxes

Under funds used for:

Decrease in bank loans of foreign subsidiaries
Increase in inventories
Increase (decrease) in cash and marketable
  securities

As the statement when presented in this form contains as integral components all changes in the individual current assets and current liability items, it is not necessary to present a supporting analysis of such changes.

Alternate forms of arranging the data

Three ways of arranging the data all enjoy substantial support from the *Accounting Trends and Techniques 1971* corporations.

The most popular arrangement, used by 213 companies, displays at the bottom of the statement the increase or decrease in working capital (or cash) during the period. This arrangement is shown in Illustration 12–1.

ILLUSTRATION 12–1

APB 19 GUIDELINES	CONSOLIDATED STATEMENT OF CHANGES IN FINANCIAL POSITION		
	✂ Hershey Foods Corporation AND SUBSIDIARIES		
1. Name changed to STATEMENT OF CHANGES IN FINANCIAL POSITION		FOR THE YEARS ENDED DECEMBER 31	
	SOURCE	1971	1970
2. The statement should begin with net income (before extraordinary items, if any) or with income before cost of goods sold and expenses. The resulting amount is the same.	Net income	$ 20,493,201	$18,857,5
	Add–Expenses not requiring outlay of working capital:		
	Depreciation	5,943,497	5,514,1
	Deferred income taxes	1,264,957	1,409,1
3. Income should be adjusted for items not requiring outlay of working capital in the current period (making clear that the adjustment items are not sources or uses of working capital or cash) and the resulting amount should be appropriately described (as it has been by Hershey).	Working capital provided from operations	27,701,655	25,780,8
	Long term borrowings	3,500,000	11,357,1
	Sale of Autopoint Company, a division of Cory Corporation, for $3,400,000 less applicable net current assets (working capital) in the amount of $1,305,367 included in sale	–	2,094,6
		31,201,655	39,232,6
	DISPOSITION		
4. The statement should prominently disclose working capital (or cash— some enterprises do not show total current assets and liabilities). The recommended wording is "working capital used in operations for the period."	Dividends paid:		
	Preferred	270,000	225,0
	Common	13,036,624	13,017,5
	Treasury stock acquired	3,652,609	1,692,7
	Additions to plant and property	22,601,768	12,012,0
	Payments of long term debt	5,514,316	3,187,3
	Other (Net)	996,648	903,5
		46,071,965	31,038,
	Increase (Decrease) in working capital	$(14,870,310)	$ 8,194,
5. If the statement shows the flow of working capital, changes within the working capital section should be shown in detail.*	CHANGES IN WORKING CAPITAL		
	Current Assets:		
	Cash	$ (3,040,314)	$ (4,134,
	Accounts receivable	2,791,853	1,827,
	Inventories	4,289,371	2,440,
	Total	4,040,910	133,
	Current Liabilities:		
	Loans payable	15,037,495	(490,
	Accounts payable	2,775,606	(6,925
	Accrued liabilities	1,567,211	(773,
	Taxes payable	(469,092)	128,
* In the 1970 annual reports of the 600 Accounting Trends and Techniques corporations only 123 presented the supporting analysis of changes in working capital items; 406 companies presented the working capital form without the analysis.	Total	18,911,220	(8,060,
	Increase (Decrease) in working capital	$(14,870,310)	$ 8,194
	The accompanying notes are an integral part of this statement.		

ILLUSTRATION 12–2

Colgate-Palmolive Company		1971	1970
	Funds Provided by:		
Thousands of Dollars	Operations:		
	Net income	$ 44,940	$ 40,312
	Depreciation	21,478	20,216
	Increase in deferred liabilities	13,610	10,794
	Total funds provided from operations	80,028	71,322
	Retirement or sale of plant and equipment	1,748	3,235
	Issuance of new long-term debt	11,655	952
	(Increase) decrease in receivables	3,138	(729)
	Increase in accounts payable	13,786	1,925
	Increase (decrease) in other accrued current liabilities net of prepaid income taxes	10,827	(6,622)
	Increase in accrued United States and foreign income taxes	3,132	9,744
	Increase—other	112	1,766
	Total	$124,426	$ 81,593
	Funds Used for:		
	Dividends declared	$ 20,718	$ 19,602
	Additions to plant and equipment	38,753	29,005
	Repayment of long-term debt	5,574	11,199
	Acquisition of treasury stock	5,074	6,444
	Decrease in bank loans of foreign subsidiaries	11,204	5,566
	Increase in inventories	8,013	23,010
	Increase (decrease) in cash and marketable securities	35,090	(13,233)
	Total	$124,426	$ 81,593

APB 19 GUIDELINES

6. If the statement shows the flow of cash (and invest-ments equivalent to cash) changes in working capital items are already shown in the statement.

ILLUSTRATION 12–3

STATEMENT OF CHANGES IN FINANCIAL POSITION

LaSalle National Bank

	Year Ended December 31	
	1971	1970
SOURCES OF FUNDS		
From Operations:		
Net Income.	$ 2,985,689	$ 2,856,243
Add (Deduct) Items Not Affecting Funds:		
Provision for Deferred Income Taxes.	(314,524)	17,917
Provision for Depreciation.	260,000	312,000
Provision for Possible Loan Losses.	305,076	319,040
Discount Accretion, Net of Premium Amortization on Securities.	(19,372)	(462,392)
Net Changes in Accrued Income and Accrued Expenses.	(1,535,408)	40,197
	1,681,461	3,083,005
Sales and Redemptions of Investment Securities,		
Net of Gains and Losses.	72,604,758	98,771,434
Deposits.	65,388,917	57,188,801
Sale of Common Stock Under Employee Stock Option Plan.	712	133,517
	139,675,848	159,176,757
USES OF FUNDS		
Purchases of Investment Securities.	74,587,847	100,598,007
Net Change in Federal Funds and Securities Agreements Position.	777,214	27,047,786
Net Change in Trading Account Securities	(2,451,516)	1,828,881
Loans.	27,870,378	9,775,548
Additions to Equipment, Furniture, and Leasehold Improvements.	1,369,816	606,797
Retirement of 4¾% Capital Debentures.	285,000	250,000
Dividends Paid on Common Stock.	1,037,953	1,036,101
Sundry—Net	1,773,622	(146,899)
	105,250,314	140,996,221
Excess of Funds Received Over Funds Disbursed.	34,425,534	18,180,536
Funds at Beginning of Year.	87,944,374	69,763,838
FUNDS AT END OF YEAR	$122,369,908	$ 87,944,374

( ) Indicates Decrease.
See Notes to Financial Statements.

ILLUSTRATION 12–4

Statement of Changes in Financial Position		The B.F.Goodrich Company and Consolidated Subsidiaries	
		YEAR ENDED DECEMBER 31	
		1971	1970
	SOURCE OF WORKING CAPITAL		
	From operations:		
	Income before extraordinary items	$ 29,834,000	$ 11,507,000
	Items not affecting working capital during the current year:		
	Depreciation and amortization	58,463,000	54,962,000
	Deferred income taxes and other	9,398,000	9,820,000
	WORKING CAPITAL PROVIDED FROM OPERATIONS EXCLUSIVE OF EXTRAORDINARY ITEMS	97,695,000	76,289,000
	Extraordinary (losses) gains	(28,094,000)	3,538,000
	Items not affecting working capital during the current year:		
	Deferred income taxes	(7,470,000)	(1,234,000)
	Reserves for future costs, expenses and losses, and to write-down assets held for sale to estimated net realizable value	34,720,000	3,500,000
	WORKING CAPITAL PROVIDED FROM OPERATIONS	96,851,000	82,093,000
	Additional long-term borrowings	2,140,000	112,350,000
	Property sold	3,004,000	12,168,000
	Investments sold	1,563,000	3,561,000
	Treasury shares reissued	1,893,000	817,000
	TOTAL SOURCE OF WORKING CAPITAL	105,451,000	210,989,000
	USE OF WORKING CAPITAL		
	Acquisition of foreign subsidiary consummated in 1971, less net current assets acquired of $9,799,000 — Note B:		
	Long-term assets at fair value	22,189,000	—
	Long-term liabilities assumed	(4,753,000)	—
	Investments made in prior years	(14,283,000)	—
		3,153,000	—
	Additions to property	61,368,000	79,169,000
	Reduction of long-term debt..................	72,047,000	10,761,000
	Cash dividends paid..........................	14,490,000	22,369,000
	Additional investments	1,167,000	18,307,000
	Treasury shares purchased	2,811,000	1,799,000
	Other items — net	4,833,000	925,000
	TOTAL USE OF WORKING CAPITAL	159,869,000	133,330,000
	(DECREASE) INCREASE IN WORKING CAPITAL	$(54,418,000)	$ 77,659,000

APB 19
GUIDELINES

7. The effects of extraordinary items, classified separately on the statement of income, as required by APB Opinion 9, should be reported separately. They should immediately follow the caption "working capital provided from (used in) operations for the period, exclusive of extraordinary items."

8. The effects of other financing and investing activities should be individually disclosed. For example, both outlays for acquisitions and proceeds from retirements of property should be reported though normal trade-ins to replace equipment should ordinarily be reported on a net basis; both long-term debt should be reported; and outlays for purchases of consolidated subsidiaries should be summarized by major categories....

The second most popular arrangement, used by 187 companies, displays an equal amount of "sources" and "applications." See Illustration 12–2.

The third arrangement, used by 168 companies, shows change during the year, add balance at the beginning, yielding balance at the end. See Illustration 12–3.

QUESTIONS AND PROBLEMS

12–1. Comment on the following questions:

a) What information can be obtained from the statement of changes in financial position that is not shown on a balance sheet?

b) What information can be obtained from the balance sheet that is not shown on a statement of changes in financial position?

c) Is it necessary to have the income statement when preparing the statement of changes in financial position? Why?

12–2. The Retained Earnings account is not shown on the statement of changes in working capital. Explain.

12–3. Explain how the following should be shown on the work sheet for the statement of changes in financial position.

 a) Net loss for the year.
 b) Depletion expense.
 c) Amortization of patents.
 d) Receipt of cash from defendant in lawsuit.
 e) Stock dividend declared and distributed.
 f) Write-off of goodwill.
 g) Loss on the sale of marketable securities.
 h) Issued for cash at a premium, 500 shares of $100 par value preferred stock.
 i) Appropriated retained earnings for sinking fund reserve.
 j) Retired bonds at face value.
 k) Profit on sale of long-term investments.

12–4. Is working capital applied when cash dividends are declared or when they are paid? Discuss.

12–5. What does it mean to say that the Accounting Principles Board, in *Opinion No. 19,* expanded the scope of the statement of changes in financial position? In what ways is this statement similar to, and in what ways does it differ from, the traditional "funds statement?"

12–6. In your opinion, why did the APB broaden the scope of the "funds statement"?

12–7. Give two examples of transactions which should be included in a statement of changes in financial position, one of which "crosses the dotted line" and one of which does not. (Give two examples which are not used as examples in the book.)

12–8. What does *Opinion No. 19* say about the effect of extraordinary items on the statement of changes in financial position?

12–9. What does *Opinion No. 19* say about acquisitions, retirements, and trade-ins of fixed assets?

12–10. What does a statement of changes in financial position do that a balance sheet and a statement of income do not do?

12–11. Why does the APB disapprove of statistics purporting to show "working capital flow per share"?

12–12. The operating data for Kent Stores, Inc., for the current year include the following:

Sales (net of returns and allowances).	$405,000
Purchases (including $6,000 acquired by issuance of stock).	200,000
Operating expenses, including $22,000 depreciation.	100,000
Interest expense	4,100
Income taxes	25,200
Cash dividends paid.	30,000
Extraordinary expenses	25,000
Net Income	50,700

The following information is taken from the year-end balance sheet:

	End of year	Beginning of year
Cash	$ 38,700	$ 18,750
Accounts receivable (net)	42,250	46,000
Merchandise	61,000	70,000
Miscellaneous current prepayments	3,000	2,200
	$144,950	$136,950
Furniture and equipment	178,000	165,000
Less: Accumulated depreciation	(135,000)	(113,000)
Land for future expansion	40,000	-0-
Total	$227,950	$188,950
Accounts payable	$ 14,150	$ 25,000
Income taxes payable	25,200	10,000
Interest payable	300	350
	$ 39,650	$ 35,350
Equipment notes payable (current at beginning of year)	47,400	58,400
Capital stock, $10 par	70,000	55,000
Additional paid in capital	12,000	2,000
Undistributed earnings	58,900	38,200
Total	$227,950	$188,950

Late in the year, 1,500 shares of capital stock were issued in exchange for assets with fair values as follows: land, $15,000; merchandise, $6,000; furniture, $4,000.

Required:

Prepare a "statement of changes in financial position" as described in Accounting Principles Board *Opinion No. 19.*

12–13. The operating data for James Stores, Inc. for the current year include the following:

Sales	$300,000
Cost of goods sold	200,000
Operating expenses (including $15,000 depreciation)	105,000
Interest expense	4,400
Net loss	9,400
Cash dividends paid	6,000

The following information is taken from the year-end balance sheet:

	End of year	Beginning of year
Cash.	$ 20,600	$ 35,000
Accounts receivable (net).	42,000	30,000
Merchandise	80,000	75,000
Prepayments	2,600	2,000
Fixed assets	190,000	160,000
Less: Accumulated depreciation	(115,000)	(100,000)
Total	$220,200	$202,000
Accounts payable.	$ 24,200	$ 12,000
Interest payable	3,400	2,000
Long-term debt (notes)	70,000	50,000
Capital stock	120,000	120,000
Retained earnings.	2,600	18,000
Total	$220,200	$202,000

During the year long-term notes were issued for $20,000 cash and fixed assets were purchased for $30,000 cash.

Required:

Prepare a "statement of changes in financial position" as described in Accounting Principles Board *Opinion No. 19.*

13

Introduction to standard ratios

THE ANALYSIS of the relationship among various financial statement items is essential to the interpretation of financial and operating data. Therefore, in addition to using comparative statements, including changes in dollars and percentages and common-size figures as well as trend data, the analyst will find that a number of individual ratios will aid him in analyzing and interpreting financial statements.

Nature of ratios

The relationship of one item to another expressed in simple mathematical form is known as a *ratio*. The relationship or ratio between current assets and current liabilities, for example, is determined by dividing the current assets, $70,000, by the current liabilities, $35,000. The answer to such a division may be stated as follows: (1) the current assets are two times the current liabilities; (2) there are $2 of current assets for every $1 of current liabilities; or (3) the current assets are 200 percent of the current liabilities. In common parlance this is a 2 to 1 current ratio.

The ratio of net income to owners' equity is determined by dividing the net income, $80,000, by the owners' equity, $1,000,000. The result of this division may be stated as follows: (1) for every $100 of owners' equity, $8 has been earned; or (2) a return of 8 percent has been realized on owners' equity.

The importance of supplementing the absolute data by ratios arises from the need to establish the relationships between related items. For

296

example, a $1,000,000 net income may appear to be favorable. However, if this amount is related to owners' equity, it might represent a net return of only 1 percent.

A single ratio in itself is meaningless—it does not furnish a complete picture. A ratio becomes meaningful when compared with some standard. Ratios, like other statistical data, merely represent a convenient means of focusing the attention of the analyst on specific relationships which require further investigation. The ratios in no way take the place of "thinking" on the part of the analyst; they are not final in any sense of the word. A change in a ratio for two given dates or periods of time must be interpreted in the light of the variations in each of the two items, the relationship of which is expressed by the ratio.

Standards of comparison

Financial and operating relationships expressed in terms of ratios or otherwise have little significance except as they are judged on the basis of appropriate standards of comparison. Therefore, in interpreting the ratios of a particular business, the analyst cannot determine whether the ratios indicate favorable or unfavorable conditions unless there are available standards to use as measuring devices. Such standards take various forms.

1. Mental standards of the analyst, i.e., a general conception of what is adequate or normal which has been gained by his personal experience and observation.
2. Ratios and percentages based on the records of the past financial and operating performance of the individual business.
3. Ratios and percentages of selected competing companies, especially the most progressive and successful ones.
4. Ratios and percentages developed by using the data included in the current budgets. Such ratios would be based on the individual company's past experience modified by anticipated changes during the accounting period. These ratios would properly be called "goal ratios."
5. Ratios and percentages of the industry of which the individual company is a member.

The latter ratios and percentages are developed by research agencies and by trade associations.[1] In most instances the best standard of com-

---

[1] See Troy, *Manual of Performance Ratios for Business Analysis and Profit Evaluation* (Englewood Cliffs, N.J.: Prentice-Hall, Inc., 1971). See also standard ratios published by Dun & Bradstreet, by Robert Morris Associates, and by trade associations. Robert Morris Associates publishes *Sources of Composite Financial Data* and *Annual Statement Studies*. See also Demarest, *Accounting, A Guide To Information Sources* (Gale).

parison is the ratios of the nearest rivals of the company or of a few carefully selected competitors whose operations are known to be similar in most respects. These data normally are available much sooner than those for the industry.

Inasmuch as each industry had its own characteristics which influence the financial and operating relationships, industry ratios are most valuable in measuring the performance of a particular company within the industry. Without information as to what may be considered to represent an adequate or favorable ratio or percentage in the particular industry, it is more difficult to form an opinion with respect to the financial and operating conditions of a specific company.

An unfavorable variation of an individual company's data from the standard for the industry indicates financial or operating weakness. However, such below-standard ratios may be a result of conditions peculiar to the individual business and not to the industry as a whole. Furthermore, a particular standard ratio may show a weak condition for the group as a whole, or it may represent unnecessary strength.

Nature of standard ratios

Assume that a banker, a credit agency, or an investor is analyzing for the first time the financial statements of a company that manufactures aircraft motors. One of the first steps in the analysis and interpretation of these statements is the development of ratios for the individual company. Similar data should be obtained for the industry as a whole. These latter ratios are known as *standards*. They might well be called *averages,* since in most instances they represent some form of an average of the data for a large number of companies within the industry. Unless they are influenced by unrepresentative extremes, standard or average ratios show representative relationships existing in an industry on a particular date or during a period of time, not ideal conditions.

Financial statements of a company are combinations of facts, accounting conventions, and personal judgments; consequently, the ratios determined therefrom cannot be considered precise or exact measures. When average ratios for an industry are computed, the effect of the foregoing combinations of facts, accounting conventions, and personal judgments is multiplied. Furthermore, some members of an industry are in an excellent financial condition and have favorable operating results, while other members show opposite characteristics.

Standard ratios are often thought of as indicating a "satisfactory condition" for the industry. However, the term "representative condition" seems more accurately descriptive. The standard ratios merely indicate to the individual company what its own ratios should be in order to be comparable to the *averages* for the industry. The "standard ratios" should never be thought of as *ideals*.

An alternative set of ratios, which may be referred to as *goal ratios,* is sometimes developed from the financial and operating data of some of the most successful and profitable companies within an industry. These ratios provide a basis for individual companies to determine in which areas they fall short of meeting, or are actually superior to, the levels attained by the most efficient competition.

One disadvantage of relying entirely or mainly on industry standard ratios is the usual delay in collecting the data. Several months are required to assemble the data from the members of the industry, to compute the ratios, and to disseminate or publish the information.

Problems involved in the preparation of standard ratios

In preparing standard ratios for a group of companies, the analyst is confronted with many problems, some of which are pointed out in the following discussion. Certain members of an industry are highly successful and most efficient; other members have an unsatisfactory financial condition and operating performance. Therefore, the decision to include or exclude low, high, or unusual ratios and amounts is an important one. Such items, if included, would bring about a lower or higher average which might not be typical or representative of the industry.

To obtain the most typical financial and operating data for an industry, the analyst must be sure that all the companies included in the summary are homogeneous, i.e., own and operate similar properties and businesses and perform almost identical functions or stages of manufacture. However, absolute homogeneity is rarely, if ever, attainable.

Variations in the financial and operating data of companies or subdivisions of companies, and, therefore, in their ratios, may be the result of one or more of the following factors:

1. Wide separation geographically, with different price levels and costs of operation.
2. Operation of "owned" or "leased" properties or a combination thereof.
3. Ownership of large or small amounts of investments in properties that are not used in connection with regular operations.
4. Different price levels reflected in noncurrent asset items.
5. New as compared with old properties.
6. Manufacture of one or a large number of products.
7. Utilization of a high or low percentage of maximum plant capacity.

8. Purchase or production of raw materials or semifinished goods.
9. Vertical or horizontal integration.
10. Maintenance of large inventories or adoption of a hand-to-mouth policy of purchasing raw materials or merchandise.
11. Valuation of inventories on a Fifo, Lifo, moving weighted average, or other basis.
12. Practice of pursuing a hand-to-mouth policy of purchasing raw materials and/or merchandise.
13. Policy of maintaining large or small inventories.
14. Sale of merchandise largely on either short- or long-term credit or mainly for cash.
15. Manufacture and sale of steel rails or steel bridges, a Ford or Continental automobile, newsprint or fine writing paper.
16. Sale of entire product to a single purchaser or to a large number of wholesalers, retailers, or consumers
17. Large or small amounts of long-term debt.
18. Dependence on creditors for financing to a greater extent than owners' equity financing, or vice versa.
19. Maintenance of working capital far in excess of normal current operating needs or maintenance of a minimum amount.
20. Marginal policies relative to discretionary decisions relative to the adoption of a high, medium, or low standard for maintenance and repair of properties in relation to depreciation.
21. Operating a profitable or nonprofitable business.
22. Policy of declaring and paying high or low rates of cash dividends and/or stock dividends.
23. Different systems of accounting and accounting procedure including classification of financial statement items, accounting periods, and depreciation methods.

Furthermore, to the extent that asset values do not represent cost or the assets have not been evaluated on a uniform basis, complete comparability does not exist. Cost may actually represent different "values," depending upon when the assets were acquired and how they were financed. For example, assets may have been paid for in cash or in capital stock which could not be sold at par; or the assets may have been purchased at a time when a low or a high price level prevailed.

It should be evident from the foregoing that the financial statements are combinations of facts, company policies, accounting conventions, and personal judgments. Furthermore, the numerous differences that may exist between companies emphasize (1) the fact that the averages of the ratios cannot be precise factual measures or standards in a strict sense and (2) the necessity of proceeding cautiously in reaching final conclusions when the data for a single company are compared with the average data.

Great stress must be placed upon the fact that average ratios merely represent summarized results which have been attained by a group of companies in the same industry. Therefore, average ratios for the industry only indicate what the ratios of a member of the industry should approximate to be representative of the industry's averages. The real value of these averages depends entirely upon the extent to which they set into action the mental processes of the analyst and result in further detailed investigation and analysis; average ratios, properly used, represent the starting point in real thinking. These averages are meaningless if the analyst merely compares them with an individual company's data and then reaches conclusions without further investigation and taking into account specific conditions of the business.

To be most meaningful and informative, i.e., reliable and representative, standard ratios should be developed for companies of an industry that:

1. Use a uniform accounting system and accounting procedures including a uniform classification of accounts and similar depreciation methods.
2. Follow a uniform accounting period preferably on a natural business year basis.
3. Follow similar asset valuation and amortization policies.
4. Represent a homogeneous group.
5. Adopt and maintain somewhat uniform managerial policies.

Inasmuch as the trade data are merely averages, the analyst may prefer to emphasize a study of historical percentages and ratios for a particular company. Certainly, such data would be more "standard" for the individual business, assuming financial and operating efficiency. The analyst may use both.

Determination of standard ratios

When standard ratios are not available in published form, the analyst can prepare his own standards. In computing standard ratios, the analyst should:

1. Assemble financial statements of comparable businesses (having homogeneous operations and uniformity of data) within each industry. The problem of determining which companies are comparable is probably the most important and difficult of the many that have to be solved in the process of computing standard ratios. In other

words, it is often stated that the incomparability of the original data represents the most serious difficulty in the development of dependable standard ratios.

2. Compute selected ratios for each business within the various industries.

3. Arrange for each industry and from high to low all pertinent ratios, such as the current ratios, ratios of net income to net sales, and ratios of owners' equity to total assets.

4. Eliminate the extreme low and high ratios in order to provide a basis for determining the most representative average.

5. Compute the arithmetic average or determine the median.

Arithmetic average. The arithmetic average of individual ratios for a group of companies engaged in the same line of business is computed by adding all of the current ratios, for example, and dividing this total by the number of ratios included. The reader will realize immediately that the arithmetic average has a major shortcoming. Extreme figures, the lowest and highest figures, affect the average so that a typical figure is not obtained. Frequently, to avoid this unfavorable result, as suggested

ILLUSTRATION 13–1

SELECTED DEPARTMENT STORES

Current Assets, Current Liabilities, and Current Ratios

(dollars in thousands)

Department Store	Current assets ($)	Current liabilities ($)	Current ratio (%)
A	52,582	21,123	250
B	72,791	31,428	232
C	43,654	41,183	106
D	32,694	11,044	296
E	53,423	21,444	249
F	712,475	84,605	828
G	26,911	8,497	317
H	27,842	9,894	281
I	10,419	1,391	749
J	7,826	2,831	276
K	1,189,473	377,610	315
L	6,924	1,505	460
M	997,153	415,480	240
N	113,990	42,218	270
O	220,121	198,307	111
P	1,019,822	886,801	115
Q	24,168	16,783	144
R	1,311,515	230,090	570
S	1,244,628	275,360	452
T	9,133	1,310	697
Average of 20			363

above, several of the lowest and highest ratios are eliminated. In this way a greater concentration of individual items will be shown and, therefore, the average of these items may be more typical or representative of the group. It should be understood that because of a wide dispersion of the data, an arithmetic average actually may not be representative of the group in spite of the fact that extreme highs and lows have been eliminated. Obviously the greater the dispersion from the average, the less significant the average becomes.

Illustration 13–1 shows current assets, current liabilities, and current ratios for a group of department stores selected at random. Illustration

ILLUSTRATION 13–2
SELECTED DEPARTMENT STORES
Current Ratios

Company	Current ratios
F	828
I	749
T	697
R	570
L	460
S	452
Q	144
G	317
K	315
D	296
H	281
J	276
N	270
A	250
E	249
M	240
B	232
P	115
O	111
C	106
Average (20 companies)	363

13–2 lists the current ratios of the 20 companies arranged from high to low and shows the average current ratio. It will be observed that the average current ratio for the 20 companies in 363 percent.

The department stores' current ratios, Illustration 13–2, range from 106 percent to 828 percent. Such a range may be a result of one or more factors such as the following: size of inventory; method of inventory costing; rapidity of the turnover of inventory and receivables; policy of maintaining high, low, or medium cash balances; classification of current items; practice of factoring or discounting receivables; and policy of maintaining a relatively large or small investment in marketable securities for emergency purposes.

Median. The median is found by listing the various ratios—for example, the current ratios—in the order of high to low, or vice versa. The median is the middle figure or mid-area in the tabulation. The median is often more representative of a group of ratios than the arithmetic average, which may reflect extreme items.

Many analysts prefer to arrange the individual ratios computed for a large number of similar companies in numerical sequence, so that the lower and upper quartiles as well as the median may be selected. The lower quartile ratio is the ratio above which 75 percent of all the other ratios lie; the upper quartile ratio is exceeded by only 25 percent of the total number of ratios; and the median ratio is the middle ratio of the series.

To illustrate this method of grouping, data for 20 companies, manufacturers of industrial machinery, have been selected. These data—current assets, current liabilities, and current ratios—are given in Illustration 13–3. The current ratios are arranged from high to low in Illustration 13–4. The upper and lower quartile and the median are also shown.

The current ratio of 553 percent is the lower limit of the upper quartile, and the ratios from 553 to 852 lie within the upper quartile; a ratio located in the upper quartile indicates a *strong current financial*

ILLUSTRATION 13–3

SELECTED MANUFACTURERS OF INDUSTRIAL MACHINERY
Current Assets, Current Liabilities, and Current Ratios
(dollars in thousands)

Company	Current assets	Current liabilities	Current ratios
A	14,296	5,052	283
B	121,306	21,024	577
C	141,682	16,629	852
D	132,883	48,321	275
E	142,681	55,735	256
F	185,982	70,716	263
G	30,715	9,715	315
H	315,833	54,267	582
I	175,934	59,841	294
J	31,892	8,505	375
K	462,888	205,728	225
L	533,725	128,608	415
M	678,642	199,015	341
N	431,411	72,506	595
O	223,975	47,352	473
P	118,472	36,453	325
Q	24,812	5,224	475
R	41,683	3,445	121
S	191,196	97,549	196
T	218,268	39,470	553
Average of 20			390

condition. The current ratios from 275 to 475 lie within the median group. A current ratio located within the upper part of the median range represents a *good current financial condition,* and a current ratio located within the lower part of the median range is considered to represent a *fair current financial condition.* The current ratios from 121 to 263 lie within the lower quartile and reflect a *weak current financial condition.*

ILLUSTRATION 13–4
SELECTED MANUFACTURERS OF INDUSTRIAL MACHINERY
Current Ratios

Company	Current ratios	
C	852	
N	595	
H	582	
B	577	
T	553	Upper quartile
Q	475	
O	473	
L	415	
J	375	
M	341	Median
P	325	
G	315	
I	294	
A	283	
D	275	Lower quartile
F	263	
E	256	
K	225	
S	196	
R	121	
Arithmetic average (20 companies)	390%	

Ratios from composite or group statements. Some analysts construct composite balance sheets and income statements for companies in an industry and prepare ratios from the combined data. The composite or group statements are prepared by adding all like items on the individual statements. Unlike the process of preparing consolidated statements, there is no attempt to eliminate intercompany transactions.

The ratios computed from composite statements are not too reliable or useful because there is no attempt to eliminate (1) extreme figures of the highly successful or the most unprofitable companies and (2) intercompany transactions. There is no way of testing whether or not the computed averages are representative as can be accomplished when dealing with a list of individual ratios.

QUESTIONS

13–1. Discuss:

    a)   The nature of standard ratios.

    b)   "Variations from standard ratios may reflect either weakness or strength."

    c)   The merits and limitations of standard ratios.

    d)   To what extent do price-level changes influence standard ratios?

    e)   "An ideal or model balance sheet and income statement may be constructed by using standard ratios."

    f)   "The best standard of comparison is the ratios of the nearest rivals of the company or of a few carefully selected competitors whose operations are known to be similar in most respects."

13–2. Is it practical to use composite statement data for an industry to prepare standard ratios? Explain.

13–3. A standard ratio is a representative common or average ratio for a large number of companies in the same line of business. Explain.

13–4. Compare the arithmetic average and the median methods of determining standard ratios. Which is preferable? Why?

13–5. "Comparability of companies must be determined before attempting to include them in a computation of standard ratios." Explain.

13–6. Discuss three factors which may account for variations in the operating and financial data of different companies in the same industry.

14

Ratio analysis of working capital

THE PURPOSE of the present chapter is to explain the various ratios and percentages which may be used in analyzing and interpreting the current financial position of a business. This approach to the analysis of financial statements is of value to both insiders (management) and outsiders (such as creditors, particularly short-term creditors, and owners.)

Commercial banks and other short-term creditors are vitally concerned with ratio analysis of working capital, as is management, to check the efficiency with which working capital is being employed in the business. It is also of importance to stockholders and long-term creditors in determining—to some extent, at least—the prospects of dividend and interest payments. The questions to be studied and answered in connection with ratio analysis of working capital include the following: Will the company be able to pay its current debts promptly? Is management utilizing working capital effectively? Is the amount of working capital adequate, excessive, or insufficient? Does the company have a favorable credit rating? Is the current financial position improving?

A business has a strong current financial position if it is able (1) to meet the claims of short-term creditors when they are due, (2) to maintain sufficient working capital for effective normal operations, (3) to meet current interest and dividend requirements, and (4) to maintain a favorable credit rating.

Current ratio

A commonly used ratio in analyzing financial statements is the current ratio, which gives a crude measure of current liquidity. If the product of dividing current assets by current liabilities is 3, the current ratio is said to be 3 to 1. It can also be stated as a current ratio of 300 percent. The current ratio is sometimes called the working capital ratio.

The current ratio is so crude a measure that except where it is unusually high (e.g., 5 to 1), it has little value unless it is accompanied by other ratios such as the number of days' operations that could be covered from available cash and liquid securities, the turnovers of receivables and inventories, and the number of days that current payables have been in hand awaiting payment. If the current ratio is unusually high, it may be unnecessary to do more than make an eye check of the components which underlie it.

A current ratio of 200 percent, i.e., a ratio of $2 of current assets to $1 of current liabilities, is sometimes considered to be a satisfactory current ratio for a commercial or industrial company. However, since the amount of working capital and the size of the current ratio depend upon many factors, a standard, or common, current ratio cannot be designated as appropriate for all businesses. For example, electric utilities and hotels can have a satisfactory working capital situation on a 1 to 1 basis. Thus, a 200 percent ratio should be used only as a starting point for further investigation. It is more practical and meaningful for comparative purposes to determine the current ratios for a specific trade or industry.

In computing the current ratio, it is important that all current assets and current liabilities, with their proper dollar amounts assigned, be included. To the extent that current asset values are not correctly shown on the balance sheet, an erroneous current ratio will result. The statement of working capital (Illustration 14–1) shows the items to be included in the current asset and current liability sections.

The current ratio indicates, in rough fashion, the degree of safety with which short-term credit may be extended to the business by current creditors. The current ratio measures to some extent the liquidity of the current assets and the ability of a business to meet its maturing current obligations. A business with a high current ratio might not be in a position to pay current liabilities because of an unfavorable distribution of current assets relative to liquidity. For example, the inventories may be excessively high relative to prospective sales; and the inventory may be turning over slowly. An increase in inventories accompanied by a decrease in sales may represent an excess of working capital; the notes receivable may represent an accumulation of past-due accounts receivable; or the accounts receivable may contain a large amount of past-due and possibly uncollectible receivables, as well as installment accounts, which usually involve long credit terms.

An increase in notes payable accompanied by a decrease in business volume may reflect the inability of a company to pay its accounts payable, an indication that working capital is inadequate. Under these circumstances, the current liabilities may be payable before the current assets are available for use in paying these obligations.

The contingent liability, notes receivable discounted, should be given thoughtful consideration by the analyst in studying the current ratio. Although it is not the most common practice, many analysts include all current notes receivable, whether discounted or not, as current assets and discounted notes as current liabilities.

ILLUSTRATION 14–1

LYNN-DALE COMPANY*
Comparative Statement of Working Capital
As of December 31, 1966–71
(in thousands of dollars)

Items	December 31					
	1966	1967	1968	1969	1970	1971
Current Assets:						
Cash	62.1	28.2	58.6	59.0	74.2	83.4
Marketable securities	33.7	105.1	39.6	39.8	39.5	44.9
Trade receivables, net	263.1	261.1	203.3	230.3	269.9	291.9
Inventories.	182.4	197.2	219.6	241.9	268.3	253.4
Other current assets	25.6	60.7	50.5	51.6	52.1	35.2
Total Current Assets (a)	566.9	652.3	571.6	622.6	704.0	708.8
Current Liabilities:						
Accounts payable	184.4	187.5	181.4	172.6	151.5	160.4
Notes payable	52.7	56.3	105.1	88.5	61.6	43.3
Other current liabilities	26.3	73.7	19.1	25.1	34.7	28.8
Total Current Liabilities (b)	263.4	317.5	305.6	286.2	247.8	232.5
Working capital (a − b) ($000)	303.5	334.8	266.0	336.4	456.2	476.3
Current ratio (a ÷ b) (%)	215	205	187	218	284	305
Trend percentages (1966 = 100%):						
Current assets (%).	100	115	101	110	124	125
Current liabilities (%).	100	121	116	109	94	88
Working capital (%).	100	110	88	111	150	157
Current ratio (%)	100	95	87	101	132	142

* Retail lumber and building supplies business.

If the business is contingently liable in the event of a default on the discounted notes at maturity, the foregoing procedure gives a more accurate and conservative picture of the current financial position. If the business is not contingently liable in case of a default—i.e., if the notes have been sold without warranty and without guaranty as to payment—the discounted notes should not be carried on the balance sheet. In general, as long as the discounted notes are shown on the balance sheet, it is assumed that the concern has a contingent liability.

The working capital, the amount of current assets after deducting current liabilities, represents a margin of safety, i.e., a "cushion" of protection for the current creditors. The larger the amount of liquid working capital in relation to current liabilities, the more favorable the position will be with reference to ability (1) to meet current debts, fixed interest charges, and dividend requirements; and (2) to absorb operating losses, declines in replacement value of inventory and temporary investments, excessive amounts of uncollectible receivables, and costs of emergency events.

In comparing the ability of two businesses to meet their current liabilities, it is sometimes assumed that the company having the larger amount of working capital has the greater liquidity or ability to pay current obligations. This is not necessarily so; the measure of liquidity is the relationship, rather than the difference, between the current assets and current liabilities. Therefore, the current ratio, rather than the amount of the working capital, is the better measure of debt-paying ability. For example, the working capital for Companies D and L, shown below, is the same. However, *assuming the same relative liquidity of the current assets,* Company D's current ratio reveals its superior working capital position:

	Company	
Items and computation	*D*	*L*
Current assets (a)...............	$300,000	$800,000
Current liabilities (b).........	150,000	650,000
Working capital (a – b)........	$150,000	$150,000
Current ratio (a ÷ b).........	200%	123%

The short-term creditors of Company L are less certain to obtain prompt or possibly full payment in the event of insolvency than those of Company D.

In the case of the Lynn-Dale Company, lumber and building material retail business (Illustration 14–1), the current debt-paying ability appears to be more favorable as of December 31, 1971 than it was on December 31, 1966. During this time the net working capital increased from $303,500 to $476,300 and the current ratio increased from 215 percent to 305 percent. The cash position, including marketable securities, has improved during the period under review. Cash and marketable securities were equal to 36 percent of total current liabilities as of December 31, 1966, and 53 percent as of December 31, 1971.

Illustration 14–4 (page 316) shows that although the trend for sales showed an increase of 84 percent, inventories increased only 39 percent; trade receivables, net, decreased or remained about the same; and accounts payable declined substantially (13 percent). The decline in the current payables at a time when sales volume was increasing may have been a result of pressure for payment from creditors. It is also possible that the company may have applied current assets to the payment of current liabilities just before the statement date to present a more favorable current ratio. This practice is commonly referred to as "window dressing." Some window dressing is legitimate, some is not. The type practiced here is legitimate.

The most efficient management of working capital, and a most important managerial objective, requires constant attention to the processes of rapid conversion of receivables and inventories into cash. The adequacy of the current ratio depends upon the number of factors, such as the credit terms received from suppliers in relation to those extended to customers, the time required to collect receivables and the turnover of the inventories, characteristics of the general financial program, the season of the year, the period of the business cycle, the length of the working capital cycle, and whether or not the business is expanding or contracting. The type and age of the business and the efficiency of management and the profitableness of operations are factors that play a major part in determining the adequacy of the current ratio. A series of current ratios that show a downward trend may indicate a developing unfavorable current financial position. On the other hand, in some cases this downward trend may be a result of more efficient utilization of working capital, thereby requiring a relatively lower amount of current assets. The real significance of the current ratio can be ascertained only by analyzing in detail the characteristics of the current assets and current liabilities.

The adequacy of the working capital may be measured approximately if customer and creditor terms are known. For example, if merchandise is purchased on 60 days' credit and sold for cash, or on account, with collections within 30 days, the working capital requirements in connection with receivables will be relatively small. On the other hand, if the creditor terms are 30 days and the customer terms 60 days, a relatively larger amount of working capital must be supplied by either the long-term creditors or the owners of the business. The amount of working capital, with respect to the purchase and sale of merchandise, depends upon the rate of turnover of current assets relative to the rate of turnover of current liabilities.

A high current ratio may represent (1) an excess of cash or its equivalent relative to the current needs of the business or (2) a preponderance of current assets having a low liquidity.

The higher the current ratio the better the creditors' position because of the greater probability that the debts will be paid when due. This conclusion is true especially if management is appropriately controlling working capital items. From the point of view of stockholders a high current ratio would not be the most profitable, especially if the company maintains excessive cash balances and has an overinvestment in receivables and inventories. Generally speaking, a low current ratio is relatively more risky than a high ratio. However, it may indicate that management is utilizing the current assets most effectively. That is, the cash balance is held to minimum requirements, and the turnovers of receivables and inventories are at a maximum. The amount of cash to be maintained depends upon the size of the business and, more specifically, upon the amount of cash that is required to meet current debts, expenses, and emergencies.

By way of emphasis, it may be stated that the analyst, in his study of the current ratio, should not draw final conclusions before considering, when available, the following factors:

1. The distribution of current assets.
2. The trend data for both current assets and current liabilities for a 5- or 10-year period.
3. The terms granted by creditors and to customers.
4. The present market value, collectible amount, or cost of replacement of the current assets.
5. The possibility and probability of value changes in the current assets.
6. The seasonal factor, if any—especially when the current ratios at different dates are being compared.
7. Inventory changes in relation to present and prospective sales volume.
8. The need for a larger or smaller amount of working capital during the following year.
9. The amount of cash and marketable securities, and whether there is an apparent excess or deficit in relation to working capital needs.
10. The extent to which bank credit has been used and is still available to the company.
11. The general credit rating of the company.
12. The amount of contingent liabilities existing as of the balance sheet date.
13. The receivables in relation to sales volume and the possible inclusion of an accumulating amount of past-due accounts.
14. The type of business—whether manufacturing, mercantile, or public utility.

The analyst must always be watchful for illegitimate forms of "window dressing," i.e., the practice of including current assets and excluding current liability items for the purpose of presenting a more favorable current ratio than actually exists. For example, the book value of the inventories may be overstated; cash receipts applicable to the next accounting period's sale of merchandise may be recorded in advance; liability for merchandise included in the inventory may be omitted; and a debt that is to be paid within the subsequent year may be classified as a long-term debt. Furthermore, the current ratio appears to be more favorable (1) when U.S. Treasury obligations are shown deducted from estimated federal income taxes payable in the current liability section, (2) when notes receivable discounted are deducted from notes receivable in the current asset section, and (3) when the company defers the replenishment of inventory or has numerous special sales to reduce its inventory at the end of the accounting period.

"Acid-test" ratio

Another ratio, which measures immediate solvency (liquidity) and supplements the current ratio, is the "acid-test" ratio. To compute this ratio, it is necessary to arrange the current assets into two groups: (1) cash and the "quick" or relatively liquid assets, such as receivables and temporary investments which are immediately available or will be available reasonably soon for the payment of current liabilities; and (2) the less liquid assets, such as inventories and prepaid expenses which will normally require some time for their realization in cash. The total of the quick assets is divided by total current liabilities to obtain the acid-test ratio, which is often called the "liquidity ratio" or the "quick ratio." It is well to bear in mind that receivables are not always liquid.

Inventories are not included as quick assets because of the time required to sell merchandise or finished goods and convert raw materials and work in process into finished goods. There is also the uncertainty as to whether or not the inventories can be sold. The acid-test ratio, the computation of which is illustrated below, represents the number of dollars of quick assets relative to the current liabilities:

$$\frac{\text{Quick assets (\$420,200)[1]}}{\text{Current liabilities (\$232,500)}} = \begin{cases} \text{The ratio of quick assets to current lia-} \\ \text{bilities (181 percent); quick assets are} \\ \text{1.81 times current liabilities.} \end{cases}$$

If a company has a quick ratio of at least 100 percent, some analysts consider it to be in a fairly good current financial condition. However, it is more practical and meaningful for comparative purposes to compare with the typical quick ratio for the specific trade or industry. Caution must be exercised in placing too much reliance on a quick ratio of 100 percent or any other fixed percentage without further investigation, since the receivables may in certain cases be relatively nonliquid and cash may be needed immediately to pay operating expenses. It must be remembered, too, that the inventories are available to a measurable

---

[1] Cash, $83,400; receivables net, $291,900; marketable securities, $44,900.

extent to meet current liabilities because of the normal conversion of merchandise into cash and receivables. In some cases the inventories may be more liquid than the receivables. Also, the sale of inventories normally results in profits, which in turn increase the amount of working capital that will be received ultimately. Quick assets, not including marketable securities, are sometimes called "dollar assets" because they are legal claims to fixed-dollar amounts and, therefore, do not change in amount with price variations, as do inventories and temporary investments in marketable securities. In interpreting the quick ratio the analyst must be aware of the fact that it does not indicate how soon the quick asset receivables will be available and when the current liabilities will be payable.

The method of arranging the quick assets, as shown in Illustration 14–2 for the Lynn-Dale Company, indicates clearly the adequacy or

ILLUSTRATION 14–2

LYNN-DALE COMPANY
Quick Assets in Relation to Current Liabilities
For the Years Ended December 31, 1966–71

Items	1966 ($000)	1967 ($000)	1968 ($000)	1969 ($000)	1970 ($000)	19 ($0
Current liabilities (a)	263.4	317.5	305.6	286.2	247.8	23
Less: Cash	62.1	28.2	58.6	59.0	74.2	8
Marketable securities	33.7	05.1	39.6	39.8	39.5	4
Current liabilities in excess of cash and marketable securities	167.6	184.2	207.4	187.4	134.1	10
Less: Trade receivables	263.1	261.1	203.3	230.3	269.9	29
Quick asset book value in excess of or less* than current liabilities	95.5	76.9	4.1*	42.9	135.8	18
Total quick assets (b) ($000)	358.9	394.4	301.5	329.1	383.6	42
Quick ratio (b ÷ a) (%)	136	124	99	115	155	18
Trend of quick ratio (%)	100	91	73	85	114	13

inadequacy of these assets in relation to current liabilities. It is here assumed that the book values of the quick assets can be realized.

In Illustration 14–2, quick assets are in excess of current liabilities except for the year 1968; and, therefore, the inventories are not needed to cover any part of the current payables. The quick ratios for the Lynn-Dale Company show improvements, with the exception of December 31, 1968 and 1969 in liquidity (although the turnover of receivables has to be studied), since they increased from 136 percent as of December 31, 1966, to 181 percent at December 31, 1971. The strengthening of the quick ratio during the period was a result of the increase in the total of cash and marketable securities; the receivables decreased during 1967 and 1968, then increased through 1971. Current liabilities declined steadily beginning December 31, 1967. Final conclusions relative to the evaluation of the quick ratio should not be made before studying the rate of turnover of receivables. Observe a different situation for the Barton Corporation in Illustration 14–3.

As suggested in the foregoing discussion, the working capital position of a company depends upon the amount of net working capital, the ratio existing between the current assets and the current liabilities, and the distribution of current assets relative to liquidity. A favorable work-

ILLUSTRATION 14–3

BARTON CORPORATION
Quick Assets in Relation to Current Liabilities
For the Years Ended December 31, 1968–71
(thousands omitted)

Items	1968	1969	1970	1971
Current liabilities	$170	$190	$250	$280
Less: Cash and marketable securities	20	30	50	10
Current liabilities in excess of cash and marketable securities.	$150	$160	$200	$270
Less: Receivables, net	190	210	160	200
Quick asset value excess (or deficit*) relative to current liabilities	$ 40	$ 50	* $ 40†	* $ 70

† In 1970, 44.44 % of the $90,000 inventory in addition to the quick assets was required to cover current liabilities.
‡ In 1971, 70.0 % of the $100,000 inventory in addition to the quick assets was required to cover current liabilities.

ing capital position may be a result of profitable current operations, a shift from current liabilities to fixed liabilities, or a shift from fixed assets to current assets. Opposite tendencies may bring about an unfavorable working capital position.

Distribution of current assets

Another approach to the analysis of working capital—also crude as explained below—is to show the individual items as percentages of total current assets. In this way, relative changes or variations from year to year in the composition of working capital may be observed. Shifts between cash, receivables, and inventories may affect the ability of the company to meet its current liabilities. A decline in the relative proportions of cash and receivables and an increase in inventories will generally result in a less liquid current condition.

The current asset common-size percentages for the Lynn-Dale Company as of December 31, 1966 and 1971 are presented in Illustration 14–4. The increase in the percentage of total cash and marketable securities indicates a somewhat more liquid composition of working capital. The data, Illustration 14–4, also reveal that trade receivables, net, increased substantially dollarwise but decreased from 46.4 percent to 41.2 percent in relation to total current assets. The increase in net accounts receivable of $28,800 in comparison with the increase in sales for the six-year period of $679,300 reflects a more effective credit and collection policy, which may or may not be a desirable development. If it is ac-

ILLUSTRATION 14–4

LYNN-DALE COMPANY
Current Assets—Amounts and Common-Size Percentages
As of December 31, 1966 and 1971

	December 31			
	1966		1971	
Items	*($000)*	*(%)*	*($000)*	*(%)*
Current Assets:				
Cash......................	62.1	11.0	83.4	11.8
Marketable Securities	33.7	5.9	44.9	6.3
Trade receivables, net	263.1	46.4	291.9	41.2
Inventory*	182.4	32.2	253.4	35.8
Other current assets	25.6	4.5	35.2	4.9
Total Current Assets	566.9	100.0	708.8	100.0
Note: Net sales	812.5		1,491.8	

* Lower of cost or market.

companied by increasing sales, it may be presumed to be a desirable trend. It will be observed that the ending inventories increased $71,000 and that the inventories were 35.8 percent of total current assets as of December 31, 1971, in comparison with 32.2 percent as of December 31, 1966. The common-size percentages indicate clearly that relative to the total current assets the inventories have increased in importance while receivables have declined. The absolute and relative increase in the inventories appear fully justifiable in view of the substantial increase in sales volume.

In spite of the fact that some indications can be gleaned from this type of ratio analysis, there are other approaches to the analysis of receivables and inventories, for example, which are sharper and more meaningful. These alternative methods involve the computation and evaluation of turnovers.

Turnover of receivables—ratio of net sales to receivables

The receivables turnover is computed by dividing total customer receivables into net sales, as shown in Illustration 14–5. Note in that illustration that the average receivable was outstanding for 122 days in 1966 (four months—an unusually long time!) but only 75 days in 1971 (still two and one-half months). The receivables turnover, which is another way of saying the same thing, was 3 times in 1966 and 4.87 times in 1971.[2]

ILLUSTRATION 14–5

LYNN-DALE COMPANY
Turnover and Age of Receivables
Years Ended December 31, 1966-71

Items		1966	1967	1968	1969	1970	1971
Net sales* (a)	($000)	812.5	853.7	859.8	1,201.2	1,341.3	1,491.8
Receivables† (b)	($000)	270.9	269.1	211.9	240.8	282.2	306.6
Days in year (c).	(No.)	365	365	365	365	365	365
Turnover of receivables (d) (a ÷ b)	(Times)	3.00	3.17	4.06	4.99	4.75	4.87
Ages of receivables (c ÷ d).	Days	122	115	90	73	77	75

* For the year.
† As of December 31. (Valuation account not offset.)

The divisor, customer receivables, should be an average for the year, is possible, because the dividend, net sales, spans the year. Frequently year-end balances do not properly represent the situation throughout the year. The sales total should not include sales for cash.

It is desirable to compare the receivables turnover of the concern with the receivables turnover typical in the industry. Sometimes it is typical in an industry to finance customers by extending long credit terms. The turnover typical in the industry is often obtainable from the industry trade association. If not, the published financial statements of competitors can be consulted.

If a turnover of 6.5 times per year was typical in the industry (slightly under two months), the Lynn-Dale turnover of 4.87 in 1971 would appear in a less favorable light.

Another way to present this ratio would be to say that sales are 487 percent of receivables or that receivables are 20.5 percent of sales. An overinvestment in receivables, which often exists in periods of depression, may necessitate borrowing on a short-term basis to pay off current liabilities. The larger the amount of receivables, in relation to net sales, outstanding at the end of the accounting period, the greater is the amount of uncollectible receivables likely to be. Furthermore, the invest-

---

[2] Three hundred sixty-five days divided by the turnover of 3 times per year yields a result of 122 days per turn.

ment in accounts receivable tends to be large in comparison to income.

A decrease in the ratio of net sales to receivables may reflect the following:

a) A decrease in sales and an increase in receivables.
b) A decrease in receivables and a proportionally greater decline in sales.
c) An increase in sales and a proportionally greater increase in receivables.
d) A decrease in sales with no change in receivables.
e) An increase in receivables with no change in sales.

A variation in the ratio of net sales to receivables from year to year or as between companies may reflect variations in the company's credit policy or changes in its ability to collect receivables. The changes may be caused by specific factors such as changes in terms of sales; inclusion or exclusion of cash and installment sales; existence of heavy or light seasonal or nonseasonal sales; special sales campaigns at the end of the accounting period; sales made directly to consumers or to middlemen; price-level changes; the effectiveness of the credit, collection, and sales departments; strikes and plant shutdowns; and the stage of the business cycle at the time the ratio is determined.

It may or may not be desirable to accomplish a reduction in average receivables, increasing turnover. Financially it is desirable to do so as demonstrated in the following analysis.

Assume that the Lynn-Dale Company increased its receivables turnover for the year 1971 from 4.87 times to 6 times as a result of improving the efficiency of its credit and collection policy. A receivables turnover of 6 times, assuming the same volume of sales ($1,491,800), would represent an investment of working capital of $248,633 or a reduction of $57,967. If working capital invested in receivables costs 5 percent, an annual saving of $2,898 would be realized. In addition, the faster the turnover of receivables, the lower the probability of bad debt losses.

Of course there may be other reasons why it may be undesirable to reduce receivables and increase turnover. For example, a more energetic collection effort may alienate customers.

Turnover of inventories—retail concern

The term "turnover of inventories" has reference to the number of times that the inventories were sold and replaced during the accounting period. The average inventory is divided into the amount of inventory sold, at cost—i.e., cost of goods sold. For the reason stated in connection with receivables turnover the average of the receivables balance at the ends of the months would be preferable, because they are more representative than the year-end balance. But in the Lynn-Dale Company (Illustration 14–4) the average inventory amount is not available so the year-end balance ($253,400) must be divided into the cost of goods sold ($1,054,700) yielding a 1971 turnover of 4.16 times (or, stated otherwise, 88 days). The comparable amounts in 1966 were 3.28 times and 111 days; in 1968, 2.86 times and 128 days. The most unfavorable year was 1968, and the most favorable, 1971.

So, though inventories have increased from 32.2 percent of current assets in 1966 to 35.8 percent in 1971, the fact seems to be that the inventory turnover has actually improved. This is a favorable trend unless the inventory gets down to a point where there are excessive inventory shorts resulting in back orders.

Trend ratios discussed in the next section should be developed to determine variations in cost of goods sold and in the inventory. Variations in cost of goods sold and in the inventories may be a result of changes in physical volume and in prices or *in the valuation method applied to the inventory.*

Caution must be exercised in drawing conclusions relative to the merchandise turnover, since the inventory represents the cost of the goods on hand at the end of the accounting period, while the cost of the goods sold represents the cost for the year. Seasonal and special sales may be involved, and costs may be affected by price changes. Furthermore, the inventory shown on the balance sheet at the end of the accounting period may not be typical of the amounts on hand during the year. Inventories may have been increased because of anticipated greater sales volume or because of anticipated higher prices of goods, or the inventories may have been reduced to a minimum because of anticipated lower prices and sales volume or in order to place the business on a more liquid basis. In comparing inventory turnovers from year to year or from company to company, it is important to have comparable data with respect to the inventory valuation basis. For example, during a period of rising prices an inventory valued on the basis of last-in, first-out would be lower in amount than one valued on the basis of first-in, first-out. If prices are rising, cost of goods sold will tend to rise; but last-in, first-out inventories will tend to retain a constant unit value. First-in, first-out inventories will tend to rise with the price level.

A difference in inventory turnover rates as between companies engaged in the same industry may reflect variations not only in inventory valuation but also in sales and merchandising policies, efficiency, and inventory control methods.

Inventories shown on statements are usually less than the average for the year, especially if the company is using the natural business year as its accounting period; therefore, the inventory turnover may be overstated.

Inventory turnovers for an entire business should be supplemented, if feasible, by turnovers of inventories by dependents. Turnovers vary to a great extent between departments.

The inventory turnover should be compared with similar turnovers of preceding years to determine whether or not an abnormal condition exists; the trend of the inventory turnover is important, although consideration must be given to the fact that two variables are involved—inventory and cost of goods sold. Excessive inventories—i.e., overstocking of merchandise—bring about higher storage costs and may result in large losses due to deterioration and changes in style, demand, and prices. Excessive inventories may also represent a dangerous financial situation, especially if the merchandise has been purchased on credit or through bank loans.

A low inventory turnover may reflect dull business; overinvestment in inventory, i.e., too large an inventory in relation to sales; the accumulation of merchandise at the end of the period in anticipation of higher prices or of greater sales volume; incorrect inventory value resulting from the inclusion of obsolete and unsalable goods; an unbalanced inventory, i.e., excessive quantities of certain inventory items in relation to immediate requirements; overstated inventory valuation; or a change in distributive functions performed by the business—the management of a retail business may be entering the manufacturing or wholesaling phase of business.

A high turnover of inventory may not be accompanied by a relatively high net income, since profits may be sacrificed in obtaining a larger sales volume. The selling price of the goods may have been lowered to increase the turnover of the inventory. A higher rate of turnover of inventory is likely to prove less profitable than a lower turnover unless accompanied by a larger total gross margin, although the rate of gross margin may well be the same or even slightly lower. Then, too, a higher rate of merchandise turnover may have been accompanied by a disproportionate increase in selling and administrative expenses. Such conditions result in a lower operating income.

A concern whose merchandise moves slowly must maintain a much higher ratio of current assets to current liabilities because of the slow conversion of merchandise into cash or receivables that must be depended upon to meet current liabilities.

The turnover of the merchandise inventory may be computed in relation to net sales when the cost of goods sold is not available. This turnover or ratio of net sales to merchandise inventory, which is determined below, shows the number of dollars of net sales for each dollar of inventory:

$$\frac{\text{Net sales (\$1,491,800)}}{\text{Merchandise inventory, end of year}} = \left\{ \begin{array}{l} \text{Inventory turnover in relation} \\ \text{to net sales (4.16 times); ratio of} \\ \text{net sales to ending merchandise} \\ \text{inventory (416 percent).} \end{array} \right.$$
$$(\$253,400)$$

Assuming that the ending inventory used in the computation is typical for the year, the higher this ratio the more rapid the turnover of the stock in trade. It should be emphasized here that in the foregoing computation the sales are shown at the selling price while the merchandise inventory is stated at cost, or the lower of cost or market. Therefore, the sales-to-inventory ratio should not be used when the cost of goods sold is available. This ratio may be used in making comparisons with statements of other companies which do not show the cost of goods sold, but the computations must use comparable methods.

The turnover of the inventories and the average age (in days) of the inventories for the Lynn-Dale Company are shown in Illustration 14–6.

During the period under review, the Lynn-Dale Company has increased the turnover of inventories (Illustration 14–6, page 322), gross margin rate, and total gross margin (Illustration 10–2, page 236). The trend of the number of days of inventory on hand shows improvement. Frequently, an increase in inventory turnover is obtained as a result of adopting a lower rate of gross margin markup. The Lynn-Dale Company should still further increase its inventory turnover, assuming that a favorable gross margin markup can be maintained. It is possible that the company has an unbalanced inventory or too large an inventory in relation to sales. On the other hand, the ending inventory may not be typical for the entire year. Greater and more effective sales promotion and activity may be desirable in attempting to improve still further the relationship between inventory and sales volume.

The advantage, from a financial point of view, of improving the turnover of inventory is shown in the following analysis: Assume that the Lynn-Dale Company increased its inventory turnover from 4.16 times to 5.16 times as a result of a lower inventory, accomplished by improving purchasing and storing and maintaining a more precise balance of items required to meet customer demands.

An inventory turnover of 5.16 times, assuming the same cost of goods sold of $1,054,700, would represent an ending inventory of $204,400 ($1,054,700 ÷ 5.16 times) or a reduction of $49,000 of working capital invested in the closing inventory. If the cost of working capital invested in inventory is 5 percent, the reduction would result in an annual saving of $2,450. An additional saving would result because of lower storage costs, spoilage, or obsolescence, and risk of price-level changes.

An internal analyst may be able to subdivide inventories and cost of goods sold by product. If so, the resulting turnover amounts will be more informative.

Turnover of inventories—manufacturing company

The turnover of inventories for a manufacturing concern is determined as shown below; in each instance, it is assumed that the inventory is representative of the inventory throughout the year:

$$\frac{\text{Raw material issued to factory (\$270,000)}}{\text{Raw material ending inventory (\$37,800)}} = \begin{cases} \text{Raw material turnover} \\ \text{(7.14), or the number of} \\ \text{times the raw material was} \\ \text{replaced during the year.} \end{cases}$$

$$\frac{\text{Cost of goods sold (\$380,000)}}{\text{Finished goods ending inventory (\$62,000)}} = \begin{cases} \text{Finished goods turnover} \\ \text{(6.13), or the number of} \\ \text{times the stock of finished} \\ \text{goods was replenished from} \\ \text{the factory.} \end{cases}$$

The inventories of a manufacturing company may be reduced to a number of days' inventory by dividing the number of days in the year by the turnover of the inventory. For example, the number of days, 365, divided by raw material turnover, 7.14, equals the number of days of inventory on hand, 51.1. Another method of computing the number of days' raw material on hand is illustrated below:

$$\frac{\text{Raw material issued to factory (\$270,000)}}{\text{Days in year (365)}} = \begin{cases} \text{Dollar volume of days'} \\ \text{consumption of raw mate-} \\ \text{rial (\$740).} \end{cases}$$

$$\frac{\text{Raw material inventory (\$37,800)}}{\text{Days' consumption (\$740)}} = \begin{cases} \text{Days' consumption represented} \\ \text{by raw material inventory (51.1).} \end{cases}$$

On the basis of 365 days the company had an average raw material inventory equal to 51.1 days' supply. With information available as to sources of supply, time involved in obtaining the material, and the rate

ILLUSTRATION 14–6

LYNN-DALE COMPANY
Turnover of Inventories and Days' Sales in Inventories*
For the Years Ended December 31, 1966–71

Items		1966	1967	1968	1969	1970	197
Cost of goods sold (a)	($000)	598.0	624.1	627.7	861.3	964.4	1,054
Ending inventory (b)	($000)	182.4	197.2	219.6	241.9	268.3	253
Days in year (c)	(No.)	365	365	365	365	365	365
Turnover of inventory (d) (a ÷ b)	(Times)	3.28	3.16	2.86	3.56	3.59	4
Age of inventory—number of days inventory on hand (c ÷ d)	(Days)	111	116	128	103	102	88

* As of December 31 (valuation account not offset).

of utilization, it is possible to determine the ideal volume of raw material to be maintained on hand. By comparing this amount with other years or other companies, an overinvestment or underinvestment in raw material may be disclosed.

Aging the receivables

The ratio of net sales to receivables represents a method of aging the receivables. A preferable method, assuming that the individual accounts are available, is to classify the accounts (as to amounts) according to (1) not yet due; and (2) past due (a) 1 to 30 days, (b) 31 to 60 days, (c) 61 to 90 days, (d) 91 to 120 days, and (e) over 120 days. Obviously, the external analyst would not have available the necessary detailed data for aging the accounts receivable in this manner, but the internal analyst may make such a schedule.

Cash available to finance operations

Another form of turnover ratio is used to make a rough evaluation of the adequacy of cash (and other fully liquid assets such as securities) in relation to current operating needs. For the external analyst this must of necessity be a rough indicator.

The heart of the calculation is a comparison of the balance of cash plus other liquid assets to operating costs and expenses that are a current drain on working capital. For example:

The balance sheet data of the Lynn-Dale Company, in Illustration 10–1, page 235, shows the following items of cash and its equivalent on December 31, 1971:

Cash	$ 83,400
Marketable securities	44,900
	$128,300

The income statement data of the Lynn-Dale Company, in Illustration 10–2, page 236, shows the following items of current expense during the year 1971:

Cost of goods sold	$1,054,700
Total operating expenses	346,100
Other expense, net.	7,500
Federal income taxes	31,300
Total Current Expenses	$1,439,600

Information as to the current annual burden of depreciation is not supplied. As depreciation is not a current drain on cash and its equivalent, we need to know this amount to eliminate it from the current expense total above. We will assume that 1971 depreciation of the Lynn-Dale

Company was $20,000—about 3 percent of the plant account net total—and make the following computation:

Total current expenses	$1,439,600
Deduct, depreciation	20,000
	$1,419,600

Cash and its equivalent ($128,300) divided into total current cash expenses ($1,419,600) goes 11.2 times. Dividing 11.2 times into 365 days in the year we find that the Lynn-Dale Company's cash and its equivalent is adequate to support current operations (without acquiring additional assets or paying down liabilities), even if there was no income whatever, for about 32 days, or slightly over one month. A cash position of this strength is found only in very strongly financed concerns.

Trend percentages for current assets and current liabilities

The changes in the individual current assets and current liabilities may be indicated by trend percentages, as shown in Illustration 14–7, below. The dollar data appear in Illustration 14–1 (page 309).

It is desirable to constantly be aware that ratios and percentages are only starting points in analyses. In interpreting the changes indicated by trend percentages for receivables and inventories, it is necessary to take into consideration the net sales. For example, an inventory increasing from year to year accompanied by stable or declining sales

ILLUSTRATION 14–7

LYNN-DALE COMPANY
Current Assets and Current Liabilities—Trend Percentages
As of December 31, 1967–71
(1966 = 100%)

Items	December 31				
	1967	1968	1969	1970	1971
Current Assets:					
Cash.	45	94	95	119	134
Marketable securities.	312	118	118	117	133
Trade receivables, net	99	77	88	103	111
Inventory	108	120	133	147	139
Other current assets	237	197	202	244	138
Total Current Assets (a)	115	101	110	124	125
Current Liabilities:					
Accounts payable	102	98	94	82	87
Notes payable	107	199	168	117	82
Other current liabilities	280	73	95	132	110
Total Current Liabilities (b).	121	116	109	94	88
Working capital (a − b)	110	88	111	150	157
Net sales	105	106	148	165	184

volume indicates, in some measure certainly, an overinvestment in inventories. A increasing receivables total with stable or declining sales volume may reflect an unfavorable credit and collection situation.

Certain observations may be made relative to the working capital position for the Lynn-Dale Company reflected by the trend data for the period from 1966 through 1971 (Illustration 14–7). Net sales increased 84 percent, whereas trade receivables decreased through December 31, 1969 and then increased as of December 31, 1970 and 1971. Inventories increased 39 percent from December 31, 1966 to December 31, 1971. Assuming that the data are properly stated, they reflect a major change in the policies relating to credit and collections and possibly to merchandising.

Note the trend of current payables (Illustration 14–5), which reflect the reduction of debt during a period of greater sales volume. As indicated above, pressure for payment from creditors may account for such an unusual situation. Assuming that all of the current items are properly shown, the total current liabilities declined to a greater extent than current assets.

A further study of the trend data reveals that in comparison with December 31, 1967, material changes took place during the year 1968 in most of the current assets and current liabilities. An expansion of the property was consummated during this year, Illustration 10–1, page 235, and in all probability, many changes in policies became effective, which fact influenced the working capital position thereafter.

Although the current ratio (the relationship between current assets and current liabilities) for the most recent date is of prime importance to the analyst, the trend of the current ratios for a number of years should be studied. It will be observed that the trend of the current ratios for the Lynn-Dale Company (Illustration 14–1) is upward except for December 31, 1967 and 1968, indicating a more favorable current financial position. Compare this situation with Company A's current ratios: 1968, 361; 1969, 340; 1970, 320; and 1971, 304. The current ratios for the end of 1971 are relatively the same for each company. However, the downward movement of Company A's current ratio may be indicative of a developing unfavorable condition, whereas the Lynn-Dale Company's showing is one of improvement. It is here assumed that in the case of each company the current assets are stated correctly and have approximately the same liquidity from year to year.

It is of prime importance to know the method of valuation that has been applied to the inventories. A more favorable interpretation would be given to the current ratio when the last-in, first-out valuation method is used during a period of price increases, since the inventory would be understated in terms of replacement cost. The understated inventory represents a "secret" or "hidden" amount of owners' equity.

Combining inventory turnover with receivables turnover

In order to analyze the efficiency of the merchandising and financial management of the Lynn-Dale Company from the point of view of minimization of the investment of working capital, the turnover of receivables and inventories may be combined. For example, the average number of days elapsing between the acquisition of inventory and the sale and conversion of the receivables into cash has been reduced substantially by the Lynn-Dale Company as shown in Illustration 14–8.

ILLUSTRATION 14–8

LYNN-DALE COMPANY
Average Number of Days from Date of Acquisition of Inventory to Date
of Conversion into Cash
For Years Ended December 31, 1966–71

Items		1966	1967	1968	1969	1970	1971
Receivables uncollected:							
Average days*		122	115	90	73	77	75
Trend	(%)	100	94	74	60	63	61
Inventories on hand:							
Average days†		111	116	128	103	102	88
Trend	(%)	100	105	115	93	92	79
Average number of days from date of acquisition of inventory to date of conversion to cash	(No.)	233	231	218	176	179	163
Trend	(%)	100	99	94	76	77	70

* Pages 317–18.
† Pages 318–19.

Comparison of inventory, sales, and working capital

The data in Illustration 14–9 are prepared to facilitate a comparison of sales, inventory, and working capital.

It can be observed from the data in the table that for 1971 relative to 1966, sales volume increased $679,300, or 83.6 percent; ending inventory (December 31) increased $71,000, or 38.9 percent; and the working capital (December 31) increased $172,800, or 56.9 percent. Furthermore, as of December 31, 1966 the ending inventory was only 60.1 percent of the working capital; at the end of 1971, it was 53.2 percent of the working capital. This comparison shows—at first glance, at least—a favorable situation, inasmuch as sales volume increased 83.6 percent, whereas the ending inventory increased only 38.9 percent. Obviously, final conclusions should not be reached until after a thorough study has been made of the data to determine the normalcy of such items; these data should be related to those of other similar companies.

ILLUSTRATION 14-9

LYNN-DALE COMPANY
Comparison of Sales, Inventory, and Working Capital
For the Years Ended December 31, 1966 and 1971

Items and computation		1966	1971	Increase ($000)	(%)
Sales..................	($000)	812.5	1,491.8	679.3	83.6
Ending inventory (a)*	($000)	182.4	253.4	71.0	38.9
Net working capital (b)*.....	($000)	303.5	476.3	172.8	56.9
Ending inventory percentage of working capital (a ÷ b).	(%)	60.1	53.2	6.9*	11.5*

* December 31.

Turnover of working capital—net sales to working capital

A close relationship exists between sales and working capital. As sales volume increases, the investment in inventories and receivables increases and, therefore, a larger amount of working capital is necessary. To test the efficiency with which working capital is utilized, many analysts determine the turnover of working capital—the ratio of net sales to working capital. The turnover shows the number of dollars of net sales the business obtained for each dollar of working capital which was not financed by current creditors. The computation of the turnover is as follows:

$$\frac{\text{Net sales (\$1,491,800)}}{\text{Working capital (\$476,300)}^3} = \begin{cases} \text{Turnover of working capital (3.13} \\ \text{times); net sales per dollar of work-} \\ \text{ing capital (\$3.13).} \end{cases}$$

The relationship between net sales and working capital reflects the extent to which the business is operating on a small or a large amount of working capital in relation to sales. Comparisons should be made with this ratio or turnover for the same company for previous years and with similar ratios for the industry.

A high turnover of working capital may be a result of inventories and receivables which required a relatively low amount of working capital. On the other hand, a high turnover of working capital may reflect an inadequacy of working capital and low turnovers of inventories and receivables. An inadequacy of working capital may be accompanied by an excess of current liabilities, which may mature before inventories and receivables are converted into cash.

A low turnover of working capital may be a result of an excess of net working capital, a slow turnover of inventories and receivables, or

---

[3] *End of year.* The *monthly average* for working capital should be used when available.

a large cash balance and investment of working capital in the form of temporary investments. Heavy investments in inventories may have been made in anticipation of higher future prices or shortages of materials or merchandise.

The larger the net sales as compared to the working capital, the less favorable the situation is likely to be if the resultant working capital turnover has been made possible by the use of an excess amount of current credit. The real danger lies in the possibility of a decline in sales due to unforeseen circumstances such as cancellation of orders, floods, fires, storms, strikes, depressions, and competition. Inventories may be accumulated even though sales have been materially reduced. In such an event, liabilities increase; and sufficient funds are not realized through sales to liquidate them when they are due.

In interpreting the working capital turnover, the analyst should exercise considerable caution. This turnover or ratio is a composite of a number of relationships. These various component elements should be analyzed individually to account for changes from year to year or between companies. There is always the possibility that the current assets and current liabilities may include items that do not relate to current operations. Trend percentages should be studied when comparing sales and working capital for a series of years.

Turnover of current assets

The efficiency and profitability of the use of working capital can be measured by determining the following relationships (see Illustration 14–8):

1. Turnover of current assets (the number of times that the average current assets were used in paying costs and expenses)—divide the total of the cost of goods sold, operating and other expenses, and federal income taxes by the average total current assets.
2. Rate of profit on average current assets—divide net income by average current assets.
3. Rate of profit per turnover of average current assets—divide rate of profit on average current assets by number of turnovers of current assets.

Illustration 14–10 shows an improvement for the Lynn-Dale Company's turnover and profitability of current assets. The exclusion of depreciation and similar nonworking capital items from cost and expenses would result in showing more accurately the turnovers and percentages.

A summary of the ratios, turnover figures, and trends that have been discussed in relation to the current financial position of the Lynn-Dale

ILLUSTRATION 14-10

LYNN-DALE COMPANY
Turnover and Profitability of Current Assets
For the Years Ended December 31, 1966-71

Items and computation		1966	1967	1968	1969	1970	1971
Net sales	($000)	812.5	853.7	859.8	1,201.2	1,341.3	1,491.8
Cost of goods sold, operating expenses, other expense in excess of other revenue deducted (including depreciation and federal income taxes) (a)	($000)	784.9	824.7	833.1	1,168.8	1,294.4	1,439.6
Net income exclusive of extraordinary items (b)	($000)	27.6	29.0	26.7	32.4	46.9	52.2
Current assets:							
Beginning of year	($000)	502.7	566.9	652.3	571.6	622.6	704.0
End of year	($000)	566.9	652.3	571.6	622.6	704.0	708.8
Total	($000)	1,069.6	1,219.2	1,223.9	1,194.2	1,326.6	1,412.8
Average amount of current assets (c)	($000)	534.8	609.6	612.0	597.1	663.3	706.4
Turnover of current assets (a ÷ c) (d)	(No.)	1.5	1.4	1.4	2.0	2.0	2.0
Rate of profit on average current assets (e) (b ÷ c)	(%)	5.16	4.76	4.36	5.43	7.07	7.39
Rate of profit per turnover of average current assets (e ÷ d)	(%)	3.44	3.40	3.11	2.72	3.54	3.70

ILLUSTRATION 14-11

LYNN-DALE COMPANY
Statistics Relative to Current Financial Position
As of, or for, the Years Ended, December 31, 1966-71

Items		1966	1967	1968	1969	1970	1971
Current ratio	(%)	215	205	187	218	284	305
Quick ratio	(%)	136	124	99	115	155	181
Trend of current assets	(%)	110	115	111	110	124	125
Trend of current liabilities	(%)	100	121	116	109	94	88
Trend of working capital	(%)	100	110	88	111	150	157
Turnover of receivables	(No.)	3.00	3.17	4.06	4.99	4.75	4.87
Collection period	(Days)	122	115	90	73	77	75
Trend of accounts receivable*	(%)	100	99	78	89	104	113
Trend of net sales	(%)	100	105	106	148	165	184
Turnover of inventory	(No.)	3.28	3.16	2.86	3.56	3.59	4.16
Days' sales in inventory	(No.)	111	116	128	103	102	88
Trend of ending inventory	(%)	100	108	120	133	147	139
Trend of cost of goods sold	(%)	100	104	105	144	161	176

* Estimated uncollectible Receivables *not* deducted.

Company is presented in Illustration 14–11. It will be observed that significant improvement has been accomplished in the current debt-paying ability of the company and in its overall current financial position. The most favorable financial position is reflected for the most recent year, 1971. However, greater improvement is desirable; the trend of progress reflected by the data may continue. The trend of the cost of goods sold is upward, but the sales volume increased at a more rapid rate. The trend of current assets is upward, and for current liabilities it is downward. Before a final conclusion is made, the analyst should study, if available, data relative to the merchandising policy, terms of sale and purchase, credit and collection policies, management in general, the individual characteristics of the company that involve sales and operations, and the averages for the year rather than the year-end information.

The computation of ratios, percentages, and turnovers has been illustrated in this chapter. In all cases, annual statement data were used. Are these statistics representative of the year? Would more accurate results be obtained by using monthly statement data?

The answers to these questions depend upon the uniformity throughout the year of factors such as production, purchases of raw material or merchandise, sales, profit on sales, collections, and payments of current liabilities. Naturally, seasonal variations in production and sales will not be revealed by annual statements but would be shown by monthly data. Inasmuch as the external analyst does not generally have access to monthly statements, he must rely on annual statements. On the other hand, the internal analyst would have all financial and operating data in detail and would in most cases prepare ratios, percentages, and turnovers at the end of each month.

QUESTIONS AND PROBLEMS

14–1. *a*) What is meant by the word "turnover"?

  b) "The greater the turnover of merchandise, the greater the profit." Explain why this statement is or is not true.

14–2. Explain:

  a) A low current ratio may reflect an inadequacy of working capital.

  b) Do long-term liabilities maturing within one year of the balance sheet affect the current ratio?

  c) Is the so-called "acid-test ratio" actually an "acid test"?

  d) How should contingent liabilities be treated in analyzing the current financial condition of the business?

  e) Is the ratio of inventory to working capital important? Explain its computation, merits, and limitations.

14–3. Discuss the "ratio of net sales to working capital" showing how it is computed and indicating its merits and limitations.

14–4. The following statements may be *true* or *false*. If false, indicate the reasons therefor.

    a) The current debt-paying ability of a company may be measured by computing the current ratio.

    b) If creditors allow 60 days' credit and customers are granted 30 days' credit, the current ratio is strengthened.

14–5. Should long-term debt, which is due and payable within one year from the date of the balance sheet, be included as a current liability even though there is no sinking fund provision for the payment?

14–6. Give the reasons for the following:

    a) The current ratio for manufacturers of tobacco products should be higher than for manufacturers of office equipment.

    b) The current ratio for telephone companies is usually lower than for department stores.

    c) The current ratio for retail furniture stores is customarily higher than for railroad companies.

    d) The current ratio is affected by the terms granted by creditors and to customers.

14–7. A corporation has $100,000 of current assets and $50,000 of current liabilities. What effect will there be on the working capital and on the current ratio if the company obtains funds for current use (1) by issuing to the bank its $5,000, 5 percent, 60-day promissory note; (2) by issuing to the bank its $10,000, 4 percent, 5-year promissory note (payable in equal annual installments); (3) by selling and issuing 1,000 shares of $100 par value common stock at par; and (4) by selling long-term investments, $25,000?

14–8. What financial and/or operating data should an analyst have, and what ratios should he compute in order to evaluate the current debt-paying ability, i.e., determine the current financial condition of a business?

14–9. The Kenmore financial statements show the following items:

December 31:	*1970*	*1971*
Accounts receivable.	$ 39,467	$ 59,172
Estimated uncollectible receivables.	1,326	2,016
For the year:		
Net sales	339,471	389,145
(2/3 of the sales were made on credit terms of 2/30, n/60)		

Required:

Compute ratios and evaluate the receivables position of the Kenmore Company.

14–10. The Harvey Company, which operates a department store, presents the following financial and operating data together with selected percentages and ratios.

HARVEY COMPANY
Comparative Balance Sheet Data
As of December 31, 1968-71
(in thousands)

	1968		1969		1970		1971	
	($)	(%)	($)	(%)	($)	(%)	($)	(%)
Assets								
Current Assets:								
Cash......................	120	6.6	135	7.1	191	11.0	174	10.
Marketable securities............	112	6.2	180	9.5	80	4.6	75	4.
Receivables, net	440	24.3	430	22.8	415	24.0	401	23.
Merchandise inventory...........	800	44.3	810	42.9	723	41.8	694	41.
Other current assets	75	4.2	80	4.2	81	4.7	70	4.
Total Current Assets..........	1,547	85.6	1,635	86.5	1,490	86.1	1,414	83.
Noncurrent tangible assets, net.......	260	14.4	255	13.5	240	13.9	275	16.
Total Assets..............	1,807	100.0	1,890	100.0	1,730	100.0	1,689	100.
Liabilities								
Current liabilities...............	510	28.2	495	26.2	471	27.2	425	25.
Long-term liabilities.............	200	11.1	200	10.6	200	11.6	150	8.
Total Liabilities............	710	39.3	695	36.8	671	38.8	575	34.
Owners' Equity								
Preferred stock	100	5.5	100	5.3	100	5.8	75	4.
Common stock	900	49.8	900	47.6	900	52.0	950	56.
Retained earnings	97	5.4	195	10.3	59	3.4	89	5.
Total Owners' Equity.........	1,097	60.7	1,195	63.2	1,059	61.2	1,114	65.
Total Liabilities and Owners' Equity	1,807	100.0	1,890	100.0	1,730	100.0	1,689	100.

HARVEY COMPANY
Comparative Balance Sheet Data
As of December 31, 1968-71
(in thousands)

	1968		1969		1970		1971	
	($)	(%)	($)	(%)	($)	(%)	($)	(%)
Sales.......................	2,824	100.0	2,900	100.0	2,991	100.0	3,364	100.0
Cost of goods sold	2,298	81.4	2,342	80.8	2,192	73.3	2,249	66.9
Gross margin	526	18.6	558	19.2	799	26.7	1,115	33.1
Net income after all taxes	81	2.9	84	2.9	119	4.0	152	4.5

HARVEY COMPANY

Selected Trend Percentages and Ratios
Trend Percentages for Financial Statements Items
(1968 = 100%)

	1969	1970	1971
Balance Sheet Items			
Cash	113	159	145
Marketable securities	161	71	67
Receivables, net	98	94	91
Merchandise inventory	101	90	87
Other current assets	107	108	93
Total current assets	106	96	91
Noncurrent tangible assets, net.	98	92	106
Total assets	105	96	94
Current liabilities.	97	92	83
Long-term liabilities.	100	100	75
Total liabilities	98	95	81
Preferred stock	100	100	75
Common stock	100	100	106
Retained earnings	201	61	92
Owners' equity	109	97	102
Income Statement Items			
Sales	103	106	119
Cost of goods sold	102	95	98
Gross margin	106	152	212
Net income after all taxes	104	147	188

HARVEY COMPANY
Ratios

	1968	1969	1970	1971
Current ratio	303	330	316	333
Quick ratio.	132	151	146	153
Net sales to receivables	642	674	721	839
Cost of goods sold to inventory	287	289	303	324
Net sales to net working capital	272	254	294	340
Days' sales uncollected:				
300 days	46.7	44.5	41.6	35.8
365 days	56.9	54.2	50.6	43.5

Required:

a) Analyze the financial and operating data, percentages, and ratios supplied by the Harvey Company.

b) Evaluate the current financial position for the four-year period.

c) Write a brief summary of your conclusions.

14–11. The Mallory Corporation presents the following financial and operating data. You are requested to analyze these data and to write a report on the current financial condition and operating results emphasizing an evaluation of favorable and unfavorable financial and operating changes that have taken place during the period.

MALLORY CORPORATION
Balance Sheet* and Income Statement** Data

	1965	1966	1967	1968	1969	1970	1971
Balance Sheet Data as of December 31							
Assets							
Cash	$ 38.2	$ 32.4	$ 25.7	$ 41.2	$ 40.1	$ 35.8	$ 30.8
Notes receivable	80.0	68.0	70.0	80.0	60.0	80.0	90.0
Accounts receivable, net . . .	205.2	210.4	251.2	260.0	240.0	270.0	300.0
Merchandise inventory	320.0	400.0	450.0	440.0	490.0	470.0	450.0
Other current assets	1.4	2.1	1.2	4.0	2.8	1.7	1.8
Total Current Assets . . .	$ 644.8	$ 712.9	$ 798.1	$ 825.2	$ 832.9	$ 857.5	$ 872.6
Noncurrent assets (net)	600.4	610.2	605.2	601.4	615.8	620.1	615.6
Total Assets	$1,245.2	$1,323.1	$1,403.3	$1,426.6	$1,448.7	$1,477.6	$1,488.2
Liabilities and Owners' Equity							
Accounts payable	$ 146.6	$ 114.9	$ 124.4	$ 148.2	$ 156.4	$ 143.1	$ 135.6
Notes payable.	75.0	95.0	105.0	92.0	80.0	90.0	85.0
Other current liabilities. . . .	2.4	2.1	1.1	1.4	2.4	3.8	5.2
Total Current Liabilities	$ 224.0	$ 212.0	$ 230.5	$ 241.6	$ 238.8	$ 236.9	$ 225.8
Noncurrent liabilities	300.0	410.0	430.0	450.0	450.0	450.0	450.0
Owners' equity	721.2	701.1	742.8	735.0	759.9	790.7	812.4
Total Liabilities and Owners' Equity . .	$1,245.2	$1,323.1	$1,403.3	$1,426.6	$1,448.7	$1,477.6	$1,488.2
Income Statement Data for the Year							
Net sales	$ 980.0	$1,140.0	$1,060.0	$ 970.0	$ 920.0	$ 890.0	$ 930.0
Cost of goods sold	581.0	610.0	592.0	575.0	561.0	584.0	681.2
Net income after all taxes and extraordinary items. .	6.2	9.1	10.4	8.2	15.7	10.2	3.2
Dividends paid	10.5	20.5	20.5	35.0	37.5	60.0	60.0

* In thousands as of December 31, 1965–71.
** In thousands for the year ended December 31, 1965–71.

MALLORY CORPORATION
Common-Size Balance Sheet

	1965	1966	1967	1968	1969	1970	1971
Assets							
Cash	3.1	2.5	1.8	2.9	2.8	2.4	2.1
Notes receivable	6.4	5.1	5.0	5.6	4.1	5.4	6.0
Accounts receivable	16.5	15.9	17.9	18.2	16.6	18.3	20.2
Merchandise inventory	25.7	30.2	32.1	30.8	33.8	31.8	30.2
Other current assets	.1	.2	.1	.3	.2	.1	.1
Total Current Assets . . .	51.8	53.9	56.9	57.8	57.5	58.0	58.6
Noncurrent assets	48.2	46.1	43.1	42.2	42.5	42.0	41.4
Total Assets	100.0	100.0	100.0	100.0	100.0	100.0	100.0
Liabilities and Owners' Equity							
Accounts payable	11.8	8.7	8.9	10.4	10.8	9.7	9.1
Notes payable	6.0	7.2	7.5	6.4	5.5	6.1	5.7
Other current liabilities. . . .	.2	.1	.0	.1	.2	.2	.4
Total Current Liabilities.	18.0	16.0	16.4	16.9	16.5	16.0	15.2
Noncurrent liabilities	24.1	31.0	30.7	31.6	31.1	30.5	30.2
Owners' Equity.	57.9	53.0	52.9	51.5	52.4	53.5	54.6
Total Liabilities and Owners' Equity	100.0	100.0	100.0	100.0	100.0	100.0	100.0

MALLORY CORPORATION
Common-Size Income Statement

	1961	1962	1963	1964	1965	1966	1967
Sales	100.0	100.0	100.0	100.0	100.0	100.0	100.0
Cost of goods sold	59.3	53.5	55.8	59.3	61.0	65.6	73.2
Net income after all taxes and extraordinary items . .	.6	.8	1.0	.9	1.7	1.2	.3

MALLORY CORPORATION
Trend Ratios
1965 = 100 Percent

	1966	1967	1968	1969	1970	1971
Balance Sheet Items						
Cash	85	67	108	105	94	81
Notes receivable	85	88	100	75	100	113
Accounts receivable	103	122	127	117	132	146
Merchandise inventory	125	141	138	153	142	141
Total current assets	111	124	128	129	133	135
Noncurrent assets	102	101	100	103	103	103
Total assets	106	113	115	116	119	120
Accounts payable	78	85	101	107	98	93
Notes payable.	127	140	123	107	120	113
Total current liabilities.	95	103	108	107	106	101
Noncurrent liabilities	137	143	150	150	150	150
Owners' equity	97	103	102	105	110	113
Income Statement Items						
Net sales	116	108	99	94	91	95
Cost of goods sold	105	102	99	97	101	117
Net income after all taxes and						
extraordinary items.	147	168	132	253	165	52

MALLORY CORPORATION
Selected Ratios

Ratios	1965	1966	1967	1968	1969	1970	1971
Current ratios	2.9	3.4	3.5	3.4	3.5	3.6	3.9
Quick ratio	1.4	1.5	1.5	1.6	1.4	1.6	1.9
Ratio of net sales to							
receivables.	343.6	409.5	330.0	285.3	306.7	254.3	238.5
Inventory turnover	1.8	1.5	1.3	1.3	1.2	1.2	1.5
Net sales times net working							
capital ✗ʘ	2.3	2.3	1.9	1.7	1.6	1.4	1.4
Days' sales uncollected*							
365 days per year	105	89	111	128	119	144	153

15

Analysis of long-term financial condition with a section on appraising bonds for long-term investment

BANKERS and current creditors are most interested in the current debt-paying ability of a business. Bondholders and stockholders are most concerned with the long-term financial position. However, neither group may logically ignore the financial aspects of primary interest to the other. Both groups concern themselves with the current and noncurrent sections of the balance sheet and with current and prospective earnings.

Essential to study both current and long-term financial position

A favorable current financial position may be sharply offset by an opposite condition reflected by the noncurrent items. For example, the recorded total amount of depreciation, depletion, and amortization may be inadequate; fixed assets may have to be replaced soon; there may be an overinvestment in fixed assets; maturities of bonds or mortgage notes may be improperly spaced; or the capital structure (long-term liabilities and owners' euity) may be overbalanced with an excess of debt.

A favorable long-term financial position may be counterbalanced by a reverse situation reflected by the current items. For example, the amount of working capital may be inadequate; receivables and inventories may be excessive and slow turning; working capital may have been depleted by unwarranted declaration of dividends or used to partially finance the acquisition of noncurrent assets; and operating or extraordinary losses may have been incurred.

From year to year, many changes may be reflected in the items included in the noncurrent sections of the balance sheet. These changes may result from various transactions, and the analyst should attempt to detect both favorable and unfavorable factors. For example, fixed operating assets may have (1) increased as a result of the acquisition, construction, or revaluation of the assets or the erroneous capitalization of ordinary repairs and maintenance; or (2) decreased because of the sale, abandonment, or revaluation of the assets or the recognition of depreciation.

Long-term investments may have increased or decreased because of additional acquisitions or sales of holdings, revaluation of investments, or recording of income and losses reported by subsidiary companies.

Intangible assets may have increased or decreased because of amortization, new inventions, purchases, sales, or revaluation.

Noncurrent debt may have increased or decreased as a result of the issuance of new obligations, the payment of long-term liabilities, or the exchange of capital stock for long-term liabilities.

Owners' equity may have increased because of the issuance of additional capital stock at par, at a discount, or at a premium, for cash or property; the retention within the business of net income; extraordinary gains; and the upward revaluation of assets. Owners' equity may have decreased because of the retirement of capital stock, the reduction in par value of stock or change from par to no-par-value stock, operating and extraordinary losses, establishment of liability accounts[1] by transfers from retained earnings, cash dividends, and downward revaluation of assets.

Net sales may have increased or decreased because of changes in physical volume of goods sold, price level, amount of gross margin included in sales prices, amount of adjustments of markup and variation in sales mix, sales returns and allowances, and customer discounts when deducted from gross sales.

Cost of goods sold and operating expenses may have increased or decreased because of changes in the physical volume of goods sold; price-level changes (including wages); changes in accounting methods; variations in efficiency of production, selling, and administrative managements, and of employees; policies with respect to uncollectible receivables, maintenance, repairs, and depreciation; and property taxation.

It is the function of this chapter to consider the ratios and comparisons that may be used in studying the long-term financial position and operating results of a business. The absolute data, trends, common-size percentages, and percentages of increase and decrease, as well as individual balance sheet and income statement ratios and comparisons, may be used to advantage in varying degrees in such a study. Financial and

---

[1] Original provision for pensions, recording of liability as a result of an anticipated unfavorable lawsuit decision, or similar transactions.

operating data for the Lynn-Dale Company, Illustrations 10–1 and 10–2 (pages 235–36), are used for illustrative purposes.

The Lynn-Dale Company data represent *book values* rather than current appraised or cost of replacement values. In computing certain ratios illustrated in the following pages, the use of current values would show more realistic relationships; however, current values are seldom available to the external analyst.[2]

Investment in assets and sources of capital

There are many questions to be answered in studying the long-term financial position of a business. Two such questions are: (1) What investment of capital has been made in the various types of assets? (2) What are the sources of this capital, i.e., borrowed funds or owners' equity?

Illustration 15–1 shows as of December 31, 1971 and 1966 the distribution of capital invested in the various types of assets of the Lynn-Dale Company in terms of dollars and percentages. The illustration also shows the sources of the capital (borrowed funds and owners' equity) in terms of dollars and percentages. It will be observed that many changes have taken place in the investment of capital in the different types of assets and that substantial changes occurred relative to the sources of capital.

One of the most significant conclusions to be made after a study of the data (Illustration 15–1) concerns the absolute and relative changes in the amounts of borrowed funds and owners' equity.

An improvement from the creditors' point of view is to be noted since borrowed funds represented only 27.0 percent of total liabilities and owners equity as of December 31, 1971 in comparison with 40.5 percent at the close of 1966. This change in the relative amounts of capital is also shown by the ratio of owners' equity to total liabilities which increased from 147 percent in 1966 to 270 percent in 1971. The margin of safety of the creditor claims has been increased substantially.

Individual ratios discussed previously or in the following pages may be utilized to determine the answers to questions such as the following:

1. Has the company the most appropriate and profitable balance between borrowed funds and owners' equity?
2. Is the investment in each group of assets properly balanced?
3. Is the investment in operating assets commensurate with current sales, prospective sales volume, and the net income?
4. Is the long-term financial strength improving? Does it give evidence of the ability of the company to expand and grow?

---

[2] However, the Accounting Principles Board has made a small beginning toward recognizing current data in financial statements.

ILLUSTRATION 15–1

LYNN-DALE COMPANY
Investment in Assets and Sources of Capital
As of December 31, 1966 and 1971

Items	December 31 1966 ($000)	(%)	December 31 1971 ($000)	(%)	Increase (decrease*) during five-year period ($000)	(%)
Assets						
Current assets	566.9	55.5	708.8	44.2	141.9	25.0
Land, plant, and equipment, net	433.5	42.4	720.1	44.9	286.6	66.1
Other noncurrent assets	21.6	2.1	174.8	10.9	153.2	709.0
Total Assets (a).	1,022.0	100.0	1,603.7	100.0	581.7	56.9
Liabilities						
Current liabilities	263.4	25.8	232.5	14.5	30.9*	12.0*
Long-term liabilities	150.0	14.7	200.5	12.5	50.5	34.0
Total Liabilities (b)	413.4	40.5	433.0	27.0	19.6	4.7
Owners' Equity						
Capital stock	400.0	39.1	620.0	38.7	220.0	55.0
Capital paid-in in excess of par value	60.0	5.9	160.0	10.0	100.0	166.7
Retained earnings.	148.6	14.5	390.7	24.3	242.1	162.9
Total Owners' Equity (c).	608.6	59.5	1,170.7	73.0	562.1	92.4
Total Owners' Equity and Liabilities	1,022.0	100.0	1,603.7	100.0	581.7	56.9
Note: Net sales	812.5		1,491.8		679.3	83.6

(a) Total investment of capital.
(b) Plus (c) equals total capital.

Ratio of owners' equity to total assets

The ratio of owners' equity to total assets shows the percentage of the total investment in assets that has been financed by the stockholders. This ratio, often called the "proprietary ratio" or "stockholders' equity ratio," is determined, as shown below, by dividing the owners' equity by total assets:

$$\frac{\text{Owners' equity (\$1,170,700)}}{\text{Total assets (net) \$1,603,700}} = \left\{ \begin{array}{l} \text{Ratio of owners' equity to} \\ \text{total assets (net) (73.0\%).} \end{array} \right.$$

The difference between this ratio and 100 percent represents the ratio of total liabilities to total assets, the percentage of the assets supplied by the creditors. Illustration 15–1 shows that as of December 31, 1971 the stockholders' equity and creditors' claims of the Lynn-Dale Company are equal to 73.0 percent and 27.0 percent, respectively, of the total assets.

The ratio of owners' equity to total assets and the ratio of liabilities to total assets reflect the relative importance of the sources of borrowed funds and owners' equity and the margin of protection for the creditor claims. Illustration 15–1 reveals that the equity of the stockholders of the Lynn-Dale Company increased and the total claims of creditors decreased from January 1, 1966 through December 31, 1971. During this period:

1. Common stock increased $220,000; capital contributed in excess of par value (premium on common stock) increased $100,000. Information relative to the amount of stock dividend is not supplied.
2. Net income before extraordinary items and after federal income taxes totaled $214,800.
3. Extraordinary gains in the amount of $195,700 occurred as a result of the disposition of property.
4. Total dividends, including stock dividends, amounted to $113,400.

The larger amount of owners' equity for the Lynn-Dale Company indicates an improvement in the long-term financial position, since there is a relatively greater margin of safety for outside creditors and less long-term debt pressure from the point of view of the owners. The most conservative, although not always the most profitable, basis of financing when bonds or other long-term obligations are used in place of capital stock is to provide for the gradual retirement of the debt. A high ratio of owners' equity to total liabilities and owners' equity is not necessarily an indication of the most profitable method of financing. The principle of trading on the equity, i.e., leverage, explained on pages 344–45, should be considered when deciding upon the relative amounts of capital to be obtained from creditors and owners.[3]

The ratio of owners' equity to total liabilities and owners' equity (or to total assets)—the proprietary ratio—is at least as important as the current ratio. It is a rough measure of the relative financial strength and reflects the long-term liquidity (solvency) by showing the presence or absence of long-term liability pressure. The current ratio gives evidence of the relative liquidity of the business, i.e., a measure of the short-term solvency or the ability to meet current debts as they mature. A relatively high proprietary ratio reflects less likelihood of financial difficulty resulting from heavy fixed interest charges and inability to meet maturing debt obligations. A relatively low proprietary ratio reflects a more speculative situation because of the possibility of high profits or losses. However, a detailed examination of debt and interest burden is superior to any ratio; the ratio tells you when your attention can be profitably given to the details.

---

[3] Large corporations that use long-term debt as a regular element in their capital structures generally do not wish to amortize it.

In comparing the percentage of owners' equity to total assets from year to year or between companies in the same line of business, differences may be a result of changes or variations in the valuation and amortization of assets and/or in financial policy. More specifically, the differences may be a result of a change or variation in:

1. The policy relating to depreciation, depletion, or amortization.
2. The recording of appreciation or extraordinary depreciation of assets.
3. The policy relating to abandonment or retirement and to additions of property.
4. The price levels obtaining when the properties under consideration were acquired.
5. The policy relating to cash and stock dividends.
6. The policy of financing asset acquisitions through the sale of stock or bonds or by using current and accumulated earnings.

From the point of view of the creditors the larger the percentage of assets that is supplied by stockholders, the more satisfactory the financial structure of the business, since owners' equity represents a margin of safety for creditors. In other words, owners' equity is a "cushion" that first absorbs losses. Periods of business inactivity which are accompanied by financial stress and greatly reduced earnings should prove less burdensome to a business that has a high proprietary ratio. Then, too, a company that has a stable profit or an experienced, successful management is able to operate on a relatively lower proprietary ratio. However, an upward trend in this ratio usually is considered by creditors to be favorable; and the larger the percentage of funds supplied by outside creditors, the less "conservative" the financial structure is likely to be, expecially in periods of poor business, because of the fixed interest obligations and the necessity of paying or refunding maturing debts. In periods of low business activity, the business may not earn its fixed interest charges or may not be able to refinance maturing obligations on favorable terms. When the stockholders' equity is quite small in comparison with the creditors' claims, a substantial decline in sales, accompanied by a large operating loss, might reduce owners' equity to a dangerously low level and require a financial reorganization. Owners' equity may be eliminated altogether and heavy losses inflicted upon the creditors.

Since World War II and the price increases following 1946–47, there has been a tendency toward more debt in large businesses. It is difficult to determine the most appropriate balance between borrowed funds and owners' equity. If a minimum amount of borrowed funds is being used, the ratio between borrowed funds and owners' equity would ordinarily reflect "too-safe" a position. On the other hand, a maximum amount of borrowed funds would usually reflect a dangerous situation. What determines how high a proportion of long-term borrowing may be resorted to with safety? The answer to this question involves an analysis of the characteristics of the industry and of the company's assets, earning capacity, and factors governing the stability of earnings.

Stability of earnings is the resultant of a number of influences. Earnings will tend to be stable when the volume of business is more or less uniform and when a fairly constant margin is maintained between selling prices and costs. Stable earnings are most likely to be enjoyed by the following industries or companies:

1. Industries supplying consumer goods or services as compared with industries supplying producer goods.
2. Old, well-established companies compared with new or young companies.
3. Companies having large unit sales volumes as compared with small unit sales volumes.
4. Companies selling goods or services that are used by habit as compared with those used on a nonhabitual basis.
5. Companies selling goods or services that are necessities as compared with those that are luxuries.

A public utility company operates large fixed properties and usually enjoys relatively stable earnings. Public service commissions regulate public utilities in detail; and as a rule, direct competition is nonexistent. On the other hand, an industrial concern which is subjected to the rigors of competition usually does not have a stability of earnings equal to that of a public utility. Less risk of loss is customarily present in the case of public utilities as compared with industrials. Consequently, a public utility may and invariably does resort to a higher proportion of bond financing.

In brief, whenever a business has a relatively low proportion of fixed tangible assets and/or unstable earnings, it is usually best to minimize or avoid bonds.

Both short- and long-term creditors may have an "equity," claim, or investment in a business. From the point of view of the business, an ideal situation exists when current operations, in excess of the minimum amount of working capital which is required permanently by the business, are financed by current creditors. If goods can be purchased on credit and converted into cash within the credit period allowed by the creditor, the business would be able to operate on the creditors' investment in the business. The stockholders, under these circumstances, would be called upon to furnish the minimum amount of current working capital and would realize the net benefit of trading on the current creditors' investment.

Stockholders may also profit by "trading on the equity." This practice involves the employment of borrowed funds in the expectation that a rate of return higher than the cost (interest and preferred stock dividends) will be realized. The common stockholders' equity is a protection for the income and principal of the creditor obligations. When earnings on the borrowed funds—which may include owners' equity obtained by the sale of preferred stock with a limited return—exceed its cost, the common stockholders benefit. the common stockholders lose when the income on the borrowed funds is less than its cost.

For example, Corporation A, as shown in Illustration 15–2, has a total invested capital (bonds, capital stock, and retained earnings) of

ILLUSTRATION 15–2

CORPORATION A

Trading on the Equity Leverage—Example

For the Years Ended December 31, 1966 and 1971

	December 31	
Items and computation	1966	1971
Bonds payable (5%).....................($000)	$ 500	$ 500
Common stockholders' equity (a)...........($000)	700	900
Total amount of funds (b)...........($000)	$1,200	$1,400
	1966	1971
Income prior to bond interest* (c)..........($000)	$ 48	$ 154
Bond interest......................($000)	25	25
Net income for stockholders* (d)...........($000)	$ 23	$ 129
Return on total amount of funds* (c ÷ b)......(%)	4.0%	11.0%
Return on common stockholders' equity (d ÷ a)............................(%)	3.3	14.3

* Before federal income taxes.

$1,200,000 and $1,400,000 as of December 31, 1966 and 1971 respectively. A lower rate of return was realized on the total capital investment for the year 1966 than the rate of interest paid on the borrowed funds. Therefore, although a 5 percent rate of return was paid to the bondholders, only a 3.3 percent rate was realized by the stockholders. In this particular year, trading on the equity was not profitable for the stockholders.

A more favorable situation exists for the year 1971. A return of 11 percent was earned on the combined investment of the bondholders and stockholders. Since only a 5 percent rate was paid to bondholders, the stockholders benefited from the use of the bondholders' investment to the extent of 6 percent. The stockholders realized a return of 14.3 percent on their equity. Trading on the equity was profitable for the stockholders in 1971.

Ratio of owners' equity to fixed assets

The ratio of owners' equity to fixed assets for the Lynn-Dale Company is determined, as shown in Illustration 15–3, by dividing owners' equity by the book value of the fixed assets. When the owners' equity exceeds the fixed (and other noncurrent) assets, a part of the net working capital is supplied by the stockholders. When the owners' equity is less than the fixed assets, creditor obligations have been used to finance a part of the fixed assets.

ILLUSTRATION 15–3

LYNN-DALE COMPANY
Ratios of Owners' Equity to Fixed Assets
As of December 31, 1966 and 1971
(dollars in thousands)

Items and computation	December 31		Increase 1971 over 1966	
	1966	1971	($000)	(%)
Fixed assets (a)............($000)	433.5	720.1	286.6	66.1
Owners' equity (b) ....($000)	608.6	1,170.7	562.1	92.4
Ratio of owners' equity to fixed assets (b ÷ a) .... (%)	140.4	162.6		

An increasing ratio indicates that expansion of fixed assets has been financed more by owners' equity than by borrowed funds. A decreasing ratio indicates that funds for the fixed assets expansion have been obtained from creditor sources to a greater extent than from the owners.

The ratios of owners' equity to fixed assets for the Lynn-Dale Company show that a significant change took place in both fixed assets and owners' equity during the years 1966 through 1971—fixed assets and owners' equity increased 66.1 percent and 92.4 percent, respectively. The new fixed assets were financed primarily by using working capital provided by current operations and the proceeds from mortgage notes and common stock.

The ratio of owners' equity to fixed assets of 162.6 percent for the Lynn-Dale Company as of December 31, 1971 may indicate an overinvestment in buildings, fixtures, equipment, and land. A heavy investment in fixed assets is disadvantageous from the point of view of the annual depreciation charges. If the excess fixed assets are not being profitably used, it is a misuse of potentially profitable capital. An overinvestment in fixed assets may have been accomplished by using current working capital, thereby causing a shortage of working capital. On the other hand, in many cases an excess of borrowed funds is used for financing the current working capital requirements. In turn, the fixed interest on the borrowed funds may be burdensome. However, the real test of over-investment in fixed assets involves the analysis of plant turnover—the plant investment in relation to sales—and earning power.

The ratio of owners' equity to fixed assets decreases or increases from year to year as a result of (1) fixed asset acquisitions and abandonments, as well as the recognition of depreciation; and (2) retention of earnings or payment of dividends, the occurrence of operating and/or extraordinary losses, and the issuance or redemption of capital stock.

Ratio of current assets to total liabilities

The ratio of current assets to total liabilities, shown in Illustration 15–4, measures the liquidity of the long-term liabilities. This ratio is

ILLUSTRATION 15–4

LYNN-DALE COMPANY
Ratios of Current Assets to Total Liabilities
As of December 31, 1966 and 1971

		December 31	
Items and computation		1966	1971
Current assets (a) ....($000)		566.9	708.8
Total liabilities (b).........................($000)		413.4	433.0
Excess of current assets over total liabilities			
(a − b) ....($000)		153.5	275.8
Ratio of current assets to total liabilities			
(a ÷ b) .... (%)		137.0	164.0

significant because the operating assets customarily have a relatively low liquidation value. The ratio is adversely affected by operating and extraordinary losses.

The ratios of current assets to total liabilities given in Illustration 15–4 indicate that the stockholders of the Lynn-Dale Company have supplied an increasing amount of the working capital since the ratio of current assets to total liabilities increased from 137.0 percent as of December 31, 1966 to 164.0 percent as of the end of 1971. It should be evident that the claims of the short-term creditors are protected to a greater extent as the amount of working capital is increased by stockholders' investments (capital stock and other owners' equity items). A high ratio indicates that if liquidation losses on current assets are not too excessive, the long-term liabilities could be paid in full out of working capital.

Ratio of fixed assets to long-term liabilities

The ratio of fixed assets to long-term liabilities reflects in some measure the security of the fixed obligations when the long-term liabilities,

ILLUSTRATION 15–5

LYNN-DALE COMPANY
Ratios of Fixed Assets to Long-Term Liabilities
As of December 31, 1966 and 1971

		December 31	
Items and computation		1966	1971
Fixed assets (a)................................($000)		433.5	720.1
Long-term liabilities (secured by fixed assets) (b)................................($000)		150.0	200.5
Ratio of fixed assets to long-term liabilities (a ÷ b)................................(%)		289.0	359.2

such as mortgage notes and bonds payable, are secured by the fixed assets. This ratio also indicates to some extent whether or not additional creditor funds may be obtained by using the same security. The computation of this ratio for the Lynn-Dale Company is shown in Illustration 15–5.

The ratios of fixed assets to long-term liabilities (Illustration 15–5) show clearly that the margin of safety of the long-term creditors increased favorably according to book values since the ratio changed from 289.0 percent as of December 31, 1966 to 359.2 percent as of the end of 1971. Another way to interpret these data is to say that as of December 31, 1966 and 1971, the business possessed $2.89 and $3.59, respectively, of fixed assets for each dollar of long-term liabilities. Plant expansion was financed almost entirely by stockholder funds. It should be understood that the computation of the ratio of fixed assets to long-term liabilities includes the assets at their book values and not at their present cost of replacement or liquidation value. The liquidation value of fixed assets is customarily low.

A more realistic ratio is determined by relating *appraised values* of the fixed assets to long-term liabilities. The protection afforded the creditors and the ability to borrow additional funds on the same properties are actually based on current replacement cost or appraised value. However, these "present values" are not always available to the external analyst.

In the final analysis, the real value of the assets depends upon the earnings of the company; profit and loss ratios and trends are of major significance to creditors and stockholders.

If a sinking fund is being accumulated and the fund does not include the company's own bonds, it should be added to the fixed tangible assets total in Illustration 15–5. If the company's bonds which are to be redeemed are included in the sinking fund, these bonds should be deducted from the liabilities before the percentage is determined.

Book value of stockholders' equity per share[4]

The book value of capital stock is the total of the owners' equity as shown by the books. Although the book value of common stock is important, it must be remembered that this information gives no indication of the current realizable value of the stock. This is true since the book values are based on cost figures rather than current economic appraisal figures. Stockholders' equity increases as a result of additional issuance of capital stock and accumulation of retained earnings and decreases when capital stock is retired, dividends are declared, and losses are incurred.

If there is no preferred stock, the book value of the common stockholders' equity per share is computed by dividing the owners' equity (capital stock and other capital items) by the number of outstanding shares of common stock. From an investment point of view, this book value, which represents the value of the assets applicable to the stock *as shown on the books,* should be compared with the current market value.

When more than one class of capital stock is outstanding, it is necessary to know, with reference to preferred stock, whether it is cumulative or noncumulative, participating or nonparticipating, or preferred or nonpreferred as to assets in the event of dissolution, and whether there are dividends in arrears. In determining book value, (1) determine the rights of each class of capital stock relative to the total owners' equity, and (2) divide the total equity assignable to each class of capital stock by the number of outstanding shares.

A method of showing the asset book value underlying preferred stock

---

[4] Refer to page 130 for a discussion of the rights of preferred stockholders.

when it is preferred as to assets is to divide the total of the assets (exclusive of intangibles), minus all outside creditor claims, by the outstanding number of shares of preferred stock. To illustrate:

Total asset book value,* exclusive of intangible assets (a) $1,000,000
  Less: Total creditor claims (b).   300,000
Net asset value* (owners' equity) (a − b)(c) .... $ 700,000
Shares of preferred stock outstanding (d).   1,000
Net assets* (exclusive of intangible assets) available to meet each
  share of preferred stock, assuming that the stock is preferred
  as to assets (c ÷ d) .... $ 700
  * Valuation and amortization accounts have been deducted.

The foregoing computation merely emphasizes that when the preferred stock is preferred as to assets, the assets of the company remaining after paying liabilities must first be applied to the liquidation of preferred stockholders' claims; it shows the margin of safety relative to the par value of the preferred stock investment.

Frequently, liquidation values are assigned to preferred stock. For example, it is rather common for a corporation to provide for a premium of $2.50 or $5 per share in the event that the preferred stock is called in during continued operations or when the concern is liquidating. Computation of book value, using preferred stock par rather than liquidation value, while theoretically improper, is more convenient and the results will be approximately the same.

Sometimes, in determining the book value of capital stock, the account, Capital Stock Subscribed, is encountered. The question arises relative to the claim on owners' equity in excess of the capital stock of the subscribers to capital stock who have not yet paid the full subscription price. Generally, the corporation has a claim against the capital stock subscriber for the unpaid amount of his subscription. Conversely, unless otherwise provided for, the subscriber is entitled to full participation in corporate assets upon the payment of the subscription balance. Therefore, the most logical procedure is to assign the surplus to the outstanding and subscribed stock.

The determination of the book value of preferred and common stock is illustrated below. The balance sheet items have been presented and arranged with special reference to:

1. The proper classification of valuation and amortization accounts, appropriations of retained earnings, and estimated liabilities.
2. The showing of the book value of the assets.
3. The determination of total owners' equity and the owners' equity of both common stockholders and preferred stockholders.
4. The computation of the book value per share of preferred stock and of common stock.

Total assets (exclusive of intangibles—before deducting valuation and amortization accounts)		$1,890,475
Less: Estimated uncollectible receivables (valuation account)	$ 18,694	
Accumulated depreciation (amortization account)	72,843	91,537
Book value of assets (exclusive of intangibles)		$1,798,938
Less: Current liabilities	$ 123,684	
Mortgage notes payable (long-term liability)	300,000	
Estimated liability for pensions (long-term liability)	30,000	453,684
Owners' equity (preferred and common stockholders' equity)		$1,345,254
Less: Preferred stockholders' equity:		
Preferred stock, par value $100	$ 300,000	
Preferred stock dividends in arrears (12% of $300,000 for two years dividends)	36,000	336,000
Owners' equity (common stockholders' equity as shown below)		$1,009,254
Common stock, par value $100	$ 600,000	
Capital paid-in in excess of par value	50,000	
Retained earnings appropriated for plant expansion	125,000	
Retained earnings unappropriated (dividends in arrears on preferred stock, $36,000)	234,254	
	$1,009,254	

Book Value

$$\frac{\text{Preferred stockholders' equity, } \$336,000}{\text{Shares preferred stock outstanding, } 3,000} = \begin{cases} \text{Book value per share of} \\ \text{preferred stock, } \$112. \end{cases}$$

$$\frac{\text{Common stockholders' equity, } \$1,009,254}{\text{Shares common stock outstanding, } 6,000} = \begin{cases} \text{Book value per share of} \\ \text{common stock, } \$168.21. \end{cases}$$

In the foregoing example, if the preferred stock had been fully participating, the owners' equity in excess of capital stock, less dividends in arrears on preferred stock, $36,000, would be assigned on a pro-rata basis to common and preferred stock in determining the book value per share.

Effect of changes in price level

At the end of a period of marked changes in the general price level, many of the balance sheet assets have values that differ widely from their book value (cost). If prices have been rising, the following items will show the most substantial understatements in comparison with the current value of the dollar:

1. Inventories (if Lifo is in use).
2. Land, plant, and equipment (unless acquired currently).
3. Components of the stockholders' equity, including outstanding common stock and retained earnings (appropriated and unappropriated).

Ratios computed by using these items will vary, depending on their statement in terms of original, or current, dollars. Other items are also affected. These matters are fully discussed in Part III.

Additional ratios for measuring long-term financial condition

The preceding discussion is devoted primarily to a study of the relative proportions of capital borrowed from various groups of creditors and contributed by, or representing the equity of, the stockholders. The following represents a discussion of the measurement of profits from the point of view of borrowed funds and owners' equity used in the business. The significant question involved is: To what extent are the assets employed profitably and the suppliers of the borrowed funds and owners' equity provided with a return on their investment which has been agreed upon or which is commensurate with the risk involved? Prospects of repaying long-term liabilities and protection of future interest and dividend payments are also considered.

Ratio of operating income to operating assets

The ratio of operating income to total operating assets shows earnings regardless of the sources of the capital invested in the assets; it is determined as shown in Illustration 15–6 for the Lynn-Dale Company by

ILLUSTRATION 15–6

LYNN-DALE COMPANY
Ratios of Operating Income to Operating Assets
For the Years Ended December 31, 1966–71

Items and computation		1966	1967	1968	1969	1970	1971
Operating income* (a)	($000)	63.4	64.9	61.9	78.1	84.5	91.0
Total operating assets† (b)	($000)	1,022.0	1,083.5	1,364.3	1,475.3	1,578.5	1,603.7
Ratio of operating income to total assets, net (a ÷ b)	(%)	6.20	5.98	4.54	5.29	5.35	5.67

* Other revenue and expenses, federal income taxes, and extraordinary items are excluded.

† Includes assets, after valuation and amortization accounts have been deducted, used in regular operation of the business (end-of-year figures). If available, the 12-month average of total operating assets owned during the year should be used. If revealed, long-term investments should be excluded in determining operating assets.

dividing operating income by total operating assets (after valuation and amortization accounts have been deducted).

The ratio of operating income to total operating assets reflects the earning ability of the company, i.e., the economic productivity of the borrowed funds and owners' equity invested in the assets, and represents an overall measure of efficiency of the business. The ratios for the Lynn-Dale Company show a downward trend through 1968 and then an upward trend through 1971. A relatively important expansion of operating assets took place during 1968; the operating income did not increase in a significant manner.

The ratio of operating income to total operating assets is useful in comparing (1) companies that have different forms of borrowed funds and owners' equity and (2) different periods of a particular company that has changed the relative amounts of borrowed funds and owners' equity; the ratio shows the earnings on the assets independently of the sources of the funds invested in them. However, caution must be exercised in studying this ratio for different companies because of the possible presence of noncomparable data. For example, there may be variations in (1) asset valuation and amortization methods; (2) inclusions of asset, revenue, and expense items; (3) accounting periods; and (4) depreciation, amortization, and maintenance policies.

A low ratio of operating income to total operating assets may reflect an overinvestment in assets in relation to sales volume; an inadequacy of sales volume from the point of view of the cost of obtaining the sales revenue; inefficiency of management in production, purchasing, merchandising, and general operations; or depressed business conditions. A high ratio of operating income to total operating assets would indicate that the company is not materially affected by the foregoing factors.

Earnings on long-term investments

Long-term investments should be compared with the income realized from them. For example, Illustration 15–7 shows long-term investments

ILLUSTRATION 15–7

COMPANY D

Comparison of Long-Term Investment and Income Thereon
For the Years Ended December 31, 1966–71

Items and computation		1966	1967	1968	1969	1970	1971
Long-term investments* (a)	($000)	150	140	160	162	175	170
Trend percentages	(%)	100	93	107	108	117	113
Income from above assets† (b)	($000)	1.7	2.1	12.5	13.1	16.3	17.8
Trend percentages	(%)	100	124	735	770	959	1,029
Rate of income on long-term investments (b ÷ a)	(%)	1.1	1.5	7.8	8.1	9.3	10.⁣

* Investment as of December 31.
† Income for the year.

and their income for Company D for the years 1966–71. The necessary data are not available for the Lynn-Dale Company.

From the data in Illustration 15–7, it may be concluded that the long-term investments held during 1966–67 were not profitable from the point of view of interest or dividend income. However, the return on the investments increased from 1.5 percent for 1967 to an average return of 8.88 percent for the years 1968–71. When appropriate data are available, the rate of return should be determined for each major long-term investment item. The cost incurred in connection with earning the revenue on the investments should be analyzed.

Ratio of net income to owners' equity

The ratio of net income (transferred to retained earnings) to owners' equity is another effective measure of the profitableness of an enterprise. In fact, this ratio is one of the most important relationships in financial statement analysis. The realization of a satisfactory net income is the major objective of a business; the ratio of net income to owners' equity reflects the extent to which this objective is being achieved.

The net income figure used in the computation of this ratio, which is shown in Illustration 15–8 for the Lynn-Dale Company, represents the net income after including all revenue items, operating, other, and

ILLUSTRATION 15–8

LYNN-DALE COMPANY
Ratios of Net Income to Owners' Equity
For the Years Ended December 31, 1966–71

Items and computations	1966	1967	1968	1969	1970	1971
Net income before extraordinary items (a) . . . . ($000)	27.6	29.0	26.7	32.4	46.9	52.2
Net income and extraordinary items (b) . . . . ($000)	27.6	28.0*	59.0	41.8	175.2	94.7
Owners' equity (end of year) (c) . . . . ($000)	608.6	603.5	792.7	948.6	1,101.8	1,170.7
Ratio of net income before extraordinary items to owners' equity (a ÷ c) . . . . (%)	4.53	4.81	3.37	3.42	4.26	4.46
Ratio of net income and extraordinary items to owners' equity (b ÷ c) . . . . (%)	4.53	4.64*	7.44	4.41	15.9	8.09

* Loss.

extraordinary expense items, and federal income taxes. The ratio is also computed in the illustration by using the net income before extraordinary items. The owners' equity figure represents the total of the stockholders' equity at the end of the year after the net income or net loss has been included in retained earnings. The average owners' equity for a year computed from monthly data should be used when the data are available.

The ratios of net income (before extraordinary items) to owners' equity for the Lynn-Dale Company reveal an unsatisfactory earnings condition. It will be observed that the ratios fluctuated from 4.53 percent for 1966 to 4.81 percent for 1967 and then from 3.37 percent for 1968 to 4.46 percent for 1971. When the rate of return on owners' equity is computed by using the net income and extraordinary items, a more profitable situation is revealed. The extraordinary gain for the Lynn-Dale Company was the result of disposing of property[5]—a gain that normally is not repeated. There appears to be an overinvestment in fixed assets in relation to the sales volume. The average return on net worth of

[5] See income statement, Illustration 10–2 (page 236).

department stores in 1968 was 11.1 percent.[6] A low ratio of net income to owners' equity may indicate that the business is not very successful because of inefficient and ineffective production, distribution, financial, or general management; unfavorable general business conditions; or overinvestment in assets. A high ratio of net income to owners' equity may be a result of efficient management throughout the company's organization, favorable general business conditions, and trading on the equity. The stockholders benefit to the extent that borrowed funds cost less than the return on these funds when invested in the business.

The ratio of net income to owners' equity, which measures the average return on the total equity of the stockholders, should be compared with the ratios for other similar companies or for the industry as a whole to determine whether the rate of return is attractive.

ILLUSTRATION 15–9

LYNN-DALE COMPANY
Earnings in Relation to Owners' Equity
For the Years Ended December 31, 1966–71

Items and computation	1966	1967	1968	1969	1970	1971
Income before federal income taxes and extraordinary items (a)..........................($000)	52.8	54.6	53.4	64.9	73.8	83
Owners' equity (end of year) (b) ....($000)	608.6	603.5	792.7	948.6	1,101.8	1,170
Ratio of income before federal income taxes and extraordinary items to owners' equity (a ÷ b)........ (%)	8.68	9.05	6.74	6.84	6.70	7

In order to determine the amount of earnings likely to be realized in the future, the analyst should exclude the federal income taxes and consider how to treat extraordinary, nonrecurring items. In Illustration 15–9, the amount of net income before federal income taxes and extraordinary items is used in estimating the probable future earnings from the operation of the business. In interpreting these ratios, the analyst should consider the fact that a portion of the income must be used to pay federal income taxes and that extraordinary items frequently recur. Although the exclusion of federal income taxes and extraordinary items is probably best suited for a comparison of the regular earning power of several companies, the analyst is in the last analysis concerned with the net earnings, i.e., the recurring income after federal income taxes. The net income before federal income taxes and extraordinary items is related to owners' equity in Illustration 15–9. The analyst should be cautious in interpreting the ratios of net income to owners' equity, since neither the assets nor the expenses are stated entirely in current values. Historical costs are reflected for most items on the balance sheet and for some of those appearing on the income statement. Therefore,

---

[6] Troy, *Manual of Performance Ratios* (Englewood Cliffs, N.J.: Prentice-Hall, Inc., 1971).

the owners' equity as well as the net income is not reported on a "current purchasing power" basis.

Trading on the equity (leverage) principle

As explained on pages 344–45, trading on the equity (leverage) involves the employment of borrowed funds (current and long-term creditor funds) in the expectation that a rate of return higher than the cost will be realized. The analyst should determine whether or not trading on the equity has been profitable by computing the average rate of return earned on the total amount of capital invested in assets

ILLUSTRATION 15–10

LYNN-DALE COMPANY
Rate of Earnings on Total Borrowed Funds and Owners' Equity
For the Years Ended December 31, 1966–71

Items and computation		1966	1967	1968	1969	1970	1971
Borrowed funds	($000)	413.4	480.0	571.6	526.7	476.7	433.0
Owners' equity	($000)	608.6	603.5	792.7	948.6	1,101.8	1,170.7
Total borrowed funds and owners' equity (a)	($000)	1,022.0	1,083.5	1,364.3	1,475.3	1,578.5	1,603.7
Income after federal income taxes before fixed interest charges and extraordinary items (b)	($000)	33.6	35.5	37.3	42.0	56.1	60.2
Income before fixed interest charges after federal income taxes and extraordinary items (c)	($000)	33.6	21.5	69.6	51.4	184.4	102.7
Rate of earnings on total borrowed funds and owners' equity, after federal income taxes, before fixed interest charges and extraordinary items (b ÷ a)	(%)	3.29	3.28	2.73	2.85	3.55	3.75
Rate of earnings on total borrowed funds and owners' equity, before fixed interest charges and extraordinary items (c ÷ a)	(%)	3.29	1.98	5.10	3.48	11.68	6.40

and comparing this rate with the average interest rate paid on borrowed funds. The rate of return is usually determined, as indicated in Illustration 15–10, by dividing the income *after* federal income taxes and *before* fixed interest charges and extraordinary items by the total of borrowed funds and owners' capital.

Illustration 15–10 shows that for each dollar of capital (borrowed funds and owners' equity) invested in the assets, the company realized (not including fixed interest and extraordinary items) an average return of 3.24 percent during the six-year period. Inasmuch as the company paid 4 percent on borrowed obligations, trading on the equity has not been profitable. This situation may be further evidence of an overinvestment in fixed assets in relation to sales volume. If the extraordinary items are included in computing the foregoing ratios, an entirely different picture is seen for the years 1968, 1970, and 1971. An average return on total capital of 4.66 percent was realized during these years. However, inasmuch as the extraordinary gain was not derived from regular operations, it normally will not be repeated. The success of trading on the equity should be judged primarily by using the regular recurring income figure.

Times fixed interest charges have been earned

The number of times that fixed interest charges have been earned is a measure of the financial strength of a company and indicates the margin of safety of the long-term creditors. In computing the interest coverage, the analyst must decide whether or not to deduct federal income taxes in determining the amount of income that is available for fixed interest charges. When a study is being made to ascertain the relative investment merits of several bonds issued by different types of businesses, the federal income tax is sometimes not deducted. The omission of the federal income tax has logical support in that (1) the tax applies only to the net income remaining after the deduction of interest charges; (2) the federal income tax rates and the amounts of capital gains and losses reflected in the total tax are different for the companies; and (3) the resultant income figure, i.e., the income available for fixed interest charges, shows the real earning power of the companies.

The credit-investor is very much concerned with the margin of safety of the income on the obligations, i.e., the number of extra times that the fixed interest has been earned. Therefore, the second—and, certainly, the more common and conservative—method of computing the fixed interest coverage is to deduct federal income taxes in determining the amount of income that is available to meet fixed interest. The foregoing method is sound, since (1) the federal income tax is very frequently classified as an operating expense, (2) the amount of the income tax is not always shown specifically, and (3) the real *margin or factor of safety* of interest coverage represents the income accruing to stockholders (net income after federal income taxes and extraordinary items).

Illustration 15–11 shows the number of times that interest charges on long-term liabilities have been earned before and after the deduction for federal income taxes by the Lynn-Dale Company for the years 1966 through 1971. Long-term liabilities increased substantially during 1968 and then were reduced from $266,000 as of December 31, 1968 to $200,500 as of December 31, 1971. Therefore, the interest on the long-term liabilities was earned a greater number of times for the years 1969, 1970, and 1971. The net income could decrease considerably without adversely affecting the payment of the fixed interest. The net income before interest and after federal income taxes exclusive of extraordinary items increased substantially—from $33,600 for 1966 to $60,200 for 1971. During the years 1969, 1970, and 1971, the interest was earned 4.4, 6.1, and 7.5 times, respectively.

ILLUSTRATION 15–11

LYNN-DALE COMPANY
Times Fixed Interest Charges Have Been Earned
For the Years Ended December 31, 1966–71

Items and computations		1966	1967	1968	1969	1970	1971
Long-term liabilities (a)	($000)	150.0	162.5	266.0	240.5	228.9	200.5
Interest on long-term liabilities (b)	($000)	6.0	6.5	10.6	9.6	9.2	8.0
Income before fixed interest, federal income taxes, and extraordinary items (c).	($000)	58.8	61.1	64.0	74.5	83.0	91.5
Income after federal income taxes, before fixed interest and extraordinary items (d)	($000)	33.6	35.5	37.3	42.0	56.1	60.2
Number of times interest earned on long-term liabilities, before federal income taxes and extraordinary items (c ÷ b)	(Times)	9.8	9.4	6.0	7.8	9.0	11.4
Number of times interest earned on long-term liabilities, after federal income taxes, before fixed interest charges and extraordinary items (d ÷ b)	(Times)	5.6	5.5	3.5	4.4	6.1	7.5

A study of the number of times that the fixed interest charges have been earned before and after the deduction for federal income taxes (Illustration 15–11) clearly reveals the adverse effect of the tax with respect to the margin of safety of the fixed interest charge. The comparison further emphasizes the necessity of deducting the federal income tax in determining the margin of safety of the interest charge.

If a corporation has more than one long-term obligation, the interest coverage may be figured for each issue, together with prior and equal liens, as well as for the total fixed interest. For example, if there are first- and second-mortgage bonds, the interest coverage for the senior bond is computed by dividing the income available for fixed interest charges (after federal income taxes) by the senior bond interest charge. The interest coverage for the junior bond is determined by dividing the income available for fixed interest charges (after federal income taxes) by the total senior and junior bond interest charges. The inclusion of the senior bond interest charge in the foregoing computation is necessary because a junior bond, by precipitating a reorganization, may interfere with interest payments on the senior bond.

Times fixed interest charges and preferred dividend requirements have been earned

The analyst may also wish to determine, as shown in Illustration 15–12 for Company A, the number of times interest charges on long-term liabilities and preferred stock dividend requirements have been earned.

ILLUSTRATION 15-12

COMPANY A
Times Fixed Interest and Preferred Stock Dividends Have Been Earned
For the Years Ended December 31, 1968-71

Items and computation		1968	1969	1970	197
Interest on long-term liabilities	($000)	3,000	3,000	8,000	9,0
Dividend requirements of preferred stock	($000)	6,000	6,000	6,000	6,0
Total fixed interest charges and preferred dividend requirements (a)	($000)	9,000	9,000	14,000	15,0
Income before fixed interest and extraordinary items, after federal income tax* (b)	($000)	37,000	48,000	56,000	74,0
Number of times interest charges on fixed debt and dividend requirements of preferred stock is earned (b ÷ a)	(Times)	4.11	5.33	4.00	4.

* Federal income taxes are deducted, since they must be included in determining the amount of income th has been realized by the stockholders.

This indicates the extent to which income may be decreased before the bondholders' and preferred stockholders' interest and dividend claims will be adversely affected.

Earnings on common stock

Illustration 15-13 shows the method of computing the earnings on common stock. The amount of net income that applies to the common stock is determined by deducting the preferred stock dividend requirements from the net income after federal income taxes and extraordinary items have been taken into account. The amount of income that applies to the common stock is divided by the number of outstanding shares of common stock in order to obtain the earnings in dollars per share

ILLUSTRATION 15-13

LYNN-DALE COMPANY
Earnings on Common Stock
For the Years Ended December 31, 1966-71

Items and computations		1966	1967	1968	1969	1970	1971
Net income, after fixed interest charges and federal income taxes, before extraordinary charges (a).	($000)	27.6	29.0	26.7	32.4	46.9	52.2
Net income, after fixed interest charges, extraordinary items, and federal income taxes (b).	($000)	27.6	28.0*	59.0	41.8	175.2	94.7
Number of shares of common stock outstanding (c).	(No.)	4,000	4,250	5,250	6,200	6,200	6,200
Earnings per share of common stock, before extraordinary items (a ÷ c).	($)	6.90	6.82	5.09	5.23	7.56	8.4
Earnings per share of common stock, after extraordinary items (b ÷ c).	($)	6.90	6.59*	11.24	6.74	28.26	15.2
Earnings per share of common stock on market value (income on common stock divided by market value of stock as of December 31).	(%)	5.10	3.10*	6.20	5.30	7.10	9.3

* Deficit.

of common stock. The analyst should compute the per share of earnings on common stock using the net income figure after deducting the preferred dividend requirements *before* and *after* extraordinary items.

The earnings per share of common stock in relation to its market value may be computed by dividing the income applicable to common stock by the market value of the common stock.

The earnings, exclusive of extraordinary items, per share of common stock for the Lynn-Dale Company, Illustration 15–13, are reasonably satisfactory for the years 1970 and 1971. The inclusion of the extraordinary items for the years 1968, 1970, and 1971 results in an unusually high earnings rate per share. However, it should be remembered that this situation may well be exceptional.

APPRAISING BONDS FOR LONG-TERM INVESTMENT

Appraising bonds for the long-term is of course a special application of the matters discussed in the preceding sections of this and prior chapters. It is important that the nature of bonds, and how they differ from stocks, be understood.

A bond is a debt of the issuing corporation; it is a specialized form of note payable. While the exact status of a bond depends on the provisions of the contract under which it was issued, the ordinary bond matures on a fixed date, carries a promise to pay interest at an agreed rate and at specified times, and permits recourse to the courts if the contract is breached. Therefore, when financial trouble appears, the ordinary bond is in a position superior to that of the stockholders, who are owners not creditors.

Therefore, investment in a bond differs from investment in a stock. The success of a stock investment depends on potential earnings, and financial position is important only to the extent that it enables or disables the owned company in its effort to achieve profits.

Investment in a bond—a debt—is made with the expectation that repayment will occur even if earnings are poor or nonexistent; in other words, financial position is of primary importance. The length of time before the debt is due for payment affects the relative importance of earnings in the bond investor's decision. A bond can be bought that matures within one or a very few years; earning power is then relatively unimportant. On the other hand, a bond can be bought which will not come due within the next 25 years; earning power is then very important because without adequate earnings a strong financial position may disappear before the due date is reached.

The basic difference between a stock and a bond as an investment vehicle can also be observed when watching their behavior on stock and bond markets. An investor who buys a stock does so expecting to receive dividends, or a rising market value, or both. Dividend rates vary; sometimes, under adverse conditions, they disappear completely. The rate of interest on a bond is fixed; it never rises, as dividends do; under adversity either one may be reduced or disappear. Stocks do not come due; they are ownership, not debt. Bonds are debt and on a certain date prescribed in the contract they fall due, and failure to pay interest when due or principal when due results in bankruptcy or receivership. So, in general, when trouble develops, the bondholder is in a position much superior to that of a stockholder.

There are stocks and bonds that fall in the middle between these patterns. Preferred stock usually has a preference on liquidation but does not participate in earnings above a fixed level. Income bonds are not obligated to pay interest unless earned. Financial managers have been busy constructing new forms of hybrid stocks and bonds that are difficult to classify.

Consequently, stock market prices fluctuate widely in response to changing expectations as to potential earnings. Bond prices fluctuate also but for a different reason: a high-grade bond will fall in price if the prevailing interest rate in the money market rises. The decrease in market price is to adjust the rate of return which the bond offers. How this mechanism works will be explained below. Of course we have been talking about high-grade bonds; a weak bond may drop in value to reflect investor doubts about its ability to pay interest and principal when due.

Let us suppose that a high-grade bond which has been outstanding for many years will mature in 12 months. Suppose also that the bond offers to pay interest at 5 percent per year and the prevailing rate in the money market for such a bond is 10 percent per year. (This disparity of rates would have been wildly unrealistic a few years ago, but in 1971 it can be observed on the public markets.) Bonds usually have a value at maturity of $1,000. This 5 percent bond, to interest a buyer, must offer 10 percent. The market price will therefore be around $954 so that an investor can expect to receive the formal interest payment of $50 plus an additional $46 from the principal value of the bond, a total of $96 on a $954 investment or approximately 10 percent. Other factors, such as the fact that the investor has to wait a full year before receiving the $46 bring about small variations in current market price.

A look at the bond quotations in the newspaper on this day in October 1971 may be useful. General Motors Acceptance Corporation 7¾ percents of 1994 are selling for $1,028.75 the maturity value is $1,000. GMAC 4 percents of 1979 are selling for $827.50; also a $1,000 bond. New York Central 4½ percents of 2013 are selling for $111.25; the Penn Central System is in receivership.

Analyzing a high-grade bond

In analyzing a high-grade bond, the investor should be concerned with:

1. The characteristics of the enterprise.
2. The terms of the bond issue contract.
3. The earnings record of the company; and, of course, if it has been in or near insolvency is important.
4. The relation of earnings to money required to pay interest charges, plus other fixed charges.
5. The relationships of the company's property and of its stockholders' equity to long-term debt.

Characteristics of the enterprise

The characteristics of an enterprise are related not only to its own operations but to the industry in which it operates and the countries under the control of which it does business.

A company which does a substantial amount of its business abroad may be subject to currency fluctuations and controls, expropriation of properties (sometimes without compensation), and other unpleasant developments. Utilities are subject to government regulation; they are unlikely to develop spectacular increases in net income; they are also much more likely to avoid spectacular decreases in profits. As a result, they carry larger amounts of long-term debt (discussed later).

Railroads used to be considered as very stable, conservative investments, but changes in transportation methods, such as airplanes, automobiles, and trucks, have changed the outlook for the industry.

There are also wide variations in the characteristics of nonregulated industries. The computer industry is rapidly growing and dynamic with one giant corporation dominating it. The automobile industry is dominated by two giant corporations with two others clinging to vulnerable segments; a feature of the industry is substantial and growing foreign competition. The aerospace industry is heavily dependent on government and grew rapidly as the government program expanded, but in 1971 it is suffering badly from cutbacks of funds. Some large corporations have gone the conglomerate route, bringing together under one top management subsidiary companies from various lines of business.

The United States is also a nation of smaller enterprises, some of which compete with the giants—such as software and specialty concerns in the computer industry—while others depend on specialties such as design, service, smaller lots, patented products, and what have you.

In short, an understanding of the industry and the ability of the concern to compete in it is important in assessing the capacity of an enterprise to survive. Other factors affecting the ability of an organization to compete are the quality of its management, the quality of its working force, the quality of its product line, the quality of its research, the quality of its plant and equipment, the relationship of its facilities to its markets, and so on.

Understanding the potential of an industry is a complex analytical problem the ability to solve which is developed by analysts by means of years of study and experience.

Here is a description of the "fundamental position" at the end of 1970 of the Iowa-Illinois Gas and Electric Company, written by analysts at Standard & Poors, investment service publishers and investment advisors.

*Fundamental Position**

Iowa-Illinois Gas & Electric supplies electricity and natural gas in Illinois and Iowa, including the cities of Rock Island, Moline and East Moline, Illinois; Davenport, Iowa City and Fort Dodge, Iowa; and natural gas only to Cedar Rapids and Ottumwa, Iowa. Population of the area served with electricity is about 346,000; gas 471,000.

These cities are important trading centers for a wide agricultural area growing corn, other grains, hops, cattle and dairy products. Urban areas produce farm and other machinery, steel products and meat and other prepared foods.

In 1969, electric and gas sales each accounted for 50% of total revenues. Residential-rural sales provided 39% of electric gross, commercial and industrial lighting 31%, industrial and commercial power 23% and other 7%. Some 53% of gas revenues was derived from residential and residential heating customers.

Rates are regulated by the Iowa State Commerce Commission and the Illinois Commerce Commission. Properties are evaluated on an original cost basis in Iowa and on a fair value basis in Illinois for rate-making purposes. Average residential electric rates at 2.69¢ per kwh. in 1969 and annual usage of 4,945 kwh. compared with 2.09¢ and 6,570 kwh. nationally. The company uses accelerated depreciation and offsets the resulting tax savings by an equal charge against income. Benefits from the 3% investment credit are treated in the same manner.

Generating capability of the company's plants will aggregate 598,000 kw. at the 1969 mid-year. Additional power is available from Iowa Power Pool members. Peak load in 1969 was 526,473 kw.

Natural gas is purchased from Natural Gas Pipeline Company of America and Northern Natural Gas. In 1969, the company paid an average price of around 33.5 cents per Mcf for gas bought from these sources.

---

* Source: Reprinted by permission of Standard & Poor's Corporation. Subsequent events have been reflected in later reports published in Standard & Poor's Stock Reports.

Dividends, paid each year since 1942, averaged 68% of available earnings in the five years through 1969.

Employees: 1,420. Shareholders: 17,142.

The terms of the contract

Some bonds are secured by liens on specific property while others are dependent on the overall soundness of the enterprise. First-mortgage bonds are of the first type, the bondholders having the right to sue for possession of the underlying property if their contractual right to interest and repayment of principal is not met. Debenture bonds are at the other extreme; the holders are general creditors with rights superior to stockholders but inferior to preferred creditors such as the mortgage bondholders, employees (for wages), and government (for taxes). Bond contracts, called indentures, are as varied in content as are other types of contracts. When investing in a bond it is well to investigate what your legal rights will be if the company develops financial difficulties.

The earnings record of the company

Forecasting the future is an inexact art. It is never possible to anticipate with precision the many difficulties that may lie around the corner. Nevertheless, an analysis of the past performance of a company is a better means of foreseeing the future than is blind faith or reliance on luck.

The Iowa-Illinois Gas and Electric Company publishes an annual statistical supplement to its annual report which gives a wealth of data for the last 12 years (1960 through 1971). The statement of income of the company, in comparative form for 11 years, is reproduced as Illustration 15–14.

This is a public utility, and we should expect steady and rising gross revenue and relatively steady and rising net income. As we shall see, the company has been enjoying the former; but in 1970, and particularly in 1971, its net income ran into heavy weather.

Adjusting the net income figures to a before (state and federal) income tax basis, and also to a before interest expense basis, we obtain the results shown in Illustration 15–15.

Notice that gross income (sales in dollars of electricity and gas) has risen steadily, as would be expected in a public utility. The growth in volume is maintaining its vigor, the increase ranging between five and seven million dollars a year.

Notice also that reported net income has risen steadily, except for a small dip in 1967, until it began falling in 1970 and skidded drastically

ILLUSTRATION 15–14

STATEMENT OF INCOME
(In Thousands)

YEAR ENDED DECEMBER 31	1960	1961	1962	1963	1964	1965	1966	1967	1968	1969	1970
OPERATING REVENUES:											
Electric	$25,366	$26,209	$27,559	$29,541	$32,167	$33,916	$36,281	$38,316	$41,538	$45,448	$48,438
Gas	25,729	28,375	31,063	32,105	35,369	36,720	38,877	41,308	42,771	45,903	49,883
	51,095	54,584	58,622	61,646	67,536	70,636	75,158	79,624	84,309	91,351	98,321
OTHER INCOME	280	215	331	352	512	405	292	265	284	329	258
	51,375	54,799	58,953	61,998	68,048	71,041	75,450	79,889	84,593	91,680	98,579
OPERATING EXPENSES, TAXES AND OTHER DEDUCTIONS:											
Operation	26,718	27,826	28,971	30,096	32,628	34,416	37,680	41,068	43,444	47,838	53,105
Maintenance	1,820	1,863	2,041	2,149	2,321	2,586	2,428	2,740	2,793	3,158	3,749
Depreciation — cost	3,728	4,325	4,927	5,080	5,314	5,496	5,682	6,120	6,794	7,460	8,462
Taxes —											
General	4,515	4,828	5,186	5,605	6,100	6,562	7,156	7,858	8,165	8,570	9,603
State income taxes paid currently	123	120	128	145	171	213	239	685	626	658	676
Federal income taxes paid currently	5,949	6,069	6,294	6,824	7,817	7,811	8,088	6,845	7,011	6,898	4,958
Income tax credit from interest on non operating activities	(119)	(122)	(29)	(26)	(21)	(39)	(98)	(210)	(484)	(997)	(1,408)
Deferred income taxes —											
Accelerated depreciation	535	799	1,023	955	923	863	818	896	1,217	1,379	1,433
Accelerated amortization	120	120	98	(19)	(22)	(22)	(22)	(22)	(22)	(22)	(22)
Deferred investment tax credit (net)			135	244	279	244	256	541	616	457	573
Interest on long-term debt	1,650	2,326	2,552	2,531	2,506	2,472	2,450	3,020	4,560	6,533	8,413
Interest on bank loans	77	84					136	422	548	801	1,306
Interest charged to construction (credit)	(544)	(438)	(36)	(78)	(46)	(83)	(358)	(861)	(1,533)	(3,239)	(4,296)
Other deductions	81	108	207	134	257	116	111	115	156	275	325
	44,653	47,908	51,497	53,640	58,227	60,635	64,566	69,217	73,891	79,769	86,877
NET INCOME	6,722	6,891	7,456	8,358	9,821	10,406	10,884	10,672	10,702	11,911	11,702
Preferred dividends	430	430	430	430	430	430	430	430	430	430	430
EARNINGS AVAILABLE TO COMMON EQUITY	6,292	6,461	7,026	7,928	9,391	9,976	10,454	10,242	10,272	10,934	10,522
Appropriation for fair value depreciation net of tax	337	337	337	337	499	544	593	635	577	577	612
EARNINGS AVAILABLE FOR DISTRIBUTION											

ILLUSTRATION 15–15

Year	Reported net income	Net income Before income tax	Net income Before tax and interest	Reported gross income
1971.	9,112	11,523	18,024	104,004
1970.	11,702	17,336	22,759	98,321
1969.	11,911	19,467	23,562	91,351
1968.	10,702	18,339	21,914	84,309
1967.	10,672	18,202	20,783	79,624
1966.	10,884	19,211	21,439	75,158
1965.	10,406	18,430	20,819	70,636
1964.	9,821	17,809	20,269	67,536
1963.	8,358	15,327	17,780	61,646
1962.	7,456	13,878	16,394	58,622
1961.	6,891	13,080	15,052	54,584
1960.	6,722	12,794	13,967	51,095

$000 omitted.

in 1971 ($9,112,000, down $4,600,000 from 1970, a drop of one third). Notice that net income before income taxes dropped nearly $6,000,000, showing the cushioning effect of income taxes, and net income before both income taxes and interest dropped only $4,750,000, showing the heavier burden of current high interest rates.

To summarize what happened in the two-year period between 1969 and 1971; the profitability of operations declined about $5,500,000 (about 23 percent), to which higher interest rates added an additional burden on profits of $2,400,000, but the final result was cushioned by a decline of $5,000,000 in the burden of state and federal income taxes, so the decline in net income was "only" $2,799,000 (nearly 25 percent).

As of December 31, 1971, the company put into effect rate increases expected to increase gross revenue by $7,000,000. However, the rate increases have not yet been approved by the regulatory state commission so it is possible that the company may have to refund the additional revenue. This shows an important characteristic of the public utility industry: unless the company can obtain increased rates to cover its increased costs, including heavy interest costs, it will not be able to maintain its former level of profitability, and security for its investors.

The total burden of interest cost has risen from $2,586,000 in 1966 to $10,648,000 in 1971. In the same period, outstanding long-term debt has risen from $63,897,000 to $159,411,000. However, not all of the interest was charged against current income; in 1971 about $4,100,000 was charged in as a cost of new construction which will, of course, flow back against future revenue through depreciation and serve to further increase the burden on net income.

Obviously these problems, wrapped up in a current decline in earning power, are not pleasing to the holders of common stock. But to bondholders they are not so directly important as the bonds carry a guaranteed interest rate and a specific maturity amount and date. Net income before income tax and interest is still running at $18,000,000 per year; and total interest burden, including interest charged to construction, is only $10,600,000. As to the potential burden of retiring outstanding bonds, the truth is that utilities do not retire their bonds—they refund them, "paying them" by issuing new bonds. This is standard practice in the utility industry, in government, and to a considerable extent in nonregulated business. Therefore, the crucial question is: what will the money markets think of their refunding securities when offered?

The relation of earnings to fixed charges

A prime test which investors in bonds customarily make in assessing the quality of a bond investment is to establish the relationship of earnings (preferably before income taxes and interest) to the burden of fixed charges ("fixed charges" is interest). As fixed charges must be satisfied whether earned or not, and as insolvency will result if they are not paid, the margin of safety afforded by ample earnings is of critical concern. While there is no magical test on which all investors would agree, the following margins are generally regarded as conservative:

	Utilities	Industrials
Average of earnings for the last 5 or 10 years (preferably the latter) in relation to fixed charges.	4 times	7 times
The year in the period which showed the poorest result	3 times	5 times

In the case of the Iowa-Illinois utility, the average of the ratios of net income before income taxes and interest, to interest on funded debt, in the period 1962 to 1971 is 6.4 times; in the period 1967 to 1971 it is 4.1 times. The year in these periods showing the poorest result is the last one, 1971, in which the multiple is 2.2 times. In the five years ended with 1971 the ratios are as follows: 1967, 7.4; 1968, 5.3; 1969, 4.6; 1970, 3.1; 1971, 2.2. The multiple in 1971 is, of course, below the "three times" standard.

Investors analyzing bonds sometimes use an alternate ratio based on after-tax net income. On this basis the requirement drops to two to one. The calculation for this company would be: net income after income taxes, $9,112,000 plus interest on long-term debt, $9,000,000, a total of $18,112,000. On this basis the ratio of after-tax net income to interest in 1971 is barely over two times and the standard is met.

The following tabulation shows the history of the factors in the times interest on long-term debt earned ratio in the period 1967 to 1971:

Year	Long-term debt	Interest on long-term debt	Net income before income taxes and interest on long-term debt
1971.	159,278	9,000	19,523
1970.	159,506	8,413	26,249
1969.	139,805	6,533	26,000
1968.	105,275	4,560	22,899
1967.	85,729	3,020	21,002

$000 omitted.

From this tabulation it can be seen that long-term debt almost doubled, interest on long-term debt tripled (interest rates rose substantially), and net income, having risen in the middle years, in 1971 dipped below 1967. The income statement shows that gross revenues rose from $79,624,000 in 1967 to $104,004,000 in 1971, up almost one third. The balance sheets show that the plant account rose from $192 million in 1967 to $318 million in 1971, up $126 million (65 percent) (requiring additional investment).

It should now be clear why this company's ratios have declined so drastically. Both sides of the computation have been involved. Substantial growth in sales has required more plant to serve the demand, which has meant larger long-term debt to pay for it. This has boosted the interest burden at a time when interest rates rose dramatically. And, again at the same time, net income has been hurt by higher operating costs not offset by higher rates charged to customers.

How serious are these developments in the eyes of a prospective bond buyer? They cannot help but be discouraging in spite of the fact that income available for interest payments is still double the sum required to avoid default. A sidelight on how the situation looks to common stock investors can be seen by comparing the quoted value of the stock on November 24, 1970 (20¼) with February 17, 1972 (18¼). Obviously the stockholders, while not enthusiastic, are not abandoning ship. Of course, the bondholders are in a much more secure position. But for the very cautious investor, there are other electric and gas utilities whose regulatory commissions have been more open-handed. Nevertheless, the current period has been a difficult one for most utilities.

The relationships of property, stockholders' equity, and long-term debt

The previous discussions have concentrated on the ability of the company to meet its interest obligations and to successfully refund the principal amount of its bonds when due. Those considerations are, of course, crucial. It is also useful, though probably somewhat less important, to test whether the relationships of property, stockholders' equity and long-term debt have been kept in balance. This is particularly important if the company is revealing on analysis any developing problem situations. In the case at hand, the Iowa-Illinois company shows the following characteristics:

Year	Property*	Long-term debt*	Debt as % of property	Stock-holders' equity*	Debt as % of debt plus equity
1971......	318,207	159,278	50.0%	107,142	60.0%
1970......	298,924	159,506	53.3	107,972	59.9
1969......	272,175	139,805	51.4	102,486	57.7
1968......	229,670	105,275	45.8	88,513	54.3
1967......	192,313	85,729	44.6	84,902	50.1

* $000 omitted.

Neither of these ratios should exceed 60 percent. The debt as a percent of property is well within the limit. The debt as a percent of total capitalization (stockholders' equity plus long-term debt) has now reached the limit, and the trend has been steadily upward.

For industrial bonds the ratio of debt to debt plus owners' equity should be substantially less, certainly not over 50 percent. In industrial companies the debt to property test is much less meaningful and tests of long-run solvency and profitability should be used instead.

QUESTIONS AND PROBLEMS

15–1. Discuss briefly: Should creditors or stockholders supply funds for financing noncurrent asset acquisitions?

15–2. a) What is the significance of the ratio of owners' equity to creditors' claims?

b) Are the long-term creditors interested in the results of trading on the equity?

c) To what extent should long-term creditors concern themselves with the current financial condition of a business?

d) To what extent should long-term creditors be interested in the income statements of a business?

15–3. Corporation X and its subsidiary Z constructed identical plants during the years 1945 and 1960, respectively. The cost and the present book value of the two buildings vary substantially. Suggest how the difference may be accounted for and indicate the importance of knowing the reasons for the variation in interpreting ratios involving the items affected.

15–4. a) Distinguish between the book value and the liquidation or real value of assets.
b) What information should be available to determine the book value of preferred stock?
c) Distinguish between the book value and the market value of stock and indicate possible reasons for a difference in the two values.
d) In determining book value of common stock, why is it desirable to deduct the carrying value of the intangible assets from owners' equity?

15–5. What ratios would be used to answer the following questions?
a) Are the claims of secured creditors adequately protected?
b) How have the assets been financed?
c) Is there a satisfactory distribution of assets?

15–6. To what extent should short-term creditors concern themselves with noncurrent assets and liabilities of a business?

15–7. The balance sheet of Corporation M showed the account, Property, Plant, and Equipment, $5,781,470. A schedule accompanying the balance sheet revealed the following details:

Plant and equipment	Patents
Improvements to leaseholds	Land
Incomplete plant construction	Leaseholds
Trademarks	Goodwill
Marine equipment	Miscellaneous fixed operating property and equipment

Required:
Do you approve the inclusion of the foregoing items as Property, Plant, and Equipment for purposes of ratio computation? Discuss.

15–8. Explain how the following are determined and indicate their importance in statement analysis:
a) How is the capital obtained from creditors and owners invested?
b) What are the sources of the invested capital?
c) What is the relation between owners' equity and total liabilities?
d) What portion of the working capital is invested in inventories?

15–9. Distinguish between "current financial condition" and "long-term financial condition." May factors exist in one which would favorably or unfavorably affect the other? Discuss.

15–10. "Generally speaking, the higher the ratio of owners' equity to total assets the stronger the financial condition of the business." Discuss.

15–11. Compute the book value per share of the preferred and common stock for the following unrelated cases.

a) Assets $600,000
Valuation and amortization accounts............   50,000
Liabilities.................................   110,000
Capital stock outstanding:
1,000 shares of 6% cumulative, nonparticipating, $100 par value, preferred stock (preferred as to assets in dissolution, dividends have been paid in full).
4,000 shares, $100 par value common stock.

b) Refer to (a) above. How would your solution be changed if preferred stock is not preferred as to assets in dissolution?

c) Owners' Equity:
Preferred stock (6%, cumulative, nonparticipating, $100 par value, preferred as to assets in dissolution, dividends have not been paid for three years), $200,000.
Common stock ($100 par value), $700,000.
Appropriated retained earnings, $150,000.
Unappropriated retained earnings, $280,000.
Capital in excess of par value, $20,000.

15–12. The Farmers Company was incorporated during the year 1956. During the year 1969 the company began a five-year expansion program by constructing new buildings and acquiring existing properties. The company's balance sheet as of December 31, 1969, 1970, and 1971 is presented on the following page.

Required:

a) Compute ratios to aid you in answering the following questions:
(1) Are the current debts likely to be paid when due?
(2) How many times has the working capital been turned over (in relation to net sales)?
(3) To what extent could all of the liabilities be paid off by using current assets?
(4) How much of the investment in the assets has been financed through the medium of borrowed funds and of owners' equity?
(5) How much of the noncurrent assets has been financed by owners' equity?
(6) Assuming that the noncurrent liabilities are secured by fixed asset mortgages, what margin of safety exists for the long-term debt creditors?

b) Determine the book value of the preferred and common stock per share as of the end of the period, under each of the following assumptions:

Assumptions:

No. 1: The preferred stock has no claim on surplus.
No. 2: The preferred stock has three years' dividends in arrears (preferred stock is nonparticipating).
No. 3: Regular dividends on preferred and common were de-

clared and paid for the year 1971 (the preferred is fully participating).

c) Analyze and study all available data in order to evaluate the current and long-term financial conditions of the company.

d) Write a report on your conclusions.

FARMERS COMPANY
Balance Sheet Data
As of December 31, 1969, 1970, and 1971
(manufacturers of farm machinery)

Items	1969 ($000)	% of total	1970 ($000)	% of total	1971 ($000)	% of total	1970 over 1969	1971 over 1969
Assets								
Current assets, net	4,731	47.2	6,645	47.9	6,670	37.6	40	41
Long-term investments	85	.9	90	.7	150	.8	6	76
Fixed assets, net	5,200	51.9	7,120	51.4	10,920	61.6	37	110
Total Assets	10,016	100.0	13,855	100.0	17,740	100.0	38	77
Liabilities								
Current liabilities	321	3.2	1,900	13.7	2,140	12.1	492	567
Deferred credit	20	.2	30	.2	35	.1	50	75
Long-term liabilities	100	1.0	500	3.6	1,500	8.5	400	1,400
Total Liabilities	441	4.4	2,430	17.5	3,675	20.7	451	733
Owners' Equity								
Common stock ($100 par)	5,000	49.9	6,700	48.4	7,000	39.5	34	40
Preferred stock (6%, $100 par)	1,000	10.0	1,000	7.2	2,500	14.1		150
Retained earnings	3,575	35.7	3,725	26.9	4,565	25.7	4	28
Total Owners' Equity	9,575	95.6	11,425	82.5	14,065	79.3	19	47
Total Liabilities and Owners' Equity	10,016	100.0	13,855	100.0	17,740	100.0	38	77
Note: Sales for the year	(7,800)		(13,460)		(21,175)		(73)	(171)

15–13.

DONALD MANUFACTURING COMPANY
Balance Sheet Data
As of December 31, 1969, 1970, and 1971
(in thousands)

	December 31						% increase (decrease*)	
	1969		1970		1971		1970 over 1969	1971 over 1969
	($)	(%)	($)	(%)	($)	(%)		
Assets								
Current assets	4,310	39.8	4,100	27.4	3,955	25.3	5*	8*
Long-term investments	300	2.8	350	2.3	340	2.2	17	13
Fixed assets, net	6,220	57.4	10,500	70.3	11,300	72.5	69	82
Total Assets	10,830	100.0	14,950	100.0	15,595	100.0	38	44
Liabilities								
Current liabilities	2,050	18.9	2,470	16.5	2,910	18.7	21	42
Deferred credit	10	.1	12	.1	16	.1	20	60
Long-term liabilities	1,000	9.2	3,500	23.4	3,500	22.4	250	250
Total Liabilities	3,060	28.2	5,982	40.0	6,426	41.2	96	110
Owners' Equity								
Common stock	6,000	55.4	7,000	46.8	7,000	44.9	17	17
Preferred stock (6%, $100 par)	1,000	9.3	1,300	8.7	1,600	10.3	30	60
Retained earnings	770	7.1	668	4.5	569	3.6	13*	26*
Total Owners' Equity	7,770	71.8	8,968	60.0	9,169	58.8	15	18
Total Liabilities and Owners' Equity	10,830	100.0	14,950	100.0	15,595	100.0	38	44
Note: Sales for the year	(7,474)		(14,742)		(15,785)		(97)	(111)

Required:

a) Compute ratios to aid you in answering the following questions for the Donald Manufacturing Company:

   (1) Are the current debts likely to be paid when due?

   (2) How many times has the net working capital been turned over (in relation to net sales)?

   (3) To what extent could all of the liabilities be paid off by using current assets?

   (4) How much of the assets has been financed through the medium of borrowed funds and of owners' equity?

   (5) How much of the noncurrent assets has been financed by owners' equity?

   (6) Assuming that the noncurrent liabilities are secured by fixed asset mortgages, what margin of safety exists for the long-term debt creditors?

b) Study the data given together with the foregoing required ratios and evaluate the current debt-paying ability and the long-term financial condition of the company.

15–14. Company M, manufacturer of iron and steel products, presents financial and operating dollar data together with trend and common-size percentages and selected ratios.

COMPANY M
Financial Statement Data
As of, or for the Years Ended December 31, 1966-71
(In Thousands)

	1966	1967	1968	1969	1970	1971
Balance Sheet Data, December 31						
Cash and cash items.	$1,738	$ 3,400	$ 501	$ 902	$ 960	$ 1,222
Marketable securities	1,042	521	10	10	10	10
Trade receivables (net)	470	670	865	532	465	965
Inventories	1,319	1,893	2,256	2,729	2,615	3,560
Prepaid expenses	43	65	212	82	58	41
Other current assets	2	2	2	6	4	8
Total Current Assets	$4,614	$ 6,551	$ 3,846	$ 4,261	$ 4,112	$ 5,806
Long-term investments.	81	106	103	127	157	150
Land, buildings, and equipment (net)	5,202	5,071	10,387	10,431	10,077	10,990
Other assets	18	19	19	20		
Total Assets	$9,915	$11,747	$14,355	$14,839	$14,346	$16,946
Notes payable			$ 560	$ 760	$ 1,038	$ 454
Accounts payable.	$ 134	$ 337	480	96	241	426
Accrued payables	206	347	342	305	241	381
Other current liabilities			661	4	9	36
Total Current Liabilities	$ 340	$ 684	$ 2,043	$ 1,165	$ 1,529	$ 1,297
Long-term liabilities				1,618	1,110	3,576
Liability "reserves".	201	201	255	175	203	269
Total Liabilities.	$ 541	$ 885	$ 2,298	$ 2,958	$ 2,842	$ 5,142
Common stock	$6,089	$ 7,213	$ 8,484	$ 8,484	$ 8,484	$ 8,484
Capital in excess of stated value	$2,293	$ 2,293	$ 2,298	$ 2,298	$ 2,298	$ 2,298
Retained earnings	992	1,356	1,275	1,099	722	1,022
Total surplus	$3,285	$ 3,649	$ 3,573	$ 3,397	$ 3,020	$ 3,320
Total Owners' Equity	$9,374	$10,862	$12,057	$11,881	$11,504	$11,804
Total Liabilities and Owners' Equity.	$9,915	$11,747	$14,355	$14,839	$14,346	$16,946
Income and Retained Earnings Statement Data, for the Year						
Net sales	$5,189	$ 8,083	$10,118	$13,234	$ 6,359	$10,212
Cost of goods sold	3,871	6,123	8,383	11,068	5,228	7,573
Gross margin on sales	1,318	1,960	1,735	2,166	1,131	2,639
Expenses charged to operations:						
Maintenance and repairs	318	432	567	759	414	688
Depreciation	360	360	360	458	471	745
Taxes (other than income). . . .	79	81	123	243	199	216
Uncollectible receivables expense	7	17	4	14	7	
Selling, general, and admin. expenses	311	393	387	423	355	406
Operating income (loss*)	243	677	294	269	315*	584
Other items, net additions deductions*	20	4	11	2*	25*	66*
Income (loss*) before federal income taxes	263	681	305	267	340*	518
Federal income taxes	65	175	78	85		130
Net income (loss*) after federal income taxes	198	506	227	182	340*	388
Extraordinary items— additions (deduction*)	373	12	1*	12	11	10
Net income (loss*) transferred to retained earnings	571	518	226	194	329*	378
Dividends declared	255	255	351	430	48	48
Fixed interest charges included above				81	56	179

16

Analysis of income

A DETAILED analysis of income statement items is of real significance because the long-run success of a business depends upon the realization of profits. The analysis of income statement items for one period of time normally is not sufficient, since unusual conditions may be reflected on the statement, and since it is impossible to determine the trends of the revenue, cost, and expense items.

A comparison of significant items such as total sales, cost of goods sold, gross margin, operating expenses, operating income, and net income for successive periods usually reveals variations that require detailed analysis and study. An analysis in depth would necessitate having the component elements of these totals itemized.

Sales

The sales figure—the number of dollars of sales shown on the income statement—reflects the fundamental, dynamic activity of a business. Where revenue from sources other than sales of merchandise is material in amount, the income statement should show the sources and amounts, separately and distinctly. If the sales volume has been obtained by increasing substantially the amount of operating expenses and thereby reducing operating income, there may not be sufficient income to meet interest charges and to provide a reasonable profit for the owners. An increase in sales volume is not necessarily favorable from a profit standpoint, and a decrease in sales volume may not be unfavorable. It is only in relation to the accompanying changes in the cost of goods sold and operating expenses that the profit significance of a variation in sales can be ascertained. It must be recognized that maximum profit does not seem to be the exclusive (and at times not even the major) interest of management. "Position in the industry," frequently judged on the basis of sales volume, can be a powerful incentive.

At the same time that sales volume was increasing, gross margin (net sales less cost of goods sold, expressed as a percentage of sales) also increased (see Illustration 16–1) from 26.4 percent in 1966 to 29.3 percent in 1971. Nevertheless, in spite of the upward trend shown in these comparative figures, the Lynn-Dale gross margins remained below those of other department stores as shown by industry averages. Lynn-Dale's gross margin in 1970 was 28.1 percent, while the average of the industry was 30.5 percent.[1]

ILLUSTRATION 16–1

LYNN-DALE COMPANY
Ratios of Cost of Goods Sold and of Gross
Margin on Sales to Net Sales
For the Years Ended December 31, 1966–71

Items and computations		1966	1967	1968	1969	1970	1971
et sales (a)	($000)	812.5	853.7	859.8	1,201.2	1,341.3	1,491.8
Trend percentages	(%)	100	105	106	148	165	184
ost of goods sold (b)	($000)	598.0	624.1	627.7	861.3	964.4	1,054.7
Trend percentages	(%)	100	104	105	144	161	176
ross margin on sales (c)	($000)	214.5	229.6	232.1	339.9	376.9	437.1
Trend percentages	(%)	100	107	108	158	176	204
atio of cost of goods sold to net sales (b ÷ a)	(%)	73.6	73.1	73.0	71.7	71.9	70.7
atio of gross margin on sales to net sales (c ÷ a)	(%)	26.4	26.9	27.0	28.3	28.1	29.3

Note also that while sales rose 84 percent between 1966 and 1971, cost of goods sold rose 76 percent—therefore gross margin increased—but operating expenses increased 129 percent (Illustration 16–1) which resulted of course in a substantial lowering of earnings. In other words, the cost of obtaining the higher sales volume was out of proportion to the increase in gross revenue.

In connection with the study of trend percentages, the analyst should consider the influence of price-level changes. If the price level has been rising, the increase in the sales figure will be due to higher prices and perhaps to a larger physical volume of goods. The problem of determining the effect of price-level changes is discussed in Part III.

The analysis of income involves a study of sales as well as an analysis of the cost of goods sold, gross margin on sales, operating expenses,

---

[1] Troy, *Manual of Business and Industrial Financial Ratios* (Englewood Cliffs, N.J.: Prentice-Hall, Inc., 1971).

operating income, and net income in relation to sales. Also, careful consideration should be given to price-level changes during the period under review.

In connection with the study of sales, the analyst should relate the sales returns and allowances to gross sales. This ratio reflects the percentage of the gross sales that either has been returned by customers or has been allowed to customers for defective or damaged goods or for "unsatisfactory" goods returned or retained. It represents a measure of dissatisfaction of customers with goods sold to them, inefficiency of employees in filling and delivering customer orders, inferior quality of goods, or a combination of these. Increases in this ratio mean more lost sales, higher transportation costs, and additional expense of handling and adjusting merchandise and customer accounts. The reasons for increases in the percentage of returns and allowances should be determined by the internal analyst so that management can put into effect remedial action.

Ratio of cost of goods sold to net sales; ratio of gross margin on net sales to net sales

The difference between the cost of goods sold and the net sales is of major importance because it represents the gross margin on net sales. Gross margin should be large enough to cover the operating and other expenses and to provide an adequate net income in relation to net sales and to owners' equity. The ratio of cost of goods sold to net sales,[2] computed (as shown in Illustration 16-1) by dividing cost of goods sold by net sales, reflects the percentage of the net sales dollars that has been absorbed by the cost of acquiring the finished goods that have been sold.

The ratio of gross margin on sales to net sales, computed (as shown in Illustration 16-1) by dividing gross margin on sales by net sales, shows the percentage of gross margin that is left after making deduction for the cost of goods sold. This ratio, which shows the average spread between the cost of goods sold and the selling price, may also be determined by deducting the ratio of cost of goods sold to net sales from 100 percent.

Gross margin is the difference between net sales (number of units sold *times* unit sales price) and cost of goods sold (number of units sold *times* unit purchase or production cost). Operating expenses are not involved at this point.

The gross margin ratios of the Lynn-Dale Company (Illustration 16-1)

---

[2] This ratio and other income statement ratios may be obtained from the income statement, common-size percentage form. See study of common-size income statement for the Lynn-Dale Company (Illustration 10-2, page 236 and pages 243-46).

increased slightly during 1967 and 1968 and then increased substantially during 1969, 1970, and 1971, but they remained below average performance in the industry. To account for the increase in gross margin, a detailed analysis must be made of (1) the quantity of units of product sold and the changes in selling prices and (2) the cost of goods sold in terms of units of the different types of product and changes in purchasing prices. The sales "mix," i.e., the sale of various priced goods having different rates of markup, is of major significance in studying the gross margin on sales. In order to analyze the gross margin most effectively, information should be available with respect to units of product and the company policies in connection with purchasing, markups and markdowns, credit extension, and general merchandising policies. These data are usually not available to the external analyst.

The increase in the gross margin of the Lynn-Dale Company may have resulted from one of the following factors:

1. Higher sales prices, cost of goods sold remaining constant.
2. Lower cost of goods sold, sales prices remaining constant.
3. A combination of variations in sales prices and costs, the margin widening.
4. An increase in the proportionate volume of higher margin items.

For example, if a company sells only one product (586,400 units) which in 1966 cost $1 per unit and sold for $1.366 per unit, the higher margin in 1971 might be due to one of the following factors:

1. Sales price higher ($1.434 per unit) and cost of goods sold the same ($1 per unit) on a volume of 959,100 units.
2. Sales price the same ($1.366 per unit) and cost of goods sold lower ($0.953) per unit on a volume of 1,006,589 units.
3. Sales price higher ($1.393 per unit) and cost of goods sold lower ($0.972 per unit) on a volume of 988,000 units.
4. The fourth example requires that the company sell at least two products and that one product carry a higher margin than the other. For example, assume that the sales volume of the company in 1966 arises from the following sales:

| | | Product A | | | Product B | | |
1966	Units	Price ($)	Total ($000)	Units	Price ($)	Total ($000)	Total ($000)
s	200,000	2.000	400	160,480	2.500	401	801
of goods sold	200,000	1.175	235	160,480	2.190	351	586
ss margin.		0.825	165		0.310	50	215
ss margin (%)		41.3	41.3		12.4	12.4	26.8

Note that the profit margin on product A is higher than the margin on product B. The increases in margin in 1971 could be due to a larger proportion of sales of product A, without any change in unit sales prices and a relatively small change in unit costs of product A as shown below:

1971	Units	Product A Price ($)	Product A Total ($000)	Units	Product B Price ($)	Product B Total ($000)	T(($(
Sales	486,900	2.000	974	160,480	2.500	401	1,3
Cost of goods sold	486,900	1.248	608	160,480	2.190	351	9
Gross margin		0.752	366		0.310	50	4
Gross margin (%)		37.6	37.6		12.4	12.4	

This example has been exaggerated to emphasize the point that the gross margin can be increased (or decreased) by a change in the "sales mix" without any variations in selling prices or unit costs, a matter of obviously major concern to a sales manager.

A low gross profit ratio may reflect unfavorable purchasing and markup policies; the inability of the management to develop sales volume, thereby making it impossible to buy goods in large volume; a price squeeze whereby selling prices are depressed not accompanied by proportionate changes in cost of goods sold; marked reduction in selling prices in an attempt to obtain a larger sales volume, not accompanied by proportionate decreases in cost of goods; and overexpansion or overinvestment in plant facilities, resulting in higher costs of production.

The level of cost of goods sold in relation to sales in a time of rising (or falling) prices will vary in accordance with the method of charging inventory costs into cost of goods sold. If the first-in, first-out method is being used, cost of goods sold will include costs brought forward from the prior (lower price-level) year; whereas if last-in, first-out is being used, cost of goods sold will consist largely of approximate replacement costs. Therefore, in a time of rising prices, Fifo will result in a higher margin than will Lifo. The "extra" margin resulting from the use of Fifo will represent, entirely or in large part, an increase in the book value of inventory which is not, however, accompanied by any increase in purchasing power. On the other hand, Lifo results in an inventory value which may vary widely from current replacement cost. These matters are considered in detail in Chapter 17.

Statement accounting for variation in gross margin

If a company manufactures and sells a single standardized product, or if gross margin data by products are available, a statement accounting for variations in gross margin will show the effect of changes in volume of sales, in selling prices, and in cost of goods manufactured and sold. In other words, such a statement shows to what extent (1) the change in sales was a result of variations in the number of units sold and in the sales price and (2) the change in cost of goods sold was a result of variations in the number of units sold and in the unit cost. That is, variations in gross margin are caused by changes in the commodity volume and price of sales and the commodity volume and cost of the goods sold. To illustrate the statement accounting for variation in gross margin, assume the following data for Company A:

Items and computation		1970	1971	Increase
Net sales (a)	($000)	3,125	3,900	775
Cost of goods sold (b)	($000)	2,375	2,955	580
Gross margin on sales (c)	($000)	750	945	195
Units sold (d)	(No.)	12,500	15,000	2,500
Unit selling price (a ÷ d)	($)	250	260	10
Unit cost (b ÷ d)	($)	190	197	7
Unit gross margin (c ÷ d)	($)	60	63	3

As demonstrated in the foregoing summary, the increase of sales in the amount of $775,000 was the result of a larger volume of goods

ILLUSTRATION 16–2

COMPANY A
Statement Accounting for Variation of Gross Margin
For the Year Ended December 31, 1971

Increase in volume:
Amount of increase in sales revenue if there had been
no change in sales price: 2,500 additional units sold
at $250 per unit $625,000
Increase in price:
Amount of increase in sales revenue if there had been
no change in sales volume: 12,500 units sold at an
increase of $10 per unit 125,000
Variation in sales revenue due to a combination of
changes in selling price and units sold: units sold
increased (2,500), unit selling price increased ($10),
thereby resulting in an increase in sales revenue 25,000
Increase in sales revenue $775,000

ILLUSTRATION 16–2 (continued)

Increase in volume:

Amount of increase in cost of goods sold if there had been no change in unit cost: 2,500 additional units cost $190 per unit.	$475,000

Increase in cost:

Amount of increase in cost of goods sold if there had been no change in units sold: 12,500 units cost an additional $7 per unit	87,500
Variation in cost of goods sold due to a combination of changes in unit cost and units sold: units sold increased (2,500), unit cost increased ($7), thereby resulting in an increase in cost of goods sold (2,500 × $10)	17,500

Increase in cost of goods sold		580,000
Increase in gross margin		$195,000

ILLUSTRATION 16–3

COMPANY B

Statement Accounting for Variation of Gross Margin
For the Year Ended December 31, 1971

The increase in sales revenue during 1971 can be accounted for as follows:

Increase in sales revenue due to increased volume:

Amount of increase in sales if there had been no change in sales price: 4,000 additional units sold at $250	$1,000,000

Decrease in sales revenue due to price change:

If there had been no change in sales volume; a decrease in sales revenue would have taken place: 16,000 units sold at a $10 decrease in unit price.	160,000
	$ 840,000

Variation in sales revenue due to a combination of changes in selling price and units sold: Units sold increased (4,000), unit selling price decreased ($10) thereby resulting in a decrease in sales revenue	40,000	
Increase in sales revenue		$800,000

The increase in cost of goods sold during 1971 can be accounted for as follows:

Increase in volume:

Amount of increase in cost of goods sold if there had been no change in unit costs: 4,000 additional units cost $212.50 per unit	$ 850,000

Increase in cost:

Amount of increase in cost of goods sold if there had been no change in units sold: 16,000 units cost an additional $3 per unit	48,000
Variation in cost of goods sold due to a combination of changes in unit cost and units sold: Units sold increased (4,000), unit cost increased ($3) thereby resulting in an increase in cost of goods sold (4,000 × $3)	12,000

Increase in cost of goods sold	910,000
Decrease in gross margin.	$110,000

sold and an increase in selling prices. In comparison with 1970 both volume and selling price were higher in 1971. The increase in cost of goods sold of $580,000 was caused by the larger volume of goods sold and a higher unit cost of goods purchased. The volume and unit costs were higher during 1971 than in 1970; however, the selling price per unit increased at a greater rate than unit costs. Although the variation in gross margin of $195,000 in the year 1967 in comparison with 1970–70 can be accounted for in detail as shown in Illustration 16–2, the analyst must search to determine who is responsible for the specific changes and to judge whether or not improvements can be made in the future.

The following data are assumed for Company B in order to demonstrate (Illustration 16–3) the accounting for a variation in gross margin when there has been an increase in the number of units of goods sold at a lower amount per unit and the cost of the units increased:

Items and computations		1970	1971	Increase (decrease*)
Net sales (a)	($000)	4,000	4,800	800
Cost of goods sold (b)	($000)	3,400	4,310	910
Gross margin (c)	($000)	600	490	110*
Units sold (d)	(No.)	16,000	20,000	4,000
Unit selling price (a ÷ d)	($)	250.00	240.00	10.00*
Unit cost (b ÷ d)	($)	212.50	215.50	3.00
Unit gross margin (c ÷ d)	($)	37.50	24.50	13.00*

Relationship of operating expenses to net sales

There is an important relationship between operating expenses and the volume of sales. The analysis of individual operating expense items in relation to the sales volume should reflect the ability of the management to adjust expense to changing sales conditions. A number of selling expenses such as advertising and sales promotion, delivery expenses, salesmen's salaries and commissions, and telephone expense usually increase or decrease with variations in the volume of sales. General and administrative expenses tend to remain approximately the same unless sales activity is considerably expanded or contracted—or unless the general price level changes.

The operating expenses will vary from one company to another or from year to year for the same company according to the operating methods, functions, and services performed. More specifically these costs depend upon volume of sales, channels through which sales are made, sales promotional programs, warehousing and storage, packaging and delivery, credit extension, facilities provided for the convenience of customers and employees, cost of owning or leasing plant facilities, wage payment plans, and the relative amount of automation employed. The ratio of each individual operating expense (selling and general and administrative expenses) to net sales shows the percentage of net sales revenue that has been consumed by the various operating expenses. These ratios, which represent a summation of changes in net sales and in the expense items, are valuable in comparing similar businesses or operating data from year to year for the same business. This method of analysis, using selling expenses as the basis, is shown in Illustration 16–4 for the Lynn-Dale Company.

ILLUSTRATION 16–4

LYNN-DALE COMPANY
Comparative Statement of Selling Expenses
For the Years Ended December 31, 1966–71
(dollar data in thousands)

Items	1966 ($)	1966 (%)	1967 ($)	1967 (%)	1968 ($)	1968 (%)	1969 ($)	1969 (%)	1970 ($)	1970 (%)	1971 ($)
Advertising expenses	17.9	2.2	21.3	2.5	23.2	2.7	40.8	3.4	55.0	4.1	67.7
Branch store expenses	25.3	3.1	26.5	3.1	27.5	3.2	39.6	3.3	44.3	3.3	50.2
Delivery expense	13.1	1.6	12.0	1.4	10.3	1.2	12.0	1.0	12.1	.9	11.7
Transportation on sales	3.8	.5	4.2	.5	4.3	.5	6.0	.5	6.7	.5	7.6
Salesmen's salaries expenses	34.7	4.3	39.3	4.6	42.2	4.9	64.9	5.4	73.8	5.5	84.5
Salesmen's traveling expenses	7.5	.9	7.7	.9	6.9	.8	14.4	1.2	17.4	1.3	25.6
Miscellaneous selling expenses	4.9	.6	4.2	.5	1.7	.2	4.9	.4	1.3	.1	6.6
Total Selling Expenses	107.2	13.2	115.2	13.5	116.1	13.5	182.6	15.2	210.6	15.7	253.6
Trend percentages— selling expenses	100		107		108		170		196		237
Net sales	812.5		853.7		859.8		1,201.2		1,341.3		1,491.8
Trend percentages— net sales	100		105		106		148		165		184

In analyzing the relationship between operating expense items and net sales, the analyst should study the common-size data, the trend percentages, the percentage changes, and the absolute data. It is shown in Illustration 16–4 that the selling expenses were equal to 13.2, 13.5, and 13.5 percent, respectively, of the net sales for 1966, 1967, and 1968. These percentages for 1969, 1970, and 1971 were 15.2, 15.7, and 17.0, respectively. During each of the six years, selling expenses absorbed a larger percentage of the net sales, which resulted in reducing the profitableness of the sales. This same situation is also reflected by the trend percentage data. Net sales increased each year—a total of 84 percent for the six-year period. During the same time, selling expenses increased each year but a higher rate than net sales—a total of 137 percent. These data may reflect several situations: (1) a greater number of sales promotional programs may have been undertaken without increasing sales in proportion to the added cost; (2) a new intensive or extensive sales program may have been put into effect, the full benefit of which has not yet been realized; (3) the merchandising manager may have been lax in increasing retail prices; and (4) the price level affecting expenses may have increased at a greater rate than retail prices.

In analyzing the relationship between operating expenses and net sales, the analyst should determine (1) whether or not the fixed costs and expenses[3] are so high that a slight decline in sales volume would result in an operating loss, (2) whether salaries of employees and officers are out of line with those of other companies, and (3) whether the salesmen are paid a salary or a commission.

If prices are rising (or falling), most expense items will tend to rise (or fall) in proportion. Depreciation, however, will remain constant or will rise at a much slower rate. This tends to distort the ratio analysis of "expenses as percentages of sales."

Ratio of maintenance and repairs to net sales

The ratio of maintenance and repairs to net sales shows the number of cents of each sales dollar that was consumed by maintenance and repairs, exclusive of depreciation. This ratio is important when maintenance and repairs expense varies in relation to sales volume. The amount of maintenance and repairs expense varies according to whether the property is new or old, owned or leased; the rate of operations (use of the plant capacity); the standard or level of the maintenance policy; economic conditions; and the practicability of closing down operations for repairs. Maintenance and repair expense to be included on the income statement also depends, as explained on pages 60–61, upon the company's policy with respect to depreciation, maintenance, and repairs. Consequently, conclusions concerning this ratio should be tentative.

The analyst may use the ratio of maintenance and repairs to net sales in comparing similar data for companies in the same industry. If comparable data are available, the ratio will serve as a guide to the relative maintenance policies of the various companies. The determination of this ratio is illustrated as follows:

$$\frac{\text{Maintenance and repairs, \$22,400}}{\text{Net sales, \$1,269,000}} = \begin{cases} \text{Number of cents expended on} \\ \text{maintenance and repairs per} \\ \text{dollar of net sales, 1.77 cents.} \end{cases}$$

In analyzing the maintenance and repair expense in relation to sales, it is necessary to have available the dollar data as well as the trend ratios for each item. These data for Company M are given in Illustration 16–5.

---

[3] Fixed costs and expenses are those that do not vary with sales volume unless a larger or smaller plant is used. Variable costs and expenses change with the sales volume. Most expenses are neither completely fixed nor completely variable.

ILLUSTRATION 16–5

COMPANY M
Comparison of Maintenance and Repairs to Net Sales
For the Years Ended December 31, 1966–71

Items and computation	1966	1967	1968	1969	1970	1.
Maintenance and repairs (a) . . . . ($000)	222	478	328	419	265	
Trend percentages. . . . . (%)	100	215	148	189	119	
Net sales (b) . . . . ($000)	10,378	14,093	20,789	26,644	18,518	22|
Trend percentages. . . . . (%)	100	136	200	257	178	
Ratio of maintenance and repairs to net sales [a ÷ b] . . . . (Cents)	2.14	3.39	1.58	1.57	1.43	

The information given in Illustration 16–5 shows that the trend for maintenance and repairs is upward, but not in proportion to the increase in sales volume. The dollar data for the years 1967 and 1969 reflect excessive maintenance and repair expense relative to the other years. Consequently, the "catching up" of deferred maintenance may be evidenced. The ratio of maintenance and repairs to net sales shows that this type of expense consumes a smaller percentage of sales as volume increases. Possibly a more logical relationship would be to compare the cost of maintenance and repairs to the gross investment in fixed assets, exclusive of land. Such a comparison which follows would tend to show whether or not the fixed assets were being maintained adequately.

Ratio of maintenance and repairs to fixed assets

The analyst should study maintenance, repairs, and depreciation in relation to fixed assets, exclusive of land, in order to detect the inclusion of an adequate or inadequate amount of expense for income determination. A discussion of these relationships follows.

The ratio of maintenance and repairs to fixed assets shows the number of cents expended for maintenance and repairs per dollar of fixed assets exclusive of land. This ratio is a guide to the policy of management in maintaining the fixed property in an efficient state. It is of special value when compared for several periods or when compared with other businesses in the same industry. For example, if this ratio is found to be declining for a period of years, and if at the same time the net income remains almost constant, the analyst has evidence of deferred maintenance. It is common practice in periods of depression for many companies to neglect or defer maintenance and repairs and to disregard depreciation so that a higher net income or a lower net loss may be shown. Obviously, such a practice merely leads to a misstatement of the expenses, net income or loss, and owners' equity. Furthermore, if this practice were continued, the property would have to be abandoned much sooner than was originally estimated; consequently, the annual depreciation charge would not properly measure the decline in the service life of the property.

The ratio of maintenance and repairs to fixed assets should be studied, together with the ratio of maintenance and repairs to net sales. When repairs and maintenance vary with sales volume, their relation to sales is important. When repairs and maintenance are independent of sales volume, their relation to fixed assets is important. In most businesses, repairs and maintenance are partly fixed (unrelated to sales volume) and partly variable (related to sales volume).

In too many cases the analyst deals with condensed financial statements, and the amount of maintenance and repairs expense may not be available. Frequently, it is impossible to obtain a breakdown of noncurrent assets, and "fixed assets" may include intangible assets as well as long-term investments. When the data are available, the ratio may be developed as follows:

$$\frac{\text{Maintenance and repair expenses } (\$222,000)}{\text{Fixed assets* } (\$13,801,000)} = \begin{cases} \text{Number of cents expended} \\ \text{on maintenance and repairs} \\ \text{per dollar of fixed assets} \\ (1.61 \text{ cents}). \end{cases}$$

* Accumulated depreciation not deducted (land excluded).

In analyzing the maintenance and repairs expense in relation to fixed assets, it is necessary to compare the dollar data as well as the trend ratios for each item. These data for Company M are given in Illustration 16–6.

ILLUSTRATION 16–6

COMPANY M

Comparison of Maintenance and Repairs and Fixed Assets
For the Years Ended December 31, 1966–71

Items and computation		1966	1967	1968	1969	1970	1971
Maintenance and repairs (a)	($000)	222	478	328	419	265	302
Trend percentage	(%)	100	215	148	189	119	136
Fixed operating assets (b)	($000)	13,801	13,905	14,287	14,281	14,777	15,770
Trend percentage	(%)	100	101	104	103	107	114
Ratio of maintenance and repairs to fixed operating assets (a ÷ b)	(Cents)	1.61	3.44	2.30	2.93	1.79	1.92
Trend percentage	(%)	100	214	143	182	111	119

The data in Illustration 16–6 show that in relation to the fixed assets, maintenance and repair expense has remained approximately the same for the years 1966, 1970, and 1971 and for 1967, 1968, and 1969. The data for 1967, 1968, and 1969 give evidence of above-normal maintenance and repair expense, assuming that the other years' expenditures are normal. In all probability, this represents the "catching up" of maintenance and repairs deferred in preceding accounting periods. The trend for the ratios of maintenance and repairs to fixed assets is upward to a greater degree than the trend for the fixed assets. This may indicate that the more advanced age of the plant is requiring a larger amount of maintenance and repairs.

The data prior to 1966 should be available to ascertain the normal expenditure for maintenance and repairs.

For comparative purposes the data in Illustration 16–7, pertaining

ILLUSTRATION 16–7

COMPANIES A, B, AND C

Ratios of Maintenance and Repairs to Fixed Assets

For the Years Ended December 31, 1966–71

(maintenance and repair cost in cents per dollar of fixed assets)

Companies	1967	1968	1969	1970	1971
A...........	.60	1.70	2.00	2.60	3.20
B...........	3.60	3.80	4.20	4.90	4.95
C...........	.40	1.05	1.80	2.71	3.70

to comparable manufacturing companies, are presented. It will be observed from these data that Company B has the most consistent ratio of maintenance and repairs to fixed assets, implying that a rather uniform policy has been in effect during the 1966–71 period. Companies A and C have evidently deferred maintenance and repairs and have not, as of 1971, attained the higher level of Company B. Assuming that these three companies are absolutely comparable, one must conclude that three companies are absolutely comparable, one must conclude that Companies A and C have a less favorable situation than does Company B.

Ratio of depreciation to net sales

The ratio of depreciation to net sales shows the number of cents of each sales dollar that was consumed by the depreciation charge. This ratio is important if depreciation is based on the rate of operation. However, most frequently the depreciation charge is not based on sales; therefore, the foregoing ratio would be of somewhat limited significance. The ratio does represent the percentage of the sales revenue that is estimated to be necessary to cover the depreciation charge. The depreciation charge may be different from one year to another for the same company or as between companies because of variations in (1) age of property; (2) depreciation methods and rates; (3) policy relative to maintenance in relation to depreciation—larger maintenance and repairs expense and less depreciation, or vice versa; and (4) composition of the fixed assets.

In view of the fact that depreciation is usually determined on the basis of the original cost of the fixed assets (exclusive of land), it is more meaningful to compute the ratio of depreciation for the year to fixed depreciable assets. This latter ratio is discussed below.

As a result of the effect of changing price levels, the analyst should be constantly aware of the relatively great impact on ratios in which depreciation is a factor. The pice-level problem is discussed in detail in Part III.

A study of depreciation—a cost of operation which does not require the use of current working capital—is important in connection with the statement of changes in financial position. This statement is discussed in Chapter 12.

Ratio of depreciation to fixed assets

The ratio of depreciation to fixed assets, exclusive of land, shows the number of cents allowed for depreciation per dollar of fixed assets. The ratio tests roughly the adequacy of the annual depreciation expense and indicates whether a uniform policy of recognizing depreciation is in effect. Furthermore, in comparing this ratio with ratios for other companies of similar size and circumstances in the same industry, the analyst may conclude that the annual depreciation expense is inadequate or excessive. Final conclusions should not be reached in analyzing this ratio without first ascertaining the makeup of the assets. The ratio of depreciation to fixed assets is computed as follows:

$$\frac{\text{Depreciation (\$460,000)}}{\text{Fixed assets* (\$15,202,000)}} = \begin{cases} \text{Number of cents allowed for depre-} \\ \text{ciation per dollar of fixed assets} \\ \text{(3.03 cents).} \end{cases}$$

* Accumulated depreciation not deducted.

The relative importance of the annual maintenance, repairs, and depreciation charges depends upon (1) whether the business operates its own plant and equipment or rents all or a portion of it; (2) the amount of the depreciable assets relative to the total assets; (3) the amount of actual maintenance, repairs, and depreciation relative to the total operating expenses; and (4) the effect upon earnings if maintenance, repairs, and depreciation are decreased or deferred. In the latter case, if the net earnings are high, the failure properly to maintain or repair the assets or to recognize depreciation would not be so adverse as in the event of a low net income. Many businesses tend to vary depreciation expense from year to year according to profits. This unfortunate practice results in overstating net income in poor years but understating it in good years—of course, this is why management does it. It should be emphasized that the policy of capitalizing or not capitalizing certain asset replacements may change the *relative amount* of depreciation and maintenance. A low depreciation rate with all replacements charged to expense may result in the same total (depreciation and maintenance) as a high depreciation rate with the larger replacements charged to the depreciation allowances.[4]

In analyzing the depreciation expense in relation to fixed assets, it is essential to have available the dollar data as well as the trend ratios for each item. These data for Company M are presented in Illustration 16–8. As shown, the trend for depreciation expense is downward, whereas

ILLUSTRATION 16–8

COMPANY M
Comparison of Depreciation and Fixed Assets
For the Years Ended December 31, 1966–71

Items and computation		1966	1967	1968	1969	1970	19
Depreciation (a)	($000)	460	477	464	395	417	
Trend percentage	(%)	100	104	101	86	91	
Fixed operating assets (b)	($000)	13,801	13,905	14,287	14,281	14,777	15,
Trend percentage	(%)	100	101	104	103	107	
Ratio of depreciation to fixed assets							
(cents) (a ÷ b)	(%)	3.33	3.43	3.25	2.77	2.82	?
Trend percentage	(%)	100	103	98	83	85	

the trend for fixed assets is upward. This decrease in depreciation may indicate that insufficient depreciation has been recognized.

The ratios of depreciation to fixed assets show a downward tendency, indicating—to some extent, at least—inadequacy of depreciation charges and variation in the depreciation policy. The ratio of depreciation to fixed assets should be studied, together with the ratio of depreciation to net sales.

For comparative purposes the data relative to comparable manufacturing companies are presented in Illustration 16–9. This information shows rather conclusively that Company B has followed a uniform depreciation policy; and since the amounts exceed those for the other companies, it may be assumed that a liberal policy is in effect. Companies A and C have not recorded depreciation on a uniform basis; therefore, their net income or loss has been computed from year to year after deducting varying amounts of depreciation.

---

[4] See discussion of relationship between the annual depreciation charge and repairs (pages 60–61 and 383).

ILLUSTRATION 16–9

COMPANIES A, B, AND C
Ratios of Depreciation to Fixed Assets
For the Years Ended December 31, 1967–71
(depreciation cost in cents per dollar of assets)

Companies	1967	1968	1969	1970	1971
A.........	1.70	2.10	4.10	4.90	5.20
B.........	6.50	6.80	6.70	6.50	6.64
C.........	1.09	2.05	2.60	3.20	3.24

Ratio of operating income to net sales

The amount of the operating income, which is one of the most important figures shown on the income statement, reveals the profitableness of the sales, i.e., the profitableness of the regular buying, manufacturing, and selling operations of the business. Many factors may bring about a variation in operating income from year to year. For example, any change in sales, cost of goods sold, and operating expenses, unless compensated for, would affect the amount of operating income. The operating income should be related to net sales by computing the ratio of operating income to net sales. This ratio is computed, as shown in Illustration 16–10, by dividing operating income by net sales. The resultant

ILLUSTRATION 16–10

LYNN-DALE COMPANY
Ratios of Operating Income to Net Sales
For the Years Ended December 31, 1966–71

Items and computations		1966	1967	1968	1969	1970	1971
t sales (a)......................	($000)	812.5	853.7	859.8	1,201.2	1,341.3	1,491.8
Trend percentages	(%)	100	105	106	148	165	184
erating income (b)................	($000)	63.4	64.9	61.9	78.1	84.5	91.0
Trend percentages..................	(%)	100	102	98	123	133	144
tio of operating income to net sales (b ÷ a)........................	(%)	7.8	7.6	7.2	6.5	6.3	6.1

percentage indicates the number of cents that remain after cost of goods sold and current operating expenses (exclusive of federal income taxes) have been deducted from the sales dollar. Operating income does not include other revenue and other expenses, federal income taxes, and extraordinary gain and loss items. When sufficient data are available, which would not be true for the external analyst, the ratio of operating income to net sales should be prepared by products, branches, or departments.

The ratios of operating income to net sales for the Lynn-Dale

Company, Illustration 16–10, reveal an unfavorable situation. The ratios declined each year from 7.8 percent for 1966 to 6.1 percent for 1971. It will be observed that both sales and operating income increased. However, the latter moved upward at a lower rate. Consequently, it is clear that the cost and expense of obtaining the larger sales volume increased at a greater rate than the sales revenue. Reference to, and study of, the trend ratios in Illustration 16–11 will verify this conclusion.

ILLUSTRATION 16–11

LYNN-DALE COMPANY
Selected Income Statement Data and Operating Ratios
For the Years 1966–71

Items		1966	1967	1968	1969	1970	1971
Net sales	($000)	812.5	853.7	859.8	1,201.2	1,341.3	1,491.
Trend percentages	(%)	100	105	106	148	165	184
Cost of goods sold	($000)	598.0	624.1	627.7	861.3	964.4	1,054.
Trend percentages	(%)	100	104	105	144	161	176
Gross margin on sales	($000)	214.5	229.6	232.1	339.9	376.9	437
Trend percentages	(%)	100	107	108	158	176	204
Selling expenses	($000)	107.2	115.2	116.1	182.6	210.6	253.
Trend percentages	(%)	100	107	108	170	196	237
General and administrative expenses	($000)	43.9	49.5	54.1	79.2	81.8	92
Trend percentages	(%)	100	113	123	180	186	211
Total operating expenses	($000)	151.1	164.7	170.2	261.8	292.4	346
Trend percentages	(%)	100	109	113	173	194	229
Operating income	($000)	63.4	64.9	61.9	78.1	84.5	91
Trend percentages	(%)	100	102	98	123	133	144
Operating ratio*	(%)	92.2	92.4	92.8	93.5	93.7	93
Trend percentages	(%)	100	100	101	101	102	102

* Cost of goods sold and operating expenses divided by net sales.

The ratio of operating income to net sales should be related to the total assets employed in obtaining the sales. The ratio of operating income to net sales and the ratio of operating income to total operating assets[5] (all assets exclusive of those not used for regular operations) are complementary. The amount of operating income may be entirely satisfactory from the point of view of the sales volume. However, the sales volume may be insufficient in relation to the plant capacity, i.e., the amount of capital invested in assets used in obtaining the sales.

The ratio of operating income to net sales should also be considered in connection with the turnover of inventory and receivables as well as the current ratio. Rapid turnovers of inventory and receivables may be a result of reduced sales prices and relatively high rates of cash discounts. When not accompanied by reduced costs and operating expenses, the smaller sales income would result in a lower operating income. A low operating income may be a result of excessive selling and general administrative expenses.

---

[5] See page 351 for discussion of the ratio of operating income to total operating assets.

The operating income is the amount of income that is available for interest, federal income taxes, dividends, and accumulations of retained earnings, assuming that there is no "other" expense or "other" revenue (exclusive of interest charges) or extraordinary gains or losses. Therefore, a small amount of operating income normally would not represent a fair return to investors. A low ratio of operating income to net sales means that a slight unfavorable change in future selling price without a proportionate change in costs probably would result in a loss instead of a profit. A low ratio may be a result of excessive costs relative to sales volume.[6]

Operating ratio

The term *operating ratio* refers to the ratio of all operating expenses—including cost of merchandise sold, selling expenses, and general and administrative expenses—to operating net revenue. The difference between the ratio of operating income to net sales and 100 percent shows the percentage of the net sales that has been absorbed by the cost of goods sold and operating expenses. This percentage, referred to as the "operating ratio," may be determined, as illustrated below, by dividing cost of goods sold plus operating expenses by net sales. The higher the operating ratio, the less favorable, since the smaller amount of operating income may not be sufficient to meet interest, dividends, and other corporate needs.

$$\frac{\substack{\text{Cost of goods sold (\$959,100) and} \\ \text{operating expenses (\$322,500),} \\ \$1,281,600}}{\text{Net sales, \$1,375,000}} = \text{Operating ratio, 93.2 percent.}$$

In interpreting the operating ratio and, therefore, the ratio of operating income to net sales, full recognition must be given to the possibility of variations in expenses from year to year or from company to company, especially those that are due to changes or differences in policies involving expenses that are subject to managerial discretion. Such expense items include uncollectible receivables, amortization, depreciation, maintenance, repairs, ordinary replacement, rents and royalties, and management and service contract fees.

Year-to-year variations in the operating ratio may be temporary, since sales or operating costs and expenses may be high or low due to short-lived conditions. More specifically, a variation in the operating ratio

---

[6] During and following a period of major price changes, operating income will be distorted (see Part III).

from year to year may be the result of one or more of the following factors: (1) variations in volume of goods sold and selling prices; (2) variation in volume and cost of goods sold and operating expenses, without a proportionate change in sales dollar volume; or (3) a change in the "sales mix." The "sales mix" refers to the proportionate shares in sales of different products or groups of products, which may, and probably will, show varying gross margins.

Although the operating ratio is a fairly good index of operating efficiency, it should be used with caution because a combination of factors are reflected therein—such as external uncontrollable factors, internal controllable items, and employee and managerial efficiency or inefficiency. The operating ratio cannot be used as a test of financial condition without taking into account other revenue and other expenses and extraordinary items. Companies with the lowest operating ratio and, therefore, the highest ratio of operating income to net sales, assuming a fair condition relative to financial and extraordinary items, have the least to fear during periods of business inactivity, since their profit can shrink considerably before a dangerous situation develops.

Revenue and expense data presented for the Lynn-Dale Company in Illustration 16–11, permit a general study of the operating ratios and their component elements. For example, the operating ratio increased slightly from 92.2 percent for 1966 to 93.9 percent for 1971. It will be observed that while sales and cost of goods sold increased, the former did so at a higher rate, thereby resulting in a more favorable change in the gross margin. However, the increase in selling expenses of 137 percent and in general and administrative expenses of 111 percent result in an adverse effect on profits. The operating income increased 44 percent; sales increased 84 percent.

The analyst can readily point out such favorable and unfavorable tendencies—the real problem is to determine the causes of the changes. A more detailed analysis requires the computation, analysis, and interpretation of individual ratios and the use of other analytical devices as explained in the preceding and following sections.

Other revenue, other expense, and extraordinary gain and loss items

The items included in the final sections of the income statement—other revenue, other expense, and extraordinary items—should be studied to determine whether favorable or unfavorable tendencies are present.

The analyst should determine the nature of the items and relate them to other appropriate financial statement accounts. For example, such items as interest and dividends on long-term investments, rental income from leased property, and interest on long-term debt should be given careful consideration. The possibility of the recurrence of extraordinary items should be forecast to determine their effect on future income.

Federal income taxes

In analyzing the various individual expense items included on the income statement, special attention should be given to federal income taxes. In the event that capital gains were realized and the federal income tax related thereto was not apportioned, the analyst should understand that the federal income tax item represents a tax on both regular and extraordinary income. The external analyst would not have the information necessary to determine the income tax which pertained to regular income. Furthermore, there may be a substantial difference between reportable income for income tax purposes and the income for accounting purposes. The differences are discussed on pages 161–62. Inasmuch as the federal income tax is not always specifically and entirely related to the current income, some ratios pertaining to income are computed before and after the tax deduction.

Ratio of net sales to total operating assets

The investment of capital in total operating assets (total assets exclusive of long-term investments) is sometimes studied in relation to net sales. The ratio of net sales to total operating assets is a measure of the utilization of the operating assets. Generally, the larger the sales volume, the greater the amount of operating assets that will be required for efficient operation. The ratio of net sales to total operating assets— which is usually referred to as the "turnover of total operating assets"—is determined, as shown in Illustration 16–12, by dividing the net sales by the total book value of the operating assets; valuation and amortization accounts are deducted in determining asset book value. This

ILLUSTRATION 16–12

LYNN-DALE COMPANY
Ratio of Net Sales to Total Operating Assets
For the Years Ended December 31, 1966–71

Items and computation		1966	1967	1968	1969	1970	1971
Net sales (a)	($000)	812.5	853.7	859.8	1,201.2	1,341.3	1,491.8
Trend percentages	(%)	100	105	106	148	165	184
Total operating assets* (valuation and amortization accounts deducted) (b)	($000)	1,022.0	1,083.5	1,364.3	1,475.3	1,578.5	1,603.7
Trend percentages	(%)	100	106	134	144	155	157
Ratio of net sales to total operating assets, net (a ÷ b)	(%)	79.5	78.8	63.0	81.4	85.0	93.0
Trend percentages	(%)	100	99	79	102	107	117

* Year-end figures. Average (preferably for 12 months) should be used, if available. Includes assets used in connection with the regular operations of the business.

ratio involves two variables: the total book value of the operating assets and the net sales. These two items, in turn, involve a great many variables.

The data for the Lynn-Dale Company (Illustration 16–12) show that the trends of net sales and total operating assets are upward, the former at the more rapid rate. This favorable tendency is also reflected by an improvement in the ratios of net sales to total operating assets beginning in 1969, since a larger volume of sales has been obtained without necessitating a relative increase in operating asset investment. The ratios decreased from 79.5 percent for 1966 to 63.0 percent for 1968 and then increased from 63.0 percent in 1968 to 93.0 percent in 1971. The turnover of operating assets in relation to sales for the Lynn-Dale Company is much lower than the average for the industry. Here is additional evidence of an overinvestment in operating assets—sales are insufficient to support, profitably, this investment.

As indicated above, the foregoing ratio may show whether there is a tendency toward overinvestment in total operating assets. For example, the volume of sales may be entirely too low in relation to the operating asset investment; or an increase in the operating asset investment may not be accompanied by a proportionate or greater change in sales volume. However, in interpreting the total operating asset turnover in relation to sales, it must be remembered that this ratio does not reveal in any manner the revenue derived from sales. A high volume of sales in relation to total operating assets does not necessarily result in profitable operations. To determine the profitableness of the total operating assets, the analyst should compute the ratio of operating income to total operating assets.[7]

Some analysts compute the plant turnover by relating net sales to total fixed assets. However, since all operating assets together with salesmen and sales promotional programs are utilized in obtaining sales revenue, it does not appear to be desirable to use only the investment in fixed plant facilities.

The analyst must also exercise caution in drawing conclusions from a study of the ratio of net sales to total operating assets. At best, the ratio is only a rough comparison or measure of the efficient use of the operating assets, since sales volume definitely depends upon the effectiveness of the salesmen and the advertising and promotional activity of management. Sales volume represents an accumulation for a period of time, usually one year, whereas the assets are stated as of a given moment of time and usually represent an accumulation of many years. The sales are ordinarily affected by factors that are beyond the control of management and that do not necessarily involve the assets. The assets are affected by factors over a period of years which do not concern

---

[7] See pages 351–52.

the sales of a single year. Plant expansion may be accompanied by a proportionate increase in sales volume, but the sales may be less profitable as reflected by the net income figure. Plant expansion may represent improvements that have no effect on sales but result in lower costs of production and, therefore, increase net income.

The influence of the price level with respect to sales may be pronounced. The trend for the physical volume of sales may be constant, upward, or downward from year to year; the dollar volume of sales may indicate the same or an opposite tendency. For example, a company that produces two million units of a single product may receive $2,500,000 or $1,700,000 for the total production, depending upon changes in production and market-price conditions. Unless price-level changes are considered, the variation in dollar sales would be attributed entirely to changes in trading profits or losses. If the price level has changed, it is desirable to adjust the profit and loss data to eliminate the influence of such variations.[8]

An overinvestment in total operating assets in relation to sales and/or profits is likely to prove far more costly than a similar situation for receivables and inventories because the receivables may be collected and the inventories may be converted into cash within a period of a few months even though a loss is involved. On the other hand, the excessive investment in total operating assets may be present for a much longer period of time. Resultant high costs—including maintenance, taxes, interest, and other fixed costs—place a heavy burden on the company. Such a condition, unless offset by commensurately larger sales volume and greater managerial efficiency, may lead to insolvency, especially if the financing has been through the medium of current liabilities or bonds.

When an analyst compares the ratio of net sales to total operating assets for several companies, it is especially important to have comparable data. For example, one company may have obtained its assets at a high or low price level; may have a preponderance of hand or machine methods which, in turn, depend on localities and upon wage levels; may have an older or a newer plant; and may have adopted liberal or nonliberal maintenance and depreciation policies. These various factors will tend to bring about a disparity in the operating asset ratios.

Ratio of net sales to "tangible" owners' equity

The ratio of net sales to "tangible" owners' equity represents the turnover of owners' equity. Tangible owners' equity is determined by deducting intangible assets from the owners' equity as shown on the balance sheet. To determine the net sales per dollar of tangible owners'

---

[8] See Chapters 17–21.

equity, divide net sales by tangible owners' equity, as follows:

$$\frac{\text{Net sales (\$98,000)}}{\text{Tangible owners' equity (\$20,000)}} = \begin{Bmatrix}\text{Net sales per dollar of} \\ \text{tangible owners' equity} \\ (\$4.90).\end{Bmatrix}$$

This computation shows the turnover of tangible owners' equity in terms of sales. The larger the net sales as compared with the tangible owners' equity, the less favorable the situation is likely to be from the point of view of conservatism and safety because the business operates too extensively on borrowed funds. From the point of view of doing a large volume of business on a small investment, the larger ratio may be favorable because it leads to higher profits. As long as sales volume and a fair net return on the sales are maintained, a minimum of owners' equity may be ample. However, when unfavorable sales conditions develop, a relatively small amount of owners' equity cannot absorb resultant losses; nor does it provide as a rule, ample working capital with which to meet maturing liabilities. A small ratio of net sales to tangible owners' equity may indicate an excessive investment in property relative to sales volume.

The foregoing ratio has definite limitations as to its reliability and significance because it is a composite ratio. To the extent that owners' equity has been invested in long-term investments and other nonoperating assets, it bears no relation to sales; and, therefore, the ratio of sales to total operating assets would be more significant than the ratio of net sales to tangible owners' equity. A large owners' equity may be necessary because of investments in slow-turning assets such as receivables and inventories as well as plant and equipment. An increase in long-term debt for plant expansion purposes—and, therefore, a proportionately lower percentage of owners' equity—would result in a higher plant turnover. The existence of an excessively high amount of debt would not be favorable.

Accounting for variation of net income for the year

Net income may vary from year to year as a result of one or a combination of the following factors:

1. An increase or decrease in unit sales volume or selling prices.
2. An increase or decrease in cost of goods sold due to variations in unit sales volume, production economies, or purchase prices.
3. An increase or decrease in operating expenses due to variations in the price level, operating efficiency, or unit sales volume.
4. An increase or decrease in other (financial) items due to variation in the price level, unit sales volume, or a change in policy as to

terms and cash discounts with respect to purchases and sales (assuming discounts are classified in this section).

5. An increase or decrease in federal income taxes due to more or less income or to higher or lower tax rates. The analyst should fully consider the fact that although the amount of the estimated federal income tax pertains primarily to current income, it is affected also by extraordinary items, including capital gains and capital losses.

6. A change of accounting method, impairing comparability.

The information normally given on an income statement is not adequate for the purpose of accounting for the variation of net income for the year, since net income may vary, as indicated above, as a result of changes in physical volume of goods sold, price levels, and economics and efficiencies of production, purchasing, and general operations. Variations in income are explained in the following pages.

Trading versus price profits

The income statement, as customarily presented, shows the net income or net loss, without any designation as to whether it includes both trading profit and a price profit or price loss. A trading profit or trading loss results from regular operations and is independent of price profits which occur because of changes in the price level.

Price profits are different from trading profits because (1) they will not be repeated unless prices continue to rise to higher levels; (2) they will be reversed into price losses if prices go down; and (3) they tend to be tied up in higher priced inventory and larger receivables and, therefore, are not available for either dividends, debt reduction, or expansion of other assets.

Furthermore, profits that arise solely from a change in the general price level are unreal. They are the result of a decrease in the purchasing power of the dollar and, therefore, lack an element that would appear essential to a "real" profit, namely, an increase in the purchasing power of the concern to acquire a larger volume of goods and services. When the general price level rises, sales, cost of goods sold, gross margin, expenses (except items like depreciation which result from historical dollar costs), and net income all tend to rise when measured in dollars. A larger "profit" results, exaggerated by factors such as inventory (which on a first-in, first-out basis tends to introduce historical dollar costs into cost of goods sold) and depreciation. The influence of price-level changes on the financial statements is discussed in detail in Part III.

The segregation of price profit or price loss is of real significance to the management, creditors, and stockholders. If the influence of price changes is not considered, management may be misled in measuring the effect of efficiency and economy of operations; creditors may be mislead in estimating future profits and debt-paying ability; and stockholders may be misled in determining profitableness of normal operations and present as well as future dividend prospects.

Price profits or losses may result not only from normal inventories but also from speculative or excess inventories which are accumulated because of anticipated higher prices or because of shortages. Where possible, price profits should be segregated in order to place the correct economic interpretation on the results of the regular or normal operating functions of the business.

Statement accounting for variation in net income— price level not changed

A comparative income statement shows the increases and decreases in revenue and expense items for two or more years. If the price level has remained approximately the same, the changes in net income from year to year are the result of (1) changes in gross margin or sales resulting from variations in the number of units sold, sales prices, and cost of goods sold; and (2) changes in operating and other expense

ILLUSTRATION 16–13

LYNN-DALE COMPANY

Comparative Income Statement

For the Years Ended December 31, 1970, and 1971

Items	1970 ($000)	1971 ($000)	Dollar increase (decrease*) 1971 ($000)	Percentage increase (decrease*) 1971 ~ (%)
Net sales	1,341.3	1,491.8	150.5	11.2
Cost of goods sold	964.4	1,054.7	90.3	9.4
Gross margin on sales	376.9	437.1	60.2	16.0
Selling expenses	210.6	253.6	43.0	20.4
General and administrative expenses	81.8	92.5	10.7	13.1
Total operating expenses	292.4	346.1	53.7	18.4
Operating income	84.5	91.0	6.5	7.7
Other revenue and expense, net (deduct)	(10.7)	(7.5)	3.2	29.9
Income for the year before federal income taxes	73.8	83.5	9.7	13.1
Federal income taxes	26.9	31.3	4.4	16.4
Net income for the year before extraordinary items.	46.9	52.2	5.3	11.3
Extraordinary items, net (add)	128.3	42.5	85.8*	66.9*
Net income and extraordinary items	175.2	94.7	80.5*	45.9*

and other revenue resulting from the variations in volume of sales and/or efficiency of operations. In order to summarize the reasons for changes in the net income, assuming no variation in the price level, the analyst may prepare a *statement accounting for variation in net income*. Data included in Illustration 16–13 are used as the basis for preparing such a statement for the Lynn-Dale Company.

The statement accounting for variation in net income, Illustration. 16–14, represents a rearrangement of the comparative income statement in Illustration 16–13.

ILLUSTRATION 16–14

LYNN-DALE COMPANY
Statement Accounting for Variation in Net Income
For the Year Ended December 31, 1971

	Amounts ($000)		Increase (%)
Items tending to increase net income:			
Increase in gross margin on sales:			
Increase in net sales:			
Net sales, 1971	1,491.8		
Net sales, 1970	1,341.4	150.5	11.2
Deduct: Increase in cost of goods sold:			
Cost of goods sold, 1971	1,054.7		
Cost of goods sold, 1970	964.4	90.3	9.4
Net increase in gross margin:			
Gross margin, 1971	437.1		
Gross margin, 1970	376.9	60.2	16.0
Decrease in other revenue and expense,			
net (Deduction): Expense, 1970.	(10.7)		
Expense, 1971.	(7.5)	3.2	
Total of items tending to increase			
net income		63.4	
Items tending to decrease net income:			
Increase in selling expenses:			
Selling expenses, 1971.	253.6		
Selling expenses, 1970.	210.6	43.0	20.4
Increase in general and administrative expenses:			
General and administrative expenses, 1971.	92.5		
General and administrative expenses, 1970	81.8	10.7	13.1
Increase in estimated federal income taxes:			
Estimated federal income taxes, 1971. . . .	31.3		
Estimated federal income taxes, 1970. . . .	26.9	4.4	16.4
Total of items tending to decrease			
net income		58.1	
Net Increase in net income:*			
Net income, 1971	52.2		
Net income, 1970	46.9	5.3	11.3

* Net income exclusive of extraordinary items.

The statement accounting for variation in net income for the Lynn-Dale Company (Illustration 16–14) shows that the $150,500 increase in net sales, accompanied by a $90,300 increase in cost of goods sold, resulted in a net increase in gross margin on sales of $60,200. Stated in terms of percentages, the net sales increased 11.2 percent during 1971; cost of goods sold increased 9.4 percent; and gross margin on sales increased 16.0 percent. The foregoing percentages clearly indicate that the increase in net sales was accompanied by a lower relative increase in cost of goods sold. Net income was further improved by the $3,200 decrease in other revenue and expense.

Net income was decreased by increases in selling expenses, $43,000, or 20.4 percent, and general and administrative expenses, $10,700, or 13.1 percent. Although net sales increased 11.2 percent, selling expenses and general and administrative expenses increased 20.4 and 13.1 percent, respectively. The greater rate of increase in selling and general and administrative expenses seems to be unfavorable and requires explanation. Estimated federal income taxes increased $4,400, or 16.4 percent.

Although the statement accounting for variation in net income indicates that changes in certain items—for example, sales, gross margin, and selling and general and administrative expenses—have occurred and that the net income has been adversely affected, it does not reveal the specific reasons for the changes.

When substantial changes have taken place, it is necessary to analyze them to determine the extent to which they have been brought about by variations in physical volume of goods sold, unit cost of goods purchased, unit markup on goods sold, price level, and economies and efficiencies of production, purchasing, selling, and general operations. The statement accounting for variations in gross margin is useful in this connection.

Break-even point analysis

Every business has a "break-even point," i.e., a volume of sales or level of operations that will produce neither a net income nor a net loss. If the sales volume is higher than this "point," there would be a profit; if lower, a loss would result.

The break-even point can be determined by preparing a graph, or it may be computed mathematically. In either case it is necessary to divide the costs, including all production, selling, general, and administrative costs, into two groups:

1. Fixed costs, which do not vary with changes in the volume of sales or level of activity. Fixed costs are incurred whether or not any sales are made or activity is completed. Property taxes and fire insurance are examples of fixed costs.

2. Variable costs, which vary approximately in proportion to the volume of sales or level of activity. Direct material or purchases and direct labor are examples of variable costs.

Of course, costs do not in reality divide so neatly into fixed and variable categories. The difference is a matter of degree, and it is necessary to be rather arbitrary in making the distribution between the two categories of cost.

For the purpose of illustrating the determination of the break-even point, the following historical data are assumed for Company A for the year 1971:

Net sales		$600,000
Less: Cost of goods sold and operating expenses:		
Fixed costs	$210,000	
Variable costs*......................	340,000*	550,000
Net Income		$ 50,000

    * Variable costs are 56.7 % of net sales.

The foregoing data are plotted on the graph presented in Illustration 16–15 below. The break-even point is located where the total cost

ILLUSTRATION 16–15

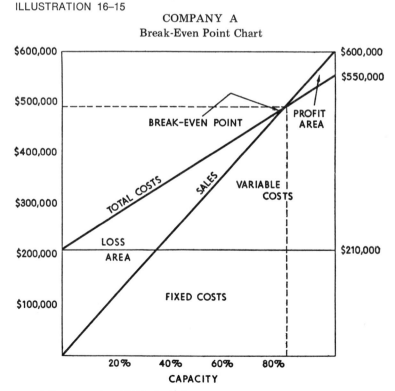

COMPANY A
Break-Even Point Chart

a) Variable costs = 56.7% of net sales.
b) Break-even point (S) = $484,988 at 81% capacity.

and sales lines intersect. Therefore, it will be seen by the graph that the break-even point is approximately $485,000. In other words, a sales volume in excess of $485,000, or operations higher than 81 percent of total sales, was required before the revenue included a profit. If the amount of fixed costs, variable costs, or sales price had increased or decreased, the break-even point would have been higher or lower.

As illustrated below, each dollar of goods that was sold represented a recovery of 56.7 cents for variable costs and 43.3 cents for fixed costs until the break-even had been attained. The fixed costs were recovered as soon as the break-even point had been reached; after that, 43.3 cents of each sales dollar represented net income.

Total sales	$600,000
Break-even point	484,988
Sales in excess of break-even point	$115,012
Variable costs, 56.7% of sales above break-even point	$ 65,212
Net income, 43.3% of sales above break-even point	49,800
Total Sales in Excess of Break-Even Point	$115,012

The historical break-even point, i.e., the break-even point at the close of an accounting period, may be computed mathematically as follows (the same data that were used in preparing the foregoing chart are assumed):

a) S = the sales at the break-even point.
b) The variable costs incurred in selling $600,000 of goods are $340,000, or 56.7 percent of the sales. The variable expenses vary in proportion to sales and should amount to 56.7 percent of any sales volume.
c) The sales at the break-even point will be the same amount as the total of fixed costs plus the variable costs, therefore:

$$S = \$210,000 \ (\text{fixed costs}) + \frac{56.7S}{100} \ (\text{variable costs})$$

$$S - 56.7S = \$210,000$$

$$\frac{43.3S}{100} = \$210,000$$

S = $484,988 (This is the break-even point. If sales are less than this amount, there will be a loss; if more, a profit will result.)

A break-even point chart is *valid* only for a relatively narrow range of production at a given time. As production increases beyond this range, some of the fixed costs must increase; and at a point below this range, some fixed costs may be reduced and some variable costs may not decline in full proportion. Only within a reasonable range will these relationships hold true.

The foregoing illustrations were based on historical accounting data. However, the determination and study of the estimated break-even point for projected future operations is just as important, if not more so, as the analysis of past and present operating performance break-even points. Many decisions concerning sales prices, sales mix, product quality, expansion, and management improvements hinge on a projected break-even point. For example, the projected break-even point would enable management to determine a sales goal. Assuming the historical variable cost relationship developed in the previous illustration, management knows that of every dollar of sales, 43.3 cents is considered to be a reimbursement for fixed costs until they have been fully recovered, and thereafter, of additional dollars of sales, 43.3 cents represents profit.

Assume that management is planning to install new showrooms that will increase fixed costs to $250,000 a year and it is decided that a 10 percent return on the owners' equity of $200,000 is required. Two questions would have to be answered: (1) What volume of sales is required to break-even? (2) What volume is necessary to yield the desired return? Using a modification of the historical break-even approach, the answers could be computed mathematically as follows:

$$a) \quad \frac{\$250,000 \text{ (fixed costs)}}{43.3 \text{ cents}} = \$577,365 \text{ (break-even sales volume)}.$$

$$b) \quad \frac{\$250,000 + \$20,000 \text{ (desired return)}}{43.3 \text{ cents}}$$
$$= \$623,556 \text{ (total sales required)}.$$

The next question management will probably ask is: "Is the required sales goal possible?" Nevertheless, the projected break-even analysis has provided the basic data.

The illustration discussed above assumes that all costs are either of a fixed or variable nature. This assumption is definitely an oversimplification. For example:

1. Some costs may be fixed so long as the sales volume does not exceed a certain amount. Once a new level of sales has been reached, additional "fixed" costs are incurred.
2. Some costs change in direct proportion to variations in sales, while others do not increase or decrease in the same manner. Many costs may be classified as semifixed or semivariable. These costs include such items as clerical salaries and rentals, which may be increased to some extent as sales volume varies.

3. If there are semivariable costs, they must be divided into their fixed and variable amounts in order to have a worthwhile break-even analysis.

It should also be noted that the break-even point may be computed most accurately when only one product is sold. If more than one product is sold it is necessary to forecast the sales mix.

The break-even point analysis may be used as a vital management tool in several ways: first, in *forecasting* such factors as the probable unit cost at varying levels of production, the sales requirements to justify a proposed plant expansion, the effect of an increase or decrease in sales volume, and the effect on profits in adjusting sales prices; second, in *evaluating management efficiency* by comparing and evaluating actual break-even results with predetermined levels; and third, in *making decisions* concerning adjustments to current operations, company policy, and further goals.

The data necessary for the determination of the break-even point are usually available to the internal analyst, especially if the business has effective systems of cost accounting and budgetary control. In case they have not been developed, the analyst will find that the most difficult

ILLUSTRATION 16–16

UNITED WALLPAPER, INC.

Net Operating Profit Realized at Various Sales Volumes
(showing years)

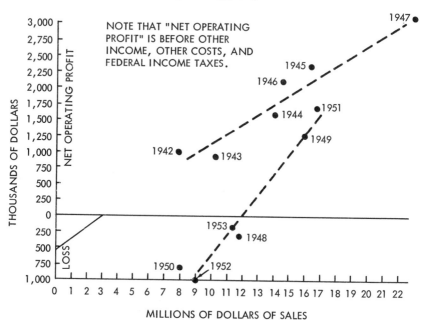

MILLIONS OF DOLLARS OF SALES

task is deciding to what extent the "fixed" costs are actually in part semivariable. The separation of costs into their fixed and variable elements at times has to be accomplished on an arbitrary assignment basis. This fact is especially true when a company sells a number of products. Although precise accuracy cannot be attained, a knowledge and study of the various costs in relation to sales revenue is of major significance in solving many managerial problems.

The external analyst ordinarily does not have access to data exact enough to permit a projection of future break-even points at substantial variations in sales volume. However, he may be able to arrive at meaningful though rough conclusions regarding the burden of fixed costs at various volumes by a comparison of operating results in the past few years. For example, an unusually graphic picture of a mistake which was fatal to the health and survival of the United Wallpaper Company can be seen in the scatter chart (a form of break-even chart) shown in illustration 16–16. It shows the substantial increase in fixed costs which resulted from the construction of a large new plant and the attendant disastrous results when an expected substantial increase in sales did not materialize.

QUESTIONS AND PROBLEMS

16–1. Should the analyst expect drastic changes in income statement ratios from year to year?

16–2. "It may easily happen that the actual sales volume of a company as expressed in physical units may increase while the total money consideration shows a downward trend." Explain the foregoing statement and indicate its importance in connection with ratio analysis.

16–3. Discuss the operating ratio with particular reference to its value as a test of the efficiency of management and of financial condition.

16–4. Give a brief discussion of the following:
  a) What are the possible causes of changes in net income?
  b) What is the difference between fixed and variable expenses? Are all expenses either fixed or variable?
  c) From the point of view of income statement ratio determination, how should the following be treated?
    (1) Federal income taxes.
    (2) Net income appropriated as a general reserve for inventories.
    (3) Amortization of bond discount and expense.
    (4) Unrealized appreciation of buildings.
    (5) Premium on serial notes retired prior to maturity.
    (6) Depreciation of buildings.
    (7) Amortization of leasehold improvements.
    (8) Gain on sale of fixed assets.
    (9) Recoveries on customer accounts previously written off.

    d)   Of what significance is ratio analysis of an income statement for a single accounting period?

    e)   What relationship does the rate of inventory turnover have (1) to the gross margin and (2) to the operating income?

    f)   Is the ratio of gross margin to sales significant? What elements of revenue and cost affect the gross margin on sales?

16–5. In preparing for ratio computations, how should the following items be treated?

    a)   Loss on sale of long-term securities:

    b)   Amortization of leasehold improvements.

    c)   Rent income.

    d)   Sales returns.

    e)   Sales discounts.

    f)   Purchases discounts.

    g)   Refund of federal income taxes.

    h)   Interest and dividend income.

    i)   Royalty income.

16–6. Distinguish between trading and price level profits and discuss the importance of accounting for each type of profit.

16–7.

BODINSON HARDWARE SALES COMPANY
Income Statement Data
For the Years Ended December 31, 1970–71
(in thousands)

Items	1970	1971
Net sales	$15,000	$16,365
Cost of goods sold	10,155	10,703
Gross margin	4,845	5,662
Selling expenses	1,170	1,178
General and administrative expenses	480	524
Total operating expenses	1,650	1,702
Operating income	3,195	3,960
Other revenue	30	33
Other expense	30	32
Income before federal income taxes	3,195	3,961
Estimated federal income taxes	1,215	1,964
Net income after federal income taxes	1,980	1,997
Expenses included in foregoing items:		
Maintenance and repairs	420	442
Depreciation	450	458
Taxes (other than income)	270	295
Uncollectible receivables expense	15	15

Required:

    a)   Compute dollar and percentage changes in the data during 1971.

    b)   Compute common-size percentages for the two years.

    c)   Write a report commenting on the changes that have taken place in the income statement items during the two-year period.

16–8.

BRIGGS STORES
Income Statement Data
For the Years Ended December 31, 1970–71
(in thousands)

Items	1970	1971
Net sales	$10,100	$13,200
Cost of goods sold...................	7,126	9,230
Gross margin	2,974	3,970
Selling expenses	976	1,128
General and administrative expenses	396	402
Total operating expenses	1,372	1,530
Operating income	1,602	2,440
Other revenues	24	23
Other expense	19	25
Income before federal income taxes	1,607	2,438
Estimated federal income taxes	915	1,080
Net income after federal income taxes......	692	1,358

Required:
Prepare a statement showing an analysis of variation in net income for the Briggs Stores for the year 1971.

16–9. The Don Leake Company presented the following data selected from its income statements:

	1967	1968	1969	1970	1971
Net sales ....($000)	13,980	17,800	16,900	14,800	13,700
Trend percentages .... (%)	100	127	121	106	98
Gross margin ....($000)	3,998	5,097	5,180	4,483	4,031
Trend percentages .... (%)	100	127	130	112	101
Operating income........($000)	352	372	911	704	651
Trend percentages .... (%)	100	106	259	200	185
Net income before extraordinary					
items ....($000)	151	159	398	330	299
Trend percentages .... (%)	100	105	258	219	198

Required:
a) Prepare charts on which you show the trend percentages.
b) Compute and chart common-size percentages.
c) Write a report in which you discuss the interpretation of the data.

16–10. The following data were selected from the income statements of the Harold Sales Corporation:

	1967	1968	1969	1970	1971
Net sales ....($000)	14,681	13,947	14,975	14,241	13,947
Trend percentages .... (%)	100	95	102	97	95
Gross margin on sales....... ($000)	4,423	4,556	4,644	4,954	4,821
Trend percentages .... (%)	100	103	105	112	109
Operating income........($000)	460	483	497	474	478
Trend percentages .... (%)	100	105	108	103	104
Net income before extraordinary					
items ....($000)	162	167	170	168	175
Trend percentages .... (%)	100	103	105	104	108

Required:

a) Chart the trend percentages.

b) Compute and chart the common-size percentages.

c) Write a report in which you discuss the interpretation of the data.

16–11. The Don Leake Company had sales and cost of goods sold for the year 1970 and 1971 as follows:

	In thousands	
	1970	*1971*
Net sales	$14,800	$13,700
Cost of goods sold	10,317	9,669
Gross margin on sales	$ 4,483	$ 4,031
Note: Units sold	1,000,000	950,000

Required:

Prepare an analysis of variation in gross margin for the Don Leake Company for the year 1971.

16–12. The following data—000's omitted—have been obtained from the financial statements of the Watson Corporation:

	As of December 31 or for the year				Increase 197 over 1968	
	1968	*1969*	*1970*	*1971*	*($000)*	*(%)*
	($000)	*($000)*	*($000)*	*($000)*		
Current assets	760	1,180	1,190	1,310	550	72.
Current liabilities	380	490	530	625	245	64.
Plant, equipment, and land	2,250	2,250	2,250	2,250		
Accumulated depreciation	730	780	840	910	180	24.
Sinking fund (long-term debt)	50	100	150	200	150	300.
Long-term debt (5%)	800	800	800	800		
Interest—long-term debt	40	40	40	40		
Preferred capital stock (6% cumulative)	500	500	500	500		
Common capital stock	1,600	1,600	1,600	1,600		
Retained earnings, appropriated	50	100	150	200	150	300
Retained earnings, free	620	730	840	910	290	46
Operating income	637	697	769	815	178	27
Other revenue	31	34	35	39	8	25
Other expense	15	21	24	23	8	53
Federal income taxes	320	350	360	380	60	18
Net income before extraordinary items	333	360	420	451	118	35

Note:

(1) Capital stock, $100 par value per share.

(2) Dividends declared and paid each year: Preferred stock, regular dividend; Common stock, 7%.

Required:

a) Compute the following dollar amounts:

(1) Net working capital.

(2) Total assets.

(3) Total liabilities.

    (4)   Total owners' equity.
    (5)   Extraordinary gain and loss, net.
    (6)   Book value of each share of common stock.
  b)   Compute the relative positions of the creditors and the owners.
  c)   After analyzing and studying all data available, write a report relative to the financial strength and operating results of the Watson Corporation.

16–13.   The Downey Corporation proposes to expand its productive facilities. It presents the following selected data relative to the present and prospective operations:

	Present facilities	Expanded facilities
Sales	$1,000,000	$1,400,000
Cost of goods sold and operating expenses:		
Fixed expenses.	$ 320,000	$ 458,000
Variable costs	560,000	612,000
	$ 880,000	$1,070,000
Net Income	$ 120,000	$ 330,000

Required:
  a)   Compute the break-even point under both of the foregoing situations.
  b)   Chart your findings.

PART III

*The Effect of Changing Price
Levels on the Interpretation
of Financial Statements*

17

Price-level changes and financial statements

It is the purpose of this chapter to discuss a problem that is particularly troublesome in periods marked by extreme price fluctuations.[1] Such a period occurred immediately after World War II when the release of

---

[1] But the cumulative effects of small price changes can also become substantial as pointed out in the following quotation from the text of the AICPA Accounting Principles Board's *Statement No. 3* (page 6) which will be discussed at length in the next few chapters.

"14. *Effects of Rate of Inflation.* Large changes in the general price level obviously have a greater effect than small changes. It is perhaps less obvious that moderate changes in the general price level may also significantly affect business enterprises and their financial statements. The nature of the income statement and the cumulative effect over time of moderate changes in the general price level tend to magnify the effects of changes in the general price level. Thus, in the income statement, differences which represent relatively small percentage changes in comparatively large revenue and expense items may be substantial in relation to net income. Also, if assets are held for a number of years the effect of inflation or deflation depends on the cumulative inflation or deflation since acquisition of the assets. The general price-level change in any one year is only a part of the total effect. Thus, the 3.8% inflation experienced in 1968 is only a small part of the total inflation effect on fixed assets appearing in 1968 statements. For fixed assets purchased in 1950, for example, there is a cumulative inflation effect of 54% (total inflation measured by the GNP Deflator from 1950 to 1968) on undepreciated cost and depreciation expense in 1968 general price-level financial statements. Furthermore, the effects of inflation compound over a period of years (for example, a constant 2% rate of inflation results in a 22% cumulative general price-level change in ten years and a 49% cumulative general price-level change in 20 years). Nonrecognition of the effects of inflation may therefore have a substantial effect on financial statement representations of assets held over long periods (such as investments, and property, plant, and equipment), even though the amount of inflation each year has been relatively small."

price controls marked the beginning of a substantial increase in the general price level. There have been wars since that time, and steadily rising prices, so that today the dollar is worth less than two thirds its value in 1947.

By "worth" we mean its ability to buy goods and services—its general purchasing power.

The problem that we are now discussing arises from the fact that company financial statements, conventionally prepared, ignore the fluctuating "value" (ability to buy) of the dollar. "Values" on such financial statements are expressed in dollars of varying size; as prices rise, the value of the dollar declines. Therefore, conventionally prepared financial statements are always distorted, and may be seriously misleading.

In June 1969, in *Statement No. 3*, the Accounting Principles Board of the AICPA suggested (but did not require) that company's issuing financial statements for the information of their stockholders and other interested readers prepare and attach supplementary financial statements constructed in such a way as to minimize the distorting effects of changes in the price level.

We will examine *Statement No. 3* in greater detail in Chapter 18. First, because of the complexity of the problem, we will explore its general nature.

The nature of the problem illustrated

The problem created by the instability of the dollar is twofold:

1. The amounts appearing on the financial statements of a given firm or of two different firms are not comparable because these amounts are expressed in dollars having different values. It is this problem that is particularly troublesome to the analyst.
2. Conventional published financial statements (relying heavily on dollar cost) fail to reflect the effect of changes in the value of the dollar upon the purchasing power of the resources of the firm.

These problems can be illustrated by simple examples. Suppose that in year 1 a real estate dealer acquires a piece of land for $1,000. Two years later, he sells the land for $1,500. If the prices of all goods and services have increased 50 percent, there is some doubt whether he has realized a profit on the sale. Obviously, he can purchase no more goods and services with the $1,500 than he could have with $1,000 two years earlier. The net income of $500 which would be shown on conventional statements results from the matching of revenue measured in year-3 dollars with costs measured in year-1 dollars.

Assume that there are two real estate dealers. One purchases land for $1,000. A year later the second dealer purchases land for $1,200.

If the prices of all goods and services rise together, it is erroneous to infer from the values of $1,000 and $1,200 shown on the financial statements of the two dealers that the second dealer holds the more valuable land, or even that the second dealer's land "cost" more. If during the intervening year the value of the dollar has declined more than 20 percent (as it did, for example, between 1946 and 1947), the land acquired for $1,200 may actually have "cost" less than the land acquired for $1,000.

These two illustrations relate to the first aspect of the problem. To examine the second aspect, assume a third hypothetical case. One real estate dealer invests $1,000 in government bonds, while another dealer purchases land for $1,000. Two years later the prices of all goods and services have doubled. Are both dealers equally well off? According to conventional accounting statements, both dealers have assets of $1,000. However, the one dealer can exchange his land for the same goods and services as he could before prices increased. The other dealer is not so fortunate; the proceeds from the bond will purchase only one half as much as at the time of purchase. Although such losses in purchasing power are difficult to measure and even more difficult to predict, the analyst must recognize the significance of such gains or losses in examining the financial statements of a firm.

The accounting conventions now in effect

Examine the problem again.

Accounting reports are stated in dollars: for example, so many "dollars' worth" of cash, plant, sales, and operating costs. The figures that make up published balance sheets and income statements are usually carried down to the cent and appear to be precise and fully comparable. The fact is that they are neither precise nor comparable.

It is an accounting convention that increases in the market values of assets (whether in inventory, investments, plant, or other assets) are not to be recognized[2] until "realized," usually by sale; this policy is known as the "realization" convention. As a result, the "value" of an asset depends primarily on the price at which it was bought, whether or not that price bears any similarity to current market conditions.

However, current assets such as inventories and short-term investments are usually "valued" at replacement cost if below original cost.[3]

---

[2] Except in parenthetical notes or footnotes—and even this is not common.

[3] Wide variations in the "value" of inventories result from the alternative use of first-in, first-out and last-in, first-out. In a period of rising prices, Fifo produces an inventory "value" which is usually only slightly under current replacement cost; Lifo, on the other hand, produces an inventory "value" which may have no relation to current market prices. These alternative inventory practices may result in marked variations in the current ratio and in the amount of working capital.

This modification of the realization convention, which applies only to losses, is known as "the lower of cost or market." It is rarely, if ever, applied to long-lived assets such as plant.[4]

In preparing the conventional balance sheet and income statement, accountants assume that the business concern will continue indefinitely; this is known as the "going-concern" convention. Consequently, it is assumed that because the company will not sell its fixed assets, the "current value" (whether liquidation value on forced sale, replacement cost, or appraised value) is irrelevant; and fixed assets are valued at "original cost" (historical dollar cost) less accumulated depreciation or depletion, if appropriate. This is known as the "original-cost" convention. It follows, therefore, that depreciation charges usually represent a proration of historical dollar cost.[5]

"Original cost," as the expression is used in this convention, means the *number* of dollars originally expended to acquire the asset and make it usable. It may require twice as many dollars in 1971 to construct a factory as would have been needed for the same purpose in 1946. Nevertheless, the "cost" of a plant built in 1946 is the number of dollars spent for the purpose in 1946, and this amount is the "cost value" of the plant (less accumulated depreciation) in a December 31, 1971 balance sheet.

These conventions have been developed over many years. They have proved their usefulness for many purposes and are defended strongly on the grounds that such "values" are "objectively determined." Opponents of price-level adjustments attack them on a number of grounds, including those described by the Committee on Concepts and Standards of the American Accounting Association in *Supplementary Statement No. 2*[6] (these objections do not reflect the opinions of the members of the Committee as the statement recommended supplementary statements adjusted for price-level change):

Conventional treatment is deep-rooted in practice, in law, and in general understanding; . . . the significance of the problem is exaggerated; . . . the

---

[4] Some companies, other than public utilities, follow a policy of charging to maintenance cost as much of the property additions and improvements as practicable. Others credit to accumulated depreciation, charges large enough to fully depreciate assets still retained in use. The result is to produce net plant values below their "depreciated original cost." On federal income tax returns "accelerated" depreciation is allowed. If these charges against taxable net income are similarly charged on the books (which they need not be), a similar understatement of the "value" of the depreciable asset results. Adjusting for price level changes will not compensate for the undervalue of the base figure.

[5] Committee on Accounting Procedure, AICPA, *Accounting Research Bulletin No. 43* (1953), p. 67, in *Accounting Research and Terminology Bulletins, Final Edition* (New York, 1961); also see, p. 73.

[6] *Accounting Review*, October 1951, pp. 468–74; *Journal of Accounting*, October, 1951, pp. 461–65.

variations in the value of money are compensated for in part by other factors; . . . any change in practice not supported by general demand will result in irregularity of application and in confusion.

Twenty years later these reasons are still among the major objections urged by opponents and new objections have been added, including: the problem is of minor importance and needs no solution; a problem exists, but accounting cannot solve it, and anyway the proposed procedures violate the "principles" of accounting; the proposed procedures have not been perfected, and action must wait until they are; price-level adjustments are not allowed for federal income tax purposes and should not be introduced into published reports until they are; in fact, if price-level adjustments are made in published statements this will lead Congress to introduce inequities into the federal income tax; there will be a problem when prices fall; and finally, accountants should not admit that unadjusted statements, on which they have issued certificates, were erroneous.

So are you surprised that it was 18 years after the issuance of Supplementary Statement No. 2 that an official body of the AICPA, the Accounting Principles Board, issued a similar recommendation in *Statement No. 3*?[7]

---

[7] In fairness to the AICPA and its committees and staff, two developments prior to 1969 should be recognized here.

In 1953 the Committee on Accounting Procedure, forerunner of the Accounting Principles Board, issued *Research Bulletin No. 43*, "Depreciation and High Costs." In this bulletin it discussed the problem created by inflation:

"The committee recognizes that the common forms of financial statements may permit misunderstanding as to the amount which a corporation has available for distribution in the form of dividends, higher wages, or lower prices. . . . Stockholders, employees, and the general public should be informed that a business must be able to retain out of profits amounts sufficient to replace productive facilities at current prices. . . . The committee therefore gives its full support to the use of supplementary financial schedules, explanations or footnotes by which management may explain the need for retention of earnings."

Six (out of twenty) members of the committee dissented, saying that the opinion did not go far enough—it should have revised the computation of net income.

In 1963 there appeared *Accounting Research Study No. 6*, "Reporting the Financial Effects of Price-Level Changes," a 278-page paperbound volume, "by the Staff of the Accounting Research Division" of the AICPA. As is customary in American Institute Accounting Research Studies, a note stated that "publication by the American Institute of CPAs does not in any way constitute official endorsement or approval. . . ." The study concluded that "financial data adjusted for price-level effects provide a basis for a more intelligent, better informed allocation of resources, whether those resources are in the hands of individuals, of business entities, or of government."

Chapter 4 discussed in detail the objections to price-level adjustments, summarized above, and concluded in each case that the objection has less validity than the advantages which would accrue. The study also discussed "the problem in perspective," various approaches to the adjustment process, price-level adjustments and generally accepted accounting principles, the index number problem, examples of

Statement No. 3 has this to say about the value of price-level adjusted financial statements:

6. Changes in the general purchasing power of money have an impact on almost every aspect of economic affairs, including such diverse matters as investment, wage negotiation, pricing policy, international trade, and government fiscal policy. The effects of changes in the general purchasing power of money on economic data expressed in monetary terms are widely recognized, and economic data for the economy as a whole are commonly restated to eliminate these effects. General price-level financial statements should prove useful to investors, creditors, management, employees, government officials, and others who are concerned with the economic affairs of business enterprises.

24. Economic data are commonly restated to eliminate the effects of changes in the general purchasing power of money. In the President's Economic Reports, National Income data of the United States, for example, have been restated in "constant" 1947–1949 dollars and "constant" 1954 dollars and are now expressed in "constant" 1958 dollars. The restatement procedures necessary for preparing general price-level financial statements are similar to those employed in restating other economic data. Some companies now use general price-level statements to report on their operations in countries in which the currency has suffered severe loss of general purchasing power.[8]

Although general price levels can and have moved both up and down, inflation has been the general rule throughout the world for the last 30 years. Some countries have experienced slowly rising prices while others have experienced rapidly rising prices. The rise in the general price level in the United States, as measured by the GNP Deflator, was approximately 22% during the period 1958–1968 or a compound annual rate of 2% in contrast to approximately 130% in the preceding 20 years or a compound annual rate of about 4%. Price indexes in Brazil rose about 3,000% from 1958 to 1966. Inflation in China, Greece, and Hungary just before and after World War II was even more spectacular. General price-level increases of 25% to 50% per year have occurred recently in several countries.

Recommendations

25. The Board believes that general price-level financial statements or pertinent information extracted from them present useful information not available from basic historical-dollar financial statements. General price-level information may be presented in addition to the basic historical-dollar financial statements, but general price-level financial statements should not be presented as the basic statements. The Board believes that general price-level information

---

what companies around the world had done in reporting the effects of price-level changes, and selected studies from the literature (including this one).

Prior to this current edition, the volume you are studying contained adjusted financial statements of the Caterpillar Tractor Company, demonstrating the dramatic effects of 20 years of inflation. In this edition the financial statements from *Statement No. 3* have been reproduced instead.

[8] This footnote is quoted from the text of *Statement No. 3*, p. 6:

is not required at this time for fair presentation of financial position and results of operations in conformity with generally accepted accounting principles in the United States.

26. The Board recognizes that the degree of inflation or deflation in an economy may become so great that conventional statements lose much of their significance and general price-level statements clearly become more meaningful, and that some countries have experienced this degree of inflation in recent years. The Board concludes that general price-level statements reported in the local currency of those countries are in that respect in conformity with accounting principles generally accepted in the United States, and that they preferably should be presented as the basic foreign currency financial statements of companies operating in those countries when the statements are intended for readers in the United States.

Outside of the United States, in countries where the currency has deteriorated at dramatic rates and conventional statements have become misleading, statements fully adjusted for price-level change have been issued. But where inflation has been of minor consequence, as in the United States, only a few concerns have introduced price-level adjusted information into their annual reports, and then on a fragmentary basis. For example, the Eastman Kodak Company showed in its annual report, in graph form, a 10-year comparison of sales "in constant dollars." The Hercules Powder Company, in the "General Statistics" section of its annual report, showed three items "in dollars of constant value": research expenditures, fixed assets, and net income. The Ayrshire Collieries showed depreciation in its primary financial statements on a price-level adjusted basis. The Reece Corporation prepares fully adjusted statements for internal use and included in its annual report a special section showing chart-form comparisons of various items in both "historical dollars" and "uniform dollars": gross income, net income, income taxes and change in invested capital.

Utilities have reason to be interested in price-level adjustment procedures because of implications relating to their rate bases and their depreciation expenses. Many have made price-level adjustment computations in connection with reports to regulatory commissions. Among those which have done so in published financial reports are the Iowa-Illinois Gas and Electric Company, which adjusted depreciation only (up 18 percent), and the Indiana Telephone Corporation, which adjusted telephone plant (up 25 percent), accumulated depreciation (up 33 percent), and depreciation expense (up 30 percent).

Statement No. 3 has this to say about "proper" and "improper" methods of measuring the effects of price level changes on financial data (page 7).

16. *Determining Combined Effects.* The effects of general price-level changes on a business enterprise and its financial statements therefore cannot

be approximated by a simple adjustment. If users attempt to adjust for general price-level changes on an uninformed basis, they are likely to draw misleading inferences. The effects of general price-level changes can only be determined by comprehensive restatement of the items which comprise its financial statements. The need for comprehensive restatement was illustrated by a field test of general price-level restatement procedures.[9] For many companies in the test, net income was a smaller numerical amount on the general price-level basis than on the historical-dollar basis for the same period; for other companies it was a larger amount. The percentage differences between the amounts of net income for each company on the two bases varied widely, even with the relatively mild inflation in the United States in recent years.

In the opinion of the authors of this volume, it is not likely that there will be any significant shift toward the use by U.S. concerns of comprehensive price-level adjustment procedures in annual reports unless and until either prices begin to rise again at a more accelerated rate or price-level adjustments are permitted for federal income tax purposes. It is not likely that the latter development will occur until and unless taxpayers use price-level adjustments in their published reports.

Even in countries which have suffered extreme inflation, such as France and Germany (see twin articles in the *Accounting Review*, April, 1963, pp. 377–88), and where revaluations were made for both statement and tax purposes under the control of government decrees, there has been a strong tendency to return to historical costs, dated of course from the official restatements.

The work of the analyst requires that he concern himself with the current status of the business. To do so, he must use current facts. If prevailing practice appears to be deficient in supplying these facts, he must secure them as best he can. If published statements bring together noncomparable figures, such as sales at year-10 prices and depreciation at year-1 prices, he must try to eliminate inconsistencies and restore comparability for purposes of his evaluation.

The significance of price-level changes

The major distortion on published statements stems from inventories and fixed asset accounts and the charges relating to these items. By expressing these assets in terms of dollars paid at different dates in the past, the balance sheet fails to provide any indication of their current value to the firm. Similarly, by stating cost of goods sold and depreciation in terms of past dollars, the income statement is distorted; current revenue is not matched with the current cost of earning it.

---

[9] See Paul Rosenfield, "Accounting for Inflation—A Field Test," *The Journal of Accountancy*, June 1969, pp. 45 to 50.

An indication of the seriousness of the distortion is revealed by such published comments as the following:

The reported net income of 30 oil companies was $763 millions in 1946 and $1219 millions in 1947, an increase of . . . 60 percent. . . . But the charges for capital extinguishments (depreciation, depletion, etc.) . . . were inadequate to replace . . . this capital. . . . The extent to which reported "profits" were thus in effect overstated can be approximately determined by adjusting the capital extinguishment charges, which are expressed in historical dollars, so that they reflect current dollars. . . . If this is done we find that the adjusted net income becomes $418 millions in 1946 and $513 millions in 1947, an increase of 23 percent. . . . It thus becomes apparent that the changing value of the dollar distorts the income account so that the reported net income ceases to be synonymous with profit.[10]

Again:

While our profits are not appreciably inflated by inventory evaluations, they are overstated because no special depreciation reserve has been set up. . . . Our depreciation allowances are based on original cost. Therefore our accounting profit does not give now, as it did before the war, a measure of the funds available for increased capacity and for dividends. Before we can even consider dividends or expansion today, a large portion of our accounting profit must be used for replacement of crude oil reserves and for replacement of worn-out and obsolete equipment.[11]

Professor Sumner Slichter, testifying before a Joint Congressional Committee, stated that during the three years 1946–48 American corporations overstated profits by $16.4 billion.[12] For the period 1946–50, the Machinery and Allied Products Institute estimated that corporate profits were overstated by $27 billion.[13]

It has been assumed by some that during periods of relatively small increases in the price level, even though steady, the effect on published statements would be negligible. This depends on both the amount of price-level change and the characteristics of the particular concern.[14]

---

[10] Joseph E. Pogue, Vice-President, Chase National Bank, quoted in Machinery and Allied Products Institute, *Bulletin No. 2138*, January 21, 1949.

[11] Eugene Holman, President, Standard Oil Company (New Jersey), quoted in Machinery and Allied Products Institute, *Bulletin No. 2138*.

[12] U.S. Congress, Joint Committee on the Economic Report, Subcommittee on Profits, 80th Cong., 2d Sess., *Corporate Profits* (Washington, D.C.: Government Printing Office, 1949), p. 3.

[13] Machinery and Allied Products Institute, *MAPI Accounting Manual* (Chicago, 1952), pp. 1003–4.

[14] A comprehensive study of the effect of price-level changes on the statements of the Caterpillar Tractor Company, 1941–60, will be found in Chapter 22 of prior editions of this volume.

A number of other analyses of the effect of price-level changes on the published reports of large concerns have been published: Westinghouse Electric, General

The Reece Corporation stated (in its 1961 annual report) that in the five-year period from 1956 to 1961 the increase in the price level was "only" about 10 percent, yet net worth, which increased about 35 percent under conventional accounting methods, went up only 25 percent on a price-level adjusted basis.[15]

The Indiana Telephone Company showed a 1961 net income on a price-level accounting basis of $320 thousand, compared with $475 thousand using conventional accounting.[16]

Firms which confined their adjustments to depreciation (Ayrshire Collieries Corporation, Iowa-Illinois Gas and Electric Company, and Sacramento Municipal Utility District) reported for various recent years in which inflation has been moderate that adjusting depreciation reduced net income by 7 percent to 14 percent.[17]

A study of the Cummins Engine Company reported that from 1953–62 the aggregate earnings of the company ($58 million) were overstated by $4 million (about 7 percent). The study stated that the disparity would have been greater had not Cummins Engine's financial strength enabled it to carry large amounts of long-term debt on which a substantial gain on fixed-dollar items was calculated.[18]

Recomputation of the depreciation of the Caterpillar Tractor Company for the year 1960 increased depreciation expense by 14 percent using the cost of construction index; by 6 percent using the wholesale price index. The distortion was partially offset by a gain on fixed-dollar items, and the use of Lifo inventory procedures presumably accomplished a substantial correction of cost of goods sold. It does not appear to the authors that the fact that an error is offset by another error

---

Electric, and the Radio Corporation of America in the *Accounting Review*, April 1951; Armstrong Cork in the *Accounting Review*, January 1953; Nine U.S. steel companies in the *Journal of Accountancy*, January 1949; three English steel companies in *Accountancy*, May and June 1959; a group of utilities in the *Accounting Review*, April 1956; a department store in the *Journal of Accountancy*, April 1954, and the *Accounting Review*, April 1955; a machinery manufacturer in the *Accounting Review*, April 1954; and a farm equipment corporation in the *Accounting Review*, July 1953. In 1955 the American Accounting Association published in monograph form the results of a study of four companies (Armstrong Cork, New York Telephone, Reece Corporation, and Sargent & Company); Jones, *Price Level Changes and Financial Statements—Case Studies of Four Companies;* and in 1961 the Washington State University Press published Hendriksen, *Price Level Adjustments of Financial Statements*, in which the statements of two utilities were adjusted using six different alternative indexes. A subsequent study is by the Institute of Chartered Accountants in England and Wales—Research Committee, Accounting for Stewardship in a Period of Inflation, 1968.

See also *Accounting Research Study No. 6*, Appendix D, pp. 169–218, and Appendix E, pp. 221–49.

[15] These data are from *Research Study No. 6*.

[16] Ibid.

[17] Ibid.

[18] *The Accounting Review*, January 1965, pp. 144–53.

justifies ignoring the inherent question of principle, or that a coincidental offset in one year necessarily will be duplicated in another.

The effect of price-level changes on fixed assets

The amounts by which the various financial statement items are affected by changes in the value of the dollar depend on (1) the amount of change in prices since the item was acquired and (2) the relative size, in dollars, of the items affected.

The first factor involves the velocity of turnover, i.e., the length of time that the item is on hand. Of all the assets of a firm, the fixed assets (plant and equipment) ordinarily have the lowest rates of turnover. It is not unusual to find a plant in use more than 25 years after its purchase. The adjustment to state this balance sheet value[19] and its related depreciation charge in terms of current dollars must take into account the entire price change during the past 25 years. Even with cyclical price fluctuations, the adjustment is likely to be significant because of the long-term upward trend in prices that has been experienced in this country.

The relatively large size, in dollars, of fixed assets and depreciation charges is a second reason why price-level adjustments of these accounts

---

[19] If prices have been rising since the date of acquisition of a fixed asset, this adjustment would of course be a "write-up." While increases in the stated balance sheet amounts of fixed assets (the result being a stated balance sheet "value" substantially above original dollar cost in dollars of the year of acquisition) are by no means unknown, the American certified public accountant manifests a deep-seated distrust and opposition to such a move. An interesting example of this attitude on the part of a leading firm of certified public accountants who have been prominent champions of the price-level adjustment of depreciation expense is contained in the following quotation:

"From a theoretical standpoint, it might be argued that if depreciation charges are increased to reflect the rise in the price level, then it would be logical to record an upward restatement of the related assets to reflect the price-level increase. Some accountants advocate such a restatement. Others say that such a restatement should not be made until the higher price level is stabilized. (In our type of economy it is doubtful that price levels will ever be stabilized.)

"Some accountants contend that upward restatements of assets, particularly those resulting from price level changes, should not require the freezing of earned surplus. However, the position of our Firm is that it would not be desirable at present to record an upward restatement of assets without following quasi-reorganization procedures, including stockholder approval and the freezing of earned surplus." A *Memorandum on Price Level Depreciation* published by Arthur Andersen & Co. in 1959, pp. 11–12: however, this firm has been strongly advocating that the accounting profession adopt price-level accounting in all respects; if and when this is done, then the price-level changes should be applied to all affected items in the financial statements, and quasi-reorganization procedures would be unnecessary—letter from the Managing Partner dated January 18, 1962.) (With regard to the thinking of the accounting profession on quasi-reorganizations, the freezing and dating of surplus, and appropriate formal disclosure, see AICPA, *Accounting Research Bulletin No. 43*, p. 45.)

frequently will be large. Although the dollar amounts of fixed assets held by any firm are somewhat dependent upon the type of business operation, it is not uncommon to 'find that in a manufacturing business such assets represent a major portion of total assets. In a study by the Machinery and Allied Products Institute, investment in plant in the typical manufacturing firm is about one half of the gross revenue, and depreciation rates average 4 percent per annum. On this basis, depreciation charges are typically 2 percent of gross revenue.[20]

Effect of price changes on inventories

Although the velocity of turnover of inventories is much more rapid than the velocity of turnover of fixed assets, the price-level adjustments required may be significant in relation to net income. This is particularly true for firms operating with a low gross margin. The exact amount of adjustment required will depend upon the inventory valuation method.

Although there is a variety of valuation methods, those most commonly used are the first-in, first-out method; the average-cost method; and the last-in, first-out method. To exemplify the effects of rising pices under these methods, the following simplified circumstances are assumed. A merchant sells one item of merchandise per year and carries in inventory one additional item, so that before each sale there are two items in inventory and after each sale there is only one item, which is supplemented by an immediate purchase of a second. Suppose that during a 10-year period the price level rose 100 percent.

In addition to one item bought for inventory in year 1 at a cost of $11, the merchant made purchases and sales as follows:

	One item	
Year	Purchases	Sales
2.	$ 12.00	$ 15.00
3.	13.00	16.25
4.	14.00	17.50
5.	15.00	18.75
6.	16.00	20.00
7.	17.00	21.25
8.	18.00	22.50
9.	19.00	23.75
10.	20.00	25.00
11.	21.00	26.25
	$165.00	$206.25

---

[20] *MAPI Accounting Manual.* See also Graham, "Depreciation and Capital Replacement in an Inflationary Economy," *Accounting Review,* July 1959, pp. 367–75.

Under the first-in, first-out assumption the merchant sold the $11 item in year 2, the $12 item in year 3, and so on, until he sold the $20 item in year 11 and showed an inventory on the last day of year 11 of $21.

Under the last-in, first-out assumption the merchant sold the $12 item in year 2, the $13 item in year 3, and so on, until he sold the $21 item in year 11 and showed an inventory on the last day of year 11 of $11. A tabular comparison of these two methods is given below:

Year	Gross margin		December 31 inventory	
	Fifo	Lifo	Fifo	Lifo
2	$ 4.00	$ 3.00	$12.00	$11.00
3	4.25	3.25	13.00	11.00
4	4.50	3.50	14.00	11.00
5	4.75	3.75	15.00	11.00
6	5.00	4.00	16.00	11.00
7	5.25	4.25	17.00	11.00
8	5.50	4.50	18.00	11.00
9	5.75	4.75	19.00	11.00
10	6.00	5.00	20.00	11.00
11	6.25	5.25	21.00	11.00
Total Margin (10 years)	$51.25	$41.25		
Fifo margin higher by	$10.00			
Fifo inventory higher by			$10.00	

The effect on working capital can be made clear by the following calculation:

Received on sales (cash and receivables). $206.25
Paid out for subsequent inventory items 165.00
Working capital produced by sales . . . . $ 41.25

Accounting results of Fifo and Lifo are compared below:

	Margin	Inventory
Fifo	$51.25	$21.00
Lifo	41.25	11.00

These amounts demonstrate that in their "pure" forms, Fifo and Lifo will produce the following results during a period of steadily rising prices:

1. The per unit "value" of a Fifo inventory rises as replacement costs increase; the per unit "value" of a Lifo inventory remains constant to the end of the 10-year period and on the final balance sheet

(in the example above), the Lifo inventory is stated at year-1 cost ($11), which is $10 less than current replacement cost.

2. The 10-year gross margin under the Fifo approach (in the example above) is $10 greater than the funds produced for working capital, other than inventory. Of the gross margin of $51.25 reported under the Fifo method, $10 is required to replace the inventory (at $21); and only $41.25 is available for operating expenses, dividends, and other purposes. Under the Lifo approach, gross margin is reported as $41.25, which agrees with the funds available for dividends and other purposes.

There are various forms of the average-cost method which give different results. In general, however, all variants of average costing should be expected to yield margin and inventory results which fall between those produced by the Fifo and Lifo approaches. It is not deemed necessary to demonstrate that fact here.

Fifo and Lifo are not standardized in practice. The last three decades, have seen the development of an unusual variety of inventory methods, all called "last-in, first-out" by the companies that use them. Of the large U.S. corporations surveyed in the AICPA's *Accounting Trends and Techniques*, only about one in five uses Lifo, and the number is slowly declining.

During a period of rising prices, cost of goods sold and depreciation (also depletion for companies in the extractive industries) are the two major distorting elements in the computation of net income under prevailing accounting conventions and methods. In some companies, where Fifo is in use and the Plant account is relatively small, cost of goods sold is the major distorting factor. In other companies, with relatively large Plant accounts and small inventories (or inventories "valued" under Lifo procedures), depreciation is the principal cost requiring evaluation and adjustment.

In a period of falling prices, depreciation tends to be excessive. Owing to the widespread use of the lower of cost or market, inventory losses tend to remain in line.

Gains or losses on "monetary" (fixed dollar) items

The purpose of the adjustments suggested for inventories and fixed assets and their related charges is to restate the values in comparable units of measure. Such adjustments do not reflect the entire effect of changes in price level upon the financial status of the firm. The extent to which a business has gained, lost, or maintained its financial position in the face of changes in the price level should be determined.

To examine additional aspects of the problem, assume that Arthur

Jones has twin sons, John and James. Upon attaining the age of twenty one, each son is given $1,000 in cash. John immediately invests his money in a piece of land, and James puts his funds in a checking account. Ten years later, the price level has doubled. If neither son has derived any income from his gift, the balance sheets of the two sons would appear as follows, *after adjustment for price-level change:*

JOHN
Balance Sheet

| Land. . . . . | $2,000 | Capital . . . . | $2,000 |

JAMES
Balance Sheet

Cash	$1,000	Capital	$2,000
		Loss in purchasing power.	1,000
			$1,000

Since there was no income, and since none of the assets was consumed, the adjustments previously described relating to charges against income have no application. The difference in these two adjusted statements stems from the types of assets held. One son held land, the value of which in dollars is dependent upon the general level of prices. The other son's assets consisted entirely of cash, the value of which in dollars is fixed at all price levels.

Land shown on John's balance sheet was adjusted upward to reflect the current value of the dollars invested in this asset. Similarly, the Capital account was adjusted to reflect the current dollar value of John's contribution to the "enterprise." John has neither gained nor lost any purchasing power. If the land has maintained its "real" value, it can be exchanged for the same goods and services that could have been purchased for $1,000 10 years ago.

But James is in a different position. The value of his asset, cash, is fixed in terms of dollars. A change in the price level increases or decreases the purchasing power of this asset. Because of this characteristic, no adjustment is made to cash on the adjusted statement. Other assets and most liabilities possess this same characteristic in that they call for receipt or payment of a fixed number of dollars regardless of the price level.

James's Capital account, however, is not unlike that of John's. It must be adjusted to $2,000 in order to state the original investment in terms of current dollars. The apparent imbalance created by such an adjustment (cash of $1,000 versus capital of $2,000) represents the loss in purchasing power that has resulted from holding cash while the price level has doubled. In terms of current dollars, the cash on hand will purchase $1,000 less goods and services that it would have purchased 10 years ago. This is a real loss to James and could be reflected in the adjusted capital thus:

Original investment (in terms of current dollars) $2,000
Loss on "monetary" items (in terms of current dollars)*. . . . .   (1,000)
    Total Capital (in terms of current dollars). $1,000

> * The terms "monetary" and "nonmonetary" are used in The Accounting Principles Board's *Statement No. 3*, and these terms will be used hereafter in this volume. A monetary asset is one the value of which is fixed in dollars.

Losses of this type will occur if as prices rise, a firm holds more monetary assets than monetary liabilities. Conversely, gains will occur if as prices rise, a firm holds more monetary liabilities than monetary assets. In recent years, public utilities have frequently benefited in this way. Conversely, if prices fall, losses will accompany net monetary liabilities; and gains will result from net monetary assets.

These gains or losses are real gains or losses to the firms. Whether or not they are shown on the income statement or statement of capital changes, they should be considered by the analyst. Although these gains or losses are difficult to predict and perhaps do not influence projections of earning power, they are important in an overall consideration of the financial position of a business.

To summarize the various counteracting and accentuating effects of price-level changes upon the various segments of the financial statements, consider one more example. Suppose that Roland Moon, Incorporated, was created by the issuance of one thousand shares of stock in exchange for a $100,000 apartment building. During the first year the company collects rent of $8,000 and pays no expenses. The only expense is depreciation of $2,500. The price level increases at a constant rate throughout the year and has tripled by the end of the year. Since the rent is received monthly, assume that all cash is received at the average price level for the year. The unadjusted and adjusted statements appear below:

ROLAND MOON, INCORPORATED
Balance Sheet
At the End of Year 1

Assets			Owners' Equity		
	Unadjusted	Adjusted*		Unadjusted	Adjusted
Cash	$ 8,000	$ 8,000	Capital stock	$100,000	$300,00
Building	100,000	300,000	Surplus: Net income	5,500	4,50
Accumulated depreciation	(2,500)	(7,500)	Losses on fixed-dollar items.		(4,00
Total Assets	$105,500	$300,500	Total Owners' Equity.	$105,500	$300,50

> * Adjusted to the price level at balance sheet date.

ROLAND MOON, INCORPORATED
Income Statement
For the Year 1

	Unadjusted	Adjusted*
Income	$8,000	$12,000
Depreciation	2,500	7,500
Net Income	$5,500	$ 4,500

* Adjusted for the average price level during the year to the price level at the end of the year.

On the adjusted statements, building, accumulated depreciation, capital stock, and the depreciation charge were all increased threefold to restate them from beginning-of-the-year to year-end dollars. Cash required no adjustment, since it is a monetary item. Income was increased by 50 percent to adjust it from average to year-end dollars. The losses of fixed-dollar items resulted from acquiring cash at the average price level and holding it while the price level increased to the year-end level.

A comparison of the unadjusted and adjusted statements reveals the following (the price level is rising):

1. If depreciation is large in relation to income, net income is reduced by price-level adjustments.
2. The ratio of net income to gross income is less if based upon the adjusted rather than the unadjusted statements.
3. Losses in purchasing power result from holding a net monetary asset balance.
4. The surplus available for distribution is less if adjustments for price-level changes are made.
5. The adjusted book value of the stock is greater than the unadjusted book value, even though surplus is reduced by adjustments to net income and by the losses on monetary items.
6. The rate of return on investment is much lower if based upon the adjusted rather than the unadjusted statements. This results from two factors: an upward adjustment to investment and a downward adjustment to net income.

This example points out some of the differences that typically may exist between unadjusted and adjusted statements if prices are rising. However, this example by no means is intended to be used to estimate the adjustments applicable in a particular case. In each instance the adjustments are dependent upon the financial characteristics of the firm and the amount of change in the price level. The methods to be employed in determining appropriate adjustments will be discussed in the chapters to follow.

The index number problem

In the discussion up to this point, reported data have been converted to a current price basis in two different ways: either by application of a general price index or by ascertainment of replacement costs. Specific indexes, which purport to measure the change in price of specific items or groups of specific items, are a rough substitute for the replacement-cost approach. These two methods are capable of producing dissimilar results. For example, in the drug-manufacturing business, the costs and selling prices of drugs have risen much less than have most other prices. Therefore, if an index of general prices is applied to the cost of goods sold of a drug-manufacturing concern, a much larger adjustment will result than if specific replacement costs are employed.

Plant assets might be adjusted by applying an index of the cost of constructing plants; construction indexes show a greater increase than does, for example, an index of consumer prices. Agricultural products in inventory might be adjusted by applying an index of agricultural prices. There is also the possibility that almost any number of specific indexes might be constructed, using available evidence as to the current replacement costs of the particular items being adjusted.

Although prices generally move together in times of inflation, they do not maintain fixed relationships. The value of the dollar declines in an inflationary period, but the measurement of the amount of the decline is a formidable theoretical problem.

Some accountants, economists, and others maintain that there is no such thing as *the* dollar; there are many dollars, one for each asset being valued. These persons maintain that adjustment for changes in the value of the dollar should be made by applying specific indexes.[21]

For the financial statement analyst the answer would seem to be that both types of adjustments are of value to him. By adjusting with a general price index, he obtains results that will demonstrate whether the resources of the concern have been maintaining their purchasing power and therefore whether the stockholders' equity has maintained its position, lost ground, or gained ground in the face of changing price levels. The use of specific indexes will enable him to evaluate the book figures in comparison with approximate current prices appropriate to the particular asset being analyzed.

The Accounting Principles Board's *Statement No. 3* is concerned with general-purpose financial statements issued to the public as supplements to basic (conventional) financial statements. For this purpose the APB states that

---

[21] For a detailed discussion of the index number problem, see *Accounting Research Study No. 6*, Appendix A.

29. *An index of the general price level, not an index of the price of a specific type of goods or services, should be used to prepare general price-level financial statements.* Price indexes vary widely in their scope; some measure changes in the prices of a relatively limited group of goods and services, such as construction costs or retail food prices in a specific city, while others measure changes in the prices of a broad group of goods and services in a whole economy. The purpose of the general price-level restatement procedures is to restate historical-dollar financial statements for changes in the general purchasing power of the dollar, and this purpose can only be accomplished by using a general price-level index.

30. Indexes which approximate changes in the general price level are now available for most countries, . . . the GNP Deflator is the most comprehensive indicator of the general price level in the United States. Consequently, it should normally be used to prepare general price-level statements in U.S. dollars.

31. The GNP Deflator is issued on a quarterly basis. The deflator for the last quarter of a year can ordinarily be used to approximate the index as of the end of the year. The Bureau of Labor Statistics Consumer Price Index has the practical advantage of being issued on a monthly basis. The consumer price index may therefore be used to approximate the GNP Deflator unless the two indexes deviate significantly.

QUESTIONS AND PROBLEMS

17–1. This chapter states that "the problem created by the instability of the dollar is twofold." The two points then made are concerned with (a) comparability and (b) purchasing power. Discuss these propositions with financial statement examples which differ from those offered in the book.

17–2. Cameron White invested $750 in U.S. savings bonds in 1958. These bonds, which did not pay interest currently, matured in 1968; and White received $1,000. Using the data on the behavior of the Gross National Product Implicit Price Deflator (Chapter 21, Appendix A), calculate the increase or decrease in purchasing power which resulted from this investment.

17–3. Discuss the following statement from ARB No. 33: ". . . accounting and financial reporting for general use will best serve their purposes by adhering to the generally accepted concept of depreciation on cost. . . ."

Is analysis of financial statements a "general use" as the term was used in this quotation?

17–4. As to the "realization convention"—
   a) Describe it.
   b) Compare it with "the lower of cost or market."
   c) Discuss the change in reported net income which would result from the abandonment of the realization convention.

17–5. If a manufacturer adopted the last-in, first-out approach to inventory valuation in 1960 and his replacement costs approximately doubled by 1970—

  a) Compare total inventory in dollars at December 31, 1970 with what it would have been had he used the first-in, first-out assumption.

  b) Describe effect on reported net income.

  c) Describe effect on net working capital and current ratio.

  d) Compare the results of average costing with Fifo and Lifo.

17–6. Describe the "going-concern" convention.

17–7. If you were a director of a company charged with the responsibility for declaring dividends, what would you think about in a period of rising prices?

17–8. In a period of rising prices, why does the first-in, first-out approach to inventory valuation result in reported gross margin figures which are in excess of the funds made available for other purposes?

17–9. Why is it that in a period of rising prices, depreciation tends to be inadequate?

17–10. "The income statement is founded on a matching of costs and revenues." Discuss current income statement practice in terms of the impact of rising prices on the matching of costs and revenues.

17–11. A public utility corporation issued $1,000,000 of bonds in 1948. In 1968 it paid them off.

  a) Has the corporation had a gain or suffered a loss? If so, how much?

  b) If so, is the gain or loss "realized"?

  c) Do the financial statements now being published reflect such gains and losses?

  (Index numbers to use in working this problem will be found in Chapter 21, Appendix A.

17–12. Enumerate the items customarily found on corporate balance sheets which, being fixed-dollar ("Monetary") items, give rise to gains and losses due to changes in the level of prices.

17–13. Discuss the pros and cons of general price indexes versus special purpose indexes.

17–14. In this chapter may be found two types of "profit" resulting from price changes: real but unrealized profits and unreal profits. Describe a situation which would give rise to both of these "profits" (or losses).

17–15. Congress has legalized, for federal income tax purposes, various depreciation methods which permit larger depreciation deductions in the early years of useful life and diminishing deductions in later years. The total deduction is limited to original dollar cost. Discuss the effectiveness of this approach in dealing with the price-level problem.

18

Ground rules for general price-level statements

The Accounting Principles Board's *Statement No. 3* presents a set of financial statements adjusted for changes in the price level (see page 451ff). Before doing so it states the "ground rules" on which the adjustments are based.[1]

28. *The same accounting principles used in preparing historical-dollar financial statements should be used in preparing general price-level financial statements except that changes in the general purchasing power of the dollar are recognized in general price-level financial statements.* General price-level financial statements are an extension of and not a departure from the "historical cost" basis of accounting. Many amounts in general price-level statements, however, are different from amounts in the historical-dollar statements because of the effects of changing the unit of measure.[2]

The cost principle on which historical-dollar statements are based is also the basis of general price-level statements. In general, amounts shown at historical cost in historical-dollar statements are shown at historical cost restated for changes in the general purchasing power of the dollar in general price-level statements. The amount may be restated, but it still represents cost and not a current value. The process of restating historical costs in terms of a specified amount of general purchasing power does not introduce any factors other than general price-level changes. The amounts shown in general price-level financial statements are not intended to represent appraisal values, replacement costs, or any other measure of current value.

---

[1] The "ground rules" concerning the index numbers to be used will be found on page 445.

[2] This paragraph and the balance of the text material in this chapter are quoted from the text of *Statement No. 3*, p. 3ff.

32. *General price-level financial statements should be presented in terms of the general purchasing power of the dollar at the latest balance sheet date.* The Board has selected current general purchasing power as the basis for presentation because it believes that financial statements in "current dollars" are more relevant and more earily understood than those employing the general purchasing power of any other period. Current economic actions must take place in terms of current dollars, and restating items in current dollars expresses them in the context of current action.

33. *Monetary and nonmonetary items should be distinguished for the purpose of preparing general price-level financial statements.* Monetary items are stated in terms of current general purchasing power in historical-dollar statements. General price-level gains and losses arise from holding monetary items. On the other hand, nonmonetary items are generally stated in terms of the general purchasing power of the dollar at the time they were acquired. Holding nonmonetary items does not give rise to general price-level gains and losses. Distinguishing monetary and nonmonetary items therefore permits (1) restatement of nonmonetary items in terms of current general purchasing power and (2) recognition of general price-level gains and losses on monetary items which are not recognized under historical-dollar accounting.

34. Assets and liabilities that have both monetary and nonmonetary characteristics should be classified as monetary or nonmonetary based on the purpose for which they are held, usually evidenced by their treatment in historical-dollar accounting. Thus, carrying debentures at acquisition cost (perhaps adjusted to lower of cost and market) and classifying them as marketable securities provides evidence that market price may be important and the debentures may be nonmonetary. On the other hand, classifying debentures held as a long-term investment and amortizing premium or discount is evidence that the debentures are held for the fixed principal and interest and therefore are monetary assets. Similarly, convertible debt is usually treated as straight debt and therefore is usually a monetary liability.

35. *The amounts of nonmonetary items should be restated to dollars of current general purchasing power at the end of the period.* Nonmonetary items are typically stated in historical-dollar financial statements in terms of the general purchasing power of the dollar at the dates of the originating transactions. They should be restated by means of the general price index to dollars of current general purchasing power at the end of the period. Restatement of nonmonetary items does not introduce current values of replacement costs. For example, restatement of the cost of land that cost $100,000 in 1958 to $123,500 in 1968 statements does not imply that the market price of the land is $123,500 in 1968. Restatement merely presents the *cost* in a unit which represents the general purchasing power of the dollar at the end of 1968.

36. Nonmonetary items are sometimes already stated in historical-dollar financial statements in dollars of current general purchasing power, for example, inventory purchased near the end of the fiscal period or assets carried at current market price. The fact that the amount of an item is not changed in restatement does not necessarily identify it as a monetary item on which general price-level gains and losses should be computed.

37. Some nonmonetary items such as inventories are stated at the lower of cost and market in historical-dollar financial statements. These items should also be stated at the lower of cost and market in general price-level financial statements. Market may sometimes be below restated cost even though it is not below historical-dollar cost, and application of the cost or market rule will therefore sometimes result in a write-down to market in general price-level statements even though no write-down was required in the historical-dollar statements.

38. *Monetary assets and liabilities in the historical-dollar balance sheet are stated in dollars of current general purchasing power; consequently, they should appear in current general price-level statements at the same amounts.* The fact that the amounts of monetary assets and liabilities are the same in general price-level and historical-dollar statements should not obscure the fact that general price-level gains and losses result from holding them during a period of general price-level change. . . . Monetary assets and liabilities which appear in financial statements of prior periods presented for comparative purposes are updated to dollars of current general purchasing power by the "roll-forward" procedure described in paragraph 44.

39. *The amounts of income statement items should be restated to dollars of current general purchasing power at the end of the period.* Revenue and expenses are typically stated in historical-dollar statements in terms of the general purchasing power of the dollar at the date of the originating transactions and should be restated by means of the general price index to dollars of current general purchasing power at the end of the period. The components of gains and losses (costs and proceeds) are also stated in terms of historical dollars and should be restated. All revenue, expenses, gains, and losses recognized under historical-dollar accounting are recognized in the same time period under general price-level accounting, but their amounts are different in the case of items that are recorded in noncurrent dollars, such as depreciation, amortization, and cost of goods sold. Transactions that give rise to gains in historical-dollar financial statements may even give rise to losses in general price-level financial statements and vice versa. Income tax amounts in general price-level statements are based on income taxes reflected in historical-dollar statements and are not computed in direct relationship to the income before taxes on the general price-level statements.

40. *General price-level gains and losses should be calculated by means of the general price index and included in current net income.* General price-level gains and losses on monetary items . . . should be calculated by restating the opening balances and transactions in the accounts for monetary assets and liabilities to dollars of general purchasing power at the end of the period and comparing the resulting restated balances at the end of the period with the actual balances at the end of the period.

41. General price-level gains and losses on monetary items arise from changes in the general price level, and are not related to subsequent events such as the receipt or payment of money. Consequently, the Board has concluded that these gains and losses should be recognized as part of the net income of the period in which the general price level changes.

42. A different viewpoint than that expressed in paragraph 41, held by

a Board member, is that all of a monetary gain should not be recognized in the period of general price-level increase. Under this view, a portion of the gain on net monetary liabilities in a period of general price-level increase should be deferred to future periods as a reduction of the cost of nonmonetary assets, since the liabilities represent a source of funds for the financing of these assets. The proponent of this view believes that the gain from holding net monetary liabilities during inflation is not realized until the assets acquired from the funds borrowed are sold or consumed in operations.[3] The Board does not agree with this view, however, because it believes that the gain accrues during the period of the general price-level increase and is unrelated to the cost of nonmonetary assets.

43. *General price-level gains and losses should be reported as a separate item in general price-level income statements.* General price-level gains and losses on monetary items are not part of the revenue and expenses reported in historical-dollar financial statements. They should be separately identified in the general price-level statements. General price-level gains may, however, be offset against general price-level losses and only a single figure representing net general price-level gain or loss for the period need be reported.

44. *General price-level financial statements of earlier periods should be updated to dollars of the general purchasing power at the end of each subsequent period for which they are presented as comparative information.* Statements of an earlier period are updated by multiplying each item by the ratio of the current general price level to the general price level of the earlier period. This "rolling forward" of earlier statements could cause confusion and convey the erroneous impression that previously reported information has been changed in substance rather than merely updated in terms of a later unit of measure.[4] Consequently, comparative general price-level financial statements and related financial information should be described in a way that makes clear that the general price-level statements of prior periods represent previously reported information updated to dollars of current general purchasing power to provide comparability with the current general price-level statements.

45. *Restatement of financial statements of foreign branches or subsidiaries of U.S. companies for inclusion in combined or consolidated financial statements stated in terms of U.S. dollars should be based on an index of the general level of prices in the United States.* General price-level financial statements stated in terms of U.S. dollars use a unit of measure that represents the general purchasing power of the U.S. dollar at a specified date. An index of changes in the general purchasing power of the U.S. dollar should therefore

---

[3] For further discussion of this view see Marvin M. Deupree, "Accounting for Gains and Losses in Purchasing Power of Monetary Items" in *Accounting Research Study No. 6*, pp. 153–65.

[4] The "roll-forward" process results in stating financial statement items at different amounts than they were stated before being "rolled forward." The differences are not gains or losses but are merely differences between the same items measured in two different units of measure. If a cost stated at 100 dollars of general purchasing power current at the beginning of the year is "rolled forward" to 105 dollars of general purchasing power current at the end of the year, the difference of 5 is not a gain. It is similar, for example, to the difference of 2 between 1 yard and 3 feet.

be used to restate the financial statements of a company and its combined or consolidated foreign branches and subsidiaries. Financial statements of foreign branches or subsidiaries to be combined or consolidated with the financial statements of their United States parent company should first be translated into U.S. dollars using presently accepted methods and then restated for changes in the general purchasing power of the U.S. dollar.

46. *All general price-level information presented should be based on complete general price-level calculations.* Financial statements in which only some of the items, such as depreciation, have been restated disclose only part of the effects of changing general price levels on an enterprise. Partially restated financial statements and information based on them are likely to be misleading and should not be presented. General price-level information should therefore be based on complete calculations, although it need not be presented in the same detail as the historical-dollar financial statements. If any general price-level information is given, at least sales, net general price-level gains and losses on monetary items, extraordinary items, net income, and common stockholders' equity should be disclosed.

Presentation of general price-level
financial information

47. Presentation of general price-level financial information as a supplement to the basic historical-dollar financial statements should be designed to promote clarity and minimize possible confusion. Because the two types of data are prepared on different bases, presentations of general price-level financial information should generally encourage comparisons with other general price-level data rather than with historical-dollar data. If general price-level financial statements are presented in their entirety, they preferably should be presented in separate schedules, not in columns parallel to the historical-dollar statements. Financial information extracted from general price-level statements . . . may be presented in either chart or narrative form, and may emphasize ratios and percentages instead of or in addition to dollar amounts.

48. The basis of preparation of general price-level information and what it purports to show should be clearly explained in the notes to the general price-level financial statements or other appropriate places. The explanation should include the following points:

a. The general price-level statements (or information) are supplementary to the basic historical-dollar financial statements.

b. All amounts shown in general price-level statements are stated in terms of units of the same general purchasing power by use of an index of changes in the general purchasing power of the dollar.

c. The general price-level gain or loss in the general price-level statements indicates the effects of inflation (or deflation) on the company's net holdings of monetary assets and liabilities. The company gains or loses general purchasing power as a result of holding these assets and liabilities during a period of inflation (deflation).

d. In all other respects, the same generally accepted accounting principles used in the preparation of historical-dollar statements are used in the preparation of general price-level statements (or information).

e. The amounts shown in the general price-level statements do not purport to represent appraised value, replacement costs, or any other
measure of the current value of assets or the prices at which transactions would take place currently.

f. The general price-level statements (or information) of prior years
presented for comparative purposes have been updated to current
dollars. This restatement of prior years' general price-level statements
is required to make them comparable with current information. It does
not change the prior periods' statements in any way except to update
the amounts to dollars of current general purchasing power.

49. Disclosure involving the following items should also be made:

a. The difference between the balance of retained earnings at the end of
the preceding year in beginning-of-the-year dollars and at the beginning
of the year in end-of-the-year dollars, which arises in the roll-forward
process discussed in paragraph 44, should be explained somewhat as
follows:

Retained earnings at the beginning of the year:
Restated to general purchasing power at the beginning
of the year xxx
Amount required to update to general purchasing
power at the end of the year xxx
Restated to general purchasing power at the end
of the year xxx

b. The fact should be disclosed that when assets are used or sold,
federal income taxes are based on cost before restatement for general
price-level changes because inflation is not recognized in the Internal
Revenue Code.

Monetary and nonmonetary items

The following analysis of the monetary and nonmonetary character
of balance sheet items is from *Statement No. 3:*

18. Assets and liabilities are called "monetary" for purposes of general
price-level accounting if their amounts are fixed by contract or otherwise
in terms of numbers of dollars regardless of changes in specific prices or
in the general price level. Holders of monetary assets and liabilities gain
or lose general purchasing power during inflation or deflation simply as a
result of general price-level changes.[5] Examples of monetary assets and liabilities are cash, accounts and notes receivable in cash, and accounts and notes
payable in cash. General price-level gains and losses on monetary items cannot
be measured in historical-dollar financial statements and are not now reported.

---

[5] See *Accounting Research Study No. 6,* page 137, for discussion of monetary
and nonmonetary items in general price-level accounting. Assets and liabilities may
be classified as "monetary" for purposes other than general price-level accounting.
Classification of assets and liabilities as monetary for general price-level accounting
purposes should be based on the fact that holders gain or lose general purchasing
power simply as a result of general price-level changes rather than on criteria
developed for other purposes.

19.   Assets and liabilities other than monetary items are called "nonmonetary" for general price-level accounting purposes. Examples of nonmonetary items are inventories, investments in common stocks, property, plant, and equipment, deferred charges which represent costs expended in the past, advances received on sales contracts, liabilities for rent collected in advance, deferred credits which represent reductions of prior expense, and common stock. Holders of nonmonetary items do not gain or lose general purchasing power simply as a result of general price-level changes. If the price of a nonmonetary item changes at the same rate as the general price level, no gain or loss of general purchasing power results. Holders of nonmonetary assets and liabilities gain or lose general purchasing power if the specific price of the item owned or owed rises or falls faster or slower than the change in the general price level. Holders of nonmonetary assets and liabilities also gain or lose general purchasing power if the specific price of a nonmonetary item remains constant while the general price level changes. Gains and losses on nonmonetary items differ from general price-level gains and losses on monetary items because they are the joint result of changes in the structure of prices (the relationships between specific prices) and changes in the general level of prices, and not the result simply of changes in the general price level. (See page 441 for additional examples of monetary and nonmonetary items.)

20.   Historical-dollar financial statements report gains and losses on nonmonetary items, usually when the items are sold, and corresponding gains and losses should also be reported in general price-level financial statements in the same time period as in the historical-dollar statements. The amounts reported as gains or losses may differ, however, because the costs and proceeds in the general price-level statements are restated for changes in the general price level. Thus, if the market price of an asset increases more than the increase in the general price level and the asset is sold, in historical-dollar statements the entire market price increase is shown as a gain in the period of sale but only the excess of the market price increase over the cost restated for the increase in the general price level is shown as a gain in the general price-level statements. The timing of reporting these gains and losses is the same in historical-dollar and general price-level financial statements but the amounts differ because of the effect of the change in the general price level. Similarly, if the asset is used instead of sold, depreciation or amortization deducted from the related revenue is reported in the same time period in both historical-dollar and general price-level statements, although the amounts differ because of the restatement made in the general price-level statements. The Internal Revenue Code does not recognize general price-level restatements for tax purposes and income taxes are therefore assessed on the basis of historical-dollar amounts rather than amounts restated for general price-level changes. The income tax expense presented in general price-level statements is not computed in direct relationship to specific amounts of gains or losses on the statements or to the amount of net income before taxes. A few members of the Board believe that federal income tax should be allocated in general price-level statements to achieve a more direct relationship between the tax and various elements presented in these statements.

21. The fact that the market price of an item does not change over long periods of time does not in itself indicate that the item is monetary. Thus gold is nonmonetary because its price can fluctuate. The fact that the price did not fluctuate for over 30 years does not make gold a monetary item. When general price levels moved upward, the holder of gold lost general purchasing power because the price of his asset did not move as much as other prices, and not simply as a result of general price-level changes. Foreign currency, accounts receivable and payable in foreign currency, and similar items are also nonmonetary. The price of foreign currency, that is, the foreign exchange rate, can change. Therefore, the holder of foreign currency items does not gain or lose general purchasing power simply as a result of general price-level changes. If the exchange rate does not change when the general price level changes because of international controls or other factors, the price of foreign currency is rising or falling at a different rate than the general price level. The effect on the holder is the joint result of a change in the structure of prices and a change in the general level of prices, and therefore the items are nonmonetary. Even though foreign currency items are nonmonetary, they may be stated at the current foreign exchange rate in general price-level financial statements. Under these circumstances they would be treated as nonmonetary items carried at current market value.

22. A different viewpoint than that expressed in paragraph 21, held by a few Board members, is that foreign currency, accounts receivable and payable in foreign currency, and similar foreign currency items are similar to domestic monetary items. Foreign currency items should therefore be stated directly at the current (closing) foreign exchange rate in the general price-level balance sheet. The effect on the income of the holder of foreign currency items is the joint result of both the change in the foreign exchange rate and the change in the domestic general price level, and the items are therefore complex. Both effects are measurable, however, and should be disclosed separately. In the general price-level income statement, the effect of the general price-level change should be reported as a general price-level gain or loss on monetary items and the effect of the change in the exchange rate should be reported as a foreign exchange gain or loss. If the foreign exchange rate does not change, only a general price-level gain or loss should be reported.

23. A few assets and liabilities have characteristics of both monetary and nonmonetary items. For example, debentures held as an investment may have both a market price and fixed interest and principal payments. The fixed interest and principal payments do not change when prices change and therefore holders have general price-level gains or losses during inflation or deflation with respect to this characteristic. On the other hand, the market price of the debentures can and does change, and this feature does not yield general price-level gains or losses. Similarly, convertible debt owed is fixed in amount when considered as debt, but may be converted into capital stock. The fixed amount of debt owed is a monetary liability, which gives rise to general price-level gains or losses when general price levels change. The conversion feature is nonmonetary in nature, and does not give rise to gains or losses of general purchasing power simply as a result of general price-level changes.

	Monetary	Non-monetary

Assets

	Monetary	Non-monetary
Cash on hand and demand bank deposits (domestic currency)	X	
Time deposits (domestic currency)	X	
Foreign currency on hand and claims to foreign currency		X
See discussion in Statement, paragraph 21.		
Marketable securities		
Stocks		X
Bonds.		(see discussion)
Bonds held as a short-term investment may be held for price speculation. If so, they are nonmonetary. If the bonds are held primarily for the fixed income characteristic, they are monetary.		
Accounts and notes receivable	X	
Allowance for doubtful accounts and notes receivable . .	X	
Inventories produced under fixed price contracts accounted for at the contract price	X	
These items are in effect receivables of a fixed amount.		
Other inventories		X
Advances to employees	X	
Prepaid insurance, taxes, advertising, rent.		X
These represent an amount of services for which expenditures have been made and which will be amortized to expense in the future. In financial statements they are substantially the same kind of item as fixed assets.		
Prepaid interest.	X	
Related to notes payable, a monetary item.		
Receivables under capitalized financing leases	X	
Long-term receivables	X	
Refundable deposits	X	
Advances to unconsolidated subsidiaries	X	
If there is no expectation that the advances will ever be collected, they are in effect additional investments and are nonmonetary.		
Investments in unconsolidated subsidiaries		(see discussion)
If an investment is carried at cost, it is nonmonetary. If, an investment is carried on the equity basis, the statements of the subsidiary should be restated for general price-level changes (in accordance with paragraph 45 of the Statement for foreign affiliates) and the equity method should then be applied.		
Pension, sinking, and other funds		(see discussion)
Depends on composition of the fund—bonds are generally monetary and stocks nonmonetary.		
Investments in convertible bonds		(see discussion)
If the bond is held for price speculation or with expectation of converting into common stock the investment is nonmonetary. If the bond is held for the fixed principal and interest, it is monetary.		
Property, plant, and equipment		X
Allowance for depreciation		X

	Monetary	Non-monetary
Cash surrender value of life insurance	X	
Advances paid on purchase contracts		X
The items to be received are nonmonetary.		
Unamortized discount on bonds payable	X	
Related to bonds payable, a monetary item.		
Deferred charges for income taxes—deferred method . . .		X
A cost deferred as an expense of future periods is nonmonetary.		
Other deferred charges which represent costs incurred to be charged against future income		X
Patents, trademarks, licenses, formulas		X
Goodwill		X
Other intangible assets		X

Liabilities

	Monetary	Non-monetary
Accounts and notes payable	X	
Accrued expenses payable (salaries, wages, etc.)	X	
Similar to accounts payable, amount is fixed.		
Cash dividends payable.	X	
Debts payable in foreign currency.		X
See Statement, paragraph 21.		
Refundable deposits	X	
Advances received on sales contracts		X
The obligation will be satisfied by delivery of goods that are nonmonetary.		
Accrued losses on firm purchase commitments	X	
Bonds payable	X	
Convertible bonds payable	X	
Treated as monetary debt until converted.		
Obligations under capitalized leases	X	
Other long-term debt	X	
Deferred taxes—deferred method		X
Cost savings deferred as a reduction of expenses of future periods.		
Deferred investment credits.		X
Accrued pension cost	X	
Reserve for self-insurance		X
Although reserve for self-insurance is nonmonetary, it may be stated in the same amount in both the historical-dollar and general price-level statements if the adequacy of the reserve in terms of current costs has been determined at year end for the historical-dollar statements.		
Deferred income		X
Provision for guarantees		X
Provision for guarantees is nonmonetary because it is a liability to provide goods or services. It may be stated in the same amount in both the historical-dollar and general price-level statements if the adequacy of the provision in terms of current costs has been determined at year end for the historical-dollar statements.		
Accrued vacation pay.	(see discussion)	
Accrued vacation pay is monetary if it is based on a fixed contract. It is nonmonetary if it is payable based on wage or salary rates that may change after the balance sheet date.		

	Monetary	Non-monetary
Owners' Equity		
Minority interest.		X
Preferred stock		X

Classifying preferred stock as nonmonetary is based on the fact that the amount accounted for is the proceeds received when the stock was issued. The proceeds must be restated to present them in terms of the general purchasing power of the dollar at the balance sheet date.

The amount of a nonconvertible callable preferred stock should not exceed the call price in the general price-level balance sheet. The periodic change in the excess of the restated proceeds over the call price, if any, should not be included in net income, but should be added to net income to determine net income to common stockholders in the same manner as preferred dividends are deducted to determine net income to common stockholders.

A different viewpoint held by some Board members is that preferred stock is a monetary item and that general price-level gains or losses from preferred stock outstanding should be included in the computation of net income.

	Monetary	Non-monetary
Common stock		X
Additional paid-in capital		X
Retained earnings	(see discussion)	

Retained earnings is a residual and need not be classified as either monetary or nonmonetary.

QUESTIONS AND PROBLEMS

18–1. What does *Statement No. 3* have to say regarding the value and proper use of financial statements adjusted for price-level changes?

18–2. Distinguish monetary from nonmonetary items and explain the effects of the difference and the appropriate procedures recommended by *Statement No. 3*.

18–3. Ignoring for the purposes of this question the differences between monetary and nonmonetary items (discussed in Question 18–2), enumerate and discuss the suggestions made by Statement 3 regarding the preparation of price-level adjusted statements.

18–4. In what areas of the financial statements would you expect to find the major distortions due to price-level changes? Explain why these areas are the most likely to show major distortions.

19

Procedures to prepare financial statements restated for general price-level changes[1]

1. [IN THE following sections] procedures for restating historical-dollar financial statements for general price-level changes are described and illustrated for two years, 1967 and 1968. Restating the statements for 1967 illustrates the procedures for the first year of restatement; restating the 1968 statements illustrates the procedures for all subsequent years. The procedures for the first year a company restates its financial statements are more time consuming than those for subsequent years.

2. Financial statements used in the illustration contain a variety of items designed to demonstrate various facets of the restatement technique. Indexes of the general price-level changes which occurred in the United States in recent years are used. For convenience, the general assumptions used in the illustration are summarized below:

a. The XYZ Company was formed in 1957, ten years before the year for which its statements are first restated.

b. All significant costs of the year-end finished goods inventory, carried at FIFO, were incurred in the last quarter of the year; costs incurred before the last quarter of the year are assumed to be not material.

c. Year-end balances of raw materials and parts and supplies inventories, carried at FIFO, were acquired fairly evenly throughout the year.

d. Market value of inventories is above the restated cost of inventories, and the market price of inventories to be delivered is below the restated amount of deferred income.

e. Depreciation is computed on the straight-line basis. A full year's de-

[1] From the Accounting Principles Board's *Statement No. 3* (June 1969).

444

preciation is taken in the year of acquisition, and no depreciation is taken in the year of sale. Depreciable assets have a ten-year life and no salvage value.

f. Sales, purchases, and selling and administrative expenses (other than depreciation, amortization of prepaid expenses, and deferred income realized) have taken place fairly evenly throughout the year, and federal income taxes accrue ratably throughout the year.

g. Interest expenses is included in selling and administrative expenses.

3. To perform restatement procedures, a company needs (1) its historical-dollar financial statements for the year, (2) index numbers, and (3) conversion factors derived from the index numbers, as described in the following paragraphs.

4. The historical-dollar financial statements needed for the first year for which statements are to be restated are balance sheets at the beginning and end of the year and the statements of income, retained earnings, and other changes in owners' equity for the year. For each subsequent year, only the balance sheet at the end of the year and the statements of income, retained earnings, and other changes in owners' equity for the year are needed. The historical-dollar balance sheet at the beginning of the first year is restated to determine the restated amount of retained earnings at the beginning of the first year.

5. The Gross National Product Implicit Price Deflator is used in the illustration as the index of changes in the general price level. This index is available on both a quarterly and annual average basis. Indexes are needed for the average and the quarters for each year since the inception of the company or 1945,[2] whichever is later. The annual average index may be used for any year in which its use would produce results not materially different from those which would be produced by using quarterly indexes. The index at the end of a year may be approximated by using the average for the last quarter of the year. To simplify the illustration, quarterly indexes are used only for 1967 and 1968.

6. Conversion factors used in restatement are computed from general price-level index numbers by dividing the index number for the current balance sheet date by each of the other index numbers. To illustrate, assume that 1957 and 1960 expenditures are to be restated to dollars of December 1968 general purchasing power. The following GNP Deflators (general price-level

---

[2] The precision of the measure of change in the general price level by any series of index numbers decreases over time because new commodities are continuously introduced and others disappear. No method has been devised to measure the percentage change in the general price level between two periods in which the bulk of commodities in either period are unique. A large portion of the dollar amount of current exchange transactions involves goods and services that originated in discoveries and innovations that grew out of the war effort (World War II) and postwar developments. Consequently, comparison of current prices with prices during and prior to World War II would probably not be reliable enough for accounting purposes because of the dissimilarity of goods and services exchanged then and now. A cutoff date is therefore indicated. The year 1945 is probably the earliest point that offers reasonable comparability of goods and services with later periods. All assets acquired, liabilities incurred, or owners' equity accumulated prior to 1945 should generally be treated as if they had originated during 1945.

index numbers) are applicable:

Average for 1957. . . . .   97.5
Average for 1960. . . . .   103.3
Fourth quarter 1968 . . . .   123.5

To compute the conversion factors for restatement to dollars of general purchasing power current at December 31, 1968, divide the index number for the fourth quarter of 1968 by each of the other index numbers:

$$1957: \quad 123.5 \div 97.5 = 1.267$$
$$1960: \quad 123.5 \div 103.3 = 1.196$$

To restate a nonmonetary item purchased in 1957, for example, its cost in 1957 dollars is multiplied by 1.267:

Cost in 1957 dollars. $1,500
                          ×   1.267
Cost in dollars current at
December 31, 1968. . . . . . $1,900

The cost of $1,500 in 1957 dollars is equal to a cost of $1,900 in December 31, 1968 dollars. The cost is not changed; it is merely stated in a larger number of smaller units of measure.

General steps to prepare general price-level financial statements

Step 1:   Identify monetary and nonmonetary assets and liabilities.

The nature of each asset and liability item must be determined inasmuch as restatement procedures for monetary items are different from those for nonmonetary items.

1967 Restatement	*1968 Restatement*
Step 1: Monetary items in the December 31, 1966 and 1967 balance sheets are: Cash Receivables Current liabilities Long-term debt Nonmonetary items are: Marketable securities Raw materials Finished goods Parts and supplies Prepaid expenses Property, plant, and equipment Accumulated depreciation Deferred income—payments received in advance* Capital stock Additional paid-in capital Retained earnings	*Step 1*: Monetary and nonmonetary items in the December 31, 1968 balance sheet are the same as in the December 31, 1966 and 1967 balance sheets.

* Deferred income—payments received in advance is a nonmonetary liability because it represents an obligation to deliver nonmonetary assets —the company's products.

Step 2:   *Analyze all nonmonetary items in the balance sheet of the current year (and the prior year for the first year of restatement) to determine when the component money amounts originated.*

Schedule the data by years, and by quarters whenever significant general price-level changes occurred during a year. If no significant general price-level changes occurred during a year, or if acquisitions were spread fairly evenly throughout a year, assume the items were acquired when the average general price level for the year was in effect. All balances accumulated prior to 1945 may be treated as if acquired in 1945. See Step 3 for treatment of special problems in restating inventories.

Retained earnings need not be analyzed. Retained earnings in the restated balance sheet at the beginning of the first year for which general price-level restatements are prepared can be computed as the balancing amount. This avoids the impractical alternative of restating all prior financial statements since the inception of the company. Retained earnings in subsequent restated balance sheets is determined from the restated statements of income and retained earnings.

1967 Restatement	*1968 Restatement*
Step 2: Analysis of raw materials, finished goods, and parts and supplies inventories is discussed in notes 3 and 4 on page 453. Marketable securities, capital stock, and additional paid-in capital are analyzed in columns 3, 5, and 7 of Table R–4 on page 454. Prepaid expenses, property, plant, and equipment, accumulated depreciation, and deferred income are analyzed in columns 3 to 6 on pages 455 and 456.	*Step* 2: Much of the analysis needed for the 1968 restatement has been prepared for the 1967 restatement and merely needs to be updated. Analysis of raw materials, finished goods, and parts and supplies inventories, capital stock, and additional paid-in capital is discussed in notes 4, 5, and 6 on page 462. Prepaid expenses, property, plant, and equipment, accumulated depreciation, and deferred income are analyzed in columns 3 to 6 of Tables R–4, 5, 6 and 7 starting on page 463.

Step 3:   *Analyze all revenue, expense, gain, and loss items in the income statements of the current year, and all dividends and other changes in retained earnings during the year, to determine when the amounts originated that ultimately resulted in the charges and credits in the statements of income and retained earnings.*

A wide range in degree of difficulty is likely to be encountered in restating inventories and cost of goods sold to dollars of current general purchasing power. Raw materials priced on a first-in, first-out basis may already be in dollars of current general purchasing power and need no restatement. If turnover is rapid and spread fairly evenly throughout the year, purchases may be in dollars whose general purchasing power can be approximated by using the average general price level for the year. Restatement of inventories of work in process and finished goods, however, can be quite complicated and time consuming. Weighted average or last-in, first-out pricing increases the amount of detail.

Shortcuts to the restatement of inventories and purchases often produce results that do not differ enough from amounts derived by detailed computation to warrant the additional effort. For example, costs of inventories based on weighted average include, in part, every expenditure ever made to buy or produce them. A shortcut would be to assume that the beginning inventory had all been acquired in one turnover period. In the case of beginning LIFO inventories, using the assumption that different layers were acquired each year when the average general price level was in effect for that year will usually approximate the results of a detailed computation, purchase by purchase. Elements of overhead costs included in work in process and finished goods inventories can usually be restated from dollars of average general purchasing power for the year when overhead was applied to that segment of the inventory. Depreciation is the overhead cost element most likely to require extensive analysis, but only when the effect would be material.

Many revenue and expense items are, of course, recognized in the accounts at approximately the same time that the receipts and expenditures occurred (for example, salaries). If these items are spread fairly evenly throughout the year, it can be assumed that the receipts and expenditures all occurred when the average general price level for the year was in effect. When peak and slack periods occur during the year, and the general price level changes significantly between periods, revenue and expense items in this category should be determined for each calendar quarter.

The restatement of revenue and expense items should, of course, reconcile with the restatement of the related balance sheet accounts, and they can be restated as part of the same computation. For example, the beginning balance of merchandise inventory plus purchases, both stated in current dollars, should equal the sum of the cost of sales and the ending balance of merchandise inventory, also stated in current dollars.

1967 Restatement	*1968 Restatement*
Step 3: Sales, cost of sales, selling and administrative expenses, and loss on sale of equipment are analyzed in column 1 on page 457. Depreciation is analyzed in column 4 in Table R-7 on page 456. Amortization of prepaid expenses is analyzed in column 5 in Table R-5 on page 455. Deferred income realized is analyzed in column 5 in Table R-8 on page 456. Federal income taxes and dividends are analyzed in Table R-3 on page 454.	*Step* 3: Sales, cost of sales, selling and administrative expenses, gain on sale of equipment, and gain or loss on sale of marketable securities are analyzed in column 1 in Tables R-8 and R-9 on pages 465-66. Depreciation is analyzed in column 4 in Table R-6 on page 464. Amortization of prepaid expenses is analyzed in column 5 in Table R-4 on page 463. Deferred income realized is analyzed in column 5 in Table R-7 on page 465. Federal income taxes and dividends are analyzed in Table R-3 on page 463.

Step 4:   Restate the nonmonetary items.

Multiply the component amounts of nonmonetary items in the balance sheet of the current year (and the prior year for the first year of restatement) and in the statement of income and retained earnings for the current year by the conversion factors applicable to the components. The restated amount of each nonmonetary item is the sum of the restated amounts of its components.

1967 Restatement	*1968 Restatement*
Step 4: Restatement of nonmonetary items is demonstrated on the pages in which the nonmonetary items are analyzed in accordance with Steps 2 and 3.	*Step* 4: Restatement of nonmonetary items is demonstrated on the pages in which the nonmonetary items are analyzed in accordance with Steps 2 and 3. Components which originated in 1967 or earlier generally are restated by merely "rolling forward" their restated amounts from the worksheets for the 1967 restatement.

Step 5: Restate the monetary items in the balance sheet at the beginning of the first year.

Monetary items in the balance sheet at the beginning of the first year for which statements are restated are stated in prior year dollars and are each restated to dollars of current general purchasing power by the conversion factor applicable to the end of the prior year. Monetary items in the balance sheet at the end of each year for which statements are restated are stated in dollars of current general purchasing power and need no restatement.

1967 Restatement	*1968 Restatement*
Step 5: Restatement of the monetary items in the balance sheet at December 31, 1966 is discussed in note 1 on page 453.	*Step* 5: (Not applicable after the first year statements are restated.)

Step 6: Apply the "cost or market" rule after restatement to the items to which it applies before restatement.

To determine that marketable securities and inventories are not stated above market in the restated statements, and that current nonmonetary liabilities are not stated below market, the restated amounts are compared with market and adjusted if necessary.

1967 Restatement	*1968 Restatement*
Step 6: Market is assumed to be higher than restated marketable securities and inventories and lower than restated deferred income.	*Step* 6: Market is assumed to be higher than restated inventories and lower than restated deferred income.

Step 7: Compute the general price-level gain or loss for the current year.

The general price-level gain or loss which arises from holding net balance sheet monetary items during inflation or deflation appears in the general price-level statements but does not appear in the historical-dollar statements. The format used to prepare a statement of source and application of net balance sheet monetary items is a convenient device to use in calculating the general price-level gain or loss. In this calculation the items which cause changes in the monetary items are analyzed and the net balance of the monetary items if there were no gain or loss is determined. A comparison of this net balance with the actual net balance of monetary items at the balance sheet date determines the gain or loss.

1967 Restatement	*1968 Restatement*
Step 7: The general price-level gain for 1967 is computed on page 458.	*Step* 7: The general price-level gain for 1968 is computed on page 467.

Step 8: *"Roll forward" the restated statements of the prior year to dollars of current general purchasing power.*

Financial statements of the prior year which were restated to dollars current at the end of the prior year are restated to dollars current at the end of the current year simply by multiplying each amount by the conversion factor applicable to the end of the prior year. This "rolling forward" serves two purposes: (1) it provides the amount of retained earnings at the end of the prior year in current dollars for the current year statement of retained earnings, and (2) it provides the prior year statements in current dollars for use as comparative statements.

1967 Restatement	*1968 Restatement*
Step 8: (Not applicable for the first year statements are restated.)	*Step* 8: The restated balance sheet at the end of 1967 is "rolled forward" in columns 1 and 2 on page 462. The restated statement of income and retained earnings for 1967 is "rolled forward" in columns 1 and 2 in Table R-3 on page 463.

QUESTIONS AND PROBLEMS

19–1. Chapter 19 enumerates and explains eight steps in adjusting financial statements for price-level changes. List the eight steps, one at a time, and explain in your own words the meaning of the step and give an example of its effect on an appropriate financial statement amount. Examples used should be different than those used in Chapter 19.

20

An example of price-level statements

IN THIS chapter will be found the price-level adjusted financial statements which resulted from the application of the procedures previously described and explained. The statements have been reproduced from The Accounting Principles Board's Statement 3 (June 1969).

XYZ COMPANY
General Price-Level Balance Sheet
December 31, 1967

	General price-level basis (restated to 12/31/67)
Assets	
Current assets:	
Cash................................	$(67) 1,700,000
Marketable securities, at cost	1,654,000
Receivables (net)	5,050,000
Inventories, at the lower of cost and market on a first-in, first-out basis:	
Raw materials	2,849,000
Finished goods	2,560,000
Parts and supplies................	578,000
Prepaid expenses	49,000
Total current assets	14,440,000
Property, plant, and equipment, at cost....	29,580,000
Less: Accumulated depreciation	21,156,000
	8,424,000
	$(67)22,864,000
Liabilities and Stockholders' Equity	
Current liabilities	$(67) 4,770,000
Deferred income—payments received in advance......................	101,000
Long-term debt....................	5,000,000
Stockholders' equity:	
Capital stock—common	2,109,000
Additional paid-in capital...........	3,785,000
Retained earnings	7,099,000
Total stockholders' equity.........	12,993,000
	$(67)22,864,000

XYZ COMPANY
General Price-Level Statement
of Income and Retained Earnings
Year Ended December 31, 1967

	General price-level basis (restated to 12/31/67)
Sales	$(67)30,424,000
Operating expenses:	
Cost of sales	23,232,000
Depreciation	2,616,000
Selling and administrative expenses	2,615,000
	28,463,000
Operating profit	1,961,000
Loss on sale of equipment.	(12,000)
General price-level gain.	138,000
	126,000
Income before federal income taxes	2,087,000
Federal income taxes	923,000
Net income	1,164,000
Retained earnings, December 31, 1966	6,137,000
	7,301,000
Less: Dividends paid	202,000
Retained earnings, December 31, 1967	$(67) 7,099,000

XYZ COMPANY
General Price-Level Restatement—1967
Gross National Product Implicit Price   12/31/67
Deflators and Conversion Factors   R-1

Year	Quarter	GNP deflators	Conversion factors 1967 (4th q.) = 1.000
Annual average			
1957		97.5	1.219
1958		100.0	1.189
1959		101.6	1.170
1960		103.3	1.151
1961		104.6	1.137
1962		105.7	1.125
1963		107.1	1.110
1964		108.9	1.092
1965		110.9	1.072
1966		113.9	1.044
1967		117.3	1.014
Quarterly			
1966	4th	115.3	1.031
1967	1st	116.0	1.025
	2nd	116.6	1.020
	3rd	117.7	1.010
	4th	118.9	1.000

Source: *Survey of Current Business*, U.S. Department of Commerce, Office of Business Economics (Deflators of 1957–1964 from issue of August 1965, page 53).

XYZ COMPANY
General Price-Level Restatement—1967
Working Balance Sheets—12/31/66 and 12/31/67   R-2

	12/31/66			12/31/67		
	Historical	Conversion factor or source	Restated to 12/31/67 $'s	Historical	Conversion factor or source	Restated to 12/31/67 $'s
Assets						
Cash	810,000	(1) 1.031	835,110	1,700,000	(2)	1,700,000
Marketable securities (at cost)	1,470,000	R-4	1,623,340	1,500,000	(2) R-4	1,654,090
Receivable—net	1,900,000	(1) 1.031	1,958,900	5,050,000	(2)	5,050,000
Inventories						
Raw materials (FIFO)	2,680,000	(3) 1.044	2,797,920	2,810,000	(3) 1.014	2,849,340
Finished goods (FIFO)	2,450,000	(4) 1.031	2,525,950	2,560,000	(4) 1.000	2,560,000
Parts and supplies (FIFO)	700,000	(3) 1.044	730,800	570,000	(3) 1.014	577,980
Prepaid expenses	50,000	R-5	52,720	48,000	R-5	49,261
Total current sales	10,060,000		10,524,740	14,238,000		14,440,671
Property, plant, and equipment (at cost)	25,400,000	R-6	29,154,200	25,900,000	R-6	29,579,550
Less: Accumulated depreciation	16,350,000	R-7	19,016,680	18,260,000	R-7	21,156,145
	9,050,000		10,137,520	7,640,000		8,423,405
	19,110,000		20,662,260	21,878,000		22,864,076
Liabilities						
Current liabilities	2,950,000	(1) 1.031	3,041,450	4,770,000	(2)	4,770,000
Deferred income—payments received in advance	120,000	R-8	125,280	100,000	R-8	100,900
Long-term debt	5,300,000	(1) 1.031	5,464,300	5,000,000	(2)	5,000,000
	8,370,000		8,631,030	9,870,000		9,870,900
Stockholders' Equity						
Capital stock—common	1,760,000	R-4	2,109,120	1,760,000	R-4	2,109,120
Additional paid-in capital	3,150,000	R-4	3,784,550	3,150,000	R-4	3,784,550
Retained earnings	5,830,000	(5)	6,137,560	7,098,000	R-3	7,099,506
	10,740,000		12,031,230	12,008,000		12,993,176
	19,110,000		20,662,260	21,878,000		22,864,076

Notes

(1) 12/31/66 monetary items before restatement are stated in 12/31/66 $'s. The conversion factor for the end of 1966 is used to restate them to 12/31/67 $'s.

(2) 12/31/67 monetary items need no restatement because they are stated in 12/31/67 $'s.

(3) Year-end balance assumed acquired fairly evenly throughout the year.

(4) Assumed that all significant costs of year-end finished goods were incurred in last quarter of the year. Costs incurred before last quarter of the year (e.g., depreciation) assumed not material.

(5) 12/31/66 retained earnings restated in the amount which makes the balance sheet balance.

XYZ COMPANY   12/31/

General Price-Level Restatement—1967   R-3

Working Statement of Income and Retained Earnings

	Historical	Conversion factor or source	Restated 12/31/67
Sales	30,000,000	R-9	30,424,2
Operating expenses:			
Cost of sales (except depreciation)	22,735,000	R-9	23,232,1
Depreciation	2,310,000	R-7	2,616,6
Selling and administrative expenses	2,577,000	R-10	2,614,7
	27,622,000		28,463,5
Operating profit	2,378,000		1,960,7
Loss of sale of equipment	-0-	R-10	(11,7
General price-level gain	-0-	R-11	137,7
	-0-		125,9
Income before federal income taxes	2,378,000		2,086,6
Federal income taxes	910,000	(1) 1.014	922,7
Net income	1,468,000		1,163,9
Retained earnings—12/31/66	5,830,000	R-2	6,137,5
	7,298,000		7,301,5
Dividends paid			
June 1967	100,000	1.020	102,0
December 1967	100,000	1.000	100,0
	200,000		202,0
Retained earnings—12/31/67	7,098,000		7,099,5

(1)   Assumed accrued ratably throughout the year.

XYZ COMPANY   12/31/6

General Price-Level Restatement—1967   R-4

Analysis of Marketable Securities, Capital Stock, and Additional Paid-in Capital

		Marketable securities		Capital stock		Additional paid-in capital	
Year acquired	Factor to restate to 12/31/67 $'s	Historical	Restated to 12/31/67 $'s	Historical	Restated to 12/31/67 $'s	Historical	Restated to 12/31/67 $
1957	1.219			1,000,000	1,219,000	2,000,000	2,438,000
1958	1.189			500,000	594,500	750,000	891,750
1959	1.170						
1960	1.151						
1961	1.137	500,000	568,500	260,000	295,620	400,000	454,800
1962	1.125						
1963	1.110						
1964	1.092	750,000	819,000				
1965	1.072	220,000	235,840				
1966	1.044						
Balances 12/31/66		1,470,000	1,623,340	1,760,000	2,109,120	3,150,000	3,784,550
1967							
1st q.	1.025	30,000	30,750				
2nd q.	1.020						
3rd q.	1.010						
4th q.	1.000						
average	1.014						
Balances 12/31/67		1,500,000	1,654,090	1,760,000	2,109,120	3,150,000	3,784,550

Note: All marketable securities assumed to be nonmonetary.

XYZ COMPANY

General Price-Level Restatement—1967
Analysis of Prepaid Expenses

12/31/67
R-5

Year acquired	Factor to restate to 12/31/67 $'s	Historical Balance 12/31/66	Additions	Amortization	Balance 12/31/67	Restated to 12/31/67 $'s Balance 12/31/66	Additions	Amortization	Balance 12/31/67
1964	1.092	5,000		5,000		5,460		5,460	
1965	1.072	10,000		7,000	3,000	10,720		7,504	3,216
1966	1.044	35,000		25,000	10,000	36,540		26,100	10,440
1967									
1st q.	1.025		25,000	8,000	17,000		25,625	8,200	17,425
2nd q.	1.020								
3rd q.	1.010		20,000	2,000	18,000		20,200	2,020	18,180
4th q.	1.000								
		50,000	45,000	47,000	48,000	52,720	45,825	49,284	49,261

XYZ COMPANY

General Price-Level Restatement—1967
Analysis of Property, Plant, and Equipment

12/31/67
R-6

Year acquired	Factor to restate to 12/31/67 $'s	Historical Balance 12/31/66	Additions	Retirements	Balance 12/31/67	Restated to 12/31/67 $'s Balance 12/31/66	Additions	Retirements	Balance 12/31/67
1957	1.219	3,000,000		200,000	2,800,000	3,657,000		243,800	3,413,200
1958	1.189	3,000,000		100,000	2,900,000	3,567,000		118,900	3,448,100
1959	1.170	4,000,000		100,000	3,900,000	4,680,000		117,000	4,563,000
1960	1.151	3,600,000			3,600,000	4,143,600			4,143,600
1961	1.137	800,000			800,000	909,600			909,600
1962	1.125	5,000,000			5,000,000	5,625,000			5,625,000
1963	1.110	3,000,000			3,000,000	3,330,000			3,330,000
1964	1.092	2,000,000		100,000	1,900,000	2,184,000		109,200	2,074,800
1965	1.072	500,000			500,000	536,000			536,000
1966	1.044	500,000			500,000	522,000			522,000
1967									
1st q.	1.025		250,000		250,000		256,250		256,250
2nd q.	1.020		300,000		300,000		306,000		306,000
3rd q.	1.010		200,000		200,000		202,000		202,000
4th q.	1.000		250,000		250,000		250,000		250,000
		25,400,000	1,000,000	500,000	25,900,000	29,154,200	1,014,250	588,900	29,579,550

XYZ COMPANY

General Price-Level Restatement—1967
Analysis of Accumulated Depreciation

12/31/67
R-7

Year assets acquired	Factor to restate to 12/31/67 $'s	Historical				Restated to 12/31/67 $'s			
		Balance 12/31/66	Depreciation (1)	Retirements	Balance 12/31/67	Balance 12/31/66	Depreciation (1)	Retirements	Balance 12/31/67
1957	1.219	3,000,000		200,000	2,800,000	3,657,000		243,800	3,413,200
1958	1.189	2,700,000	290,000	90,000	2,900,000	3,210,300	344,810	107,010	3,448,100
1959	1.170	3,200,000	390,000	80,000	3,510,000	3,744,000	456,300	93,600	4,106,700
1960	1.151	2,520,000	360,000		2,880,000	2,900,520	414,360		3,314,880
1961	1.137	480,000	80,000		560,000	545,760	90,960		636,720
1962	1.125	2,500,000	500,000		3,000,000	2,812,500	562,500		3,375,000
1963	1.110	1,200,000	300,000		1,500,000	1,332,000	333,000		1,665,000
1964	1.092	600,000	190,000	30,000	760,000	655,200	207,480	32,760	829,920
1965	1.072	100,000	50,000		150,000	107,200	53,600		160,800
1966	1.044	50,000	50,000		100,000	52,200	52,200		104,400
1967									
1st q.	1.025		25,000		25,000		25,625		25,625
2nd q.	1.020		30,000		30,000		30,600		30,600
3rd q.	1.010		20,000		20,000		20,200		20,200
4th q.	1.000		25,000		25,000		25,000		25,000
		16,350,000	2,310,000	400,000	18,260,000	19,016,680	2,616,635	477,170	21,156,145

(1) Depreciation basis: Straight line
10 year life
No salvage value
Full year's depreciation in year of acquisition
No depreciation in year of disposition

XYZ COMPANY

General Price-Level Restatement—1967
Analysis of Deferred Income

12/31/67
R-8

Year acquired	Factor to restate to 12/31/67 $'s	Historical				Restated to 12/31/67 $'s			
		Balance 12/31/66	Additions	Realized	Balance 12/31/67	Balance 12/31/66	Additions	Realized	Balance 12/31/67
1966	1.044	120,000		120,000		125,280		125,280	
1967									
1st q.	1.025		40,000	40,000			41,000	41,000	
2nd q.	1.020		50,000	30,000	20,000		51,000	30,600	20,400
3rd q.	1.010		50,000		50,000		50,500		50,500
4th q.	1.000		30,000		30,000		30,000		30,000
		120,000	170,000	190,000	100,000	125,280	172,500	196,880	100,900

XYZ COMPANY
General Price-Level Restatement—1967
Analysis of Sales and Cost of Sales

12/31/67
R-9

	Historical	Conversion factor or source	Restated to 12/31/67 $'s
Sales			
Current sales	29,810,000	(1) 1.014	30,227,340
Deferred sales realized	190,000	R-8	196,880
Total sales	30,000,000		30,424,220
Cost of sales (except depreciation)			
Inventories 12/31/66			
Raw materials	2,680,000	R-2	2,797,920
Finished goods	2,450,000	R-2	2,525,950
Parts and supplies	700,000	R-2	730,800
Purchases during 1967	22,845,000	(1) 1.014	23,164,830
	28,675,000		29,219,500
Inventories 12/31/67			
Raw materials	2,810,000	R-2	2,849,340
Finished goods	2,560,000	R-2	2,560,000
Parts and supplies	570,000	R-2	577,980
	5,940,000		5,987,320
	22,735,000		23,232,180

(1) Spread fairly evenly throughout the year.

XYZ COMPANY
General Price-Level Restatement—1967
Analysis of Expenses

12/31/67
R-10

	Historical	Conversion factor or source	Restated to 12/31/67 $'s
Selling and administrative expenses			
Amortization of prepaid expenses	47,000	R-5	49,284
Other	2,530,000	(1) 1.014	2,565,420
	2,577,000		2,614,704
Loss on sale of equipment			
Cost	500,000	R-6	588,900
Accumulated depreciation	400,000	R-7	477,170
	100,000		111,730
Proceeds, December, 1967	100,000	1.000	100,000
Loss	-0-		11,730

(1) Spread fairly throughout the year.

XYZ COMPANY
General Price-Level Restatement—1967
General Price-Level Gain or Loss

12/31/67
R-11

	Source	12/31/66 Historical	Restated to 12/31/67 $'s	12/31/67 Historical (stated in 12/31/67 $'s)
Net monetary items				
Cash	R-2	810,000	835,110	1,700,000
Receivables	R-2	1,900,000	1,958,900	5,050,000
Current liabilities	R-2	(2,950,000)	(3,041,450)	(4,770,000)
Long-term debt	R-2	(5,300,000)	(5,464,300)	(5,000,000)
		(5,540,000)	(5,711,740)	(3,020,000)

	Historical	Source	Restated to 12/31/67 $'s
General price-level gain or loss			
Net monetary items—12/31/66	(5,540,000)	as above	(5,711,740)
Add:			
Current sales	29,810,000	R-9	30,227,340
Additions to deferred income.	170,000	R-8	172,500
Proceeds from sale of equipment	100,000	R-10	100,000
	24,540,000		24,788,100
Deduct:			
Purchases	22,845,000	R-9	23,164,830
Selling and administrative expenses—other	2,530,000	R-10	2,565,420
Federal income taxes	910,000	R-3	922,740
Dividends	200,000	R-3	202,000
Purchase of marketable securities.	30,000	R-4	30,750
Purchases of property, plant, and equipment	1,000,000	R-6	1,014,250
Additions to prepaid expenses	45,000	R-5	45,825
	27,560,000		27,945,815
Net monetary items—historical— 12/31/67 (as above)	(3,020,000)		
Net monetary items—restated— 12/31/67 (if there were no gain)			(3,157,715)
Net monetary items—12/31/67 (as above)			(3,020,000)
General price-level gain.			137,715

XYZ COMPANY
Comparative General Price-Level
Balance Sheets
December 31, 1968 and December 31, 1967

	General price-level basis (restated to 12/31/68)	
	Dec. 31, 1968	*Dec. 31, 1967*

Assets

Current assets:

Cash.	$(68) 2,120,000	$(68) 1,766,000
Marketable securities, at cost		1,719,000
Receivables (net)	6,170,000	5,247,000
Inventories, at the lower of cost and market on a first-in, first-out basis:		
Raw materials	2,575,000	2,960,000
Finished goods	2,390,000	2,660,000
Parts and supplies.	621,000	601,000
Prepaid expenses	43,000	51,000
Total current assets	13,919,000	15,004,000
Property, plant, and equipment, at cost	31,208,000	30,733,000
Less: Accumulated depreciation.	24,253,000	21,981,000
	6,955,000	8,752,000
	$(68)20,874,000	$(68)23,756,000

Liabilities and Stockholders' Equity

Current liabilities.	$(68) 2,521,000	$(68) 4,957,000
Deferred income—payments received in advance	51,000	105,000
Long-term debt.	4,700,000	5,195,000
Stockholders' equity:		
Capital stock—common	2,191,000	2,191,000
Additional paid-in capital.	3,932,000	3,932,000
Retained earnings.	7,479,000	7,376,000
Total stockholders' equity.	13,602,000	13,499,000
	$(68)20,874,000	$(68)23,756,000

XYZ COMPANY
Comparative General Price-Level Statements
of Income and Retained Earnings
Years Ended December 31, 1968 and
December 31, 1967

	General price-level basis (restated to 12/31/68)	
	1968	1967
Sales............................	$(68)27,381,000	$(68)31,611,000
Operating expenses:		
Cost of sales..................	21,379,000	24,138,000
Depreciation	2,408,000	2,719,000
Selling and administrative expenses...................	2,658,000	2,717,000
	26,445,000	29,574,000
Operating profit	936,000	2,037,000
Gain (or loss) on sale of equipment....	41,000	(12,000)
Loss on sale of securities...........	(118,000)	
General price-level gain............	85,000	143,000
	8,000	131,000
Income before federal income taxes ...	944,000	2,168,000
Federal income taxes	639,000	959,000
Net income	305,000	1,209,000
Retained earnings, beginning of year.....................	7,376,000	6,377,000
	7,681,000	7,586,000
Less: Dividends paid	202,000	210,000
Retained earnings, end of year.......	$(68) 7,479,000	$(68) 7,376,000

XYZ COMPANY   12/31/68
General Price-Level Restatement—1968   R-1
Gross National Product Implicit Price Deflators and Conversion Factors

Year	Quarter	GNP deflators	Conversion factors 1968 (4th q.) = 1.000
Annual average			
1957		97.5	1.267
1958		100.0	1.235
1959		101.6	1.216
1960		103.3	1.196
1961		104.6	1.181
1962		105.7	1.168
1963		107.1	1.153
1964		108.9	1.134
1965		110.9	1.114
1966		113.9	1.084
1967		117.3	1.053
1968		121.8	1.014
Quarterly			
1966	4th	115.3	1.071
1967	1st	116.0	1.065
	2nd	116.6	1.059
	3rd	117.7	1.049
	4th	118.9	1.039
1968	1st	120.0	1.029
	2nd	121.2	1.019
	3rd	122.3	1.010
	4th	123.5	1.000

Source: *Survey of Current Business*, U.S. Department of Commerce, Office of Business Economics.

XYZ COMPANY
General Price-Level Restatement—1968
Working Balance Sheets—12/31/67 and 12/31/68

12/31/68
R-2

	12/31/67		12/31/68		
	Restated to 12/31/67 $'s (1)	Restated to 12/31/68 $'s (2)	Historical	Conversion factor or source	Restated to 12/31/68 $'s
Assets					
Cash	1,700,000	1,766,300	2,120,000	(3)	2,120,000
Marketable securities (at cost)	1,654,090	1,718,600			
Receivables—net	5,050,000	5,246,950	6,170,000	(3)	6,170,000
Inventories					
Raw materials (FIFO)	2,849,340	2,960,464	2,540,000	(4) 1.014	2,575,560
Finished goods (FIFO)	2,560,000	2,659,840	2,390,000	(5) 1.000	2,390,000
Parts and supplies (FIFO).	577,980	600,521	612,000	(4) 1.014	620,568
Prepaid expenses.	49,261	51,182	42,000	R-4	43,030
Total current assets	14,440,671	15,003,857	13,874,000		13,919,158
Property, plant, and equipment					
(at cost).	29,579,550	30,733,153	26,400,000	R-5	31,208,277
Less: Accumulated depreciation.	21,156,145	21,981,235	20,210,000	R-6	24,253,021
	8,423,405	8,751,918	6,190,000		6,955,256
	22,864,076	23,755,775	20,064,000		20,874,414
Liabilities					
Current liabilities	4,770,000	4,956,030	2,521,000	(3)	2,521,000
Deferred income—payments					
received in advance	100,900	104,835	50,000	R-7	50,490
Long-term debt	5,000,000	5,195,000	4,700,000	(3)	4,700,000
	9,870,900	10,255,865	7,271,000		7,271,490
Stockholders' Equity					
Capital stock—common	2,109,120	2,191,376	1,760,000	(6)	2,191,376
Additional paid-in capital	3,784,550	3,932,147	3,150,000	(6)	3,932,147
Retained earnings	7,099,506	7,376,387	7,883,000	R-3	7,479,401
	12,993,176	13,499,910	12,793,000		13,602,924
	22,864,076	23,755,775	20,064,000		20,874,414

Notes

(1) From R-2 of 12/31/67.
(2) Each item "rolled-forward" from 12/31/67 $'s to 12/31/68 $'s by using conversion factor for the last quarter of 1967—1.039.
(3) Monetary items—no restatement needed.
(4) Year-end balance assumed acquired fairly evenly throughout the year.
(5) See note 4 in R-2 of 12/31/67.
(6) No change in historical balances during 1968. The restated balances in the 12/31/68 balance sheet are therefore the same as the balances in the 12/31/67 balance sheet restated to 12/31/68 $'s in column 2 of this worksheet.

XYZ COMPANY
General Price-Level Restatement—1968
Working Statements of Income and Retained Earnings

12/31/68
R-3

	Restated to 12/31/67 $'s (1)	Restated to 12/31/68 $'s (2)	Historical	Conversion factor or source	Restated to 12/31/68 $'s
	1967			*1968*	
Sales	30,424,220	31,610,764	27,000,000	R-8	27,381,735
Operating expenses:					
Cost of sales (except depreciation)	23,232,180	24,138,235	20,856,000	R-8	21,379,109
Depreciation	2,616,635	2,718,684	2,070,000	R-6	2,407,937
Selling and administrative expenses	2,614,704	2,716,677	2,620,000	R-9	2,658,412
	28,463,519	29,573,596	25,546,000		26,445,458
Operating profit	1,960,701	2,037,168	1,454,000		936,277
Gain or (loss) on sale of equipment	(11,730)	(12,187)	61,000	R-9	41,354
Gain or (loss) on sale of securities			100,000	R-9	(118,600)
General price-level gain	137,715	143,086	-0-	R-10	84,703
	125,985	130,899	161,000		7,457
Income before federal income taxes	2,086,686	2,168,067	1,615,000		943,734
Federal income taxes	922,740	958,727	630,000	(3) 1.014	638,820
Net income	1,163,946	1,209,340	985,000		304,914
Retained earnings—beginning of year	6,137,560	6,376,925	7,098,000	R-2 (1967, 8)	7,376,387
	7,301,506	7,586,265	8,083,000		7,681,301
Dividends paid					
June 1968	102,000	105,978	100,000	1.019	101,900
December 1968	100,000	103,900	100,000	1.000	100,000
	202,000	209,878	200,000		201,900
Retained earnings—end of year	7,099,506	7,376,387	7,883,000		7,479,401

(1)   From R-3 of 12/31/67.
(2)   Each item "rolled-forward" from 12/31/67 $'s to 12/31/68 $'s by using conversion factor for the last quarter of 1967—1.039.
(3)   Assumed accrued ratably throughout the year.

XYZ COMPANY
General Price-Level Restatement—1968
Analysis of Prepaid Expenses

12/31/68
R-4

		Historical					Restated to 12/31/68 $'s			
Year acquired	Factor to restate 1968 additions	Balance 12/31/67	Additions	Amortization	Balance 12/31/68	Balance 12/31/67 in 12/31/68 $'s (1)	Balance 12/31/67 (2)	Additions	Amortization	Balance 12/31/68
1965		3,000		3,000		3,216	3,341		(3) 3,341	
1966		10,000		8,000	2,000	10,440	10,847		(3) 8,678	2,169
1967										
1st q.		17,000		10,000	7,000	17,425	18,105		(3) 10,650	7,455
3rd q.		18,000		12,000	6,000	18,180	18,889		(3) 12,593	6,296
1968										
3rd q.	1.010		14,000	3,000	11,000			14,140	3,030	11,110
4th q.	1.000		20,000	4,000	16,000			20,000	4,000	16,000
		48,000	34,000	40,000	42,000	49,261	51,182	34,140	42,292	43,030

(1)   From R-5 of 12/31/67.
(2)   Each item restated by factor for 4th quarter 1967—1.039.
(3)   Restated amortization is same percentage of restated 12/31/67 balance as historical amortization is of historical 12/31/67 balance.

XYZ COMPANY
General Price-Level Restatement—1968
Analysis of Property, Plant, and Equipment

12/31
R-?

Year acquired	Factor to restate 1968 additions	Historical Balance 12/31/67	Additions	Retirements	Balance 12/31/68	Balance 12/31/67 in 12/31/67 $'s (1)	Restated to 12/31/68 $'s Balance 12/31/67 (2)	Additions	Retirements	Balance 12/31/68
1957		2,800,000			2,800,000	3,413,200	3,546,315			3,546,31
1958		2,900,000			2,900,000	3,448,100	3,582,576			3,582,57
1959		3,900,000			3,900,000	4,563,000	4,740,957			4,740,95
1960'		3,600,000			3,600,000	4,143,600	4,305,200			4,305,20
1961		800,000			800,000	909,600	945,074			945,07
1962		5,000,000			5,000,000	5,625,000	5,844,375			5,844,37
1963		3,000,000			3,000,000	3,330,000	3,459,870			3,459,87
1964		1,900,000		300,000	1,600,000	2,074,800	2,155,717		(3) 340,376	1,815,34
1965		500,000			500,000	536,000	556,904			556,90
1966		500,000			500,000	522,000	542,358			542,35
1967										
1st q.		250,000			250,000	256,250	266,244			266,24
2nd q.		300,000			300,000	306,000	317,934			317,93
3rd q.		200,000			200,000	202,000	209,878			209,87
4th q.		250,000			250,000	250,000	259,751			259,75
1968										
1st q.	1.029		300,000		300,000		308,700			308,70
2nd q.	1.019		200,000		200,000		203,800			203,80
3rd q.	1.010		300,000		300,000		303,000			303,00
4th q.										
		25,900,000	800,000	300,000	26,400,000	29,579,550	30,733,153	815,500	340,376	31,208,27

(1) From R-6 of 12/31/67.
(2) Restated to 12/31/68 $'s by factor for 4th quarter 1967—1.039.
(3) Restated retirement amount is same percentage of restated 12/31/67 balance as historical retirement amount is of historical 12/31/67 balance.

XYZ COMPANY
General Price-Level Restatement—1968
Analysis of Accumulated Depreciation

12/31
R-?

Year assets acquired	Factor to restate to 12/31/68 $'s	Historical Balance 12/31/67	Depreciation (1)	Retirements	Balance 12/31/68	Balance 12/31/67 $'s (2)	Restated to 12/31/68 $'s Balance 12/31/67 (4)	Depreciation (1)	Retirements	Balance 12/31/68
1957		2,800,000			2,800,000	3,413,200	3,546,316			3,546,31
1958		2,900,000			2,900,000	3,448,100	3,582,576			3,582,57
1959		3,510,000	390,000		3,900,000	4,106,700	4,266,861	474,096		4,740,95
1960		2,880,000	360,000		3,240,000	3,314,880	3,444,160	430,520		3,874,68
1961		560,000	80,000		640,000	636,720	661,552	94,507		756,05
1962		3,000,000	500,000		3,500,000	3,375,000	3,506,625	584,437		4,091,06
1963		1,500,000	300,000		1,800,000	1,665,000	1,729,935	345,987		2,075,92
1964		760,000	160,000	120,000	800,000	829,920	862,287	181,534	(3) 136,151	907,67
1965		150,000	50,000		200,000	160,800	167,071	55,690		222,76
1966		100,000	50,000		150,000	104,400	108,472	54,236		162,70
1967										
1st q.		25,000	25,000		50,000	25,625	26,624	26,624		53,24
2nd q.		30,000	30,000		60,000	30,600	31,793	31,793		63,58
3rd q.		20,000	20,000		40,000	20,200	20,988	20,988		41,97
4th q.		25,000	25,000		50,000	25,000	25,975	25,975		51,98
1968										
1st q.	1.029		30,000		30,000			30,870		30,87
2nd q.	1.019		20,000		20,000			20,380		20,38
3rd q.	1.010		30,000		30,000			30,300		30,30
4th q.										
		18,260,000	2,070,000	120,000	20,210,000	21,156,145	21,981,235	2,407,937	136,151	24,253,02

(1) Depreciation basis: Straight line
10 year life
No salvage value
Full year's depreciation in year of acquisition
No depreciation in year of disposition
(2) From R-7 of 12/31/67.
(3) Restated accumulated depreciation on assets retired is same percentage of restated 12/31/67 balance as historical accumulated depreciation on retirements is of historical 12/31/67 balance.
(4) Restated to 12/31/68 $'s by factor for 4th quarter 1967—1.039.

XYZ COMPANY
General Price-Level Restatement—1968
Analysis of Deferred Income

12/31/68
R-7

| | | Historical | | | | Restated to 12/31/68 $'s | | | | |
| | | | | | | Balance 12/31/67 in 12/31/67 $'s | Balance 12/31/67 | | | |
Year acquired	Factor to restate to 12/31/68 $'s	Balance 12/31/67	Addi-tions	Realized	Balance 12/31/68	(1)	(2)	Addi-tions	Realized	Balance 12/31/68
1967										
2nd q.		20,000		20,000		20,400	21,196		21,196	
3rd q.		50,000		50,000		50,500	52,469		52,469	
4th q.		30,000		30,000		30,000	31,170		31,170	
1968										
1st q.	1.029		20,000	20,000				20,580	20,580	
2nd q.	1.019		10,000		10,000			10,190		10,190
3rd q.	1.010		30,000		30,000			30,300		30,300
4th q.	1.000		10,000		10,000			10,000		10,000
		100,000	70,000	120,000	50,000	100,900	104,835	71,070	125,415	50,490

(1) From R-8 of 12/31/67.
(2) Each item restated by factor for 4th quarter 1967—1.039.

XYZ COMPANY
General Price-Level Restatement—1968
Analysis of Sales and Cost of Sales

12/31/68
R-8

	Historical	Conversion factor or source	Restated to 12/31/68 $'s
Sales			
Current sales	26,880,000	(1) 1.014	27,256,320
Deferred sales realized	120,000	R-7	125,415
Total sales.	27,000,000		27,381,735
Cost of sales (except depreciation)			
Inventories 12/31/67			
Raw materials	2,810,000	R-2 (1967, 8)	2,960,464
Finished goods	2,560,000	R-2 (1967, 8)	2,659,840
Parts and supplies.	570,000	R-2 (1967, 8)	600,521
Purchases	20,458,000	(1) 1.014	20,744,412
	26,398,000		26,965,237
Inventories 12/31/68			
Raw materials	2,540,000	R-2	2,575,560
Finished goods	2,390,000	R-2	2,390,000
Parts and supplies.	612,000	R-2	620,568
	5,542,000		5,586,128
	20,856,000		21,379,109

(1) Spread fairly evenly throughout the year.

XYZ COMPANY
General Price-Level Restatement—1968   12/31/
Analysis of Expenses   R-9

	Historical	Conversion factor or source	Restated to 12/31/68 $
Selling and administrative expenses Amortization of prepaid			
expenses	40,000	R-4	42,292
Other	2,580,000	(1) 1.014	2,616,120
	2,620,000		2,658,412
Gain or (loss) on sale of equipment			
Cost	300,000	R-5	340,376
Accumulated depreciation	120,000	R-6	136,151
	180,000		204,225
Proceeds, June 1968	241,000	1.019	245,579
Gain	61,000		41,354
Gain or (loss) on sale of marketable securities			
Cost	1,500,000	R-2 (1967, 8)	1,718,600
Proceeds, December 1968	1,600,000	1.000	1,600,000
Gain (loss)	100,000		(118,600)

(1) Spread fairly evenly throughout the year.

XYZ COMPANY
General Price-Level Restatement—1968   12/31/68
General Price-Level Gain or Loss   R-10

		12/31/67		12/31/68
	Source	Historical	Restated to 12/31/68 $'s	Historical (stated in 12/31/68 $'s)
Net monetary items				
Cash................	R-2	1,700,000	1,766,300	2,120,000
Receivables..........	R-2	5,050,000	5,246,950	6,170,000
Current liabilities	R-2	(4,770,000)	(4,956,030)	(2,521,000)
Long-term debt	R-2	(5,000,000)	(5,195,000)	(4,700,000)
		(3,020,000)	(3,137,780)	1,069,000

General price-level gain or loss	Historical	Source	Restated to 12/31/68 $'s
Net monetary items—12/31/67	(3,020,000)	as above	(3,137,780)
Add:			
Current sales	26,880,000	R-8	27,256,320
Additions to deferred income	70,000	R-7	71,070
Proceeds from sale of equipment	241,000	R-9	245,579
Proceeds from sale of securities	1,600,000	R-9	1,600,000
	25,771,000		26,035,189
Deduct:			
Purchases	20,458,000	R-8	20,744,412
Selling and administrative expenses— other..........................	2,580,000	R-9	2,616,120
Federal income taxes...............	630,000	R-3	638,820
Dividends	200,000	R-3	201,900
Purchases of property, plant, and equipment	800,000	R-5	815,500
Additions to prepaid expenses...........	34,000	R-4	34,140
	24,702,000		25,050,892
Net monetary items—historical—12/31/68 (as above)........................	1,069,000		
Net monetary items—restated—12/31/68 (if there were no gain).................			984,297
Net monetary items—12/31/68 (as above)			1,069,000
General price-level gain................			84,703

QUESTIONS AND PROBLEMS

20–1. The sales of the Gardner Company were as follows: year 1, $700,000; year 2, $875,000. The company has constructed an index which in their opinion reflects average sales prices of their products during the two years, as follows: year 1, 100; year 2, 110.

Required:
Adjust the company's sales figures for price-level change.

20–2. Explain why, in Problem 20–1, you used the method employed and also what alternative approach was available and why you did not use it.

20–3. Explain what problem or problems you might expect to encounter in constructing an index of average sales prices, as in Problem 20–1.

20–4. If two manufacturers build identical plants in 1970 at costs of $100,000 and $110,000, respectively, how is the competitive advantage of the one manufacturer over the other manufacturer reflected in his income statements?

20–5. What is meant by "the matching of cost and revenue"?

20–6. If an analyst proposes to convert an income statement for the year 1970 into 1971 dollars, should he convert to the average dollar for the year 1971 or the dollar at December 31, 1971? Why?

20–7. During the year 1971, a corporation derived income from the following sources:

The common stock of a 100% owned subsidiary, being the entire net income of the subsidiary (no dividends paid or declared)	$250,000
Investment in 1% of the common stock of a good customer:	
Proportion of book income	50,000
Dividends declared (proportionate share)	20,000
Dividends received	25,000
Interest on loans to wholly owned subsidiary	10,000

Required:
To what extent do these income amounts require adjustment for changes in the value of the dollar?

20–8. It is frequently stated that statements for a month or a quarter are nothing more than tentative measurements. Prepare a brief statement concerning this conclusion.

21

Results of adjusting for price-level changes

THIS CHAPTER is an analysis of the differences which resulted when the conventional financial statements were adjusted for price-level changes in the Accounting Principles Board's *Statement No. 3.*

In Illustration 21–1 (balance sheets) and Illustration 21–2 (statements of income and retained earnings) the historical and general price-level statements are presented in comparative form and the differences are computed on an item-by-item basis.

Balance sheets

Cash and receivables. These items are "monetary" (their value is hooked to the value of the dollar) so adjustment is not appropriate.

Inventories: Raw materials and parts and supplies. The small upward adjustments of these two inventory items (about 1½ percent) are due to adjusting the average price level of the year to bring it up to the price level at the end of the year. The inventories were assumed to have been acquired gradually throughout the year.

Inventory of finished goods. It was assumed that this inventory was acquired during the last quarter of the year and that adjustment is not necessary.

Prepaid expenses. Small increase (about 1½ percent) is due to various adjustments to bring 1966, 1967, and 1968 balances up to the price level at December 31, 1968.

Property, plant and equipment. This substantial upward adjustment

ILLUSTRATION 21–1

XYZ COMPANY
Historical and General Price-Level
Balance Sheets
December 31, 1968
(in comparative form)

	Balance sheet		Differences	
	Historical	Price level	Debt	Credit
Assets				
Current Assets:				
Cash	$ 2,120,000	$ 2,120,000		
Receivables, net	6,170,000	6,170,000		
Inventories, at the lower of cost and market on a first-in, first-out basis:				
Raw materials	2,540,000	2,575,000	$ 35,000	
Finished goods	2,390,000	2,390,000		
Parts and supplies	612,000	621,000	9,000	
Prepaid expenses	42,000	43,000	1,000	
Total Current Assets	$13,874,000	$13,919,000		
Property, plant, and equipment, at cost	$26,400,000	$31,208,000	4,808,000	
Less: Accumulated depreciation	20,210,000	24,253,000		$4,043,000
	$ 6,190,000	$ 6,955,000		
Total Assets	$20,064,000	$20,874,000		
Liabilities and Stockholders' Equity				
Current liabilities	$ 2,521,000	$ 2,521,000		
Deferred income—payments received in advance	50,000	51,000		1,000
Long-term debt	4,700,000	4,700,000		
Stockholders' Equity:				
Capital stock—common	1,760,000	2,191,000		43,000
Additional paid-in capital	3,150,000	3,932,000		782,000
Retained earnings	7,883,000	7,479,000	404,000	
Total Stockholders' Equity	$12,793,000	$13,602,000		
Total Liabilities and Stockholders' Equity	$20,064,000	$20,874,000	$5,257,000	$5,257,000

(about 18 percent) results from adjusting each item from its historical cost in the dollars of the year of its acquisition to the same cost in the less valuable dollar at the end of 1968.

Accumulated depreciation. The accumulated depreciation balances for each year were adjusted to the price level at the end of 1968 using the same procedures as were employed in adjusting property, plant, and equipment.

Net fixed assets after adjustment to the price level at December 31, 1968. General price-level net cost is about 12½ percent higher than historical cost. This substantial increase is due to the varying numbers of years between acquisition and the balance sheet date.

Payments received in advance. This deferred income item was adjusted up to the year-end price level. The actual increase before being rounded was $490, about 1 percent.

Capital stock and additional paid-in capital. These two items were adjusted from the price levels of the years in which paid in, to the price level at December 31, 1968. The relevant increases in the price level (as measured by the deflator) were: from 1957, about 22 percent;

ILLUSTRATION 21–2

XYZ COMPANY
Historical and General Price-Level
Statements of Income and Retained Earnings
Year Ended December 31, 1968
(in comparative form)

	Statements of income and retained earnings		Differences	
	Historical	Price level	Debit	Credit
Sales.	$27,000,000	$27,381,000		$ 381,000
Operating expenses:				
Cost of goods sold (except depreciation).	$20,856,000	$21,379,000	$ 523,000	
Depreciation	2,070,000	2,408,000	338,000	
Selling and administrative expenses	2,620,000	2,658,000	38,000	
	$25,546,000	$26,445,000		
Operating profit	$ 1,454,000	$ 936,000		
Gain (or loss) on sale of equipment.	$ 61,000	$ 41,000	20,000	
Gain (or loss) on sale of securities.	100,000	(118,000)	218,000	
General price-level gain.	—	85,000		85,000
	$ 161,000	$ 8,000		
Income before federal income taxes	$ 1,615,000	$ 944,000		
Federal income taxes	630,000	639,000	9,000	
Net income	$ 985,000	$ 305,000	To balance	680,000*
Retained earnings, beginning of year.	7,098,000	7,376,000		
	$ 8,083,000	$ 7,681,000		
Less: Dividends paid	200,000	202,000		
Retained Earnings, End of Year	$ 7,883,000	$ 7,479,000	$1,146,000	$1,146,000

Decreases in net income.

from 1958, about 19 percent; and from 1961, about 14 percent; overall about 20 percent.

Retained earnings. The general price-level balance of retained earnings at December 31, 1967, was determined to be the amount necessary to produce a balance of the two sides of the general price-level balance sheet as of that date. Net income for the year 1968 was then added and dividends were deducted.

	Historical	Price level
Retained earnings, balance at end of 1967	$7,098,000	$7,376,387
Net income, 1968	985,000	304,914
	$8,083,000	$7,681,301
Dividends, 1968	200,000	201,900
Retained earnings, balance at end of 1968	$7,883,000	$7,479,401

The difference between the historical net income and the general price-level net income in 1968 will be analyzed below. The small difference (about 1 percent) in the two dividend figures is due to adjustment from average 1968 price level to end of 1968 price level.

Statements of income and retained earnings

Sales. The difference between the historical and price-level amounts (less than 1½ percent) is from adjusting to the December 31, 1968 price level.

Cost of goods sold (except depreciation). This substantial difference ($523,000) is due to: (1) adjusting 1968 purchases ($20,458,000) to the end of 1968 price level ($286,000) and (2) carrying about $6,000,000 of inventory through a year of rising prices ($235,000).

Depreciation. Adjusting the "costs" of the depreciable assets from the price levels of the years of their acquisition to the $338,000 (about 16 percent).

Selling and administrative expenses. Adjusted to end of 1968 price level (up 1½ percent).

Gain on sale of equipment. Equipment was bought in 1964 for $300,000 which, in 1968 dollars, would be a cost of $340,000. However, this difference has to be adjusted for a $16,000 increase in depreciation, and the result, after adjustment to end of 1968 prices, is a $20,000 decrease in the gain.

Gain or (loss) on sale of securities. Adjustment of this item for changes in the price level turns a $100,000 gain (on a conventional income statement) into a $118,000 loss (on a general price-level income statement) a whopping swing of $218,000. This difference arises from a $218,000 increase in "cost." One third of the securities were bought in 1961; two thirds were bought in 1964 and 1965. The historical cost of $1,500,000 increased by about 14½ percent, which converted a substantial gain, as originally computed, into a substantial loss after adjustment for the price level.

General price-level gain. This gain, arising from a preponderance of debt over monetary assets during a period of rising prices, was computed to total $85,000. (See page 471.)

AN OVERVIEW

What can we learn from the results of the analysis described above?

Statement of income

Operating profit, computed as $1,454,000 on a conventional historical cost income statement, dropped to $936,000 when price-level adjustment procedures were applied. This is a decrease of $518,000 (down 35½ percent). This decrease arose out of cost of goods sold. Forty percent came from a recomputation of depreciation which was understated when based on historical costs. Sixty percent came from squeezing out apparent but unreal inventory profits which are always present when Fifo is used in a time of rising prices.

Below operating income, there were three extraordinary items. Gains on sales of equipment and securities, amount to $161,000, turned into a net loss of $77,000 when the increasing price level was taken into account. Most of this "swing" was on the securities transaction.

A general price-level gain contributed $85,000 to net income on the general price-level income statement.

As a result of these changes, net income dropped $680,000, from $985,000 to $305,000.

On the conventionally prepared income statement, operating profit was 11.3 percent of stockholders' equity; net income was 6.9 percent. On the general price-level statement of income, operating profit dropped to 7.7 percent of stockholders' equity and net income declined to 2.25 percent.

Balance sheet

While there were some other items, such as inventories, that showed minor differences on the general price-level balance sheet, the major changes were in fixed assets and stockholders' equity.

Property, plant, and equipment increased from $26,400,000 to $31,208,000, up $4,808,000 (18 percent). Accumulated depreciation increased from $20,210,000 to $24,253,000, up $4,043,000 (20 percent). Therefore, net fixed assets increased from $6,190,000 to $6,955,000, up $765,000 (12 percent).

Common stock and additional paid-in capital, together, rose from $4,910,000 to $6,123,000, up $1,213,000 (nearly 25 percent). Retained earnings declined from $7,883,000 to $7,479,000, down $404,000 (5.1 percent).

Both statements

Note that the increasing price level increased stockholders' equity (capital contributions rose as the dollar declined in value) but depressed operating income and net income (due to elimination of unreal inventory "profits," and heavier depreciation.) The ratio of income to stockholders' equity suffered at both ends. The balance sheet offset to the increased stockholders' equity is primarily in the adjusted cost of fixed assets.

While the XYZ Company example from *Statement No. 3* is fictitious, the distortions it reflects are realistic. The decline in 1968 net income was perhaps unusually large because of a conjunction of three major distorting factors: unreal inventory profits, depreciation, and extraordinary losses, primarily on securities. In the Caterpillar Tractor Company example in previous editions of this book, the effects of price-level adjustments were less severe. The effect of depreciation was the same, but the use of Lifo eliminated the inventory distortion, and the extraordinary losses were not present.

APPENDIX A. GROSS NATIONAL PRODUCT IMPLICIT PRICE DEFLATOR

Annual Averages, 1929–68

Year	Deflator (1958 = 100)	Percent increase (decrease) from previous year
1929	50.6	
1930	49.3	(2.6)
1931	44.8	(9.1)
1932	40.3	(10.0)
1933	39.3	(2.5)
1934	42.2	7.4
1935	42.6	.9
1936	42.7	.2
1937	44.5	4.2
1938	43.9	(1.3)
1939	43.2	(1.6)
1940	43.9	1.6
1941	47.2	7.5
1942	53.0	12.3
1943	56.8	7.2
1944	58.2	2.5
1945	59.7	2.6
1946	66.7	11.7
1947	74.6	11.8
1948	79.6	6.7
1949	79.1	(.6)
1950	80.2	1.4
1951	85.6	6.7
1952	87.5	2.2
1953	88.3	.9
1954	89.6	1.5
1955	90.9	1.5
1956	94.0	3.4
1957	97.5	3.7
1958	100.0	2.6
1959	101.6	1.6
1960	103.3	1.7
1961	104.6	1.3
1962	105.7	1.1
1963	107.1	1.3
1964	108.9	1.7
1965	110.9	1.8
1966	113.9	2.7
1967	117.3	3.0
1968	121.8	3.8

Quarterly Averages, 1947–72

Year	Quarter	Deflator
1947.	1	73.0
	2	73.7
	3	74.9
	4	77.0
1948.	1	78.2
	2	79.2
	3	80.6
	4	80.3
1949.	1	79.7
	2	79.1
	3	78.8
	4	78.9
1950.	1	78.3
	2	79.0
	3	80.8
	4	82.3
1951.	1	84.8
	2	85.4
	3	85.6
	4	86.7
1952.	1	86.7
	2	87.1
	3	87.7
	4	88.3
1953.	1	88.4
	2	88.3
	3	88.4
	4	88.4
1954.	1	89.5
	2	89.6
	3	89.5
	4	89.8
1955.	1	90.2
	2	90.6
	3	91.0
	4	91.6
1956.	1	92.6
	2	93.4
	3	94.6
	4	95.4
1957.	1	96.4
	2	97.1
	3	98.0
	4	98.5
1958.	1	99.3
	2	99.7
	3	100.1
	4	100.6
1959.	1	101.1
	2	101.4
	3	101.9
	4	102.1

Quarterly Averages, 1947–72 (continued)

Year	Quarter	Deflator
1960........	1	102.6
	2	103.0
	3	103.4
	4	104.0
1961........	1	104.3
	2	104.5
	3	104.5
	4	105.1
1962........	1	105.4
	2	105.5
	3	105.8
	4	106.2
1963........	1	106.6
	2	107.0
	3	107.1
	4	107.8
1964........	1	108.3
	2	108.4
	3	109.0
	4	109.6
1965........	1	110.1
	2	110.7
	3	111.0
	4	111.6
1966........	1	112.6
	2	113.5
	3	114.4
	4	115.3
1967........	1	116.0
	2	116.6
	3	117.7
	4	118.9
1968........	1	120.0
	2	121.2
	3	122.3
	4	123.5
1969........	1	125.7
	2	127.2
	3	129.0
	4	130.5
1970........	1	132.6
	2	134.0
	3	136.0
	4	138.1
1971........	1	139.9
	2	141.3
	3	142.2
	4	142.7
1972........	1	144.9

Source: United States Department of Commerce, *Survey of Current Business*, issued monthly. Quarterly figures are available only since 1947. The deflators for 1929 to 1964 were recapitulated on pages 52 and 53 of the August 1965 issue of the *Survey*.

PART IV

*Analysis and Interpretation of the
Financial Statements of Several
Regulated Industries*

22

Statements of air carriers

THE UNITED STATES today possesses one of the most efficient and modern air-transportation industries in the world. Scheduled air transportation was established in 1926, when the Post Office Department contracted with private aviation companies for transporting airmail. Scheduled passenger service became important in 1930, when the Post Office Department began to require the establishment of scheduled passenger service by those companies holding airmail contracts.

The policy put into effect in 1930 was for the benefit of the economy of the United States and the postal service. Furthermore, civil aviation was encouraged and developed from the point of view of national defense. Civil aviation affords a system of high-speed communications which may be used in an emergency; a highly trained body of personnel is in existence which may be drawn upon in the event of war; support is given to aviation production, which also constructs military and naval equipment; military and naval aviation is benefited by experimental work carried on by civil aviation; and the nationwide system of lighted and radar- and radio-equipped airways is available to military and naval aviation. Civil aviation proved to be of tremendous value to the war effort during World War II.

Uniform system of accounts

The Civil Aeronautics Board, which regulates interstate commercial aviation, adopted on July 1, 1938, a uniform system of accounts, records, and reports. This uniform system of accounts has been revised from time to time, the last comprehensive revision was made as of January 1, 1957. It is unlawful for air carriers to keep any records other than those prescribed by the Board, without specific approval. Approval may be obtained (1) if the integrity of the accounts, records, or memoranda prescribed or approved by the Board is not impaired; and (2) there is no undue financial burden on the air carrier.

Monthly, quarterly, and annual financial and operating data[1] for commercial aviation companies must be filed with the Civil Aeronautics Board and are available to the public. The availability of these uniform data is of considerable importance, especially to the aviation companies, investors, bankers, the Congress, and the Civil Aeronautics Board.

Uniform financial and operating data are used to determine the relative financial and operating efficiency and investment value of different air-carrier companies and in regulating such matters as airmail, express and freight, and air-passenger rates; carrier and noncarrier property; capital and revenue expenditures; depreciation; services; reorganizations; combinations; and abandonment of air routes. The Civil Aeronautics Board does not have authority to regulate air-carrier securities issues or the incurrence of liability of any nature.

The major sources of financial and operating data include the Civil Aeronautics Board, the Air Transport Association of America, and the annual reports of individual air-carrier companies.

Comparison of balance sheets of air carriers and nonregulated businesses

The balance sheet accounts prescribed for air carriers are designed to show the financial condition of an air carrier as of a given date, reflecting the asset and liability balances carried forward subsequent to the closing or constructive closing of the air carrier's books of account. The balance sheet of an air carrier (Illustration 22–1) differs slightly from a balance sheet prepared for a nonregulated business with respect to the order of presentation and the terminology used. These differences may be seen in the following comparison of the main sections appearing on the two types of balance sheets. The balance sheet items of an air carrier are explained beginning on page 481.

---

[1] Air carriers are required to keep their accounting books and records on a quarterly basis; full accruals and adjustments must be recorded for each quarter. The books are closed at the end of each calendar year.

Nonregulated Business	*Air Carrier*[2]

Assets:
  Current assets (includes short-term prepayment of expense)
  Long-term investments
  Fixed assets
  Intangible assets
  Deferred charges
  Other assets

Assets:
  Current assets (includes short-term prepayments)
  Investments and special funds
  Property and equipment:
    Operating
    Nonoperating
  Deferred charges (includes long-term prepayment of expense)

Liabilities:
  Current liabilities (includes unearned revenue)
  Deferred credits to expense
  Long-term liabilities

Liabilities:
  Current liabilities
  Noncurrent liabilities
  Deferred credits

Owner's Equity:
  Capital stock
  Paid-in surplus
  Retained earnings:
    Appropriated
    Unappropriated
  Appreciation surplus

Stockholders' Equity:
  Paid-in capital:
    Capital stock
    Other paid-in capital
  Retained earnings:
    Reserve for self-insurance
    Other appropriations of retained earnings
    Unappropriated retained earnings
  Treasury stock

ASSETS

Current assets

All resources which may reasonably be expected to be realized in cash or sold or consumed in one year are classified as current assets.

In the current asset section of the balance sheet are included such items as unrestricted cash; working funds and special deposits; U.S. government securities; other short-term securities; current receivables, including subscriptions to capital stock; material and supplies; accrued revenue; and other similar items of a current nature. Materials and supplies[3] include flight equipment—expendable parts, motor fuels, and lubricating oils. The classification of accounts specifically provides for including (as a part of the cost of materials, parts, and supplies) all transportation charges, custom duties, excises, special insurance, taxes, and other applicable charges. It is also provided that any losses sustained or gains realized upon the abandonment or other disposition of flight equipment expendable parts should be recognized as capital gains or

---

[2] Accounts prescribed by the Civil Aeronautics Board, effective January 1, 1957.

[3] A perpetual inventory is required to be maintained for all materials, supplies, lubricating oils, motor fuels, and flight equipment expendable parts. These inventories must be verified by physical count at least annually.

ILLUSTRATION 22–1

AMERICAN AIRLINES INC. AND CONSOLIDATED SUBSIDIARY
Consolidated Statement of Operations
(in thousands)

Assets

	December 31
	1971	1970

Current Assets

Cash	$ **44,858**	$ 33,236
Marketable securities, at cost	**9,000**	2,800
Receivables	**198,318**	203,856
Spare parts, materials and supplies, at average cost less obsolescence reserve (1971—$6,882; 1970—$7,036)	**45,296**	40,315
Prepaid expenses	**4,917**	4,231
Total Current Assets	**302,389**	284,438

Operating Equipment and Property (Notes 3 and 5)

Flight equipment, at cost	**1,294,937**	1,276,639
Less: Accumulated depreciation and obsolescence	**439,610**	465,855
	855,327	810,784
Cash deposits with manufacturers for purchase of flight equipment	**134,930**	184,632
	990,257	995,416
Land, buildings and other equipment, at cost	**225,956**	231,183
Less: Accumulated depreciation	**75,023**	65,473
	150,933	165,710
Total Operating Equipment and Property—Net	**1,141,190**	1,161,126

Investments and Other Assets

Investment in and advances to Sky Chefs, Inc. (Note 1)	**28,212**	27,312
Aircraft held for resale and receivable on sale of aircraft and other equipment (less reserves, including deferred income: 1971—$24,032; 1970—$21,392) (Notes 4 and 7)	**130,843**	27,786
Route acquisition costs (Note 2)	**36,500**	—
Miscellaneous investments	**7,976**	7,606
Deferred charges	**15,504**	16,678
Total Investments and Other Assets	**219,035**	79,382
Total Assets	**$1,662,614**	$1,524,946

Liabilities and Stockholders' Equity	December 31	
	1971	1970
Current Liabilities		
Accounts payable	**$ 137,568**	$ 151,606
Accrued salaries and wages	**48,151**	46,383
Other accrued liabilities	**32,600**	25,284
Long-term debt maturing within one year	**30,949**	19,171
Air travel plan subscribers' deposits	**9,372**	9,781
Unearned transportation revenue	**30,863**	25,386
Total Current Liabilities	**289,503**	277,611
Long-Term Debt (Note 7)		
Senior	**453,530**	430,200
Subordinated convertible debentures	**172,508**	282,870
Total Long-Term Debt	**626,038**	713,070
Deferred Credits		
Federal income tax (Note 6)	**146,616**	146,266
Self-insurance	**20,669**	18,344
Employee stock purchase plan (Note 10)	**—**	8,977
Other	**1,690**	—
Total Deferred Credits	**168,975**	173,587
Stockholders' Equity (Notes 2, 7, 8, 10 and 14)		
Preferred stock—no par value 5,000,000 shares authorized; none issued		
Common stock—$1 par value 60,000,000 shares authorized (1970—40,000,000); 28,311,000 shares issued and outstanding (1970—20,281,000)	**28,311**	20,281
Additional paid-in capital	**311,188**	96,576
Retained earnings	**238,599**	243,821
Total Stockholders' Equity	**578,098**	360,678
Total Liabilities and Stockholders' Equity	**$1,662,614**	$1,524,946

losses. Such gains or losses may take place when the flight equipment remains on hand at the time of disposing the airframe or aircraft engine to which the parts are related. A reserve for inventory obsolescence may be approved by the Civil Aeronautics Board.

Working funds are in the nature of revolving funds; special deposits include funds specifically providing for the payment of debts, dividends and interest, and other items of a current nature.

Short-term securities include readily marketable securities exclusive of U.S. government securities. Investments maturing within one year from the date of the balance sheet should be transferred from the Investments account to the Short-Term Securities account.

Receivables represent debts due primarily from the U.S. government for airmail transportation and air travel, other lines and agents, and subscribers to air-travel plans. Most travel plans provide for a deposit of cash, so that receivables from this kind of travel are more than matched by deposit liabilities. Receivables should not include uncollectible or doubtful accounts. The uncollectible accounts should be written off to a preestablished valuation account, Reserve for Uncollectible Accounts.

Short-term prepayments include prepaid rent, insurance, taxes, interest, and similar items. Prepayments extending beyond one year when material in amount should be included as long-term prepayments under the heading of deferred charges.

Investments and special funds

The air carrier is required to include as investments (1) the ledger value of loans and notes maturing in more than one year from the date of the balance sheet, securities of nonassociated companies, individuals, state and municipal governments held as long-term investments; and (2) net investment in separately operated divisions such as schools of instruction, crop-dusting service, and manufacturing division. Long-term investments in securities of associated companies are shown separately from the investments stated above. Investments in associated as well as nonassociated companies, which must be stated at cost as of the acquisition date, are shown in detail as stocks, bonds, notes and mortgages, and advances. Any discount or premium on investments having fixed maturities must be amortized over the remaining life of the securities. When securities of others owned by the air carrier suffer a permanent impairment in value, the book value may be written down by a charge to nonoperating Income and Expense—Net; ordinary fluctuations in market value are not recorded.

Special funds include those to cover uninsured losses (self-insurance), sinking funds, cash and securities posted with courts of law pending settlement of lawsuits, employees' funds for purchase of capital stock, pension funds under the control of the air carrier, equipment purchase funds, and depreciation funds when specifically established.

Operating property and equipment

Operating property and equipment (flight equipment and ground property and equipment) accounts include those relatively permanent assets used by the air carrier in air transportation services and services incidental thereto. The following accounts are under this heading:

Airframes
Aircraft Engines
Aircraft Communication and Navigational Equipment
Aircraft Propellers
Miscellaneous Flight Equipment
Improvements to Leased Flight Equipment
Flight Equipment Rotable Parts and Assemblies
Passenger Service Equipment
Hotel, Restaurant, and Food Service Equipment
Ramp Equipment

Communication and Meteorological Equipment
Surface Transport Vehicles and Equipment
Furniture, Fixtures, and Office Equipment
Maintenance and Engineering Equipment
Storage and Distribution Equipment
Miscellaneous Ground Equipment
Maintenance Buildings and Improvements
Land
Construction Work in Progress

The accounting classification requires that the air carrier record in operating property and equipment accounts the cash purchase price or the actual money value of the consideration given in exchange for the assets. Specific provision is made within the accounting classification for the capitalization of transportation costs, taxes, legal fees, inspection and testing costs before use, and all other expenditures properly applicable to the cost of asset acquisition.

Reserves for depreciation and maintenance

The accounting classification provides for accumulating, in accounts titled Reserves for Depreciation of Property and Equipment, all provisions for losses occurring in property and equipment from use and obsolescence. More specifically such reserves are established to record current lessening in service value due to wear and tear from use and the action of time and the elements which are not replaced by current repairs, as well as losses in capacity for use or service occasioned by obsolescence, supersession, discoveries, change in popular demand, or the requirement of public authority.

Maintenance reserves are required to be established by each air carrier for the estimated cost of all periodic airframe maintenance operations of material amount in such manner as will equitably apportion the total airframe direct maintenance costs to the different accounting years. The objective is to effect an appropriate matching of total airframe maintenance costs with the operation of airframes and thereby prevent a distortion of the operating and financial statements by reason of a peak in maintenance cost in one accounting year. The carrier has the option of establishing maintenance reserves for aircraft engines. The estimated maintenance costs are charged to maintenance Reserve Provisions (Profit and Loss account).

The foregoing reserves for depreciation and maintenance are offset against their respective asset accounts on the balance sheet.

Nonoperating property and equipment

Property and equipment not used in the carrier's air transportation services, and services incidental thereto or in separately operated divisions, are listed under the caption of "nonoperating property and equipment." Property and equipment held for future use are also included as nonoperating property and equipment. Specific items includible under this heading are real estate, property held for investment or future use, and the book value of abandoned airports. Air carriers are required to establish reserves for depreciation for depreciable assets listed in this section.

Deferred charges

The *deferred charges* classification for air carriers includes all debit balances in general clearing accounts[4] which are held in suspense pending receipt of information necessary for final disposition, prepayments chargeable against operations over a period of years, capitalized expenditures of an organizational or developmental character, property acquisition adjustments, discount and expense on long-term debt, capital stock expense, and the cost of patents, copyrights, and miscellaneous intangibles. The foregoing items that have a definite time incidence are amortized over the periods to which they apply. The property acquisition adjustment item mentioned above represents the unamortized difference between the purchase price to the air carrier of property and equipment acquired as a part of an air-carrier business from another air carrier and the depreciated cost to the predecessor company at the date of such acquisition.

Unlike commercial businesses, air carriers classify intangible assets

---

[4] A clearing account is one used as a medium for temporary accumulation of costs that are redistributable to appropriate applicable accounts.

as deferred charges rather than provide a special intangible asset classification.

Contingent assets and contingent liabilities

A contingent asset is one the existence, value, or ownership of which depends upon the occurrence of nonoccurrence of a specific event or upon the performance or nonperformance of a specified act. A contingent liability is a possible source of liability of an air carrier dependent upon the fulfillment of conditions regarded as uncertain.

It is provided in the accounting classification that contingent assets and contingent liabilities are not to be included in the body of the balance sheet but are to be referred to and shown in detail in footnotes appended to the statements.

LIABILITIES AND CAPITAL

Current liabilities

Current liabilities represent all debts or obligations the liquidation or payment of which is reasonably expected to require the use, within one year, of existing resources of a type which are properly classifiable as current assets or the creation of other current liabilities.

Current liabilities include, in addition to the usual accrued and current payables, the following accounts: Collections as Agents—Traffic, the amounts collected by the air carrier for the account of other air carriers or surface transport carriers for transportation services over their lines; Air-Travel Plan Liability, the liability for deposits received by the air carrier from the sale of air-travel plan contracts; and Unearned Transportation Revenue, the amount of transportation revenue collected, the service for which has not been performed or a refund has not been made.

Noncurrent liabilities

Noncurrent liabilities include all debts or obligations the liquidation or payment of which is not reasonably expected to require the use within one year of current assets or the creation of current liabilities. These liabilities include such items as mortgage notes, equipment trust certificates, bonds, receivers' certificates, and notes. Pension liability, when the pension plan is administered by the air carrier, is classified as a noncurrent liability. The face value of the long-term debt is recorded as is discount or premium, and is entered in appropriate discount or premium accounts, to be amortized.

Advances from Associated[5] Companies, which is listed on the balance sheet under the heading of noncurrent liabilities, include amounts due associated companies on open accounts and loans and notes payable.

Deferred credits

Deferred credits include credits held in suspense pending receipt of information necessary for final disposition, and premiums on long-term debt securities of the air carrier. Deferred credits that have a definite time incidence are required to be amortized over the periods to which they apply. Under the caption of "deferred credits" are listed the following accounts:

Unamortized premium in debt. This account is the unamortized premium on all classes of long-term debt securities issued or assumed by the air carrier.

Deferred federal income taxes. This account is the difference between the federal income tax computed in accordance with the income tax law and the amount determined on the basis of regular accounting purposes. That is, the income tax law provides for the rapid depreciation of properties at rates in excess of those that are prescribed for regular accounting purposes. In subsequent years the higher tax liability for accounting purposes is charged in part against Deferred Federal Income Taxes.

Self-insurance—clearing. This account is credited for all accruals by the air carrier for uninsured losses and debited for all losses actually sustained. At the close of the accounting year the credit (or debit) balance is transferred to the profit and loss account Over or Under Self-Insurance Accruals. The net debit or credit in Self-Insurance—Clearing prior to clearing at the end of the year is simultaneously reflected in appropriated retained earnings by crediting or debiting Reserve for Self-Insurance and debiting or crediting unappropriated Retained Earnings.

Stockholders' equity

Stockholders' equity includes all items which record the aggregate interests of holders of the air carrier's capital stock. The classification of accounts requires that stockholders' equity be subdivided as shown on page 489.

---

[5] An associated (or affiliated) company is one that is controlled solely by the air carrier or controlled jointly by the air carrier and others.

Paid-in capital:
Capital stock (preferred, common, and subscribed)
Other paid-in capital—net

Retained earnings
Reserve for self-insurance
Other appropriations
Unappropriated

Treasury stock (offset at cost)

Paid-in capital includes (1) the par or stated value of capital stock issued or the cash value of the consideration actually received in case of no-par or no-stated-value stock; and (2) the excess (premium) or deficiency (discount) of the cash value of the consideration received from the issue of any capital stock having par or stated value, donations by stockholders, adjustments of capital resulting from reorganization or recapitalization, and gains or losses from reacquisition and resale or retirement of the air carriers' capital stock.

Discounts applicable to a particular class or series of capital stock should not be offset against premiums applicable to another class or series of stock.

The *retained earnings* balance sheet classification reflects the net profits, income, and gains of the air carrier from the date of incorporation after deducting losses and distributions of stockholders. Retained earnings is subdivided into appropriated and unappropriated amounts. Appropriated retained earnings include reserve for self-insurance. The amount of this item is increased or decreased each year through the Retained Earnings account, depending upon the balance in the Self-Insurance Accruals—Clearing account prior to the closing process at the end of the accounting year.[6]

Comparison of operating statements of air carriers and commercial businesses

The profit and loss accounts (income statement) are designed to reflect the elements entering into the derivation of income or loss accruing to the proprietary interests during each accounting period. The system of accounts prescribed provides for the grouping of all revenues and expenses in terms of both major natural objectives and functional activities and for subdivision of both to provide varying degrees of detail for air carriers of differing accounting capacities and/or requirements.

The air carrier's income statement (Illustration 22–2) varies in form and terminology from the commercial or industrial income statement. These differences may be seen in the comparison of the sections appearing on the two types of statements on page 491.

---

[6] See page 488.

ILLUSTRATION 22-2

AMERICAN AIRLINES INC. AND CONSOLIDATED SUBSIDIARY
Consolidated Balance Sheet
(in thousands)

	Year Ended December 31	
	1971	1970
Revenues		
Passenger	**$1,111,973**	$1,014,668
Freight	**97,751**	86,564
Mail	**22,445**	22,433
Express	**5,219**	6,349
Other (Note 12)	**7,943**	2,765
	1,245,331	1,132,779
Expenses		
Flying Operations	**364,513**	340,577
Maintenance	**189,104**	175,610
Passenger Service	**129,248**	122,519
Aircraft and Traffic Servicing	**233,762**	217,374
Promotion and Sales	**133,432**	123,778
General and Administrative	**56,817**	54,718
Depreciation and Obsolescence	**108,813**	106,068
	1,215,689	1,140,644
Operating Income (Loss)	**29,642**	(7,865)
Interest and Miscellaneous		
Interest on long-term debt	**38,055**	34,231
Interest income	**(5,497)**	(4,487)
Interest capitalized	**(8,791)**	(14,060)
Loss from Reservations World (Note 13)	**—**	3,176
Miscellaneous—net (Note 12)	**2,271**	10,386
	26,038	29,246
	3,604	(37,111)
Federal Income Tax (Credit), including deferred tax: 1971— $350; 1970—$(476) (Note 6)	**275**	(10,350)
	3,329	(26,761)
Other Income (Loss)		
Net earnings of Sky Chefs, Inc. (Note 1)	**900**	804
Loss on disposal of property and equipment, net of federal income tax effect: 1971—$(400); 1970—$(180)	**(1,200)**	(441)
	(300)	363
Net Earnings (Loss) for the Year	**$ 3,029**	$ (26,398)
Earnings (Loss) Per Share of Common Stock (Note 9)	**$.13**	$(1.30)

Unregulated Business	*Air Carrier*

Sales
Cost of goods sold
Gross margin
Selling expenses
General and administrative expenses
Operating income
Other revenue
Other expense
Net income before extraordinary items
Extraordinary gains
Extraordinary losses
Income before federal income taxes
Federal income taxes
Net income after federal income taxes
Net income

Operating revenues:
  Transport:
    Passenger
    United States mail
    Foreign mail
    Property
    Charter
    Other
  Nontransport:
    Federal subsidy
    Incidental revenue—net
Operating expenses:
  Flying operations
  Maintenance
  General services and administration
  Depreciation and amortization
Operating profit or loss
Nonoperating income and expense—net
Income before income taxes
Income taxes for current period
Net income before special items
Special items:
  Special income credits and debits—net
  Special income tax credits and debits—net
Net income after special items

OPERATING REVENUES

Transport revenue; nontransport revenue

Operating revenues of an air carrier are subdivided into two groups—transport and nontransport revenues. Transport revenues include revenue of a character usually and ordinarily derived from the performance of air transportation which relate to services performed during the current accounting year or during prior periods if the amounts are not material. Transportation revenue derived from scheduled and nonscheduled services is recorded on the books of the air carrier in the following accounts: First-Class and Coach Passenger Revenue, including both scheduled and chartered flights; United States and Foreign Mail Revenue; Express Revenue; Freight Revenue; Excess Baggage Revenue; and Other Transportation Revenue, which includes revenue from special types of air services such as aerial photography, advertising flights, and the transportation of articles not classified as express, freight, or excess baggage.

Nontransport revenue includes incidental revenue derived from federal subsidy and net revenues from services performed incidental to the performance of air transportation. Subsidy revenue is realized for the carriage of U.S. mail if the air carrier receives mail compensation in excess of the amounts accruing to it under service mail rates. Incidental revenue accounts include Hotel, Restaurant, and Food Service—Net; Service Sales—Net (sale of supplies, parts, and repair service); Rental from Operating Property—Net; Surface Transportation Service—Net (transportation of passengers and baggage to and from airports); and other similar incidental revenue accounts. These accounts are shown after related expenses have been deducted.

OPERATING EXPENSES

Operating expenses include expenses of a character usually and ordinarily incurred in the performance of air transportation which are attributable to services performed during the current accounting year or in prior periods if the amounts are not material.

Flying operations

Expenses of flying operations include those expenses incurred directly in the in-flight operation of aircraft and expenses attaching to the holding of aircraft and aircraft operational personnel in readiness for assignment to an in-flight status. Flying operations accounts show wages of flight personnel; supplies and expenses of flight crews; aircraft engine oils and fuels, including taxes; rents for flight equipment; damage to flight equipment; other loss and damage; and employees' compensation and other insurance.

Maintenance

Maintenance includes all expenses, both direct and indirect, specifically identifiable with the repair and upkeep of property and equipment as may be required to meet operational and safety standards; in inspecting or checking property and equipment in accordance with prescribed operational standards; and in polishing and cleaning property and equipment. These expenses include (1) direct costs such as costs of labor, materials, and outside services consumed directly in periodic maintenance operations and the maintenance and repair of property and equipment of all types and classes; and (2) maintenance burden which is specifically identified with activities involved in periodic maintenance operations and the maintenance and repair of property and equipment.

General services and administration

This function includes expenses incurred on the ground in controlling and protecting the in-flight movement of aircraft; landing, handling, or servicing aircraft on the ground; selling transportation; servicing and handling traffic of all classes; promoting the development of traffic; and administering operations generally.

Depreciation and amortization

Depreciation and amortization include all charges to expense to record losses suffered through current exhaustion of the serviceability of property and equipment—due to wear and tear from use and the action of time and the elements—which are not replaced by current repairs. Air carriers also recognize losses in serviceability occasioned by obsolescence, supersession, discoveries, and changes in popular demand or action by public authority.

Separate accounts are maintained for depreciation of airframes, aircraft engines, airframe parts, aircraft engine parts, and other flight equipment. Airframes and engines are depreciated on a unit basis.

Capitalized developmental and preoperating costs and other intangible assets applicable to the performance of air transportation are amortized.

Nonoperating income and expense—net

The nonoperating income and expense—net item includes income and loss incident to commercial ventures not inherently related to the performance of the common carrier air transport services; other revenues and expenses attributable to financing; and special recurrent or nonrecurrent items of a nonperiod or extraordinary nature of a magnitude which will not significantly distort the net income of the current year.

Nonoperating income includes cash discounts for the prompt payment of accounts, interest and dividend income, amortization of premium on debt, nonoperating property and equipment income, and income from nontransport ventures. Nonoperating expense includes the following items: interest expense, amortization of discount and expense on debt, nonoperating property and equipment expense, and losses from separately operated divisions. Expenses pertaining to extension and development projects, at the option of the air carrier, may be charged directly to the expense account, Extension and Development, or accumulated in the asset account, Extension and Development Projects, and subsequently written off or amortized to the expense account.

Nonoperating income and expense also include foreign exchange adjustments (debits and credits) and capital gains and losses when relatively minor in amount.

Income taxes for current period

The item, income taxes for the current period, includes provisions for excess profits taxes, federal, state, local, and foreign taxes which are based upon the net income of the air carrier for the current year together with refunds for excess profits or carry back of losses and increases or reductions of income taxes of prior years of a magnitude which will not distort net income of the current accounting year.

Special items

This primary classification includes debits and credits which relate to prior accounting years and extraordinary special items that are of sufficient magnitude to significantly distort current financial results.

23

Statements of air carriers (continued)

Analysis of financial and operating data of an air carrier

IN ANALYZING the financial and operating condition of an individual air carrier, it is essential to consider several important factors in addition to the data appearing on the balance sheet and statement of profit and loss. A study of the territory and cities now being served by the air carrier is desirable to determine traffic potentialities. The territory and routes having the most dense population, the highest degree of economic and industrial development, and the most favorable meterological and topographical characteristics should prove most profitable. Other significant factors are the extension and addition of operations, both intensive and extensive; the amount and type of equipment in use; and the quality of service offered to passengers.

The relative financial strength of an air carrier and the efficiency and economy of its operation and management may be measured and evaluated by comparisons with its own operating and financial data from year to year or by comparisons with similar data for other air carriers. In order to make comparisons most practical and effective, the data, which are obtained largely from accounting and special operating reports, must be reduced or summarized to common units. These statistics are more comprehensive, readable, and comparable than the absolute figures.

In analyzing the financial and operating condition of an air carrier, the analyst should know (1) the various statistical units used to express commercial air carriers' operating and financial data, (2) the manner in which the statistics are developed, (3) the causes of fluctuations in the units, (4) the qualifications to which each unit must be subjected, and (5) the relationship existing between and among the different units under review.

The same techniques and statistical units used in analyzing commercial financial statements cannot be used without modification in analyzing air-carrier financial statements. An entirely different type of asset is used by air carriers; also, a different type of service is performed.

Methods used in analyzing the financial statements of air carriers, together with an explanation of the statistical units used, are presented in this chapter.

Trend ratios

The use of trend percentages (index numbers) is often a valuable aid in analyzing financial and operating data. In this manner the direction of the movement of the items may be noted and studied. Increases and decreases in percentages may readily be determined from the trend figures. The dollar and trend data (Illustration 23–1) reveal that American Airlines expanded its property between 1968 and 1971. Fixed operating assets (net of valuation and amortization reserves) increased $115 million, or 11 percent; total assets (net) increased $245 million, or 17 percent.

ILLUSTRATION 23–1

AMERICAN AIRLINES
Selected Data: Dollar Amounts and Trends
For the Years Ended December 31, 1968–71
(index numbers: 1968 = 100%)

Items	1971	1970	1969	1968
Fixed operating assets—net ($000,000)	$1,141	$1,161	$1,101	$1,026
Trend (%)	111	113	107	100
Total assets—net ($000,000)	1,663	1,525	1,491	1,418
Trend (%)	117	108	105	100
Total liabilities (including deferred credits) ($000,000)	1,085	1,164	1,088	1,038
Trend (%)	105	112	105	100
Stockholders' equity ($000,000)	578	361	403	380
Trend (%)	152	95	106	100
Passenger revenue ($000,000)	1,112	1,015	903	834
Trend (%)	133	122	108	100
Mail revenue ($000,000).	22	22	21	21
Trend (%)	105	105	100	100
Freight and express revenue ($000,000).	103	93	84	98
Trend (%)	105	95	86	100

The net assets acquired by American Airlines were financed by retained current earnings. Stockholders' equity increased $198 million, or 52 percent; total debt decreased $56 million, or 8 percent.

It will be observed (Illustration 23–1) that passenger revenue increased $278 million, exactly one third, between 1968 and 1971.

In order to determine the profitableness of the asset expansion and of the operations involving passenger and mail services, it is necessary to analyze operating costs. A comprehensive analysis of these and similar data requires the computation and interpretation of individual financial and operating ratios. This is done below.

Common-size percentage statements

Financial and operating data may be stated in common-size or percentage form as illustrated by the comparative balance sheets shown in Illustration 23–2. This method of presentation shows the ratio of each individual asset or group of assets to total assets and the ratio of each of the liability and stockholders' equity items or groups of items to total liabilities and stockholders' equity.

An examination of Illustration 23–2 points up the following facts: In the three-year period between December 31, 1968 and December 31, 1971, American Airlines' current assets have declined from 23.3 percent to 18.2 percent of total assets; current liabilities rose from 14.8 percent to 17.4 percent; so working capital declined nearly 8 percent,

ILLUSTRATION 23–2

AMERICAN AIRLINES AND UNITED AIRLINES
Comparative Condensed Balance Sheets
As of December 31, 1968, and 1971

	American Airlines				United Airlines			
	December 31				December 31			
	1971		1968		1971		1968	
Items	($000)	(%)	($000)	(%)	($000)	(%)	($000)	(%)
Assets								
Current assets..........................	302,389	18.2	330,701	23.3	425,609	19.1	317,397	16.9
Operating property and equipment, net.......	1,141,190	68.6	1,025,706	72.3	1,724,607	77.2	1,522,497	80.8
Other assets..........................	219,035	13.2	62,072	4.4	82,454	3.7	43,219	2.3
Total Assets....................	1,662,614	100.0	1,418,479	100.0	2,232,670	100.0	1,883,113	100.0
Liabilities and Stockholders' Equity								
Current liabilities	289,503	17.4	209,391	14.9	355,929	15.9	269,169	14.3
Noncurrent liabilities..................	795,013	47.8	829,084	58.4	1,231,613	55.2	1,016,065	54.0
Total Liabilities..................	1,084,516	65.2	1,038,475	73.3	1,587,542	71.1	1,285,234	68.3
Capital stock:								
Preferred.........................	None		None		29,669	1.3	12,538	.6
Common..........................	28,311	1.7	20,238	1.4	104,619	4.7	92,120	4.9
Retained earnings.....................	238,599	14.4	264,186	18.6	173,576	7.8	208,847	11.1
Other paid-in capital	311,188	18.7	95,580	6.7	337,264	15.1	284,374	15.1
Total Stockholders' Equity	578,098	34.8	380,004	26.7	645,128	28.9	597,879	31.7
Total Liabilities and Stockholders' Equity	1,662,614	100.0	1,418,479	100.0	2,232,670	100.0	1,883,113	100.0

and the current ratio dropped from nearly 1.6 to 1 to 1.3 to 1. United's current assets rose from 16.9 percent to 19.1 percent; current liabilities went up from 14.3 to 15.9 percent; so working capital increased about .6 percent and stands at the current ratio of 1.2 to 1. In the air carrier industry a current ratio of 1.5 to 1 is average.

The most interesting development shown by Illustration 23–1 is the 52 percent increase, from 1968 to 1971, of American Airlines' stockholders' equity. The same table shows that passenger revenues rose 33 percent while other revenues rose only 5 percent. In the same period, United Airlines' stockholders' equity went up about 10 percent.

In spite of this obvious prosperity, American's working capital went down (Illustration 23–2) by about $100 million; its operating equipment (net) went up about $140 million and its long-term debt went down about $35 million; so we can see where the earnings were applied. During the same period, United Airlines' working capital went up almost $20 million; its operating assets rose about $200 million; both of these increases were financed by additional long term debt.

At the end of 1971 American's proprietary ratio stood at 52 percent debt, 48 percent stockholders' equity. United's proprietary ratio stood at 60 percent debt, 40 percent proprietary ratio. Airlines are public utilities and tend, therefore, to maintain a higher ratio of debt though their instability of earnings makes them less popular with bond buyers. In general, public utilities of all types like to trade on the equity but this is beneficial to the stockholders only if earnings are in excess of the cost of interest on the bonds. American and United have both had recent loss years and years of poor earnings:

	American		United	
	($000)	(%)	($000)	(%)
1971.	3,029	.4	(5,071)	
1970.	(26,398)		(40,877)	
1969.	38,468	6.7	47,682	7.4
1968.	35,456	6.1	46,421	7.2

Trading on the equity is of little or no value or even detrimental[1] under these conditions. American has been reducing its noncurrent liabilities, from 58.4 in 1968 to 47.8 in 1971. In the same period, United increased its noncurrent liabilities from 54.0 to 55.2 percent (Illustration 23–2).

---

[1] Trading on the equity is explained on page 355.

Until the second half of the 1950's, air carriers were financed largely by common stockholders, for the following reasons:

1. The development of commercial air transportation, dating from 1926, has involved an element of risk which bondholders normally will not assume.
2. The operating assets are converted at a relatively rapid rate into working capital through the depreciation process.
3. The bulk of the operating assets consists of direct and indirect flying equipment. Airports and airways are in most instances furnished by the local, state, or federal governments and, therefore, do not require capital investment, on the part of the air carrier.

Operating ratio

The operating ratio is determined by dividing operating expenses by operating revenues. The operating ratio is regarded as an index of operating efficiency, although variations in this ratio may be a result of changes in operating revenues, operating expenses, or both. Many factors that affect the operating ratio are beyond the control of management. Such factors include income and property tax assessments and rates, the price level, and emergency and war conditions.

A detailed study of both operating expenses and operating revenues is necessary in determining the reasons for variations in the operating ratio from year to year or between air carriers. The data in Illustration

ILLUSTRATION 23–3
AMERICAN AIRLINES AND UNITED AIRLINES
Selected Operating Data
For the Years 1969–71

Items	1971	1970	1969
Operating revenue:			
American Airlines ($000).	1,245,331	1,132,779	1,052,960
United Airlines ($000).	1,617,570	1,590,070	1,567,891
American Airlines (trend %)	118	110	100
United Airlines (trend %).	103	101	100
Operating expenses:			
American Airlines ($000).	1,215,689	1,140,644	969,998
United Airlines ($000).	1,275,099	1,603,111	1,438,283
American Airlines (trend %)	125	118	100
United Airlines (trend %).	110	112	100
Operating ratio*:			
American Airlines (%)	97.6	100.6	93.9
United Airlines (%)	97.4	100.8	91.7

* Operating expenses divided by operating revenues. United's hotels are included.

23–3 show that American Airlines' operating revenues rose $192 million, or 18 percent; and operating expenses increased $171 million, or 25 percent. United Airlines' operating revenues rose $61 million, or 3 percent, and operating expenses rose $137 million, or 10 percent.

The trend of the operating ratios of both carriers has been unfavorable.

A favorable trend in the operating ratio may be the result of increases in rates of fare or an increase in traffic volume without a comparable increase in operating expenses, or it may be the result of a decrease in operating expenses without a corresponding decrease in revenues.

Operating revenues vary from year to year or between air carriers because of changes or differences in (1) rates of pay received for rendering transportation services, (2) amount of traffic volume, and (3) distances involved in rendering transportation services.

Operating expenses vary from year to year or between air carriers because of changes or differences in (1) the price level, which may affect such major items as personnel compensation and material and supplies; (2) traffic density; (3) old and new routes operated; (4) terrain and operating conditions; (5) competition; (6) the character and frequency of the service rendered; (7) the depreciation and maintenance policies; (8) the efficiency of maintaining and operating the property; and (9) the type and size of airplanes used.

Final conclusions relative to an apparent favorable or unfavorable operating ratio should not be reached until other individual ratios and data have been analyzed and interpreted. The operating ratio alone does not represent a reliable financial index because the data exclude consideration of nonoperating income and nonoperating expense items.

Sources of operating revenue

The most important sources of operating revenue for air carriers are passenger, mail, and express and freight traffic. The distribution of operating revenues for American Airlines and United Airlines, in dollars and in percentage form, is shown in Illustration 23–4.

It will be observed that United derived a slightly larger percentage of its operating revenues from passenger revenue than did American Airlines. The latter, in turn, showed a larger relative volume of cargo revenue. A comparison with Illustration 23–5 shows that United's passenger traffic results are above the average performance of all domestic passenger-cargo carriers and American Airlines' results are below the average, but the differences are of minor significance.

The period from 1930 through 1938 was a period of heavy subsidiza-

ILLUSTRATION 23–4

AMERICAN AIRLINES AND UNITED AIRLINES
Distribution of the Sources of Operating Revenue
For the Years 1968 and 1971

| | American Airlines | | | | United Airlines | | | |
| | 1968 | | 1971 | | 1968 | | 1971 | |
Items	($000)	% of total	($000)	% of total	($000)	% of total	($000)	% of total
Passenger revenue	834,240	87.2	1,087,670	87.3	1,115,544	89.5	1,347,640	89.5
Cargo revenue	91,351	9.5	89,215	7.2	85,687	6.9	115,857	7.7
Other revenue	31,607	3.3	68,446	5.5	45,826	3.6	41,585	2.8
Total Operating Revenue	957,198	100.0	1,245,331	100.0	1,247,057	100.0	1,505,082	100.0

ILLUSTRATION 23–5. Total revenues, by classes, of all passenger-cargo domestic airline operations for the year 1971

	($000)	% of total
Passenger revenue	6,364,522	88.4
Cargo revenue	411,581	5.7
Other revenue (except subsidies)	421,273	5.9
	7,197,376	100.0
Subsidies	58,283	
Total Operating Revenues	7,255,659	

Source: Civil Aeronautics Board, *Air Carrier Financial Statistics.*

tion of commercial aviation companies, paid for transporting airmail. The federal government's purpose was to foster the development of civil aviation for the benefit of the nation at peace, and also its wartime potential. American Airlines and United Airlines were no longer receiving subsidies in 1971 though they were, of course, being paid at regular rates for hauling mail. Illustration 23–5 shows that in 1971 other airlines were receiving $58 million in subsidies.

Operating expenses

Illustrations 23–6, 23–7, and 23–8 show the operating expenses for 1971 of American Airlines, of United Airlines, and of all passenger and cargo carrying domestic airline operations, in terms of (1) the absolute dollar amounts, (2) cents per revenue ton-mile, (3) percentage of operating

ILLUSTRATION 23–6

AMERICAN AIRLINES
Distribution of Operating Expenses
For the Year 1971

Items	($000)	% of operating revenue	% of operating expense	Cents per revenue ton-mile	Dollars revenu aircra mile flo
Flying and ground operations	727,523	58.4	59.7	28.7	2.4
Maintenance	189,104	15.2	15.6	7.4	.6
Promotion and sales	133,432	10.7	11.0	5.2	.5
General and administration	56,817	4.6	4.7	2.2	.2
Depreciation and amortization	108,813	8.7	9.0	4.3	.4
Total operating expense	1,215,689	97.6	100.0	47.8	4.1
Total operating revenue ($000)	1,245,331	100.0			
Overall revenue ton-miles (000,000)	2,542				
Revenue aircraft-miles flown (000,000)	297				

ILLUSTRATION 23–7

UNITED AIRLINES
Distribution of Operating Expenses
For the Year 1971

Items	($000)	% of operating revenue	% of operating expense	Cents per revenue ton-mile	Dollars per revenue aircraft-mile flown
Flying and ground operations	888,093*	58.2	58.9	28.3	2.2
Maintenance	209,067	13.7	13.9	6.7	.5
Promotion and sales	159,764	10.5	10.6	5.1	.4
General and administration	81,429	5.3	5.4	2.6	.2
Depreciation and amortization	168,099	11.0	11.2	5.4	.4
Total operating expense	1,506,452	98.7	100.0	48.1	3.7
Total operating revenue ($000)	1,527,050*	100.0			
Overall revenue ton-miles (000,000)	3,129				
Revenue aircraft-miles flown (000,000)	411				

* Hotels omitted.

revenue, (4) percentage of operating expenses, and (5) cents per revenue-mile flown.

A comparison of these three tables of operating revenue brings out the following facts:

Operating expenses of American Airlines and United Airlines in 1971 are superior to the 100.9 percent average of all passenger-cargo air carriers, American being 97.6 percent and United 98.7 percent; the industry as a whole showed an operating loss. A closer look shows that American had slightly higher flying and ground operations expense, materially higher maintenance expense, lower administrative cost, and lower depreciation. A comparison of depreciation characteristics of the

ILLUSTRATION 23–8

DOMESTIC OPERATIONS OF ALL PASSENGER-CARGO AIR CARRIERS
Distribution of Operating Expenses
For the Year Ended June 30, 1971

Items	($000)	% of operating revenue	% of operating expense
Flying and ground operations	4,244,078	58.5	58.1
Maintenance	1,129,172	15.6	15.4
Promotion and sales	814,049	11.2	11.1
General and administration	360,330	5.0	4.9
Depreciation and amortization	770,972	10.6	10.5
Total operating expense	7,318,601	100.9	100.0
Total operating revenue ($000)	7,255,659	100.0	
Overall revenue ton-miles (000)			
Revenue aircraft-miles flown (000)			

two airlines shows that American is actually following a more conservative depreciation policy than is United:

1971 ($000)	American		United	
Operating plant and equipment	$1,520,893		$2,456,806	
Depreciation and amortization.	108,813	7.1%	168,099	6.8

American shows a slightly lower cents per revenue ton-mile; United shows a more substantial advantage in dollars per revenue aircraft-mile flown. Information useful in explaining these differences is not available. Obviously, the types of aircraft used has a major impact on these costs.

Current ratio

As in any other business enterprise, the current ratio is helpful in judging short-term debt-paying ability. On December 31, 1971, American Airlines had a current ratio of 1.3 to 1 and United 1.2 to 1. The average current ratio of all domestic trunk air carriers was 1.5 to 1. The other two "Big Four" airlines, Eastern and TWA, had current ratios of 1.3 to 1 and 1.0 to 1; TWA has had serious (though not fatal of course) financial difficulties. Like other public utilities, airlines usually show low current ratios; but 1.3, 1.2, and particularly 1.0 to 1 are low indeed.

Relative earnings

The relative profitability of operations can be assessed by expressing net income as a percentage of stockholders' equity or as a percentage of total assets, or, preferably, both. The former is primarily an index of the success of the shareholders' investment; the latter is an index of the management's success in profitably employing assets. The year 1970 was a poor year for American and United which both showed losses (Illustration 23–9). The industry also showed a loss. The year 1971 was better.

Earnings of 5 or 6 percent on stockholders' equity are not sufficient to content a stockholder; bonds are currently paying more than that. Both airlines have earned more at times in the past, but not often, and obviously earnings are very erratic.

Measuring revenue and expense against ton-miles flown

Dollars of operating revenue, of operating expense, and of the resulting operating income, in absolute amounts are not as informative in appraising operating effectiveness as are the same data expressed in

ILLUSTRATION 23-9
AMERICAN AIRLINES AND UNITED AIRLINES
Net Income Ratios
1970 and 1971

	Company	1971	1970
Earnings from operations before income taxes as percent of stockholders' equity	American United	5.13% 6.58	(2.18)% (2.29)
Net income as percent of total assets	American United	.18 .23	(1.73) (1.87)

relation to a factor showing service rendered, such as ton-miles flown. In this way it is possible to dispense with the distinction between passengers and cargo and appraise the results of operations overall. These data are shown in Illustration 23–10.

In both cases expenses per revenue ton-mile have gone up faster than revenue but United has suffered more than American. Both rate levels and cost levels can affect this comparison, and we are not in a position to measure their relative contributions to diminishing profitability. Again the precariousness of profitability in this industry is demonstrated.

The passenger-carrying side of the business

Both companies have substantially increased the number of seat-miles flown, and American has increased more than United; but the proportion of occupancy on the average flight has dropped, more in the case of

ILLUSTRATION 23–10
AMERICAN AIRLINES AND UNITED AIRLINES
Operating Revenue and Expense per Revenue Ton-Mile Flown
For the Years 1968 and 1971
(in cents)

Items	American Airlines		United Airlines*	
	1968	1971	1968	1971
Per revenue ton-miles flown (cents):				
Operating revenue.	44.2	49.0	44.5	48.1
Operating expense.	41.2	47.8	41.6	47.8
Operating income	3.0	1.2	2.9	.3

* Hotels omitted.

ILLUSTRATION 23–11

AMERICAN AIRLINES AND UNITED AIRLINES
Selected Passenger-Traffic Data
For the Years 1968 and 1971

				Increase (1968 over 197▪	
Items	Company	1968	1971	Amount	(%
Seat-miles flown	American	27,748	35,182	7,434	26.▪
(000,000)	United	40,477	47,325	6,848	16.▪
Revenue passenger load	American	55.7%	49.8%	(5.9)	(9.▪
factor.	United	54.8%	49.9%	(4.9)	(7.▪

American than United. Of course, planes have steadily increased in size and it is well known that airline companies are having difficulty keeping them occupied; the Boeing 747 is a well-publicized example. Larger planes are more costly to run; and if occupancy drops, profits suffer (Illustrations 23–11 and 23–12).

Source of statistics

The financial and operating statistics used in connection with analyzing the statements of air carriers are readily obtained from two publications of the Civil Aeronautics Board called *Air Carrier Financial Statistics* and *Air Carrier Traffic Statistics*. These publications contain numerous statistical measures, many of which were used in this analysis but

ILLUSTRATION 23–12

AMERICAN AIRLINES AND UNITED AIRLINES
Selected Passenger-Traffic Data
For the Years 1968 and 1971

				Increase (decrease) (1971 over 1968	
Items	Company	1968	1971	Amount	(%)
Revenue passengers carried	American	19,079	19,245	166	.9
(000,000)	United	27,221	26,048	(1,173)	(4.3
Passenger revenue	American	834	1,088	254	30.5▪
($000,000)	United	1,109	1,345	236	21.3
Revenue passenger-miles	American	15,457	17,535	2,078	13.4
(000,000)	United	22,183	23,602	1,419	6.4
Passenger revenue per	American	5.4	6.2	.8	14.8▪
passenger-mile (cents)	United	5.0	5.7	.7	14.0▪

some of which were not. The statistics used and the ways they are used depend to some extent on the situation and the objectives of the analyst.

External factors affecting air carriers

When a complete and detailed analysis is being made of an individual air carrier or of a group of air carriers, special consideration must be given to certain external factors which are beyond the control of management. The most important of these factors are discussed below.

Regulation. Interstate commercial aviation[2] as well as all other interstate civil aviation is regulated by the Civil Aeronautics Board with respect to safety measures. Commercial aviation regulation also includes control by the Civil Aeronautics Board of mail and passenger rates, establishment and abandonment of air routes, service, equipment, facilities, competition, accounts and reports, and consolidations and mergers.

Regulation of air transportation is essential to the orderly development of a sound and stable industry. Consistent and effective governmental regulation makes possible the perfection of equipment, organization and operation, and the adoption of long-term plans for adequate financing. Excessive competition is prevented through efficient control of the establishment of new air routes. It should be emphasized that although regulation is essential, it frequently is so restrictive that progress is retarded.

Competition. Commercial aviation companies have as competitors other airline companies, the railroads, buses, and automobiles. Under effective regulation, competition between airline companies involves primarily service rather than rates. However, competition between airlines, railroads, and buses involves rates as well as service, including the time element. As the distance involved increases, and as time becomes of the essence, the airlines have the advantage.

Business cycle. In interpreting commercial aviation's traffic trends and operating revenues and costs for a period of time, it is necessary to study general business activity. Commercial aviation companies may be adversely affected in periods of depression because of the relatively high fixed costs which cannot be varied in proportion to the inevitable reduction in revenues.

---

[2] Commercial aviation includes scheduled mail, passenger, and express airlines as well as charter and fixed-base airplane operators.

QUESTIONS AND PROBLEMS

23–1.   Explain what is meant by "passenger-load factor" and indicate how it may be improved. Why is it so important to improve the passenger-load factor?

23–2.   Relative to a commercial air carrier:
  a)   What financial statement items are used in determining current debt-paying ability?
  b)   Is the current ratio of major significance?
  c)   Does an air carrier treat income taxes as an operating expense?

23–3.   What reasons may be given to account for changes over a period of years in each of the following?
  a)   Revenue passenger-miles.
  b)   Average revenue per passenger.
  c)   Passenger density.
  d)   Passenger revenue.
  e)   Mail revenue.
  f)   Seat-miles flown.
  g)   Operating expense per seat-miles flown.
  h)   Revenue plane-miles.
  i)   Working capital.
  j)   Passenger-load factor.
  k)   Depreciation expense.

23–4.   What data should be available to compute the following statistics?
  a)   Revenue passenger-load factor.
  b)   Passenger density.
  c)   Revenue passenger-miles.
  d)   Revenue ton-miles.
  e)   Operating ratio.
  f)   Current ratio.
  g)   Trend percentages.
  h)   Common-size percentages.

23–5.   Discuss briefly the following:
  a)   Commercial air carriers in comparison with manufacturing concerns operate with a different type of asset and perform a different type of service.
  b)   The difference between a valuation reserves and an operating reserve.
  c)   The "operating ratio" and its merits and limitations with respect to commercial air carriers.

23–6.   What are the advantages and disadvantages of a uniform accounting system for commercial air carriers from the point of view of the air carriers, the investor in air carrier securities, the regulatory agency, and Congress?

23–7.   Compare the major financial statement items of commercial air carriers and industrial companies.

23–8. To what extent is the financial data of commercial air carriers influenced by price level changes? Discuss.

23–9. What information may be obtained by studying the following comparative data for a five-year period?
   a) Average number of seats operated per revenue plane-mile flown.
   b) Revenue passenger-load factor.
   c) Average length of journey.
   d) Passenger density.
   e) Average operating revenue and operating expense per revenue plane-mile flown.
   f) Operating revenue and operating expense per mile of route operated.
   g) Trend percentages.

23–10. Give a brief answer to the following:
   a) What are the major sources of revenue for commercial air carriers?
      What is the relative importance of these sources?
   b) What financial and operating data would you use to show air-carrier growth and in what form would you present them to show the growth of an air carrier?
   c) How do the operating expenses of commercial air carriers differ from those of manufacturing companies?
   d) What is the significance of reducing certain dollar data to a per mile of route-operated basis?

23–11. Distinguish between:
   a) Current asset items for air carriers and manufacturing companies.
   b) Property and equipment items for air carriers and a retail store.
   c) Operating reserves and amortization reserves.
   d) Operating expenses of an air carrier and a manufacturing business.
   e) Revenue items of an air carrier and a retail store.

23–12. Comment on the following statements:
   a) The operating ratio represents a useful indication of operating efficiency and of financial condition.
   b) The current ratio is considered more significant for air carriers than for commercial businesses.
   c) An increase in operating revenue per mile of line operated should be considered favorable.
   d) An increase in operating expense should be viewed with alarm.
   e) Substantial increases in revenue results in an improvement in net income.
   f) Air carriers do not follow the "clean-retained earnings principle."

23–13. Match each of the following with the appropriate phrase listed to the right.

(1) Relationship of passenger-miles to miles of route operated.

(2) Passenger-miles divided by number of passengers carried.

(3) Working capital.

(4) Relationship between operating expense and operating revenue.

(5) Freight revenue.

(6) Flying operations expense.

(7) Relationship between working capital and current liabilities.

(8) Revenue passenger-load factor.

a) Current ratio.

b) Operating revenue.

c) Operating ratio.

d) Operating expense.

e) Average number of seats occupied compared with seats available.

f) Excess of current assets over current liabilities.

g) Average length of journey.

h) Passenger density.

23–14. Study the following statistics and develop additional information as appropriate. Rank the companies in accordance with their operating position.

	December 31, 1971 air carriers		
	A	B	C
Passenger revenues (000's)	$ 16,200	$ 11,442	$ 8,343
Mail revenues (000's)	4,230	4,461	1,967
Express revenues (000's)	560	617	249
Total operating revenues (000's)	21,467	16,849	10,682
Operating expenses (000's)	16,782	14,782	8,151
Net income (000's)	3,473	1,711	1,894
Revenue plane-miles flown (000's)	26,700	23,472	14,211
Seat-miles flown (000's)	461,421	349,168	256,425
Revenue passenger miles flown (000's)	315,671	226,981	154,629
Average number of seats per plane-mile flown	18.3	18.4	14.8
Average number of revenue passengers per plane-mile flown	12.8	9.5	10.9
Miles of route operated	6,843	6,994	5,800

23-15.   Financial and operating data for Companies C, E, and F (air carriers) are presented below:

	C	E	F
Balance Sheet Data (000's),			
December 31, 1971			
Current assets	$ 1,260	$ 394	$ 571
Plant, property, and equipment (net).	1,620	771	959
Other assets	213	155	26
Current liabilities	1,052	390	291
Long-term notes	143	175	203
Other liabilities	51	14	52
Capital stock	1,359	793	410
Capital surplus	42	55	648
Earned surplus	446	107*	48*
Profit and Loss Data (000's),			
for the Year 1971			
Passenger revenues	2,324	878	1,056
Mail revenue.	1,852	408	849
Express and freight revenue	115	30	84
Other operating revenue	47	4	31
Operating expenses	3,901	1,504	2,025
Other income	31	93	11
Other deductions	40	21	
Estimated income tax	100		
Operating Statistics			
Revenue miles flown (000's)	6,076	2,894	3,137
Revenue passengers.	174,250	58,260	69,791
Passenger seat-miles flown (000's)	121,526	40,137	48,592
Revenue passenger miles (000's)	52,659	19,426	22,892
Miles of route operated	5,764	6,015	6,416

* Denotes deficit.

Required:

a)   Prepare comparative statements for Companies C, E, and F.

b)   Compute additional statistics as appropriate.

c)   Study all data available and write a report evaluating the financial condition and operating result of the companies.

23-16.   The following financial and operating data was obtained from the records of Air Carrier L:

	1968	1969	1970	1971
Balance Sheet Data (000's),				
December 31				
Current assets	$1,965	$3,269	$ 6,990	$ 9,159
Property and equipment (net).	1,339	1,567	3,481	3,591
Other noncurrent assets	490	116	447	607
Current liabilities	655	1,102	1,924	2,650
Noncurrent liabilities.	47	48	50	51
Common stock	2,083	2,149	2,813	2,866
Capital surplus	784	544	3,444	3,497
Earned surplus	225	1,109	2,687	4,293
Profit and Loss Data (000's),				
for the Year				
Operating revenues	3,805	7,600	10,701	13,667
Operating expenses	3,495	6,473	8,949	11,466
Miscellaneous income	7	15	359	311
Provision for federal income tax	65	230	535	901

Required:

a) Prepare comparative statements.

b) Compute ratios and percentages that will aid in studying the financial condition and operating results of the company.

c) After studying all data available, write a report in which you evaluate the company's financial position and operating results.

d) What additional data should be available to make a more complete analysis?

24

Statements of public utilities

A PUBLIC UTILITY is a business that is required to perform safe and adequate service at reasonable and nondiscriminatory prices to all who apply. A public utility renders a service which, in general, is not duplicated and upon which the public at large becomes dependent. Because of the ruinous nature of public utility competition, public utilities are looked upon and treated in the eyes of the law as "natural monopolies." Governmental regulation is used to minimize conflicts between the public and the utility.

Public utilities—in accordance with a narrow classification assumed in the present chapter—include electric light and power, manufactured and natural gas piped to the customer, water, telephone, telegraph, and local transportation (bus and street railway) companies. Based on a broad classification, railroads are considered public utilities. However, due to competition from other forms of transportation, the railroads no longer have the same monopoly characteristics which they formerly possessed. Airlines are also regulated as public utilities.

Public utilities differ from transportation companies in the following respects:

1. The services of public utilities are consumed, for the most part, in the home or in the place of business.
2. The public, in general, is dependent upon these services; substitute services are *not* available to most of the public, as is the case in the field of transportation.

3. Regulation by federal, state, and municipal authorities plays a greater part in the determination of public utility rates, charges, and services than does competition. Rates and charges may be established by public utilities with greater reference, as compared to transportation agencies, to a fair return on the fair value of the property used and useful for the performance of the service. Competition between or among like public utility agencies is, as a rule, of no consequence.

4. Electric light and power, manufactured gas, and water companies operate generally on a smaller scale basis than do railroads, telephones, and telegraph.

5. Public utilities, excluding street railways, enjoy a greater stability of earnings than do transportation companies. The reasons for this include the following: (a) protection from competition; (b) more effective regulation of consumer rates and, therefore, of the fair return, which is possible because, in effect, there is a division of territory in which competition between like utilities is generally not authorized; and (c) the public is dependent upon utility services, and the demand does not fluctuate to the same extent as does general business activity.

6. Because of their stable earnings, public utilities are able to capitalize on the advantages of trading on the equity by using bonds and preferred stocks as major sources of long-term investment funds. They customarily raise as much as one half (and sometimes more) of their long-term investment funds by selling fixed-dollar securities. Consequently, public utilities commonly derive large gains on the excess of fixed-dollar liabilities and preferred stocks over fixed-dollar assets during periods of rising prices. (See Chapters 17 through 21, Part III.)

Uniform accounting systems prescribed for public utilities

Uniform accounting systems and reports have been prescribed by the Federal Power Commission for all interstate electric light and power and natural gas companies;[1] by the Federal Communications Commission for interstate telephone and telegraph companies;[2] and by many state utility commissions for intrastate utility companies. These regulatory bodies enforce uniformity of accounting and reporting which has value to all who analyze public utility statements including the regulatory bodies, investors, and the company.

State commissions generally have adopted, with modifications in cer-

---

[1] The latest regulations, for electric utilities, went into effect March 1, 1965, and for natural gas companies February 1, 1964.

[2] Effective August 31, 1965.

tain instances, the uniform accounting system prescribed by the Federal Power Commission, or the one required by the Interstate Commerce Commission. The uniform accounting system adopted by the Federal Power Commission was developed by the Commission in collaboration with the National Association of Railway and Utilities Commissioners.

Public utility balance sheet accounts

The following pages are devoted to an explanation and discussion of the most important balance sheet accounts provided for in interstate public utility accounting classifications. Differences in account content of electric power, gas, and telephone companies will be explained. Balance sheet accounts for these utilities appear in Illustrations 24–1 and 24–2. Accounts prescribed for natural gas companies are identical to those prescribed for electric companies with a few minor changes because of the different business involved.

ASSETS

Utility plant

The item utility plant represents a summary of condensation of fixed operating assets, both tangible and intangible. For electric power companies, it includes generating power plants—steam, hydraulic, and internal-combustion engine—electric transmission and distribution systems, land and buildings, and intangibles.

For gas companies, utility plant includes the gas wells, production plants, storage plants, transmission and distribution systems, and intangibles. From the gas well or the production plant, natural or manufactured gas (or a combination of the two) is forced into transmission pipelines or into storage tanks. The transmission lines, getting the gas either from the production plants or from the storage plants, transmit it to the consuming area, where the transmission pipeline is connected with the distribution system which, in turn, distributes the gas to the place of consumption. Although the asset values of the production and storage plants are shown separately, the expense of maintaining the storage plant is considered a production cost.

For telephone companies, plant, property, and equipment includes land and buildings, rights of way, poles, wire, cable, underground conduits, switchboards, telephones, office furniture, vehicles, tools, and intangibles.

Intangible assets for public utilities may include organization expense and cost of franchises, patent rights, licenses, consents, privileges, and

ILLUSTRATION 24-1

CLASS A* AND B† INTERSTATE ELECTRIC LIGHT AND POWER COMPANIES

Balance Sheet Accounts‡

Assets and Other Debits

Utility Plant

Electric Plant, Less Depreciation
Electric Plant Adjustments
Other Utility Plant

Other Property and Investments

Nonutility Property, Less
  Depreciation
Investments
Special Funds

Current and Accrued Assets

Cash
Special Deposits
Working Funds
Temporary Cash Investments
Notes Receivable
Accounts Receivable
Receivables from Associated Companies
Material and Supplies
Prepayments
Other Current and Accrued Assets

Deferred Debits

Unamortized Debt Discount and Expense
Extraordinary Property Losses
Preliminary Survey and Investigation
  Charges
Clearing Accounts
Other Deferred Debits

Liabilities and Other Credits

Proprietary Capital

Common Capital Stock
Preferred Capital Stock
Stock Liability for Conversion
Premiums on Capital Stock
Installments Received on Capital Stock
Discount on Capital Stock
Capital Stock Expense
Appropriated Earned Surplus
Unappropriated Earned Surplus
Reacquired Capital Stock

Long-Term Debt

Bonds
Advances from Associated Companies
Other Long-Term Debt

Current and Accrued Liabilities

Notes Payable
Accounts Payable
Payables to Associated Companies
Dividends Declared
Matured Long-Term Debt
Matured Interest
Customers' Deposits
Taxes Accrued
Interest Accrued
Other Current Accrued Liabilities

Deferred Credits

Unamortized Premium on Debt
Customers' Advances for Construction
Other Deferred Credits
Accumulated Deferred Investment Tax
  Credits

Operating Reserves

Reserve for Amortization of Limited-Term
  Electric Investments
Reserve for Amortization of Electric Plant
  Acquisition Adjustments
Reserve for Depreciation and Amortization
  of Other Property
Reserve for Uncollectible Accounts
Property Insurance Reserve
Injuries and Damages Reserve
Pensions and Benefits Reserve
Amortization Reserve—Federal
Miscellaneous Operating Reserves

Contributions in Aid of Construction

Contributions in Aid of Construction

Accumulated Deferred Income Taxes

Accumulated Deferred Income Taxes—
  Accelerated Amortization
Accumulated Deferred Income Taxes—
  Liberalized Depreciation

* Utilities whose annual electric operating revenues amount to $2,500,000 or more.
† Utilities whose annual electric operating revenues amount to more than $1,000,000 but less than $2,500,000. Class B electric utilities are not required to maintain all of the classification accounts.
‡ Federal Power Commission, *Uniform System of Accounts for Public Utilities Subject to the Provisions of the Federal Power Act—Effective January 1, 1937* (Revised to March 1, 1965), pp. 20 and 21.

ILLUSTRATION 24–2

CLASS A* AND B† TELEPHONE COMPANIES
Balance Sheet Accounts ‡

Assets	*Liabilities*
Plant and Other Investments:	Capital Stock:
Telephone Plant	Stock Liability for Conversion
Telephone Plant Adjustments	Premium on Capital Stock
Other Utility Plant	Capital Stock Subscribed
Investments in Affiliated Companies	Installments Paid on Capital Stock
Advances to Affiliated Companies	
Other Investments	Long-Term Debt:
Miscellaneous Physical Properties	Funded Debt
Sinking Funds	Funded Debt Subscribed
	Receivers' Certificates
Current Assets:	Advances from Affiliated Companies
Cash	Other Long-Term Debt
Special Cash Deposits	
Working Funds	Current Liabilities:
Temporary Cash Investments	Notes Payable to Affiliated Companies
Notes Receivable from Affiliated Companies	Other Notes Payable
Other Notes Receivable	Accounts Payable to Affiliated Companies
Due from Customers and Agents	Other Accounts Payable
Reserve for Uncollectible Accounts— Credit	Customers' Deposits
Accounts Receivable from Affiliated Companies	Matured Interest and Dividends
Other Accounts Receivable	Matured Long-Term Debt
Interest and Dividends Receivable	Advance Billing and Payments
Material and Supplies	Other Current Liabilities
Other Current Assets	
	Accrued Liabilities Not Due:
Other Assets:	Taxes Accrued
Subscriptions to Capital Stock	Unmatured Interest, Dividends, and Rents Accrued
Subscriptions to Funded Debt	
	Deferred Credits and Reserves:
Prepaid Accounts and Deferred Charges:	Premium on Long-Term Debt
Prepaid Rents	Insurance Reserve
Prepaid Taxes	Provident Reserve
Prepaid Insurance	Depreciation Reserve
Prepaid Directory Expenses	Amortization Reserve
Other Prepayments	Employment Stabilization Reserve
Discount on Capital Stock	Other Deferred Credits
Capital Stock Expense	Other Capital Surplus
Discount on Long-Term Debt	
Provident Funds	Earned Surplus Reserved
Insurance and Other Funds	
Extraordinary Maintenance and Retirements	Earned Surplus Unappropriated
Other Deferred Charges	

* Telephone companies having average annual operating revenues exceeding $250,000.
† Telephone companies having average annual operating revenues exceeding $50,000 but not more than $250,000. Class B companies are not required to keep all of the accounts.
‡ Federal Communications Commission, *Uniform System of Accounts, Effective January 1, 1937, as Revised to August 3, 1956, for Class A and B Telephone Companies.*

other intangible items, all of which are necessary or valuable in the performance of utility service.

On the books of each electric utility the operating property (electric plant) is classified as follows:

1. In service.
2. Leased to others.
3. Construction work in progress.
4. Held for future use.
5 In process of reclassification.
6. Plant acquisition adjustments.

The regulatory authorities having jurisdiction over gas, electric power, and telephone companies require each company to state the value of its properties at the original cost to the person who first devoted such property to public utility service. Excess payments for such property must be recorded in a Plant Acquisition Adjustment (Electric, Gas, or Telephone) account. This individual account may or may not be shown separately on the balance sheet. The balance in this adjustment account is amortized over a period of time designated by the utility commission and charged to operating expense.

Utilities are required to record in a Plant Adjustments account any write-up (appreciation) of plant that had been recorded as of the effective date of the classification of accounts.

Reserves for depreciation and amortization

The electric utility account classification provides for a single composite Reserve for Depreciation and Amortization[3] which should be shown as an offset to the Utility Property account on the balance sheet. For purposes of analysis each utility is required to maintain records for showing accumulated depreciation relative to steam production, internal-combustion-engine production, transmission, distribution, and general.

The foregoing account also includes accumulated amortization of limited-term electric investments, franchises, licenses, patent rights, and plant acquisition adjustment.

Other physical property

Land, structures, and equipment owned but not used in utility service are classified as other physical property. These investments are referred to as nonoperating assets.

---

[3] Under the practice now current among Certified Public Accountants, the word "Reserve" is not used in nonregulated statements. The account carries a title such as Accumulated Depreciation and Amortization.

Fund accounts

Like other types of businesses, public utilities accumulate funds consisting of cash, securities, or other assets for special purposes. For example, a sinking fund may be established to provide funds to pay a debt at its maturity; a depreciation fund may be accumulated to provide funds for the purchase of assets that must be replaced; and special funds may be provided for insurance, employees' pensions, savings, relief, and hospitalization.

The telephone accounting classification shows provident and insurance funds are prepaid accounts and deferred charges.

Investments

Public utilities have investments in physical property which are not used in the utility service, and in the stocks and bonds of associated and nonassociated companies. Advances to associated and nonassociated companies are also classified as investments. These investments may be in companies that (1) are being acquired as subsidiaries, (2) are depended upon for a supply of utility service, or (3) conduct incidental or subordinate operations such as gas, transportation, or heating services. Utilities may also advance, on a noncurrent basis, money and credit to associated as well as nonassociated companies. The uniform accounting classifications require that separate and detailed accounts be maintained by the utilities to show these various kinds of property, investments, and advances.

It is generally provided that investments in securities shall be recorded at cost, which may be subsequently written off or written down if a permanent impairment in value materializes. Ordinary market fluctuations are disregarded.

When securities with a fixed maturity date are purchased at a discount or premium, such discount or premium may be amortized over the remaining life of the securities.

Marketable securities or temporary investments of cash should not be included under the heading "investments"; these represent current assets.

Current and accrued assets

Current and accrued assets are cash, those assets which are readily convertible into cash or held for current use in operations or construction, current claims against others, collection of which is reasonably assured, and amounts accruing to the utility which are subject to current settlement. Various subheadings are used in published statements to denote the current assets section, some of which are as follows: current assets, current and accrued assets, and current and working assets. Regardless of the caption, the utilities customarily include in this section the accounts explained below:

Cash. The cash item includes current cash funds, with the exception of working funds.

Special deposits. Special deposits of cash may be made for the current payment of interest and dividends, as a guaranty for the fulfillment of obligations, and for other special purposes. Special deposits also include cash realized from the sale of the accounting utility's securities deposited with trustees to be held until invested in property.

Working funds. Cash advanced to officers, agents, employees, and others as petty cash or working funds is included under the capation of "working funds."

Temporary cash investments. Temporary cash investments include demand and time loans, U.S. Treasury certificates, marketable securities, and other similar temporary investments. An appropriate record must be maintained for pledged temporary investments.

Notes receivable. Promissory notes and other similar evidences of money due on demand or within one year from the date of the balance sheet are shown as notes receivable. The utility accounting classifications require that the contingent liability resulting from discounting promissory notes be shown as notes receivable discounted under the caption of "current liabilities."

Accounts receivable. On the books of the utility, accounts receivable are shown separately (1) for customers who owe for utility service and merchandise, (2) for miscellaneous accounts receivable such as amounts due personally from officers and employees, and (3) for amounts due from associated companies within one year on open accounts, notes, and drafts.

Utility accounting classifications provide that receivables shown on the balance sheet must not be of doubtful value, unless an adequate reserve has been provided.

Subscriptions to capital stock. Subscriptions to capital stock represents the balance due from subscribers upon legally enforceable subscriptions to capital stock of the utility. Telephone companies show subscriptions to capital stock as other assets rather than current assets.

Interest and dividends receivable. Interest and dividends receivable represents the amount of interest due but not received.

Rents receivable. Rents receivable includes rents receivable or accrued on property rented or leased by the utility to others.

Accrued utility revenues. Electric power and gas utility accounting classifications provide for an account, Accrued Utility Revenues, in which may be recorded, at the option of the company, the estimated amount of accrued revenue for services rendered but not billed. If the accrued utility revenue is recorded, the accrued cost of the revenue must also be taken into account.

Material and supplies. Material and supplies may include merchandise for resale, office and selling supplies, material and supplies for construction and maintenance, fuel, and unissued small tools. The cost includes the invoice price, customs duties, excise and other taxes on purchases, insurance, costs of inspection, special tests prior to acceptance, loading and unloading, transportation, and other directly assignable costs.

Other current and accrued assets. Current and accrued items not properly includible elsewhere are shown as other current and accrued assets. Gas companies have an additional current asset in the form of gas stored underground. The utility company may elect to use one of the usual inventory valuation methods: Fifo, Lifo, or weighted average.

Deferred debits

Deferred debits include such items as unamortized debt discount and expense, extraordinary property losses, preliminary survey and investigation charges, and miscellaneous work in progress other than construction work.

Public utilities are frequently authorized by a commission to show as a deferred debit (1) property that has been abandoned but not fully depreciated and (2) extraordinary losses such as unforeseen damages to property which could not reasonably have been anticipated and which are not covered by reserves or by insurance. These items would normally be written off to Earned Surplus. However, the Federal Power Commission may authorize the amortization of these deferred debits over a fixed period. Preliminary survey and investigation charges represent the expense of determining the feasibility of utility projects. If construction results, this amount will be transferred to the appropriate utility asset account; if the work is abandoned, the cost should be written off to Earned Surplus.

The telephone accounting classification provides for *prepaid Accounts and Deferred Charges,* under which caption are shown prepayments of expense, discount on capital stock, capital stock expense, discount on long-term debt, provident funds, insurance and other funds, extraordinary maintenance and retirements, and other deferred charges.

Capital stock discount and expense

Discount on capital stock and capital stock expense are shown separately on the records of the utility. These two items may be amortized over a period of time by debiting Earned Surplus.

Discount on capital stock is preferably classified as an offset in the capital stock and surplus section of the balance sheet. Although shown separately, capital stock expense is in the nature of a deferred charge (to Earned Surplus).

Contingent assets

Contingent assets represent a possible source of value to the utility contingent upon the fulfillment of conditions regarded as uncertain. An investment in properties located in an "enemy" country which has been written off may be considered a contingent asset. Such "assets" may be indicated by a footnote to the balance sheet.

Reacquired securities

Capital stock and long-term obligations that have been issued and later reacquired and not retired or canceled by a utility are shown at par or face value in separate accounts for reacquired capital stock and long-term debt. Instead of showing reacquired securities as assets, it is more desirable to list them as deductions in their respective balance sheet sections. That is, reacquired capital stock should be offset against issued stock; and reacquired long-term debt should be offset against issued long-term debt.

The difference between the par value of the reacquired capital stock and the amount paid therefor is recorded in capital surplus. The difference between the face value of the reacquired long-term debt obligations and the amount paid therefor adjusted for unamortized discount, expense, and/or premium, is recorded as Earned Surplus.

If the securities have been reacquired for sinking or other funds, they would be turned over to the trustee and considered as actually outstanding. In this event the securities are included in the Sinking Fund or Other Fund accounts and shown on the balance sheet under the caption of "investments."

LIABILITIES

Capital stock and surplus

The owners' equity of a public utility company, as in the case of other industries, is the excess of assets over liabilities. The owners' equity accounts are listed and explained below.

Capital stock. The utility classification of accounts requires that capital stock be shown at par value or at stated value in the case of no-par-value stock. When no-par-value stock has no stated value, the cash value of the consideration received for such stock is to be recorded in the Capital Stock account. Separate accounts are to be maintained for each class of capital stock.

The difference between the par value or the stated value of the stock and the actual cash value of the consideration received for the stock is shown as a premium or discount, as the case may be. A premium and discount account is required for each particular class of stock.

Stock liability for conversion. Frequently, utility companies agree· to exchange their own securities for outstanding securities of other companies whose properties are being required. The par, stated, or cash value of the securities to be issued is reflected in the Stock Liability for Conversion account until the transaction is completed.

Premiums and assessments on capital stock. When stock is sold for more than the par or stated value, the excess is shown on the books of the utility as Premium and Assessments on Capital Stock. Assessments on capital stock should also be entered in this account.

Capital stock subscribed. The Capital Stock Subscribed account includes legally enforceable subscriptions to capital stock shown at the par or stated value or the subscription price when no-par-value stock has no stated value.

Installments received on capital stock. If installments are received in payment for capital stock and an enforceable legal contract does not exist, such amounts are entered in the Installments Received on Capital Stock account.

Contributions in aid of construction. Included in the account, Contributions in Aid of Construction, are donations or contributions in cash, services, or property from states, municipalities, or other governmental agencies, individuals, and others for construction purposes. The balance or a portion of the balance may be transferred to Earned Surplus if specifically approved by the public utility commission.

Earned surplus. Earned surplus consists of earnings from operations and extraordinary gains. On the records of the utility, earned surplus may be shown as appropriated or unappropriated earned surplus. Appropriated earned surplus represents earned surplus that has been appropriated or reserved for a specific purpose and temporarily is unavailable for dividend purposes. Unappropriated earned surplus represents the amount of earned surplus that is available for dividend and other corporate purposes.

Unappropriated earned surplus may be increased during an accounting period by such items as net income, profits on retirement of debt securities, credit corrections of income and expense items of preceding accounting periods, amounts previously written off through charges to

Earned Surplus and now returned to Unappropriated Earned Surplus, and gain on sale of assets.

Unappropriated earned surplus may be decreased during an accounting period by such items as net loss; debit corrections of income and expense items of preceding accounting periods; dividend appropriations; reservation or appropriation of surplus; adjustments for depreciation, amortization, and depletion for past periods; and loss on reacquirement of the utility's debt securities.

Capital surplus. Capital surplus includes all surplus not classified as earned surplus. More specifically, capital surplus (preferably referred to as paid-in surplus) includes profit on the sale of reacquired capital stock, surplus arising from the retirement and cancellation of the utility's capital stock, donations received from stockholders, surplus originating from a reduction of the par or stated value of the utility's capital stock, and surplus resulting from a recapitalization of the public utility.

Long-term debt

Long-term debt includes all of the utility's obligations which normally will not be paid within one year subsequent to the balance sheet date. Long-term debt includes such obligations as bonds, receivers' and trustees' certificates, and advances from associated companies. Separate accounts are required for the various debt obligations.

Current and accrued liabilities

Current and accrued liabilities are those obligations which have either matured at the date of the balance sheet or will become due within one year from the date thereof. The accounting classifications provide specifically that bonds, receivers' certificates, and similar obligations shall be classified as long-term debt until their maturity date. Accrued taxes, such as income taxes, are classified as accrued liabilities even though payable more than one year from the balance sheet date. The following current and accrued liability accounts, which are self-explanatory, are maintained by a utility:

> Notes Payable
> Notes Receivable Discounted
> Accounts Payable
> Payables to Associated Companies (Current)
> Dividends Declared
> Matured Long-Term Debt
> Matured Interest
> Customers' Deposits (security for payment of bills)
> Taxes Accrued
> Interest Accrued
> Other Current and Accrued Liabilities

Deferred credits

Deferred credits include such items as unamortized premium on debt, customers' advances for construction, and amounts that cannot be entirely cleared or disposed of until additional information has been received, or that should be credited to income or surplus accounts in the future.

The account, Customers' Advances for Construction, represents amounts that have been paid by customers for construction. These amounts will be partially or wholly refunded to the customers. If retained by the utility, the amount is transferred to the account, Contributions in Aid of Construction.

Reserves

Public utility accounting classifications provide for the establishment of a number of reserves. Included in this group are reserves for depreciation, amortization,, and uncollectible accounts; insurance (self-insurance against losses through accident, fire, flood, or other hazards to property); injuries and damages; and employees' pensions, accident and death benefits, savings, relief, hospital, and other provident purposes.

These reserves—with the exception of the reserve for uncollectible accounts, which is offset against accounts receivable—are shown in public utility balance sheets under the caption of "reserves." The reserve for depreciation and amortization (accumulated depreciation and amortization) would be better classified as a deduction from the related asset.

Contingent liabilities

Contingent liabilities include items that become obligations of the utility but which are neither direct nor assumed liabilities as of the balance sheet date. The utility is required to explain in detail in a footnote or on a separate statement the nature of its contingent liabilities including cumulative dividends on preferred stock. However, the contingent liability, notes receivable discounted, is included in the current and accrued liabilities section of the balance sheet.

Public utility income statement accounts

The following pages are devoted to an explanation and discussion of the most important income statement items provided for in interstate public utility accounting classifications. Typical income statement accounts for electric power, gas, and telephone companies appear in Illustrations 24–3 and 24–4, following. Accounts prescribed for natural gas companies are identical to those prescribed for electric companies with a few minor changes because of the different business involved.

The income accounts are designed to show for each month and each calendar year the operating revenues and expenses, and other income,

ILLUSTRATION 24–3
CLASS A AND B* INTERSTATE PRIVATE ELECTRIC LIGHT
AND POWER COMPANIES
Income Accounts

Utility Operating Income

Electric Operating Income:
  Operating Revenues
  Operating Revenue Deductions:
    Operating Expenses
    Maintenance Expense
    Depreciation Expense
    Amortization of Limited-Term Electric Investments
    Amortization of Other Electric Plant
    Amortization of Electric Plant Acquisition Adjustments
    Taxes Other than Income Taxes
    Income Taxes
    Provision for Deferred Income Taxes
    Investment Tax Credit Adjustments
      Total Operating Expenses
  Net Operating Revenues
  Income from Electric Plant Leased to Others
Other Utility Operating Income
  Total Operating Income

Other Income

Income from Merchandising, Jobbing, and Contract Work
Income from Nonutility Operations
Nonoperating Rental Income
Interest and Dividend Income
Miscellaneous Nonoperating Income
  Total Other Income
  Gross Income

Income Deductions

Interest on Long-Term Debt
Amortization of Debt Discount and Expense
Amortization of Premium on Debt—Credit
Taxes Assumed
Interest on Debt to Associated Companies
Interest Charged to Construction—Credit
Other Interest Charges
Miscellaneous Amortization
Miscellaneous Income Deductions
  Total Income Deductions
  Net Income

Disposition of Net Income

Miscellaneous Reservations of Net Income
  Balance Transferred to Earned Surplus

* See page 516, Illustration 24–1, nn. * and †, for definition of Class A and B companies.

ILLUSTRATION 24–4
CLASS A AND B* TELEPHONE COMPANIES
Income Accounts

Operating Revenues:
  Local Services
  Toll Services
  Revenue from Services Incidental to the Utility Operations
  Uncollectible Operating Revenues (Debit)
Operating Expenses:
  Maintenance Expenses
  Depreciation and Amortization Expenses
  Traffic Expenses
  Commerical Expenses
  General Office Salaries and Expenses
  Other Operating Expenses
Other Income:
  Dividend Income
  Interest Income
  Income from Funds
  Income from Miscellaneous Physical Properties
  Miscellaneous Income
Deductions from Income:
  Fixed Charges (interest, discount, etc.)
  Miscellaneous Taxes
  Miscellaneous Income Charges

  * See page 517, Illustration 24–2, nn., for definition of Class A and B Telephone Companies.

the income deductions, the net income, the miscellaneous reservations of net income, and the amount of income or loss remaining for transfer to earned surplus.

REVENUES

Operating revenue accounts show the amounts of money which the utility has received or accrued for furnishing utility service and services incidental thereto for a period of time, usually for each month and for the calendar year.

Operating revenues for utility companies are shown on the records as follows:

ELECTRIC LIGHT AND POWER COMPANIES

Operating Revenues:
  Sales of electric energy:
    Residential or domestic sales
    Commercial and industrial sales
    Sales to railroads and street railways
    Public street and highway lighting
    Other sales to public authorities
    Sales to other electric companies
    Interdepartmental sales
    Other sales

Revenue from services incidental to the utility operation:
Rent from electric property
Interdepartmental rents
Customers' forfeited discounts and penalties (amounts forfeited by customers because of failure to pay their accounts within the specified time)
Sales of water for irrigation, domestic, industrial, or other uses
Servicing of customers' electrical installations (charges to customers for the maintenance of appliances, wiring, piping, and other electrical installations on customers' premises)
Miscellaneous electric revenues

GAS COMPANIES

Operating Revenues:
Sales of gas:
Residential
Commercial and industrial
Public street and highway lighting
Municipal and governmental
Other sales to public authorities
Sales to other gas companies
Interdepartmental
Other
Revenue from services incidental to the utility operation:
Rent from gas property
Interdepartmental rents
Customers' forfeited discounts and penalties (amounts forfeited by customers because of failure to pay their accounts within the specified time)
Servicing of customers' installations (charges to customers for the maintenance of appliances, piping, or other installations on their premises)
Revenue from transportation of gas of others
Sales of products extracted from gas
Miscellaneous

TELEPHONE COMPANIES

Operating Revenues:
Revenues from:
Local services (local exchange service)
Toll services (long-distance and local toll services)
Revenue from services incidental to the utility operation:
Directory advertising
Rent of properties
Telegraph commissions
Other operating revenue

OPERATING EXPENSES

Operating expense accounts show in detail the cost of furnishing the utility service (except for depreciation, amortization, extraordinary property losses, and taxes). Depreciation, taxes, amortization, and extraordinary property losses are generally shown for the plant as a whole rather than being distributed as production, transmission, distribution, or other expense.

Operating expenses ("operating revenue deductions") for utility companies are shown on the records as follows:

Operating Expenses:
  Production Expenses:
    The cost of generating electric energy by steam, hydraulic, and internal combustion engine, and nuclear power.
  Transmission Expenses:
    The cost of transmitting electric energy from power station to the area of distribution to consumers.
  Distribution Expenses:
    The cost of distributing electric energy to consumers.
  Customers' Accounting and Collecting Expenses:
    The cost of supervising, directing, and performing work on customers' contracts, orders, inquiries, and accounts, and in meter reading, credit investigations, and collecting.
  Sales Promotion Expenses:
    The cost of the sales department, including the solicitation of new business.
  General and Administrative Expenses:
    The cost of the general administrative offices.

Depreciation and Amortization:
  Depreciation expense on plant and equipment used in performing the electric utility service, and amortization of utility property when a limited-term franchise is involved. Amortization charged to operations may also include amortization of electric plant acquisition adjustments. The write-off of this value, which is in excess of the cost of plant to the original purchaser, over a short period of time against operations is authorized by the utility commission. Depreciation is defined in the account classification as loss in service value not restored by current maintenance caused by current operation and against which the utility is not protected by insurance. Among the causes to be given consideration are wear and tear, decay, action of the elements, inadequacy, obsolescence, changes in the art, and changes in demand and requirements of public authority.

Property Losses Chargeable to Operations:
  Extraordinary property losses may be amortized by charges to operations upon the approval of the utility commission.

Taxes:
  Federal, state, county, municipal, and other taxes, which are properly chargeable to electric operations.

GAS COMPANIES

Operating Expenses:
  Production Expenses:
    The cost of producing, manufacturing, and storing gas. Production expense includes cost of raw materials used in making gas and cost of gas purchased from other gas companies.
  Transmission Expenses:
    The cost of transmitting gas from the production or storage plant to the consuming areas.
  Distribution Expenses:
    The cost of distributing gas from the transmission lines to the customers.
  Customers' Accounting and Collecting Expenses:
    The cost of supervising, directing, and performing work on customers' contracts, orders, inquiries, and accounts, and in meter reading, credit investigations, and collecting.

Sales Promotion Expenses:
The cost of the sales department, including the solicitation of new business.
General and Administrative Expense:
The cost of the general administrative offices.

Depreciation and Amortization:
Depreciation applicable to utility properties and amortization of limited-term utility investments, including utility plant acquisition adjustment.

Property Losses Chargeable to Operations:
The utility commission may authorize the utility to amortize the extraordinary property losses by charges to operations.

Taxes:
Federal, state, county, municipal, and other taxes which are properly chargeable to utility operations.

TELEPHONE COMPANIES

Operating Expenses:
Maintenance Expenses:
The cost of inspection, repairs, and rearrangements required to keep the plant and equipment in an efficient operating condition.
Traffic Expenses:
Costs incurred in handling messages.
Commercial Expenses:
The cost incurred in business relations with customers; public telephone commissions; and the cost of directories, sales activities, and advertising.
Operating Rents:
Rents for the use of buildings and other telephone facilities.
General and Miscellaneous Expenses:
Costs of the following: general administration; accounting and treasury departments; development and research; provision for employees' accident and other benefits.

Depreciation and Amortization Expense:
Depreciation applicable to the telephone plant and amortization of intangible property and of the telephone plant acquisition adjustment account balance.

Taxes, Other then Income Taxes:
Federal, state, and other governmental taxes which are properly chargeable to utility operation.

OTHER INCOME AND INCOME DEDUCTIONS

Income earned on nonutility assets or on assets not being used in the utility service is known as other income. The sources of other income for utility companies include nonutility operations, lease of other physical property, dividends and interest on bond and stock investments, and earnings on sinking and other funds. For gas and electric power companies, other income may include income from merchandising, jobbing, and contract work.

Income deductions

Electric power, gas, and telephone utilities deduct from gross income such items as the following: interest on long-term debt, amortization of debt discount and expense, taxes assumed on interest payments, interest on debt to associated companies, and decline in value of investments and donations.

Disposition of net income

Net income is disposed of by transferring appropriations to Miscellaneous Reservations of Net Income and the balance to Earned Surplus. Miscellaneous reservations made out of current income before the net income balance is transferred to Earned Surplus include those required under the terms of mortgages, deeds of trust, orders of courts, contracts, and other agreements.

25

Statements of public utilities (continued)

Analyzing public utility financial data

THE RELATIVE financial strength of a public utility and the efficiency and economy of its operations and management may be measured and evaluated by comparing its operating and financial data from year to year or in comparison with similar data of other utility companies. In order to make the comparisons most practical and effective, however, the data should be reduced to common units. The absolute data are valuable in obtaining a picture of the magnitude of a utility industry; and, too, these data must be studied in connection with the interpretation of ratios and trends.

When data for different periods of time or for various public utilities are analyzed, it is necessary to determine variations in the items under review and, in turn, to ascertain the causes of the fluctuations. The analyst should know the various statistical units or phrases used to express public utility operating and financial data, the manner in which the statistics are developed, the causes of fluctuations in the units, the qualifications to which each unit must be subjected, and the relationship existing between and among the different units under review.

The following pages are devoted to the presentation and discussion of public utility ratios, trends, and comparisons. Data for two electric light and power companies are presented in Illustration 25–1, comparative balance sheets as of December 31, 1971, and in Illustration 25–2, comparative income statements for the year 1971.

ILLUSTRATION 25–1

IDAHO POWER COMPANY AND
ROCHESTER GAS AND ELECTRIC CORPORATION
Comparative Balance Sheets
December 31, 1971
(thousands of dollars)

	Rochester		Idaho	
	($000)	(%)	($000)	(%)
Assets				
Utility Properties, at Original Cost:				
Electric.	443,785		515,273	
Gas.	139,295			
Steam	15,327			
	598,407	119.0	515,273	115.0
Less: Accumulated depreciation	134,419	26.7	87,158	19.4
Utility Properties, Net	463,988	92.3	428,115	95.6
Investments, at cost.			283	...
Current Assets:				
Cash and equivalent investments	12,463		6,867	
Deposits			451	
Accounts receivable, net.	12,999		7,113	
Materials and supplies, including construction materials, at average cost	10,828		1,674	
Prepayments and other assets	610		2,055	
Total Current Assets	36,900	7.3	18,160	4.0
Deferred Debits:				
Unamortized debt discounts and expense	1,640		626	
Other.	398		1,053	
	2,038	.4	1,679	.4
Total Assets.	502,926	100.0	448,237	100.0
Capital and Liabilities				
Capitalization:				
Common stock	106,434		33,000	
Capital surplus, principally premium on preferred stock, less expense	(2,405)		47,818	
Preferred stock	67,000		21,500	
Retained earnings.	44,624		67,967	
	215,653	42.9	170,285	38.0
Long-term debt	236,677	47.1	217,772	48.6
Total Capitalization	452,330	90.0	388,057	86.6
Deferred Credits:				
Unamortized premium, less expense, on debt	233		91	
Deferred taxes on income			24,298	
Other	96		551	
	396	.1	24,940	5.6
Current Liabilities:				
Notes payable.	21,500		21,200	
Accounts payable.	10,181		1,495	
Taxes accrued.	5,018		5,303	
Other current liabilities	7,027		4,355	
Total Current Liabilities	43,726	8.6	32,353	7.2
Contributions by customers for construction			2,887	.6
Operating reserves	854	.2		
Nuclear fuel contract.	5,687	1.1		
Total Capital and Liabilities	502,926	100.0	448,237	100.0

ILLUSTRATION 25–2

IDAHO POWER COMPANY AND ROCHESTER GAS
AND ELECTRIC CORPORATION
Comparative Income Statements
For the Year 1971

	Idaho		Rochester	
	($000)	(%)	($000)	(%)
Operating income:				
Operating revenues	81,810	100.0	175,879	100.0
Operating expenses:				
Operating expenses including maintenance and repairs	21,299	26.0	104,234	59.3
Depreciation and amortization	7,498	9.2	14,106	8.0
Taxes.	23,580	28.8	25,280	14.4
Total Operating Expenses	52,377	64.0	143,620	81.7
Net operating revenue	29,433	36.0	32,259	18.3
Other income and deductions	383	.4	656	.4
Net income before interest	29,816	36.4	32,915	18.7
Interest	10,409	12.7	14,906	8.5
Net Income	19,407	23.7	18,009	10.2

Common-size percentages and percentages of increase and decrease

Financial and operating data may be shown in percentage form, as in Illustration 25–3 (which compares an electric utility with a telephone company). This method of presentation brings to light sharply one of the characteristics of public utilities as compared to commercial companies—fixed operating assets and the capitalization (long-term debt, capital stock, and surplus) are of major importance. The data in Illustration 25–3 show that as of December 31, 1971 the electric company and the telephone company had 95.6 percent and 93.6 percent, respectively, of their total resources invested in fixed operating assets. Illustration 25–3 also shows that the electric company obtained 62.0 percent of its resources from creditors; the telephone company, 39.7 percent.

The relatively large amounts of long-term debt are common for public utilities because of their more stable income and the continuous need for fixed capital, but less for telephone than for electric concerns.

Illustration 25–4 compares the balance sheets of an electric utility at the end of 1971 and 1968 and the dollar and percentage increases or decreases during the period. Current assets increased $16 million, or 43 percent, whereas current liabilities increased only 21.5 percent. It is interesting to note the $42 million, or 19.4 percent, increase in

ILLUSTRATION 25-3

IDAHO POWER COMPANY AND ILLINOIS BELL TELEPHONE COMPANY
December 31, 1971

Items	Idaho Power Company Amount ($000)	% of total	Illinois Bell Telephone Company ($000)	% of total
Assets				
Utility plant, net.	428,115	95.6	2,679,994	93.6
Other assets	20,122	4.4	183,561	6.4
Total Assets	448,237	100.0	2,863,555	100.0
Liabilities and Owners' Equity				
Paid-in capital.	170,285	38.0	1,726,128	60.3
Long-term debt.	217,772	48.6	851,500	29.7
Total Capitalization	388,057	86.6	2,577,628	90.0
Other liabilities.	60,180	13.4	285,927	10.0
Total Liabilities and Owners' Equity	448,237	100.0	2,863,555	100.0

ILLUSTRATION 25-4

ROCHESTER GAS & ELECTRIC CORPORATION
Comparative Balance Sheets
As of December 31, 1968, and 1971

Items	December 31 1971 ($000)	% of total	1968 ($000)	% of total	Increase (decrease) ($)	(%)
Assets						
Current assets	36,900	7.3	20,979	5.1	15,921	43.1
Property and plant, net	463,988	92.3	386,056	94.5	77,932	16.8
Other assets	2,038	.4	1,593	.4	445	21.8
Total Assets.	502,926	100.0	408,628	100.0	94,298	18.7
Liabilities and Stockholders' Investment						
Current liabilities	42,954	8.5	33,699	8.2	9,255	21.5
Bonds	236,677	47.2	200,000	49.0	36,677	15.5
Other liabilities and reserves.	7,642	1.5	1,105	.3	6,537	85.5
Total Liabilities	287,273	57.2	234,804	57.5	52,469	18.3
Stockholders' Investment:						
Preferred stock	67,000	13.3	47,000	11.5	20,000	29.9
Common stock	106,434	21.2	89,581	21.9	16,853	15.8
Paid-in surplus less expense	(2,405)	(.6)	(2,040)	(.5)	(365)	(15.2)
Retained income	44,624	8.9	39,283	9.6	5,341	12.0
Total Stockholders' Investment. . .	215,653	42.8	173,824	42.5	41,829	19.4
Total Liabilities and Stockholders' Investment	502,926	100.0	408,628	100.0	94,298	18.7

ILLUSTRATION 25-5

IDAHO POWER COMPANY AND ROCHESTER GAS & ELECTRIC CORPORATION
Trends of Selected Data (1968 = 100%)
Years Ended December 31, 1968-71
($000 omitted)

		1971	1970	1969	1968
Utility plant, net	Rochester	598,407	569,641	527,917	485,48(
	Trend %	123	117	109	100
	Idaho	428,116	413,654	409,657	404,60"
	Trend %	106	102	101	100
Long-term debt	Rochester	236,677	236,677	221,677	200,00(
	Trend %	118	118	111	
	Idaho	217,772	218,019	218,268	218,51(
	Trend %	100	100	100	100
Stockholders' Equity	Rochester	215,653	209,479	202,074	173,82(
	Trend %	124	121	116	100
	Idaho	170,285	162,628	157,285	153,93]
	Trend %	111	106	102	100
Operating revenue	Rochester	175,879	152,966	132,315	123,36!
	Trend %	143	124	107	100
	Idaho	81,810	74,735	69,377	66,92(
	Trend %	122	112	104	100
Operating expenses including taxes and depreciation	Rochester	143,620	123,344	106,840	100,31!
	Trend %	143	123	107	100
	Idaho	52,377	47,340	44,158	43,02!
	Trend %	122	110	103	100
Net income	Rochester	18,009	19,005	19,126	17,11!
	Trend %	105	111	112	100
	Idaho	19,407	16,763	14,773	14,97!
	Trend %	130	112	99	100
Operating expenses exclusive of depreciation	Rochester	129,514	110,838	96,375	90,059
	Trend %	144	123	107	100
	Idaho	45,040	40,298	37,218	36,272
	Trend %	124	111	103	100
Taxes	Rochester	25,280	19,355	18,513	18,571
	Trend %	136	104	100	100
	Idaho	23,579	22,369	20,944	19,177
	Trend %	123	117	109	100
Depreciation	Rochester	14,106	12,506	10,465	10,259
	Trend %				
	Idaho	7,337	7,042	6,940	6,756
	Trend %	109	104	103	100

stockholders' investment in comparison with the $52 million, or 18.3 percent, increase in total liabilities. In other words, the asset expansion of $94 million was financed by using funds obtained from creditors, 52 million, and the additional investment of stockholders, 42 million, 58.4 percent debt. A reliance on 60 percent debt is not unusual in electric utilities.

Trend percentages

Trend percentages or ratios may be used advantageously in analyzing financial and operating data for a period of years. In this way the growth or increase and decline or decrease in the data over a period of several years may be studied.

The trends for selected data for the Idaho Power Company for the years 1968–71 are shown in Illustration 25–5. During the period the increase of $23,500,000, or 6 percent, in the utility plant (plant, property, and equipment) was financed entirely by owners' equity. Long-term debt actually declined slightly.

The trend for operating revenues—an increase of $14,800,000, or 22 percent—was matched by the trend for operating expenses—an increase of $9,300,000 or 24 percent. Idaho Power has an unusually low operating ratio (Illustration 25–6). Net income increased $4,500,000, or 30 percent. Taxes and depreciation expense increased $4,400,000, or 23 percent, and $580,000, or 9 percent, respectively.

ILLUSTRATION 25–6

IDAHO POWER COMPANY AND
ROCHESTER GAS AND ELECTRIC CORPORATION
Operating Ratios 1968–71

		December 31			
	Company	1971	1970	1969	1968
Operating expenses as percent of operating revenue	Rochester	81.7%	80.6%	80.7%	81.3%
	Idaho	64.3	63.3	63.6	64.0

Current ratio

The relationship between the current assets and current liabilities is not so important for a public utility as the proportion between the capitalization and the fixed operating assets. A public utility should have working capital sufficient to meet current obligations such as accounts and notes payable, interest charges on funded debt, dividends on capital stock, and emergencies. An electric light and power utility does not have an inventory problem, and credit risks in connection with receivables are minimized. A gas utility company acquires an inventory problem if gas is stored.

A turnover of receivables from utility services is relatively rapid and certain because (1) the utility services are essential to the customer and the utilities exercise the right to discontinue the service if the bill is not paid within a certain time; and (2) a discount is customarily offered by utility companies for prompt payment of the bill, or a penalty is added if the bill is not paid when due. Telephone companies collect in advance of service except for toll charges.

While the working capital of a public utility is ordinarily of minor importance, a study of current ratios will show whether debt-paying ability in the short run has been impaired or is deteriorating. For example, the following figures show that whereas the Rochester Gas & Electric Corporation ordinarily has a current ratio of around 1 to 1, the Idaho Power Company does not. This is a signal which should lead to a more careful examination of the Idaho Power Company's current position.

		December 31		
Company	1971	1970	1969	1968
Idaho Power Company........(%)	56.1	62.5	52.6	47.3
Rochester Gas & Electric Corporation.............(%)	85.9	116.7	107.7	62.2

Ratio of funded debt to net fixed operating property[1]

The ratio of funded debt to net property is determined by dividing funded debt by net fixed operating property.

		December 31		
Company	1971	1970	1969	1968
Idaho Power Company........(%)	53.2	53.9	53.3	54.0
Rochester Gas & Electric Corporation.............(%)	51.1	52.5	52.5	51.8

A low percentage of funded debt to net fixed operating assets is most favorable from the point of view of the long-term creditors because of the greater asset value underlying the funded debt and the lower resultant fixed charges. However, from the point of view of the common stockholders a relatively high ratio of funded debt to fixed operating

---

[1] Property less depreciation reserve equals net property.

assets may be more favorable because of the possibility of benefiting from trading on the equity (leverage).

Ratio of capitalization (including surplus) to net property

The ratio of capitalization (long-term debt, capital stock, and surplus) to net property is determined by dividing capitalization by net property.

Company	December 31			
	1971	1970	1969	1968
Idaho Power Company........(%)	90.5	92.0	91.7	92.1
Rochester Gas & Electric Corporation.............(%)	97.5	99.1	100.4	96.8

The foregoing ratios are more favorable for Rochester Gas & Electric than for Idaho Power, since the latter company's captilization fell well short of the cost of its property. This fact indicates that Idaho Power financed 8 to 10 percent of its fixed property by using funds from sources other than long-term debt, capital stock, and surplus, mostly current liabilities.

In analyzing the capitalization and net operating property, consideration should be given to (1) the distribution of borrowed funds and owners' equity, (2) the spacing of bond maturities, (3) the probable current commercial value or cost of replacement of the operating property, (4) the market or present estimated value of the investments, and (5) the nature of the investments, whether they are held for income and/or control purposes.

Public utility property is valued by public utility commissions to determine the amount of fair return that may be included in the charge to the consumer. The valuation may be based on original cost, cost of reproduction, or prudent investment cost of the property presently used or useful for rendering the utility service. When this valuation is available, it may be used in connection with the study of the value of the operating property as shown on the books.

Sources of capital invested in total assets

The data in Illustration 25–7 clearly indicate that from the standpoint of the creditors Rochester Gas & Electric is in a much more favorable and conservative position that Idaho Power. Rochester's total liabilities are only 57 percent of total liabilities plus capital, while the comparable

ILLUSTRATION 25-7

IDAHO POWER COMPANY AND
ROCHESTER GAS & ELECTRIC CORPORATION
Sources of Funds Invested in Total Assets
As of December 31, 1971 and 1968

	Company	1971 ($000)	1971 (%)	1968 ($000)	1968 (%)
Total assets, net	Rochester	502,926	100.0	408,628	100.0
	Idaho	448,237	100.0	418,603	100.0
Current liabilities	Rochester	42,954	8.5	33,699	8.3
	Idaho	32,353	7.2	23,927	5.7
Long-term and other non- current liabilities	Rochester	244,318	48.6	201,105	49.2
	Idaho	245,599	54.8	240,745	57.5
Total liabilities	Rochester	287,273	57.1	234,804	57.5
	Idaho	277,952	62.0	264,672	63.2
Preferred stock	Rochester	67,000	13.3	47,000	11.5
	Idaho	21,500	4.8	21,500	5.1
Capital surplus	Rochester	(2,405)*	(.5)	(2,040)*	(.5)
	Idaho	47,818	10.7	47,818	11.4
Common stock and retained earnings	Rochester	151,058	30.1	128,864	31.5
	Idaho	100,967	22.5	84,614	20.3
Total stockholders' equity	Rochester	215,653	42.9	173,824	42.5
	Idaho	170,285	38.0	153,931	36.8

* Capital stock expense net of premium.

percentage for Idaho Power in 62 percent. The Rochester creditors have therefore a buffer against hard times of 75 percent while the comparable margin of safety in Idaho Power is only 61 percent.

Times funded debt interest is earned

The number of times that funded debt interest is earned represents an important ratio. This ratio is determined by dividing net income (after all taxes), before deducting fixed interest charges, by the amount

Company	1971	1970	1969	1968
Idaho Power Company . . . . .(times)	3.1	2.8	2.6	2.5
Rochester Gas & Electric Corporation. . . . .(times)	2.4	2.7	3.1	3.2

of funded debt interest. Until recently, Rochester Gas & Electric has enjoyed a superior margin of safety with respect to the payment of fixed interest charges, but in the four years 1968 to 1971 its advantage steadily declined until in 1970 and particularly in 1971 Idaho Power moved into a superior position. The reason is the spectacular rise in interest rates. Rochester borrowed money at a rate as high as $9\frac{1}{8}$ percent whereas Idaho Power borrowed no money during the high rate period— expansion was financed out of earnings—so that its highest rate was $6\frac{1}{8}$ percent. However, neither company is really in an unsound position with regard to this ratio (see the discussion below).

One should also note in Illustration 25–5 that Idaho is booking substantially less depreciation than Rochester. It should be remembered however that depreciation charges do not involve the use of working capital and do not result in the incurrence of a liability. Therefore, a company that has not fully earned its fixed charges may develop sufficient working capital—for a few years, at least—to meet interest charges, if depreciation charges are in excess of expenditures for new fixed assets.

Times fixed interest charges and preferred dividend requirements are earned

The number of times that fixed interest charges and preferred dividend requirements are earned is determined by dividing net income (after all taxes) before fixed interest charges and preferred dividends by fixed interest charges and preferred dividend requirements. The high

Company	1971	1970	1969	1968
Idaho Power Company . . . . .(Times)	2.8	2.6	2.4	2.3
Rochester Gas & Electric Corporation. . . . .(Times)	1.9	2.1	2.3	2.6

interest rate situation has had a similar effect on Rochester's ratios in this table. Free of the burden of additional interest, Idaho's position has steadily improved.

The number of times that fixed interest charges and preferred dividend requirements are earned is important not only to the bondholders and preferred stockholders but also to common stockholders. Common stockholders are not entitled to a dividend until after the fixed interest and preferred dividend requirements have been paid. The greater the number of times that fixed interest and preferred dividend requirements are earned, (1) the greater the amount of earnings that may be apportioned as dividends to the stockholders or accumulated in earned surplus for their benefit; (2) the more favorable the credit rating that will be assigned to the company; (3) the more favorable the prospects of financing future requirements on a low-cost basis; and (4) the greater the investment value of the company's securities.

The average rate of interest on funded debt and the average dividend rate on preferred stock reflect the credit standing of a company as well as the relative cost of financing. For example, during 1971 the funded debt interest for Rochester Gas & Electric averaged 5.8 percent and the average preferred stock dividend rate was 5.3 percent. The funded debt interest for Idaho Power averaged 4.6 percent, and the preferred stock dividend rate averaged 4.0 percent. Back in 1964 Rochester's average interest rate was 3.5 percent; Idaho was 4.0 percent.

Inasmuch as interest has to be provided for before preferred dividends are declared, the total net income should be related to the preferred dividend to determine the number of times that the preferred dividend was earned. This is accomplished by dividing the net income (after all taxes and interest charges) by preferred dividend requirements.

Company	1971	1970	1969	1968
Idaho Power Company . . . . .(Times)	22.6	19.5	17.2	17.4
Rochester Gas & Electric Corporation. . . . .(Times)	5.1	5.4	6.2	8.4

Return earned per share of common stock

The return earned on common stock is most commonly determined by dividing net income, after deducting preferred stock dividend requirements, by the number of outstanding shares of common stock. The return is stated in dollars and cents per share.

Company	1971	1970	1969	1968
Idaho Power Company . . . .($)	2.81	2.41	2.11	2.14
Rochester Gas & Electric Corporation. . . . .($)	2.08	2.22	2.31	2.17

When a study of earnings is being made, special consideration should be given to the problem of depreciation, inasmuch as public utilities depreciate asset original costs on a straight-line basis. Current property costs are much higher than the cost of most of the assets that are owned and used by the public utility companies. Consequently, the depreciation charges do not represent equivalent amounts necessary for the asset replacement at current costs. As a result it should be evidence that in many cases a substantial portion of the reported profits are required for the purpose of maintaining the same physical quantity of fixed assets.

Ratio of net income after preferred dividend requirements to common stock and surplus

The ratio of net income, after deducting preferred dividend requirements, to common stock and surplus shows the percentage of net earnings on common stock and surplus. This ratio, which represents the net earnings on the total equity of the common stockholders, is determined by dividing net income after preferred dividend requirements by common stock and surplus. During the year 1971 Idaho Power earned 12.5 percent on the common stockholders' equity and Rochester realized a return of 9.6 percent.

In interpreting this ratio, the analyst should give consideration to the "tentative" book value of capital stock and surplus, which reflects the valuation of all assets and the "tentative" nature of the net income figure, especially if it represents the results for an abnormal year (war, for example). The net income for any year may be overstated because of deferred maintenance and other adjustments which are assignable at a later date to a specific prior year.

A high rate of return may be a result of greater efficiency of operations, increased volume of business, a favorable change in the price level, or an overstatement of net income due to deferred maintenance.

A low rate of return indicates that the business is not successful, some of the reasons for which may be inefficient financial, production, or sales management; general business conditions; overinvestment in assets; or disproportionate distribution of bonds and preferred stock relative to the total capitalization.

Ratio of fixed operating property (net) to operating revenue

The ratio of fixed operating property (net) to operating revenue shows the number of dollars invested in operating property for each dollar of revenue. This ratio is determined by dividing fixed operating property (after deducting accumulated depreciation) by operating revenue. It will be observed that the foregoing ratio is the reverse of the ratio of net sales to operating assets which is used by commercial and industrial companies. In public utilities the fixed plant investment is much larger than the annual revenue; in commercial and industrial companies, annual sales exceed the operating assets.

Company	1971	1970	1969	1968
Idaho Power Company . . . .($)	5.2	5.5	5.9	6.0
Rochester Gas & Electric Corporation. . . . .($)	7.0	6.6	6.0	6.0

Variations in this ratio may be the result of one or more of the following practices or situations by one of the companies:

1. Purchases of a large volume of electric power at a price lower than the cost of producing the energy in the company's own plant.
2. Expansion of the plant at the end of the period; therefore, the productive capacity would not be reflected in earnings, although the cost would be included in property.
3. Greater concentration of demand—that is, a greater density of distribution—thereby requiring a relatively lower investment in the distribution system.
4. Operation of a hydroelectric power plant.
5. Construction of plant during a period of high or low prices as compared to other companies.
6. More or less favorable rate structure.
7. Appreciation of property.
8. Unfavorable plant utilization and load factors.
9. Age of plant, as well as the price level as of the date of construction.

The last two factors require brief explanation.

A public utility must serve the public 24 hours per day and, therefore, must have utility facilities to supply service whenever demanded. Some time during each day, season, or year the demand made on the utility facilities will be at its highest point. This point of demand or production is known as the "peak load." The utilities commonly have reserve capacity, i.e., capacity that is not needed to serve the highest peak of demand.

The ratio of the peak load of a utility plant to the rated generator capacity of that plant is known as the "plant utilization factor." In other words, this ratio shows the percentage of the total plant that is used at the peak. The lower this ratio, the more unfavorable the situation becomes because of the current unproductiveness of the idle facilities.

The "load" factor represents the relationship between the average demand on the production plant and the peak demand made on the utility facilities. Expressed in terms of a ratio, the load factor represents the percentage of the average load to the peak load. The lower this ratio, the less favorable the situation because the facilities of the utility would be in use a relatively short period of time and, therefore, will be less profitably used. The load factor of a utility is improved by offering special rates for off-peak service, thereby "ironing out" or "leveling off" the peak demand. In other words, the special rates encourage customers to diversify their demand; off-peak demand is thereby raised, thus giving better average use and increasing the load factor. The diversity factor receives much attention by public utility management.

A utility company is able to operate on the most profitable basis when it has high plant utilization and load factors. When a utility has a low plant utilization factor as well as a low load factor, a relatively large portion of the plant investment is nonproductive.

It should be understood that the external analyst, in most instances, would not have available data with respect to the plant and load factors. Even so, he should understand these terms, since the factors have a profound effect upon the operation of the utility.

Ratio of income before interest charges to total assets

The ratio of income (after all taxes) before interest to total assets, which is determined by dividing income before interest charges by total assets, shows the rate of income on the investment in total assets. This ratio indicates the average rate of return on the total asset investment and, therefore, indicates the relative income-producing capacity of such assets.

Company	1971	1970	1969	1968
Idaho Power Company........(%)	6.0	6.4	5.7	5.5
Rochester Gas & Electric Corporation............(%)	6.5	6.7	6.8	6.5

One utility may be inferior to another because it has:

1. A productive plant capacity in excess of the current demand for the utility service.
2. A less efficient plant.
3. An inefficient management.
4. Operating costs that are increasing at a more rapid rate than operating revenues.

Operating revenues

Operating revenues represent the amount of money which the utility has received or accrued for furnishing utility service and services incidental thereto. Whenever available, the breakdown of operating revenues should be studied to determine the reasons for changes in the amounts from year to year. For example, an increase in operating revenue may have been a result of (1) a normal, wartime, or emergency plant expansion and a larger volume of business, (2) a larger normal, wartime, or emergency volume of demand not accompanied by an increase in facilities, (3) a change in the class of service performed, or (4) a favorable change in the rate structure. The larger volume of demand may be almost entirely from the old customers or from old and new temporary or permanent customers. For example, the new demand may originate from military installations and other government-operated agencies and commercial and war-production centers.

A decrease in operating revenue may be a result of a lower volume of demand, an unfavorable change in the rate structure, or both. The lower volume of business may be caused by a depression or a decrease in demand from temporary defense activities.

Frequently, the analyst will have at hand data similar to those shown in Illustrations 25–8, 25–9, and 25–10, which may be used in studying the revenues of an electric utility. Comparable data for other utilities are often published. Detailed records of plant facilities and the rate structure should also be available if a complete analysis is to be undertaken.

The data in Illustrations 25–8 through 25–10 should be studied and compared. Similar data for several years, reduced to trend percentages, would indicate improvement or decline. For example, analysis of Idaho Power's residential customers (Illustration 25–8) shows that the annual average consumption of kilowatt-hours per customer increased from 9,171 in 1968 to 10,595 in 1971. During the same period of time the annual price per kilowatt-hour increased from 1.72 cents to 1.75 cents. Illustration 25–10, using Rochester Gas & Electric, shows how consumption of electricity by the individual customer has dramatically increased.

The operating revenues of public utilities are generally more stable than those of other businesses. This stability, which is largely a result

ILLUSTRATION 25–8

IDAHO POWER COMPANY
Comparative Data
For the Years Ended December, 1968–1971

Items	Residential customers			
	1971	1970	1969	1968
Annual average per residential customer:				
Kilowatt-hours per customer..........	10,595	9,995	9,499	9,171
Price per kilowatt-hour (cents)	1.75	1.70	1.71	1.72

ILLUSTRATION 25–9

ROCHESTER GAS AND ELECTRIC CORPORATION
Sources and Comparison of 1968 and 1971 Revenues

	Revenue ($000)		1971 over 1968 (%)	% of total revenue	
	1968	1971		1968	1971
Residential.	61,635	74,355	20.6	50.0	42.3
Commerical	27,499	38,625	40.4	22.2	22.0
Industrial.	23,996	32,334	34.7	19.4	18.4
Other utilities.	457	16,892	*	.4	9.5
Other	9,775	13,673	39.8	8.0	7.8
	123,362	175,879	42.5	100.0	100.0

* Not meaningful.

ILLUSTRATION 25–10

ROCHESTER GAS AND ELECTRIC CORPORATION
Electric Customers and Kilowatt-Hours
Comparison of the years 1968 and 1971

	No. of Customers			Kilowatt-hour sales		
				(000 omitted)		
	1968	1971	% increase	1968	1971	% increase
Residential	220,074	232,558	5.7	1,078,434	1,339,847	24.2
Commercial	21,599	22,712	5.2	847,080	1,076,457	27.1
Industrial.	1,395	1,382	(1.0)	1,073,170	1,216,411	13.2
Other	1,735	2,039	1.8	356,863	2,462,361	590.0
	244,803	258,691	5.7	3,355,547	5,095,076	51.8

of the fact that utility services are "necessities" in everyday life, aids the utility company in maintaining its credit and the standing of its securites in periods of recession.

The stability of the electric power and gas companies has been increased during the past several years because of the demand for the services of utilities for residential heating, refrigeration, and air conditioning. Naturally, if a public utility serves heavy industries almost exclusively, in periods of recession its operating revenue will be reduced very substantially.

The public utility that is able to increase its operating revenue without expanding its plant facilities is in a most favorable position because the additional revenue will not involve a proportionate increase in operating expense. Increased demand that can be supplied with the present plant facilities means less unproductive plant capacity.

Operating expense

Operating expense—including maintenance, taxes, depreciation, and amortization—represents the cost of furnishing the utility service. Variations in expense from year to year should be studied, if the data are available, to determine the reasons therefor. Operating expense may increase because of expanded facilities, increased demand for services, a higher price level, a change in maintenance and depreciation methods and policies, and imposition of new taxes or financial burdens by regulatory authorities. Trend ratios of the various operating expenses for a number of years should be studied to detect, if possible, whether maintenance and repairs have been deferred.

Operating expenses may be studied in relation to gross revenue and in terms of production units. For example, the analyst would usually determine, as illustrated in the following section, the percentage of operating revenue that has been consumed by operating expenses. Production units include the kilowatt-hour for electric power companies and one thousand cubic feet of gas for gas companies. The expense situation is brought out by a ratio called the operating ratio.

The operating ratio is determined by dividing operating expenses, including taxes and depreciation, by operating revenue.

Company	1971	1970	1969	1968
Idaho Power Company . . . .(%)	64.3	63.3	63.6	64.0
Rochester Gas & Electric Corporation. . . . .(%)	81.7	80.6	80.7	81.3

The operating ratio

Variations in the operating ratio from year to year or from company to company depend upon changes in operating revenues and in operating expenses as well as upon changes or variations in policy with reference to service charges, maintenance, and depreciation policies. A high operating ratio may be the result of reductions in service charges or a decline in demand for the services without a corresponding increase in revenues. It should be understood that a detailed study of both operating revenues and operating expenses is necessary before final conclusions are reached with respect to the favorableness or unfavorableness of the operating ratio.

The operating ratio does not represent a conclusive index of the financial condition of a public utility because nonoperating income and expense items are not included. In fact, the operating ratio often does not reflect taxes and depreciation. The most important nonoperating items are interest and dividend income on investments and fixed interest charges.

Ratio of maintenance to operating revenue

The ratio of maintenance to operating revenue shows the percentage or cents of operating revenues that have been used in maintaining the property. This ratio, which is determined by dividing maintenance expense by operating revenue, may vary from year to year for the following reasons: (1) maintenance may be higher than usual as a result of "catching up" on deferred maintenance or adverse changes in expense charges not proportionately offset by increases in revenue; (2) maintenance may be lower than usual because of deferred maintenance or favorable changes in expense charges; and (3) operating revenues may have decreased or increased without proportionate changes in maintenance expense. The following data show maintenance as a percent of revenue:

Company	1971	1970	1969	1968
Idaho Power Company.......(%)	26.0	23.8	23.2	24.9
Rochester Gas & Electric Corporation.............(%)	8.0	7.4	7.6	7.7

This dramatic difference probably explains why Idaho Power takes less depreciation than Rochester. Maintenance appears to be elaborate.

Ratio of depreciation to operating revenue

The ratio of depreciation to operating revenue, which is determined by dividing depreciation expense by operating revenue, shows the percentage of the operating revenue that is consumed by depreciation charges. This ratio will vary from year to year, depending upon changes in depreciation policy and depreciation methods used and the increases or decreases in operating revenues.

At the present time, most utilities use some form of the straight-line method of determining annual depreciation charges. The application of the straight-line method will result in a more uniform depreciation charge from year to year, regardless of changes in operating revenue. Other methods of recognizing depreciation, formerly used, result in fluctuating depreciation charges. These latter methods include the retirement reserve and renewal or replacement methods.

The retirement reserve method, which is being discarded by electric and gas utilities, is not an acceptable method of recognizing depreciation. For each accounting period the utility debits Retirement Expense and/or Earned Surplus and credits Retirement Reserve for an amount deemed sufficient to cover current retirements of depreciable property. Attention should be called to the fact that the entry suggested above includes a debit *either* to Retirement Expense, a current expense account, to Surplus, or to both. The amount debited to Earned Surplus would not be reflected in the current operating expenses.

The retirement reserve method has disadvantages, as follows: *First,* current expense for depreciation varies from year to year, depending upon anticipated retirements or upon the desire of management to increase or decrease "reported" net income. *Second,* the book value of depreciable assets is overstated because "depreciation" is based on retirements rather than the decline in service value due to such causes as wear, tear, use, and the elements. The Reserve for Retirement seldom exceeds 10 to 15 percent of the asset cost. *Third,* the retirement reserve may be accumulated by debits to Earned Surplus. *Fourth,* the retirement reserve is created for the property as a whole rather than for specific assets.

The renewal or replacement method, which is seldom used at the present time, is an unsatisfactory substitute for depreciation. At the time of renewing or replacing property, Renewal Expense is debited for the cost of the new acquisition. The cost of the old asset is retained in the asset account. This method has very definite shortcomings. *First,* expense is shown only when assets are replaced; therefore, a uniform charge from year to year for "depreciation" is not made. *Second,* the depreciable assets are shown on the books at an overstated value, since depreciation has not been recorded. *Third,* renewals or replacements are decided upon by management; therefore, reported current income or loss may be varied, depending upon the desire of management to do so. *Fourth,* the cost of the old asset, rather than that of the new asset, is shown in the property account.

Since public utilities have the bulk of their capital invested in depreciable fixed assets, depreciation is an expense of the greatest importance. Furthermore, increases in the general price level produce a progressively increasing understatement of depreciation expense, which is based on historical cost.

In a study of the ratios of depreciation to operating revenue for a selected group of state and interstate operating electric power and gas companies, it was found that from 6.94 cents to 13.95 cents of the revenue dollar were consumed by depreciation. Such a range indicates an attempt on the part of some of the utilities to vary depreciation charges in accordance with their desire to show a larger or smaller "net income" figure. Depreciation as a percentage of operating revenue:

Company	1971	1970	1969	1968
Idaho Power Company.........(%)	9.0	9.4	10.0	10.1
Rochester Gas & Electric Corporation...............(%)	8.0	8.2	7.9	8.3

Ratio of depreciation reserve to property

The ratio of depreciation reserve to property is determined by dividing depreciation reserve by property. This ratio shows the percentage of property that has been recognized as depreciation expense and which is accumulated in the Reserve for Depreciation account. The adequacy of the reserve cannot be judged by the external analyst, since he would not have available information with respect to the different types of properties and the original cost, the estimated life, and the present age of each individual depreciable asset.

Ratio of depreciation expense to property

The ratio of depreciation expense to property is determined by dividing depreciation expense by property (plant and equipment).

Company	1971	1970	1969	1968
Idaho Power Company.........(%)	1.7	1.7	1.7	1.7
Rochester Gas & Electric Corporation...............(%)	3.0	2.8	2.5	2.7

Note that Idaho is booking less depreciation but more maintenance.

These ratios show the average rate of depreciation in relation to operating revenue that has been currently recorded. The trend of the ratio is important because the analyst can judge whether or not a consistent depreciation policy is being followed. In analyzing these data, it must be remembered that *property* includes both land and intangibles, no portion of the value of which is included in depreciation. Land and intangibles if shown separately should be excluded.

Other factors affecting public utilities

In addition to analyzing the financial statements of public utilities, it is essential to consider other factors which may affect the utilities either favorably or unfavorably. The more important of these factors may be summarized as follows:

Government regulation. Public utilities are "affected with a public interest" and, therefore, are regulated in detail by government agencies. Interstate electric light and power and natural gas companies are regulated by the Federal Power Commission; interstate telephone and telegraph companies by the Federal Communications Commission; intrastate utilities by state commissions; and local utilities by either local or state authorities. The Securities and Exchange Commission has authority over the issuance of all public utility securities which enter interstate commerce.

Without effective regulation, unwise consolidations and combinations may be undertaken; unsound accounting and reporting practices and methods may be followed; financial abuses may develop; a short-sighted policy with reference to rates, services, and dividends may be adopted; and a weak credit rating may result which would increase the cost of funds. All of these factors tend to be unfavorable over a period of time not only to the public utility but also to the investor who seeks sound investments.

However, the regulation to which public utilities are subjected may adversely affect them. For example, in periods of rising prices the commission may now allow consumer rate increases in proportion to rising production costs. Also, in periods of declining prices the commission, as a result of public agitation, may require greater reductions in consumer rates than the decrease in production costs warrants.

Although public utilities are regulated in a comprehensive manner, there is no guarantee that a fair return will be realized. Income may be related, and therefore adjusted, to the cost of plant constructed during a low price level period; or insufficient revenue may be obtained because of a low demand for the company's product.

Government competition. Local municipal electric and gas plants frequently compete with private properties, and the federal government competes on a large scale in certain areas with privately owned electric light and power companies. Examples of the latter include power projects such as the Tennessee Valley Authority, Hoover Dam, and Grand Coulee Dam. In this connection the analyst must think in terms not only of current government competition but also of prospective competition.

Government franchises issued to utilities. Public utility companies, almost without exception, operate under a franchise, which is a contract between the public and the utility. The franchise makes provision with respect to (1) the use of public property; (2) the right to acquire property under eminent domain; (3) exclusion of other similar utility companies from the area; (4) the term of the grant; and (5) other rights, privileges, and obligations of both parties.

The franchise may be perpetual, for a limited period of time, or for an indeterminate period of time. In most states, franchises are controlled directly by state commissions, with a limited amount of authority exercised by local governments.

The indeterminate franchise is the most desirable from all points of view, since it remains in effect only as long as the utility performs adequate service at reasonable rates or until the municipality purchases the property. This type of franchise also provides for current adjustments of rates, charges, and services; and if regulatory provisions are included, they are general in nature, the detailed rules and regulations being promulgated and put into effect by a commission.

Government taxation of utilities. Public utilities are taxed rather heavily; therefore, the tax policy should be carefully analyzed. Furthermore, the trend of taxation with special reference to utilities should be considered; prospects of future higher taxes must be carefully studied.

Public utilities during a period of defense or war. Public utilities are affected in many ways by war and defense conditions. *First,* the demand for utilities services by military installations and other government-operated war agencies and greatly accelerated business and production activities increase to such an extent that the public utility is placed under extraordinary pressure; facilities are used to their maximum capacity, and properties are expanded to the extent that new construction is permitted and additional equipment is obtainable. *Second,* inasmuch as new equipment is restricted, old and less efficient and more costly equipment is continued in operation or is reclaimed from retired property. *Third,* many of the materials, supplies, and repair parts ordinarily used in the operation, maintenance, and construction programs are vital for war production; and their use is restricted by the federal government. In spite of shortages of material, supplies, and labor, the utilities try to maintain operations in behalf of the war effort without shutdowns or delays; consequently, properties are not maintained on a normal scale. *Fourth,* the higher price level increases operating costs for wages, fuel, and material and supplies; both property and income taxes absorb a larger proportionate share of the gross income. *Fifth,* labor turnover is unusually high and costly. *Sixth,* sales promotion activities, the load-building efforts of the utilities, are discontinued; and great emphasis is placed upon helping customers get the fullest benefit possible from their utility installations. *Seventh,* utilities, especially electric and gas companies, usually provide additional equipment and personnel as a protective measure for plants and properties. *Eighth,* whenever it is desirable in the public interest to aid in the war effort, electric power companies are permitted to arrange for interconnections of transmission systems to provide large power pools.

It should be evident from the foregoing discussion that the analysis of public utility financial statements covering a war period requires more than ordinary attention. The full impact and effect of the war on the public utilities cannot be reflected in the financial and operating data until some time after the war's end. Consequently, the financial statements are in many respects tentative to a still greater extent than they are during normal peacetime.

It is essential that public utility management retain in the business a large portion of the reported income, so that deferred maintenance and postwar adjustments may be taken care of without delay as soon as war or defense shortages no longer prevail.

Price-level changes. Public utility consumer rates and charges are determined in advance; and generally, they are not changed until after the expiration of one or more years. On the other hand, costs of production, operation, and financing, with the exception of depreciation and interest, vary in accordance with price-level changes. Therefore, the longer the rates remain in effect, the more likely it is that price-level changes will be adverse either to the public or to the utility. For example, when the price level moves upward, the utility cannot immediately increase consumer rates. Frequently, when the price level moves downward, consumer rates remain the same.

Price-level changes affect the fair-return valuation base to the extent that the cost-of-reproduction method of valuation is permitted.

Growth or decadence of cities and communities. Many cities and communities show substantial growth or decadence over a period of time. In a growing city the utility must anticipate demand and expand its property accordingly. The city of Washington, and the community surrounding it, is an outstanding example of the necessity for management of the electric light and power as well as gas and telephone companies to anticipate the utility needs of a rapidly growing area. The city of Washington is the focal point of the nation's administrative, defense, war, and peace activities; its population as well as its commercial and industrial activities have grown tremendously in recent years.

In analyzing the financial condition of a public utility, one must take into account the diversity and type of business activity, the general nature and prospects, and the growth or decadence of the territory in which the company operates. Investment value decreases in an area that shows a decline in population as well as in commercial and industrial activities.

The trends of the past development of a company as shown by the financial statements should be supplemented, if possible, with a study of the territory served. This latter study will show to what extent the area is adequately served and also the potentialities for further development.

QUESTIONS AND PROBLEMS

25–1. The following factors are of importance in connection with the analysis and interpretation of public utility financial statements. Discuss each factor:
  a) Public regulation.
  b) Plant utilization factor.
  c) Taxation.
  d) Load factor.
  e) Competition.
  f) Price-level changes.
  g) Economic development of the territory in which the utility operates.
  h) Growth or decline of cities and communities in which the utility operates.
  i) Public utility property and nonpublic utility property.
  j) The volume of general business activity.
  k) A war period or a manpower period.

25–2. What is the importance of each of the following ratios?
  a) Times funded debt interest is earned.
  b) Times funded debt interest and preferred stock dividend requirements are earned.
  c) Rate of return earned on total of borrowed funds and owners' equity.
  d) Rate of return earned on common stockholders' equity.
  e) Earnings per share of common stock.

25–3. Give a brief answer or discussion for the following:
  a) Is the current ratio for a public utility as significant as that for an industrial business?
  b) The long-term debt of public utility companies is usually less complicated than that of railroad companies.
  c) The operating revenues of public utilities are generally more stable than other businesses.
  d) What financial statement data, and in what form, would you present to show the growth of a public utility company?
  e) Should public utilities treat taxes on income as an operating expense?
  f) What are the advantages of commission control over public utility accounting?

25–4. Study the following data and state the reasons that may account for the changes in the amounts or ratios. Is it possible to determine

from the data given whether or not the changes have been favorable?
Explain.

	1968	1971
Ratio of funded debt to property (%)	48.5	60.2
Ratio of current liabilities to total liabilities and owners' equity (%)	5.0	6.4
Plant, property, and equipment ($000)	70,475	94,680
Operating ratio (%)	78.2	70.5
Net income (after taxes) applicable to common stock and surplus (%)	5.80	7.40

25–5. Some of the financial statement items of a public utility are similar
to, or differ from, those of an industrial company. Discuss.

25–6. Distinguish between:
  a) Plant utilization and load factor.
  b) Contributions in aid of construction and earned surplus.
  c) Materials and supplies of public utilities and inventories of a
      manufacturing business.
  d) The current ratio of public utilities and commercial businesses.
  e) Problems involving the analysis of the financial statements of
      public utilities and manufacturing business.

25–7. Comment on the following statements:
  a) The long-term debt of public utilities is usually more compli-
      cated than railroads.
  b) There is no such item as a *contingent asset*.
  c) Revenues for public utilities are entirely different than for railroads.
  d) Trend percentages and common-size percentages are more useful
      in analyzing public utility financial statements than they are in
      analyzing commercial companies.
  e) In evaluating the operating ratio it is necessary to study varia-
      tions in both operating revenues and operating expenses.

25–8. What information may be obtained by studying the following comparative data for a five-year period?
  a) Operating ratio.
  b) Common-size percentages.
  c) Times fixed interest charges earned.
  d) A detailed list of liabilities and owners' equity.
  e) Ratio of creditor claims to total assets.
  f) Trend percentages.
  g) Ratio of net income to total assets.

25–9. Match each of the following with the appropriate phrase listed to
the right.

(1) Public utilities.	a) Times fixed interest earned minus *one*.
(2) Ratio of maintenance to operating revenue.	b) Percentages of investment in assets financed by owners' equity.
(3) Percent of operating revenue absorbed by operating expenses.	c) Borrowed funds and owners' equity.
(4) Margin of safety of long-term debt interest charges.	d) Reflects growth or decline.
(5) Relationship of owners' equity to total assets.	e) Fixed charge.
(6) Funded debt.	f) Affected with a public interest.
(7) Interest on funded debt.	g) Current liability.
(8) Debt maturing within one year.	h) Capital invested in assets.
(9) Trend percentages.	i) Operating ratio.
(10) Sources of capital invested in assets.	j) Percent of operating revenue absorbed by maintenance.

25–10. *a*) Prepare condensed financial statements for Gas Companies D and Y.

	Gas Companies	
	D	Y
Balance Sheet Data (in Thousands), December 31, 1971		
Property, plant, and equipment	$88,452	$88,227
Less: Accumulated depreciation	10,438	9,411
	$78,014	$78,816
Investments	2,026	214
Other assets	22,277	18,053
Preferred stock (6%, cumulative, nonparticipating)	10,243	19,216
Common stock	22,990	16,637
Surplus	2,138	7,152
Mortgage bonds	40,000	37,500
Debenture bonds.	11,700	
Notes		2,860
Other liabilities.	15,246	13,718
Additional Data (in Thousands) for the Year 1971		
Operating revenues	18,297	20,992
Operating expenses:		
Operations	7,877	7,801
Taxes	2,482	3,253
Maintenance	642	1,661
Depreciation	1,432	2,333
Funded debt interest	1,889	1,425
Other income and expense—net deduction	441	115
Preferred stock dividends paid (includes full depreciation for 1971)	670	1,172
Common stock dividends paid	2,897	2,231

b) Prepare the following ratios and percentages for Gas Companies D and Y:
   (1) Source of funds invested in total assets (%).
       Capital stock.
       Surplus.
       Total liabilities.
   (2) Fixed operating property to operating revenue (times).
   (3) Net income to total assets (%).
   (4) Maintenance to net property (%).
   (5) Depreciation to net property (%).
   (6) Times fixed interest earned.
   (7) Times fixed interest and preferred dividend earned.
   (8) Average rate of interest on funded debt.
   (9) Earnings on common equity (%).
   (10) In relation to total operating expenses (%):
        Operations.
        Taxes.
        Maintenance.
        Depreciation.
   (11) In relation to total operating revenues:
        Operations.
        Taxes.
        Maintenance.
        Depreciation.
   (12) Operating ratio (%).
c) After studying all available data, answer the following questions:
   (1) Which company has the stronger financial and operating position? Give reasons for your conclusions.
   (2) What is the difference between a mortgage and a debenture bond?
   (3) What is the nature of the item, "Investments"?

25–11. a) Prepare condensed financial statements for Gas Company B.

	1968	1969	1970	1971
Balance Sheet Data, December 31				
Utility plant...................	$588,461	$589,997	$606,374	$827,400
Investments and advances...........	70,475	40,499	39,360	30,170
Current and working assets.........	48,672	52,584	54,974	61,480
Special funds and deposits.........	840	967	1,711	1,924
Capital stock, preferred, 5%, cumulative, nonparticipating*..............	$ 50,000	$ 50,000	$ 50,000	$110,000
Capital stock, common.............	122,000	122,469	132,175	166,482
Long-term debt..................	220,460	183,393	177,715	279,827
Current and accrued liabilities........	34,467	25,196	45,923	55,729
Reserves for retirements and depreciation......................	141,670	148,732	157,889	169,470
Capital surplus	105,550	105,369	105,261	105,200
Earned surplus	34,301	48,888	33,456	34,266

Profit and Loss Data, for the Year

Operating revenues	99,935	109,998	119,598	152,896
Operating expenses:				
Operations	46,508	48,917	52,237	71,691
Maintenance	5,938	5,978	6,221	8,925
Retirements and depreciation	17,198	13,015	14,326	27,894
Taxes	8,711	9,370	9,975	12,473
Other income and expense—net addition	250	231	252	242
Fixed charges	9,748	9,788	9,583	13,942
Preferred dividends	2,500	2,500	2,500	6,100

* $60,000 preferred issued during 1971 was 6 %, cumulative, nonparticipating.

b) Prepare the following ratios and percentages for Gas Company B:
(1) Fixed operating property to operating income (times).
(2) Net income to total assets.
(3) Maintenance to net property.
(4) Depreciation to net property.
(5) Sources of funds invested to total assets:
Capital stock.
Surplus.
Total liabilities.
(6) Times fixed interest earned.
(7) Times fixed interest and preferred dividends earned.
(8) Average rate of interest on funded debt.
(9) Earnings to common stockholders' equity.
(10) Operating ratio.
(11) In relation to total operating expenses:
Operations.
Taxes.
Maintenance.
Depreciation.
(12) In relation to total operating revenues:
Operations.
Taxes
Maintenance.
Depreciation.
c) After studying all available data, answer the following questions:
(1) Has the financial position of the company improved?
(2) Were the operating results more favorable for 1968 than for the other years?
(3) Is there any current or long-term debt pressure?
(4) Is there an appropriate balance between borrowed funds and owners' equity?
(5) Is the long-term debt a good investment?

26

Financial statements of commercial banks

COMMERCIAL banks occupy a position of economic importance in the communities in which they serve. The major functions performed by such banks include (1) the receiving of funds from individuals, business concerns, and other organizations who later will withdraw the deposits; and (2) the investing of funds in readily marketable, interest-bearing securities and the loaning of funds on a secured or an unsecured short-term basis. Nonbanking departments, such as trust, safe-deposit, and foreign departments, are also customarily operated by commercial banks.

All national as well as most state banks are members of the Federal Reserve System, which consists of 12 regional Federal Reserve banks. The Federal Reserve banks serve as banks for the commercial banks which are members of the system; they are often referred to as "bankers' banks."

Members of the Federal Reserve System are required, and nonmember banks may elect, to insure their deposits with the Federal Deposit Insurance Corporation. Deposits of individual depositors in banks which are members of the Federal Deposit Insurance Corporation are protected up to a maximum of $20,000. As of December 31, 1970 the corporation insured deposits in 13,840 commercial and savings banks. These represented 97 percent of the 14,199 banks in operation in the United States.[1] Deposits in insured banks totaled $483 billion. As shown by a survey

---

[1] *Annual Report of the Federal Deposit Insurance Corporation for the Year Ended December 31, 1970,* pp. 203 and 206.

in 1970, 99 percent of the accounts in insured banks were fully protected and 64 percent of total deposits were insured.[2]

National banks are required to submit uniform reports of their "financial condition" and of "income and dividends" when requested by the Comptroller of the Currency. The Directors of the Federal Deposit Insurance Corporation and the Board of Governors of the Federal Reserve System receive financial and operating statements from all members of the Federal Reserve System. The published annual reports of these regulatory agencies constitute the most important source of financial and operating data pertaining to commercial banks. Other sources of such data include the American Bankers Association, Rand McNally (*Bankers Directory*), *Moody's Manual of Investments,* and state banking associations. Banks are required by law to publish, in at least one newspaper, their reports of financial condition.

The report of financial condition as of December 31, 1971 of The First National Bank and Trust Company of Evanston, as published in the newspaper, is reproduced as Illustration 26–1.

All banks of deposit are required to submit to examination and regulation under the laws of the United States or of the state, territory, or district in which the bank is located.

Depositors, bank stockholders, and the general public have shown a much greater interest in bank statements since the closing of all U.S. banks in 1933. Bank officials recently have published more detailed statements in the hope of gaining greater public favor and trust.

There is also a trend toward annual audits by independent Certified Public Accountants.

Although commercial banks have been subjected to detailed governmental supervision and control for a long period of time, a uniform accounting system has not been prescribed for them. In general, a great many banks have neglected the development of sound and adequate accounting records, especially with respect to revenue and expense items. Cost records and analyses are essential to provide adequate information for satisfactory control of bank affairs and operations.

Report of condition—form

The most important financial statement prepared for a bank is the "report of condition." This report contains three main sections: *assets, liabilities,* and *capital accounts,* and a minor section, *reserves.* Unlike commercial balance sheets the balance sheet items are not classified as current and fixed assets and liabilities, long-term investments and intangible assets.

---

[2] Ibid., p. xii.

ILLUSTRATION 26–1

(OFFICIAL PUBLICATION)

REPORT OF CONDITION,
CONSOLIDATING DOMESTIC
SUBSIDIARIES, OF THE

FIRST NATIONAL BANK AND TRUST COMPANY OF EVANSTON

In the State of Illinois, at the close of business on December 31, 1971. Published in response to call made by Comptroller of the Currency, under Title 12, United States Code, Section 161.

Call No. 480

Charter No. 13709

National Bank Region No. 7

	Dollars Cts.
ASSETS	
Cash and due from banks	20,937,905.33
U. S. Treasury securities	14,416,397.57
Obligations of other U. S. Government agencies and corporations	10,249,052.94
Obligations of States and political subdivisions	33,951,575.72
O t h e r securities (including $192,000.00 corporate stock)	6,466,860.40
Loans	96,429,166.37
Bank premises, furniture and fixtures, and other assets representing bank premises	2,660,854.77
Real estate owned other than bank premises	28,435.13
Other assets	1,999,683.78
TOTAL ASSETS	187,139,932.01
LIABILITIES	
Demand deposits of individuals, partnerships, and corporations	46,772,434.75
Time and savings deposits of individuals, partnerships, and corporations	103,277,033.08
Deposits of United States Government	843,028.39
Deposits of States and political subdivisions	8,891,932.00
Certified and officers' checks, etc.	1,670,215.00
TOTAL DEPOSITS ... $161,454,643.22	
(a) Total demand deposits $ 52,760,210.14	
(b) Total time and savings deposits $108,694,433.08	
Federal f u n d s purchased and securities sold under agreements to repurchase	5,933,000.00
Other liabilities	5,000,155.83
TOTAL LIABILITIES	172,387,799.05

RESERVES ON LOANS AND SECURITIES	
Reserve for bad debt losses on loans (set up pursuant to IRS rulings)	2,179,015.01
TOTAL RESERVES ON LOANS AND SECURITIES	2,179,015.01
CAPITAL ACCOUNTS	
Capital notes and debentures 6½% Due Jan. 1, 1990 $3,000,000.00	3,000,000.00
Equity capital-total	9,573,117.95
Common Stock - total par value	2,800,000.00
No. s h a r e s authorized 647,311	
No. shares outstanding 560,000	
Surplus	3,600,000.00
Undivided profits	3,173,117.95
TOTAL CAPITAL ACCOUNTS	12,573,117.95
TOTAL LIABILITIES, R E S E R V E S, AND CAPITAL ACCOUNTS	187,139,932.01
MEMORANDA	
Average of total deposits for the 15 calendar days ending with call date	153,166,813.66
Average of total loans for the 15 calendar days ending with call date	92,057,945.93

I, Howard B. Silverman, Vice President and Comptroller, of the above-named bank do hereby declare that this report of condition is true and correct to the best of my knowledge and belief.

HOWARD B. SILVERMAN.

We, the undersigned directors attest the correctness of this report of condition and declare that it has been examined by us and to the best of our knowledge and belief is true and correct.

CLIFFORD J. PETERSON,
E. A. HORSCH,
J. ROSCOE MILLER,
Directors.
Jan—28

A report of condition, showing the assets, liabilities, and capital accounts for all national banks as of December 31, 1970 and 1969 is presented in Illustration 26–2. It should be understood that the items on the report of condition are controlling or summary accounts and that detailed information would appear on the books of the bank. The statement of condition as of December 31, 1971 and 1970 of

ILLUSTRATION 26–2.   Assets, liabilities, and capital accounts of national banks, 1969 and 1970 (dollar amounts in millions)

	Dec. 31, 1969, 4,669 banks		Dec. 31, 1970, 4,621 banks		Change, 1969–1970	
	Amount	Percent distribution	Amount	Percent distribution	Amount	Percent
ASSETS						
Cash and due from banks..........................	$54,727	17.43	$56,040	16.44	$1,313	2.40
U.S. Treasury securities.............................	29,589	9.42	34,223	10.04	4,634	15.66
Securities of other U.S. Government agencies and corporations.......................................	4,640	1.48	6,681	1.96	2,041	43.99
Obligations of States and political subdivisions........	34,526	10.99	41,542	12.19	7,016	20.32
Other securities...................................	1,362	.43	1,800	.53	438	32.16
Total securities...........	70,117	22.32	84,246	24.71	14,129	20.15
Federal funds sold and securities purchased under agreements to resell...................................	5,809	1.85	10,436	3.06	4,627	79.65
Direct lease financing..............................	696	.22	790	.23	94	13.52
Loans..	171,702	54.67	177,202	51.98	5,500	3.20
Fixed assets......................................	5,280	1.68	5,911	1.73	631	11.95
Customers' liability on acceptances outstanding........	1,838	.59	2,054	.60	216	11.75
Other assets......................................	3,879	1.24	4,227	1.24	348	8.97
Total assets...............................	314,048	100.00	340,906	100.00	26,858	8.55
LIABILITIES						
Demand deposits of individuals, partnerships, and corporations.......................................	$105,961	33.74	$107,768	31.61	$1,807	1.70
Time and savings deposits of individuals, partnerships and corporations..................................	103,238	32.87	119,843	35.15	16,605	16.08
Deposits of U.S. Government........................	3,175	1.01	5,061	1.48	1,886	59.40
Deposits of States and political subdivisions..........	19,569	6.23	25,053	7.35	5,484	28.02
Deposits of foreign governments and official institutions, central banks, and international institutions.........	2,138	.69	3,386	.99	1,248	58.37
Deposits of commercial banks.......................	16,649	5.30	18,494	5.43	1,845	11.08
Certified and officers' checks, etc....................	5,696	1.81	4,179	1.23	−1,517	−26.63
Total deposits...............................	256,426	81.65	283,784	83.24	27,358	10.67
Demand deposits..........................	141,092	44.93	145,122	42.57	4,030	2.86
Time and savings deposits....................	115,334	36.72	138,662	40.67	23,328	20.23
Federal funds purchased and securities sold under agreements to repurchase...............................	9,947	3.17	11,830	3.47	1,883	18.93
Liabilities for borrowed money......................	2,284	.73	1,280	.38	−1,004	−43.96
Acceptances executed by or for account of reporting banks and outstanding..........................	1,880	.60	2,096	.61	216	11.49
Other liabilities...................................	16,472	5.24	13,204	3.87	−3,268	−19.84
Total liabilities.............................	287,009	91.39	312,194	91.57	25,185	8.77
Minority interest in consolidated subsidiaries..........	—	—	1	ட	1	—
RESERVES ON LOANS AND SECURITIES						
Reserves on loans.................................	3,698	1.17	3,747	1.10	49	1.33
Reserves on securities..............................	87	.03	89	.03	2	2.30
CAPITAL ACCOUNTS						
Capital notes and debentures.......................	1,120	.36	1,161	.34	41	3.66
Preferred stock...................................	62	.02	63	.02	1	1.61
Common stock....................................	6,166	1.96	6,457	1.89	291	4.72
Surplus..	10,488	3.34	10,659	3.13	171	1.63
Undivided profits.................................	4,707	1.50	5,864	1.72	1,157	24.58
Reserves...	711	.23	671	.20	−40	−5.63
Total capital accounts.......................	23,254	7.40	24,875	7.30	1,621	6.97
Total liabilities and capital accounts...............	314,048	100.00	340,906	100.00	26,858	8.55

NOTES: The 1969 and 1970 data reflect consolidation of all majority-owned bank premises subsidiaries and all significant domestic majority-owned subsidiaries, with the exception of Edge Act subsidiaries.
    Data may not add to totals because of rounding. Dashes indicate amounts of less than $500,000.

the First National Bank and Trust Company of Evanston (Illustration 26–3), which is representative of the statements being issued currently by progressive banks, is less confusing to the average reader than the report of condition called for by the Comptroller of the Currency. At the same time, it is evident that these reports contain less information than the report submitted to the Comptroller.

The Comptroller of the Currency is required to *call* for *a report of condition* from all national banks a minimum of three times each year; usually, four calls are made. The call is made without advance notice to the banks, and the report must be made as of a designated

ILLUSTRATION 26–3

FIRST NATIONAL
BANK AND TRUST COMPANY **of EVANSTON**

Statement of Condition

1971

	December 31		
	1971	**1970**	**Change**
Assets			
Cash and Due from Banks	$ 20,937,905	$ 17,501,247	+$ 3,436,658
Investment Securities: (Note 2)			
United States Treasury Securities	14,416,398	12,169,877	+ 2,246,521
Securities of Other U.S. Government			
Agencies and Corporations	10,249,053	11,186,562	− 937,509
Obligations of States and Political Subdivisions	33,951,576	26,269,234	+ 7,682,342
Other Securities	6,466,860	208,000	+ 6,258,860
Federal Funds Sold	—	5,000,000	− 5,000,000
Loans (Note 3)	95,015,315	90,986,794	+ 4,028,521
Bank Premises and Equipment (Note 4)	2,689,290	2,848,500	− 159,210
Other Assets	1,999,684	1,553,480	+ 446,204
Total Assets	**$185,726,081**	**$167,723,694**	**+$18,002,387**
Liabilities			
Demand Deposits	$ 52,760,210	$ 53,769,360	−$ 1,009,150
Time Deposits	108,694,433	94,952,644	+ 13,741,789
Total Deposits	**$161,454,643**	**$148,722,004**	**+$12,732,639**
Federal Funds Purchased and			
Securities Sold Under Agreements to Repurchase	5,933,000	1,419,000	+ 4,514,000
Mortgage Payable	—	60,444	− 60,444
Other Liabilities	3,586,305	3,753,687	− 167,382
Total Liabilities	**$170,973,948**	**$153,955,135**	**+$17,018,813**
Reserve for Loan Losses (Note 5)	$ 2,179,015	$ 2,075,313	+$ 103,702
Capital Accounts			
Capital Notes (Note 6)	$ 3,000,000	$ 3,000,000	$ —
Equity Capital:			
Common Stock (Note 7)	$ 2,800,000	$ 2,700,000	+$ 100,000
Surplus	3,600,000	3,400,000	+ 200,000
Undivided Profits	3,173,118	2,593,246	+ 579,872
Total Equity Capital	**$ 9,573,118**	**$ 8,693,246**	**+$ 879,872**
Total Capital Accounts	**$ 12,573,118**	**$ 11,693,246**	**+$ 879,872**
Total Liabilities, Reserves and			
Capital Accounts	**$185,726,081**	**$167,723,694**	**+$18,002,387**

date which is prior by several days to the date of call. The report must be submitted within a certain time and signed and attested to under oath by designated bank officials.

Report of condition—description of accounts

The following several pages are devoted to an explanation and discussion of the various items appearing on a bank report of condition, more commonly referred to as a statement of condition, shown in Illustration 26–3.

U.S. government obligations, direct and guaranteed

U.S. government securities, which are practically as liquid as cash itself, are of a high grade and are readily marketable. Investment securities should be restricted in most cases to short maturities, either short-term obligations such as Treasury bills and certificates or maturing obligations like Treasury notes and bonds.

Long-term securities tend to fluctuate in price to a greater extent than the short-term obligations because of variations in interest rates. Consequently, market-price stability is more likely to be attained when short-term investments are made.

U.S. government securities consist of (1) Treasury bills and notes and U.S. bonds, including war bonds, all of which are issued directly by the U.S. government; and (2) obligations of U.S. government corporations and agencies which are guaranteed by the U.S. government and consist of obligations issued by the Home Owners' Loan Corporation, the Federal Farm Mortgage Corporation, and other similar agencies.

Obligations of states and political subdivisions

Securities issued by states and political subdivisions include state and municipal bonds, notes, and warrants. Highway bonds and special district improvement bonds such as irrigation bonds, levee bonds, and drainage bonds are also municipal bonds.

Other securities

Securities include those issued by (1) U.S. government agencies such as the federal land banks and the federal intermediate credit banks, the obligations of which are not guaranteed by the United States; (2) railroads, public utilities, and industrial corporations; (3) Federal Reserve and other banks; and (4) foreign, public, and private organizations. Corporate stocks include those issued by the Federal Reserve bank, affiliates of the reporting bank, other domestic banks, other domestic corporations, and foreign corporations are also shown under this heading.

Each member bank of the Federal Reserve System is required to subscribe to the stock of its district Federal Reserve bank in the amount of 6 percent of its paid-in capital and surplus. Fifty percent of the stock has to be paid for at the time of the subscription; the balance of the stock must be paid for when called by the Board of Governors of the Federal Reserve System. With each increase of capital stock and surplus the ownership of Federal Reserve bank stock is required to be increased. The banks receive a 6 percent cumulative dividend on the paid-up amount of the stock.

Loans, including rediscounts and overdrafts

Two types of loans made by banks are included in the item *loans*. The former represents loans of funds the interest on which is due at the maturity of the loan. The latter represents loans of funds the interest on which is deducted as of the loan date. Thus, a business may borrow on its own interest-bearing promissory note or obtain funds by discounting its customers' negotiable paper or its own noninterest-bearing promissory notes. The effective rate of interest is slightly higher when a business discounts its own noninterest-bearing note than when it borrows on its own interest-bearing note.

Bank loans, which are customarily for short periods of time, often less than three months, may be classified according to the type of customer or paper. Schedule A (Illustration 26–4) is from the current official Report of Condition form.

Bank loans may be classified as to whether they are secured or unsecured. The customer may or may not have been required to deposit pledged assets or conditional title to pledged assets as security for the payment of the loan. Such security may take the form of stocks, bonds, merchandise or other warehouse receipts, conditional title to real estate, or the assignment of insurance policies to the bank.

Bank loans are required, by good financial management and by law, to be liquid. Fixed or long-term loans on real estate are definitely restricted by law. First mortgages are most frequently required as security for real estate loans; second-mortgage loans are generally frowned upon. National banks and many state banks are not permitted to make loans to any individual borrower in excess of 10 percent of the bank's unimpaired capital and surplus (not including undivided profits).

Bank overdrafts represent customer withdrawal of funds in excess of

ILLUSTRATION 26–4

SCHEDULE A - LOANS (including rediscounts and overdrafts)	DOLLARS			CTS.	
1. Real estate loans (include only loans secured primarily by real estate):	x x x	x x x	x x x	x x	1
(a) Secured by farm land (including improvements)					(a)
(b) Secured by 1- to 4-family residential properties (other than farm):	x x x	x x x	x x x	x x	(b)
(1) Insured by the Federal Housing Administration					(b)(1)
(2) Guaranteed by the Veterans Administration					(b)(2)
(3) Not insured or guaranteed by FHA or VA (conventionally financed)					(b)(3)
(c) Secured by multifamily (5-or-more) residential properties (other than farm):	x x x	x x x	x x x	x x	c
(1) Insured by the Federal Housing Administration					(c)(1)
(2) Not insured by FHA (conventionally financed)					(c)(2)
(d) Secured by nonfarm non-residential properties (e.g., business, industrial, hotels, office buildings, churches)					d
2. Loans to financial institutions:	x x x	x x x	x x x	x x	2
(a) To domestic commercial and foreign banks					(a)
(b) To other financial institutions (include loans to sales finance, personal finance, insurance and mortgage cos., factors, mutual savings banks, savings and loan assoc., Federal lending agencies, and all other business and personal credit agencies)					(b)
3. Loans for purchasing or carrying securities (secured or unsecured):	x x x	x x x	x x x	x x	3
(a) To brokers and dealers in securities					(a)
(b) Other loans for the purpose of purchasing or carrying stocks, bonds, and other securities					(b)
4. Loans to farmers (secured and unsecured except loans secured by real estate above, but including loans for household and personal expenditures)					4
5. Commercial and industrial loans (include all loans for commercial and industrial purposes, secured or unsecured, except those secured by real estate above)					5
6. Loans to individuals for personal expenditures:	x x x	x x x	x x x	x x	6
(a) Loans to purchase private passenger automobiles on installment basis (include purchased paper)					(a)
(b) Credit cards and related plans: (1) Retail (charge account) credit card plans					(b)(1)
(2) Check credit and revolving credit plans					(b)(2)
(c) Loans to purchase other retail consumer goods on installment basis (include purchased paper-exclude credit card plans) (1) Mobile homes, not including travel trailers	x x x	x x x	x x x	x x	c (1)
(2) Other retail consumer goods					c (2)
(d) Installment loans to repair and modernize residential property					d
(e) Other installment loans for household, family, and other personal expenditures (exclude check/credit plans)					e
(f) Single-payment loans for household, family, and other personal expenditures					f
7. All other loans (incl. overdrafts). (To churches, hospital, charitable or educational institutions, etc., not secured by real estate above)					7
8. Total loans (total of items 1 to 7) (must agree with item 8 of "Assets")					8

deposits; overdrafts are forbidden by the National Bank Act, but they occur nevertheless. If an overdraft is specifically arranged for in advance, it is in effect a loan to the customer. Bank overdrafts must be shown separately from regular loans and discounts.

Banks commonly establish a valuation account, Reserve on Loans (preferably titled Estimated Losses on Loans), to match cost and revenue more appropriately and to avoid overstating undivided profits.

Cash on hand, balances with other banks (including statutory reserve balance), and cash items in process of collection

Cash and cash items include (1) currency and coin on hand in the bank vaults; (2) cash balances due from other banks which are maintained to establish a line of credit for present or possible future requirements and to facilitate the financing of bank or customer operations; (3) coupons and matured bonds in the process of collection; (4) checks on other banks not yet put through the clearing house or otherwise collected, usually shown on the bank books as Exchange from Clearings; and (5) *statutory reserves* held on deposit with the Federal Reserve bank, correspondent banks, or other authorized reserve agents.

Statutory or "legal" reserves

The term "statutory or legal reserves" requires explanation. Every member of the Federal Reserve System is required by law to keep on deposit with the Federal Reserve bank of its district a sum bearing a specified relation to its deposits. The fundamental purpose of these legal reserves is to afford some protection for depositors by forcing a certain limited degree of liquidity upon the member banks. However, this *liquid* asset cannot be used for meeting deposit withdrawals except to the extent that such withdrawals result in excess legal reserves. The amount of the legal reserve depends upon the location of the bank, the nature of the bank's deposits, and the policy of the Board of Governors of the Federal Reserve System.

State banks are also required by state law to maintain minimum reserves against deposits. However, unlike member banks of the Federal Reserve System, state banks are permitted to have a portion of the required reserves in their own vaults, the balance being on deposit with approved depository banks.

In accordance with the National Bank Act, member banks are required to maintain reserves in the form of vault cash plus deposits in the Federal Reserve bank of their district, as shown in Illustration 26–5.

Primary reserve. The primary reserve of a bank is the total of cash items—cash on hand; balances due from other banks, including legal reserves on deposit with a Federal Reserve bank; and cash items in the process of collection. There is no legal requirement with reference to the amount of primary reserves to be maintained by a bank except

ILLUSTRATION 26–5

	Reserves	
Class of bank	Against net demand deposits	Against savings and time deposits
Designated "reserve city" banks and nonreserve city banks with average demand deposits exceeding $400 million:		
Up to $5 million.	17 %	3%
Excess over $5 million	17½%	6
Nonreserve city banks unless average net demand deposits exceed $400 million:		
Up to $5 million.	12½	3
Excess over $5 million.	13	6

"Reserve cities" are large financial centers such as Boston, Chicago, Cleveland, Dallas, New York, and San Francisco.

These rates are effective as of September 27, 1972.

that which represents the statutory reserve. Primary reserves are maintained in accordance with the judgment of the bank officers.

The primary reserve possesses two of the three characteristics of a bank asset—liquidity and safety. The third characteristic—earning power—is not present because interest is not received on deposits with other banks. The primary reserve may be expanded or replenished by borrowing from other banks or by converting a portion of the secondary reserve into cash.

The objectives of the primary reserve are (1) to enable a bank to meet the current cash withdrawal demands of its deposits; (2) to serve as a protection for deposits by maintaining a certain amount of liquidity of the assets; (3) to maintain a minimum control of the extension of bank credit by governmental authority (the legal reserve); and (4) to provide cash necessary for current bank operations.

Secondary reserve. The secondary reserve—the second line of defense for the protection of deposits—consists of short-term marketable investments which normally will or can be quickly converted into cash through sale without material loss. It is composed of income-producing assets such as government obligations; nongovernment short-term securities of the highest quality and marketability; and that portion of loans and discounts consisting of bankers' acceptances, call loans, and prime commercial or other paper which is eligible for rediscount at Federal Reserve banks.

The secondary reserve fulfills two functions: *First,* it provides protection for the deposits, since the assets are selected on the basis of safety and marketability with price stability; and, *second,* but subordinate to the first and unlike the primary reserve, it yields income to the bank. The major objective of the secondary reserve is to give a bank liquidity. The secondary reserve may be drawn upon to replenish the primary reserve.

The management of the secondary reserve portfolio requires a high degree of skill and experience. This is true not only because it is necessary properly to select the securities but also to determine the appropriate amount to be maintained. Additional seasonal primary reserve requirements and possible higher legal reserve requirements represent two important considerations in establishing the secondary reserve amount.

Investments. Published statements of condition customarily do not distinguish between secondary reserve and investment assets. Assets that have the following characteristics, and in the order listed, are suitable for the secondary reserve: safety, liquidity, and income-earning capacity.

Investments should not be depended upon to replenish the primary reserve. The Investment account does not represent a reserve; its amount has no direct relationship to deposits. The amount of the Investment account depends upon the available funds remaining after establishing the primary and secondary reserves and the investment in the bank premises and other noncurrent assets. Bonds that are "not distinctly or predominantly speculative," which include securities having the highest grade established by rating agencies, are most suitable for this account; diversification of investment assets is of major importance. Banks are not permitted to purchase securities that are in default or that are predominantly speculative. These securities may be owned as a result of a default on secured loans.

Securities owned by a bank are customarily carried on the books at cost or market, whichever is lower.

Bank premises and furniture and fixtures. Under the heading Fixed Assets are shown the buildings, furniture, fixtures, and land owned and used by the bank in conducting its banking business. Occasionally, a bank may follow the policy of depreciating the foregoing property items to a nominal sum within a period of a few years. As a result of this policy the assets and undivided profits of the bank are understated, and a secret reserve is created.

In published bank statements, fixed assets are as a rule shown net, i.e., the Accumulated Depreciation account is not specifically listed.

Real estate owned, other than bank premises. Because of the need for high degree of liquidity, banks are restricted as to the ownership of real estate other than their banking premises. However, title to farm, business, and residential property is obtained by banks through foreclosure proceedings. Generally, such property must be sold within a relatively short time.

Customers' liability to the bank on acceptances outstanding. Under this title is to be included the amount of trade acceptances drawn on and accepted by the bank on behalf of customers. Instead of loaning funds in such cases, the bank loans its credit. The customer obligates himself to pay the bank the necessary funds before the maturity date, or he authorizes the bank to charge his account at the maturity of the acceptance.

The liability of the bank with respect to these acceptances is shown under the title of "acceptances executed by or for account of this bank and outstanding." Thus, the bank asset is the liability of the customer; and the bank liability is, in effect, the guaranty of the payment of the debt. The asset may be less than the liability in the event that customers have paid their liability and the acceptance has not yet been presented to the bank for payment.

Other assets. Other assets include interest, commissions, rent, and other income earned or accrued but not collected; prepaid expenses and other assets that a bank may have obtained in settlement of a loan; or assets that cannot be otherwise classified.

LIABILITIES

Deposits

Deposits represent the major source of funds for a commercial bank. In effect, they are loans to the bank, for the most part noninterest-bearing, and are definitely a liability of the bank. To a considerable extent, demand deposits result from credit granted by the bank to customers. It is a common practice for customers to receive credit in their bank accounts rather than cash when loans are negotiated.

Deposits are usually classified as either demand or time deposits. Demand deposits of individuals, partnerships, and corporations are payable at any time on the demand of the depositor. Time deposits and savings are those that are not payable within 30 days or those that require 30 days' notice of withdrawal.

The deposits of individuals, partnerships, and corporations are shown separately from those of the U.S. government, state, and political subdivisions, and other banks. Also, it is customary for a bank to segregate certified and officers' checks, letters of credit and traveler's checks sold for cash, and amounts due to the Federal Reserve bank.

Other deposit accounts are Special Deposits, such as deposits in escrow and deposits under court jurisdiction; Garnishee Deposits, or those deposits which have been garnisheed by a creditor and are at least temporarily unavailable to the depositor; and Trust Department Deposits, which represent the uninvested funds held by the trust department.

Most published bank statements show all deposits as *Deposits,* the details of which are omitted.

Other liabilities for borrowed money

Banks may borrow money from other commercial banks or, if members of the Federal Reserve System, from their Federal Reserve bank.

Rediscounted customer paper represents a contingent rather than a primary liability. Such paper will be presented for payment to the maker or acceptor at maturity. In the event that the one primarily liable does not pay, the bank contingently liable on the instrument would be called upon to reimburse the holder of the paper.

Banks make a practice of showing rediscounts not as contingent liabilities but as regular liabilities. The contingent asset—the rediscounted paper—is shown in "loans."

Banks have not found it necessary in recent years to borrow funds on a large scale because their excess primary reserves have been more than sufficient to meet demands of customers for funds.

Acceptances executed by or for account of the bank and outstanding

Under this heading will appear the bank's liability assumed when it executes acceptances for customers. On the asset side of the statement of condition will appear the asset, customers' liability on acceptances outstanding.

Other liabilities

Other liabilities may consist of such items as accrued interest, taxes, and other expenses; unearned discounts; unpaid declared dividends; and the bank's own outstanding checks, known as cashier's checks.

CAPITAL (OWNERS' EQUITY) ACCOUNTS

Capital accounts

The term "capital accounts" as used on the report of condition which is submitted to the Comptroller of Currency may consist of debentures, preferred stock, and common stock. Capital notes and income debentures may be issued by national banks and by state banks, which in some cases are denied the privilege of issuing preferred stock, for purposes of borrowing funds. This class of capital liability has a preference as to dividends and assets over preferred and common stock if both have been issued. Income debentures are subordinate to other liabilities.

National bank preferred stock was first issued generally as a result of the recommendation and requirement of the Reconstruction Finance Corporation and a provision in the Emergency Banking Act of March 9, 1933, which legalized such stock. The preferred stock is usually cumulative and callable in whole or in part at par and accumulated dividends; there is generally a provision for the establishment of a retirement fund. Furthermore, the holders of preferred stock customarily have a right to vote. National banks, which numbered 4,621, had $63,000,000 of preferred stock outstanding as of December 31, 1970. The total capital stock amounted to $6,520,000,000, and total owners' equity, $23,714,000,000.

Common stockholders prefer the retirement of capital notes, debentures, and preferred stock as soon as possible because of the prior claims on income and assets. Dividends on common stock cannot legally be declared and paid for any semiannual dividend-paying period until after 10 percent of the net income for the previous six-month period has been transferred to surplus. This restriction does not apply to preferred stock or to common stock if the surplus equals the common stock. The proceeds of newly issued common stock may be used to retire these prior-claim obligations.

The Emergency Banking Act of 1933 and an amendment to the national banking law eliminated the *double* liability[3] requirement formerly attached to national bank capital stock. State regulations have also been relaxed.

Surplus and undivided profits

The Surplus account as used by banks represents paid-in capital (premiums on capital stock) and amounts transferred from the Undivided Profits account. National banks are required to have surplus equal to 20 percent of their outstanding capital stock before they are permitted to declare dividends on common stock. Member banks of the Federal Reserve System are required to base stock subscriptions to Federal Reserve bank stock on their own capital stock and surplus (not including undivided profits).

The Surplus account is stated in round amounts; and the balance does not fluctuate, as it does in the Undivided Profits account. The latter account is used to record the net income or net loss, dividend payments, and all other changes in capital (owners' equity) that do not involve capital stock or Surplus as described above. The Undivided Profits account, which is "free surplus," remains open from one accounting period to another; it is not closed as is the Revenue and Expense Summary account in commercial businesses.

Surplus, which is not used for dividends, is regarded as more or less permanent capital. However, to the extent that surplus exceeds 20 percent of the par value of the common stock, the board of directors may transfer the excess back to Undivided Profits and use it to meet extraordinary losses or for other corporate purposes.

Many individuals have the impression that capital stock and surplus are invested in a particular form of asset such as bank building, land, furniture, or fixtures. However, such as not the case; capital stock, surplus, and undivided profits represent an excess of assets over customer deposits and other creditor claims. In other words, the stockholders' equity represents a margin of safety to outside creditors, including the depositors.

Report of income and dividends—form

While some banks still do not make public detailed statements of earnings, there is a strong trend running toward this disclosure. It has

---

[3] The owners of double liability capital stock were contingently liable to an assessment equal to the par value of their stock.

long been a requirement of regulatory authorities that such information be sent to them annually. The number of banks being audited annually by independent CPAs is steadily increasing; and in March 1969, in APB *Opinion No. 13,* the Accounting Principles Board made the provisions of APB *Opinion No. 9,* "Reporting The Results of Operations," applicable to commercial banks audited by members of the AICPA.

A report of income and dividends prepared by a bank for the Comptroller of Currency, is divided into the following sections:

Current operating revenue
Current operating expenses
Net current operating earnings
Recoveries, transfers from valuation reserves, and profits on securities and loans, and other gains
Losses, charge-offs, and transfers to valuation reserves on securities, loans, and other items
Net income before related taxes
Taxes on net income
Net income
Dividends on capital
Net income after dividends

The bank report of income and dividends, which is generally prepared annually, is relatively simple as compared with the income statement of a manufacturing or a merchantile business. Banks merely list revenue and expense items, whereas commercial and manufacturing concerns determine cost of goods manufactured and/or sold. The real difference in the businesses mentioned is that banks sell *services;* the manufacturer processes goods and then sells them.

The statement of earnings for the years 1971 and 1970 of the First National Bank and Trust Company of Evanston (Illustration 26–6) is representative of such statements being currently prepared and presented under the provisions of Accounting Principles Board *Opinion Nos. 13* and *9.*

Report of income and dividends—description of items

The following pages are devoted to an explanation and discussion of the various items appearing on the bank report of income and dividends submitted to the Comptroller of Currency.

Current operating revenue

Interest and dividends. The item interest and dividends includes income earned on investments in U.S. obligations and obligations of states and political subdivisions; other bonds, notes, and debentures; and corporate stocks owned by the bank.

ILLUSTRATION 26–6

FIRST NATIONAL
BANK AND TRUST COMPANY of EVANSTON
Statement of Earnings

	1971	1970	Change
Operating Income			
Interest and Fees on Loans	$ 6,673,244	$ 7,018,600	−$345,356
Income on Federal Funds Sold	74,404	185,391	− 110,987
Interest and Dividends on Investments:			
United States Treasury Securities	536,436	747,797	− 211,361
Securities of Other U.S. Government Agencies and Corporations	657,899	275,635	+ 382,264
Obligations of States and Political Subdivisions	1,275,324	884,088	+ 391,236
Other Securities	296,517	19,417	+ 277,100
Trust Income	441,004	405,554	+ 35,450
Service Charges on Deposit Accounts	282,352	297,852	− 15,500
Other Operating Income	232,524	206,576	+ 25,948
Total Operating Income	$10,469,704	$10,040,910	+$428,794
Operating Expenses			
Salaries	$ 1,801,392	$ 1,791,788	+$ 9,604
Pension and Other Employee Benefits (Note 8)	323,224	301,257	+ 21,967
Interest on Deposits	4,856,096	4,265,853	+ 590,243
Interest on Borrowed money	118,323	157,249	− 38,926
Interest on Capital Notes	195,000	146,611	+ 48,389
Net Occupancy Expense of Bank Premises	248,453	186,176	+ 62,277
Furniture and Equipment Expense	214,714	200,813	+ 13,901
Provision for Loan Losses (Note 5)	399,000	420,000	− 21,000
Other Operating Expenses	973,507	970,510	+ 2,997
Total Operating Expenses	$ 9,129,709	$ 8,440,257	+$689,452
Income before Income Taxes and Securities Gains	$ 1,339,995	$ 1,600,653	−$260,658
Applicable Income Taxes (Note 9)	21,447	343,959	− 322,512
Income before Securities Gains	$ 1,318,548	$ 1,256,694	+$ 61,854
Securities Gains less Related Income Tax effect of $49,159 in 1971 and $12,462 in 1970	54,918	955	+ 53,963
Net Income	$ 1,373,466	$ 1,257,649	+$115,817
Earnings per Share (Note 10)			
(based on 560,000 shares)			
Income before Securities Gains	$ 2.35	$ 2.24	+$ .11
Net Income	$ 2.45	$ 2.25	+$ .20
Earnings per Share assuming Full Conversion of Capital Notes (Note 10)			
Income before Securities Gains	$ 2.19	$ 2.07	+$ .12
Net Income	$ 2.28	$ 2.07	+$ .21

Interest and discount on loans. The term "interest" is used to designate the amount of income earned on loans when the income is received as of the maturity of the loan. The income on a 6 percent, 60-day, $1,000 loan would normally be received 60 days after the date of the loan. This income, amounting to $10, is called "interest." Interest on installment loans also would be included; i.e., the installment payments might, and often do, include both a payment on principal and a payment of interest. Interest earned but not yet collected would be recorded.

The term "discount" is used to denote the amount of income earned on loans when the income is received on the date of the loan or discount. In other words, the income on a noninterest-bearing, 60-day, $1,000 loan would be received as of the date of the loan; the proceeds, $990, would be given to the borrower. This income, amounting to $10, is known as a "discount." Interest collected in advance should be carried forward on the balance sheet.

Service charges and other fees on bank's loans. Service charges made, and fees collected, in connection with loans are summarized in the item service charges and other fees on bank's loans.

Service charges on deposit accounts. The maintenance of each customer's deposit account involves a certain amount of expense for the bank. These expenses include deposit insurance and costs involved in the maintenance of the bank building, equipment and records, and wages of the personnel. The credit balance of many customer accounts is sufficiently large to enable the bank to earn income to offset partially or completely the cost of maintaining the account. On the other hand, this is not true of numerous small accounts. At the present time, it is the custom of banks to make a service charge against customer deposit accounts in the event that the account balance is not large enough to enable the bank to earn a *net return* on the account.

Service charges may be levied in one of the following ways:

1. A flat charge may be made against those accounts whose average balances fall below a fixed amount.
2. The service charge may be levied on a measured basis, i.e., a per item charge against all debits above a prescribed maximum number. This maximum number is customarily varied, depending upon the average balance.
3. Each individual account may be analyzed in detail to determine the cost of maintaining the account; services charges would be levied on the basis of this cost. A knowledge of bank costs would be essential for this last analysis.

Other service charges, commissions, fees, and collection and exchange charges. Banks perform services for customers by making collection at maturity on drafts, acceptances, notes, and interest coupons. Other services of a similar nature may be performed by a bank.

Trust department (net earnings). The trust department's net earnings represent the excess of the amount of fees earned by the trust department over the expenses of the department. The activities of a trust department include acting as executor and trustee under wills, trustee in personal and corporate matters, transfer agent, registrar, and in other similar fiduciary capacities.

Banks most commonly use the cash rather than the accrual basis of accounting for the trust department fees. The reasons for such a policy are that in many cases the fees are collected only after a relatively long-term commitment has been completed or the fee to be received may not be determinable at the time the trust agreement is entered into.

Other current operating revenue. The foreign department of a bank handles financial matters arising between the bank's customers and foreign banks. The income from fees and exchange services less the expenses of conducting the foreign department represents its net earnings. Rent on real estate temporarily held is shown as rent received.

All other income pertaining to current operations which cannot be otherwise classified is shown as other current operating revenue.

Current operating expenses

Salaries. wages, and benefits. The total of officers' and employees' salaries, wages, and benefits represents the largest and, therefore, the most important item of current expense. These costs are recorded as:

Salaries—officers
Salaries and wages—employees
Officer and employee benefits—pensions, hospitalization, social security, insurance, and similar items.

Fees paid to directors and members of executive, discount, and advisory committees. The honoraria paid directors and others who assist in the management and operation of the bank, but who are not paid on a salary or wage basis, are shown as fees paid to directors and members of executive, discount, and advisory committees. Ordinarily, the bylaws of the bank will specify the fee to be paid per meeting and whether the expense of the director or committee member incurred in connection with the meeting should be included. In the majority of banks, directors' fees account for most of the total of this item of expense. Some banks are known to pay a per annum honorarium regardless of the number of meetings attended.

Interest on time and savings deposits. Banks allow interest on time and savings deposits but are prohibited by law from doing so with respect to demand deposits.

Interest and discount on borrowed money. Banks may borrow money on their own interest-bearing promissory notes, in which case interest expense would be involved. On the other hand, if the bank discounts its customers' paper, the "interest" would be known as "discount expense."

Interest and discount on borrowed money are of no real consequence, since the bank customarily depends upon customer deposits as the primary source of loanable funds.

Net occupancy expense of bank premises. All costs of occupying, maintaining, managing, and owning bank premises are shown on the report of income and dividends as occupancy expense of bank premises. Rental income from bank premises or other related credits are deducted to obtain net occupancy expense. The individual occupancy expense items are listed below:

Salaries and wages of building employees:
  a) Officers (number on payroll at end of period)
  b) Employees (number on payroll at end of period)
Building officer and employee benefits
Recurring depreciation on bank premises and leasehold improvements
Maintenance, repairs, and uncapitalized alteration costs of bank premises and
    leasehold improvements
Insurance, utilities (heat, light, and water)
Rents paid on bank premises
Taxes on bank premises and leasehold improvements
Gross occupancy expense
Less:
  a) Rental income from bank premises
  b) Other credits
Net occupancy expense

Furniture and equipment expense. The various costs of maintaining, using, and renting or owning furniture and equipment include depreciation, rents, servicing, and other similar uncapitalized items.

Other current operating expenses. Miscellaneous operating expenses that cannot be classified in any of the foregoing categories are shown as other current operating expense.

Net current operating earnings

The excess of current operating revenue over current operating expenses represents the net current operating earnings. This net amount, however, does not represent the *net income* as the term is used in general accounting, since income taxes are shown after net earnings.

Recoveries, transfers from valuation reserves, and profits

Recoveries on loans. Banks often make collections on loans after they have been written off as uncollectible. These amounts are recorded as Recoveries on Loans and added to the Reserve for Loan Losses.

Recoveries on bonds, stocks, and other securities. Banks may write down the costs of bonds, stock, and other securities to recognize losses due to a decline in market value. Banks are not now so likely to do so as they were in the past because such a write-down must be taken into account in computing net income. Of course, if the decrease in value is expected to be permanent a write-down is mandatory. If, later, events cause a write-up back to original cost, income will be increased accordingly; such a write-up might be recorded as Recoveries on Securities. The same situation may be encountered in connection with securities which are deemed to have become worthless.

Profits on securities sold. Banks invest funds in securities and frequently realize a profit when they are sold. It should be clearly understood that banks are not supposed to speculate in securities and that speculative profit is not considered here.

Securities are purchased, held, and sold by banks as a regular part of the banking function; whereas for most nonbanking businesses, such transactions are merely incidental to the regular business operations. Consequently, in the case of banks the interest and dividends on, and the gain or loss on the sale of, the securities represent operating profit or loss. For nonbanking businesses, interest and dividends are considered financial or nonoperating income, and the gain or loss on the sale of the securities is usually shown below net operating income but before net income.

All other profit. Under the heading "all other profit," would be included profit from sources other than those listed above. Profit on the sale of real estate or other property owned by the bank should be shown here.

Losses, charge-offs, and transfers to valuation reserves

Charge-offs on loans. The extension of credit always involves the risk of loss, and some such losses will occur in spite of the exercise of the soundest judgment in making loans. When such losses do occur, the amount is charged to the Reserve for Loan Losses. This reserve, which is similar to the provision for doubtful accounts found in industrial and commercial balance sheets, is set up by annual charges to income in amounts regulated by governmental authorities. Recoveries are credited to the reserve.

Losses on bonds, stocks, and other securities. When banks sell owned securities at a loss, the amount may be charged to Loss on Securities which is deducted in computing net income. It usually appears below operating income.

Net income

The statement of earnings (or income) is now prepared in keeping with the prescriptions of APB *Opinion No. 9* and therefore includes in the computation of net income virtually all income credits and expense and loss debits except those which qualify as "prior period adjustments" under the restrictive provisions of APB *Opinion No. 9*.

27

Financial statements of commercial banks (continued)

Bank statement analysis is of value to several groups

THE ANALYSIS of bank statements is undertaken by analysts, depositors, regulatory authorities, stockholders, borrowers, the bank management, and authors of books like this one. A depositor is interested in the solvency of the bank, i.e., the safety and availability of his funds. The regulatory authorities desire to assure themselves that banks are operating in accordance with the requirements of the law and are in sound financial condition. Stockholders are primarily interested in the general financial condition of the bank and the earnings, the dividends, and the management's policy with reference to the accumulation of surplus. The borrower is interested in knowing the extent of available funds and the use that is made of the bank's resources.

The management of a bank has several obligations the fulfillment of which is made easier and more certain with the aid of financial statement analysis. These major obligations are: to meet the demands of the depositor, both for financial services and for safekeeping of funds; to satisfy the sound credit needs of the community; to earn a fair return on the equity of the stockholders; and to fulfill the legal requirements as reflected by laws and the rules and regulations of the regulatory authorities.

Analyzing bank financial statements

A detailed analysis of bank financial and operating data sometimes cannot be made by an external analyst because only condensed bank statements are available to him. However, if he has the data usually available in the current annual report, the analyst may make a reasonably satisfactory analysis of the present financial condition and operating results of a bank. To analyze and interpret the financial and operating data of an individual bank, the analyst should know (1) the various ratios, trends, and percentages which may be used to the best advantage in expressing the data; (2) the manner in which these statistics are determined; (3) the reasons for fluctuations in the units; (4) the qualifications to which each unit must be subjected; and (5) the relationship existing between and among the different units under review. The analyst should also assemble financial and operating data for a number of similar banks. The strength or weakness of an individual bank can be determined more accurately by making comparisons with a group of similar banks. Data for all national banks are also useful for comparative purposes.

The analyst must always bear in mind that a single ratio or trend, regardless of its nature or importance, cannot be used as conclusive and complete evidence of financial or operating conditions. Furthermore, not all significant data are set forth in financial statements, even when supplemented by figures of productivity or other units of physical measurement of activity.

In interpreting and evaluating bank ratios and relationships, the analyst must consider many external factors, some of which are the type of community or territory served; the general business activity, industrial production, and credit conditions; political factors; the type and diversification of clientèle dealt with—whether retail, wholesale, manufacturing, mining, agricultural, or financial; the size of the city in which the bank is located—whether it has a small, medium, or large population; the possible occurrence of an extraordinary event, such as a disastrous flood, a serious fire, the establishment of a new corporation, the transfer of business to another community, or the dissolution of a large business; and the existence or nonexistence of national emergency of war conditions. In brief, it is necessary to study and interpret the economic, business, and political forces which are affecting the banking business.

The ratios and relationships that are discussed in the following pages are valuable for purposes of determining the relative liquidity and solvency of a bank, judging the effectiveness of a bank's reserve and investment policies, measuring and analyzing a bank's earning capacity, and analyzing and evaluating the efficiency of the management. As each ratio and relationship is explained, the statements of two banks are presented for illustrative purposes. Their respective comparative statements, as of December 31, 1968–71, appear in Illustrations 27–1 and 27–2. The two banks are comparable in size.

ILLUSTRATION 27–1

FIRST NATIONAL BANK OF EVANSTON AND BOULEVARD NATIONAL BANK OF CHICAGO
Selected Data Showing Trend
December 31, 1971, 1970, 1969, 1968
($000 omitted; base year = 1968)

	Bank	1971	1970	1969	1968
Cash and due from banks	First Nat.	$ 20,938	$ 17,501	$ 23,253	$ 17,009
	Trend %	123	103	137	100
	Boulevard	54,615	47,307	50,343	37,495
	Trend %	146	126	134	100
Marketable securities	First Nat.	65,084	49,833	38,998	49,295
	Trend %	132	101	79	100
	Boulevard	82,043	71,162	47,463	62,706
	Trend %	131	114	76	100
Loans and discounts	First Nat.	95,015	90,987	103,756	92,636
	Trend %	103	98	112	100
	Boulevard	151,473	128,133	125,479	121,898
	Trend %	124	105	103	100
Total cash, securities, and	First Nat.	181,037	158,321	166,007	158,940
loans	Trend %	114	100	104	100
	Boulevard	288,131	246,602	223,285	222,099
	Trend %	130	111	101	100
Total assets	First Nat.	185,726	167,724	169,767	164,826
	Trend %	113	102	103	100
	Boulevard	304,855	261,467	232,023	228,121
	Trend %	134	115	102	100
Deposits	First Nat.	161,455	148,722	151,662	153,720
	Trend %	105	97	99	100
	Boulevard	268,350	232,110	214,502	206,699
	Trend %	130	112	104	100
Capital stock	First Nat.	2,800	2,700	2,600	2,500
	Trend %	112	108	104	100
	Boulevard	3,500	3,000	3,000	3,000
	Trend %	117	100	100	100
Surplus, undivided profits	First Nat.	8,952	8,069	7,664	6,777
and reserves	Trend %	132	119	113	100
	Boulevard	14,068	13,292	12,267	11,242
	Trend %	125	118	109	100
Total stockholders' equity	First Nat.	9,573	8,693	8,542	7,697
	Trend %	124	113	111	100
	Boulevard	14,455	13,180	11,404	10,379
	Trend %	139	127	110	100

ILLUSTRATION 27–2

FIRST NATIONAL BANK OF EVANSTON AND BOULEVARD NATIONAL BANK OF CHICAGO
Selected Data Showing Trend
Years 1971, 1970, 1969, and 1968
($000 omitted; base year = 1968)

	Bank	1971	1970	1969	1968
Current operating revenue	First Nat.	$10,470	$10,041	$ 9,592	$ 8,294
	Trend %	126	121	116	100
	Boulevard	14,754	14,426	12,322	10,121
	Trend %	146	143	122	100
Current operating expenses	First Nat.	9,130	8,440	7,946	6,868
	Trend %	133	123	116	100
	Boulevard	13,863	12,614	10,458	9,282
	Trend %	149	136	113	100
Net operating income	First Nat.	1,340	1,601	1,646	1,426
	Trend %	94	112	115	100
	Boulevard	890	1,812	1,864	839
	Trend %	106	216	222	100
Other income and (expense) including gains and losses on securities, and income taxes	First Nat.	33	(343)	(342)	(414)
	Trend %	Not meaningful—see below			
	Boulevard	718	(384)	(539)	231
	Trend %	Not meaningful—see below			
Net income before dividends	First Nat.	1,373	1,258	1,304	1,012
	Trend %	136	124	129	100
	Boulevard	1,608	1,428	1,325	1,070
	Trend %	150	133	124	100
Dividends	First Nat.	488	471	422	396
	Trend %	123	119	107	100
	Boulevard	350	300	300	300
	Trend %	117	100	100	100
Net income retained in the business	First Nat.	885	787	882	616
	Trend %	144	128	143	100
	Boulevard	1,258	1,128	1,025	754
	Trend %	167	150	136	100
Percent retained in the business	First Nat.	64%	63%	68%	61%
	Boulevard	78%	79%	77%	70%

Key Factors in Other Income and Expense

First National Bank:

	1971	1970	1969	1968
Securities gains less related income tax	55	1	(33)	(93)
Income taxes	(22)	(344)	(309)	(321)
Other income and expense	33	(343)	(342)	(414)

Boulevard National Bank:

	1971	1970	1969	1968
Securities gains less related income tax	728	210	122	352
Income taxes	(10)	(594)	(661)	(121)
Other income and expense	718	(384)	(539)	(231)

Common-size percentages

Financial and operating data may be stated in common-size (percentage) form, as shown in Illustrations 27–1 and 27–2. Each of the percentages may be thought of as a ratio to the total of the group of items. For example, for the First National Bank at December 31, 1968, the ratio of deposits to total liabilities and capital accounts (owners' equity) was 93 percent; the same ratio as of December 31, 1971, was 87 percent. This method of presentation sets forth sharply the most important items appearing on the statements of commercial banks. Deposits represent the major item of the liabilities and capital, whereas cash, U.S. government securities, and loans and discounts are the major assets. The changes in the amounts of these items relative to the statement totals are shown in the comparative statements.

On December 31, 1968 the First National and Boulevard had, respectively, cash in the amount of $17,000 and $37,500, which was equivalent to 10.3 percent and 16.4 percent of their total assets. As of December 31, 1971, these amounts were $21,000 and $54,600, or 11.3 percent and 17.9 percent, respectively, of their total assets.

Relative changes may also be noted in the asset, marketable securities. First National and Boulevard possessed this type of asset on December 31, 1968 equal to 30 percent and 27 percent of its total assets, respectively. Similar percentages for 1971 were 35 percent and 27 percent.

The highly liquid condition as of December 31, 1971 of First National and Boulevard is reflected by their respective ratios of cash and marketable securities to total assets: 46 percent and 45 percent. The ratio of cash and securities to total assets for all national banks as of December 31, 1970 was 41 percent.

To determine whether or not the relative changes have been favorable, the analyst must compute ratios and trends for the period of time under review and also make detailed comparisons with a group of similar banks. Common-size data are valuable in making the latter analysis.

The comparative common-size statement of earnings (Illustration 27–2) reveals that in the case of The First National Bank a relatively larger amount of the gross revenue from current operations was absorbed by current operating expenses during 1971 than during 1968: 1971 operating expense was 133 percent of 1968, while revenue was only 126 percent of 1968, and net operating income went down 6 percent. By contrast, Boulevard's net operating income went up 6 percent even though expenses rose somewhat faster than revenue.

To analyze and account for variations, it is essential that individual ratios and comparisons be made.

ILLUSTRATION 27–3

NATIONAL BOULEVARD BANK OF CHICAGO AND
FIRST NATIONAL BANK AND TRUST COMPANY OF EVANSTON
Comparative Balance Sheets
As of December 31, 1968 and 1971

	Boulevard National Bank December 31				First National Bank December 31			
	1971		1968		1971		1968	
	$000	%	$000	%	$000	%	$000	%
Assets								
Cash and due from banks	54,615	17.9	37,495	16.4	20,938	11.3	17,009	10.3
Investment securities	82,043	26.9	62,706	27.5	65,084	35.0	49,295	29.9
Federal funds sold	12,450	4.1	2,215	1.0	—		2,750	1.7
Loans and discounts	151,473	49.7	121,898	53.4	95,015	51.2	92,636	56.1
Bank premises and equipment	1,657	.5	1,017	.5	2,689	1.4	1,569	1.0
Other assets	2,616	.9	2,790	1.2	2,000	1.1	1,567	1.0
Total	304,854	100.0	228,121	100.0	185,726	100.0	164,826	100.0
Liabilities and capital accounts								
Demand deposits	159,485	52.3	117,845	51.7	52,760	28.4	50,770	30.8
Time deposits	108,865	35.7	88,854	39.0	108,694	58.5	102,949	62.5
Other liabilities	11,436	3.8	7,180	3.1	9,520	5.1	1,830	1.1
Total	279,786	91.8	213,879	93.8	170,974	92.0	155,549	94.4
Reserve for loan losses	3,113	1.0	3,113	1.4	2,179	1.2	1,580	1.0
Capital notes	7,500	2.5	—		3,000	1.7	—	
Common stock	3,500	1.2	3,000	1.3	2,800	1.5	2,500	1.5
Surplus	7,500	2.5	7,000	3.1	3,600	1.9	3,000	1.8
Undivided profits	2,587	.8	261	.1	3,173	1.7	2,197	1.3
Reserve for contingencies	118	—	118		—		—	
Reserve for securities	750	.2	750	.3	—		—	
Total Capital Accounts	21,955	7.2	11,129	4.8	12,573	6.8	7,697	4.6
Total	304,854	100.0	228,121	100.0	185,726	100.0	164,826	100.0

ILLUSTRATION 27–4

NATIONAL BOULEVARD BANK OF CHICAGO AND
FIRST NATIONAL BANK AND TRUST COMPANY OF EVANSTON
Condensed Statements of Earnings and Dividends
For the Years ended December 31, 1968 and 1971

	National Boulevard Bank				First National Bank			
	1971		1968		1971		1968	
	$000	%	$000	%	$000	%	$000	%
Current operating revenue	14,754	100.0%	10,121	100.0%	10,470	100.0%	8,294	100.0%
Current operating expenses	13,864	93.9	9,282	91.7	9,130	87.2	6,868	82.8
Income before income taxes and securities gains	890	6.1	839	8.3	1,340	12.8	1,426	17.2
Applicable income taxes								
Current	156				35			
Deferred	(146)				(14)			
Total	10	.1	121	1.2	21	.2	321	3.9
Income before securities gains	880	6.0	718	7.1	1,319	12.6	1,105	13.3
Securities gains less related income taxes	728	4.9	353	3.5	55	.5	(93)	1.1
Net income	1,608	10.9	1,070	10.6	1,373	13.1	1,012	12.2
Cash dividends	350	2.4	300	3.0	488	4.7	396	4.8
Net income retained	1,258	8.5	770	7.6	885	8.4	606	7.4
Percent of net income retained		78.2%		72.0%		64.5%		59.9%

So it may be observed that ratios (trend percentages) may be used advantageously in analyzing financial statements for a number of years. In this manner the direction of the movement of related items—favorable or unfavorable tendencies over a period of time—may be determined and more easily analyzed and interpreted. The current favorable or unfavorable financial position and operating results may have been attained because of abnormal conditions which are not likely to be repeated. Trend analysis will lead to the discovery of the inclusion of unusual increases or decreases which require further detailed study.

In Illustration 27–1 it may be observed that total stockholders' equity increased in both banks over the four-year period, but Boulevard's four-year growth was 39 percent while First National grew only 24 percent. If the increase in total assets were used, the indicated difference would be greater; but this is not a satisfactory measure as assets can be increased by incurring additional liabilities. However, the amount of growth in current operating revenue (Illustration 27–2) is a satisfactory measure, and it will be observed that Boulevard's growth was only slightly less than twice that of First National. However we will later see that a material amount of Boulevard's 1971 revenue is not of the annually recurring type.

As previously noted, First National's expenses got out of control and net operating income actually declined 6 percent during the four years, while Boulevard's net operating income went up 6 percent; this result, while superior to First National's decline, was actually rather poor also considering the fact that revenue went up 46 percent. It can also be seen that this is misleading by noting the low level of net operating income that Boulevard enjoyed in 1968, the base year. In 1969 Boulevard's net operating income was more than twice its level in 1968. The following comparison may clarify the matter:

	Net operating income as a percent of gross revenue			
	1971	1970	1969	1968
First National Bank	8.9%	15.9%	17.1%	17.2%
Boulevard National Bank	6.0	12.5	15.1	8.3
For comparison, Continental Illinois Bank (the largest in Chicago).	13.8	10.9	11.8	14.5

So it becomes clear that First National did better in realizing net operating income out of the gross revenue it had available, though Boulevard's rate of revenue growth was superior. But Boulevard made up for its poorer showing above net operating income by realizing gains on securities of nearly $1,400,000; during the same four-year period First National showed a loss on securities. (However, it must be realized that the gains and losses on securities were *realized* gains and losses and we have no way to know what gains, as yet unrealized, the two banks have in their portfolios.)

The gains and losses from both operations and securities transactions combine to produce the net income figures shown in Illustration 27–2. The following comparisons are of interest:

| | Growth of net income | | | |
| | 1971 | | 1968 | |
	Trend (%)	% of gross revenue	Trend (%)	% of gross revenue
First National Bank	136	13.1	100	12.2
Boulevard National Bank	150	10.8	100	10.5

So we can see that even after the great difference in net income due to the gains on securities realized by Boulevard, First National's percent of gross revenue saved for net was substantially more. It appears that First National's primary difficulty is in the area of gross revenue growth: in the four-year period First National's gross revenue went up 26 percent; Boulevard's gross revenue went up 46 percent. In Illustration 27–1 look at the following.

| | Growth 1968 to 1971 | | |
	Deposits	Loans	Cash, loans and securities
First National Bank	Up 5%	Up 3%	Up 14%
Boulevard National Bank	Up 30	Up 24	Up 34

Going back to the annual reports for more detailed information on the sources of revenue, we obtain the following information:

		First National		Boulevard	
		Amount	Trend	Amount	Trend
Interest from loans and	1971	$ 9,439	125	$12,017	133
securities	1968	7,561	100	9,010	100
All other operating income	1971	$ 1,081	148	$ 2,737	246
	1968	733	100	1,111	100
Current operating revenue	1971	$10,470	126	$14,754	146
	1968	8,294	100	10,121	100

($000 omitted)

Unfortunately, it is not possible for the external analyst to determine percentage return on loans and securities, because only year-end balances are available. It appears that Boulevard has been more successful than First National insofar as interest income is concerned. But the most striking feature is the 146 percent increase in all other operating income so we now seek an analysis of the components of those totals.

	Other operating income 1971 ($000 omitted)		
	First National	Boulevard	Differ- ence
Trust income	$ 442	$ 542	$ 100
Service charges on accounts.	282	280	(2)
Income on federal funds sold.	74	511	437
Trading account income	. . . . . .	967	967
Other	233	437	204
	$1,031	$2,737	$1,706

Federal funds are funds on deposit with the Federal Reserve bank. Some are in excess of the amount required to satisfy the legal reserve requirements; they are "sold" to other banks for a fee. On its December 31, 1971, statement of condition, the Boulevard Bank shows "trading account securities" $10,691,986; the trading account income amount is apparently gains from trading in these securities. Information about "other" is not available.

The conclusions of this study may be summarized as follows:

	First National	Boulevard
In the four-year period:		
Interest income from loans and securities	Up 25%	Up 33%
Gross operating revenue from all other sources.	Up 1	Up 13

The principal factors accounting for Boulevard's superiority in the category of "all other sources" were:

Trading account income	6.8%
Federal funds sold	3.1
Trust income	.7
Miscellaneous	1.4
	12.0%
Boulevard's "all other sources"	13.0%
First National's "all other sources".	1.0
	12.0%

First National was superior in retaining gross operating revenue for net operating revenue; in other words, its expenses were lower. In 1971 the superiority was 2.9 percent, a dollar value of about $300,000. This offset Boulevard's higher trust income ($100,000) and miscellaneous income ($204,000). But Boulevard remains superior in growth of deposits, in yield from interest on loans and securities, in gains on securities transactions, and in federal funds sold. First National appears to be a cost cutter and lacking in aggressiveness (these two frequently go together) while Boulevard is actively and effectively seeking income and very possibly spending money to make money, characteristics which also often go together.

Ratio of cash and marketable securities to deposits

Federal and state bonds and some other highly liquid, low-risk securities may be regarded as the equivalent of cash, so in making a comparison of cash and deposits, they are taken into account as cash. The amount of cash that a bank should keep on hand depends on the portion legally required for deposit with the Federal Reserve bank as reserves, and the likelihood of customer demands for cash. Time and savings account balances are much less subject to withdrawal than are checking account balances. The ratios of cash and securities to deposits of the First National and Boulevard National banks are shown in the following tabulation:

	1971	1970	1969	1968
First National Bank				
Deposits:				
Demand deposits	52,760	53,769	52,702	59,770
Time and savings deposits.	108,694	94,953	98,960	102,949
Total deposits.	161,454	148,722	151,662	162,719
Cash, due from banks, securities.	86,022	67,334	62,251	66,304
Ratios:				
Cash and equivalents as percent of:				
Demand deposits	163%	125%	118%	111%
Time deposits and savings	79	71	63	64
Total deposits.	53%	45%	41%	41%
Boulevard National Bank				
Demand deposits.	159,485	141,394	143,875	117,845
Time and savings deposits	108,865	90,716	70,628	88,854
Total deposits.	268,350	232,110	214,503	206,699
Cash, due from banks, securities.	136,658	118,469	97,806	100,201
Ratios:				
Cash and equivalents as percent of:				
Demand deposits	86%	84%	68%	85%
Time deposits and savings	126	131	138	113
Total deposits.	51%	51%	46%	48%

($000 omitted)

Cash is sometimes called the primary reserve. It alone may be deposited with the Federal Reserve bank to satisfy legal reserve requirements. Unless it is in excess of the amount legally required it is in effect frozen, not usable for other operating purposes. The Federal Reserve bank pays interest on the reserve balances.

Cash in the hands of the First National and Boulevard National banks does not produce bank income, as for example loans and securities do. Therefore, banks are anxious to keep their cash at the lowest possible safe level.

Ratio of quick assets to total deposits

One of the best tests of bank liquidity is the ratio of quick assets to total deposits. Quick assets are cash and those assets that that can be readily converted into cash; they include the primary reserve, that portion of the secondary reserve and investments that has ready marketability, and those loans and discounts whose maturity is short or which can be rediscounted. Assets already pledged are not available as quick assets.

The external analyst has no way of determining the dollar amounts of the quick assets because the published report of condition in practically all cases reveals neither the nature and liquidity of loans and securities nor the valuation method that has been applied to these assets. Unrealized gains should not be reflected except by way of a footnote in the statement of condition. On the other hand, unrealized losses should be anticipated and recorded. In this manner the assets as well as the capital of the bank will be more accurately stated.

The quick-asset ratio is determined by dividing total quick assets,[1] evaluated at realizable amounts, by total deposits. The higher this ratio, the greater the liquidity of a bank. However, the highest quick-asset ratio does not necessarily represent the most favorable ratio from an income point of view, since cash and very low income-producing assets may predominate. A bank has a favorable quick-asset ratio when it has sufficient liquidity to meet current demands even though loan liquidation proves slow.

As there is no way to know that any of the securities held by the First National and Boulevard banks would not qualify as quick assets, the comparison previously made of cash and securities with deposits qualifies as the quick ratio.

Total deposits times capital

The relationship between total deposits and capital is of concern to both depositors and stockholders. Capital, the stockholders' equity, represents a margin of safety for the depositors, i.e., a protection for bank customers in the event of loss or shrinkage in the value of assets. The deposit funds, to the extent that they are invested by the bank in income-producing assets, represent a major source of earnings for the stockholders.

The ratio of total deposits to capital is determined by dividing total deposits by capital. To be of most significance, this relationship should be determined after all known or anticipated losses have been written off against Undivided Profits. The external analyst can do little, if anything, with respect to this problem. The results of computing this ratio for the First National and Boulevard National banks are shown in the following tabulation:

---

[1] Quick assets include cash and due from banks, government securities, loans and discounts, and other investments.

	1971	1970	1969	1968
Total deposits divided by stockholders' equity (times):				
First National Bank	16.9	17.1	17.7	21.1
Boulevard National Bank	18.5	17.6	18.8	19.9

Total deposits of all national banks in the United States as of December 31, 1970, were equal to 11.4 times their capital. Assuming that for a particular bank a relationship of $14 of deposits to each $1 of capital is ideal, in that adequate protection is afforded depositors and satisfactory earnings are realized in behalf of the stockholders, a lower figure would indicate greater security for depositors and less income on investments of funds for stockholders. A figure higher than $14 to $1 would mean less protection for depositors and greater earnings for stockholders, assuming the same rate of return on funds and no emergency which might result in losses. It should be noted that the ratio of total deposits to capital varies between cities and in accordance with size of banks.

In the final analysis the adequacy or inadequacy of the amount of capital relative to deposits depends upon the amount of cash and the safety and liquidity of the assets, the economic condition of the times, the nearness of the bank to a Federal Reserve bank, the existence of federal deposit insurance protection for the deposit customers of the bank, and the effectiveness of management in its loan and investment policies. To the extent that the foregoing factors are favorable, a much higher ratio of deposits to capital will be justifiable.

The comparison of total deposits and capital furnishes a clue to probable earnings and risks; the principle of "trading on equity" is evidenced. Stockholders benefit by the investment of customer deposits when the realized income is greater than the cost of funds to the bank. Consequently, the greater the amount of customer deposits that are profitably invested and the lower the amount of capital, the higher the return will be to the stockholders.

The extent to which the First National and Boulevard National banks trade on equity is also reflected in the following data:

	1971	1970	1969	1968
Loans, and securities divided by stockholders' equity (times):				
First National Bank	16.7	16.2	16.7	18.4
Boulevard National Bank	10.6	15.1	15.2	17.8

Other things being equal, the bank that has the higher ratio of loans, discounts, and securities to capital will earn the higher return for stockholders. However, the factors of *safety, liquidity, rate of income,* and *expenses of operations* must all be considered in determining the feasibility and profitability of the trading on equity by each particular bank.

Ratio of capital to total assets

The safety of customer deposits depends upon the adequacy of the capital if it is necessary to absorb losses. And, of course, the ability to absorb losses is also affected by the existence or absence of federal deposit insurance.

The ratio of capital to total assets is computed by dividing capital by total assets (in the following amounts, reserves and capital notes have not been included in total capital). As of December 31, 1968 and 1971, this ratio for the First National Bank & Trust Company of Evanston was 5.0 percent and 5.2 percent; for the Boulevard National Bank, 4.6 percent and 4.7 percent. The depositors in the First National Bank of Evanston will be protected up to $20,000 by the Federal Deposit Insurance Corporation and in addition up to 5.2 percent of the total assets; the Boulevard Bank is also insured by the FDIC and has 4.7 percent capital.

The smaller the ratio, the more likely it is that substantial losses will be accompanied by drastic action in regard to the capital structure of the bank. The larger the ratio, the greater is the degree of safety enjoyed by the bank. Some analysts compute the foregoing ratio as the ratio of total capital to total assets *less cash* on the basis that normally there will be no loss on cash.

ILLUSTRATION 27-3

FIRST NATIONAL BANK OF EVANSTON AND
BOULEVARD NATIONAL BANK OF CHICAGO
Selected Ratios for the years 1968-71

		1971	1970	1969	1968
Net income to total stockholders' equity	First Nat.	14.3%	14.4%	15.2%	13.1%
	Boulevard	11.1	10.8	11.6	10.3
Net income to total assets	First Nat.	7.3%	7.5%	7.6%	6.1%
	Boulevard	5.2	5.4	5.7	4.6
Dividends to net income	First Nat.	35.5%	37.4%	32.3%	39.1%
	Boulevard	21.7	21.0	22.6	28.0
Stockholders' equity as a percent of liabilities (proprietary ratio)	First Nat.	5.3%	5.6%	5.4%	4.9%
	Boulevard	7.8	5.4	5.3	4.8

The relatively small amount of capital in comparison with total assets emphasizes the absolute necessity for banks to be ultraconservative with respect to their primary and secondary reserve and investment policies. This conservatism is evidenced by three characteristics of a sound bank asset: *First,* it must be safe; *second,* it must possess liquidity; and *third,* it must be income producing.

Another factor of prime importance in analyzing the assets and capital of a bank is the determination of the relative amounts of capital invested in the bank building or other real estate, fixtures, and other nonincome-producing assets. A relatively large investment in the foregoing type of assets reduces the liquidity of capital; and, therefore, management has a smaller amount of funds which are subject to its discretionary investment policy.

Analysis of income statement data

The internal analyst has available, assuming adequacy of accounting records, a detailed classification of the sources of income and expenses for both banking and nonbanking functions. Banking functions or operations include the acceptance of deposits and the making of loans and investments. Nonbanking functions consist of the operations of departments such as the trust, safe-deposit, and safekeeping departments. Although the operation of nonbanking departments may not add directly to the earnings of a bank, it may result in profitable business for the banking departments of a bank.

Banks should analyze the costs of obtaining revenue in the interest of more satisfactory and effective control of operations. For example, the cost of performing various services should be known, so that (1) when practicable, a proper charge may be made against the customer; and (2) a comparison may be made of income from different sources with the cost of obtaining that income. The cost analysis reveals the extent to which the operation of nonbanking departments is a source of profit or a drain on the earnings of a bank.

A particular individual bank should compare its revenue and expense data with averages computed for a group of banks operating under comparable conditions or with standards of performance established on the basis of ideal accomplishments. In order to control operations effectively, a bank should maintain a cost accounting system and develop comparative and analytical reports.

The internal analyst or others in possession of a detailed bank income statement should make comparisons with various studies of earnings by the Comptroller of the Currency, the Federal Deposit Insurance Corporation, and the Federal Reserve banks. These data present average earning and expense figures of groups of banks by localities and by sizes.

When data are available, the analyst should compute, study, and make comparisons as suggested below:

> Average rate of income on—
> Loans
> U.S. government obligations
> Other securities
> Total owners' equity
> Total assets
> Average service charges on demand deposits
> Average interest paid on time and savings deposits
> Current operating expenses to current operating revenue

The external analyst does not have available sufficient data to make a comprehensive analysis and interpretation of the sources of bank income and the cost of obtaining that income. In fact, some banks publish only the net income and dividend figures.

The assets of a bank should earn income sufficient in amount to meet all expenses and losses, to provide a reasonable rate of interest on time deposits, to permit the declaration and payment of reasonable dividends to the stockholders, and to provide periodic additions to surplus.

The profitability of the bank's operations is revealed by the ratios of net income to total capital (owners' equity) and to total assets. To account for the variations in the ratios which involve changes in net income and owners' equity the analyst would require detailed information in regard to the bank's established policies with respect to primary and secondary reserves, investments, loans, discounts, and services and all other elements affecting net income and owners' equity.

Using the data contained in Illustrations 27–3 and 27–4, it is possible to determine that in 1971 the net income of the First National Bank as a percentage of total stockholders' equity was 14.3 percent. The comparable figure for Boulevard National was 11.1 percent and Comptroller General's Report shows an average for all National banks of 11.75 percent (in 1970). First National paid 35.5 percent of its net income in dividends; Boulevard National paid 21.8 percent; all National banks averaged 5.3 percent (in 1970).

Investors are vitally interested in a comparison of earnings, dividends, and book and market value of the capital stock.

When the amount of net income is not published, the analyst may attempt to ascertain this figure by comparing the capital items appearing on consecutive statements of condition. This is a simple and reliable method of determining net income, *assuming* that the only change in these items has been a result of dividend declaration and the net income for the period.

The analyst must exercise care in determining net income in the manner suggested above because of the possible inclusion in the surplus items of surplus paid in during the period, a write-off of asset value, or an abnormal loss charged directly to Undivided Profits.[2]

Gains and losses from fixed-dollar ("monetary") items

The statements of financial condition of banks reveal an unusually high proportion of debt in relation to capital stock, surplus, and undivided profits. An increasing price level produces gains arising from this factor. However, even a larger proportion of assets is of the fixed-dollar type; the banks generally lose when the price level rises. In other words, the stockholders' equity in a bank remains relatively stable irrespective of price-level changes. Banks do not have inventories; and their depreciation expense is relatively insignificant, so that earnings are not distorted materially by changes in the price level (see Part III, Chapters 17–21).

QUESTIONS AND PROBLEMS

27–1. Discuss briefly:

    a) What financial statement data, and in what form, would you present to show the growth of a commercial bank?

    b) Is a depositor of a bank a creditor of the bank?

    c) "The capital of a bank serves as a margin of safety to depositors." Explain.

    d) Distinguish between a bank's Surplus and Undivided Profits accounts.

27–2. Distinguish between:

    a) Statutory reserves and primary reserves.

    b) Valuation reserves and secret reserves.

    c) Secondary reserves and primary reserves.

    d) Secondary reserves and investments.

    e) Surplus and undivided profits.

27–3. What is the major interest in commercial bank financial statements of the depositor, the stockholder, and the outside creditor (excluding depositors)?

27–4. Give a brief answer to the following:

    a) To what extent are banks faced with problems in connection with depreciation?

    b) To what extent is a study of trend ratios important in analyzing the financial statements of a bank?

    c) Is the study of a bank's statement of condition more important than the study of its statement of earnings?

    d) What is the significance of each of the following?

---

[2] Under APB *Opinion No. 9* only "prior period" adjustments may be charged to Undivided Profits.

(1) Ratio of cash (including balances due from other banks) and U.S. government securities to total deposits.

(2) Total deposits to capital.

(3) Loans, discounts, and securities to capital.

(4) Ratio of capital to total assets.

(5) Liquidity, safety, and earnings power.

27–5. *a*) Discuss the relative importance of borrowed funds and capital for a commercial bank and an industrial concern.

   b) Discuss "trading on the equity" with respect to commercial bank operations.

27–6. Explain the significance of the following statements:

   a) "In analyzing bank financial statements, it is necessary to study and interpret the economic, business, and political forces which affect the banking business."

   b) "Commercial banks assemble capital from a large number of individuals and businesses and also manufacture credit within certain limits."

27–7. Most of the financial statement items of a commercial bank differ from those of a commercial business. Explain.

27–8. Compare the major sources of revenue and the major cost and expense items of commercial banks, public utilities, air carriers, railroads, and manufacturing businesses.

27–9. Distinguish between:

   a) Liabilities of banks and commercial businesses.

   b) A bank's report of condition and a retail store's balance sheet.

   c) Loans and discounts.

   d) Bank surplus and undivided profits.

   e) Resources of banks and commercial businesses.

   f) The services performed by banks and railroads.

   g) An overdraft and a loan.

27–10. Comment on the following statements:

   a) The deposits of all commercial banks are guaranteed by a governmental agency.

   b) Commercial banks classify financial statement items in a manner similar to the classification followed by retail businesses.

   c) Payment of dividends by banks is restricted by law.

   d) Bank earnings are distorted because of the failure to consider the influence of price-level changes.

   e) Trend percentages are not too useful in analyzing bank statements.

27–11. What information may be obtained by studying the following comparative data for a five-year period?

   a) Primary reserves in relation to total deposits.

   b) Common-size percentages.

   c) Owners' equity in relation to total assets.

   d) Loans and discounts in relation to total deposits.

   e) Trend percentages.

  f) Cash in relation to total deposits.

  g) Net income in relation to total assets.

27–12. Match each of the following with the appropriate phrase listed to the right.

(1)	Undivided profits.	*a*)	Protection of depositors.
(2)	Relationship of owners' equity to total assets.	*b*)	Depositors.
		c)	Bank balance sheet.
(3)	Margin of safety for depositors.	*d*)	Bank statement of earnings.
		e)	Bank capital stock.
(4)	Deposit insurance.	*f*)	Margin of safety for creditors.
(5)	All national banks.	*g*)	Revenue earned on loans.
(6)	Report of condition.	*h*)	Members of Federal Reserve System.
(7)	Income statement.		
(8)	Interest and discount.	*i*)	Owners' equity.
(9)	Capital.	*j*)	Relationship between total deposits and owners' equity.
(10)	Creditors.		

27–13. The following financial data were obtained from the reports of condition for Banks L and D. Which of the two banks has the more favorable financial position?

	December 31, 1971 (in thousands)			
	L	(%)	D	(%)
Loans and discounts	$ 22,150	14.5	$ 61,830	39.8
U.S. government obligations	38,960	25.5	44,940	28.9
Federal Reserve bank stock	300	.2	350	.2
Cash	64,970	42.6	37,640	24.2
Bank premises, net	8,940	5.9	2,600	1.7
Other securities and investments	15,000	9.8	7,000	4.7
Other assets	2,200	1.5	1,000	.6
Total	$152,520	100.0	$155,360	100.0

27–14. The following financial data were obtained from the records of Banks B and L:

	December 31, 1971 national banks	
	B	L
Cash and due from banks	$ 87,301	$ 87,276
U.S. government securities—direct and fully guaranteed	50,387	44,691
State, municipal, and other public securities.	12,589	10,109
Other bonds and securities	1,427	890
Loans and discounts.	91,112	82,362
Federal Reserve bank stock.	325	420
Bank buildings, vaults, furniture, and fixtures	2,541	2,368
Interest earned not received	418	325
Customers' liability under letters of credit and acceptances	817	1,075
Capital stock	8,000	7,000
Surplus	5,000	7,000
Undivided profits	851	4,060
Reserves for interest, taxes, and contingencies.	3,753	1,803
Discount collected not earned	448	344
Letters of credit and acceptances	817	1,606
Deposits	228,048	207,299
Dividends payable		150
Miscellaneous liabilities		254

Required:
a) Reconstruct the report of condition including dollar amounts and common-size percentages.
b) Compute the following ratios:
(1) Cash and due from banks to total deposits.
(2) Cash and due from banks plus U.S. securities to total deposits.
(3) Total deposits times capital.
(4) Capital to total assets.
c) Analyze all available data.
d) Write a report evaluating the financial position of the two banks.

27-15. The data presented below were obtained from published reports of Banks X, Y, and Z:

(1)   (*Data in thousands*):

	December 31, 1971 national banks		
	X	Y	Z
Cash and due from banks	$ 46,600	$ 89,938	$ 69,533
U.S. government securities	62,873	50,028	71,544
State and municipal securities	5,967	905	6,275
Other securities (including stock in Federal Reserve bank)	2,435	6,052	2,958
Loans and discounts	23,378	27,339	48,544
Banking houses and fixtures	1,455	3,107	3,310
Other real estate and other resources.	476	405	681
Capital stock	2,100	3,750	4,500
Surplus	6,000	3,500	4,500
Undivided profits (including appropriated reserves)	1,753	3,104	2,551
Reserves for taxes and interest	348	141	343
Dividends payable	106	75	158
Deposits	132,658	167,099	190,568
Other liabilities	219	105	225

(2)   *Ratios:*

	X	Y	Z
Cash and due from banks to total deposits	35.1	53.8	36.5
Cash and due from banks plus U.S. securities to total deposits	82.5	83.8	74.0
Total deposits times capital	13.5	16.1	16.5
Capital to total assets	6.9	5.8	5.7

(3)

BANKS X, Y, AND Z
Common-Size Percentages
As of December 31, 1971

	X	Y	Z
Assets			
Loans and discounts	16.3	15.4	23.9
U.S. government securities	43.8	28.1	35.3
State and municipal securities	4.2	.5	3.1
Other securities (including stock in federal Reserve bank)	1.7	3.4	1.5
Cash and due from banks	32.6	50.6	34.3
Banking house and fixtures	1.1	1.7	1.6
Other real estate and other resources	.3	.3	.3
Total Assets	100.0	100.0	100.0
Liabilities and Capital			
Liabilities:			
Deposits	92.7	94.0	93.9
Dividends payable	.1		.1
Reserve for taxes and interest	.2	.1	.2
Other liabilities	.1	.1	.1
Total Liabilities	93.1	94.2	94.3
Capital:			
Capital stock	1.5	2.1	2.2
Surplus	4.2	2.0	2.2
Undivided profits (including appropriated surplus)	1.2	1.7	1.3
Total Capital	6.9	5.8	5.7
Total Liabilities and Capital	100.0	100.0	100.0

Required:

a) Analyze and interpret all available data.

b) Write a report in which you evaluate the financial positions of the two banks.

Index

Index